An *Abaris* Companion

OPERA

A PICTORIAL GUIDE

by Quaintance Eaton

ABARIS BOOKS • NEW YORK

To John Owen Ward

Design: Andor Braun
Layout and Research: Barbara Sorel
Photography: Abaris Productions, Ltd.
Cover Design: Ken Meads

Copyright © 1980 by Abaris Books, Inc.
International Standard Book Number 0-913870-71-4
Library of Congress Card Number 80-68675
First published 1980 by Abaris Books, Inc.
24 West 40th Street, New York, NY 10018
Printed in the United States of America

Beverly Sills Greenough

Dear Quaintance,

Rare is the book which combines so much intellectual and visual appeal as yours. Having known you for such a long time, I can appreciate how this book grew from day to day through thousands of musical experiences and through endless research and collecting of material.

I'm sure this book will be a joy for many music lovers as well as a guide for others who are on the verge of discovering the world of opera. Congratulations!

Beverly Sills

Look up an opera

Check the *List of Operas* on pages 7-8. All operas are listed by title in the original language as well as in English. Or turn to the *composer* of the opera in the main section, where all the composers are listed alphabetically, followed by their operas in the order that they were composed. For each major opera, both a synopsis and a historical and critical essay are provided. For less frequently performed works, only a brief synopsis is given.

Look up a composer

All composers of the operas in this volume are listed alphabetically in the main section of this book, as well as in the *General Index.*

Look up a librettist

Consult the *General Index.*

Look up a singer

Consult the *General Index.* Most famous performers are pictured in their principal roles.

Look up a conductor

Consult the *General Index.*

Look up outstanding opera houses

Consult the *General Index* for the page number of the illustration.

Look up the first performance of an opera.

You will find it below the *Cast of Characters* for each opera.

Look up a stage designer of famous productions

Consult the *General Index.*

OPERAS

ADOLPHE-CHARLES ADAM (Paris, 24 July 1803 – 3 May 1856). It seems ironic that one of the most popular composers of light opera in France was expressly forbidden, by his father, to write music for the stage — indeed, to enter the musical world at all. But young Adam's wishes and talent finally prevailed, and he was allowed to study at the Conservatoire at the age of fourteen. He came under the influence of one of the most respected opera composers of the time, François Boïeldieu, and began to make his way in the Paris Opéra-Comique, which thereafter produced most of his fifty-three operas. His earliest substantial success was *Danilowa*, but his fame today rests on *Le Postillon de Longjumeau*, although *Si j'étais Roi* is occasionally heard. In the world of ballet, his *Giselle* is a classic. An attempt to manage a theater, where young composers would be encouraged, was frustrated by the revolution of 1848, and he was left in debt, which he industriously managed to clear up in five years. His music is noted for the charm of its melodies, a characteristic apparent in another of his still-popular songs, *Cantique de Noël* (Christmas Song).

ACT I.   In the early nineteenth century, Chappelou, the coachman of Longjumeau, is lured away from his new bride, Madeleine, by the impresario of the Paris Opéra, the Marquis de Courcy, who has heard him sing a song about the happy fate of a postillion (this is the most famous piece in the opera, calling for a tenor who can imitate the posthorn and negotiate some high D's). True to his promise, the Marquis makes Chappelou the leading tenor at the Opéra, under the name of St. Phar. Chappelou's friend Bijou also seeks his operatic fate in Paris.

ACT II.   Ten years have elapsed. Madeleine, still in love with her absent husband, has also come to Paris after receiving a large legacy, and now is prominent in the fashionable world as Madame La Tour. Both the Marquis and St. Phar are in love with her. Even face to face, St. Phar does not recognize his wife, and persuades her to marry him. To avoid actually committing bigamy, he induces Bijou (now head of the opera chorus and known as Alcindor) to impersonate a priest. But Madame, learning of this, has Bijou locked up, and the ceremony is performed by a real priest.

ACT III.   The Marquis, knowing of the trickery, plans to have St. Phar arrested for bigamy. But Madame forestalls this by producing her own denouement — appearing in peasant dress and holding a conversation with herself in her two characters. When the police come, she reveals the truth, and we have the proper happy ending.

DOMINICK ARGENTO (York, Pennsylvania, 27 October 1927 –). One of America's most distinguished opera composers, he came to the lyric theater at thirty, after a career of considerable achievement and many honors in other musical fields. Even throughout his earlier years, he considered the human voice the supreme instrument, and wrote many works around it, a notable example being his 1975 Pulitzer Prize-winning song cycle, *From the Diary of Virginia Woolf*. He frequently works and lives in Florence, Italy, which he considers his spiritual home.

Le Postillon de Longjumeau, Act I, Scene 2.

Le Postillon de Longjumeau

9
ADAM

(*The Coachman of Longjumeau*)

Text by A. de Leuven and L.L. Brunswick.

MADELEINE	*Soprano*
CHAPPELOU	*Tenor*
LE MARQUIS DE CORCY	*Tenor*
BIJOU	*Bass*
ROSE (A MAID)	*Soprano*
BOURDON	*Bass*

First Performance
Paris, 13 October 1836.

Dominick Argento.

Argento's American home since 1958 is Minneapolis, particularly the University. He was associated with Sir Tyrone Guthrie in the theater named after that English producer, and helped to found the Center Opera Company (now the Minnesota Opera), where most of his works have been produced. These include:

The Boor, libretto by John Olon-Scrymgeour after Chekhov (1957).

Colonel Jonathan the Saint, libretto by Olon-Scrymgeour (1971).

The Masque of Angels, a humorous religious fable, libretto by Olon-Scrymgeour; commissioned by the Community Center Arts Council of Walker Art Center, Minneapolis (1964).

Christopher Sly, based on Shakespeare's *Taming of the Shrew*, libretto from John Manlove (1967).

The Shoemaker's Holiday, libretto from Thomas Dekker's seventeenth-century ballad opera, with additional lyrics by Olon-Scrymgeour. Commissioned by the Minnesota Theater Foundation (1967).

Postcard from Morocco, libretto by John Donahue. Commissioned by Center Opera, Minneapolis. Premiere: Minneapolis, 14 October 1971. One Act. Symbolic fantasy set in a waiting room in Morocco, where the passengers reveal themselves by the contents of their baggage — hats for the soprano, shoes for the baritone, a cornet for the bass, and so on. A temporary romance between Mr. Owen (the only one with a name) and the soprano leads to the revelation of Owen's empty suitcase. The others, their curiosity appeased, revert to their own preoccupations, watch a puppet show, then depart for the train. Owen acts with the puppets in a fantasy until the puppet curtain falls. Has been widely performed.

A Water Bird Talk, monodrama based partly on Chekhov and also on Audubon's *The Birds of America*. One act. Premiere: Brooklyn, 19 May 1977. A henpecked professor gradually reveals his unhappy condition during an illustrated lecture on water birds.

The Voyage of Edgar Allan Poe, libretto by Charles Nolte. Commissioned by the University of Minnesota for the Bicentennial. Two acts. Premiere: Minneapolis, 24 April 1976. Argento's most impressive opera to date. The poet, shadowed and driven by his nemesis, Griswold (in real life the author's vindictive literary executor), embarks on an imaginary voyage where hallucinations beset him, bearing him in madness to the tomb. He sees a vision of his dying young wife Virginia; later she comes to life, then dies again. A bizarre trial finds him guilty; a macabre auction produces women to supplant Virginia as his muse. He sees himself alone in the center of a maelstrom, and in a delirium he dies. On the dock, from which he is supposed to have embarked on the fantastic voyage, his body is found by the Doctor and Griswold. The latter steals his manuscripts and vanishes.

Miss Havisham's Fire, libretto by Olon-Scrymgeour, based loosely on an incident from Dickens's *Great Expectations*. Two acts, prologue and epilogue. Commissioned by the New York City Opera. Premiere: New York, 22 March 1979. The action centers around the death in a fire of Miss Havisham, eccentric recluse, and an inquest into its circumstances. The chief characters are Pip, the orphan who is

Scene from Argento's The Voyage of Edgar Allen Poe with George Livings and Karen Hunt.

befriended by the old lady; Estella, the girl Miss Havisham has adopted and trained to lure and then repel men; the attorney Jaggers, the nurse Nannie; the drunken gardener Orlick, several relatives, who expect but are denied an inheritance, and Bentley Drummle, the coldhearted dandy who marries Estella, then leaves her. The scenes shift back and forth in time, suggesting cinematic technique. A very long mad scene for Miss Havisham ends the opera. The chief characters are each represented by two singers portraying them in youth and maturity.

Severely criticized for its length and confusing structure, the opera was in the process of being revised by its composer shortly after its premiere.

DANIEL FRANÇOIS AUBER (Caen, 29 January 1782 – Paris, 12 May 1871). Auber, who has been called the last great exponent of *opéra-comique*, began to write music at eleven. He later moved to London and lived there until 1804. His reputation as a "drawing-room" composer grew, and he wrote several instrumental works for friends. His first attempts at dramatic composition made no impression, and it was not until *La Bergère châtelaine* appeared at the Paris Opéra-Comique that he scored any success. This was in 1820; a stream of works followed rapidly, sometimes several in one year. He owed much to his friend and collaborator, Eugène Scribe, whose well-wrought librettos underlay most of Auber's triumphs. These included the operettas *Le Cheval de bronze (The Bronze Horse)*, 1835, later made into an opera-ballet; *Le Domino noir (The Black Domino)*, 1837; *Les Diamants de la couronne (The Crown Diamonds)*, 1841; and Auber's most prominent effort in serious opera, *La Muette de Portici (The Dumb Girl of Portici)*, also known as *Masaniello* after its hero. The last, like the others, is seldom heard, although a company in Boston presented it in 1915, with Anna Pavlova as the dancer-heroine.

Auber's fame today rests largely on the comic opera, *Fra Diavolo*. It is interesting to note that in choice of libretto he anticipated four composers better known today: Verdi with *Gustav III ou Le Bal masqué* (1883); Debussy with *L'Enfant prodigue* (1850); and Massenet and Puccini with *Manon Lescaut* (1856).

ACT I.   In Matteo's inn near Terracina, in the mountains between Rome and Naples, the brigadier Lorenzo is fretting because he may lose his sweetheart Zerlina to a wealthy farmer whom her father, the innkeeper, has chosen for her. Lorenzo hopes to capture the notorious bandit, Fra Diavolo, on whose head a reward has been placed. A further reward is offered by a wealthy English traveler, Lord Cockburn, who arrives with the tale of a daring robbery on the road. His wife Pamela's jewels have been taken, although a cache of gold has escaped the bandit's notice. Lord Cockburn is also upset by the attentions of a certain Marquis of San Marco to Lady Pamela. Matteo goes off to complete wedding arrangements with the farmer, leaving matters to Zerlina, who explains in a pretty ballad the story of Fra Diavolo. The "Marquis" (who is actually the bandit himself) joins in the last verse.

Fra Diavolo
(*Brother Devil*)

Text by Scribe.

12
AUBER

FRA DIAVOLO	*Tenor*
LORD COCKBURN	*Tenor*
LADY PAMELA	*Mezzo-Soprano*
LORENZO	*Tenor*
ZERLINA	*Soprano*
GIACOMO	*Bass*
BEPPO	*Tenor*

First Performance
Paris, 28 January 1830.

Le Postillon de Longjumeau, Act III, after Schoeller.

Then he admits two "beggars," really Giacomo and Beppo, members of his band—who confess to having missed the gold. Fra Diavolo vows to learn its whereabouts from Lady Pamela, who providentially appears to join him in a passionate duet. This turns into a barcarolle at the appearance of the jealous husband, who, nevertheless, is flattered by the "Marquis" into revealing that the gold is sewn into various garments.

Lorenzo and his carabiniers bustle in, reporting that they have killed at least twenty of the bandits and recovered the stolen property. Pamela gives him the reward immediately so that he may marry Zerlina. The furious Fra Diavolo swears to avenge his slain followers.

ACT II. By an awkward arrangement, the Cockburns' bedroom may be reached only through Zerlina's. The latter, preparing for bed while singing a brilliant aria, is observed by the two bandits, who have hidden in a closet. After she is asleep, the plan for the robbery is interrupted by the arrival of Lorenzo. The noise awakens everyone. The Marquis gets out of his predicament by explaining to Lord Cockburn that he has a rendezvous with Lady Pamela, and, conveniently, to Lorenzo that he has a date with Zerlina. Lorenzo challenges him to a duel.

ACT III. In the mountains, Fra Diavolo sings of the jolly life of a bandit, and awaits the signal from his henchmen that the coast is clear to rob the inn while the others are at an Easter celebration. Lorenzo, sadly recalling his lost love, suddenly remembers the duel, and reproaches Zerlina in song. Beppo and Giacomo, in hiding, recognize the girl and laugh a little too loudly at the memory. They are captured, and a diagram of the projected crime discovered. Fra Diavolo, responding to the false signal of a church bell pealing, is surrounded. Two alternative endings are possible: a relatively happy one has the bandit merely captured; a relatively tragic denouement is to have him shot in ambush.

Tito Schipa as Fra Diavolo.

13
BARBER

SAMUEL BARBER (West Chester, Pa., 9 March 1910 –) turned to opera late, although he had been influenced by his famous aunt, the contralto Louise Homer, and studied singing at the Curtis Institute with Emilio De Gogorza along with piano and composition. He first gained notice with chamber and orchestra works (especially the *Overture* to *The School for Scandal* and the *Adagio for Strings*), then went on to compose many works in various forms. In the early fifties, Barber's close friend Gian Carlo Menotti, himself an established man of the theater, offered to write a libretto for Barber. The result was *Vanessa*, which, when given its premiere by the Metropolitan in 1958, was the first full-length native work to be heard in that house since Hanson's *Merry Mount* in 1934. With its splendid cast (Eleanor Steber, Rosalind Elias, Nicolai Gedda, Regina Resnik, and Giorgio Tozzi), Dimitri Mitropoulos in the pit, and handsome settings and costumes by Cecil Beaton, the opera scored a substantial success. It was later heard in Salzburg with virtually the same personnel, and then revived at the Met in 1965 and at the American Spoleto Festival in Charleston, S.C. Barber

World premiere of Vanessa: Left to right, Eleanor Steber, Nicolai Gedda, George Cehanovsky, Regina Resnik, Rosalind Elias; 1958, Metropolitan Opera, New York.

Vanessa

Text by Gian Carlo Menotti.

VANESSA	*Soprano*
ERIKA, HER NIECE	*Mezzo-Soprano*
THE OLD BARONESS,	*Contralto*
VANESSA'S MOTHER	
ANATOL	*Tenor*
THE OLD DOCTOR	*Baritone*
MAJOR-DOMO	*Bass*
FOOTMAN	*Bass*

First Performance
New York, 15 January 1958.

won his first Pulitzer Prize for the opera. He went on to write a miniature work, *A Hand of Bridge* (1959), and was commissioned by the Metropolitan to do an opera for the opening of its new house in Lincoln Center in 1966. This, *Antony and Cleopatra*, with libretto, direction, and settings by Franco Zeffirelli, was a pronounced failure. The production had the dubious distinction of breaking down some of the elaborate machinery that was to be the pride of the new house, and locking the prima donna (Leontyne Price) in a miniature pyramid for hours at dress rehearsal. Barber has since revised and simplified *Antony and Cleopatra* but so far it has not found favor. *Vanessa*, however, continues to hold audiences, and was successfully televised at its Spoleto performance.

THE ACTION TAKES place in an unnamed northern country, in Vanessa's sumptuous mansion, about 1905. Vanessa, having dismissed her lover many years in the past, has become a recluse, covering all the mirrors and drawing the curtains. Now, on a snowy evening, she expects his return. The old Baroness, her mother, watches with the stony silence she has maintained in disapproval of her daughter, but Erika, Vanessa's niece, eagerly helps the preparations. It is not Anatol who arrives, but his son, also named Anatol, who is curious to see the lady who jilted his father. Vanessa cannot face him, but Erika stays, attracted and eventually seduced by the insouciant young man. She keeps this secret from Vanessa, who gradually becomes warmly attached to Anatol and determines to marry him. When their betrothal is announced at a ball, Erika flees wildly into the icy night, and loses the child she is carrying. The Baroness, furious now at the younger girl, retreats into silence once more as Vanessa gaily departs with her new husband for Paris, and Erika remains, to draw the curtains, cover the mirrors, and sink into her own silent watchfulness.

The opera is in four acts and five scenes. The music is lyrical, with many dramatic effects, and a particularly fine quintet at the end.

BÉLA BARTÓK (Nagyszentmiklós, Transylvania, 25 March 1881 — New York, 26 September 1945) whose creative spirit was a watershed in twentieth century music, like Debussy's (to whom he has been compared in originality); whose explorations of folk music extended far beyond the reaches of his own Hungarian music and "spoke of the brotherhood of peoples," as one authority put it; whose six string quartets remain unparalleled in their fresh, personal energy; who revolutionized the study of the piano; who wrote one, and only one, stunning opera — was not hailed worldwide for all of this marvelous work until after his death. Now his position is so secure that it is difficult to remember how strange the creations of this frail, dedicated composer-pianist seemed at first.

Bartók studied at the Royal Conservatory of Music and later taught there. After World War I he was a member of the Music Directorate with Dohnányi and Kodály. The latter joined him in research into folk music, which remained a stirring influence in Bartók's music, along with French impressionism. The two enthusiasts transcribed and recorded more than eight thousand folk tunes. Although Bartók did not yield to the rigid twelve-tone system, he opened conventional harmony and rhythm, believing in the availability of every note in the chromatic scale, and freely employing old modal systems.

During the Nazi supremacy he came to America in 1940 with his second wife Ditta, frequently his partner in two-piano concerts. They lived in great want, fiercely refusing what they deemed to be charity from concerned friends. Only slowly did his great works emerge as solid repertoire items: the six volumes of piano studies called *Mikrokosmos*; the forty-four violin duos; the *Music for Strings, Percussion, and Celesta*; the *Concerto for Orchestra*, the piano, viola, and violin concertos, and many works in smaller forms. His chief choral work was a *Cantata Profana*, his two ballets were *The Wooden Prince* and the more famous *Miraculous Mandarin*.

The sole one-act opera is *Duke Bluebeard's Castle (A Kékszakállú Herceg Vára)*, composed in 1911 but not performed until 1918. The libretto by Béla Balázs does not conform to the Perrault fairy tale except that it concerns a grim character in a haunted castle with an unusually large number of wives.

The opera can convey many meanings, perhaps chief among them the loneliness of the human soul, the power of a redemptive woman (but that power destroyed, like Elsa's in *Lohengrin*, by her fatal curiosity), and the conflict between rational man and emotional woman. A narrator asks the audience to relate their own lives to the myth about to be unfolded.

Bluebeard was performed occasionally in Europe after its premiere in Budapest, and has been revived there. First heard in America as a concert performance in Dallas in 1946, the first stage performance was at the New York City Center in 1952; the Metropolitan mounted it in an anachronistic,

Béla Bartók.

15
BARTÓK

James pease and Ann Ayars in scene from Duke Bluebeard's Castle.

over-realistic production in June 1974. The City Opera's production employed ballet dancers to represent the heroine's inner self and each of Bluebeard's wives, in an attempt to add drama to the rather static story. The drama, however, lies in the music, which fully expresses each stage of the fate of Bluebeard's last wife and the growing sorrow of the man himself.

Duke Bluebeard's Castle

Text by Béla Balázs.

DUKE BLUEBEARD   *Bass*
JUDITH   *Mezzo-Soprano*

First Performance
Budapest, 24 May 1918.

DUKE BLUEBEARD brings his newest wife Judith to his dark, forbidding castle, in which there are seven closed doors. In a desire to bring light into the gloomy place, Judith asks that the doors be opened. Bluebeard reluctantly yields the keys to each in turn, but as the woman's insatiable curiosity grows, the man's despair increases. One by one his innermost secrets and his past life are revealed: the first room is a torture chamber, the terrors and suffering of youth; the second an armory, his mature defenses; the third a treasure house, his worldly success; the fourth a beautiful garden, his poetic life; the fifth a limitless horizon, his power; the sixth a lake of tears, the sorrows of age. Judith is at first exultant, then repelled by the blood that covers and taints all.

It is Bluebeard's blood; but she does not understand and sympathize, instead she demands the seventh key. True to her suspicion, the fateful chamber shows Bluebeard's first three wives, those who represent the morning, the noon, and the twilight of his life. Now Judith must join them, as the night, and Bluebeard remains in his solitary grief, perhaps to seek understanding again (like the Flying Dutchman) or perhaps too old to do so.

Scene from Duke Bluebeard's Castle with Edmund Kossowskis and Khrystyne Szostek — Radhoeva, Warsaw

JACK BEESON (Muncie, Indiana, 15 July 1921 –). A full life as a creator as well as a scholar has yielded Jack Beeson seven operas to date and numerous significant positions — among the latter, MacDowell Professor of Music at Columbia University, where he headed the Music Department for several years, an association begun in 1945. That same year he worked with Béla Bartók. Two years in Europe proved fruitful; his first opera, *Jonah*, was composed during that stay, to a play by Paul Goodman. Among many honors and responsibilities, he was elected to the National Institute of Arts and Letters. His other six operas, all of which have earned favorable attention, are:

Hello Out There, one act, to a libretto by William Saroyan based on his play (1954).

The Sweet Bye and Bye, two acts, libretto by Kenward Elmslie (New York, 1957; revised and performed in Muncie, the first contemporary opera to have been performed in Beeson's birthplace). The story is reminiscent of the highly colored career of Aimée Semple McPherson.

Lizzie Borden, three acts and prologue, libretto by Kenward Elmslie based on a scenario by Richard Plant. Commissioned by the Ford Foundation for the New York City Opera, which gave its premiere 25 March 1965 and revived it a decade later. Subtitled "A Family Portrait," the story presumes that Lizzie was guilty of the axe murders (although she was in fact acquitted). There are powerful confrontations between the girl and her stepmother and her father, who ignores her after his second marriage.

Lizzie helps her sister Margaret elope with Captain Jason MacFarlane, after Borden has mockingly offered Lizzie as a bride instead, and forbidden Margaret to see him. He also bars from the house the Reverend Harrington, who has been friendly to Lizzie. Lizzie dresses up in her own mother's wedding dress, and is caught and taunted by Abbie, the stepmother. Lizzie's fantasies about Margaret's fiancé, and her realization that she is now alone with her "family," unhinge her mind. After a visit to the bedroom where Abbie is napping, she greets her father in the bloodstained wedding dress and follows him to the bedroom. In the epilogue, Lizzie is a virtual prisoner in the house, scorned and mocked by everyone, in spite of her acquittal.

My Heart's in the Highlands, libretto by the composer, based on the William Saroyan play. Composed especially for television, premiere on NET Opera Theater, 18 March 1970. Essentially a confrontation between a charming, indigent family and an eccentric bugle-playing refugee from an old people's home. A "fullbodied musical setting of Saroyan's euphoric extravagance," according to one critic.

Captain Jinks of the Horse Marines, three acts, libretto by Sheldon Harnick after a play by Clyde Fitch. Aided by grants from the National Endowment for the Arts and the Missouri State Council on the Arts. Premiere: Kansas City Lyric Theater, 20 September 1975. The witty story deals with the arrival of opera singer Aurelia Trentoni in New York during the 1870s to make her American debut as Violetta in *La Traviata* (the opportunity for quotation is cleverly seized by the composer). Jonathan Jinks, young lawyer and man-about-town, wagers that he can make a successful pass at the foreign prima donna, but falls in love with her. Their romance is blossoming when Colonel Mapleson, the impresario, and Papa Bellarti, her vocal coach, discover the wager and inform her. She is furious, but

Jack Beeson.

after her triumph in *Traviata* forgives her lover. Many operatic allusions in the score earned *Jinks* the title, "a valentine to opera."

Dr. Heidegger's Fountain of Youth, one act, commissioned by the National Arts Club, New York. Premiere: 17 November 1978. Old Dr. Heidegger summons four friends to try his newly discovered elixir of youth. They experience a regression to younger days, one girl winning the attentions of her fiancé's friend (to the annoyance of her fiancé), precipitating a fight. In the struggle, the bottle of elixir is spilled, and all return to their mournful middle age.

LUDWIG VAN BEETHOVEN (Bonn, 15/16 December 1770 – Vienna, 26 March 1827). When he began work on his only opera, Beethoven was already suffering the deafness that would become total. His true maturity as a composer was already evident. The *Eroica* Symphony had been introduced to the public; the Fourth Piano Concerto, the Violin Concerto, and the immortal Fifth Symphony waited in the wings. In 1803 an oratorio, *Christus am Ölberg (Christ on the Mount of Olives)*, was produced with immense success at the new Theater an der Wien, which, under the impresario Emanuel Schikaneder (the very one who had provided the libretto for Mozart's *Zauberflöte*) was competing with the Kärntnerthor Theater under Baron von Braun.

The closest Beethoven had previously come to lyric drama was the ballet music for *The Creatures of Prometheus*. Before he could be put to test, however, Baron von Braun took over the Theater an der Wien, reinstating Schikaneder as manager and giving Beethoven a new contract, this time definitely specifying an operatic work. The composer chose a story that had been made into a libretto by Jean Bouilly from an actual incident, during the French Revolution. *Léonore, ou l'Amour conjugal* had been set by Ferdinando Paër in an Italian translation, which was produced in Dresden in 1804. Beethoven probably knew of Paër's opera, but it has been established that he was working on *Fidelio*, as the work came to be called, before the Italian's production.

The glorification of conjugal love (which Beethoven was never to experience) and the freedom of the human spirit were sentiments that profoundly stirred the composer. The opera might serve solely as a moral tract, were it not for the genius of the musical setting. The libretto was given to Joseph Sonnleithner, secretary of the imperial theaters, who added a third act to the original two and so made the opera too long for a favorable reception. Indeed, *Fidelio* suffered an unhappy early life. It was Beethoven's misfortune to see the premiere of his difficult brainchild take place in the time of Napoleon's occupation of Austria. Three performances were given before audiences largely composed of French officials.

Then close friends of the composer persuaded him to restore the work to the play's original two acts, which necessitated cutting three numbers. Stephan von Breuning rearranged the libretto. In its new form, *Fidelio* was given on 29 March 1806, and again 10 April, but Beethoven quarreled with Baron von Braun and again withdrew his opera. In 1814 *Fidelio* was revived again, at the Kärntnerthor Theater, this time in its final form. Georg Friedrich Treitschke, official poet and stage manager of the theater, was entrusted with the dramatic changes, which included in the opening of the sec-

Melanie Kurt as Leonore.

ond act a believable justification for Florestan's aria. In addition, the concluding scene took place in daylight instead of the gloom of the dungeon, a change that delighted Beethoven and pleased audiences as well.

The complications of the several overtures written for what Beethoven called the "dearest child of my sorrow" may be unraveled thus: at the premiere, the work now known as *Leonore* No. 2 was played; in 1806 it was *Leonore* No. 3. An overture was not ready for the first 1814 performance; but for the second, the one now known as *Fidelio* was played. *Leonore* No. 1 was for many years believed to have been composed for a Prague performance—after Nos. 2 and 3—but later evidence seems to show that it was actually the first, and that Beethoven discarded it as too "light." Often today the *Fidelio* overture is played before the opera and the imposing *Leonore* No. 3 is inserted between the first and second scenes of Act II—a procedure which effectively holds up the action but invariably arouses a storm of applause.

Beethoven's usual painstaking habits are plainly shown in the notebooks for *Fidelio*; there are almost twenty sketches for Florestan's aria and ten for the chorus *Wer ein solches Weib*. This industry illustrates the fallacy of the idea that Beethoven wrote in "outbursts of feeling awakened by unfortunate love affairs," as it has been said of his creative work. Beethoven was composer first, man second.

Despite music which has made it immortal, *Fidelio* has had to overcome two disadvantages that hamper its acceptance by contemporary audiences. It is a *Singspiel*; that is, the action is advanced by spoken dialogue, while the emotions are expressed in music. The change from singing to speaking in opera is often a wrench to American sensibilities, in spite of the resemblance to the most typical American lyric form, the musical comedy.

Second, more than ordinary "suspension of disbelief" is necessary to accept the dramatic soprano vital to the role of Leonore as a man. Other "trouser" roles such as Octavian or Cherubino are more plausible, for they are supposed to be striplings, but Leonore is a mature woman who must masquerade as a man of twenty-five.

One political note is interesting: it seems that all is forgiven if the scene of the libretto is shifted out of its original country. Witness *Rigoletto* and *Un ballo in maschera*. Bouilly set his story in Spain, although it was said to be based on a Paris incident during the Reign of Terror following the French Revolution, when he himself occupied an official post.

That Beethoven never wrote another opera was not from want of trying. The wreckage of hopes and poet's offerings lies strewn from 1808 on—Goethe's *Faust*, Shakespeare's *Romeo and Juliet*, and a half dozen others. Beethoven's appetite for the stage was whetted by composing incidental music for Goethe's *Egmont* and August von Kotzebue's *The Ruins of Athens*, and he asked the latter for a libretto in 1812. But the two poets who commanded most of his attention were Heinrich von Collin (the author of *Coriolan*) and Franz Grillparzer. Collin's version of *Macbeth* absorbed Beethoven for several years, but the libretto was never finished. Collin's *Bradamante* contained too much supernatural material for the composer, who wanted real and heroic personages. Grillparzer also offered *Macbeth*; but it was his *Dragomira* that Beethoven brooded over longest. This was abandoned, however, in favor of his *Melusine*, eventually rejected

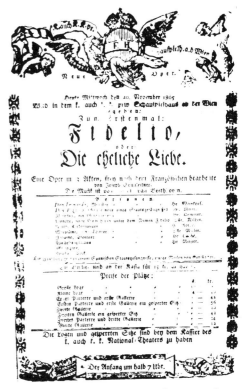

Playbill announcing the first performance of Fidelio.

19
BEETHOVEN

Fidelio

Text by Joseph Sonnleithner and
Georg Friedrich Treitschke.

LEONORE, KNOWN AS FIDELIO	*Soprano*
FLORESTAN	*Tenor*
DON PIZARRO	*Bass*
ROCCO	*Bass*
MARCELLINA	*Soprano*
JACQUINO	*Tenor*
DON FERNANDO	*Bass*

First Performance
Vienna, 20 November 1805.

by opera management as being too much like E.T.A. Hoffmann's *Undine*.

So *Fidelio* stands alone, its merits explained, according to Thayer, by Beethoven's "inborn genius, untiring industry, and the ambition to rival Cherubini;" its defects stemming from "want of practice and experience in operatic writing."

The composer in those years was already withdrawing into the introspection that would endure until his death. There was no place in that soul-searching for the artificialities of the stage; string quartets became the final testament.

ACT I. Ten years before the opera opens, the evil prison Governor Don Pizarro has incarcerated the young Spanish nobleman Florestan with no other cause than personal enmity. The arrest has not been recorded. Florestan's wife, Leonore, does not believe Pizarro's report that Florestan has died. She determines to find and rescue her husband, at last narrowing down the possibilities of his place of confinement to Pizarro's castle-fortress. She dons man's clothing and, calling herself Fidelio, is accepted as assistant by the jailor Rocco. Rocco's daughter Marcellina, though courted by the turnkey Jaquino, has

Fidelio Act II with Birgit Nilsson and Jon Vickers.

turned her affections to the newcomer, a fact not unobserved by her father.

The setting is the lodge of the prison. As the scene opens, Jacquino is quarreling with Marcellina about the date for their wedding. They are interrupted by visitors for whom Jacquino must open the gate. Marcellina deplores Jacquino's suffering, but at the same time expresses in a simple aria her hope for connubial bliss with Fidelio. The object of her affections enters, burdened with the post and provisions. Jacquino begins to realize that he is losing Marcellina's affections. In a celebrated quartet, Fidelio despairs at the misunderstanding, Marcellina is blissful, Rocco lenient, and Jacquino brokenhearted.

Rocco now announces that his daughter's marriage to Fidelio will take place the day after Don Pizarro departs for Seville, and injects some practicality into the emotional scene by extolling the power of money (the "Gold aria"). Fidelio professes to be delighted, but begs another boon: she would like to relieve Rocco of some of the heavy work inspecting the prison cells. Rocco protests that it is against orders; but yields as Marcellina joins in the plea. However, one dungeon remains out of bounds. Fidelio's further discreet questioning is interrupted by the ceremonious entrance of Don Pizarro and his guards. Pizarro reads a letter that informs him of the Minister's intention to release the victims of his arbitrary power; in a tempestuous aria he utters his resolve to plunge a dagger into Florestan's heart before the Minister arrives. He orders a guard to give a trumpet signal at the approach of Don Fernando, the Minister, then summons Rocco and orders him to kill the secret prisoner and dig a grave in the cell. When Rocco balks at murder, Pizarro claims that privilege for himself. But Rocco is to prepare the grave.

Fidelio overhears this plot. As the two men leave, she bursts into an agitated recitative, *Abscheulicher! Wo eilst du hin?* ("Fiend incarnate! What monstrous evil are you planning?") followed by an aria in which she invokes hope and love, determining to rescue Florestan.

Now a rather intrusive scene of bickering between Jacquino and Marcellina ensues, cut short by Rocco's return. Fidelio avoids any more discussion of marriage by begging Rocco to release the prisoners for an hour or so; the Governor will not return, she says, and the weather is fine. At last, Rocco agrees, and the cells are opened to admit the ragged, feeble wretches. Their joy at freedom is cut short by Pizarro's unexpected return; he has been warned by a guard. Fidelio has not found her husband among the horde, so concludes he must be the occupant of the secret dungeon. The acts ends with a big ensemble, everyone revealing his innermost feelings.

ACT II.   In the deep dungeon, Florestan, chained to the wall and almost at the end of his resistance, flares up in what he senses may be his last protest at his fate. His aria is a final roseate vision of his beloved wife. He sinks exhausted as Rocco and Fidelio descend the steep stairway. They begin to clear the opening of an old cistern that shall be Florestan's grave. At last, Fidelio manages to see the prisoner's face and hear his voice. With Rocco's permission, she gives the pitiful

Margarete Matzenauer as Leonore.

21
BEETHOVEN

Scene from Fidelio with Elizabeth Fretwell, John Hargreaves and Owen Brannigan, Sadler's Wells, London.

man a little wine and a bit of bread. Rocco is visibly moved by Florestan's suffering and Fidelio's kindness, but he must do his duty. He blows the whistle that will inform Pizarro all is ready. The Governor descends, wrapped in a great cape.

Confronting Florestan, he reveals his identity, and is about to perform the murder, when Fidelio intervenes, producing a pistol, proclaiming herself Florestan's wife. As she holds the villain at bay, the trumpet sounds, announcing the Minister's arrival. Jacquino and officers appear at the cell grating to confirm the prisoner's deliverance. After a vigorous quartet, Pizarro slinks away, followed by Rocco. The reunited couple proclaim their joy in a triumphant duet ("O namenlose Freude").

The scene changes to the castle courtyard (or variously to a great hall or an open space near the castle), where the populace has gathered to greet the Minister and the freed prisoners. Rocco begs for clemency for Florestan, who is immediately recognized by the Minister, and introduces Leonore, who is given the happy task of freeing her husband from chains. In a great chorus, the prizes of freedom and wifely loyalty are praised, while presumably Pizarro meets his fate, and Marcellina is reconciled to Jacquino.

VINCENZO BELLINI (Catania, Sicily, 3 November 1801 — Puteaux, near Paris, 23 September 1835). Like several other musical creators, Bellini died young, possibly with many achievements lost to the world, although he accomplished prodigious amounts of work and left a legacy of opera that is unique in its ravishing melody. He composed eleven operas within ten years, and although only three of them can boast currency in the world's repertoires — *La Sonnambula, I Puritani,* and most of all *Norma* — several others, notably *Il Pirata, I Capuleti e i Montecchi,* and *Beatrice di Tenda* are occasionally revived, most often in concert form.

After their initial successes, these operas went out of fashion as the number of singers capable of coping with their *bel canto* dwindled, and composers of more dramatic music came along. More recently, as singers of the caliber of Callas, Sutherland, Sills, and Caballé took up the cause of Bellini, Donizetti, and Rossini, these treasurable operas came back into favor. *Bel canto* requires not only a command of florid style but also a smooth legato line, variety of shading, and, in spite of opinions to the contrary, a keen dramatic sense. Prima donnas may no longer simply stand still and pour out glorious sounds (although some of them attempt to revert to this old-fashioned practice), but must bring out the passionate nature of most of these heroines, a few of whom, indeed, verge on madness.

Bellini's father was an organist and his grandfather a rather indifferent composer. The young man found a patron in the Sicilian Duke of Sammartino, who sent him to the Naples Conservatory, where Donizetti had studied. He composed two operas before meeting the distinguished librettist Felice Romani, who wrote librettos for seven Bellini operas, all of the better known ones except *I Puritani.* An unfortunate quarrel with Romani was not patched up until too late. Soon after *I Puritani's* premiere in Paris, Bellini died of an intestinal ailment that had plagued him over the years.

At the time of his death, he was working on three projects, all, ironically, later and more or less successfully set by other composers: *Maria di Rohan* (Donizetti), *Gustav III* (Verdi's *Un ballo in maschera*), and *Rienzi* (Wagner) — but all called by one authority "Projects like Phantoms."

Bellini's own description of how he worked, as quoted by William A.C. Lloyd, is worth looking at. After the choice of an interesting subject, "I study carefully the characters, the passions that dominate them, their sentiments, and their minds . . . knowing that music results from a variety of feelings and that passion can be expressed in many different modifications. . . . Shut in my room, I commence to declaim the parts of each person with all the heat of passion [observing] the inflections of my voice, the haste or languor which the situation demands, the accent, tone, and expression . . . and I find the motives and musical rhythms appropriate . . . . Then I write these and try them at the piano, and if I find that they correspond with the emotion that I feel, I judge that I may proceed, but in the contrary case I recommence and return to the work."

BELLINI'S FIRST REAL success, *La Sonnambula,* met with unrestrained enthusiasm from the Teatro Carcano in Milan on 6 March 1831, its two principals, Pasta and Rubini, veritable "angels" in the composer's sight. The opera traveled immediately to London with the same singers, and reached New York (in English) in 1835. It had the honor of being the first grand opera to be heard in two important American cities: Chicago in 1850 (after

Vincenzo Bellini.

the second performance, Chicago's first opera house, the Rice Theater, burned down), and San Francisco in 1851. Gerster and Patti graced the leading role in intervening years, then the Metropolitan performed it in its first season, 1883-84, with Sembrich and Campanini, and repeated it occasionally until 1935, when Lily Pons stitched her best *petit-point*, according to one critic. Then came a hiatus until 1962 when Sutherland provided a "Gobelin tapestry" by comparison. Bellini's music shows charm and a sweet innocence as befits the subject.

ACT I.   The scene is a Swiss village in the early nineteenth century. Amina and Elvino, a rich young landowner, are celebrating their betrothal, congratulated by everyone except the jealous Lisa, the innkeeper, who had hoped to marry Elvino herself. A stranger (actually Count Rodolfo, lord of the castle, returning after a long absence) pays marked attentions to Amina, arousing Elvino's anger. Teresa, Amina's stepmother, disperses the crowd by reminding them of the nocturnal apparition that frightens everyone. Rodolfo enters the inn, where Lisa visits him. She has discovered his identity and flirts shamelessly. Rodolfo is all too willing to meet her halfway, but they are interrupted by Amina, who enters Rodolfo's room through the window, obviously sleepwalking. Lisa retreats, leaving her handkerchief, which Rodolfo carelessly places on the bed post, then leaves Amina, feeling it would be tactless, if not dangerous, to waken her. But Lisa is bent on revenge, and summons Elvino and the villagers to witness Amina's shame. Elvino immediately repudiates her, mistaking her confusion upon awaking for guilt. A striking duet for the two estranged lovers is the climax of the act.

La Sonnambula

(*The Sleepwalker*)

Text by Felice Romani.

AMINA	*Soprano*
ELVINO	*Tenor*
LISA	*Mezzo-Soprano*
COUNT RODOLFO	*Bass*
ALESSIO,	*Bass*
A VILLAGER	

First Performance
Milan, 6 March 1831.

Scene from Act II of La Sonnambula.

ACT II.   In the first scene, villagers visit the castle to ask the Count to intercede with Elvino for Amina. But the young man, meeting his former fiancée, takes back the ring he'd given her. The second scene, near Teresa's mill, brings Rodolfo to plead with Elvino, explaining that Amina is a somnambulist. But Elvino now plans to marry Lisa. The enraged Teresa pulls out the handkerchief she has found in the Count's bedroom and it is identified as Lisa's. In the midst of this confusion, Elvino gets the proof he needs to believe in Amina's unconcious perambulations: the girl appears, sleepwalking, at the mill wheel. It is a perilous moment, and brings the villagers to prayer. A plank breaks (not always possible to show safely in production) but the girl (all too often a rather hefty specimen) reaches the other side. She kneels to pray for Elvino, then sings the most famous aria in the opera, "Ah, non credea mirarti" (scarcely could I believe it — that the flowers he gave me would wither so soon). When she wakens, her sorrow turns to bliss, for Elvino has replaced the ring on her finger and is gazing tenderly at her. Her joy is expressed in the brilliant cabaletta, "Ah! non giunge," one of the showpieces of Italian opera. Its tender sweetness and radiance have made it a favorite on the prima donna's concert program, even when the opera does not appear.

THE ROLE OF NORMA has been the pinnacle to be scaled by every soprano who claims to have the *bel canto* requirements, backed by the necessary dramatic force and extraordinary stamina. Lilli Lehmann once declared that she would rather sing three Brünnhildes than one Norma. Giuditta Pasta was the first to take it on; rather surprisingly, since she had previously been the lighter and even more florid heroine of *La Sonnambula*. But in those days, and through the times of Lehmann, singers were not compartmentalized as they are today, and even Nordica undertook both *Traviata* and the heavier Wagner. Giulia Grisi was the splendid Adalgisa of the first performance, then herself sang Norma at the New York Academy of Music in 1854, with her husband, Mario, as Pollione. The Metropolitan premiere was on 27 February 1890, with Lilli Lehmann singing the title role in German.

Norma calls for deeper characterization than previous Bellini operas, and more dramatic confrontations. Some of the music between the exalted solos, duets, and ensembles is not of the highest inspiration, but the listener is swept along by the power and the beauty of expressive vocalism.

ACT I.   The high priest Oroveso calls the Druids to the sacred grove, where he implores the gods to rouse his people to the destruction of the Romans, who occupy Gaul. He expects Norma to issue a call to war with the rising of the moon. As this group disperses, Pollione, Roman Pro-consul, and his confidant, Flavio, appear. Pollione confesses that he has cooled in his love for Norma, who has broken her priestess's vow and borne him two children. He has turned his affections to the younger temple virgin Adalgisa. The two men exit as the Druids return, Norma in their midst. She ascends the sacred altar, cuts mistletoe with a golden sickle and distributes it among her priestesses. She does not issue the expected call to arms, but rather invokes

Montserrat Caballé and Giorgio Tozzi in Norma.

Norma

Text by Felice Romani.

NORMA	*Soprano*
ADALGISA	*Soprano or Mezzo-Soprano*
POLLIONE	*Tenor*
OROVESO	*Bass*
FLAVIO	*Tenor*
CLOTILDE, NORMA'S NURSE	*Mezzo-Soprano*

First Performance
Milan, 26 December 1831.

Scene from Norma with Maria Callas, Mario Del Monaco, Cesare Siepi

peace — for she does not wish to harm her lover. She sings the most famous aria in the opera (and one which is the goal of every soprano): "Casta Diva," an invocation to the Queen of Heaven. Privately she prays that her love may be restored — Pollione has been evading her.

Still in the sacred grove, Adalgisa comes to meet Pollione, and against her better judgment is persuaded to flee with him to Rome.

ACT II. Outside Norma's dwelling, Adalgisa comes to confess her transgression. Norma, herself having sinned, sympathizes until she learns the identity of the girl's lover as Pollione enters. The trio that follows is one of the most exciting spots in the opera.

ACT III. Alone in her dwelling, Norma contemplates killing her two children, but repents of the idea. When Adalgisa arrives and, from loyalty to Norma, will renounce Pollione, the two sing the incandescent duet, "Mira, o Norma."

ACT IV: Oroveso and the chorus await Norma in the sacred grove. Norma, learning that Pollione has refused to return to her, calls for war, then as Pollione is dragged in (he has attempted to carry off Adalgisa and been caught), relents and asks to be left alone with him. Their two great duets are the climax of the opera. Realizing that Pollione is lost to her, Norma mounts the altar and announces a new victim — herself. To the horror of the crowd, she goes to the funeral pyre. Pollione, moved to pity and renewed love by her nobility, joins her in death.

IT WAS AT THE suggestion of Gioacchino Rossini, who befriended the younger composer in Paris, that Bellini submitted I Puritani to the Théâtre des Italiens, where it immediately became popular after its premiere and was soon heard in other operatic centers. For the first time in years, Bellini had to find a librettist other than Romani, and this proved discouraging. He finally settled on the rather dilettantish Count Pepoli; it was his slightly absurd story and undistinguished poetry that Bellini redeemed with what is perhaps his most beautiful score. The opera suffered the fate of other *bel canto* examples, going neglected for many years. One of its most recent revivals, at the Metropolitan in 1975-76, boasted singers — Joan Sutherland, Luciano Pavarotti, Sherrill Milnes, and James Morris — who rivaled in illustrious singing the original quartet: Grisi, Rubini, Tamburini, and Lablache — although of course as no living person had heard these early divinities, the comparison is purely speculative.

Although coloratura sopranos can more easily be tempted into the higher realm of birdsong that *Puritani* offers, tenors are not so easily found to render the high (and inevitable) D's (and one impossible high F for a Dauntless Dan). Tenors have taken suddenly ill before performances of *Puritani*, and replacements are not easy to come by. Still, a good, even if not perfect, performance is rewarding for Bellini's long, flowing, supple, sinuous lines, and glittering fioritura.

ACT I, Scene 1. The time is the English Civil War, the place, near Plymouth, in and near a fortress held for Cromwell by Lord Walton (Gualtiero). Sir Richard Forth (Riccardo), another Cromwell adherent, has been promised the hand of Walton's daughter, Elvira, but Walton's brother, Sir George (Giorgio) persuades her father to allow the girl to marry Lord Arthur Talbot (Arturo), a Stuart cavalier, whom she passionately loves. Soldiers greet the day; a prayer is heard from within the castle. In an aria and a duet with the officer, Bruno, Riccardo expresses his grief and rage at the situation. A fine martial duet, "Suoni la tromba" ends the scene.

Scene 2. In Elvira's apartment, the distraught girl (already showing signs of instability), still believes that she will have to marry Riccardo, but her uncle reassures her — she will wed her true love. In one of the meltingly lovely arias assigned to this sympathetic character, Giorgio relates how he has pacified his brother, and Elvira joins in his joy.

Scene 3. The third scene brings the whole assembly together in the Hall of Arms, as wedding preparations are afoot. Arturo sweetly tells his love in "A te, o cara" ("To thee, beloved"), and the other principals

Grisi as Norma.

I Puritani
(*The Puritans*)

Text by Count Pepoli.

LORD WALTON (GUALTIERO)	*Bass*
SIR GEORGE WALTON (GIORGIO)	*Bass*
LORD ARTHUR TALBOT (ARTURO)	*Tenor*
SIR RICHARD FORTH (RICCARDO)	*Baritone*
SIR BRUNO ROBERTSON (BRUNO)	*Tenor*
QUEEN HENTIETTA (ENRICHETTA)	*Soprano or Mezzo-Soprano*
ELVIRA	*Soprano*

First Performance
Paris, 25 January 1835.

Act II, Scene 4 from I Puritani.

and the chorus join in. Lord Walton hands Arturo a safe conduct for himself and Elvira through the Puritan lines; he will not attend the wedding as he must escort a prisoner to appear before Parliament. To Arturo's dismay the prisoner is discovered to be Queen Henrietta (Enrichetta), widow of Charles I, to whom he owes loyalty. He undertakes to save her, using the safe conduct. Elvira, reappearing in her wedding dress, sings the delicious polacca, "Son vergine vezzosa" ("I am a joyous maiden"), and generously places her wedding veil on Enrichetta's head, a rehearsal. But foolishly she leaves it there and although no one in the audience is fooled, this provides the disguise for Enrichetta's escape, after all have retired for final preparations. Riccardo gleefully observes Arturo's "defection" and makes the most of it when Elvira returns, heartbroken, and showing signs of her ensuing madness. A tremendous finale ensues, including some brilliant fireworks from the delirious heroine.

ACT II.   In the hall in the castle, there is general mourning for Elvira, and Giorgio (in the manner of Raimondo telling of Lucia's madness) informs the gathering in a beautiful and sorrowful aria "Cinta di fiori" ("Garlanded with flowers") how his niece is grieving. Riccardo enters in time to witness the girl herself, entering after a pitiful offstage plea either for hope or death. She sings one of the most beautiful melodies ever composed — the "Qui la voce" ("Hither his dear voice"), and a dazzling cabaletta. Riccardo and Giorgio are devastated, but the former will not yield to pleas that he forgive Arturo, and the two agree that if the culprit is present when the Puritan army attacks, he must be killed, although his ghost, along with Elvira's, will haunt Riccardo. This is one of the stentorian male duets of all time, "Suoni la tromba" ("Sound the trumpet!").

ACT III.   In a garden, during a storm, soldiers fail to capture Arturo, who has returned to his country and his beloved. He hears her voice but is forced by the presence of soldiers to hide himself, then reemerges to sing a pretty romance. At last Elvira enters, and regains her sanity almost at once when Arturo assures her of his faithfulness. The impassioned duet, "Vieni fra questa braccia" ("Come to these arms") requires two high D's from the tenor, and in the ensemble that follows the entrance of the company occurs that unique high F (which no tenor attempts today). Everyone (except Riccardo) is restored to happiness by the sudden news that the Stuarts are defeated and all prisoners forgiven. The volatile Elvira, threatened once more with madness at Arturo's capture, can now return to full sanity and joy.

ALBAN BERG (Vienna, 9 February 1885 – 24 December 1935). Three of Berg's best works — the Three Orchestral Pieces (Op. 6), the Kammerkonzert (Chamber Concerto), and the opera *Lulu* — are dedicated to Arnold Schönberg, the Viennese master who exerted the greatest influence on the younger composer. In his works Berg combined the tradition of Viennese music with newer forms, and exemplified the transition from past to present.

Wozzeck, Berg's first opera, was suggested by a performance in 1914 of a dramatic fragment by Georg Büchner (which in turn was based on an actual incident — Franz Wozzeck, the poor soldier, was a real person). The libretto occupied Berg for two years. The music shows a formal plan, each scene a musical form. The first act includes five "character pieces," the second a symphony in five movements, and the third contains six "inventions," (noted here at the beginning of each scene). The continuous music often allows only a few bars between scenes for scene changes. Unlike *Lulu*, *Wozzeck* cannot be said to be dodecaphonic, although with one exception there are no key signatures. The one exception is in the long interlude between the scene of Wozzeck's death and the finale, the musical and philosophical climax of the opera. There, a tonality (D minor) is noted.

Berg makes considerable use of *Sprechstimme* (musically defined speech), until then best known from Schönberg's *Pierrot Lunaire*: rhythm and pitch are prescribed, but each note is only "defined in the moment when it is articulated; immediately afterward the voice drops or rises as in natural speech" in the words of Erwin Stein, another pupil of Schönberg's.

Berg finished the music in 1921 but no performance seemed possible. As a compromise, the composer made a cycle of three musical fragments, which was performed at the festival of the Allgemeiner Deutscher Musikverein at Frankfurt-am-Main on 11 June 1924, under Hermann Scherchen. Berg immediately found himself the center of controversy, which was only heightened after the premiere of the complete opera under Erich Kleiber at the Berlin State Opera the following year. Long a storm center, *Wozzeck* is at last considered a "repertory" opera throughout the world.

For *Lulu*, Berg turned to Frank Wedekind's two tragedies, *Erdgeist* (Earth Spirit), and *Die Büchse der Pandora* (Pandora's Box); the characters of Lulu and several others appear in both works. At Berg's death, only the first two acts were finished in full score. International curiosity about the third act, which was kept hidden by Berg's widow — the opera being given with a skeletal form of action — has at last been appeased. The third act has been released, discovered to be almost complete, and realized for performance by Friedrich Cerha after the vocal score by Erwin Stein. The entire opera as Berg intended it had its world premiere at the Paris Opéra on 24 February 1979. The American premiere was given at Santa Fe, and occurred on 28 July 1979. *Lulu*, like *Wozzeck*, is composed in various set forms, but unlike the earlier opera it is entirely dodecaphonic, although with many expressive lyrical passages.

In the spring of 1935, Berg began work on a violin concerto, inspired by the death of the young daughter of Alma Mahler. Shortly after finishing the work in August, Berg suffered from a carbuncle, and after intense pain, died on Christmas Eve, at the zenith of his powers.

Alban Berg.

Wozzeck

Text by the composer.

WOZZECK	*Baritone*
DRUM MAJOR	*Tenor*
ANDRES	*Tenor*
CAPTAIN	*Tenor*
DOCTOR	*Bass*
MARIE	*Soprano*
MARGRET	*Contralto*
TWO APPRENTICES	*Baritone, Bass*
IDIOT	*Tenor*
MARIE'S CHILD	*Treble*

First Performance
Berlin, 14 December 1925.

ACT I. Musical form: *Five character pieces.*

Scene 1. *Suite.* In a German provincial town at the beginning of the nineteenth century, the Captain, sentimental, shallow, and given to empty moralizing, talks nervously to his soldier-servant Wozzeck, who is shaving him. Wozzeck is roused to protest when the Captain scolds him for having a child out of wedlock.

Scene 2. *Rhapsody on three chords.* Wozzeck's friend Andres is singing cheerfully while gathering sticks in a field near town, but Wozzeck believes the place to be cursed, and cries that the ground is quaking beneath his feet. He sees in the sunset only an all-consuming fire.

Scene 3. *Military March—Lullaby—Scena.* Marie, Wozzeck's sweetheart, looks longingly out her window at the swaggering Drum Major, who is leading the approaching band. When her neighbor Margret accuses her of promiscuity, she slams the window shut, takes her child in her arms, and sings a beautiful lullaby. Wozzeck knocks at the window, but refuses to come in or even to look at the child. He is full of wild fancies, and rushes off, leaving Marie terrified.

Scene 4. *Passacaglia (Theme and Variations).* The Doctor promises Wozzeck a pittance if he will play guinea pig for fantastic dietary experiments. He sadistically torments Wozzeck, and raves wildly about his own prospects for fame.

Scene 5. *Andante affetuoso (quasi Rondo).* In the street, Marie again admires the resplendent Drum Major. He embraces her, and she breaks away. But at his second attempt she does not resist; she disappears with him into her house.

ACT II. Musical form: *Symphony in Five Movements.*

Scene 1. *Sonata movement.* In a broken mirror, Marie admires her new earrings, a gift from the Drum Major. She frightens the child with a wanton song. Wozzeck enters unobserved, and questions her suspiciously about the earrings. She stammers that she has found them, but he does not believe her. He hands her money and goes out, leaving her remorseful.

Geraint Evans as Wozzeck.

Scene 2. *Invention and Fugue.* The Doctor, hurrying along the street, cautions the Captain about his flushed appearance and a possible stroke. As Wozzeck passes by both men turn their spleen on the unhappy man, taunting him with his "wife's" unfaithfulness. To their astonishment, Wozzeck reacts violently.

Scene 3. *Largo for chamber orchestra.* Wozzeck accuses Marie of infidelity, and when she gives a pert reply, moves as if to strike her. "Better a knifeblade in my heart than lay a hand on me!" she cries. In a dazed whisper, Wozzeck repeats the words: "Better a knifeblade."

Scene 4. *Scherzo with three trios and recapitulation* (two orchestras). In a beer garden, apprentices sing drunkenly while soldiers and girls dance. Wozzeck sees Marie and the Drum Major among the dancers and starts for the dance floor as the music ends and the couple lose themselves in the crowd. Andres conducts the soldiers in a lusty hunting ballad, after which an inebriated apprentice preaches a rambling sermon which reels with drunken logic. An Idiot creeps up to Wozzeck, who has kept apart from the jollity, and intones: "Joyful . . . joyful . . . and yet it reeks of blood!" Wozzeck cries out that there is a red mist before his eyes. The Drum Major and Marie resume their dance.

Scene 5. *Introduction and Rondo marziale.* In his barrack room, Wozzeck complains that he cannot sleep. The dance hall scene haunts him. Very drunk, the Drum Major staggers in, bragging of his conquest. He commands Wozzeck to drink with him. Wozzeck ignores him, whistling, and the Drum Major drags him out of bed. They wrestle, and Wozzeck is thrown to the floor. Andres mutters sleepily: "He bleeds . . . ." "One time after another," says Wozzeck, as the obsession with blood once again possesses him.

ACT III. Musical form: *Six inventions.*

Scene 1. *Invention on a Theme.* Marie compares the story of Mary Magdalene to her own life as she reads the Bible by candlelight. She alternately fondles and repels the child, then cries: "Savior . . . as Thou hadst mercy on her, have mercy now on me!"

Scene 2. *Invention on one note.* Reluctantly, Marie accompanies Wozzeck on a walk beside a pond away from town. He forces her to sit beside him on a bench, reflecting on their relationship. He kisses her, but so strangely that she trembles. She observes the moon rising; to Wozzeck it is like a blood-red iron. He takes out a knife and stabs her in the throat.

Scene 3. *Invention on a rhythm.* In the tavern, Wozzeck drinks wildly and roughly persuades Margret to dance with him. She sings; then, frightened, sees blood on his hand. "Blood! Blood!" is echoed by the girls and apprentices, as Wozzeck blunders out.

Scene 4. *Invention on a chord of six notes; invention on a key (D minor).* Wozzeck looks for his knife by the side of the pond, but stumbles on Marie's corpse, and cries: "What is that so like a crimson necklace? And was it well earned? The price of sinning? Murder! Murder! They'll soon be searching for me!" He finds the knife and throws it into the pond. Now it seems to him that the whole world is bathed in blood, and he walks into the pond to wash it off. "The water is blood!" he cries. He drowns.

The Captain and the Doctor enter and comment on the sound they have heard. "It groans like a dying man!" exclaims the Doctor. "The moon is red," comments the Captain. They depart quickly.

(The orchestral interlude here—in D minor—is a climax and a lament for the hero; seeming, according to Erwin Stein, to "address us directly instead of through the drama.")

Scene 5. *Invention on a continuous quaver-movement.* Marie's child plays apart from a group of children in the street. Others run in, telling him that his mother is dead. But the child does not comprehend. He continues his solitary game, calling out, "Hopp-hopp, hopp-hopp, hopp-hopp," as the curtain falls.

Lulu

Text by the composer,
after Frank Wedekind plays.

LULU	*Soprano*
COUNTESS GESCHWITZ	*Mezzo-Soprano*
WARDROOM MISTRESS	*Contralto*
(ACT I)/SCHOOLBOY	
(ACT II)/GROOM	
(ACT III)	

32
BERG

DR. GOLL (ACT I)/	*Speaking Role*
PROFESSOR (ACT III)	
PAINTER (ACT I)/	*Tenor*
NEGRO (ACT III)	
DR. SCHÖN (ACTS I,	*Baritone*
II)/JACK THE RIPPER	
(ACT III)	
ALWA	*Tenor*
SCHIGOLCH	*Bass*
ANIMAL TRAINER	*Bass*
(PROLOGUE)/RODRIGO	
(ACTS II, III)	
THE PRINCE (ACT I)/	*Tenor*
SERVANT (ACT II)/	
MARQUIS (ACT III)	
THEATER DIRECTOR	*Bass*
(ACT I)/POLICE COM-	
MISSIONER (ACT II)/	
BANKER (ACT III)	
15-YEAR OLD GIRL	*Soprano*
(ACT III)	
HER MOTHER	*Contralto*
(ACT III)	
DESIGNER (ACT III)	*Mezzo-Soprano*
SERVANT (ACT III)	*Baritone*

First Performance
Zurich, 2 June 1937.

First Complete Performance
Paris, 24 February 1979.

PROLOGUE.   An animal trainer introduces his circus troupe. His star is Lulu, whom he calls his "serpent." She has also been called the Eternal Feminine, a female Faust, a latter-day Lilith, a creature beyond good and evil.

ACT I, Scene 1. A Painter's studio where Lulu (now called Eva) is posing for her portrait, and Dr. Schön is watching the process. Alwa, the doctor's son, a writer, comes to take his father to a rehearsal of his play. The Painter is distracted from his easel, and begins to make advances to Lulu, who even climbs a ladder to avoid him. When she comes down, the Painter is once more in pursuit, and in this compromising situation they are discovered by Lulu's husband, Dr. Goll. He promptly dies of a stroke. The Painter is horrified, but Lulu is interested only in her inheritance. She goes to change into street clothes from the Pierrot costume she has worn for the painting.

Scene 2. Lulu and the Painter have been married for two years. Lulu is in a bleak mood when her husband joins her, for she has read the news that Dr. Schön has become engaged. The doorbell rings, the Painter admits a beggar, then goes off to work. The newcomer is Schigolch, an enigmatic old street musician, who is commonly supposed to be Lulu's father, but has probably been one of her lovers. The old man leaves as Dr. Schön enters. While realizing that Lulu still retains her hold on him, he tells her they must not meet again. She says: "If I belong to anyone on this earth, I belong to you." Schön has taken her off the streets a as child and taught her everything. But now he wants freedom. When the Painter returns, Schön reveals Lulu's sordid past. She has had several lovers, all of whom call her by a different name: to Schön, she is Mignon; to the Painter, Eva; and to Dr. Goll, Nelly. The Painter, unable to bear the revelation, locks himself in a room and cuts his throat. Lulu and Schön break in and find him. Alwa now returns with news—of a revolution in Paris—that his father will want to attend to in his newspaper, and Schön gratefully allows himself to be taken away; he fears a scandal from the present situation. Lulu sings to her own motive, as the curtain falls: "You'll marry me in the end!"

Scene 3. An extended orchestral interlude leads to a scene in Lulu's theater dressing room. She is dressing behind a screen for her dance performance, while Alwa pours champagne. She wonders if Dr. Schön will be in the audience; then she tells Alwa that a Prince wants to marry her and take her away. Alwa reminds her that he had begged his father to marry her after his mother's death. She goes on stage. The Prince enters, but soon there is a commotion outside. Lulu has seen Dr. Schön and his fiancée in the audience and has faked a faint. She is carried in, then revives as Dr. Schön enters hurriedly. He upbraids Lulu, then sending the others away, continues his tirade. But Lulu eventually breaks down his resistance and forces him to write a letter to his fiancée, in which he breaks their engagement.

ACT II, Scene 1. Lulu has married Dr. Schön, and in their elegant town house is now receiving the severely tailored Countess Geschwitz, who is obviously attracted to Lulu. Dr. Schön is jealous and resentful of this latest incursion, and when the Countess takes Lulu away with her, he feverishly imagines that he senses intruders and hunts vainly for them, pistol in hand. Lulu returns, showing unusual affection for her husband, so that he leads her away (presumably) to a bedroom. The Countess stealthily returns and hides, as Schigolch, Rodrigo (an athlete), and a Schoolboy enter. The boy is in love with Lulu, and Schigolch has promised to arrange a meeting. Schigolch now reveals that he is not Lulu's father, but a "suitor." The three hide as Lulu returns, and Alwa is announced. A servant, who also evinces a hopeless passion for Lulu, interrupts the intimate conversation between Lulu and Alwa, as the latter at last confesses his love for Lulu and kneels with his head in her lap. She responds by revealing that it was she who had years ago poisoned his mother. Dr. Schön, who has been observing all this, reveals himself and leads Alwa away, then returns as Rodrigo scuttles off. In a fury, Schön gives Lulu his gun, ordering her to shoot herself.

Stage design for Lulu by Gianni Ratto.

She fires a shot at the ceiling, and Schön takes the gun away from her. The suspicion that Rodrigo is still there and the discovery of the Countess Geschwitz further enrage him, and he thrusts the gun at Lulu, renewing his command to use it on herself. She counters with the suggestion of a divorce, and breaks away as he tries to wrest the gun from her. In a dramatic passage of great virtuosity, she defends herself: "If men have killed themselves for my sake, that does not lower my value . . . I have never pretended to be anything other than what I am." As her husband twists the gun in her hand toward her head, he is startled by the Schoolboy's appearance and turns away. Lulu fires five shots at his back. Still on her knees, she declares that he is the only man she has ever loved. Alwa, who enters, is horrified at Lulu's crime, and turns her over to the police. (A long orchestral interlude is accompanied in some productions by motion pictures or slides symbolically or realistically depicting Lulu's trial, condemnation, imprisonment, and escape.)

Scene 2. Two years later. The same room in Schön's house, but now shabby and neglected. Alwa, Countess Geschwitz, and Rodrigo (dressed as a footman to aid the escape plans) are waiting for Schigolch, who brings the necessary papers to get Lulu out of the country. Rodrigo plans to make Lulu his partner in an acrobatic turn and take her to Paris. Schigolch leads out the Countess, who will substitute for Lulu in the cholera ward of the hospital; the Countess has deliberately contracted cholera in order to do so. The Schoolboy rushes in, released from reform school, with a plan to rescue Lulu, but he is sent away believing her to be dead of cholera. Alwa and Rodrigo quarrel over the expenses and trouble in securing Lulu's release. At last she appears, supported by Schigolch. But she is so pale and wasted that Rodrigo disowns her as an athlete and rushes off. Schigolch gives Lulu the train tickets to Paris and exits. Now Lulu relates the circumstances of her escape through the Countess's heroic sacrifice. Lulu repays this typically: "And now the old horror will be shipped back to prison in my place."

Lulu begs Alwa to come to Paris with her. Responding to her ardor he begins to make passionate love to her. She murmurs: "Isn't this the sofa where your father bled to death?" But he either does not hear her or does not want to.

ACT III, Scene 1. In a Paris gambling salon, Alwa, Rodrigo, the Marquis, the Banker, the Journalist, Lulu, a fifteen-year-old and her Mother, the Designer, and the Countess Geschwitz are in animated conversation. Many of them have invested in the Jungfrau Cable Railway on the Banker's advice. The Marquis, a "Mädchenhändler," i.e. a trafficker in white slavery, threatens Lulu with exposure to the police for the murder of Dr. Schön if she will not go to Egypt as a highly paid prostitute. She protests that she cannot sell the only thing she has ever owned. She is further blackmailed by Rodrigo, and Schigolch comes in also to ask for money. Schigolch promises to "take care" of Rodrigo if Lulu will persuade the Countess Geschwitz to make a rendezvous at Schigolch's place with Rodrigo—and the Countess, still obsessed with Lulu, agrees. Now the Banker learns that all his—and the others'—investments have failed. Everyone leaves except Alwa. Lulu tells her young Groom to exchange clothes with her and escapes with Alwa as the Marquis brings the police.

*Joan Carroll as Lulu with
one of her victims, 1963,
Santa Fe Opera.*

Scene 2. London, a wretched attic, dark and fusty. Making her debut as a streetwalker, Lulu brings her first customer to the dishevelled
room as Alwa and Schigolch (who have fled with her) hide. This customer is a Professor, who comes and goes without speaking. The
Countess Geschwitz suddenly appears, having followed and found
them at last. She brings the portrait of Lulu which she has cut out of its
frame. For a moment, memories of a brighter life hold them all. The
Lulu takes to the street again, the Countess following her. Alwa refuses
to hide when Lulu brings in her next client, a Negro. When Alwa protests, the Negro fells him with a blow. Lulu rushes out into the street
once more. Schigolch emerges from hiding and goes out to a pub, thus
becoming the only survivor in the sad tale — possibly a hint that Lulu's
story will begin all over again. Geschwitz, having returned, is alone in
the room when Lulu brings in Jack the Ripper. Uncomfortable because
of the presence of Geschwitz, who is kneeling before Lulu's portrait,
and because of Lulu's suggestion that he stay the night, Jack turns to
leave, but Lulu persuades him to remain. They discuss money; Lulu
ends up giving *him* cash. When they are in the other room, Geschwitz
determines to go back to Germany, to fight for women's rights and to
study law. When she hears Lulu screaming: "No! No! No! No!"

Gerschwitz forces open the door, but Jack, coming out, stabs her as well. He washes his hands in a bowl, and complains that these people don't even have a towel. As he leaves, Geschwitz gasps: "My angel! I will stay near you—for eternity," and dies.

N.B. Berg intended that the characters in the third act should mirror the previous ones, so that Dr. Goll and the Professor are the same singer; as are the Painter and the Negro; and so on (see cast). The symmetry of the work is established as Lulu, who has killed Dr. Schön, is murdered in her turn by Jack the Ripper.

The Ghost of Hector.

Dido.

Costume designs for Les Troyens (1873-74 Metropolitan Opera Company Prod.). Sketches by Peter Wexler.

HECTOR BERLIOZ (Côte-Saint-André [Isère], 11 December 1803 – Paris, 8 March 1869). "A prophet is not without honor save in his own country." St. Matthew said it, and it applies most forcibly to the giant creator, Hector Berlioz, who never in a storm-torn, volatile life, found the respect—indeed, the adulation—due him from his compatriots or his adopted city, Paris. They could not understand his credo: "I belong to the religion of Beethoven, Weber, Gluck, and Spontini." This great liberator (from Wagner) of nineteenth century French music, the undoubted founder of French Romanticism, was too far ahead of his time in French eyes. He was greatly honored in Germany, where that prodigious patron of new musical thoughts, Franz Liszt, embraced and performed his music; and he associated in a kind of wary friendship with Wagner in London. He stubbornly maintained his integrity, trying to keep out of the way of "fools and madmen, and of the sophisticates who are able to make folly look like reason."

His emotional life was as troubled as his professional career; a disastrous marriage to the English actress Harriett Smithson caused him grief and humiliation, and added to his deep, lifelong sense of tragedy.

His non-operatic works made their way more easily in the world, although the difficulty of his orchestrations, with their emphasis on originality of color and complexity, daunted some early performers. Of his five symphonies, the *Symphonie Fantastique* is most widely played today, while violists find *Harold in Italy* a grateful vehicle. His "dramatic symphony" on *Romeo and Juliet*, with its solos and chorus, is occasionally heard. Quite popular is his oratorio, *L'Enfance du Christ*, and his "secular oratorio," *La Damnation de Faust*, has even been staged, although it does not lend itself entirely comfortably to dramatic presentation.

His three operas have not had their due, perhaps because, as he wrote to a patron, he was always succumbing to the temptation to make music "free and wild and sovereign," which usually meant sacrificing dramatic values. He insisted that the music "forcibly contain both the design and the coloring."

Benvenuto Cellini (1838) is a complex, elaborate work of some melodic appeal, seen in Europe today but rarely in America. Shakespeare (to whom Harriet introduced him) inspired his comedy based on *Much Ado About Nothing* and titled *Béatrice et Bénédict*. But his unqualified masterpiece is *Les Troyens*.

BECAUSE OF ITS overwhelming length (more than four hours for the complete duality of *La Prise de Troie* and *Les Troyens à Carthage*) and the almost insuperable difficulties of production, this grandest of operas has not been performed very often. Indeed, at its premiere in 1863, only the second half was given, and a complete showing was not possible until 1890, in Karlsruhe, Germany. Later performances occurred in several German cities, in England, and in American concert versions. Milan and Paris followed at last, in 1961 and 1962, San Francisco in 1966 and 1968, but the honor of the American premiere of the true "complete" version fell to Sarah Caldwell and her Opera Company of Boston in 1972. The Metropolitan mounted an elaborate production in 1973-74, with a later revival. The brilliant, subtle, and colorful orchestration and the severity of Part I yield to richness in Part II. The text is set with extreme felicity.

PART I. *La Prise de Troie.* The Trojans, rejoicing at the apparent withdrawal of the Greek army after ten years of siege, come out onto the plain, examining with great curiosity the gigantic horse the Greeks have left behind. Although Cassandra, daughter of King Priam, who has been given the gift of prophecy, urges her compatriots to "beware of the Greeks bearing gifts," the Trojans lug their new prize within the gates. A priest, Laocoön, also forsees doom and tries to destroy the horse, but he and his sons are crushed to death by two serpents—the gods are obviously favoring the Greeks. Those soldiers within the horse admit their army through the gate, and Troy is sacked. Cassandra's lover, Choroebus, is slain. Only Aeneas, warned by the ghost of Hector, escapes with his son, Ascanius. Cassandra persuades the women to take their own lives and as the invading army appears, stabs herself. All but a craven few follow suit.

Les Troyens
(*The Trojans*)

Text by the composer after Virgil.

Part I—La Prise de Troie
(*The Sack of Troy*)

CASSANDRA	*Soprano*
ASCANIUS	*Soprano*
HECUBA, WIFE OF PRIAM	*Mezzo-Soprano*
POLYXENA, DAUGHTER OF PRIAM	*Soprano*
AENEAS	*Tenor*
CHOROEBUS	*Baritone*
PANTHEUS, TROJAN PRIEST	*Bass*
GHOST OF HECTOR	*Bass*
PRIAM, KING OF TROY	*Bass*
ANDROMACHE, WIDOW OF HECTOR	*Mime*
ASTYNAX, HER SON	*Mime*
HELENUS, SON OF PRIAM	*Tenor*

37
BERLIOZ

Hector Berlioz, caricature by E. Carjat.

The Trojans, Part I finale with Nell Carter (center), La Scala, Milan.

Part II—Les Troyens à Carthage (*The Trojans in Carthage*)

DIDO	*Mezzo-Soprano or Soprano*
ANNA	*Contralto*
IOPAS, POET	*Tenor*
HYLAS, TROJAN	*Tenor*
SAILOR	
NARBAL	*Bass*
MERCURY	*Baritone*

(AENEAS, ASCANIUS, AND PANTHEUS APPEAR
ALSO. SMALLER PARTS
INCLUDE SOLDIERS AND GHOSTS.)

First Performance
Part II only, Paris, 4 November 1863.

Complete Performance
Karlsruhe, Germany, 5 and 6 December 1890.

PART II. *Les Troyens à Carthage*. Queen Dido, who has fled from Tyre with her court, has established a flourishing city on the African coast, and remains unmarried after the death of her husband, Sichaeus, although her sister Anna urges her to find another mate. The Trojans, on their way to found a new state, arrive under assumed identities. But when Narbal, Dido's minister, tells of a Numidian invasion, Aeneas reveals his identity and repels the invaders. Dido falls in love with the hero, to the disquiet of Narbal.

In a symphonic interlude, The Royal Hunt and Storm (often played on symphonic programs), naiads and satyrs disport themselves in the forest, dispersed by the royal hunting party. Dido is dressed as Diana, goddess of the hunt. A sudden storm drives Dido and Aeneas into a cave, and the music suggests that their love is consummated.

Aeneas is lulled into inactivity by Dido's love, and reclines beside her as they watch a ballet and listen to a song by the poet Iopas. Aeneas tells of Troy's history and downfall, then engages in a lengthy love duet with Dido. As they depart, the vision of Mercury appears, striking Aeneas's shield and crying: "Italy!" Aeneas must be summoned back to duty. The ghosts of Priam, Choroebus, Cassandra, and Hector appeal to him and he yields. Some of his men are reluctant to leave the comforts of Carthage, and Aeneas himself is torn between his obligation and his love for Dido. But at last the fleet is ready, and in spite of Dido's last plea, Aeneas commands the departure. Dido, in a tremendous outburst, determines to die. A great pyre is erected, Dido throws upon it her own veil and Aeneas's accoutrements, then mounts it herself and plunges her lover's sword into her breast.

There is magnificent music, both vocal and instrumental, in each of the two parts, and one noticeable feature is the Trojan March, which is heard first as the horse is dragged within the Trojan walls, and recurs at salient junctures. It is also a concert piece of great popularity.

GEORGES BIZET (Paris, 25 October 1838 — Bougival, 3 June 1875). In spite of the overwhelming popularity of *Carmen*, Georges Bizet was not a one-opera man. *Les Pêcheurs de Perles* (1863), charming but flawed, and the perhaps unjustly neglected one-act *Djamileh* (1872) both showed talent, but between them and the masterpiece *Carmen* is an almost unbelievable gulf. But an intervening work offers some clue to Bizet's sudden development: a set of twenty-seven pieces of incidental music to Alphonse Daudet's *L'Arlésienne*. The orchestration, for twenty-six players, is masterly. Some of the music still survives, notably as a ballet suite sometimes used in the last act of *Carmen*.

Nineteen stage works were projected but left unfinished. However, ten completed operas remain, of which the three mentioned above and the one-act operetta *Le Docteur Miracle* (1856-57) seem viable. *La Jolie Fille de Perth* (1866-67) is not only neglected but possibly negligible. Bizet wrote works in other forms, of which only a few retain currency—for chorus, for orchestra, for piano, and songs. The early Symphony in C is notable, both in the orchestral repertoire and as a Balanchine ballet.

Georges Bizet.

Célestine Galli-Marié, the original Carmen.

Gertrud Wettergren as Carmen.

Carmen

Text by Henri Meilhac
and Ludovic Halévy.

CARMEN	*Soprano, Mezzo-Soprano, or Contralto*
DON JOSE	*Tenor*
ESCAMILLO	*Baritone*
MICAELA	*Soprano*
ZUNIGA	*Bass*
EL DANCAIRO	*Baritone*
EL REMENDADO	*Tenor*
MORALES	*Baritone*
FRASQUITA	*Soprano*
MERCEDES	*Soprano or Mezzo-Soprano*
LILLAS PASTIA	*Mime*

First Performance
Paris, 3 March 1875.

Bizet's personal life, his doubt of his own abilities, his uncertainties and disappointments probably dictated the confused pattern of his output. His three years of early freedom in Rome as a Prix de Rome winner were succeeded by periods of trial and discouragement, alternating with occasional lighter moments. Only unhappiness resulted from his marriage to Genevièv Halévy—daughter of the composer of *La Juive* and cousin of Bizet's librettist, Ludovic Halévy—herself to serve later as the model for Proust's charm ing, heartless Duchesse de Guermantes.

The crowning irony of Bizet's career lies in his death at the moment his true masterpiece was gaining favor. He was just under thirty-seven, and thus joins the ranks of those geniuses cut off in full flower—Schubert, Mozart, Bellini. . . .

Meilhac and Halévy based the libretto for *Carmen* on a novelette by Prosper Mérimée. For the premiere in Vienna, 23 October 1875, the origina spoken dialogue (customary at the Opéra-Comique) was supplanted by reci tatives written by Ernest Guiraud. The original version, with dialogue, did not gain ground anywhere except in France until recently.

The Paris audience at the premiere was shocked by the "immoral" story and the unhappy ending. But *Carmen* soon captured the world and has been hailed as a masterpiece. With *Aida* and *La Bohème* as A and B, it is the C in popularity in the United States. Spain is the only Western country that does not approve, not recognizing any native flavor in the music. *Carmen* has been called the "perfect opera": it is said to contain no false note, no boring interlude, no intrusive or unimportant character. Even the whole some Micaela, not in Mérimée's story and considered by some critics to be an unnecessary sweetening, makes a good foil to the voluptuous, amoral Carmen.

José was central to Mérimée, but the librettists and Bizet bring Carmen front and center. She is never offstage after her reentry in the first act. Her character holds the deepest fascination for singers and audience alike. Galli-Marié was the first to sing the role, which lies within the vocal range of almost all women singers, although the temperamental demands cannot so easily be met by all. A woman can make a career out of Carmen, but migh find herself typecast forever. Emma Calvé, one of the most illustrious Carmens, had difficulty in getting any other role in America.

The dialogue of the original contains many details valuable to a more complete understanding of the story and characters. Several of these bits are included [in brackets] in the synopsis, where they occur in the original.

THE OVERTURE brings us immediately into the colorful world o Seville; the toreador's song is introduced, and then the threatenin theme that has been labeled "fate" leads into the first scene.

ACT I.   The crowd bustles to and fro in the Seville square which is flanked by a guardhouse and a cigarette factory. Moral es, a dragoon, hails the pretty young girl who is approaching. She i Micaela, who has come from the country to give a message to one of th corporals, Don José. Learning that he will soon be there, she leaves, bu promises to return. The relief guard arrives, preceded by a band o street boys imitating soldiers. As the guard changes, Morales tells Jos of his visitor. José replies that she is the one he loves—he has no interes in the cigarette girls Captain Zuniga asks him about. [Zuniga has just been assigned to this post, and is innocent of the neighborhood. In the course of their conversation, José tells Zuniga the story of his past: he is a Navarrais by the name of Lizzarabengoa, and an "old Christian." His Basque origin probably accounts for his pride and stubbornness. He once studied for the priesthood, but a weakness for a game of ball betrayed him into a quarrel with a lad from l'Alava. He won—possibly even killing his opponent—but was banished from his village. His mother accompanied him to a spot near Seville, and brought along the young orphan Micaela, whom she had befriended.] (In Mérimée's novel, José had already committed two murders before he killed the married Carmen: presumably at her instigation, he killed her ugly husband, García le Norgne, while the officer—Zuniga in the opera—also fell victim to his knife. To have adhered to Mérimée's plot in the opera would have considerably weakened the otherwise taut structure and the progress of the drama.)

The factory bell rings, and the cigarette workers spill into the square. [The "Cigarette Chorus" is followed, in the original dialogue, by a diverting sequence in which the men appeal to the girls for attention but are rejected in favor of their fragrant tobacco.]

Carmen enters, the cynosure of all eyes—except José's. Singing of the fickleness of love in the "Habanera," (which was adapted from a song by the Spanish-American Sebastian Yradier), she advances ever closer to the indifferent corporal, finally flinging a rose at his feet. After she and the others have returned to the factory, José picks up the flower, calling the girl a witch, but guiltily thrusting the flower within his jacket as Micaela approaches. The girl has brought a letter and a kiss from his mother. After a melodious duet, Micaela leaves, but promises to return. [He has begun to read the letter aloud, and knowing its contents, a suggestion that he marry her, Micaela is embarrassed.]

Program for Carmen with Enrico Caruso as Don José, Hamburger Stadt-Theater.

41
BIZET

Enrico Caruso and Geraldine Farrar in Carmen.

Scene from Act I of the first production of Carmen, 1875, Paris.

A commotion inside the factory erupts into the square. Carmen, it seems, has wounded another worker. A free-for-all ensues. Zuniga sends José into the factory to report. Carmen is brought out. [In dialogue, the women tell the story: Manuelita said that when she was rich, she would buy an ass to ride. Carmen jeered: "Why not get a broom instead?" Manuelita retorted that when further information about asses was needed, they would ask Carmen. Then the fight broke out. Approximately two additional pages of chorus excitement are in the original.]

Zuniga goes into the barracks to issue a warrant for Carmen's arrest, leaving her in José's charge. This is a fatal mistake; Carmen secures her freedom by singing the seductive "Seguidilla," promising to meet José at Lillas Pastia's inn. As they exit, Carmen breaks loose and escapes. José's breach of duty earns him a jail sentence.

ACT II. The gypsies and the soldiers are enjoying themselves at Lillas Pastia's, Carmen, Frasquita, and Mercédès prominent among them. Carmen sings the vivacious "Gypsy Song," joined by the others. Zuniga asks her to come with him, but she refuses. [Lillas Pastia, a speaking character in the original, has tried several times to get the officers to leave, and has given a signal to the girls not to go with them. Zuniga reminds Carmen that he once consigned her to prison; perhaps that is why she is cold to him.] Zuniga reveals to Carmen that the dragoon who went to prison for two months in her place is now free, though he has been demoted to the rank of a simple soldier. All are about to depart when the noise of a procession reaches them. It is Escamillo, the famous toreador. Zuniga asks him to join the company [in spite of Pastia's protests]. The hero of the ring is persuaded to sing a rousing salute to bravery and love (the "Toreador Song"). [In this all-too popular piece Bizet requested the baritone to sing the refrains "softly and fatuously," which would have further revealed the bullfighter's shallow character. But few singers obey.] Escamillo's attempts to win Carmen's favor are met with indifference; she also snubs Zuniga when he threatens to return.

The smugglers Dancairo and Remendado enter. [Pastia explains that they have come from Gibraltar and have hidden some English merchandise near the coast.] They need the girls—not to carry the bales, but to use their feminine wiles on any guards they meet. This is expressed in a sprightly quintet. Suddenly, Carmen asks to be left behind—she is in love. To their expostulations, she explains that he is a dragoon who has done her a service. Dancairo suggests that he may not come, but Carmen is triumphant as a jaunty marching song is heard outside. The others peer out the window and admire the approaching José, then the four retire as José enters. Carmen is delighted to see him. [She asks what became of the gold piece and the file she sent him. The latter, he says, he used to sharpen his lance, but he could not betray his honor by escaping. As for the gold piece—he tosses it on the table. Carmen cries out that it is a miracle, and summons Pastia to bring delicacies and wine. She gobbles the bonbons greedily, "like a child of six," as José comments.]

Carmen's careless mention that she has danced for his superior officers arouses his jealousy. She promises to dance for him also—at once. [She cannot find her castanets, so she breaks a plate and uses the fragments instead.] As she dances and sings "la, la, la," José hears a bugle sounding across the street and interrupts her. He must go. She upbraids him and tells him to go if he must be so law-abiding, but not to expect her to believe in his love. To prove it to her, he sings an impassioned avowal ("Flower Song"), but still she pretends to doubt him, saying that if he truly loved her, he would go with her far away into the mountains. He is appalled, yet ready to leave with her, when his retreat is cut off by the return of Zuniga. At the Captain's peremptory command that he depart at once, José stubbornly stands his ground and challenges his superior officer to a duel, a reckless act of insubordination. He is saved by the smugglers, who pinion Zuniga while José escapes with Carmen.

ACT III.   The smugglers rest at a mountain pass. They sing a lively song about the dangers and joys of their business. The moody José confesses that he worries about his mother, who lives close by. Carmen jeers, bidding him to go home. He threatens her, but she faces him down.

Frasquita and Mercédès draw out their fortune-telling cards and enter into a happy duet about the good luck they are promised. Carmen takes out her own cards, but her fortune is dark. Fatalistic, she knows her death is certain (the "Card Song"). Dancairo bids the smugglers to get ready to go, and tells José to watch behind them. The three girls sing

Emma Calvé as Carmen.

Lawrence Tibbett as Escamillo.

a merry song about their power to charm the customs officials. As everyone exits, a guide escorts Micaela in. She is looking for José. [The paid guide indulges in a lengthy dialogue with Micaela, warning her of a probable guard left behind, and praising her for her courage — she did not even show fright when they encountered a troupe of savage bulls, led by Escamillo.]

After the guide goes, Micaela confesses in an aria that invariably draws loud ovations, that she was indeed terrified but that God will protect her ("Je dis que rien ne m'épouvante"). (Bizet is supposed to have lifted this aria from an unfinished work of 1868, *La Coupe du Roi de Thulé*, which also contains strong evidence of the splendid third-act finale. Some believe the aria to have come from another abortive attempt, *Grisélidis* (1870-71).)

Micaela spies José about to fire his rifle, and quickly hides. But he is shooting at a stranger, now revealed as Escamillo. José welcomes the toreador warmly, but learning that he has come to seek Carmen, challenges him to a fight. The men draw their knives. [In the original are approximately five additional pages, in which Escamillo taunts José, saying that he knows Navarraise style and that José cannot win. He proves his point, but refuses to deal the death blow. After a breathing spell, they resume the duel; this time José's luck turns.] José breaks Escamillo's knife, and is about to complete his victory when the smugglers return. Carmen's intervention saves the toreador, who departs jauntily, inviting all those who love him — here he looks pointedly at Carmen — to come to his next bullfight. Carmen would follow him, but José restrains her. Micaela is discovered and pleads with José to come home, for his mother is dying. Carmen bids him contemptuously to leave, and he goes, but with a final threat that they will meet again.

Carmen Act IV with James McCracken and Marilyn Horne.

ACT IV [Scene 2 of Act III in the original].   After an entr'acte which shows a strong Spanish strain, the curtain rises on the space in front of the bullring. (A lavish ballet is often inserted here, accompanied by numbers from the *L'Arlésienne* Suite.) There is a brief dialogue between Zuniga and fruit vendors, omitted when the ballet is not performed.

The crowd jubilantly hails the bullfighters, chief among them Escamillo, who enters proudly with Carmen on his arm. The two join in a melodious love duet, after which everyone goes into the arena except Carmen and her two friends. Frasquita and Mercédès warn that José has come to find her, and that he looks desperate. They leave her at last.

José, ragged, unshaven, wild-eyed, slinks in. He piteously pleads with Carmen to return to him, but she rejects him with scorn. As his tone mounts feverishly, her stubbornness grows, until finally she flings his ring at him, enraged to the point of utter rashness. It is an irresistible challenge to José. As she attempts to push past him to enter the arena, where shouts of triumph for Escamillo are rising, he stabs her. She falls to the ground as the crowd pours out, stunned at the tragedy. José throws himself on Carmen's body, crying in despair: "You can arrest me! It is I who have killed her! Oh, my adored Carmen!"

Mary Garden as Carmen.

ARRIGO BOITO (Padua, 24 February 1852 – Milan, 10 June 1918). Although the opera world thinks of Boito mainly as the distinguished librettist for Verdi's *Otello* and *Falstaff* (and indeed they are considered his masterpieces), he is also highly regarded as the composer (and librettist) of *Mefistofele*. The idea of an opera on the Faust legend was conceived by Boito in Paris, where he had just heard Gounod's work (destined to be more popular than his.) *Mefistofele* created a *scandale* at its premiere at La Scala in 1868, pro and con factions becoming wildly disorderly and continuing the riot onto the street after the performance. One more hearing, and Boito withdrew the work, revising it considerably, so that it proved a success from then on, having, in 1880 alone, performances in Hamburg, London (in both Italian and English), Boston, and New York. The Metropolitan produced it in 1883 and revived it periodically for a time, as did La Scala and Covent Garden. With the Chicago Opera in earlier days, Chaliapin was a flamboyant devil, his figure, nude to the waist, painted grey. The spectacular production of the New York City Opera, remaining current, also reinforced the stardom of Norman Treigle, a "sniveling, malevolent impersonation of evil" (*Newsweek*) in a skin-tight, strategically decorated bodystocking; Samuel Ramey succeeded notably to the part.

Boito labored for almost half a century on another opera, *Nerone*, based on the Emperor Nero's misdeeds, but never brought it to completion. After his death, Arturo Toscanini revised its score and conducted it at La Scala in 1924. *Nerone* has been revived in Italy but has found no favor elsewhere.

The son of an Italian miniature painter and a Polish countess, Boito occupied an enviable place in the cultivated circles of the world. Greatly honored by his country not only for his musical prowess but for his poetic achievements, Boito came to the attention of Verdi first when he wrote the words for the conductor's *Hymn of the Nations*. But the literary man's caustic remarks about Italian opera alienated the proud composer, and a rapprochement was not effected until *Otello* was proposed. Among Boito's

Arrigo Boito.

Boris Christoff as Mefistofele, 1961, Lyric Opera of Chicago.

Mefistofele
(*Mephistopheles*)

Text by the composer.

MEFISTOFELE	*Bass*
FAUST	*Tenor*
MARGHERITA	*Soprano*
MARTA	*Contralto*
WAGNER	*Tenor*
ELENA	*Soprano*
PANTALIS	*Contralto*
NEREO	*Tenor*

Note: The roles in the second part are sometimes doubled with those in the first part.

First Performance: Milan, 5 March 1868.
Revised: Bologna, 1875.

other librettos is the complicated story of *La Gioconda* to Ponchielli's score. He also made excellent translations of Wagner's *Tristan und Isolde* and *Rienzi.*

BOITO, WRITING his opera in a prologue, four acts, and epilogue, endeavored to encompass the depth of Goethe's philosophy and at the same time tell the story of Faust and Marguerite, as Gounod had restricted himself to doing. Thus the opera sometimes seems to break into two dissimilar parts, and only a dazzling production and superb cast can draw it together.

PROLOGUE. In the nebulous regions of space, the invisible legions of angels, cherubs, and seraphs lift their voices in praise of the Creator. Mefistofele enters, sardonically echoing the greeting, and mocking the small human creatures on earth. He undertakes to lure the learned Faust to avowed evil; the wager is accepted by the angels; annoyed by the pious cherubs, Mefistofele vanishes. The five divisions of the music, between splendid choruses and the solo invective, sustain dramatic interest throughout.

ACT I. On Easter Sunday in Frankfurt-am-Main, festive crowds move in and out of the city gates. The aged Doctor Faust and his pupil Wagner are among them, followed by a mysterious Friar clad in grey, who disturbs the old philosopher. Wagner, however, scoffs, and Faust returns to his laboratory.

This scene opens with the serenely beautiful aria, "Dai campi, dai prati" ("From fields and meadows"). (The tune detective can notice a slight resemblance to a theme in Beethoven's *Kreutzer Sonata.*) As Faust opens a Bible, a horrid shriek is heard from the Friar, who has followed and hidden himself. When Faust makes the sacred sign of Solomon, the Friar throws off his cloak and reveals himself as the Devil, clad as a cavalier and carrying a black cloak. He introduces himself as "the spirit that denies all things," and whistles violently to illustrate his power to hiss at the world. He offers to take Faust with him, and obey all his commands on earth, reversing the conditions in afterlife. Faust, weary of life, agrees, saying that if one hour can be given him when he would ask it to stay, he will cheerfully let Hell engulf him. Mefistofele spreads his cloak so that they may fly through the air.

ACT II. In a garden, Faust (now called Henry) strolls with Margherita, while Mefistofele pairs off with Marta (variously called Margherita's mother, companion, and duenna). Margherita, in spite of misgivings about "Henry's" irreligious attitude, professes her love for him and accepts a sleeping draught to immobilize her overprotective mother. The scene ends with a delightful quartet.

Now Mefistofele whisks Faust off to the heights of the Brocken, where they witness a Witches' Sabbath amid raging elements, and Mefistofele is acknowledged ruler. The weird sisters present him with a glass globe to which he sings "Ecco il mondo" ("Behold the earth") and smashes it to bits.

Mefistofele, Act II, Scene 2, Witches' Sabbath, with Boris Christoff, Ilva Ligabue, Carlo Bergonzi, Vera Magrini, Christa Ludwig, 1961, Lyric Opera of Chicago.

Faust sees a vision of Margherita with a thin line of blood around her throat. The demons celebrate the destruction of the world.

ACT III.   In prison, Margherita lies half-crazed. She sings the exquisite "L'altra notte in fondo al mare" ("To the sea one night")—she has drowned her baby and is accused of poisoning her mother. Faust, observing, begs Mefistofele to save her, and enters to persuade her to fly. But Margherita is determined to die for her sins, and after a beautiful duet full of love and regret, "Lontano, lontano" ("Far, far away"), she expires and is saved, while the Devil claims Faust.

ACT IV.   The split in Boito's plan appears here, taken from the second part of Goethe's tragedy. Mefistofele escorts Faust to the shores of the Vale of Tempe, where he is enchanted by the beauty of Helen of Troy as she relates the history of her ill-fated city, and they pledge their love in an ecstatic duet. Mefistofele is miserable in the light and joy of this classical Sabbath.

EPILOGUE.   Mefistofele attempts to secure his bargain with Faust, who is now at the point of death, but the old man forestalls his evil genius by an appeal to the Holy Book, and dies, redeemed, while Mefistofele writhes under a shower of roses and beams of heavenly light. The chorus of Cherubim hails the happy outcome.

ALEXANDER PORFIRIEVITCH BORODIN (St. Petersburg, 11 November 1833–27 February 1887) was one of the most fascinating characters in musical history. A study in opposites, he divided his time, energy, and talents between science—in which he rose to lofty professional heights as a

Chaliapin as Mefistofele.

Program from 1935 performance of Prince Igor, Covent Garden, London.

48
BORODIN

Prince Igor

Text by the composer
after a play by V.V. Stassov.

PRINCE IGOR SVIZTOSLAVITCH	*Baritone*
YAROSLAVNA (HIS WIFE)	*Soprano*
VLADIMIR IGORI-VITCH (HIS SON)	*Tenor*
VLADIMIR YAROSLAVITCH, PRINCE GALITZKY	*Bass*
KHAN KONTCHAK	*Bass*
KHAN GZAK	*Bass*
KONTCHAKOVNA (KONTCHAK'S DAUGHTER)	*Mezzo-Soprano*
OVLOUR	*Tenor*
SKOULA	*Bass*
EROSHKA	*Tenor*
YAROSLAVNA'S NURSE	*Soprano*
YOUNG POLOVTSIAN MAIDEN	*Soprano*

First Performance
St. Petersburg, 4 November 1890.

chemist, lecturer, and author—and music, which absorbed him from age eight. He should have been a Gemini instead of a Scorpio. Although his total musical output was slender, its quality earned him a fine reputation and inclusion in the powerful Russian "Mighty Five," the others being Balakirev, Mussorgsky, Cui, and Rimsky-Korsakoff. Although happily married, he was often bombarded with with the attentions of young ladies; his serious side was lightened by his love of musical jokes. Liszt befriended him, as he had so many other gifted men. His symphony, songs, chamber and piano music had distinction and charm. Of several unfinished stage works, *Prince Igor* is the only one current, and even that had to be completed by Rimsky-Korsakoff and Glazounov after Borodin's death. Ill health beset him for years; he wrote his wife that it was "difficult to be a scientist, commissioner, artist, government official, philanthropist . . . doctor, and invalid—one ends by becoming only the invalid."

His original duality arose from his parentage—he was the illegitimate son of an elderly Prince and the young wife of an army doctor—the former Caucasian, the latter Russian. According to the law of the time, he was registered as the lawful son of his father's serf, Porfiry Borodin, and carried that name. This multi-talented man died of a heart attack at midnight after joyous high jinks at a fancy-dress ball.

Borodin's delightful music has received the distinction of serving as basis for a Broadway musical, *Kismet*, adapted by George Forrest and Robert Wright. One hit song, *Stranger in Paradise*, was taken from one of the Polovtsian Dances; another, *This Is My Beloved*, is based on the Nocturne from the String Quartet in D.

PROLOGUE. In the marketplace of Poutivl in 1185, Igor, Prince of Seversk, sets off with his son Vladimir to put down an attack by the Polovtsi, a Tartar tribe, in spite of an eclipse of the sun which the populace regards as an evil omen.

ACT I. Prince Vladimir Galitzky, the brother of Igor's wife Yaroslavna, has been left in charge and betrays his trust by carousing and trying to usurp power. His vigorous aria shows his aggressive character. Skoula and Eroshka, who have deserted the army, aid in stirring up the mob.

The scene changes to Yaroslavna's room, where she sings a beautiful arioso. She receives a group of girls, one of whose number has been abducted by Galitzky, who has refused their pleas for mercy. His triumph is complete when news comes that Igor has been defeated, and the Polovtsians are besieging the city.

ACT II. In the Polovtsian camp, Igor has given his word to Khan Kontchak that neither he nor his son will try to escape—and he keeps this word even when Ovlour, a convert to Christianity, offers him the opportunity. Vladimir has fallen in love with the Khan's daughter and she with him. In a great aria, the Khan offers his "guests" amusement, and soon the dancers appear for the series of dances that have become a part of every concert program. They end the act thrillingly.

Dance of the Polovetski.

ACT III.   A savage march precedes the entrance of Khan Gzak, full of his victory over the Russians. In the ensuing wild celebrations, another opportunity to escape is offered Igor and Vladimir. In spite of Kontchakovna's pleas, Vladimir leaves his love behind, and she vengefully informs the guard. Vladimir is recaptured, but the Khan, out of respect for Igor's point of view, keeps Vladimir as hostage, allowing him to live and marry his daughter. (In a recent New York City Opera version, Vladimir is killed trying to escape, and his body brought on as a warning to his father.)

ACT IV.   Yaroslavna mourns the loss of her husband and the sack of her city, but soon is comforted by the sight of Igor's approach. Eroshka and Skoula repent their evil ways and ring the town bell to summon the people to welcome their leader. Great rejoicing ends the opera.

Khan Kontchak.

Benjamin Britten as a young man.

BENJAMIN BRITTEN (Lowestoft, Suffolk, England, 22 November 1913 – 3 December 1976). It was 1941, and Benjamin Britten was in self-imposed exile from his native England in the United States, because of anti-war sentiments. He had already written several major works when he came across an article by E.M. Forster, about George Crabbe, a peculiarly English poet writing about a peculiarly English strip of East Coast, centering on the town of Aldeburgh. Britten's only operatic venture thus far had been that same year, an operetta entitled *Paul Bunyan*, based on a text by W.H. Auden and performed at Columbia University, then set aside until much later in Britten's life.

He reacted strongly to Crabbe's *The Borough*, which vividly portrayed the Suffolk coast where Britten had always lived. He and Peter Pears, the tenor and long-time companion who shared his exile, began to construct a scenario.

Serge Koussevitzky performed Britten's *Sinfonia da Requiem* with the Boston Symphony soon afterward, and commissioned an opera through the Koussevitzky Foundation. Britten began work on *Peter Grimes* after arriving home in April, 1942. He revised it after the premiere at Sadler's Wells in 1945, and it soon found favor all over the world.

Britten was forced by economics for several years to compose works on a smaller scale, producing the chamber operas *The Rape of Lucretia*, 1946 (concerning Tarquinius's violation of the virtuous matron); *Albert Herring*, 1947 (in which a village boy is chosen "King of the May"); a new realization of *The Beggar's Opera*, 1948; and *The Little Sweep*, or *Let's Make an Opera*, 1949, "an entertainment for young people." In 1951 he reset Purcell's *Dido and Aeneas* and also wrote the first large opera since *Peter Grimes*, an adaptation of Melville's *Billy Budd*. This dramatic tale of a sweet-tempered young seaman, who falls beneath the evil generated by a cruel master-at-arms on a British ship, was first seen in the United States in an NBC-TV production in 1952, then given at Indiana University. Professional productions appeared in Chicago in 1970, and revivals were mounted by both the Metropolitan and San Francisco Operas in 1978-79.

Britten's next opera, *Gloriana*, was composed in honor of Queen Elizabeth's coronation in 1953. It dealt frankly with the first Elizabeth's love for Essex, arousing a great deal of hostility. *The Turn of the Screw*, which set Henry James's enigmatic tale of the governess obsessed with the evil influences surrounding her two charges, has been hailed for its skill and atmosphere of eeriness. American companies, especially the New York City Opera, have mounted it with enthusiasm.

Other stage works were added: *Noye's Fludde*, 1958, a deceptively simple piece designed to be performed in church with few resources; *A Midsummer Night's Dream*, 1960, elaborate except for the "lean" Britten orchestra; and three church parables: *Curlew River*, *The Prodigal Son*, and *The Burning Fiery Furnace*. *Owen Wingrave*, on another Henry James story, was composed for television (1971) but also staged later. *Death in Venice*, based on Thomas Mann, was Britten's last opera.

This most gifted of British modernists has been prolific in other genres as well, writing for orchestra, chorus, chamber groups, instrumental soloists, and solo voice (very often for Peter Pears). Faithful to his birthplace, and to Crabbe's own locale, Britten founded the Aldeburgh Festival

Peter Pears in Britten's Curlew River, 1964, Covent Garden, London.

in 1948. Each year his and other composers' music is played in congenial surroundings, where his genius is commemorated since his death.

BECAUSE OF HIS obligation to Koussevitzky, Britten had to allow the American premiere of *Peter Grimes* to take place at the Berkshire Music Festival in 1946. He was obviously distressed at the idea of performance by "students," although he had brought along a favorite librettist-director, Eric Crozier, to assist Frederick Cohen in the direction, and a powerful, rising young conductor named Leonard Bernstein was in the pit. Britten was particularly disturbed because the Grimes played his scene of madness flat on the floor. "It is, after all, the climax of the opera," the composer complained.

The Metropolitan Opera produced the work in 1948 and 1949, and has revived it periodically since, as tenors come along who are able to cope with the exacting role—Jon Vickers notably.

Britten wrote in 1945: "For most of my life I have lived closely in touch with the sea. In *Grimes* I wanted to express my awareness of the perpetual struggle of men and women whose livelihood depends on the sea."

He rejected the Wagnerian "permanent melody" in favor of the classical "separate numbers." "One of my chief aims is to try to restore to the musical setting of the English language a brilliance, freedom, and vitality that have been curiously rare since the death of Purcell."

From the *Grimes* music, the composer drew a suite of "Sea Interludes," which is popular in orchestral repertoires.

The sea is the final antagonist for Peter Grimes, but the bigotry and spite of the villagers generate an enmity as strong and as vicious as the storms.

Before the opera opens, Peter is in trouble with the villagers. It takes two to manage a boat, but no one in the village will help Peter, so he hires young boys, then mistreats them brutally. The village is callous to this—"Grimes is at his exercise," is their comment—although they despise

Peter Grimes

Text by
Montague Slater.

PETER GRIMES	*Tenor*
APPRENTICE	*Mime*
ELLEN ORFORD	*Soprano*
CAPTAIN BALSTRODE	*Baritone*
AUNTIE	*Contralto*
TWO NIECES	*Sopranos*
BOB BOLES	*Tenor*
SWALLOW	*Bass*
MRS. SEDLEY	*Mezzo-Soprano*
REV. HORACE ADAMS	*Tenor*
NED KEENE	*Baritone*
HOBSON	*Bass*
DR. THORPE	*Mime*

First Performance
London, 7 June 1945.

him for his independence and pride. But now one of the boys has died, and the village sits in judgment.

PROLOGUE.   It is around the year 1830. In a room in the Moot Hall, Lawyer Swallow is cross-examining Peter about his apprentice's death after exposure at sea. The village characters are called on one by one for evidence, a device which serves to introduce them sharply. The widow, Mrs. Sedley, is particularly spiteful, provoking a chorus, "When women gossip, the result is someone doesn't sleep at night." Ellen Orford, the schoolmistress, has tried to help the boy and his master. Swallow announces a verdict of accidental death, but warns Peter not to get another boy; he should ask a woman's help instead. That is Peter's wish, but not until he has "stopped people's mouths" of their gossip. Ellen and Peter are left alone. She attempts to console him, and he is momentarily diverted from his rage and pain.

ACT I, Scene 1. In a street by the sea, Moot Hall, The Boar Tavern, the church porch, and Keene's Apothecary Shop are visible. The kindly, retired Captain Balstrode watches as fishermen come ashore and make for The Boar; the landlady, Auntie, greets them at the door; the Rector, Mrs. Sedley, and Ned Keene enter; Swallow calls "Good Morning!"; Bob Boles, Methodist, warns the ungodly — it is a typical Borough morning. (The chorus that describes the village life is one of two direct quotations from Crabbe: "O hang at open doors the net . . ."; the other is the closing chorus of Act III.) Balstrode and Keene go to help Peter with his boat. Keene says he has found a new apprentice for Peter, but Hobson, the carter, refuses to fetch the boy from the workhouse. Ellen offers to accompany Hobson and take care of the boy. The crowd mutters: "Because the Boro' is afraid, you who help will share the blame." Ellen answers sharply in an aria: "Let her among you without fault cast the first stone," and exits. Mrs. Sedley asks Keene in a whisper if he has secured her sleeping draught, laudanum. The quack says it will be in Hobson's next delivery. Balstrode excitedly points to an impending storm, and the crowd prays: "O tide that waits for no man, spare our coasts." Balstrode, alone with Peter, suggests that he leave the Borough. Peter, accustomed to his life there, refuses, and reveals his burning ambition to gain wealth and marry Ellen. As Balstrode angrily leaves him, Peter sings passionately: "What harbour shelters peace?" The wind rises.

Scene 2. The interior of The Boar, battened against the storm. Auntie admits Mrs. Sedley and pushes her into a corner to await Keene. Boles bursts in, shouting that the tide has broken over the Northern Road. The two Nieces, of ambiguous status, but conscious that they are the chief attraction of The Boar, tumble downstairs in their nightclothes — the storm has blown their windows in. Balstrode speaks slightingly of the two, and Auntie answers wrathfully: "A joke's a joke, and fun is fun, but say your grace and be polite for all that we have done." Bob Boles makes drunken advances to one of the Nieces, but is restrained by Balstrode, who begins a song, joined by the chorus: "We live and let live, and look, we keep our hands to ourselves." Keene forces the door open against the wind to announce that Grimes's hut has been undermined by the cliff falling. Grimes himself now enters, drenched and wildeyed. The others move away from him. He sings introspectively: "Now the Great Bear and Pleiades where earth moves are drawing up the clouds of human grief . . . . Who can turn skies back and begin again?" In the silence that follows, Boles tries to assault Grimes, but is again overpowered by Balstrode, who calls for a song. Keene begins a round, "Old Joe has gone fishing," in which three tunes are combined in an extraordinary tour de force in 7/4 time. Peter breaks in wildly but the others recover the original tune. At its climax, the door bursts open to admit Ellen, the carter, and the new apprentice, John, soaked and weary. Peter takes the boy roughly out into the storm in spite of Ellen's protests.

ACT II, Scene 1. A fine, sunny morning several weeks later.
The street is deserted until Ellen comes in with young John. She questions him about his life with Peter, but he does not answer and draws away, trying to hide a bruise under his torn shirt. Peter rushes in

Set Svanholm as Peter Grimes.

to take the boy, for the fish are running. As the church service is occasionally heard in the background, Peter and Ellen argue about the boy. Ellen cries desperately: "Were we wrong in what we planned to do?" When, in spite of his protests, she concludes that they have failed, he strikes her, and hurriedly takes the boy away. Auntie, Keene, and Boles, who have watched the scene from their windows, come out to join the church crowd, the men proposing a visit to Grimes to punish him. The mob's temper grows as its chant recurs: "Grimes is at his exercise." They set off to find him, led by Hobson beating his drum. Auntie, Ellen, and the Nieces (who sing as one) are left to ponder, in a lyrical trio, the relationship of woman to man: "Shall we smile or shall we weep or wait quietly until they sleep?"

Jon Vickers as Peter Grimes.

The Villagers in a scene from Act III of Peter Grimes, 1947, Covent Garden, London.

Scene 2. Peter's hut — an overturned boat on the edge of the cliff, with two doors, one leading to the road, the other giving onto the cliff. Grimes begins a long monologue, developing into an aria, which ranges in mood from chastisement of the boy, through urgency to get money and marry Ellen, to a thoughtful reverie on the hope of a more peaceful life. He grows wilder as he thinks he sees the ghost of the former apprentice, and the noise of the approaching crowd becomes louder.

John watches him in horror. Suddenly, as if to defy the investigating crowd, Grimes thrusts the boy out the cliff door, admonishing him to be careful. But a pitiful scream is heard as he falls. Grimes clambers after him, leaving only the quiet, shipshape hut to confound the villagers, who begin to believe their suspicions were unfounded.

ACT III, Scene 1. On a summer night, a dance is in progress in Moot Hall; we hear first a polka, then a barn dance. At first the stage is deserted, but a little later men are constantly seeking refreshment in The Boar. One of the Nieces runs down the steps of the Hall, pursued by Swallow, whose refrain is "Assign your prettiness to me; I'll seal the deed and take no fee." The second Niece joins and sings with the first that they are safe "provided the tête-à-tête's in threes." The disappointed Swallow reenters the inn, as Keene comes out. His pursuit of the girls is halted by Mrs. Sedley, who venomously accuses Grimes: "Murder most foul it is!" She continues to fulminate, nearly hidden by the darkness, as various characters call good-nights, and is still hidden when Ellen and Balstrode approach. They have seen Peter's boat, but he has disappeared. Worse, Ellen recognizes the boy's jersey, on which she had embroidered an anchor; it has been washed up by the tide. She sings the meditative aria: "Embroidery in childhood was a luxury of idleness." As they exit, Mrs. Sedley summons Swallow, and seeing Peter's boat, he once again, as Mayor of the Borough, forms a posse to hunt out Grimes. Sedley resumes her muttering: "Crime — that's my hobby," as the mob sets off, threatening: "Him who despises us we'll destroy . . . Peter Grimes!"

Scene 2. Peter is discovered near his boat, some hours later. A fog horn sounds distantly, and the weird calls of the crowd echo eerily. Grimes is wet and anguished, almost insane. He begins a poignant monologue: "Steady! There you are. Nearly home. What is home?" He suffers hallucinations about the dead apprentices, recalls the enmity of the village, the round about "Old Joe," and his love for Ellen. He curses the Borough, and is almost raving when Ellen and Balstrode find him. Peter echoes his previous question: "What harbour shelters peace?" Balstrode urges him towards his boat, commanding him to sail out until he loses sight of shore, then to sink the boat. The captain leads the sobbing Ellen away. The orchestra returns after the eerie silence, punctuated only by the voices and the fog horn.

Now dawn breaks. The posse returns, acknowledges failure, and disperses. The village regulars straggle in. Swallow notices a boat sinking at sea, but everyone else is indifferent. The chorus echoes Crabbe's original words: "To those who pass the Boro' sounds betray the cold beginning of another day . . . . In ceaseless motion comes and goes the tide." The Borough is back to normal.

Peter Grimes's adversaries, the citizens of the village.

55
BRITTEN

Portrait of Emmanuel Chabrier by Manet.

Louise Bérat as the mother in Louise.

(ALEXIS) EMMANUEL CHABRIER (Ambert, Puy de Dôme, 18 January 1841 – Paris, 13 September 1894). Really an amateur in music, forced by his father to practice law for eighteen years, Emmanuel Chabrier nevertheless attained a reputation in the illustrious circle of musicians and artists around him – Duparc, D'Indy, Debussy, Fauré, Messager, and the Impressionist painters, whose works he collected. His work took on a tinge of Wagnerism after he fell under the spell of Bayreuth, and this conflict with his strong French feeling is thought to have contributed to his later mental disorder. His most famous work today is the orchestral rhapsody, *España*, and the popular ballet, *Bourrée fantasque*, orchestrated from its original piano form. Of two light operas, *L'Education manquée* (one act, 1879) is performed by colleges and workshops, while the more elaborate *L'Etoile*, a mélange of mistaken identities, revenges, pardons, misadventures, and mixed love affairs, is not often heard in America. His *Gwendoline* (1886), showed heavy German influence. Best known is *Le Roi malgré lui*. Chabrier's brilliance, wit, and flair for comedy all find expression in this sparkling score.

Le Roi malgré lui (The King in Spite of Himself) is in three acts, with a libretto by Émile de Najac and Paul Burani, based on a comedy by F. Ancelot. It had its premiere at the Opéra-Comique, 18 May 1887. Like *L'Etoile*, it has a vastly complicated plot, in which Henri de Valois, the French king of Poland, tries to get out of his job and the Poles are all too willing to help. Henri changes identities with his close friend Comte de Nangis, and they go to a ball at Count Laski's, where Polish conspirators plan to kill the king, but are foiled by his disguise as Nangis. Alerted by Nangis's sweetheart, the slave Minka, and distracted by the presence of an old flame from Venice (the wife of the foolish Duc de Fritelli), Henri goes through a number of wild adventures before reaching an inn on the way to the Polish border. There the confusion is sorted out, and Henri, now favored by the Polish lords because of his gallantry, returns to the throne, in spite of himself. The music is lively, full of character, and brilliant, with some lovely arias and spirited ensembles.

GUSTAVE CHARPENTIER (Dieuze, Lorraine, 25 June 1860 – Paris, 18 February 1956). Looking like the true Bohemian, with flowing bow tie, pointed beard, and long hair, Gustave Charpentier lived the Bohemian life as well, in Paris, to which he had moved in 1885 from a small town. A pupil of Massenet at the conservatoire, he won the Prix de Rome in 1887 for his cantata *Didon*. One of the required works he sent home turned out to be the first act of his opera *Louise*. A cantata composed for a huge demonstration of workers, and the "coronation of the Muse" were also incorporated into the opera. In his Montmartre hideaway, he would have starved while composing the opera except for the unlimited credit extended him by a bakery. Strongly socialistic in opinion, he brought French music further along the path to independence from foreign influence by his use of naturalism. A man of the people, a consistent bard of democracy, he founded a conservatory for working girls and got them free tickets to concerts. He called *Louise* a "musical novel," rather than an opera. His only important work, it was an immense success at and after its premiere at the Opéra-Comique. Marthe Rioton, who created the title role, had to give way because of illness, and Mary Garden stepped in to her blazing first success. The opera has been extensively popular ever since. Garden sang it at the Manhattan Opera House in 1918; the Metropolitan mounted it in 1921 with Farrar; many have sung it since — Bori, Moore, Kirsten; Sills, Neblett, and Saunders have taken the role at the New York City Opera; Edvina was a charming Louise in London and Boston. Charpentier's sequel, *Julien*, which carries on the adventures of the hero, has not found much success.

ACT I.   In their modest apartment in Paris, the Father, the Mother, and their daughter Louise live out their drab lives. Louise has fallen violently in love with the poet Julien, whose window is opposite hers, and contrives to see him whenever her parents are out. They strongly disapprove; the Mother calls Julien "a pillar of the saloon"; the Father is secretly jealous of any man who approaches. Julien is serious and writes to ask for Louise's hand, but the Mother will not hear of it, and the Father puts off any further discussion. Louise dissolves in tears.

ACT II.   At five in the morning, the street at the foot of the hill of Montmartre is deserted. Various citizens go about their business, and Charpentier has used the actual street cries of peddlers — the coal woman, the ragpicker, the old-clothes man, and many others — to give the scene reality. The Night-Prowler, a symbol of the pleasures of Paris that Louise longs for, returns home from his revels. Julien and some friends approach the place where Louise works, but hide as the Mother brings the girl to work, looking suspiciously around her. Julien drags her

Mary Garden as Louise.

Louise

Text by the composer.

LOUISE	*Soprano*
HER MOTHER	*Contralto*
HER FATHER	*Bass*
JULIEN	*Tenor*
IRMA	*Soprano*
CAMILLE/ AN ERRAND GIRL/ ELISE/ BLANCHE/ A MILK WOMAN/ A NEWSPAPER GIRL/ MARGUERITE	*Sopranos*
A STREET-SWEEPER/ A YOUNG RAGPICKER/ A FOREWOMAN/ A COAL-GATHERER	*Mezzo-Sopranos*

57
CHARPENTIER

GERTRUDE/ SUZANNE/ MADELEINE	*Contraltos*
A NIGHT-PROWLER (NOCTAMBULE)/ A STUDENT/ AN OLD-CLOTHES MAN/ A KING OF FOOLS/ A PHILOSOPHER	*Tenors*
AN OLD BOHEMIAN/ A SONG WRITER/ A YOUNG POET/ A SCULPTOR/ TWO POLICEMEN/ AN APPRENTICE	*Baritones*
A RAGMAN/ A JUNKMAN/ A PAINTER/ A PHILOSOPHER	*Basses*

First Performance
Paris, 2 February 1900.

Vanni-Marcoux as the Father in Louise, Chicago Civic Opera.

out of the dressmaker's house, but is discouraged at the response to his letter and at her lack of spunk. In the work room of the dressmaker's establishment, the girls chatter and gossip and tease Louise about her lover, Irma singing a charming little song. Louise can stand it no longer; when Julien comes again to serenade, she walks out to join him.

ACT III.   The lovers rest in front of a small house at the top of Montmartre, with Paris spread before them. Louise sings the song that lingers most clearly in the memory: *Depuis le jour* ("Ever since the day when I gave myself to love"). The two rejoice in their freedom, then prepare for the Coronation of the Muse — in this case, Louise herself. Their mirth is interrupted by the entrance of the Mother. She tells Louise that the Father is ill, and promises Julien that Louise will be free to return to him if she will only come home now.

ACT IV.   The scene is the same as Act I. Louise is openly rebellious at the promise broken — she has been restrained and not allowed to rejoin Julien. The Father is grumpy and dissatisfied — he has been ill, and no longer shows the tenderness of other days to Louise, until she is about to retire; then he takes her on his knee and sings lovingly to her. But she demands her freedom. Paris itself is calling her, and at last she no longer resists. As she rushes out of her parents' home forever, the Father curses the city, and the curtain falls on his cry: "O Paris."

LUIGI CHERUBINI (Florence, 14 September 1760 — Paris, 15 March 1842) (christened Maria Luigi Carlo Zenobio Salvatore), whose music Beethoven admired above that of all others writing for the theater at that time, and who laid the foundation for the grand opera style in Paris, lived three distinct lives in composition. In the first, from 1780-91, he wrote motets and masses *a cappella* and light operas *à la* Neapolitan; the second, 1788-1816, produced the more serious operas, of which *Médée (Medea)* is the prime example. Another opera of this period, *Les Deux Journées* (in English known as The Water Carrier), being a "rescue opera," influenced Beethoven's *Fidelio* — indeed, the librettist, Bouilly, was the same for both.

The third phase of Cherubini's career was devoted almost entirely to religious music. His influence on French opera did not last very long, as he was soon supplanted by the livelier Boïeldieu and Auber, but through his Conservatoire position he molded most of the French composers of the first half of the nineteenth century. He wrote several operas for London, but none of lasting quality. Honors came to him late in life, and then all at once. He had been slighted by Napoleon, and this soured his already dour disposition.

Medea is not too frequently performed (and then almost always in Italian) because of its severity and the imperious demands of the soprano lead. Mme. Scio, the original protagonist, is supposed to have died from the exertions of the part; but it was a soaring triumph for Teresa Tietjens in the 'seventies and 'eighties. Maria Callas made a supreme Medea; Eileen Farrell a tremendously powerful one.

The spoken dialogue which peppered the original was set to music by Franz Lachner in 1854; it is his version which is generally used today.

Maria Callas in the title role of Medea, revived 1953 at the Florence Festival.

Médée
(*Medea*)

Text by François
Benoit Hoffman after Euripides.

MEDEA	*Soprano*
JASON	*Tenor*
GLAUCE	*Soprano*
CREON	*Bass*
NERIS	*Mezzo-Soprano*
TWO MAIDSERVANTS	*Sopranos*
CAPTAIN OF THE GUARD	*Baritone*

First Performance
Paris, 13 March 1797.

BEFORE THE OPERA begins, the fabulous Argonauts, with Jason at their head, have, after many tribulations, been successful in retrieving the Golden Fleece, which was appropriated by King Aetes of Colchis after he had killed its owner, Phrixus. (Phrixus is a relation of Jason, and also of the treacherous King Pelias, who had usurped the kingdom of Jason's father, and who sent Jason on this perilous quest). The climax of the voyage came when Medea, Aetes's daughter, who had saved Jason from many perils by her magic, and was condemned by the gods to love him forever, enabled him and the Argonauts to escape by killing her own brother and dismembering him, knowing that her father would stop to retrieve the pieces in order to give him decent burial. Then, married to Jason and with two sons, she found him wearying of her and turning to the daughter of King Creon of Corinth. (Jason and Medea had been forced to flee to Corinth from their home in Iolcos because Medea had wreaked a particularly vicious revenge on King Pelias: she had tricked his daughters into murdering him, ostensibly to restore him to youth.)

ACT I.   Creon's daughter Glauce is preparing for her wedding to Jason, still fearing Medea's vengeance although both Jason and Creon try to reassure her. Medea enters, and Creon threatens to

Painting for the curtain of Medea by Lucien Coutaud.

imprison her if she remains another day. He leaves her alone with Jason. In a duet of mounting power and classic splendor, she rails at his cruelty and faithlessness; with her he curses the Golden Fleece that lies at the root of their troubles; finally, he departs.

ACT II. Creon's palace to one side, the Temple of Hera to the other. Medea, fuming at her fate, determines to stay and face it for her children's sake, although her confidante, Neris, warns her that the mob is demanding her life. Creon enters, and urges Medea to flee, as he cannot guarantee her safety. Medea pleads her case strongly, but realizes she must lose, and begs just one day's delay. Creon reluctantly agrees, and after he departs, Medea sinks into brooding silence while Neris sings a beautiful aria, the last moment of tranquility before the denouement.

Jason appears, and touched by Medea's pretence of anguish for her children, permits them to stay with her until she leaves. She determines to kill them as well as her rival. To the latter end, she sends a poisoned crown and robe, once blessed by Phoebus Apollo, to the bride. The wedding procession begins and Medea curses it, seizes a burning brand from the altar of Hera, and vanishes.

ACT III. Medea appears in her true guise as a sorceress before the Temple of Hera, hears of Glauce's grateful reception of her gift, and gleefully notes the terrible outcome, as the bride's screams are heard. Neris takes the two children into the Temple, as Medea's resolve falters. But she regains her venom, and enters after them, knife drawn. As Jason appears with the crowd, Medea reemerges, terrible in her vengeance. The Temple bursts into flame as her last stroke.

The opera does not treat of Jason's life after the tragedy, but the legend has it that, aged and broken, he is sitting beside his old ship, the Argo, and is killed by the fall of a rotting beam — by the same agent that made him famous.

FRANCESCO CILÈA (Palmi, Calabria, 26 July 1866 — Varazza, 20 November 1950). *Adriana Lecouvreur* is the one opera of Cilèa's to hold the boards. Also an excellent composer for the piano, as well as a respected professor in Florence, Cilèa wrote four additional operas: *Gina* (1889); *La Tilda* (1892); *L'Arlesiana* (1897, to Daudet; Caruso scored an early success in the leading role); and *Gloriana* (1907). All were favorably received in their time.

Caruso also created the leading tenor role in *Adriana*, which brought him and the opera to international notice. Based on real characters, the opera is like a patchwork quilt: some pretty pieces but many dull ones. It is a favorite with prima donnas, who, in addition to singing a ravishing aria, get to enact a gripping death scene and recite at some length the *Phaedra* of Racine. Ada Giachetti, later to become Caruso's wife, sang the first London Adriana; the beautiful Lina Cavalieri was the Metropolitan's first. Revivals at the Met brought Renata Tebaldi (after a great deal of dissension) to her beloved role; Renata Scotto and Montserrat Caballé have also delighted in it there. Magda Olivero, herself a supreme actress, is one of the most refulgent Adrianas.

Montserrat Caballé as Adriana Lecouvreur.

Act III, Judgement of Paris ballet, Adriana Lecouvreur.

61
CILÈA

Adriana Lecouvreur

Text by Colautti from the play by Scribe and Legouvé.

ADRIANA LECOUVREUR	*Soprano*
MAURIZIO	*Tenor*
MICHONNET	*Baritone*
PRINCESSE DE BOUILLON	*Mezzo-Soprano*
PRINCE DE BOUILLON	*Bass*
L'ABATE DI CHAZEUIL	*Tenor*
MAJOR-DOMO	*Tenor*
MEMBERS OF THE COMPANY:	
MLLE. JOUVENOT	*Soprano*
MLLE. DANGEVILLE	*Mezzo-Soprano*
QUINAULT	*Bass*
POISSON	*Tenor*

First Performance
Milan, 26 November 1902.

ACT I.   The green room of the Comédie Française, Paris, 1730.
Adriana confesses to her mentor, the stage director Michonnet, that she loves a soldier (in reality the Count of Saxony), forestalling Michonnet's own declaration of love for her. Maurizio, however, is playing a double game: the Princesse de Bouillon is his mistress. Adriana, in a passionate interview, gives him violets for his buttonhole.

Renata Tebaldi and Aurelio Colzani in scene from Adriana Lecouvreur.

Pierrette Alarie and Gérard Souzay in scene from Il matrimonio segreto.

The prince himself, with an actress for a mistress, invites the company to the actress's villa after the show. Maurizio breaks a date with Adriana to be with the princess, but he is very upset because by now he loves Adriana.

ACT II.   At the villa, Maurizio hides the princess as the others enter. Adriana discovers his true identity and, unsuspecting, helps him smuggle the princess away from the villa. But he has given Adriana's violets to the princess, to calm her jealous suspicions. Michonnet gives Adriana a bracelet that the princess has dropped in her flight. And the princess has learned from Adriana herself that Maurizio is faithless.

ACT III.   Maurizio is on a secret government mission when the prince gives a great ball. The princess, recognizing Adriana by her voice, tells her that Maurizio is wounded, and gets the reaction she expects. Maurizio returns during this tense scene. A ballet intervenes, in which the Judgment of Paris gives the prize to the princess instead of to Venus. The princess now begins to goad Adriana, who produces the bracelet in revenge. The princess shrugs it off. Now Adriana is asked to recite, and declaims the speech from *Phaedra*, using Racine's words to brand the princess a strumpet. She is escorted out in disgrace and retires from the theater.

ACT IV.   Alone in her home and almost suicidal, Adriana receives Michonnet and members of the company who celebrate her birthday. She receives a gift — violets, the very ones she has given Maurizio. In their shriveled appearance, she sees the death of Maurizio's love. She presses the flowers to her face — a fatal gesture, for the princess has poisoned them. As Maurizio appears, protesting his love and proposing marriage, she forgives him. But it is too late; the princess's poison has worked, and Adriana dies in her lover's arms.

DOMENICO CIMAROSA (Aversa, Naples, 17 December 1749 — Venice, 11 January 1801). Of the sixty operas this gifted composer wrote, *Il matrimonio segreto (The Secret Marriage)* is the only one we know today, although others are doubtless worth reviving. Cimarosa lived and worked for several years in both Rome and Naples, composing for their operas, and having the satisfaction of seeing his works performed also in London, Paris, Vienna, and Dresden. In 1787 he was invited to be chamber composer to Catherine the Great of Russia; later he succeeded Salieri as Kapellmeister at the Viennese court. It was in Vienna that his most famous work had its premiere — which was so successful that at the end the emperor had supper served to the entire company, then demanded a repetition of the opera. Cimarosa's last years, after a triumphant return to Naples, were passed in sadness: he was imprisoned for favoring Napoleon when the French marched into Naples. After his release, he attempted to reach St. Petersburg, but died in Venice on the way.

IN BOLOGNA IN THE eighteenth century, the wealthy Geronimo lives with his sister, Fidalma, and his two daughters, Elisetta and Carolina.

Scene from Il matrimonio segreto.

Il Matrimonio Segreto

(*The Secret Marriage*)

Text by Giovanni Bertati after Colman's *The Clandestine Marriage.*

GERONIMO	*Bass*
ELISETTA	*Soprano*
CAROLINA	*Soprano*
FIDALMA	*Mezzo-Soprano*
COUNT ROBINSON	*Bass*
PAOLINO	*Tenor*

First Performance
Vienna, 7 February 1792.

The latter, the more attractive of the two, is secretly married to her father's bookkeeper, Paolino. Count Robinson, Paolino's former employer, arrives from England with the intention of marrying Elisetta. When he sees Carolina, however, he changes his mind. For obvious reasons, Elisetta and Fidalma plot to send Carolina away to a convent so that the coast will be clear for Elisetta to marry the count. Fidalma, for her part, has set her cap for Paolino. Geronimo, who has been promised by the count that he will require only half the dowry to marry Carolina, is happy with the situation and sends Paolino off with a letter to the mother superior of the convent. There is a scene of general confusion, with comings and goings and hidings and revelations, until at last Caroline and Paolino are able to reveal their marriage and all ends happily.

LUIGI DALLAPICCOLA (Pisino, 3 February 1904 – Florence, 19 February 1975). One of the most celebrated twelve-tone composers of Italy, Dallapiccola was highly respected for his solo, chamber, and orchestral music, in which he used the formal understructure of dodecaphonism but still conveyed decided lyricism. He wrote especially well for the voice, and at least one of his three operas, *Il Prigioniero*, is current. The one-act *Volo di notte* (*Night Flight*), based on Antoine de Saint-Exupéry's *Vol de nuit* (premiere, Florence, 18 May 1940), is a highly emotional account of the tension in a small airline office in Buenos Aires, where three mail flights are expected to

Il Prigioniero
(*The Prisoner*)

Text by the composer after "La Torture par l'espérance" by Count Villiers de l'Isle-Adam and "La Légende d'Ulenspiegel et de Lamme Goedzak" by Charles de Coster.

THE PRISONER	*Baritone*
JAILER/GRAND INQUISITOR	*Tenor*
THE MOTHER	*Soprano*
TWO PRIESTS	*Tenor, Baritone*
FRA REDEMPTOR	*Mime*

First Performance
Turin, 1 December 1949.

land, proving that night flying is feasible. Two are safe, but the third, despite the feverish, personal instructions of the radio operator, is lost. The pilot's wife and the staff condemn him for the disaster, but the director sternly sends out another mail plane "another crew up into the unknown . . . maybe to their death . . . certainly into the future."

Dallapiccola's third opera, *Ulisse* (premiere Berlin, 20 September 1969), is an account of the hero's wanderings after the fall of Troy.

IL PRIGIONIERO has had several United States performances since its premiere at the Juilliard School, 16 March 1951. Notable among these were the New York City Opera's production, 29 September 1960, and the San Francisco Opera's revival, 3 October 1979. The story reflects the composer's sympathy for prisoners.

In Saragozza, Spain, in the second half of the sixteenth century, a Flemish patriot has been imprisoned and tortured by the Spanish Inquisition. His mother visits him, and he tells her of the kindly Jailer, who has called him "brother," and filled him with hope. The Jailer reinforces this sanguinity by relating a Flemish victory. Then the Prisoner finds his cell door open, and cautiously creeps down a long, dark passageway. No one stops him, as he reaches a beautiful garden and believes himself free. But now the Grand Inquisitor (who was the Jailer), holds him fast, repeating "My brother." His final torture has been hope, he realizes, as he is led to the stake.

Scene from Il Prigioniero with Scipio Colombo as the Prisoner and Amy Delorie as the Mother, 1962, Holland Festival.

(ACHILLE) CLAUDE DEBUSSY (Saint-Germain-en-Laye, 22 August 1862 – Paris 25 March 1918). No artist in the history of French music ever arrived more precisely at his appointed time than Claude Debussy (he dropped the Achille at about the time he completed *Pelléas et Mélisande*). His new sounds and new harmonies launched Debussy into the forefront of French music, established him there as unique, and left him without a successor – or even important imitators. This music was grounded in a workmanlike precision that stamped him as a classicist, though he was not recognized as such for quite a while. He scorned the appellation "impressionist," which was descriptive only of the new theories of the contemporary painters about the effects of light and vision on color and forms. "What I am trying to do, he explained, "is create a kind of reality."

Several musicians of the day were his friends – Satie, himself an original to the point of eccentricity, exerted great influence; and Debussy had friendly contact with Chabrier, Chausson, and others. Several were totally unsympathetic, even antagonistic, as is understandable. For a long time deeply influenced by Wagner, Debussy eventually overcame the "ghost of old Klingsor"; the Russians – whom he first encountered in visits to Tchaikovsky's patroness the wealthy Nadezhda von Meck – lingered with him, especially after his acquaintance with Mussorgsky's exhibition, and found their way into his creative imagination.

But it was the "Symbolist" poets who affected him most deeply – Mallarmé, Verlaine, Louÿs, De Régnier, Mourey, Baudelaire; and above all, the brooding shadow of the American poet, Edgar Allen Poe.

After his disillusionment with Bayreuth, Debussy wrote to his composition teacher Ernest Guiraud of his longing for "a poet-librettist who will only hint at things . . . who will create characters whose history and abode belong to no place or period . . . who will not despotically impose set scenes upon me, but will allow me, here and there, to surpass him in artistry, consummate his work." He wanted no long, ponderous acts, but brief, fluid episodes, and his characters should not "argue endlessly" but should submit to life and to destiny. The music he meant to create should be "a universal and essential psychic conception . . . for music begins where speech fails." He wanted to express the inexpressible, to create new forms "in which musical voices will be wedded to instruments tuned to those voices, discreetly mingling with their harmonious periods the echoes of dreams and the plaintive murmur of music."

What more perfect description of the opera that eventually evolved: *Pelléas et Mélisande!*

Tailored to fit Debussy's requirements was the Belgian poet-dramatist Maurice Maeterlinck. Debussy had known of him before he came across a copy of *Pelléas* in 1892 and saw a performance of the play in 1893. He paid a visit to Ghent to get formal permission from the author to set *Pelléas*, even securing the proud Maeterlinck's agreement to several large cuts. (Because these are important omissions of symbolic scenes, they will be noted in their places in the synopsis.)

Although initially fired by the idea, Debussy took almost a decade to finish the opera, reworking parts of it many times. After it had been accepted by the Opéra-Comique, the composer's affinity with the playwright suffered a complete collapse because of the choice of the young Scottish soprano Mary Garden to sing Mélisande. Maeterlinck had counted on his

Claude Debussy.

65
DEBUSSY

Pelléas and Mélisande, drawing by J. Quentin Jaxon.

Martial Singher as Pelléas.

common-law wife Georgette Leblanc singing the role. The playwright was furious and did everything he could to ensure the ruin of the opera. It was a period of agitation for the composer. During rehearsals he was forced to add orchestral interludes to allow for scene changes, among other trying vicissitudes. However, these turned out to be most telling and beautiful elements, each foreshadowing the events and emotions of the scene to come.

There were many hostile reactions to *Pelléas* after its premiere, but very soon the work was accorded a *succès fou,* not the less by virtue of a fanatical following contemptuously dubbed "Pelléastres,"—who rendered a kind of adulation that sickened Debussy and affected his entire future. Never afterward did he complete a work for the lyric stage, although he made many abortive attempts (but two of his most famous orchestral works—*La Mer* and *Images,* as well as many piano and solo voice works and the incidental music, and the *Martyr de Saint-Sebastien* were issued between 1902 and his death).

Poe's haunting tale, *The Fall of the House of Usher,* preoccupied him most deeply. He had completed setting only part of it when he died, and that part was considered undecipherable. Yet it has been reconstructed and found to be extremely interesting and beautiful.

PELLÉAS IS ONE of the few operas to be set directly to a play; two others are Richard Strauss's *Salome* (to Oscar Wilde), and *L'Amore dei tre re,* by Italo Montemezzi, to Sem Benelli's play.

Mary Garden remained for many years the perfect embodiment of Mélisande; in voice and appearance she was the mysterious being who moved in shadows to an inevitable goal—death through love. Her long golden hair became a symbol, an indispensable talisman. Garden and Debussy, on a visit to London to see Sarah Bernhardt (who often played men's parts) as Pelléas and Mrs. Patrick Campbell as Mélisande in the play, were outraged by the latter's long black tresses. A New York City Opera soprano also violated tradition by donning a black wig—but for one time only.

At Garden's insistence, Oscar Hammerstein imported virtually the entire original cast to New York for the American premiere of the opera in 1908: Jean Périer (Pelléas), and Hector Dufranne (Goulaud) among them. Garden and Louise Edvina were the heroines of the Boston Opera productions, 1911-13, and Georgette Leblanc at last got to sing Mélisande, also performing in the play given in tandem with the opera in Boston. Vanni Marcoux, the remarkable baritone, made his American debut at one of these performances. André Caplet, Debussy's close friend, conducted. Garden then sang the work with the Chicago Opera, but the Metropolitan did not display it until 1925. Maggie Teyte, who succeeded Garden in Paris, did not do the role in the United States until 1948, when she was long past believability and the New York City Opera production was one of the most awkward on record; nevertheless it served to introduce a charming Pelléas, Theodor Uppman. Other high baritones have assumed this role with success, notably Martial Singher, who partnered Bidu Sayao in many Metropolitan performances—after the first series, which starred Lucrezia Bori and tenor Edward Johnson. Richard Stilwell is another baritone Pelléas, as is Dale Duesing. Famous Goulauds have been Lawrence Tibbett and John Brownlee; Alexander Kipnis was a treasurable Arkel. *Pelléas* continues to be a jewel in the repertory of almost every world opera, and new young singers come along to vie for honors: Teresa Stratas and Frederica von Stade among them. The two star-crossed lovers should never cease to draw wondering, rapturous attention from audiences.

The overall setting is Allemonde, which may be taken to mean "Everyland," or none known at all—Debussy's exact specification. Garden placed it in dreary Northland, but nothing so specific is desirable, since symbolism plays so weighty a part in this story.

ACT I, Scene 1. Prince Golaud has been sent by his grandfather Arkel to seek alliance with Princess Ursula, thus to mend fortunes. He has lost his way in a strange land while hunting, and in a deep forest comes upon a well beside which crouches a beautiful maiden. She responds with terror to his questions, shrinks away from his comforting hand, and threatens to throw herself in the well if he tries to retrieve a crown which sparkles deep in the water. He urges her to go with him, but she refuses; however, as he moves away, she runs after him.

(A Prologue was omitted, in which a group of servants calls to a castle porter to open the great doors.)

Scene 2. In Arkel's castle, Geneviève, the mother of Golaud and Pelléas, reads the old king a letter from Golaud. He has married the mysterious Mélisande and asks permission to come home in spite of having disobeyed his grandfather's wishes. If he is welcome, a light is to be shown in the tower nearest the sea. Arkel, in spite of his disappointment, remarks that he has never put himself at cross purposes with destiny; perhaps there are no useless events. The lamp is to be lighted. Pelléas enters reading a letter from his friend Marcellus, who is fatally ill. He wishes to go to him, but Arkel restrains him, commenting that Pelléas's own father is also gravely ill, and the young man must remain. Thus fate is sealed.

Pelléas et Mélisande
(Pelléas and Mélisande)

Text by Maurice Maeterlinck.

MELISANDE	*Soprano*
PELLEAS	*Tenor or High Baritone*
GOLAUD	*Baritone*
ARKEL	*Bass*
GENEVIEVE	*Contralto*
YNIOLD	*Soprano or Boy Soprano*
A PHYSICIAN	*Bass*

First Performance
Paris, 30 April 1902.

67
DEBUSSY

Dale Duesing and Maria Ewing in the title roles of Pelléas and Mélisande, 1979, San Francisco Opera.

Mary Garden as Mélisande, 1902,
Opéra-Comique, Paris.

Scene 3. In the gardens, Mélisande notices the gloom surrounding the castle; Geneviève attempts to lighten her mood. Pelléas finds them and there is immediate tension. Fog and mist hide the coast, but a great ship sets out — it is the very vessel that brought Mélisande there. Geneviève bids Pelléas to escort Mélisande back to the castle. He would take her hand, but her arms are full of flowers, so he gently supports her arm. As they go, he remarks that he may go away the next day. Plaintively, she asks why.

ACT II, Scene 1. Pelléas has brought Mélisande to a deserted fountain in the park, and tells her that the waters had formerly made the blind see. But since the king himself is nearly blind, no one goes there anymore. Mélisande lies at the edge of the fountain, attempting to reach the bottom with her hand, but instead her long hair falls into the water. Pelléas is astounded at its length: Yes, it is longer than I, she says. He questions her about her meeting with Golaud, but she is evasive and leans further over the water, beginning to toss her wedding ring into the air. Inevitably this bond with her husband falls into the water, irretrievable. Nor should they find others, she remarks strangely. Pelléas advises her to tell the truth to Golaud.

Scene 2. At the very moment that Mélisande has lost the ring, Golaud has been wounded by his horse's sudden plunge against a tree. He refuses the ministrations of Mélisande, and is distressed as she begins to weep. She says she is ill — she is not happy there. Who has made her unhappy? He names everyone — she catches his reference to Pelléas and says, No, it is not he. It is something beyond her, stronger than herself. Pelléas does not like her, she believes. Golaud reassures her; he is young, he will change. And the dark days are gone, so that she can see the sky as she wishes. He takes her hands and with horror notes the absence of the ring. Now she tells her first lie: she has lost it in a grotto while gathering sea shells for the little Yniold, Golaud's son by a former wife. Golaud immediately tells her to take Pelléas and go search for the ring. She echoes her cry: "I am not happy!"

Scene 3. In their futile quest, the two young people have penetrated into a deep grotto, where the darkness is palpable. Pelléas in some excitement describes it as beautiful, but Mélisande feels only fright. A sudden shaft of moonlight reveals three bodies huddled asleep against a boulder. Pelléas explains that there is a famine and the poor seek shelter there. They leave, their problem unresolved.

(Scene 4 of the play was omitted. In it Arkel renews his disapproval of Pelléas's journey to his friend, who is now dead. Pelléas agrees to stay.)

(ACT III, Scene 1 of the play was also omitted. It shows the possibly mischievous character of Yniold, who as a lonely child pokes and pries into his elders' actions and feelings. He enters a room where Pelléas and Mélisande are alone, distracts them with his chatter, and voices his premonition that Mélisande is going away. Golaud, who has been hunting, returns unexpectedly, is met by Yniold, and joins the others. Yniold carries a lamp which he thrusts up into the faces of the young people, saying that both have been weeping.)

ACT III, Scene 1. In the window of a tower, Mélisande is comb-
ing her long hair and singing (the song she sings is not the one in
the play, but a verse about her hair, and a phrase picked up from one of
the omitted scenes.) Pelléas enters and is immediately bewitched by the
long golden strands, which he claims love him a thousand times more
than she does. His ardor, plainly revealed, frightens Mélisande, the
more so now that she hears Golaud approaching. But her hair is now
caught in vines, and disengaged only with difficulty. Golaud, inwardly
seething, merely calls them children, and laughs nervously.

Scene 2. For no apparent reason, Golaud leads Pelléas into a deep
vault, where stagnant water exudes the odor of death. He forces Pelléas
to lean over the abyss, but holds his arm. Pelléas chokes, then the two
ascend.

Scene 3. After the menace of the vault, Pelléas rejoices in the fresh
air. As they see Mélisande and Geneviève in the distance, Golaud warns
Pelléas not to repeat the "childish games" of the night before. Mélisande
is about to become a mother, and to spare her upsetting emotion,
Pelléas must avoid her. (It is possible that Mélisande was already preg-
nant by the unknown who gave her the crown even before she met Golaud: another mystery in this cobwebby story.)

Scene 4. Golaud questions Yniold about Pelléas and Mélisande but
cannot obtain satisfactory answers. At last the child agrees that Pelléas
and Mélisande have kissed (but it is possible that he said only what he
knew Golaud wanted to hear; other evidence in the story suggests that
their kiss happens only later.) Finally, Golaud lifts Yniold up high
enough to spy into Mélisande's window. Pelléas is with Mélisande but
they do not speak, only look at the light. Yniold's complaints at last
force Golaud to take him away.

ACT IV, Scene 1. Pelléas asks for a rendezvous with Mélisande; his father has improved and he is going away. She agrees
to meet him by the fountain. Old King Arkel addresses Mélisande in a
long passage, expressing joy at the new situation, but pity for Mélisande, who, however, protests that she is not unhappy. But the entrance of Golaud, in a towering rage, changes the mood. He has at last
given way to insane jealousy, and drags the weeping Mélisande about
by the hair, to Arkel's distress as well. The old man says: "Were I God, I
would have pity on the hearts of men."

Scene 2. Yniold has lost his ball, and tries to recover it from under a
heavy stone. He sees a flock of sheep in the distance — the Shepherd tells
him they are not going home: they are going to the slaughter. (This
scene, often omitted, has been restored in some recent productions. It
interrupts the continuity of the preceding orchestral passage, which is
the most vivid and emotionally charged in the opera, and should lead
directly to the scene following.)

Scene 3. By the fountain. Pelléas and Mélisande at last avow their
love, in a magic instant of silence when the orchestra has no comment.
It is a famous moment in the opera, one of breathtaking effect. As the
two embrace, Golaud is heard approaching, but they pay no attention.
The infuriated husband stabs his brother in the back and pursues the
fleeing Mélisande.

*Jean Alixis Périer, the first Pel-
léas, 1902, Opéra-Comique,
Paris.*

69
DEBUSSY

John Macurdy as Arkel, 1979, San Francisco Opera.

(ACT V, Scene 1, omitted. Servants are gossiping, and reveal that Golaud, after killing Pelléas and wounding Mélisande, has tried to commit suicide. This is never indicated in the opera. The servants prepare to enter Mélisande's chamber, as a signal of her approaching death.)

ACT V, Scene 1. Mélisande's bedchamber. She has given birth to a daughter, but does not seem to realize it. Golaud begs her to forgive him, but soon loses control and demands to know her true feelings for Pelléas. Her answers are vague and unsatisfactory. Bitterly he complains that it was not his fault. Arkel reassures him, but asks him to leave Mélisande—"The human soul likes to go away alone." Golaud must live for the child.

LÉO DELIBES (Saint-Germain du Val, Sarthe, 21 February 1836—Paris, 16 January 1891). Better known today for his ballets (among which *Coppélia* and *Sylvia* are outstanding), Delibes nevertheless wrote many operettas popular in their day in Paris; but among his few endeavors in a larger musico-dramatic form only *Lakmé* is remembered. A young American soprano, van Zandt, who had found high favor in Paris (Herman Klein called her "the spoiled child of the Opéra-Comique") created the role of Lakmé, and sang it again with the Metropolitan, making her debut on tour in Chicago, where she was called "this dainty, delicate, captivating dreamer." The role has attracted many coloratura sopranos since, from Pons to Sutherland. Pons, perhaps, caused the greatest sensation when her Metropolitan costume left off far above the waist and resumed far below.

Lily Pons in her Paris debut in the title role of Lakmé, Paris Opéra.

IN NINETEENTH-century India, Gérald, a British officer, comes upon Lakmé in a forbidden Hindu garden, where her father, the priest Nilakantha, jealously guards her. Lakmé and Gérald are deeply attracted to each other, and he lingers too long in spite of her warning. Nilakantha vows death to the desecrator of holy ground, whose identity, however, he has not discovered. He forces Lakmé, disguised, to sing, then to sing again during a religious procession that night in the public square, where Gérald and his British companions, Frédéric, Ellen (Gérald's fiancée), Rose, and Mrs. Benson (governess of the young ladies) are watching. Gérald recognizes Lakmé and rushes to her, whereupon Nilakantha stabs him. Lakmé, however, with the help of her faithful servant Hadji, spirits him away and nurses him back to health. But their idyll is short-lived; Gérald hears martial music in the distance and knows he must return to duty. Lakmé eats the leaf of a poisonous flower and dies.

The captivating song which Lakmé sings to lure her lover is of course the Bell Song ("Où va la jeune Hindoue?"), a prime favorite with prima donnas. When well sung, it is a remarkable tour de force, full of glittering runs and tinkling bell sounds. There are other pretty numbers as well, especially a duet for Lakmé and her slave Mallika, and an aria for Gérald.

GAETANO DONIZETTI (Bergamo, 29 November 1797 – 8 April 1848). Among Donizetti's more than seventy operas, *Lucia di Lammermoor* remains the most consistently popular, although the comedies, *Don Pasquale*, *L'Elisir d'amore*, and *La Fille du régiment* hold their place. Only recently have several serious works been rediscovered—*Anna Bolena*, *Lucrezia Borgia*, *Maria Stuarda*, *Roberto Devereux*, and *La Favorita*. All are subject to tides caused by such moon goddesses as, in recent times, Lily Pons, Maria Callas, Joan Sutherland, and Beverly Sills.

Before *Lucia's* successful premiere in 1835, the high spots for Donizetti had been *Anna Bolena* in 1830, *Elisir* in 1832, and *Lucrezia Borgia* in 1833—only three hits out of fifty-one tries! This member of the supreme Italian opera triumvirate of the first half of the nineteenth century averaged almost three operas a year from 1816 to 1843. Chronologically between Rossini and Bellini, he began to emerge after the former mysteriously retired from creating new operas; and Bellini died three days after the premiere of *Lucia*. Donizetti's facility ran away with him when he was hard pressed by deadline.

Donizetti's was a generous character, free from envy. Bellini, to whom Donizetti was often unfavorably compared, wrote bitterly resentful letters against his colleague, who appeared not to know about them, and who gave back only love and loyalty. Even when he was critically ill, Donizetti produced Verdi's *Ernani* in Vienna, earning its composer's gratitude and respect.

Other composers were less appreciative. Wagner wrote: "Rossini's strong and opulent nature outlived the consumptive variations of Bellini and Donizetti on his own voluptuous themes." William Apthorp later attributed the curious inconsistency of Donizetti and Bellini to the "inbreeding in Italy, the decadence that had already set in before Rossini," when Italy was "shut up within her own boundaries, immune from the German development."

Lakmé

Text by Gondinet and Philippe Gille, after the former's *Le Mariage de Loti*.

LAKME	*Soprano*
GERALD	*Tenor*
NILAKANTHA	*Bass-Baritone*
MALLIKA	*Mezzo-Soprano*
ELLEN	*Soprano*
ROSE	*Soprano*
MRS. BENSON	*Mezzo-Soprano*
FREDERIC	*Baritone*
HADJI	*Tenor*

First Performance
Paris, 14 April, 1883.

71
DONIZETTI

Gaetano Donizetti.

Fernando Corena as Dr. Dulcamara floating down in his big balloon, from L'Elisir d'Amore.

The case for the defense was ably put by H.M. Ticknor, who insisted that Donizetti was "well grounded in departments that Bellini ignored," that his melodies were "sometimes superficial but never trivial . . . [full] of true sentiment, variety, and purely musical quality; the outlines of his scoring correct even when badly filled in; his accompaniments, though thin, often full of rich harmony and tone color."

Simon Mayr, Donizetti's mentor, himself wrote more than sixty operas and was, until Rossini appeared, the toast of Italy. He was said to have introduced the orchestral crescendo made famous by Rossini. Of the writing habits of his star pupil, Donizetti, we know that he never used a piano, but wrote rapidly, never making corrections. He always kept by his side, but seldom used, a small ivory scraper, the gift of his father. The latter, a poor caretaker of a pawnshop, counseled his son to "Write as little rubbish as possible."

Signs of Donizetti's illness probably appeared even when he was working on *Lucia,* for he complained of a blinding headache while writing the last act (disaffection for tenors cannot have been wholly responsible). In 1845 he suffered hallucinations during the rehearsals for his next-to-last opera, *Don Sebastiano,* and said, half in jest: "I think I shall go mad yet." Grief at loss of his father and of his wife Virginia also took its toll. His last few years were spent in hopeless melancholia, and Donizetti died in his home town, as "mad" as his hapless *Lucia.*

Scottish and English subjects held a peculiar fascination for Donizetti, as they did, indeed, for other Italian composers — and even for French, German, South American and North American ones. Donizetti's preoccupation with the misty, withdrawn North can easily be seen, for in addition to

Self caricature signed by Donizetti.

Lucia, he set several librettos of English or Scottish origin, not to mention the trilogy of English queens.

Salvatore Cammarano, who was to write six additional librettos for Donizetti, did not stick too closely to history for *Lucia*, but no matter. Nor was he faithful to Sir Walter Scott's *The Bride of Lammermoor*. In the later, Arturo (Frank Hayston) Laird of Bucklaw, is not killed but goes abroad. Edgardo (Ravenswood) is lost in the quicksands of Kelpies on his way to a duel with Henry. The malignant character of the companion-duenna Alisa has been suppressed in the opera.

Scott is said to have based his heroine on one Janet Dalrymple, who murdered her bridegroom in 1669. According to an American descendant, Jean Dalrymple, the family were powerful landowners in the lowlands, not entitled to a tartan. (The assorted tartans assigned to both Ravenswoods and Lammermoors in the opera would probably horrify a Scottish historian.)

The composer made two interesting changes before the first performance. He had intended to use the glass harmonica—the quaint instrument perfected by Benjamin Franklin—in the Mad Scene, but substituted the flute instead. He changed a weak ending of the second act after the sextet, so that the tenor and baritone end, as they begin, that marvelous ensemble.

Many changes were made by composer and librettists for a performance in French at the Théâtre de la Renaissance in Paris in 1839, the most important being the substitution of a double aria from *Rosamonda d'Inghilterra* (a work with libretto by Felice Romani, 1834) for Lucia's grand *scena* in the first act. The substitutions have been recorded by Joan Sutherland, but they did not last long.

Even odder scene changes affected *Lucia* in the New World. When Melba reigned at the Metropolitan, she insisted that the last scene be cut, thus ruining the evening for the tenor. *Cavalleria Rusticana* would end the bill. Quite often Melba would appear in flowing gown with tresses let loose to sing the *Lucia* Mad Scene after a performance of *La Bohème*—Mimi as a role for the diva was not quite enough.

A passage recently restored after the first section of the Mad Scene, in which Raimondo restrains Enrico from harming Lucia, and the two join in expressions of pity and sorrow, gives the soprano a chance to catch her breath before embarking on further flights. When Lucia collapses, Raimondo turns on Normanno, blaming him for the original fault of telling Enrico about Edgardo, thus salving his own conscience.

The first performance of *Lucia* in the Teatro San Carlo in Naples was one of the most sensational in that theater. The audience wept freely and applauded frantically. But this triumph was hard won, for up until curtain time, it was not known if the theater could pay its bills, and the King himself had to intervene. Donizetti called them all "a cage of madmen."

The original Lucia was Fanny Tacchiniari-Persiani. Within eight years, *Lucia* was at home in the opera houses of the world. It was the second work to be produced in the new Metropolitan Opera House, 24 October 1883, when Marcella Sembrich made her debut, with Italo Companini as Edgardo and Giuseppe Kaschmann as Enrico.

Several other operas of Donizetti not included here are occasionally revived, the "serious" works usually in concert form or merely recorded. These include *Parisini* (to a libretto by Felice Romani, based on Byron's

Luisa Tetrazzini as Lucia di Lammermoor.

Nellie Melba.

poem); *Gemma di Vergy* (based on Dumas), and *Linda di Chamounix*, noted principally for its coloratura *scena*. *Il furioso all' isola di San Domingo* (based on an episode in *Don Quixote*) has recently been produced. Two short comedies, *Il campanello di notte* (one of the few to Donizetti's own libretto), and *Rita* (posthumously produced in 1860 at the Paris Opéra-Comique), have also enjoyed popularity in workshops and colleges.

L'Elisir d'Amore
(*The Elixir of Love*)

Text by Felice Romani.

ADINA	*Soprano*
NEMORINO	*Tenor*
DOCTOR DULCAMARA	*Bass*
SERGEANT BELCORE	*Baritone*
GIANNETTA	*Mezzo-Soprano*

First Performance
Milan, 12 May 1832.

IN A LITTLE village in the early nineteenth century, Nemorino, a poor and simple-hearted peasant, despairs of winning the love of Adina, the rich girl of the place. She rather favors him, but is piqued by his backwardness, and teases him unmercifully. To further add to his misery, she flirts shamelessly with Sergeant Belcore, the swaggering head of a troop of soldiers. At last he sees a ray of hope: the ebullient quack, Doctor Dulcamara, visits the village with his famous elixir. Nemorino buys a bottle with the money he receives from Belcore for entering the armed services. The potion, being only a strong wine, immediately brings out the bravado in the timid, erstwhile Nemorino, and a second application only increases his self-esteem. Adina is piqued when, now surrounded by girls who have heard that he has just inherited a fortune, he snubs her. Noticing a "furtive tear" on her lashes, Nemorino apostrophizes it in the "hit" song of the opera, *Una furtiva lagrima*. Adina then decides that he is her choice after all, and buying back his commission from Belcore and dismissing the Sergeant (although marriage prepara-

Final scene from L'Elisir d'Amore.

tions are already under way for the two), she makes her peace with her rustic lover.

The music is a little masterpiece, animated, sparkling, witty, melodious in both solo and ensemble pieces.

BECAUSE HE WROTE *Lucrezia Borgia* (three years after his first real success with *Anna Bolena*) on a Felice Romani libretto based on Victor Hugo, Donizetti "anticipated the Italian—and not only the Italian—appetite for gory melodrama that would lead through Verdi to the verismo operas," as Henry Pleasants pointed out. This really marked a watershed in Italian opera, although Donizetti did not follow up the melodramatic line himself to any great extent. *Lucrezia* has only recently reappeared as a vehicle for the mid-twentieth century crop of virtuoso sopranos, although the ballata *Il segreto per esser felici* ("The Secret of Happiness") has been a contralto warhorse since the beginning, being especially beloved of Ernestine Schumann-Heink.

PROLOGUE.   Lucrezia Borgia, the villainess of the Renaissance, has done away with three husbands and married a fourth, Alfonso d'Este, Duke of Ferrara. She has come to Venice seeking her son by a former marriage, Gennaro, whom she has kept secret from Alfonso. She finds Gennaro asleep after revels with his companions, and delights in his beauty. Awakening, he falls immediately under her spell, but is soon disillusioned by his companions, who reveal that she is a Borgia. She vows vengeance on all but Gennaro.

ACT I.   Alfonso, jealous of Gennaro and unaware that he is Lucrezia's son, is overjoyed when the boy hacks away the first letter from the "Borgia" on the escutcheon of the palace in Ferrara. He arrests the youth. Lucrezia demands the death of the perpetrator; then, discovering that it is Gennaro, pleads for his life. Alfonso cynically condemns him to die by poison handed him by Lucrezia herself. Unwittingly, Gennaro drinks it, but is saved by Lucrezia, who urges the antidote upon him and begs him to flee Ferrara.

ACT II.   Gennaro has meant to leave, but is persuaded by his friend Orsini to stay for a banquet at the Princess Negroni's palace. The gaiety is at its height when Orsini (a trouser role) sings the charming ballata, "Il segreto." As he finishes, the doors open to admit a chorus of chanting monks, five coffins are disclosed, and Lucrezia reveals herself as the poisoner of the company. But a sixth coffin is needed; Lucrezia had not reckoned on Gennaro's presence. Heartsick, she begs him to swallow the antidote, but he attempts to stab her. Then she discloses her relationship to him and he dies in her arms, acknowledging her as his mother. But it is doubtful that he forgives her. She herself then seizes the poisoned cup he has drunk from and drains it, falling dead with her son.

DONIZETTI HAD ALREADY had thirty-two operas produced when his first sensational success came along: *Anna Bolena*, given at Milan's Teatro Carcano on 26 December 1830. The second of the "Queen" sagas was *Maria Stuarda*, at San Carlo, Naples, 19 October 1834. This was originally produced as *Buondelmonte*, because the censors could not allow certain trespasses (the word "bastard"; a queen kneeling; and worst of all, the execution of a queen in plain view, which had caused Maria Cristina, Queen of

Lucrezia Borgia

Text by Felice Romani
after Victor Hugo.

LUCREZIA BORGIA	*Soprano*
GENNARO	*Tenor*
DON ALFONSO	*Bass*
MAFFIO ORSINI	*Contralto*
LIVEROTTO	*Tenor*
VITELLOZZO	*Bass*
RUSTIGHELLO	*Tenor*
GUBETTO, ASTOLFO	*Basses*

First Performance
Milan, 26 December 1833.

75
DONIZETTI

The Three Queens

Anna Bolena
Maria Stuarda
Roberto Devereux

the two Sicilies, to faint dead away at dress rehearsal). It was not given as intended until 30 December 1835, at La Scala.

Preoccupation with English royalty continued, with *Roberto Devereux, Conte d'Essex*, first heard at the San Carlo on 29 October 1837. *Anna Bolena* has had some currency in recent years, but the other two remained obscure (except for scattered concert performances) until Beverly Sills was persuaded by Julius Rudel to take on the three queens in a row, in the early seventies at the New York City Opera. While this feat has not encouraged other prima donnas to sing all three heroines, Joan Sutherland at least is noted for her Maria Stuarda.

In two of the operas, Donizetti's librettists were fortunate to have as foundations excellent plays: Schiller's for *Maria Stuarda* was a particularly strong base for Giuseppe Bardari to build upon. François Ancelot's *Elisabeth d'Angleterre* formed the basis for Salvatore Cammarano's *Devereux*. It is possible that Felice Romani derived his *Anna Bolena* from a French play; certainly it was not based on Shakespeare's *Henry VIII*. Historical accuracy did not bother any of these gentlemen, and rightly so, if dramatic urgencies are to be considered. For example, the famous meeting of Mary and Elizabeth in *Maria Stuarda* never took place.

Giuditta Pasta was the first Anna Bolena, with Giovanni Battista Rubini as Percy. The prima donnas in *Maria Stuarda* were bitter rivals in life as on stage: Giuseppina Ronzi-De Begnis and Anna Delserre even indulged in fist fights. When *Stuarda* was given in its original form at La Scala, Maria Malibran graced the title role. De Begnis showed up again as Elizabeth in *Roberto Devereux*. Donizetti himself supervised four productions of *Devereux*, for the one in Paris adding three new numbers. The singers were Grisi, Rubini, and Tamburini. The public in London did not take to the dumpy Grisi as Elizabeth, as they compared her to the tall historical queen.

Giuditta Pasta was the first Anna Bolena.

Anna Bolena

(*Anne Boleyn*)

Text by Felice Romani.

ANNE BOLEYN (ANNA)	*Soprano*
JANE SEYMOUR (GIOVANNA)	*Mezzo-Soprano*
LORD RICHARD PERCY	*Tenor*
HENRY VIII (ENRICO)	*Bass*
SMEATON (SMETON)	*Mezzo-Soprano*
LORD ROCHEFORT	*Bass*
SIR HERVEY	*Tenor*

First Performance
Milan, 26 December 1830.

ACT I, Scene 1. Outside the Queen's apartments in Windsor Castle, Jane Seymour (Giovanna), expresses her remorse at having won the love of King Henry (Enrico); she is still loyal to her mistress. Anne Boleyn (Anna) enters and asks her favorite musician Smeaton (who is secretly in love with her) for a song, but when the singer comes too close to the actuality—that the Queen is sighing for a former love—she stops him. Now the king finds Jane alone, and presses his attentions on her. Still remorseful, she leaves him unsatisfied.

Scene 2. In the park at Windsor Castle, Anne's brother, Lord Rochefort, encounters Anne's former admirer, Lord Percy, who has been summoned from banishment by Henry. As the king rides by on a hunt, he observes the nervousness of both Percy and Anne, and orders his courtier Sir Hervey to keep a close watch on Percy. The scene ends with a fine ensemble, during which only Henry is ominously silent.

Scene 3. As in Scene 1. Smeaton, kissing a portrait of the Queen, sings of his love for her, then hides as Rochefort and Anne appear. Anne consents to a meeting with Percy, who eventually breaks down and confesses that he still loves her. She refuses to listen, and he threatens to kill himself. Mistaking his drawn sword, Smeaton rushes out to defend Anne, who promptly faints. Henry comes upon this scene, outraged, and orders the offenders to prison. Smeaton, pleading his innocence and willingness to die, tears open his jacket, whereupon the portrait of Anne falls at Henry's feet — a damning bit of evidence. Henry curtly dismisses Anne's plea. She realizes that her fate is sealed and begins the concluding sextet, in which her premonitions are echoed: by Henry with scorn, by the other with pity and remorse.

ACT II. Scene 1. Left alone in the Tower of London by her ladies-in-waiting, Anne kneels and prays, an affecting moment. Jane enters, and pleads with Anne to confess, and so save her life. Anne refuses haughtily, especially when she realizes for the first time that it is Jane herself who has supplanted her. After a stormy scene, she sends Jane away, promising to pray for her. Jane protests that Anne's forgiveness is harder to bear than her scorn.

Scene 2. Outside the Council chamber, the courtiers are dismayed to learn that Smeaton has confessed to intimacy with the queen, thinking it may save her and him. When Anne and Percy are led in to confront the king, he accuses them of adultery; Anne, outraged, flings the accusation in his face. A fierce trio ensues, in which each tells of his rage or sorrow. Henry, alone, is confronted by Jane, who wishes to renounce him. Henry will not hear of it, even after the announcement comes that his marriage to Anne has been annulled and she and her "conspirators" are condemned to death.

Scene 3. In the Tower, Percy and Rochefort both refuse pardon when they learn Anne is to die. Percy sings the famous tenor aria, "Vivi tu," begging Rochefort to accept the pardon, but he refuses. Then Anne has a scene of pitiful madness. Ringing bells proclaim the new queen, as the opera ends on a note of passionate denunciation from Anne Boleyn.

Montserrat Caballé as Maria Stuarda.

Maria Stuarda
(*Mary Stuart*)

Text by Giuseppe Bardari
(after Schiller).

QUEEN ELIZABETH I (ELISABETTA)	*Soprano*
MARY STUART (MARIA STUARDA)	*Soprano or Mezzo-Soprano*
ANNA	*Mezzo-Soprano*
ROBERT DUDLEY, EARL OF LEICESTER (ROBERTO)	*Tenor*
CECIL, LORD BURGHLEY	*Bass*
TALBOT, EARL OF SHREWSBURY	*Baritone*
HERALD	*Bass*

First Performance (as *Buondelmonte*) Naples, 19 October 1834.

ACT I. In the Palace of Westminster, Queen Elizabeth, although still in love with Leicester (Robert Dudley), thinks of marrying the king of France. She discusses Mary Stuart with Lord Talbot, who asks her to be merciful, and with Lord Cecil, who reminds her of Mary's perfidy. Leicester enters, and Elizabeth orders him to go as ambassador to France. She demands to see a letter he has just received from Mary, and realizes that Mary would steal both her throne and her lover. In spite of her anger, she agrees to Leicester's suggestion that she visit Mary at Fotheringay Castle, where Mary is being held prisoner.

ACT II. The encounter is disastrous. Mary is at first humble, but when Elizabeth accuses her of murdering her husband Darnley, she reacts furiously, calling Elizabeth the bastard of Anne Boleyn. This seals her fate.

ACT III, Scene 1. After some indecision, the Queen signs Mary's death warrant, and spitefully orders Leicester to watch the execution.

Scene 2. In the famous confession that caused Maria Cristina, Queen of the Two Sicilies, to faint, Mary tells Talbot that she sees Darnley's ghost and that Darnley has died because of Elizabeth's jealousy. Cecil announces that Mary may have one last wish; it is that her faithful companion Anna accompany her to the end. Leicester too is present, and Mary goes to her death protesting her innocence and her devotion to the good of both England and Scotland.

Roberto Devereux
(*Robert Devereux*)

Text by Salvatore Cammarano based on Ancelot's *Elisabeth d'Angleterre*.

QUEEN ELIZABETH I (ELISABETTA)	*Soprano*
DUKE OF NOTTINGHAM	*Baritone*
SARA, DUCHESS OF NOTTINGHAM	*Mezzo-Soprano*
ROBERT DEVEREUX, EARL OF ESSEX (ROBERTO)	*Tenor*
LORD CECIL	*Tenor*
SIR WALTER RALEIGH	*Bass*

First Performance
Naples, 29 October 1837.

Lucia di Lammermoor
(*Lucy of Lammermoor*)

Text by Salvatore Cammarano after Sir Walter Scott's novel.

LUCIA DI LAMMERMOOR	*Soprano*
LORD ENRICO ASHTON	*Baritone*
EDGARDO OF RAVENSWOOD	*Tenor*
RAIMONDO	*Bass*
LORD ARTURO BUCKLAW	*Tenor*
ALISA	*Mezzo-Soprano*
NORMANNO	*Tenor*

First Performance
Naples, 26 September 1835.

ACT I, Scene 1. Queen Elizabeth confides in Sara that she still loves Essex, even though she suspects that he has turned to another woman. He is being recalled from Ireland. The queen does not realize that the other woman in Essex's life is actually Sara, who has been forced during his absence to marry the older Duke of Nottingham. Refusing Lord Cecil's demand that Robert be tried for treason, Elizabeth receives him, and despite his vows of loyalty, perceives that his affection has cooled. Enraged, she leaves him. Nottingham, still his friend, offers what support he can give, but Robert is unresponsive.

Scene 2. Robert visits Sara, and discovers that she still loves him. He tears off the ring Elizabeth has given him as talisman, and leaves it with Sara. She in turn gives him a blue scarf she has been embroidering (which her husband has seen).

ACT II. In the great Hall of Westminster, news comes that Essex has been arrested by Raleigh, and condemned to death; the blue scarf has been taken from him. When Nottingham identifies it, he would kill Essex, but the queen stays him. She will have her own vengeance. She signs the death warrant.

ACT III, Scene 1. Sara receives the news, and plans to take the ring to the queen, and so to intercede for Essex, but she is prevented by her husband, now aflame with fury and jealousy.

Scene 2. In the Tower, Robert vainly waits for the expected pardon to arrive.

Scene 3. Elizabeth, waiting either the presentation of the ring or the notice of execution, is disposed to forgive Essex, but even Sara's breathless arrival with the ring is too late. Elizabeth turns on the Nottinghams and orders them away. Then she longs only for death and the accession of James to the throne.

BEFORE THE CURTAIN rises, Lord Enrico has incurred the enmity of the reigning monarch and lost his fortune as well. In his ruthless drive for power, he has made lifelong enemies of the Ravenswood family, whose only surviving member, Edgardo, is nevertheless in love with Enrico's sister Lucia. Enrico, however, plans to marry his sister to Lord Arturo Bucklaw, thus repairing his fortunes and smoothing over a touchy political situation.

ACT I, Scene 1. After a short prelude, the curtain rises on a grove near the Castle of Lammermoor. The officious Normanno, one of Enrico's followers, has told Enrico that a mysterious person seen in the vicinity is Edgardo, who he suspects has been meeting Lucia secretly. Enraged, Enrico sends men out to find Edgardo, sings a powerful aria (*Cruda funesta smania*—"Each nerve with fury trembles"), then a cabaletta of revenge.

Scene 2. Lucia comes to keep a tryst with Edgardo. As she waits, she tells her companion Alisa about the spooky Ravenswood fountain nearby. The ghost of a murdered Ravenswood woman has appeared to warn her of her own danger (*Regnava nel silenzio*—"Silence all about was reigning"); then anticipation of her lover's coming lightens her gloom (*Quando rapita in estasi*—"Then swift as thought"), and as he enters, they join in a rapturous duet. Edgardo must go to France immediately, but desires first to ask Lucia's brother for her hand. Knowing Enrico's attitude, she begs him not to speak; he reluctantly agrees, and they pledge their undying love (*Verranno a te sull' aura*—"My sighs shall on the balmy breeze") ending this melodic scene in a burst of passion.

ACT II, Scene 1. Enrico's apartment. Enrico plans to trick Lucia into marriage with Bucklaw by showing her a letter from Edgardo that he has forged (having already intercepted and destroyed previous letters). Believing herself abandoned, she is vulnerable to this approach. A dramatic duet between brother and sister leads in some productions to the scene in which the unctuous chaplain Raimondo counsels Lucia to give in to her brother. He does not, however, know that the letter has been forged. When she capitulates, he congratulates her in a jaunty cabaletta, piously reassuring her that she will find her reward in heaven. This scene is traditionally cut, although more recent versions, among them the N.Y. City Opera's, have included it.

Scene 2. In a great hall, the Lammermoors are rejoicing at their new prospects (*Per te d'immenso giubilo*—"For you the festive glee"). At last Lucia appears, and against her will is forced to sign the marriage contract. Edgardo enters dramatically just as she has accomplished the deed. Amid the ensuing consternation, Enrico begins the splendid Sextet, in which the principals express their individual anger, bewilderment, anguish, and pity. Edgardo draws his sword against the Lammermoors, but is restrained by Raimondo; then Enrico shows Edgardo the contract, and the bitter young man, denouncing his love, storms out.

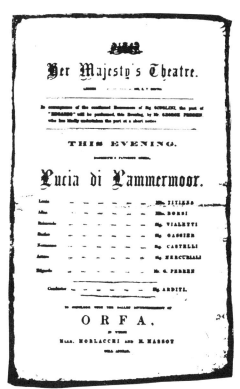

Program for Lucia di Lammermoor.

Scene from Act III of Lucia di Lammermoor, Budapest State Opera House.

Lily Pons and Enzo Mascherini in Lucia di Lammermoor.

Scene 3. The tower at Wolf's Crag on a stormy night immediately after the preceding scene. Enrico comes to challenge Edgardo to a duel at dawn, in a wild and melodramatic scene of great power, also traditionally cut but recently restored.

ACT III, Scene 1. In a great hall, the Lammermoors, still jubilant in spite of the previous brouhaha, are reduced to silence and terror as Raimondo brings them the horrid news—Lucia has murdered her bridegroom with his own sword (or dagger) and has undoubtedly lost her wits. The tale is all too true. The terrified crowd shrinks back as the distraught bride appears (in some versions carrying the bloody knife, with blood streaked down her gown; in others, with a more squeamish management, perfectly immaculate). Lucia's madness as a character study is authentic, veering from one mood to another; it is marvelously organized as music, a *scena* of cunningly wrought contrast and climax, a challenge to the singer both in technique and sensitivity. As one writer said: "Whatever the state of her mind may be, she has her voice under perfect control." When performed with the necessary brilliance and emotional empathy the scene becomes an awesome evocation of beauty and tragedy, and not merely a virtuosic show.

Scene 2. Edgardo waits near the tomb of his Ravenswood ancestors (for his antagonist, as we saw in the Wolf's Crag scene). He has already decided to fall on Enrico's sword, and thus the mood of suicide is set. When he learns of Lucia's madness and death, he sings of his beloved (*Tu che a Dio spiegasti l'ali*—'Tho' from earth thou'st flown before me"), stabs himself, and bids death take him to her.

Two famous Lucias, left: Amelita Galli-Curci; right: Joan Sutherland.

WHEN *LA FAVORITA* is performed nowadays it is most often sung in Italian than in the original French. It has occasional revivals for a virtuoso pair, soprano or mezzo-soprano and tenor.

Leonora, the mistress of Alfonso XI, King of Castile, has captured the affections of Fernando, a young novice in the Monastery of St. James, who renounces his vocation for her. Not realizing her position, he accepts a commission from the king and is victorious in battle with the Moors. He asks for the hand of Leonora as reward. The king, though reluctant to give her up, realizes that this will resolve his own difficulty, for he has been threatened with papal excommunication if he continues his liaison with Leonora and ignores his wife. Leonora trembles at the thought of Fernando's discovery of this liaison and sends her maid Ines with a letter to prepare him. But Ines is captured by the king's men, and the letter never reaches Fernando. After the marriage, the taunts of the courtiers enlighten him, and he returns to the monastery in disgust and disillusionment. Baldassare, the prior (in some editions his father and also the king's father-in-law), welcomes the prodigal. Leonora, disguised as a novice, seeks him out and wins his pardon—but too late. She dies in his arms.

Rosine Stolz and Gilbert Duprez, the first Leonora and Fernando in La Favorita.

La Favorita

Text by Alphonse Royer and Gustave Vaëz, after Arnaud; reworked by Scribe.

(Italian names used)

LEONORA DI GUSMAN	*Soprano or Mezzo-Soprano*
FERNANDO	*Tenor*
ALFONSO XI, KING OF CASTILE	*Baritone*
BALDASSARE	*Bass*
INES	*Soprano*
DON GASPARO, THE KING'S MINISTER	*Tenor*

First Performance
Paris, 2 December 1840.

La Fille du Régiment
(*The Daughter of the Regiment*)

Text by Alphonse Reyer and Gustav Vaëz
after a play by Baculard d'Arnaud.

MARIE	*Soprano*
°TONIO	*Tenor*
SERGEANT SULPICE	*Bass*
MARQUISE DE BIRKENFELD	*Mezzo-Soprano*
HORTENSIO, STEWARD	*Bass*
DUCHESSE DE CRAKENTHORP	*Soprano*

First Performance
Paris, 11 February 1840.

LA FILLE DU RÉGIMENT contains many lively, delightful melodies for the principals, and Tonio has a particularly notorious aria in which he must emit a series of nine clear, ringing high C's. Luciano Pavarotti is possibly the only tenor of this generation who accomplishes it gracefully, without the strangled tone which that note often evokes. The Duchess of Crakenthorp is a small character part, which the famous Ljuba Welitsch delighted in playing at the Metropolitan during one revival.

IN THE SWISS TYROL in 1815, Marie, the darling of the Twenty-first Regiment of Grenadiers, which adopted her after finding her abandoned on the battlefield as a child, happily lives with her comrades. She is especially fond of her foster father, the merry Sergeant Sulpice. Her delight is

Finale to Act I of La Fille du Régiment with Jenny Lind and Lablache, drawing by J. Branard, c.1847.

expressed in the "Rataplan" duet, in which she drums with rolls and flourishes. Into her life now has come a young Swiss named Tonio, who has rescued her from falling over a precipice. But she cannot marry him, because he is not of the regiment. He remedies the situation by joining it. But fate, in the person of the Marquise of Birkenfeld, takes Marie away from him; she claims Marie as her long-lost niece. The girl is introduced to high society and refined behavior, and a marriage is promised with the son of the Duchess of Crakenthorp. But she languishes in these surroundings and longs for the regiment. Suddenly, to her delight, it appears. The Marquise, touched by her loyalty, confesses that Marie is really her own love child, and allows her to follow her true wishes.

Don Pasquale

Text by the composer and Giacomo Ruffini, based on Anelli's *Ser Marc' Antonio.*

NORINA	*Soprano*
ERNESTO	*Tenor*
DOCTOR MALATESTA	*Baritone*
DON PASQUALE	*Bass*
A NOTARY	*Baritone*

First Performance
Paris, 3 January 1843.

DON PASQUALE contains much admirable and amiable music, including brilliant tunes for Norina, a beautiful serenade for Ernesto, and buffo fireworks for Pasquale. It was Donizetti's virtuoso work.

ERNESTO, THE NEPHEW of Don Pasquale, a rich old bachelor, has fallen in love with Norina, a young widow. But Pasquale has determined to take a bride himself, and angrily refuses his nephew the same privilege, disinheriting him. Ernesto seeks the advice of Dr. Malatesta, his friend (and Pasquale's), who introduces Norina to the old man as his sister, just out of a convent. The old man marries her on the spot, unaware that the ceremony is a fake. She immediately turns into a virago, indulges in all sorts of extravagances, and provokes the intimidated Pasquale to the point of demanding a divorce. At this point Malatesta reveals the hoax, and Pasquale, relieved of his distress, sanctions Ernesto's marriage to Norina.

Bidu Sayao as Norina in Donizetti's Don Pasquale, San Francisco Opera.

ANTONIN DVOŘÁK (Nelahozeves o/Vltava near Prague, 8 September 1841–Prague, 1 May 1904), the most widely celebrated nationalist Czech composer, followed in Bedřich Smetana's footsteps in absorbing and utilizing Czech folk song to the highest degree. His music in all forms is distinctive, melodious, harmonically rich, vivid and colorful. Befriended by Liszt and Brahms, with whom he became intimately associated, he was also welcomed many times in England as well as visiting Germany and Russia, and during a three-year period (1892-95) was in America as director of the National Conservatory of Music in New York. He spent his summers in Spillville, Iowa, and absorbed many facets of Indian and Negro music. Some of this is reflected in his most famous symphony, "From the New World." His versatility is apparent in the many beautiful chamber works, songs, choruses, concertos, and works for solo instruments, as well as substantial orchestral compositions. Well beloved are his haunting Slavonic Dances, first written for piano duet, then scored for orchestra by the composer.

Dvořák's early operas are not seen in America, nor are four later much more familiar ones: *Dimitri*, an imposing work which follows the later fortunes of the Pretender to the Russian throne; *The Jacobin*, a folk drama;

Antonin Dvořák.

Scene from Dvořák's Rusalka.

Rusalka

Text by Jaroslav Kvapil.

RUSALKA	*Soprano*
JEZIBABA	*Mezzo-Soprano*
THE SPIRIT OF THE LAKE	*Bass*
THE PRINCE	*Tenor*
THE FORESTER	*Baritone*
THE KITCHEN BOY	*Mezzo-Soprano*
THE FOREIGN PRINCESS	*Soprano*
WOOD NYMPHS	*Two Sopranos, Contralto*
WATER NYMPHS	*Dancers*

First Performance
Prague, 31 March 1901.

The Devil and Kate, a comedy in which the shrewish Kate is gratefully returned to earth by the beleagured Satan; and *Armida,* one of the many versions of Tasso's poem, *Gerusalemme liberata. Rusalka* is the work most performed in the United States, having premiered under Slav auspices in Chicago in 1935. Later performances were at the University of Southern California, Ravinia (concert form), the Washington Civic Opera, and the Juilliard Opera Center, New York.

ACT I.   Rusalka is a version of the legend of Undine, the water sprite who yearns to be a mortal. The heroine asks her father, the wise old Spirit of the Lake, for advice, but he sends her to the witch, Jezibaba, who can better advise her in her predicament: she has fallen in love with the handsome prince who visits the wood. Rusalka sings to the moon of her love, in the tender aria that is the most famous portion of the opera. Jezibaba promises to grant Rusalka human form that she may marry the prince, but she will not be able to speak, and must remain forever silent. Now the prince arrives in pursuit of a white doe, and is enchanted by the appearance of Rusalka, whom he takes with him to be his bride.

ACT II.   The wedding festivities are being celebrated, and the forester and kitchen boy gossip about the palace — it seems that a foreign princess has already attracted the prince, rather understandable since he cannot draw a word of affection from his bride-to-be. At a brilliant ball, Rusalka feels herself neglected, and runs to her father when he is heard singing sorrowfully. The prince and his new favorite appear and engage in a spirited, fiery duet, driving Rusalka to despair. She flings herself into the lake.

ACT III.   Jezibaba reveals that Rusalka is doomed to wander forever as a ghost unless human blood is shed for her. The forester and the kitchen boy come to plead with Jezibaba for the prince, who is apparently under a magic spell. Jezibaba turns them out. Wood nymphs dance gracefully, but are interrupted by the Spirit of the Lake, who cannot bear their frivolity in the face of Rusalka's trouble. Now the prince appears, calling for Rusalka. He begs forgiveness for his infidelity toward her, and she tenderly reproaches him. But she cannot give him the embrace he craves — it would mean his death. He pleads ecstatically for the boon, and she kisses him, drawing him into her own domain to share her fate.

MANUEL DE FALLA (Cadiz, 23 November 1876 — Alta Gracia, Argentina, 14 November 1946). Falla's two operas, *La Vida Breve* and *El Retablo de Maese Pedro,* are about equally known in America, but both are less performed than his two ballets, *El Amor Brujo (Love, the Sorcerer)* and *El Sombrero de tres Picos (The Three-Cornered Hat).* He won the prize in an open competition for a national opera with *La Vida Breve (The Short Life)* in 1905, but the short two-act work was not performed until 1913 in Nice. He had gone to Paris to live in 1907, and was urged to take French citizenship, but refused, and returned to Madrid at the outbreak of war. Other distinguished works of this sensitive, accomplished musician are *Noches en los Jardines de España (Nights in the Gardens of Spain)* for piano and orchestra, colorful piano pieces, and the set of seven popular Spanish songs.

Stage design for La Vida Breve by S. David.

El Retablo de Maese Pedro (Master Peter's Puppet Show) was suggested by an episode in Cervantes' *Don Quixote*. It was given in 1979 by the Opera Company of Boston among scattered American performances, many for children. *La Vida Breve* is more often performed by larger companies, such as Santa Fe (1975).

Falla spent the last two decades of his life in retirement, going to Argentina to stay with a sister in 1940.

IN A GYPSY corner of Granada, the girl Salud fears that her betrothed Paco is unfaithful. Her grandmother tries to console her, but the girl sings sadly that those who laugh live long; those who cry have a short life. Paco does come to her, but meets her wholehearted sincerity with rather stiff formality. Salud's uncle wants to interfere—for he knows that Paco is going to marry a rich girl the very next day.

An intermezzo intervenes before the second act, which shows a small street in Granada, and courtyard where the wedding of Paco and Carmela is being celebrated. A singer sings an Andalusian tune and then there is a dance, which is often excerpted for concert performances. Salud enters, and, realizing what is going on, sings a lament in which she longs for death. Her uncle and grandmother arrive, and try to prevent Salud from entering the patio, but she will not be restrained. Confronting Paco, she will not believe his stammered excuses, and drops dead at his feet—ending the short life of one who sorrows.

FRIEDRICH VON FLOTOW (Teutendorf, Mecklenburg-Schwerin, 26 April 1812—Darmstadt, 29 January 1883). The son of a landed nobleman, Flotow found his way into professional music-making via Paris, where his early works were performed privately. His first public success was in 1839; after that he did not cease until 1878 to produce operas and light operas in several countries. The only one of the more than two dozen works from his facile pen that remains current is *Martha*, although *Alessandro Stradella* may be remembered as the tale of the real composer-singer who, by his singing, charmed the villains who were sent after him by the old man whose ward he eloped with.

La Vida Breve
(*A Short Life*)

Text by Carlos Fernandez Shaw.

85
FLOTOW

SALUD	*Soprano*
HER GRANDMOTHER	*Mezzo-Soprano or Contralto*
HER UNCLE	*Bass or Baritone*
PACO	*Tenor*
CARMELA	*Mezzo-Soprano*
HER BROTHER	*Baritone*
A SINGER	*Baritone*

First Performance
Nice, 1 April 1913.

Sembrich as Martha.

AFTER ITS premiere in Vienna, *Martha* quickly found acceptance in London and in New York, at Niblo's Garden, in 1852. Its first performance by the Metropolitan was on 4 January 1884, in the first season's tour (it was later repeated in a spring post-season), with Alwina Valleria, the first American on the Met's roster, in the title role. Adelina Patti sang it at the Met in 1887, although not as a member of the company. The opera possesses the dubious distinction of offering one of the very rare occasions in which a singer dropped dead during actual performance. This happened on 10 February 1897, when Armand Castlemary, the jovial bass who was singing Sir Tristan, staggered and fell; the audience supposed it was only extremely realistic acting.

In a Metropolitan revival in 1961, *Martha*, most often sung in Italian, was subjected to a rather illiterate English translation. Whether in rebellion against this, or for the reason he gave as "wanting his fans to know how Caruso sounded," Richard Tucker sang the famous aria, "M'appari," in Italian, to the delight of the audience and the distress of the management.

Martha is that rare, if not unique specimen, an opera that was adapted from a ballet, *Henriette, ou la Servante de Greenwich*, for which Flotow wrote the first-act music. It was given in Paris in 1844.

Another distinction is the fact that its most favorably received sections were both interpolations. "The Last Rose of Summer," the beloved Irish song, served as a showpiece for the heroine; and "M'appari " (originally

Beniamino Gigli as Lionel in Martha.

Act I, Scene 1 of Martha with (l. to r.) Rosalind Elias, Lorenzo Alvary and Victoria de los Angeles.

"Ach, so fromm"; the Italian is better known), the delight of tenors the world over even today, was inserted in a Paris performance in 1865, lifted from Flotow's earlier *L'Ame en peine.*

Martha

Text by Wilhelm Friedrich after the French ballet-pantomime, *Lady Henriette ou la Servante de Greenwich.*

LADY HARRIET DURHAM (MARTHA)	*Soprano*
NANCY (JULIA)	*Mezzo-Soprano*
LIONEL	*Tenor*
PLUNKETT	*Baritone or Bass*
SIR TRISTAN MICKLEFORD	*Bass*
A SHERIFF	*Bass*

First Performance
Vienna, 25 November 1847.

ACT I.   The bored Lady Harriet Durham, maid of honor to Queen Anne, yields to the suggestion of her pert maid Nancy that they offer themselves as servants at the Richmond Fair. In Scene 2, they are bid for at the fair by the well-to-do young farmer Plunkett and his foster brother Lionel, and are forced to accept. They try to escape with Harriet's cousin, Sir Tristan Mickelford, but the two young men carry them away.

ACT II.   At the farm, the joke has turned into a sore trial. The girls are good for no farm work, not even spinning (which, however, produces one of the opera's most winning pieces, a quartet). Martha and Julia (these are the names they have assumed) are distraught, although the latter has begun to fancy Plunkett. To put Lionel off, Martha sings "The Last Rose of Summer," but this only arouses warmer feelings in the young man's breast. The girls are sent to bed after a most affecting and charming "Good-night" quartet. But Sir Tristan arrives with a carriage and they make their escape.

ACT III.   Lionel spots "Martha" at a hunt, but she refuses to recognize him. Plunkett also sees "Julia." The music here consists of a drinking song by Plunkett, the "M'appari," and a song for Julia. Lionel is declared mad and arrested, but luckily chooses this time to produce a ring given him by his father, which proves he is of noble

Phyllis Curtin and Norman Treigle in the 1956 New York City Opera premiere of Susannah.

Susannah

Text by the composer.

SUSANNAH POLK	*Soprano*
OLIN BLITCH	*Bass-Baritone*
SAM POLK	*Tenor*
ELDER MCLEAN	*Bass*
ELDER GLEATON	*Tenor*
ELDER HAYES	*Tenor*
ELDER OTT	*Bass*
MRS. MCLEAN	*Mezzo-Soprano*
MRS. GLEATON	*Soprano*
MRS. HAYES	*Soprano*
MRS. OTT	*Contralto*
LITTLE BAT	*Tenor or Speaking*

First Performance
Talahassee, Florida, 24 February 1955.

birth. Now it is his turn to scorn Harriet for her snobbishness.

In the last scene, she steals back to the farm, arranging everything the way it was on the day of the fair. The two pairs of lovers are united, to universal joy.

CARLISLE FLOYD (Latta, South Carolina, 11 June 1926 –). Brought up as a pianist and almost entirely ignorant of opera even as late as the mid-'fifties, when he wrote his most favored work, *Susannah,* Carlisle Floyd has since become one of the most popular American composers for the lyric stage. It began in college when he wrote a one-act piece called *Slow Dusk* (1949). *Susannah,* which came along in 1955, brought such favorable attention that he has worked virtually only on commission ever since. *Wuthering Heights* (Santa Fe commission, 1958) is one of only two subjects he has chosen that are not American; the other is *Markheim* (1966), to a story by Robert Louis Stevenson. The influence of the South is very strong in many of his operas, and a folk element is often present. Other works are *The Passion of Jonathan Wade* (New York City Opera, 1962); *The Sojourner and Mollie Sinclair* (1963); *Of Mice and Men* (to Steinbeck's book, a Seattle Opera commission, 1970); *Flower and Hawk* (1972), and *Bilby's Doll* (a 1976 Houston Opera commission). In preparation is an opera based on Robert Penn Warren's "All the King's Men," titled *Willie Stark.*

The composer writes his own librettos.

The New York City Opera premiere of the work in 1956 brought Phyllis Curtin and Norman Treigle, in the leading roles, to wide attention. Both of these singers have taken part in succeeding Floyd operas.

IN THE PRIMITIVE Tennessee mountain town of New Hope Valley, Susannah Polk, innocently beautiful, attracts all the men, even the itinerant minister Olin Blitch, thereby incurring the hatred of all the women. One day the pious church elders discover Susannah bathing in the creek they wish to use for baptism; they ostracize her. In spite of her misgivings, she heeds the advice of her loving but ineffectual brother Sam, and attends a prayer meeting. She is deeply impressed by the impassioned eloquence of Blitch, who notices her and follows her home. When he attempts to seduce her, she does not resist, out of lethargy and despair. Sam kills the preacher in revenge, and the outraged congregation storms Susannah's home. She repulses them with a shotgun. Then, utterly demoralized, she makes advances to the weak-witted Little Bat, but slaps him when he responds. Now she is left alone, embittered for life.

GEORGE GERSHWIN (Brooklyn, New York, 28 September 1898 – Beverly Hills, California, 11 July, 1937). It is rather dismaying to consider what *Porgy and Bess* might have been if Al Jolson had taken the leading role, even with songs and lyrics by Jerome Kern and Oscar Hammerstein II. Because of his extreme need, Du Bose Heyward, the author of the original book and the play from which a musical show was to be derived, had given the rights to Jolson even while Gershwin was considering the project. Gershwin, too busy to get to work immediately, generously allowed Heyward to make the commercial connection. Fortunately for everyone, no doubt, Jolson's interest lapsed, and *Porgy* went ahead to become the worldwide smashing success as the "first real American opera," with the qualification "folk" attached in its first years. But this success was not immediately forthcoming.

Gershwin had blazed a trail through Tin Pan Alley and Broadway with more than fifteen show hits (most with his brother Ira as lyricist), innumerable imperishable songs, the watershed *Rhapsody in Blue* (introducing the element of jazz into "concert" music), and the subsequent ventures into the classical realm, particularly with the *Piano Concerto* and *An American in Paris.* Never one to deprecate his own talent, he had naively expressed the hope that the new stage work "would be a serious attempt to put into operatic form an American theme. If I am successful, it will represent a combination of the drama and romance of *Carmen* and the beauty of *Meistersinger*" (Edward Jablonski and Lawrence D. Stewart, *The Gershwin Years,* N.Y.: Doubleday, 1973).

But the acceptance of *Porgy* as an "opera" was slow in coming. Boston gave it all the acclaim Gershwin could have wished at the tryout opening, 30 September 1935 (there had been a concert run-through at Carnegie Hall previously, and in uncut form the work ran more than four hours, so cuts were mandatory). But New York critics after the premiere on 10 October were confused, even chilly. They couldn't get used to the Catfish Row folk singing their joys and troubles, just like kings, queens, gods, and ghosts. The Broadway production lost its capital of $70,000, and royalties were slim.

The true force of *Porgy's* popularity began to be felt in its first revival, in Los Angeles in 1938. Momentum picked up with a New York revival in 1942, then accelerated with a tour in the early fifties that took the opera (now called by that name) to Milan, London, Vienna, and Russia. It was the first time an American musical production had penetrated the Iron Curtain. In this cast were William Warfield and young Leontyne Price (later married, then divorced). Miss Price had not yet made her "real" operatic debut and become an international diva.

The original cast had been an illustrious one: Todd Duncan and Anne Brown in the title roles, John W. Bubbles as Sportin' Life, Ruby Elzy as Serena, Warren Coleman as Crown, Edward Matthews as Jake, and Helen Colbert as Clara (who opens the show singing the now immortal "Summertime"). Rouben Mamoulian directed; Alexander Smallens conducted. Avon Long and Cab Calloway were later embodiments of Sportin' Life. A 1976 revival, full scale, in New York, clinched the opera's position for all time, it seemed. Restoring the original recitatives (for which dialogue had previously been substituted), this *Porgy and Bess* (with Donnie Ray Albert and Clamma Dale) was termed very high class, whether musical or opera.

GERSHWIN VISITED Du Bose Heyward and his wife Dorothy in Charleston, S.C., to observe at first hand the "Gullah" folk whose individuality had informed the novel and play. The scene of the opera is Catfish Row, once an aristocratic neighborhood but now a tumbledown Negro quarter on the waterfront at Charleston; the time, "contemporary." Street cries, hymns, and folk tunes all played a part in Gershwin's thought, and their influence may be heard.

William Warfield as Porgy. Mr. Warfield appeared frequently in this title role in both Europe and the United States.

Porgy and Bess

Text by Du Bose Heyward.
Lyrics by Heyward and Ira Gershwin.
Based on Heyward's play and book.

PORGY	*Bass-Baritone*
BESS	*Soprano*
SPORTIN' LIFE	*Tenor*
CROWN	*Baritone*
CLARA	*Soprano*
SERENA	*Soprano*
JAKE	*Baritone*
MINGO	*Tenor*
ROBBINS	*Tenor*
PETER	*Tenor*
FRAZIER	*Baritone*
LILY	*Mezzo-Soprano*
STRAWBERRY WOMAN	*Mezzo-Soprano*
JIM	*Baritone*
UNDERTAKER	*Baritone*
NELSON	*Tenor*
CRAB MAN	*Tenor*

First Performance
New York, 10 October 1935
(Previous Boston tryout).

90
GERSHWIN

ACT I.   In the circle of crapshooters on a summer evening in Catfish Row are Robbins, a stevedore who joins the game in spite of the protests of his wife Serena; Porgy, a crippled beggar who goes around on a little cart drawn by a goat; Crown, a mean stevedore, accompanied by his woman, the flashy Bess (who is disdained by the respectable housewives in the Row), and Sportin' Life, a dope peddler from Harlem, who on his visit to Catfish Row has cast a lustful eye on Bess. Crown, sniffing some of Sportin' Life's "happy dust," quarrels with Robbins and kills him with a stevedore's hook. The game breaks up as a policeman's whistle is heard; Crown runs away to the jungles of Kittewah Island, and Bess seeks shelter. Porgy, who has long admired her from a distance, takes her in to his little hovel under the apartment house. (In this scene occur "Summertime," "A Woman Is a Sometime Thing," and "Crap Game Fugue.")

In a wake in Serena's room, money is collected to bury Robbins. The white undertaker says it is not enough, but agrees to bury the dead man anyway, so that he will not be turned over to medical students. ("My Man's Gone Now," and "Leavin' fo' de Promis' Lan'.")

Some weeks later, Porgy is happily settled down with Bess and expounds his philosophy: "I Got Plenty O' Nuttin'." A white lawyer offers to make a lady out of Bess for fifty cents (she has already considered a divorce from Crown for a dollar—except that she was never married to Crown). Sportin' Life tries to tempt Bess with happy dust, but she and the other women chase him away. Although she is reluctant to go on a picnic to Kittewah Island without Porgy, he persuades her, and she leaves with the crowd, after singing the duet with Porgy: "Bess, You Is My Woman Now."

ACT II.   Sportin' Life tries to turn the innocent picnic into something evil, citing all the fallacies in the Bible stories in "It Ain't Necessarily So." The whistle sounds for the departure of the boat, but

The circle of crapshooters from Act I of Porgy and Bess.

Scene from the 1935 production of Porgy and Bess of the Theater Guild, New York.

Bess is prevented by Crown from leaving, and yields weakly to him.

A week later, Bess has returned, feverish, and Porgy is distraught. The fishermen depart, the street cries of vendors are heard, and Bess recovers, to be reassured by Porgy and to sing "I Loves You, Porgy." But the peace of the afternoon is broken by hurricane warnings. The neighbors huddle in Serena's room and pray. Suddenly Crown bursts in, demanding that Bess go with him. In a lull, Clara looks out the window and sees her husband's boat overturned. She hands her baby to Bess and runs out, followed by Crown.

ACT III.   It is night and the storm has blown over. Bess nurses Clara's baby, while Sportin' Life predicts trouble between Porgy and Crown. Crown enters stealthily, but Porgy, with the enormous strength of his shoulders and arms, overcomes the bully, and chokes him to death.

Next morning, the neighbors all pretend ignorance of Crown's murder as white policemen interrogate them. Porgy is taken away as a "witness," and Sportin' Life seizes the opportunity to play on Bess's fears and persuade her to go with him: 'There's a Boat That's Leavin' Soon for New York."

When Porgy is freed and returns to Catfish Row, he asks "Where's My Bess?" and learning the truth, does not despair but sets off himself in his little cart to find her: "I'm On My Way."

ALBERTO GINASTERA (Buenos Aires, 11 April 1916 –), is one of the most distinguished of contemporary composers, respected and performed in all Western countries. His parents were Argentinian, his grandparents Italian and Catalonian. In spite of influences from Stravinsky to folklore, his innovative mind and willingness to experiment have always been operative. Although his own influence is still deeply felt in his native country, he has lived in Geneva for several years. His works range widely from solo piano pieces and songs to concertos and choruses, chamber works, and large orchestral compositions. His completed operas are three. *Don Rodrigo* was first heard in Buenos Aires in 1964, then given its North American premiere by the New York City Opera in 1966 (on the occasion of the company's move to Lincoln Center). *Bomarzo* was commissioned by the Washington Opera Society and performed in Washington on 19 May 1967, then given by the City Opera in 1968. Shockingly, it was banned in Buenos Aires without being examined. *Beatrix Cenci* was also commissioned and performed in Washington and New York by the same forces, 1971 and 1973. All three operas are melodramatic, murderous, and imbued with sex. *Don Rodrigo* is the story of a Spanish conqueror who is himself conquered by his own rash and traitorous nature. *Beatrix Cenci* relates the cruelty and violence perpetrated upon his daughter by the evil Count Francesco Cenci. *Bomarzo* is most often performed among the three.

BOMARZO, THE PARK of Monsters, actually exists in a villa near Viterbo, Italy. It was the property of Pier Francesco Orsini, Duke of Bomarzo. The park is sometimes called Vicino; the horrifying stone sculptures are still to be seen: fanciful animals, a giant tearing a maiden limb from limb, and

*The Spanish soprano Isabel Perragos as Bomarzo's wife in the premiere
performance of Bomarzo, Lisner Auditorium, Washington D.C.*

the Mouth of Hell among them. But mystery still surrounds their original conception and execution.

The story of their owner, who was judged to be a monster himself, was made into a book by the Spanish author Manuel Mujica Lainez, who also fashioned the libretto.

The action takes place in the 16th century. The opera is in two acts and fifteen scenes, each appropriately named.

ACT I.   The humpbacked Duke lies dying in his Garden of Monsters, having swallowed a potion that his Astrologer, Silvio di Narni, said would make him immortal. Instead, it was a deadly poison. His secret past unfolds before him. In his miserable childhood, his brothers, Girolamo and Maerbale, force him to wear women's clothes; his father, instead of rescuing him, thrusts him into a secret room where a dancing skeleton seems to pursue him until he faints. His grandmother, Diana Orsini, hails him as the most glorious of the Orsinis and the Astrologer predicts eternal life for him. But a peacock screams, although there are no peacocks in the garden — a sure omen of death. A messenger brings the news that his father has been wounded; the forecast seems to be coming true.

Now the young man is sent to the courtesan Pantasilea in Florence, but the experience of seeing his misshapen body reflected thousandfold in the mirrored chamber completely unnerves him and he flees, once again accompanied by peacocks' screams. His grandmother soothes him by telling him the story of the Orsinis and that he has nothing to fear, being protected by the ancestral She-bear. Girolamo falls to his death from a high rock, and Pier Francesco succeeds to the Dukedom. He yearns for the beautiful Julia Farnese, but she seems to prefer Maerbale. An erotic ballet, dreamlike, turns into a nightmare. He visits his new portrait by Lotto, but is so shocked by his actual image in a mirror as contrasted with the idealized painting that he smashes the glass.

ACT II.   Courting Julia, he spills a glass of wine on her gown, a premonition of death. He marries Julia, but is impotent on their wedding night, and sees the face of the Devil in a painting. Obsessed by nightmares, he envisions the future sculptures in a frenzied dance. He flees to the sculpture court and recognizes his remaining brother in the Minotaur. Several years later he has this brother killed by his slave. Maerbale's son Nicholas witnesses the slaying, and later drops the poison in the cup prepared by the Astrologer to ensure Orsini's "immortality." Orsini begs his monsters to save him, in vain. As he dies, a shepherd boy kisses his forehead, the only forgiveness for a monster.

UMBERTO GIORDANO (Foggia, 27 August 1867 – Milan, 12 November 1948) came along in the torrid wash of volcanic "reality" stimulated by Mascagni's *Cavalleria Rusticana*. While still a student in Naples, he attracted the publisher Sonzogno, who commissioned an opera, *Mala vita*, from him. This was *verismo* with a vengeance. All of his subsequent operas display that sense of real life, but none has lasted as long as *Andrea Chénier* (1896). *Fedora* (Milan, 1898), to Sardou's play, had its vogue, and in its American premiere at the Metropolitan in 1906 featured what W.J. Henderson called

Bomarzo

Text by Manuel Mujica Lainez after his novel.

PIER FRANCESCO ORSINI	*Tenor*
SILVIO DE NARNI	*Baritone*
GIAN CORRADO, FATHER OF PIER	*Bass*
GIROLAMO	*Baritone*
MAERBALE	*Baritone*
NICHOLAS	*Contralto or Tenor*

JULIA FARNESE	*Soprano*
PANTASILEA	*Mezzo-Soprano*
DIANA ORSINI	*Contralto*
MESSENGER	*Baritone*
SHEPHERD BOY	*Treble*
PIER FRANCESCO, GIROLAMO AND MAERBALE AS CHILDREN	*Speaking Roles*
ABUL, SLAVE OF ORSINI	*Mime*
SKELETON	*Dancer*

First Performance
Washington, D.C., 19 May 1967.

Umberto Giordano.

Andrea Chénier

Text by Luigi Illica.

MADDALENA DI COIGNY	*Soprano*
ANDREA CHENIER	*Tenor*
CARLO GERARD	*Baritone*
COUNTESS DI COIGNY	*Mezzo-Soprano*
BERSI	*Mezzo-Soprano*
FLEVILLE	*Baritone*
THE ABBE	*Tenor*
MATHIEU	*Baritone*
INCREDIBILE	*Tenor*
ROUCHER	*Baritone*
MADELON	*Mezzo-Soprano*
DUMAS, PRESIDENT OF THE TRIBUNAL	*Baritone*
FOUQUIER-TINVILLE, ATTORNEY-GENERAL	*Baritone*
SCHMIDT, JAILER	*Baritone*
MAJOR-DOMO	*Baritone*

First Performance
Milan, 28 March 1896.

the "Hogarthian curves" of the beauteous Lina Cavalieri; later Maria Jeritza made it seductive. *Siberia* (Milan, 1903) came to the New Orleans Opera in 1906 and to Hammerstein's Manhattan Opera in New York in 1908. *Madame Sans-Gêne* (Sardou-Moreau) was accorded a world premiere by the Metropolitan, attractive for Toscanini in the pit and Geraldine Farrar supremely appealing on stage.

La Cena delle Beffe (The Jest) was the last to be heard in America. Based on the play by Sem Benelli, it had its premiere in Milan in 1924, and came to the Metropolitan in 1926, with Alda, Gigli, and Ruffo.

Gigli also favored *Andrea Chénier,* which he sang in most of its incarnations at the Met, with Muzio, Ponselle, and Rethberg as his Maddalenas. The opera has had periodic revivals in New York and elsewhere (even the New York City Opera tackled it), and its trio of principal singers revel in the dramatic situations and arias provided for them. Maddalena was Zinka Milanov's farewell role at the Met in 1966.

THE HERO OF the opera was a real person, the poet André Marie de Chénier, who did protest the excesses of the Revolution and was guillotined in 1794.

ACT I.   In the salon of the Chateau de Coigny in 1789, the servants are preparing for a reception. Carlo Gérard, one of the servants, bitterly resents the hardships suffered by his old father, who is also a menial in the house. Gérard, at the same time, is torn by hopeless love for Maddalena, the daughter of the Countess de Coigny. The guests gather, among them a sycophantic Abbé and Fléville, a cavalier. The latter introduces the poet Andrea Chénier, who, after some pretty choruses and dances, agrees to Maddalena's request to read a poem. This is the *Improvviso di Chénier,* "Un dì, all' azzurro spazio," in which his extremist

Scene from Act I of Andrea Chénier with Mario del Monaco, San Francisco Lyric Opera.

Act II of Andrea Chénier with Jon Vickers in the title role (center foreground) and Shakeh Vartenissian as Maddalena, 1961 season, Chicago Lyric Opera.

denunciation of authority arouses antagonism among the guests. The resumption of frivolity is interrupted by an incursion of beggars headed by Gérard, who then tears his livery from his back and goes to join the Revolution. The gaiety recommences as if nothing had happened.

ACT II.   At the Café Hotto in Paris, Chénier sits alone while Bersi, Maddalena's mulatto maid, revels in the new freedom of the Revolution. The spy Incredibile is suspicious of both Chénier and Bersi. Chénier's friend Roucher arrives with a passport, which Chénier refuses in a passionate "Credo a una possanza arcana." The poet is determined to stay in Paris, not the least because he has received mysterious letters from a lady in distress.

After a cheering band of revolutionaries headed by Robespierre has passed, Bersi brings Maddalena to Chénier — it is she who has written the letters. Meanwhile, Gérard is searching for Maddalena, and Incredibile, noting the absorbed couple, decides this is Gérard's lady and goes off to tell him. Gérard interrupts a passionate duet by Chénier and Maddalena, and in an ensuing duel is wounded by Chénier. Gérard professes not to recognize his former friend, but nonetheless warns him of danger.

ACT III.   At the Revolutionary Tribunal, Mathieu exhorts the crowd for contributions to the common fund. An old woman, Madelon, advances with her young son, whom she relinquishes to serve the revolution — she has already lost two boys. Incredibile reports that Chénier has been arrested and asks for the indictment against him.

Elizabeth Rethberg as Maddalena in Andrea Chénier.

Mikhail Ivanovich Glinka.

Haunted by conscience and former respect for Chénier, Gérard sings the famous "Nemico della patria"—can Chénier really be an enemy of his country? Then, thinking of Maddalena, he reverses his opinion and signs the fateful paper. At this moment Maddalena arrives to plead for Chénier. She even offers her love to Gérard in exchange, and sings of her mother's horrible death in flames as the mob stormed the chateau— "La mamma morta." Gérard, touched, promises to try to help, but it is obvious as the crowd gathers and the Tribunal begins, that the judges will be swayed by the bloodlust of the mob. Chénier is condemned along with others.

ACT IV.   Chénier, in prison, reads to Roucher the poem he has just written, the beautiful aria "Come un bel dì di Maggio" (Like a beautiful day in May). Gérard, at last moved to pity for the lovers, brings Maddalena to Chénier. She will go to the guillotine under an assumed name, to accompany him. But meanwhile, they indulge in a duet on a grand scale, "Vicino a te"—they will be together. The phrases mount ever higher to a great dramatic and lyrical climax, as the two walk to their death, hand in hand.

MIKHAIL IVANOVICH GLINKA (Novospasskoye, 1 June 1804—Berlin, 15 February, 1857). Although he spent some formative years in Italy and Berlin (in the latter city learning to formalize his somewhat unsophisticated and amateur talents), Glinka became the founder of the nationalist Russian school, the first to bring a native musical flavor to the attention of the educated public. His works consist of hundreds of songs and piano pieces and some larger compositions, but he completed only two operas. The first of these, *A Life for the Tsar*, an intensely patriotic tale, was first called *Ivan Susanin* after its hero and later under the Soviet regime restored to that title. It is still a favorite in Russia, although not heard widely elsewhere except on records. The second opera, *Russlan and Ludmila*, a brilliant fairy tale, did not at first win favor in Russia, but gradually found its place, and is occasionally performed outside Soviet borders.

Discouraged by its original failure, Glinka left Russia and spent some time in Paris (where he renewed acquaintance with Berlioz) and in Spain. At the outbreak of the Crimean War he returned to St. Petersburg, but left again for Paris and Berlin, where he passed his last days.

As he had introduced Polish music in *A Life for the Tsar*, so did he bring to *Russlan* an oriental flavor that was to influence Borodin, Mussorgsky, and Rimsky-Korsakov—and even Tchaikovsky.

THE OVERTURE IS an extremely popular concert piece.

ACT I.   Three suitors seek the hand of Ludmila, daughter of the Grand Duke Svietosar of Kiev: Russlan, a knight (and the favorite), the Oriental poet Ratmir, and Farlaf, a blustering but cowardly Scandinavian warrior. A thunderclap interrupts the festivities at a ball and when the sudden darkness lightens, Ludmila has disappeared. The three suitors set out to find her, Svietosar promising her hand to the victor.

ACT II.   In the cave of Finn, the wizard, Russlan learns that his love has been abducted by Tchernomor, the dwarf, at the behest

Russlan waking Ludmila with the magic ring from the last act of the opera, 1846 Moscow Production.

Russlan and Ludmila

Text by V.F. Shirokov and
K.A. Bakhturin after Pushkin.

LUDMILA	*Soprano*
RUSSLAN	*Baritone*
SVIETOSAR	*Bass*
RATMIR	*Contralto*
FARLAF	*Bass*
GORISLAVA	*Soprano*
FINN	*Tenor*
NAINA	*Mezzo-Soprano*
TCHERNOMOR	*Tenor*
BAYAN, A BARD	*Tenor*

First Performance
St. Petersburg, 9 December 1842.

of the wicked fairy Naina. A second scene shows Farlaf with Naina, who advises him to allow Russlan nearly to recapture Ludmila, then whisk her away. Here occurs Farlaf's famous patter song, *Rondo.* In another scene, Russlan meets a gigantic and terrible disembodied head (with a chorus singing inside it) and vanquishes it with a lance he finds nearby.

ACT III.   In the enchanted palace of Naina, Ratmir appears, with his slave, Gorislava, who loves him. He sings a beautiful ballad. But he, as well as Russlan, is imperilled by Naina's magic sirens; Russlan manages to escape through Finn's intervention.

ACT IV.   Ludmila, a captive of Tchernomor, is put into a trance by the dwarf, and although Russlan rescues her by the power of his magic sword, he cannot awaken her.

ACT V.   Now Russlan with Finn's help uses a magic ring to awaken his love, and to break the dwarf's spell. The happy pair are united.

CHRISTOPH WILLIBALD GLUCK (Ritter von) (Erasbach near Barching, Upper Palatinate, 2 July 1714 — Vienna, 15 December 1787). Gluck's *Orfeo ed Euridice* is the oldest opera to remain in the current repertory. More than thirty operas preceded *Orfeo,* most written in Italian, and produced in Italy, also in London, France, and Vienna. The others were in French and

The finale of Russlan and Ludmila, 1953 Bolshoi Theater, Moscow.

Christoph Willibald Gluck, painted in 1775 by Parisian artist Duplessis at the time of the Paris production of Orfeo.

Giulia and Sofia Ravogli, who launched the Metropolitan Opera tour of Orfeo in Chicago, 1891.

mostly given in or near Vienna. Today we know only the light *Cadi Dupé* of 1761, and, after *Orfeo*, the splendid *Alceste, Paride ed Elena, Armide,* and the two *Iphigénies,* one "in Aulis," the other "in Tauris."

Gluck's so-called "reform" of opera owes mainly to a change in librettists. At first he relied for some seventeen operas on the most famous poet-librettist of the time, Metastasio (Pietro Trapassi), with stories based on ancient history and mythology. Then in mid-eighteenth century, *opera seria,* with its stiff succession of recitatives (accompanied by harpsichord) and airs — an unnatural structure that restricted musical expression, with its florid singers, the dominant *castrati* — was replaced by more natural forms, and more human and dramatic expression.

Gluck turned to Raniero da Calzabigi (spelled variously), an Italian who had been a crony of Casanova's and was described by him as "a great conniver, familiar with financial dealings, acquainted with the business of all countries, well versed in history, a *bel esprit,* poet, and great lover of women." But Gluck did not entirely abandon Metastasio; indeed, he set three of his librettos after *Orfeo.*

Orfeo still showed traces of *opera seria*: a weak overture; the unreal character of Amor as *deus ex machina;* too much in too short a time for Euridice; the constant presence of Orfeo that makes the role virtually a monologue; and the feeble happy ending. These mistakes were avoided in *Alceste,* yet that opera has never supplanted *Orfeo* in popularity.

The "reform" heralded in *Alceste* was made evident in the famous preface to the score. Though no doubt Calzabigi's work, it was sanctioned, even signed, by Gluck. In part, it read:

"I have striven to restrict music to its true office of serving poetry by means of expression and by following the situations of the story, without interrupting the action or stifling it with a useless superfluity of ornaments . . . Thus I did not wish to arrest an actor in the greatest heat of dialogue to wait for a tiresome *ritornello,* nor to hold him up in the middle of a word on a vowel favorable to his voice, nor to make display of the agility of his fine voice in some long-drawn-out passage, nor to wait while the orchestra gives him time to recover his breath for a cadenza. . . in short, I have sought to abolish all the abuses against which good sense and reason long have cried out in vain."

Orfeo and *Alceste* were translated into French and performed in Paris, but not until *Iphigénie in Aulide* (libretto by François du Roullet based on Racine after Euripides) had a smashing success at the Opéra in 1774.

Several enemies now appeared, resenting Gluck's seeming invincibility in Paris. These incited a talented Italian composer, Nicola Piccinni, to move to Paris and challenge Gluck. He was given the same libretto that Gluck, now in Vienna, was working on — *Roland,* by Philippe Quinault, a famous seventeenth-century poet and playwright who had supplied a dozen librettos for Lully, many of which were set again by later composers.

Gluck learned of the plot and destroyed what he had already written, but continued with the Quinault *Armide.*

The French version of *Alceste* had only a moderate success after this brouhaha; later, however, it became fully appreciated. *Armide* also was received coolly in 1777, while Piccinni's *Roland* was a hit in 1778. Gluck returned with *Iphigénie en Tauride* in 1779, his reputation once more secure with the Paris public. This great work was written to a text by Nicole-François Gillard based on Euripides.

Scene from Gluck's Alceste, 1941, Metropolitan Opera Company, New York.

The composer's last opera, *Echo et Narcisse*, to a libretto by Baron Ludwig von Tschudi, failed in Paris in September, 1779. Embittered, Gluck returned to Vienna, where he suffered a long illness. He drank a liqueur forbidden him by his doctors, and collapsed from a stroke while riding in his carriage.

"THE CONCISE OXFORD Dictionary of Opera" lists a full seven-inch column of operas on the Orpheus legend, from the very first by Peri (1600), through Monteverdi (1607) to Offenbach and, later, Milhaud and Casella. But it is Gluck's revolutionary work that holds the boards — revolutionary in both its musical and dramatic aspects. Musically, Gluck forswore the *opera seria* rigidity in favor of a flowing, uninterrupted style that foreshadowed Wagner; dramatically, as we have seen, he held the poet's contribution to be equal if not superior. For Paris in 1774, Gluck revised the score and Moline the libretto; the role of Orfeo was sung by the tenor Legros. Hector Berlioz made another revision in 1859, which combined both earlier versions, with the famous mezzo-soprano Pauline Viardot-Garcia in the title role. Ever since, the question of which voice should sing Orfeo has plagued producers, but America seems most likely to hear a woman's voice in the part.

The opera was given in English in New York in 1863; the Metropolitan launched it on tour in Chicago in 1891, with the sisters Giulia and Sofia Ravogli. Several Metropolitan revivals followed, one by Toscanini in 1909 introducing a fourth character, the Happy Spirit, sung by Alma Gluck with Homer and Gadski in the leading roles. The Spirit was later dropped. In 1935-36, the ballet took over the action, with singers in the pit. A new Metropolitan production in 1970-71 retained the ballet action but placed the singers on the stage. The ballet is, of course, vital to any production, as is the chorus.

The original myth, in which Orpheus's grief is turned against all women and he is torn to pieces by the Maenads, is not followed by Calzabigi (other

Alma Gluck appeared as the Happy Spirit in the 1909 Toscanini revival of Orfeo at the Metropolitan Opera Company, New York.

Frontispiece of the original score of Orfeo ed Euridice from a painting by C. Monnet engraved by N. le Mire, 1774.

Orfeo ed Euridice

(*Orpheus and Eurydice*)

Text by Raniero da Calzabigi.

ORFEO	*Contralto*
EURIDICE	*Soprano*
AMOR	*Soprano*
(A HAPPY SPIRIT)	*(Soprano)*

First Performance
Vienna, 5 October 1762.

operas prefer various versions of the tragedy). Orpheus was the son of the Muse Calliope by Oeagrus (some authorities say Apollo); it was Apollo who gave him the magical lure that charmed even the beasts. He was one of the company of Argonauts who, with Jason, sought the Golden Fleece.

ACT I.   Euridice has been bitten by a serpent as she was fleeing from an embodiment of the god Pan, and has died. At her tomb in Thessaly, nymphs and shepherds are mourning with Orfeo. The bereaved husband resolves to seek Euridice, and to this end is aided by the God of Love, Amor, who promises to allow Orfeo to enter the Underworld and rescue his beloved. There is one condition: he must not look upon her face until they have reached the River Styx on the return journey. (A florid aria Gluck composed for the tenor Legros is no longer sung although it remains in most vocal scores.)

ACT II.   In the first scene, the Furies greet Orfeo with a tremendous chorus of rejection, their shouted "No!" repeatedly chilling the rash pilgrim, together with the orchestral growls of Cerberus, the three-headed monster watchdog of the Underworld. But Orfeo gradually softens their adamant position, and is allowed to proceed.

In the second scene the Happy Spirits dance in the Elusian Fields to an entrancing flute solo (added by Gluck for the Paris version). A solo for Euridice, "E quest'asilo" (In this refuge) is taken by the Happy Spirit when that character is introduced. Orfeo's beautiful aria, "Che puro ciel" (What pure light) is the final version of an air that had already appeared in three previous Gluck operas, *Tigrane, Endo,* and *Antigone.* A chorus brings Euridice to him, and he begins to lead her to the Upper World, never looking at her.

ACT III.   Euridice at first follows her husband joyfully, but at last piqued by his seeming coldness, insists, woman-like, that he look at her. At last he can no longer resist her, but his first glance brings death to her. Now indeed his grief is inconsolable. He expresses it in the famous aria, "Che farò senza Euridice?" (How can I live without my Euridice?), and attempts to kill himself. Once more the gods relent and bring Euridice back to life.

In the final scene, the Temple of Amor, the paean to love and to the god is lovely, but seems bland, especially when we remember the original legend. Occasionally a chorus from Gluck's *Echo et Narcisse* (first interpolated in Berlioz's version) is substituted.

Kathleen Ferrier in her famous role as Orfeo.

Risë Stevens as Orfeo and Marvel Biddle as Euridice in the Julliard production of the opera, New York.

CHARLES-FRANÇOIS GOUNOD (Paris, 18 June 1818 — Saint-Cloud, 18 October 1893). Although Gounod's preference was for church music — and he was to write a great deal of it — he was forced by the circumstances of the day to try to make his living in the theater. His first venture was at the urging of Pauline Viardot-Garcia, the renowned mezzo-soprano, for whom he wrote *Sapho* at the Opéra in 1851. Her appearance in the title role created more enthusiasm among the critics than the work deserved, and it soon faded. Three years later, *La Nonne sanglante* (*The Bleeding Nun*), a rather feeble piece, found complete oblivion. *Faust* was supposed to have been Gounod's next stage work, but a grand melodrama on the same subject beat him to it, and at the advice of Léon Carvalho of the Théâtre-Lyrique, he shelved the serious work and composed instead a comedy based on Molière, *Le Médecin malgré lui*. For the first time in what was to be a partnership in seven operas, Gounod worked with the well known librettists, Jules Barbier and Michel Carré — they would aid him in *Faust* (1859);

Nellie Melba as Juliette in Gounod's Romeo and Juliette, composed 1867.

Philémon et Baucis (1860), a diversion which contains some pretty music but no action; *La Colombe* (*The Dove* – 1860); *La Reine de Saba* (*The Queen of Sheba* – 1862), a failure; *Roméo et Juliette* (1867); and *Polyeucte*, after Corneille (1878). Carré was also responsible for the text of *Mireille*, based on the Provençal poem, produced in 1864, and today occasionally revived for its melodic charm and a certain excitement of plot.

When Gounod changed librettists, it did not improve his prospects, for no sucess attended *Cinq-Mars* (1877), with text by Gallet and Poirson; *La Tribut de Zamora* (1881), text by D'Ennery and Brésil; and his final effort, the unfinished *Maître Pierre*, for which he again sought Gallet.

Faust remains the landmark work for Gounod, over all his other operas and works in many forms. At the time of his death in 1893, his masterpiece had reached its thousandth performance in Paris; there is no counting its subsequent representations all over the world.

FAUST, WRITTEN originally with spoken dialogue in five acts, was revised ten years after its premiere by Gounod for Christine Nilsson at the Opéra. He added accompanied recitatives and the ballet, the version since universally performed (in four acts or even three acts), although sometimes without the ballet, which depicts Walpurgis Night. Mme. Miolan-Carvalho, wife of the impresario Léon Carvalho, was the original Marguerite; the role has since been sung by practically every lyric soprano in the world. Faust is a favorite of lyric tenors, and Méphistophélès has been cherished by virtuoso basses, from Edouard de Reszke and Pol Plançon to Feodor Chaliapin, Ezio Pinza, Cesare Siepi, Jerome Hines, Boris Christoff, and Norman Treigle.

When Charles Santley, the famous baritone, sang an English version in London in 1864, he requested a new aria for Valentin. Gounod obliged with

"Even Bravest Heart Must Swell" (later translated into French as "Avant de quitter ses lieux"). *Faust* was first given in New York at the Academy of Music in 1863 in Italian, then was chosen to open the new Metropolitan on 22 October 1883. The cast included Nilsson, Italo Campanini, Sofia Schalchi, and Franco Novara. The opera had so many performances in subsequent years that the critic William J. Henderson nicknamed the Metropolitan the "Faustspielhaus."

Selling one's soul to the Devil is a theme as old as mankind, the basis of legend and a boon to literature. The first real embodiment of the age-old superstition was John Fust of Württemburg, who inherited enough money to study at the University of Cracow, and was reviled by authoritative religious figures for his supposed dealings with the Prince of Darkness. He first appears in print in Frankfurt in 1587 in a book by Spiess, which, in translation, formed the source for Marlowe's *Dr. Faustus*. After hundreds of versions, Goethe took up the story. His remains the model for Faust's struggle with Satanic powers. The romance of Faust and Gretchen (Marguerite) was entirely Goethe's invention.

Dozens of operas have been composed around the legend, the most famous being Boito's *Mefistofele,* Busoni's *Doktor Faustus,* and Berlioz's *La Damnation de Faust* (really a dramatic cantata, although sometimes staged). "Faust" works have been written by Robert Schumann, Franz Liszt, and Richard Wagner, among others.

Gounod's work was destined for easy popularity; today after hearing countless performances, we are apt not to realize how fresh and charming the tunes sounded at first. The Soldier's Chorus, a shouting banality to us, seemed "a thrilling expression of communal feeling."

Faust Inaugural program, 1883 Metropolitan Opera, New York.

Emma Eames as Marguerite in Faust.

Faust

Text by Jules Barbier and Michel Carré.

FAUST	*Tenor*
MARGUERITE	*Soprano*
MEPHISTOPHELES	*Bass*
VALENTIN	*Baritone*
SIEBEL	*Mezzo-Soprano*
MARTHE	*Mezzo-Soprano*
SCHWERLEIN	*or Contralto*
WAGNER	*Baritone*

First Performance
Paris, 19 March 1859.

As one production follows another, and new viewpoints in staging are pushed forward, together with omissions of one scene or another, we revert here to the complete score, noting the more common omissions.

ACT I.   After a short prelude, the curtain rises on Faust's cluttered study. The aged philosopher-magician, completely disillusioned, is ready for death. He is about to drink poison and is temporarily distracted by offstage choruses of girls and men extolling life and love and God. Faust utters curses and calls for Satan's help. *"Me voici!"* ("Here I am") comes the answer. (The demon describes his costume, so that the designer should provide a sword, a plumed hat, and a rich cloak.) Faust at first is indifferent to the riches offered him; he wants only the pleasures of youth. Méphistophélès persuades him to sign a binding contract (he will be master on earth, but will revert to Hell's slavery after a certain time), by showing him a vision of the young Marguerite. Faust drinks a potion and is young again. (This transformation is awkward to handle; it was solved at least once by providing two Fausts, one old, one young.) The two conspirators depart for their fantastic adventures.

ACT II.   In a city market place, a fair is in full swing. The student Wagner sings a short solo in praise of drink; the soldiers, old men, girls, and youths join in. Valentin enters, looking at an amulet given him by his sister Marguerite to keep him from harm in the war he is about to join. (A short scene showing the exchange was cut at the in-

*George Baklanoff
as Méphistophélès.*

The Garden Scene from Faust with Mirella Freni and Nicolai Gedda, Paris Opéra at the Metropolitan Opera, New York.

Charles Gounod, drawing by Ingres.

sistence of Carvalho, but is occasionally restored in pantomime.) Valentin is worried about leaving Marguerite alone, but the love-smitten youth Siébel (played by a mezzo) promises to look after her. Valentin sings the aria "Avant de quitter ces lieux," then Wagner leads the crowd in "The Song of the Rat." But a stranger interrupts. It is Méphistophélès, who sways the crowd with the "Calf of Gold" aria, then reads Wagner's palm, predicting early death. He viciously informs Siébel that flowers will wither in his grasp. Valentin comes forward, to be told that he will be killed. Swaggering, Méphistophélès then tries the wine, but spits it out and magically produces his own (from some appropriate piece of scenery or prop). He toasts Marguerite, ignoring Valentin's anger, and all the others draw their swords. Méphistophélès inscribes a circle around himself with his sword, which breaks Valentin's at the first attack. Now realizing the evil force among them, the men reverse their swords, so that the handles are crosses. The Devil usually cowers and trembles at this, but occasionally shows complete arrogance.

The crowd disperses, and Méphistophélès is joined by Faust, who is impatient to meet Marguerite. Now the crowd returns, having forgotten the sinister incident, and indulges in a merry waltz. As Marguerite enters, Siébel tries to approach her but is brushed aside by Méphistophélès. Faust offers her his arm, but she modestly disclaims any need for escort. Faust is crestfallen, but Méphistophélès promises him eventual success. The crowd soon resumes the dance, the beat of which has never ceased.

ACT III.   Siébel, deeply troubled by the stranger's prophecy, tests it out in Marguerite's garden. His little song dedicates the flowers to his beloved, but the posies do indeed wither in his hand. Dipping his fingers in the holy water under the shrine of the Virgin in the garden, he finds he can pluck a fresh bouquet safely, and leaves it for Marguerite. The Devil, watching, runs off to get a richer gift, leaving Faust to contemplate in ecstasy the house of his loved one in the aria

Saléza as Faust.

Christine Nilsson as Marguerite.

Mary Garden as Marguerite.

Vanni-Marcoux as Méphistophélès in Faust, Chicago Civic Opera Company.

"Salut! demeure chaste et pure" ("All hail, thou dwelling pure and lowly"). Satan returns with a casket of jewels. Faust, now touched by Marguerite's obvious innocence, draws Méphistophélès away.

Marguerite enters, distracted by remembering the handsome stranger. She sings a ballad, "The King of Thule," several times interrupting it with her own thoughts. There is no evidence that the spinning wheel at which the soprano is usually found here belongs in this spot. It appears later in a scene often omitted. (In Goethe's play, Gretchen sings the ballad as she undresses in her bedroom, a staging employed in a New York City Opera production.) As she ends her song, she notices the flowers and beside them the jewel box. Surprise gives way to curiosity and curiosity to experiment. She bedecks herself, happy at the beauty revealed in the mirror she finds in the casket. This is the brilliant "Jewel Song." As she finishes it, Marthe enters. This character is variously called a duenna, a neighbor, or merely a local gossip. Faust and Méphistophélès return, the former to woo his chosen lady, the latter to bedevil the older woman and keep her occupied. A cunningly written quartet follows. Méphistophélès finally manages to escape Marthe, and in a sinister monologue calls on Night to work its magic. The lovers grow more ardent; Marguerite plucks daisy petals with the inevitable result: "He loves me!" She suddenly recovers her modest demeanor, and sends Faust away. But he, egged on by Satan, returns to her as she appears languishing in her window. The Devil's mocking laughter punctuates the orchestral postlude.

ACT IV.   The first scene is often omitted, although part of it was restored in a recent mounting by the Metropolitan. At her spinning wheel, Marguerite mourns the departure of her lover. Behind the scene, a chorus of girls mocks her situation. She sings a ballad (the same music that was played under Faust's first vision of her). Siébel comes to comfort her and sings of his love (this was another addition for the London performance of 1884). Marguerite goes to the church to pray for her unborn child. (This part of the scene is valuable to the plot; without it, we are asked to take too much for granted.)

In the church, it is the Devil who confronts the sinner, denying her the solace of prayer. Choruses of demons and priests vie for her soul, but Méphistophélès has the last word.

In the last scene, before Marguerite's house, the soldiers gather, triumphantly singing of their return from the war. Siébel evades Valentin's questions about Marguerite, and the brother rushes into the house. Méphistophélès and Faust come upon the scene, Faust remorseful, but the Devil arrogantly singing a mocking serenade to his own guitar accompaniment. This brings Valentin to the door. A splendid trio precedes the inevitable duel: Valentin vengeful, Faust sympathetic, Méphistophélès rejoicing in the (to him) known outcome. The Devil makes sure Faust's blade finds Valentin's heart, then the two miscreants flee. The crowd gathers, parting to allow Marguerite to fall beside her brother. Dying, he curses her.

Nellie Melba as Marguerite.

Basso Léon Rothier as Méphistophélès,
Metropolitan Opera, New York.

Charles Kullman as Faust.

ACT V. The scenes in the Hartz Mountains were added by Gounod and his librettists for the Paris Opéra. Heretofore the opera used only the first part of Goethe's *Faust*; now episodes from the second part were drawn upon: the revels of Walpurgis Night, the eve of 1 May, on the Brocken, highest peak. In a lush landscape, Faust is introduced to legendary courtesans: Aspasia, Helen of Troy, Cleopatra, Laïs, Phryne, and Astarte. In the midst of an ensuing orgy, the vision of Marguerite appears to Faust, a thin red line around her throat, as if drawn by a knife. He demands to be taken to her.

Méphistophélès and Faust find Marguerite in prison, where she has been immured for killing her child. There is little time to rescue her before the gallows claim her. At first she is happy to see her lover, but immediately sinks into a daze, and recoils violently when she spies the Devil in the shadows. As she calls on the angels for help, the grand trio begins, the voices mounting higher and higher, Faust despairing, Méphistophélès impatient, Marguerite supplicating. When the splendid climax is reached, the heavens open to receive Marguerite's soul. Faust's fate is left uncertain; presumably he keeps his bargain with the Devil, although some productions hint that he shares Marguerite's redemption.

JACQUES-FRANÇOIS-FROMENTHAL-ÉLIE HALÉVY (Paris, 27 May 1799 – Nice, 17 March 1862). From a Jewish family, his real name was Lévy. His musical talents were evident very early, and he progressed diligently, eventually winning a Grand Prix de Rome. But operatic success did not come easily; several ventures either failed or met with moderate acclaim before *La Juive*, which remains the masterpiece by which he is remembered. At the same time he was working on this typical example of French "grand opera," in which he ranked possibly only second to Meyerbeer, he composed a trifling musical comedy. This versatility and eagerness to do too much at once led him to careless habits. At one time he was producing works for three Paris theaters. But he was also a respected teacher, a man of superior intellect, and a musician whose great worth shows in many passages of his numerous operas.

Halévy's brother, Léon, was a librettist, and Léon's son, Ludovic, was a dramatist who supplied the texts for several Offenbach operettas as well as for Delibes, Bizet, Lecocq and others.

HALÉVY AND HIS librettist Scribe originally planned to set the opera in Spain at the time of the Inquisition, and to give the role of Eléazar to a high bass, but the famous tenor Adolphe Nourrit eventually got the role and the opera's locale was switched to Constance, Switzerland. Nourrit is said to have aided considerably in the composition, especially the aria that has been a favorite with tenors, "Rachel, quand du Seigneur." Eléazar was the last role of Caruso before his death, and the one most coveted by Richard Tucker, who, however, sang it only in concert performances. The Metropolitan revived it occasionally after its premiere there in 1885.

Before the opera opens, we should know that De Brogni as chief magistrate of Rome had banished Eléazar from Rome, thus saving his life after he had been condemned to death as a usurer. In a siege by Neapolitans, Brogni's house was burnt, his wife killed and his daughter lost. Brogni joined the church, and became Cardinal, president of the Council.

ACT I. A church choir sings a *Te Deum* in honor of the Emperor's visit. Léopold, a young prince and general, who has been victorious over the Hussites (thus encouraging the Emperor to endeavor to unite all Christians), has visited the city and fallen in love with Eléazar's daughter Rachel. Now he has been accepted under the name of Samuel as a workman in the Jewish jeweler's shop. Ruggiero, provost of the town, is angry at the work still going on in Eléazar's shop during a proclaimed holiday, and calls the jeweler and his daughter to account. Brogni, passing by, recognizes Eléazar, and saves him once more. At last left alone, Léopold serenades Rachel, who invites him to the Passover celebration that evening.

A crowd gathers to make the most of the holiday in song and dance, and once more the Jew and his daughter are imperilled. This time, Léopold comes to the rescue, having been recognized by one of his own soldiers, Albert. His authority puzzles Rachel.

ACT II. This is an impressive scene of the Passover celebration, at the end of which "Samuel" drops the unleavened bread uneaten, an alien gesture noticed only by Rachel. An imperious knock at the door causes Eléazar to send all away except "Samuel." It is the Princess

Caricature of Halévy by Chs. Joseph Travies des Villers.

La Juive
(*The Jewess*)

Text by Eugène Scribe.

PRINCESS EUDOXIA	*Soprano*
RACHEL	*Soprano*
ELEAZAR	*Tenor*
LEOPOLD (SAMUEL)	*Tenor*
RUGGIERO	*Baritone*
CARDINAL DE BROGNI	*Bass*
ALBERT	*Bass*

First Performance
Paris, 23 February 1835.

*Rosa Raisa in the title role of La Juive
(The Jewess).*

Eudoxia, who wishes to buy an antique chain for her husband Léopold. Hearing this, the false "Samuel" is overcome with remorse. A meeting with Rachel, in which he confesses that he is a Christian, is interrupted by Eléazar, who furiously denounces them. Only Rachel's piteous plea moves him; he will consent to the marriage. But father and daughter are thunderstruck when Léopold confesses that he cannot marry.

ACT III.   In a scene often omitted, Rachel follows Léopold to the palace, although she does not know his identity. She begs Eudoxia to be allowed to serve as a slave for one day only; the Princess agrees.

In the gardens of the Emperor's palace, the festival begins. Eléazar brings the chain to Eudoxia, who is about to place it on Léopold's shoulders when Rachel denounces him. Brogni condemns the two Jews and Léopold to death.

ACT IV.   Rachel agrees to withdraw her charge in order to save her lover. The Cardinal then implores Rachel to save herself by renouncing Judaism. She refuses. Eléazar similarly is obdurate, and reminds the Cardinal of his previous tragedy. His daughter still lives, the Jew tells the Cardinal. But he will not reveal her identity, although of course she is Rachel, and the old man is troubled at allowing her to go to death under false pretences. As the crowds howl for vengeance, Eléazar makes up his mind to let her die. This is the climax of the opera, and brings the great tenor aria.

ACT V.   Léopold's sentence has been commuted to banishment, but the two Jews are brought forward for execution. A last-minute offer of pardon is offered to Rachel, but she proudly refuses, and is thrown into a flaming cauldron. Eléazar calls to the Cardinal: "There is your daughter!" and mounts to his own death.

GEORGE FRIDERIC HANDEL (Halle, 23 February 1685—London, 14 April 1759). For almost two hundred years, the name of Handel would not have appeared on concert or opera programs except for his *Messiah* or one or two other oratorios that remained popular with sacred and secular choruses. But recently more and more of the fabulous body of operatic works by this genius are being produced, with joyous discovery of their beauty and vitality. Germany began the revivals; England soon followed, and now America has its own affection for Handel.

What was the reason for the long neglect? Perhaps the incredible difficulty of many of the roles, which were originally written for *castrati*. When the vogue for these strange beings died out, Handel himself rewrote some of the roles, fearing the imbalance of voices that would result from mere transposition.

In this country we have heard *Giulio Cesare, Alcina, Amadigi, Deidamia, Il Pastor fido, Rodelinda, Serse*, and several others, most often in concert form. *Alcina*, in a splendid production by Franco Zeffirelli, was the opera of Joan Sutherland's debut, in Dallas, 1960. *Susanna*, long considered impossible to stage, was successfully produced in New York and turned out to be a jewel of a comic opera. Many of the other so-called oratorios are no doubt capable of being staged as well, certainly if they are given the fantastic and all-out dramatic treatment that best suits them. We shall consider only *Giulio Cesare* here.

Francesco Senesino, the leading male soprano of Handel's time, sang the title role in the premiere of Julius Caesar in London, 1724.

111
HANDEL

Georg Frideric Handel from an engraving on the published score of his Oratorio, Alexander's Feast, 1738.

Joan Sutherland in the title role of Handel's Alcina.

Handel's first public impression was scored by the oratorio *Saint John Passion* in 1704 in Hamburg, where he was violinist and harpsichordist in the opera. His father had wanted him to be a lawyer, but the pull of music was too strong, and he left home to follow it. His first operas were also given in Hamburg—*Almira Nero,* and *Florindo and Daphne.* After a few years in Italy, he became Kapellmeister to the court of Hanover, but visited England ever more frequently. *Rinaldo* was produced in London in 1711. His long absences infuriated the Elector of Hanover, who, when he became King George I of England in 1714, did not heal the breach for several years. It is said that the famous *Water Music* acted as a peace offering.

Handel remained in London the rest of his life, active in many fields, and turning out operas steadily for twenty-one years. When George I died, the influence of the Pepusch-Gay *Beggar's Opera* turned the public away from Italian opera, and Handel was neglected. He suffered a stroke in 1737, but recovered and composed several more operas until his last, *Deidamia,* in 1741. *Messiah* had its triumphant premiere in Dublin in 1742; many others followed. Eight days before his death, and now totally blind, he led a performance of *Messiah* from the organ, and immediately after took to his bed, dying on April 14. He was buried in Westminster Abbey, an honor richly deserved.

AT THE PREMIERE of *Giulio Cesare* in London in 1724, the title role was sung by the famous castrato Senesino. Almost 200 years later, Germany revived the longforgotten masterpiece, which then was dormant for another thirty years. Appropriately, the buried city of Pompeii heard a revival in 1952 with Renata Tebaldi, Cesare Siepi, and Elena Nicolaidi among others; La Scala picked it up in 1956-57. The most celebrated revival recently was that of the New York City Opera, which brought Beverly Sills to acknowledged stardom, in 1966. Norman Treigle was the Cesare. The practice of substituting a bass voice for the castrato has been deplored by Handel authorities, but persists. The story follows that employed by George Bernard Shaw in *Caesar and Cleopatra* rather than Shakespeare's *Julius Caesar*.

ACT I.   In Alexandria, after he has conquered Pompey, Caesar receives Cornelia, Pompey's wife, and promises peace. But Achillas, an Egyptian lord, comes in and shows Pompey's severed head, which Ptolemy, King of Egypt, has cut off. Caesar is furious. Pompey's son Sextus vows revenge. Curio, Caesar's companion, prevents Cornelia from killing herself, then inappropriately tries to woo her.

In the second scene, the rivalry and jealousy between Cleopatra and her brother Ptolemy is revealed. When Ptolemy is alone, Achillas enters and informs him of Caesar's attitude. He promises to defeat Caesar with Cornelia's hand the prize.

In the third scene, Caesar receives Cleopatra, in disguise as her maid Lydia. He is immediately smitten with her beauty. As he leaves for

Giulio Cesare in Egitto

(*Julius Caesar in Egypt*)

Text by Nicola Haym.

JULIUS CAESAR	*Contralto or Bass*
CURIO	*Bass*
CORNELIA	*Contralto*
SEXTUS	*Soprano or Tenor*
CLEOPATRA	*Soprano*
PTOLEMY	*Bass or Contralto*
ACHILLAS	*Bass-Baritone*
NIRENUS	*Bass or Contralto*

First Performance
London, 20 February 1724.

113
HANDEL

Beverly Sills and Norman Treigle in Handel's Julius Caesar, New York City Opera.

Contralto Maureen Forrester sang the role of Cornelia in the New York City Opera production of Julius Caesar.

court, she hides with Nirenus, her confidant, and witnesses a scene between Cornelia, who again tries to commit suicide, and Sextus. She reveals herself and promises to help Sextus in his revenge, in order to get rid of her brother.

In the fourth scene, Ptolemy receives Caesar, each outwardly cordial but expressing to themselves their antagonism. After Caesar leaves, Achillas brings in Cornelia and Sextus, and Ptolemy joins the list of aspirants for Cornelia's favors. But he promises her to Achillas, who then has Sextus arrested.

ACT II.   In the first scene, Cleopatra appears to Caesar, still in the guise of Lydia, and the two sing a love duet. In the seraglio garden, Cornelia again is buffeted by rival claims for her affection. Nirenus tells her she must be immured in Ptolemy's harem, but secretly promises to smuggle in Sextus.

Again alone with "Lydia," Caesar confesses that he wants her for his wife. Nirenus comes to tell Caesar he is betrayed. Cleopatra reveals her true identity. Each sings a brilliant aria, Caesar in warlike spirit, Cleopatra no less militant.

ACT III.   On the shore, a fierce battle rages, accompanied by a warlike *Sinfonia*. Ptolemy, the victor, orders Cleopatra imprissoned. Caesar is saved, though his troops are killed. Sextus, Nirenus, and then Achillas appear, the last mortally wounded and confessing his misdeeds. He gives Sextus a seal that will command a hundred men in a cave nearby and enable him to rescue the women. Caesar enters and takes the seal from Sextus. They set off on their mission.

In the second scene, Caesar frees Cleopatra from her brother's camp. The next scene shows Ptolemy pressing his unsuccessful suit for Cornelia. Sextus rushes in and kills the tyrant. The final scene shows Caesar and Cleopatra entering Alexandria triumphantly, accompanied by Cornelia and Sextus. All rejoice in the happy outcome of events.

Franz Josef Haydn, painting by C.L. Seehas.

FRANZ JOSEF HAYDN (Rohrau, 31 March 1732 — Vienna, 31 May 1809). Although Haydn is beloved today more for his symphonies, chamber music, and choral works, he was fascinated by opera and wrote quite a few works, most of them now forgotten. Several puppet operas were among his output; one, *Philemon and Baucis,* is occasionally seen. The conductor Antal Dorati is in the process of restoring many of these works to currency, and they may soon become repertory novelties, if not regulars. *L'infedeltà delusa* (Deceit Outwitted) has been quite popular with American universities, and was also given by the Opera Society of Washington in 1966. *Lo speciale, La vera costanza, L'isola disabitata, Armide,* and *L'anima del filosofo* are others we may expect to see, while *Il mondo della luna* has been given in an edition by the scholar Robbins Landon. John Gutman did the translation for an English version as *The Man in the Moon* seen in Hollywood in 1958.

L'INFEDELTÀ DELUSA'S two acts take place in early eighteenth-century Italy, in and near the country houses of Don Filippo and Vespina and Nanni. The plot is one of those tangled webs of conflicting loves. The elderly Filippo wants his daughter Sandrina to marry Nancio, a wealthy countryman. She agrees, although she loves Nanni, her swain for three years. Nanni and his sister Vespina overhear Sandrina advise Nancio to marry her (Vespina) and is enraged when he says he now loves Sandrina. Vespina dresses as an old woman and assures her brother that she will stop the match. She does this by telling Filippo that his daughter has already married Nancio and been betrayed by him. Nancio is now thoroughly confused.

Vespina assumes another disguise, that of a German servant whose master seeks Sandrina's hand. Filippo is pleased, but Nancio is upset. Now Vespina appears as the master, the Marquis of Ripafratta, who tells Nancio he has no intention of marrying Sandrina but will pass her on to his servant. But Nancio does not enjoy his revenge for long. Vespina, now in the appearance of a notary, marries Sandrina to Nanni, disguised as the servant. Then she casts off all pretense, and Nancio, charmed by her resourcefulness, agrees to make the wedding a double one.

L'Infedeltà Delusa
(Deceit Outwitted)

Text by Marco Cotellini.

VESPINA	*Soprano*
SANDRINA	*Soprano*
FILIPPO	*Tenor*
NANCIO	*Tenor*
NANNI	*Bass*

First Performance
Esterhazy, 26 July 1773.

115
HENZE

Painting of a scene from Haydn's opera The Improvised Meeting *with the composer shown conducting from the cembalo in the foreground.*

HANS WERNER HENZE (Gütersloh, 1 July 1926–) was the leading composer of the generation after the Second World War, reviving contemporary thought that had been suppressed by the Nazi regime. He has undoubtedly exercised enormous influence over the operatic life of the past few decades, although he has said that the form is dead. Still he continues to produce works for the theater and ballet, as well as in almost all other genres. His left-wing sympathies have been extreme, and he strongly emphasizes the responsibility of the artist to his world.

George Shirley in the American premiere of Henze's The Stag King, Santa Fe Opera.

Henze's long list of operas began with the one-act *Das Wundertheater* (1948) after Cervantes; then came a radio opera *Ein Landarzt* (1951) and his first real hit, *Boulevard Solitude* (1952), a contemporary version of the Manon Lescaut story. Another radio opera, *Das Ende einer Welt*, followed, a stinging satire on snobbism with comic overtones. Next was *König Hirsch* (produced 1956) based on a Gozzi fairytale and suffused with the Italian feeling that dominated the composer at the time. It is the story of the responsibilities of a monarch, told in magical terms. *Der Prinz von Homburg* (1960) is an indictment of military ideas expressed through a soldier-dreamer. *Elegy for Young Lovers* (1961) cynically explores the ego of a famous poet who will sacrifice anything and anybody for his career. *Der junge Lord* (1965) is a satire on German bourgeois pretensions. For *The Bassarids*, perhaps Henze's most imposing opera, see below. More recent works have included *El Cimarrón* (1970); *Der langwierige Weg* (*The Tedious Way to the Place of Natasha Ungeheuer* – 1971); *La Cubana* (1974), and *We Come to the River* (1976).

Santa Fe Opera has given three Henze operas, all American premieres: *König Hirsch* (*The Stag King* – 1965); *Boulevard Solitude* (1967), and *The Bassarids* (1968). San Diego had the American premiere of *Der junge Lord* (*The Young Lord*) in 1967; the New York City Opera production of 1973 brought the stage debut (in a non-speaking role) of Sir Rudolf Bing, general manager of the Metropolitan. The Juilliard School in New York gave the American premiere of *Elegy for Young Lovers*.

Set for Henze's Boulevard Solitude, Rome Opera production designed by Jean-Pierre Ponnelle.

The Bassarids

Text by W.H. Auden and
Chester Kallman, based on
The Bacchae, by Euripides.

DIONYSUS (ALSO VOICE AND STRANGER)	*Tenor*
PENTHEUS	*Baritone*
CADMUS	*Bass*
TIRESIAS	*Tenor*
AGAVE	*Mezzo-Soprano*
AUTONOE	*Soprano*
CAPTAIN OF THE GUARD	*Baritone*
BEROE	*Mezzo-Soprano*
YOUNG SLAVE	*Mute*
CHILD	*Mute*

First Performance
Salzburg, 6 August 1966.

CADMUS, SON OF the King of Tyre, founded Thebes with the assistance of five warriors, known as the Sown Men because they sprang from dragon's teeth sown by Cadmus's daughter Agave, whose son Pentheus is about to assume the throne, Cadmus having retired. Semele, another of Cadmus's daughters, supposedly has been loved by Zeus and been consumed by fire through a trick of the god's wife Hera. Zeus rescued Semele's unborn, the baby Dionysus, whose cult grew to rival Apollo's and represent the sensual, even brutal, side of human nature.

The opera is divided into four movements, with an Intermezzo in the third. As the scene opens, the people of Thebes are gathered to greet their new king, who has proclaimed the power of reason over superstition and rejected the cult of Semele, whose tomb stands near with a flame burning on an altar. But when a voice offstage announces the arrival of Dionysus, the crowd disperses. Cadmus, Agave, the ancient, blind prophet Tiresias, and the old slave Beroe enter, concerned about Pentheus, who has shut himself away to fast and pray. A handsome Captain of the Guard, with whom both Agave and her sister Autonoe are fascinated, proclaims Pentheus's edict denouncing Semele's immortality, and Pentheus himself comes to snuff out the flame on the tomb with his own cloak. He is furious at the defection of the people, and rushes off. Meanwhile, the voice of Dionysus is heard offstage inviting everyone to Mount Cytheron. Agave and Autonoe depart, hypnotized by the seduction of the god.

In the second movement, Pentheus orders the Captain of the Guard to arrest everyone he can find on Mount Cytheron, determined to stamp out the cult of Dionysus. The Captain brings prisoners, among them Autonoe, Tiresias, a woman slave and her daughter, and a young stranger. All are still in a daze; the two royal women are sent into the palace, the slaves tortured, and the young man questioned by Pentheus, who does not recognize him as Dionysus himself.

The third movement finds Pentheus completely taken in by the stranger, the fire on Semele's tomb is revived, the prisoners freed, and an earthquake shakes the palace. In an Intermezzo, the audience witnesses a travesty on love in an eighteenth-century French court, with the characters performing "The Judgment of Calliope," using Roman names for the gods. Pentheus, whose repressed desires it illuminates, is outwardly disgusted, but, still under the influence of the stranger, allows himself to be dressed as a woman and goes to observe the revels on Cytheron. He is soon surrounded and torn apart by the Bassarids, worshipers of Dionysus. Thus reason yields to superstition. In the fourth movement, Agave is forced to recognize the severed head she carries as that of her own son. Her repentance and defiance of Dionysus are to no avail; the palace is set aflame, and the god rejoices in his vengeance for his mother.

Detail from Scene 4 of Paul Hindemith's Mathis the Painter, 1959, Städische Opera, Berlin. Scenery and costumes by Rochis Gliese.

PAUL HINDEMITH (Hanau, 16 November 1896 — Frankfurt, 28 December 1963). Hindemith's half-dozen viable operas (three early one-acters have been forgotten) are but the tip of the iceberg of this prolific and influential composer's *oeuvre*. The violist-composer wrote in all forms, and was particularly noted for a neo-classicism that rejected conventionalism and even the later twelve-tone rigidity. His method was to use the chromatic scale as a basis, with the notes being fixed by the science of acoustics. His predilection for contrapuntal style often made his operas seem "dry," yet they are invariably interesting for their skill and musicianship. *Cardillac* (1926 — revised in 1952), his first large-scale work for the theater, was based on Ferdinand Leon's play, drawn from E.T.A. Hoffman's grisly story, "Mademoiselle de Scudéry." The goldsmith Cardillac so loves his beautiful works that he cannot bear others possessing them. He murders one buyer after another, until at last, half-mad, he confesses. *Hin und Zurück* (There and Back) (1927) reverses the plot midway, the unfaithful wife slain by her husband comes to life, her lover retreats, and the husband puts away his gun. The music of the last half also mirrors the first half. This opera, which had its premiere in Baden-Baden, has been quite popular in the United States since its premiere in Philadelphia in 1928.

Neues vom Tage (News of the Day), a satire on the press, was seen first in Berlin in 1928 and had its American premiere in Santa Fe in 1961. (Santa Fe was also responsible for the first hearing in the United States of *Cardillac* in 1967; the outdoor theater burned to the ground after the first performance, but no significance was attached to this.)

Mathis der Maler (Mathias the Painter), Hindemith's most imposing stage work, caused Nazi objections to its glorification of the peasants after

its premiere in Zurich in 1938. It is based on the life of the painter Grüne-
wald. Boston University boasted its American premiere in 1956. *Die Har-
monie der Welt*, based on the life of the astronomer Kepler, was first heard
in 1957. *Der lange Weihnachtsmahl* (The Long Christmas Dinner), Hindemith's last opera (1961), depicts a Christmas dinner that lasts over 90 years,
with several generations of family appearing. The Juilliard School in New
York gave it in 1963.

Paul Hindemith, painting by R. Heinisch.

John Reardon as Cardillac in the American premiere of the opera, 1967, Santa Fe Opera.

Engelbert Humperdinck, drawing by Von Orlik.

ENGELBERT HUMPERDINCK (Siegberg, 1 September 1854 — Neustrelitz, 27 September 1921) met Richard Wagner in Italy and was invited to Bayreuth to assist in the preparation of *Parsifal* during 1880-81. It was thought for a while that he had even composed a few bars for a transformation scene, but these were dropped. His ties with the Wagner family were close and the son Siegfried received his musical education from Humperdinck. A half dozen operas followed *Hansel and Gretel,* but none made an impression except, briefly, *Königskinder,* which Humperdinck enlarged from incidental music to a play. Geraldine Farrar scored a great hit as the Goosegirl who loves a Prince — and appears on the stage with live geese — when the opera had its premiere at the Metropolitan in 1910. It is only occasionally revived here and there. *Hansel and Gretel* continues to be one of the most popular operas in the Western world, charming children and grownups alike. It is most often given in English in the United States. Many famous singers have graced the roles of the children; memorable are Queena Mario and Editha Fleischer, a team for many years; Nadine Conner and Risë Stevens, and more recently Teresa Stratas and Rosalind Elias. The Witch of former days was either Louise Homer or Dorothee Manski; later Thelma Votipka was a notable hag. Tenors have taken to this part as well, among them Karl Dönch and Paul Franke.

The music has often been scornfully termed too "Wagnerian," and indeed it is heavy for the slight story, but its sweet tunes and luscious harmonies continue to beguile audiences. The librettist Adelheid Wette was the composer's sister.

Andrea Velis as the Witch and Rosalind Elias as Hansel.

Hansel and Gretel

Text by Adelheid Wette after Grimm.

HANSEL	*Mezzo-Soprano*
GRETEL	*Soprano*
THE WITCH	*Mezzo-Soprano or Tenor*
GERTRUDE	*Soprano*
PETER	*Baritone*
SANDMAN	*Soprano*
DEW FAIRY	*Soprano*

First Performance
Weimar, 23 December 1893.

The Witch's Home, stage set for Humperdinck's Hansel and Gretel.

THE OVERTURE, embodying all the favorite tunes, is a popular piece.

ACT I. In the cottage of a broom-maker in the Hartz Mountains, Hansel and Gretel play, sing a charming duet and dance a merry dance. Their mother Gertrude, angry at their idleness, inadvertently knocks a pitcher of milk on the floor. Because there is no supper, she sends the children out into the woods to gather berries. The husband Peter enters to a rousing song, and placates Gertrude with his basket of food. But the children have been gone too long, and there is a witch in the wood. They rush off to hunt for Hansel and Gretel.

ACT II. Berries are gathered—but eaten, and darkness falls. The fearful children fall asleep with the aid of the Sandman, first singing their evening prayer.

ACT III. The Dew Fairy wakens the children, and they notice the gingerbread house. Of course they nibble at it, but the Witch catches them, forces them inside with a magic spell and prepares to make a meal of them. Gretel soon frees her brother from the cage where the Witch has put him to fatten him up, and when the Witch demonstrates how to light the oven, the girl thrusts the old dame into its flaming depths. At once all spells are broken; the gingerbread children return to life; Peter and Gertrude catch up with their wayward pair, and the angels come down to bless everyone.

121
JANÁČEK

LEOŠ JANÁČEK (Hukvaldy, 3 July 1854—Prague, 12 August 1928) came late to concentrated composition of opera, for during many years he was confined by the necessity to teach in order to make a living. Furthermore, he suffered under a miserably unhappy marriage. Some choral works, piano pieces, and folk-song arrangements came from his pen in those years, as well as three operas—*Sarka*, *The Beginning of a Romance*, and *Fate*, only the second having contemporary performances in Brno. The others waited until later successful works brought about their resurrection, notably in a Janáček Festival in Brno in the fall of 1978.

Janáček was over sixty when the spotlight of fame finally fell upon him. His third opera, *Jenůfa*, (proper title *Her Foster Daughter*) was performed in Brno in 1904 and became a fixture there; but only in 1916, through the in-

Leos Janáček.

Sylvia Fisher and Gré Brouwenstijn in Jenůfa, Lyric Opera of Chicago, 1959.

tervention of a literary gentleman from Prague, was the opera produced by the National Theater in Prague. It had been sent in 1904 to the intendant, Kovarovic, who was furious at something Janáček had written about him, and rejected the opera. But he was prevailed upon in 1916 to do it, and suddenly the obscure composer found himself a national hero. At the same time, he fell deeply in love with a younger married woman, Kamila Stösslova, and the affair lasted to the end of his life, no doubt contributing to the flow of marvelous music that, unprecedented in history, came from him—four operas and another produced posthumously, one in Prague, the others in Brno. Two-thirds of his important work came from this twelve-year period.

There is something so singular, so individual, about Janáček's music that one feels an immediate strangeness when first hearing it, then a sense of recognition of his particularity comes with hearing each new work. In high expressiveness, there is little to rival *Jenůfa* and *Katya Kabanova*, his third important work. *The Excursions of Mr. Brouček*, which came between the two (1920), is not often heard in America, although it deserves performance for its fantastic tale of a man who learns nothing though he goes to the moon then back to fifteenth-century Hussite times, and it contains some treasurable music, midway between early and mature styles of the composer.

The Cunning Little Vixen, with its searching look into animal and human nature, and its exceptionally melodious score, is becoming a popular favorite, although it is difficult to retain the special character of the animals. *The Makropoulos Affair* marks a new stage in the composer's development—a score less melodic, more fragmentary, relying more on declamation; a heroine who must convey seductiveness at the age of 327. But it also is gaining wide acceptance. Only *From the House of the Dead*, a masterpiece based on Dostoyevsky's novel, has yet to be staged in America, aside from an NBC-TV representation. The English National Opera has given it a stunning production, exemplifying Dostoyevsky's words that stand at the head of the score: "In every human being there is a spark of God."

What is so special about Janáček's music? In the first place, he reflects the Czech language in sound, inflection, and habits of repetition, its soft endings, and variations so very faithfully—part of the strangeness stems from this close marriage with a strange language. In this devotion to 'The Word," he resembles most closely Mussorgsky and Debussy; the intent is similar, the flavor different; each thus reflects a "nationalism" that is true and unmistakable, although their music bears little similarity. (Quite natural when we think of the gulfs between the three languages.) Secondly, Janáček employs unusual harmonies and progressions of harmonies, uses a few instruments at a time out of a large orchestra to create unusual effects; employs passionate melody in totally emotional effect; draws on a color palette of exceptional and occasionally exotic variety.

It is easy to become a Janáček addict. Those who visited the American Spoleto Festival in Charleston, S.C., in 1979 had a taste of this alluring stuff; those who go to Brno at almost any season are fortunate indeed.

Scene from Janáček's Jenůfa, Covent Garden, London.

THE SOMEWHAT complicated Moravian family tree of *Jenůfa's* characters should be made clear: before the time of the action, Grandmother Buryja's two sons are already dead. The elder, who owned the family mill, married a widow who had a son, Laca. The couple had another son, Števa, the heir of the family. The Grandmother's second son had a daughter, Jenůfa, by his first wife, who died; he then married Kostelnička.

ACT I.   Old Grandmother Buryja, peeling potatoes in front of the mill, watches Laca nearby and Jenůfa, standing by the stream, a pot of fading rosemary (a sinister sign) in her hands, bitterly wondering if Števa has been taken by the army. She has foolishly yielded to him and will bear his child. Laca is bitterly jealous of his secondary position in the family; furthermore, he is secretly in love with Jenůfa. The mill foreman has noticed this, and disapproves Laca's harsh words about Jenůfa, then causes a small sensation by announcing that Števa has been spared induction. Števa struts in, already drunk from celebrating his freedom. The imperious Kostelnička interrupts a scene of merriment with a severe lecture directed at Števa, and demands a year of sobriety before he can think of marriage. This is a deadly blow to Jenůfa. After a vivid ensemble, Jenůfa and Števa are left alone. He drunkenly shrugs off her anguished pleas for love and understanding, and reels into the house. Laca finding Jenůfa alone, taunts her with Števa's shallowness, and then in a rage slashes her rosy cheek with his newly sharpened knife. She runs screaming into the house, and the Foreman rightly accuses Laca of intentionally committing the crime.

Jenůfa

(Její Pastorkyna)

Text by the composer founded on a story by Gabriella Preissova.

JENŮFA	*Soprano*
KOSTELNIČKA	*Soprano*
GRANDMOTHER BURYJA	*Contralto*
LACA	*Tenor*
ŠTEVA	*Tenor*
FOREMAN	*Baritone*
MAYOR	*Bass*
MAYOR'S WIFE	*Mezzo-Soprano*
KAROLKA	*Mezzo-Soprano*
A MAID	*Mezzo-Soprano*
BARENA, SERVANT	*Soprano*
JANO, SHEPHERD BOY	*Soprano*
AUNT	*Contralto*

First Performance
Brno, 21 January 1904.

Lone Koppel as Jenufa, Australian Opera.

ACT II.   In Kostelnička's house, Jenůfa has been in seclusion for weeks; the baby has been born, to her own joy but the shame of her stepmother, cruelly hurt in her pride of Jenůfa and too conventional to forgive. Jenůfa goes into her room to sleep, with the aid of a narcotic potion given her by her stepmother. Števa comes to call, confessing he had not known of the baby, and refusing to marry Jenůfa. Indeed, he has become engaged to Karolka, the Mayor's daughter. Now Laca comes, hoping that Jenůfa has returned from Vienna (the subterfuge given for her absence), and still longing for her love. Kostelnička feels she must tell him of the baby. At his revulsion, the woman makes up her mind, and says that the baby is dead. Then in an agony of irresolution and despair, she takes the child away and drowns it. When Jenůfa awakes, Kostelnička tells her the baby has died during her long unconsciousness. After Jenůfa's initial grief, and learning of Števa's faithlessness, she agrees to marry Laca. Kostelnička is reassured, but cringes in terror as the window crashes open and lets in an icy blast.

ACT III.   The wedding preparations are in full swing, and everyone is joyous except Kostelnička, who is deeply troubled by her conscience. The mayor's family, and even Števa, are present, and a group of gaily dressed girls sing a wedding song. Suddenly a tumult is heard outside — the baby's body has been discovered. Jenůfa's shock and horror that the baby has not been properly buried bring vengeful actions from the crowd, who believe the murder was hers, but Kostelnička tells the truth, and with dignity goes to meet justice. Jenůfa at first commands Laca to leave her, but he convinces her that their love can heal all wounds, and she gladly agrees over her sorrow; their suffering has led to greater and deeper happiness.

JANÁČEK'S LIKING for Russian texts is shown especially in his choice of Ostrovsky's stormy tale of the generation gap in a small provincial city which could be anywhere in Europe. The older, conservative segment is represented by Marfa Kabanova (Kabanicha), the widow of a rich man, whose son Tikhon has married Katya; and also by the wealthy merchant Dikoy, whose charming but weak nephew, Boris, has fallen in love with Katya. The younger element, ready for change and a new life, includes Barbara, foster child in the Kabanov family, and her sweetheart Vanya, Dikoy's clerk. The two lovers at the center of the plot are caught in the meshes of convention and propriety; the result is inevitably tragic. The music is laden with melody, and repeated motifs that characterize situations and individuals.

ACT I.   Outside the Kabanov's house by the Volga River, Vanya and Glasha, a Kabanov servant, are arguing, interrupted by the arrival of Dikoy, who complains about Boris's laziness. He leaves and Boris enters. He confides to Vanya that he must stay with his tyrannical uncle because of the provisions in his grandmother's will. As the people return from church, Boris admits to Vanya his love of Katya. Kabanicha orders Tikhon to go to the market at Kazan, and insults Katya. Although Tikhon protests, he cannot stand up to his domineering mother. Barbara, highly indignant, turns on Tikhon for his weakness and comments on Katya's unhappy state.

The second scene is inside the Kabanov's house, where Katya confides in the sympathetic Barbara. When Tikhon enters with the news that he must depart, Katya would have him make her swear not to see another man. He refuses, but yields to his mother in exacting the very same oath. Kabanicha taunts Katya as the younger woman almost breaks down.

ACT II.   Kabanicha continues her taunts. When she leaves, Barbara gives Katya the key to the garden she has purloined. Katya struggles with the temptation to meet Boris and yields to it. Dikoy comes to visit Kabanicha, and drunkenly asks her to scold him for the sin of cursing a peasant who asked for money. Money is all that matters to the old miser and hypocrite.

In the hot summer night in the garden, Vanya sings a peasant song to balalaika accompaniment. Boris enters; Barbara gives him the message that Katya will soon be there, and when she comes, the two lovers disappear into the darkness. Vanya and Barbara sing a simple duet, which is climaxed by the reentry of Katya and Boris.

ACT III.   Ten days later, a storm drives many into an old summer house by the river. Vanya and his friend Kolgin comment on the tyranny that infects the country — 'There is one in every family." As if on cue, Dikoy appears, followed by Boris. At the end of the rain, all leave except Vanya and Boris. Barbara comes to tell Boris that Tikhon is home and Katya is distracted to madness. The Kabanovs all come in as the storm begins again, and Katya wildly confesses her affair to Tikhon. Kabanicha gloats.

The last scene takes place by the river. Katya has disappeared, and Tikhon, who still loves her, is searching. Barbara and Vanya, loathing their circumstances, agree to run away. Katya reenters, hoping once

Katya Kabanova
(*Káta Kabanová*)

Text by the composer after the translation by Cervinka of Ostrovsky's *The Storm.*

KATERINA KABANOVA (KATYA)	*Soprano*
MARFA KABANOVA (KABANICHA)	*Contralto*
DIKOY	*Bass*
TIKHON IVANOVICH KABANOV	*Tenor*
BORIS GRIGORIVICH	*Tenor*
VANYA KUDRJAS	*Tenor*
BARBARA	*Mezzo-Soprano*
GLASHA	*Mezzo-Soprano*
FEKLUSHA, A SERVANT	*Mezzo-Soprano*
KULIGIN	*Baritone*

First Performance
Brno, 23 October 1921.

The final scene of Katya Kabanova, 1947, National Theater, Prague.

The Cunning Little Vixen

(Peíhody lisky Bystrousky)

Text by the composer
after stories by Tesňohlídek.

BYSTROUSKA, THE VIXEN	Soprano
AS A CUB	Child Soprano
GOLDENMANE, THE FOX	Soprano
LAPAK, THE DACHSUND	Mezzo-Soprano
THE COCK	Soprano
CHOCKOLKA, THE HEN	Soprano
THE BADGER	Bass
THE SCREECH-OWL	Contralto
THE WOODPECKER	Soprano
CRICKET,	Boy Sopranos

more to see Boris. He comes to her, and after some almost hallucinatory wandering of her mind, she bids him goodbye. She throws herself into the river. Her body is recovered by Dikoy. Kabanicha has the last word, thanking friends and neighbors for their kindness.

THE WONDERFUL MIXTURE of human and animal lives and characters in Janáček's opera owed its existence to newspaper articles by Rudolf Tesňohlídek about a half-tamed vixen, called by the composer Sharp-Ears. He wrote the libretto in the Brno dialect, which hampered early productions, but a stunning show by the East German director Walter Felsenstein launched the opera on a reign of popularity in the late fifties. It has been performed by the Santa Fe Opera with great success, and is on the schedule of the New York City Opera.

The music, like the text, is strongly rooted in Moravian folklore. A Forester, scattering the wild creatures he has caught in a dance, falls asleep, then wakens and catches the vixen, Sharp-Ears. He takes her home, where she is tormented by the dog Lapák and the Forester's son Pepík and his friend Frantík, as well as by the cock and hens. At last she escapes, and chases the badger out of his den.

In the human world, the unpopular Priest, a counterpart of the badger, has seduced a pretty gypsy girl. She is also pursued by the Schoolmaster, but marries the poacher Harašta. Back among the animals, Sharp-Ears is married to the handsome fox, Goldenmane. Their brood of cubs feast on chickens which Sharp-Ears has lured from the poacher. But he returns and kills the Vixen. The Forester hears that the poacher has given his bride a fox muff and mourns the Vixen. Once again he

Portion of the score for Janáček's The Cunning Little Vixen, written in the composer's own hand.

The Cunning Little Vixen, drawing for publicity poster, Australian Opera.

GRASSHOPPER,	
MOSQUITO,	
FROG,	
HUMANS	
THE FORESTER	*Bass-Baritone*
HIS WIFE	*Contralto*
THE SCHOOLMASTER	*Tenor*
HIS WIFE	*Soprano*
PEPIK,	*Boy Sopranos*
FRANTIK	

First Performance
Brno, 6 November 1924.

falls asleep in the forest and upon waking sees again a fox cub. It is Vixen's. The cycle is complete.

PERHAPS THE Makropoulos "Secret" would be a better title for the opera; the Czech word "věc" means "thing," and undoubtedly refers to the formula for eternal life which was concocted by Hieronymus Makropoulos in 1565. The Habsburg Emperor Rudolf II made the physician's daughter Elina drink the potion to test it. Her father wound up in jail, but Elina lived on through 327 years, assuming different identities, but always keeping the initials E.M.

The San Francisco Opera gave the American premiere of the work in 1966; multimedia contrivances featured the New York City Opera production in 1970.

AS THE OPERA OPENS, the opera singer Emilia Marty comes to the law offices of Kolenatý, whose chief clerk Vitek is absorbed in the case of Gregor *vs* Prus, which has dragged on for a century. Marty seems familiar with it, as well she may have been, for as Ellen MacGregor she had had an affair with Baron Prus and borne him a son, Ferdinand MacGregor, whom she registered as Makropoulos. Now Marty advances the claims of (Mac) Gregor and reveals the probable hiding place of written proof. (Her father's formula is supposed to be with the hidden letters, and she feverishly wants to retrieve it, as her youth must be re-

The Makropoulos Affair
(*Věc Makropoulos*)

Text by the composer
based on Karol Čapek's play.

EMILIA MARTY	*Soprano*
ALBERT GREGOR	*Tenor*
DR. KOLENATY	*Bass-Baritone*
VITEK	*Tenor*
CHRISTA	*Mezzo-Soprano*
JAROSLAV PRUS	*Baritone*
JANEK	*Tenor*
COUNT HAUK-SENDORF	*Operetta-Tenor*
STAGEHAND	*Bass*
DRESSER	*Contralto*
CHAMBERMAID	*Contralto*

First Performance
Brno, 18 December 1926.

newed periodically.) Albert Gregor, the claimant, his adversary Jaroslav Prus, and the latter's son Janek all fall violently in love with the mysterious lady, and Christa, Vitek's daughter, admires her extravagantly. At the opera house where Marty is singing, she receives her admirers irritably; among them is an old roué, Count Hauk-Sendorf, who notes her resemblance to a Spanish singer long ago. He realizes that they are one and the same.

Prus now almost penetrates her secret; he has the important paper which obsesses her, but only agrees to give it to her after she has tried tempting his son and failed—the father also falls under her spell. He spends the night with her in her hotel, and though disillusioned by her coldness, gives her the paper she wants. A message comes for him: his son has committed suicide for love of Marty. Soon all the principals are gathered in the room and Marty, tired of life and drinking heavily, at last reveals her secret. To the horror of everyone, she ages before their eyes, and dies. They all shudder away from the formula, and it is burned—symbolically by the young singer Christa.

Scene from Act III of the Makropoulos Affair with Maria Podvalová and Zdenek Otava, 1955, National Theater, Prague.

ÉDOUARD LALO (Lille, 17 January 1823—Paris, 22 April 1892), whose brilliant *Symphonie espagnole* for violin and orchestra and beautiful *Cello Concerto* have remained treasurable repertory choices, completed only one significant opera, *Le Roi d'Ys* (1888). It was heard in New Orleans two years after its premiere, and was given at the Metropolitan with Ponselle and Gigli in 1922, but has been seldom performed since.

LE ROI D'YS, set to a libretto by Édouard Blau based on Breton legend, concerns the kingdom of Ys, which has won peace at the price of the betrothal of the King's daughter Margared to the enemy leader Karnac, although she is in love with the soldier Mylio, who is presumed lost at sea. Her sister Rozenn also loves Mylio, who, reappearing, returns her affections. In revenge, Margared agrees with Karnac, who has been de-

Drawing of Édouard Lalo.

Drop curtain for stage set of Lalo's Le Roi d'Ys, Auditorium of Charles Garnier's palatial Opera, 1888.

feated by Mylio in battle, to open the floodgates and drown the city. When the deed has been done, she repents, kills Karnac, and offers herself to the sea as a sacrifice. The city is saved. The overture to the opera contains many melodious moments, and there are several notable arias, among which the *Aubade* is still a tenor favorite.

RUGGIERO LEONCAVALLO (Naples, 8 March 1858 — Montecatini, 9 August 1910). It is perhaps inevitable that those twin operas in the style known as "verismo" should wind up as partners in double bill wherever opera is given — *Cavalleria Rusticana* and *Pagliacci* are indeed well mated. (The nickname "Ham and Eggs" describes them irreverently.) The affinity goes beyond the character and style of the two short operas to the similarity of the two composers' careers. Both Mascagni and Leoncavallo were saved from dire poverty by the stupendous success of these operas; both had the misfortune of composing little else that left a mark.

The réclame of *Pagliacci* led to a production of the earlier *Medici*, which had been designed as the first of a trilogy on Italian Renaissance history, but after its failure Leoncavallo never completed the attempt to parallel Wagner's *Ring*. Another early work, on the life of the poet Chatterton, was also produced, with no success. Ill luck continued to pursue the composer, who adapted Murger's scenes of Bohemian Paris just at the time Puccini's opera was widely accepted — Leoncavallo could be justifiably bitter, as he had sent Puccini a libretto based on Murger long before the latter let it be known he was composing *La Bohème*. One opera among the dozen or so after *Pagliacci* that achieved fleeting fame was *Zazá*, which served

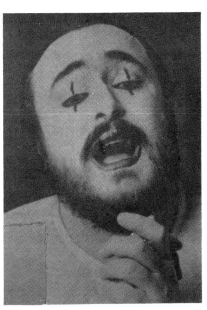

Luciano Pavarotti as Canio in Leoncavallo's Pagliacci.

Geraldine Farrar for three seasons at the Metropolitan, and was indeed her choice for her final performance, packed with emotion and shenanigans by her fans, the Gerry Flappers, in 1922. *Edipo Re*, composed specially for Titta Ruffo, also had a brief spell in the limelight in 1920. It was Leoncavallo's last opera.

Pagliacci did not bring unalloyed happiness to the composer at first, because Catulle Mendès, a flamboyant librettist, sued him for plagiarizing the plot from one of his own plays. Leoncavallo countered by defending the common use of a murder occurring in a play within a play as a story line, and substantiated his defense by citing a real case that his father had tried in Calabria. Mendès withdrew his suit. Some authorities prefer the title without the plural article, "I." The term "Pagliaccio" in Italian has come to mean "clown."

Fritzi Scheff as Nedda.

Two Canios, Enrico Caruso (right) and Beniamino Gigli (below).

The final scene of Pagliacci with Tito Gobbi as Tonio, Giuseppe de Stefano as Canio, Mariano Caruso as Beppe, 1958, Lyric Opera of Chicago.

Both tenors and baritones have found *Pagliacci* a happy hunting ground, for its stirring arias as well as its heated drama. The first Tonio was that great Victor Maurel for whom Verdi had written Iago and would write Falstaff. It was his suggestion that the famous Prologue be added to the story, to the delight of ensuing generations of baritones. Tenors who don the clown costume with gusto range from Caruso to the present day. The first conductor of this splendidly surviving opera was a young man named Arturo Toscanini.

TONIO, ONE OF a troupe of itinerant players who have come to a small town in Calabria, appears before the curtain to say that the actors are real human beings in spite of the superficiality of their play. One of his melodies will appear again in the Intermezzo between the two acts. Finally, he signals for the play to begin.

ACT I.   All is not well in the troupe headed by Canio. He is insanely jealous of his pretty young wife Nedda, and with reason; in this very town she has found a lover, Silvio. After the villagers have welcomed the players, Canio goes off into town and Nedda, musing happily on her love, sings about the birds above — the "Ballatella." Tonio clumsily tries to make love to her, but she scorns him, whipping him offstage. He hides, and witnesses a love scene between Nedda and Silvio, then rushes off to inform Canio. In a blind rage, the betrayed husband tries to catch the lovers, but Silvio escapes unidentified. Tonio advises Canio to watch for the lover in the night's audience. Canio, heartbroken, sings one of the most famous arias in opera, the "Vesti la giubba" (On with the motley), with its tragic climax, "Ridi Pagliaccio!" (Laugh, Clown!). The Intermezzo leads into the next act.

Pagliacci
(*Clowns*)

Text by the composer.

NEDDA (COLUMBINE IN THE PLAYLET)	*Soprano*
CANIO (PAGLIACCIO IN THE PLAYLET)	*Tenor*
TONIO (TADDEO IN THE PLAYLET)	*Baritone*
BEPPE (HARLEQUIN IN THE PLAYLET)	*Tenor*
SILVIO	*Baritone*

First Performance
Milan, 21 May 1892.

Antonio Scotti as Tonio in Leoncavallo's Pagliacci.

ACT II. The play within the play is a Commedia dell'Arte farce, depicting the very circumstances of real life: the faithless wife, the escaping lover (the clown Beppe), the vengeful husband. But Canio makes it real, to the growing terror of Nedda, who refuses to reveal her lover's name. The audience has begun to be uneasy, and as the tension mounts, Nedda tries to escape, but Canio catches her and stabs her. Silvio rises in anguish, and is himself stabbed. "The comedy is finished!" mutters Canio, dropping his knife.

ALBERT LORTZING (Berlin, 23 October 1801—Berlin, 21 January 1851), actor, singer, cellist, producer, theater manager, conductor—all these and a composer of thirteen comic operas as well. Three of these survive hardily in Germany and are occasionally picked up elsewhere for their light-hearted stories, tuneful music, and general attractiveness. The librettos are the composer's own.

The best known is *Zar und Zimmerman* (Tsar and Carpenter), which had its premiere at Leipzig in 1837. Based on a French play by J.T. Merle, it describes the adventures of Peter the Great, who is working under an assumed name as a shipwright in Holland, and befriends a young man who is taken for him when his true identity is suspected. The Tsar escapes and returns to Russia.

Der Wildschütz (The Poacher) was also heard at Leipzig for the first time in 1842. The source of the libretto was a play by A. von Kotzebue, which concerns a schoolmaster Baculus, who is arrested for poaching dur-

Albert Lortzing, painting by von Souchay.

ing the celebration of his betrothal to Gretchen. A merry mix-up follows, in which the Baroness at Eberbach disguises herself as a peasant, and she and Gretchen are pursued by the Count (brother of the Baroness) and the Baron (the Count's brother-in-law). Eventually all is straightened out, and Baculus is forgiven—after all, instead of the deer he is supposed to have shot, he has killed his own donkey.

Der Waffenschmied (The Armorer), based on a comedy by Von Ziegler, had its premiere in Vienna in 1846. The Count of Liebenau has disguised himself as Konrad, a journeyman with the armorer Stadlinger, in order to pay court to the latter's daughter Marie. The father, however, decides to betroth her to another journeyman, actually the count's valet, also in disguise. But as the lesser of two evils, he settles on Konrad, and is pleasantly surprised at the result.

The billiard scene from Lortzing's Wildschütz.

PIETRO MASCAGNI (Leghorn, 7 December 1863 — Rome, 2 August 1943). Mascagni's fierce little opera, the winner in a contest sponsored by the Sonzogno publishing house, rescued him from the desperate situation in which he found himself in 1890. Long before, he had left the routine of the Milan Conservatory and become first a vagabond, then a struggling married man, in the little town of Cerignola, where he gave piano lessons and managed a municipal school of music. Hearing about the competition, Mascagni chose to set a story by Giovanni Verga (who had made it into a play that Eleanora Duse starred in). On the very night before he intended to start work, his wife gave birth to a son, but in spite of the distraction, Mascagni toiled at his score and had it ready for the competition. He managed to scrape up the money to get to Rome for the finals, and heard his prize-winning work cheered to the roof of the Teatro Costanzi. Thus was the style known as *verismo* launched, a predictable reaction to the closing of the Verdian era. The Victorian primness of the turn of the century was outraged by what one critic called "The piquant contemplation of adultery, seduction, and murder amid the reek and stench of the Italian barnyard." Today we view it indulgently as far less scarifying than television.

Pietro Mascagni.

Enrico Caruso and Emmy Destinn as Turridu and Santuzza in an historic performance of Cavalleria Rusticana, uniting Caruso and conductor Arturo Toscanini for the first time since their La Scala days, 1908, Metropolitan Opera, New York.

Mascagni never again composed a winner to parallel *Cavalleria*. Like Leoncavallo, he turned out a series of semi-successes, momentary meteors, and downright flops. On the mid-plateau are *L'amico Fritz* (1891), a light and rather charming tale of pastoral Jewish life; *Iris* (1898), a grisly story with some interesting music; *Le maschere* (1901), produced simultaneously in six Italian cities but hissed in all but Milan (with Toscanini conducting) and in Rome (Mascagni conducting); *Isabeau* (1911), which, based on the legend of Lady Godiva, was bound to cause a sensation in Chicago in 1917 when Rosa Raisa appeared in flesh-colored tights under her long hair.

Several of Mascagni's works might bear revival. Some critics admire *Parisina* (1913), setting a baroque text by D'Annunzio; and by some Italians *Il piccolo Marat* (1921) is considered his best opera. *Lodoletta* (1917), the setting of Ouida's sentimental *Two Little Wooden Shoes*, came to the Metropolitan as a potential vehicle for Geraldine Farrar, but the prima donna withdrew after one performance. Mascagni went on to write more operas, his penultimate work, *Nerone* (1935), being a eulogy of Mussolini; his devotion to the Fascist cause shadowed his last years. He made a tour of the United States in 1902, a fiasco because of bad management and his own irresponsibility, but a South American tour was more successful.

THREE IMPRESARIOS vied for the American premiere of Mascagni's shocker, and Gustave Hinrichs of Philadelphia won; the date was 9 September 1891 (Hinrichs was also responsible for the U.S. premieres of *Pagliacci* and *Manon Lescaut*). Then Rudoph Aronsen of the Casino, across the street from the old Metropolitan, beat Oscar Hammerstein with a matinee on 1 October; Hammerstein perforce took the evening spot. (Aronsen had as director the future general manager of the Met, Heinrich Conried.) The Met trailed a poor fourth, on 30 December. But it boasted Emma Eames as Santuzza. Stars have studded the casts ever since, from Calvé of yesterday to today's Bumbry. Partners in double bills have not always been the other of the "Heavenly Twins," *Pagliacci,* but have ranged even into the realms of absurdity with the maimed torsos of such as *Lucia di Lammermoor* or *Il Barbiere di Siviglia,* or a steady procession of novelties, ballets, and more respectable one-acters. Still, *Cav* and *Pag* are the norm.

AFTER A PRELUDE culminating in a "Siciliana," which the tenor Turiddu sings behind the curtain as a serenade to his former love, Lola, the curtain rises on Easter morning in the Sicilian village. Men and women sing as they enter the church. Santuzza enters and talks briefly with Turiddu's mother, Mamma Lucia. When Alfio, the teamster (and Lola's husband), swaggers in, singing a rousing ditty about the joys of teamster life, and mentions that he has seen Turiddu in the village (when he

Cavalleria Rusticana

(*Rustic Chivalry*)

Text by G. Menasci and G. Targioni-Tozzetti, based on a story by G. Verga.

SANTUZZA	*Contralto*
TURIDDU	*Tenor*
LOLA	*Mezzo-Soprano*
ALFIO	*Baritone*
MAMMA LUCIA	*Contralto*

First Performance
Rome, 17 May 1890.

135
MASCAGNI

*Morag Beaton as Santuzza,
Umberto Borso as Turridu,
1972, Australian Opera.*

Scene from Cavalleria Rusticana; the villagers greeting the arrival of Alfio, played here by Matteo Managuerra, 1977-78 season, New York.

Grace Bumbry and Franco Corelli in a scene from Franco Zeffirelli's realistic setting of Mascagni's work.

was supposed to have gone to fetch wine), Santuzza restrains the older woman from speaking. When Alfio has gone, Santuzza bursts out with a recital of her woes in the tempestuous aria, "Voi lo sapete" (Now you shall know), describing her affair with Turiddu after he returned from war to discover that his former sweetheart Lola had married Alfio. Now Turiddu has left her and is pursuing Lola again. Turiddu enters, and a stormy scene between him and Santuzza is interrupted by the entrance of Lola, who distracts the man and mocks the scorned woman. She enters the church, and when Turiddu would follow, Santuzza drags him back. In a highly dramatic duet, Turiddu finally repulses Santuzza and goes into church. Furious, Santuzza takes her revenge. She tells Alfio all about it. Now the action quiets, while the orchestra recalls the joys of Easter in the famous "Intermezzo."

After church, Turiddu invites the villagers to drink his wine. All join in the gaiety and Turiddu's drinking song except Alfio, who challenges Turiddu to a duel. In the Sicilian fashion, Turiddu bites his rival's ear as acceptance. Then, realizing what he has done, he says sobbing farewell to his mother, and bids her to look after Santuzza. He goes off to the dueling place, and for a few moments, nothing is heard. Santuzza comes in and waits fearfully with Mamma Lucia. Suddenly a woman screams: "They have murdered Turiddu!" Santuzza swoons. The bloody tale is over. At least, there is no murder on stage; but Cavalleria's twin, Pagliacci, makes up the lack.

JULES MASSENET (Montaud near Saint-Étienne, 12 May 1842 – Paris, 13 August 1912). *Manon* is undoubtedly Massenet's masterpiece; yet many others of this typically French composer's works are finding their way into current repertories – indeed, there seems to be a Massenet Renaissance. *Werther* and *Thaïs* have been slightly less popular than the favorite, but now we are seeing *Cendrillon, La Navarraise, Le Jongleur de Notre Dame, Don Quichotte,* and *Portrait de Manon,* a one act "sequel" to the famous work. *Sapho* has been brought out in concert form at least, and we may even yet experience some others – *Cléopâtre* (a favorite, along with other operas by this composer, of Mary Garden), and *Grisélidis.* The work that first brought the composer to fame, a sacred drama called *Marie Magde-leine* (launched by the noted mezzo-soprano Pauline Viardot-Garcia in 1873) was given in New York as recently as 1976 by the Sacred Music Society of America. *Thérèse* (1907) has been recorded by Richard Bonynge, an ardent Massenet exponent. Note on *Le Jongleur de Notre Dame:* Massenet disagreed heartily with Mary Garden's assumption of the part he intended for a tenor: the young Juggler Jean, who plies the only art he knows as a

Mary Garden as Jean in Le Jongleur de Notre Dame, Chicago Civic Opera.

Jules Massenet in his Paris home.

tribute to the Virgin. Garden sang the part with Oscar Hammerstein's Manhattan Opera in New York in 1908-09, then insinuated the opera into the Chicago repertory in 1911-12, no doubt feeling justified when a critic called the role one of her very best. A 1979 recording restored the role to a tenor, Alain Vanzo.

The composer of these fascinating operas, most of them boasting alluring heroines, studied composition at the Paris conservatoire with Ambroise Thomas (composer of *Mignon* and *Hamlet*) who was influential in securing his pupil's first stage performance, the one-act *La Grande Tante,* at the Opéra Comique. When it came time to choose a heroine for *Manon,* Massenet spied in a theater one evening the singer who had graced this early performance, and tapped her for the part. Her name was Marie Heilbronn, and she sang more than eighty performances of *Manon* before her death. The sentimental Massenet then withdrew the opera until he met the captivating little American, Sybil Sanderson, who so entranced him with her per-

Emma Calvé in the title role of Massenet's Sapho, a role she created in 1897 in Paris.

Sybil Sanderson as the first Thaïs.

Manon

Text by Henri Meilhac
and Philippe Gille, based
on the Abbé Prévost's novel.

MANON LESCAUT	*Soprano*
LESCAUT	*Baritone*
CHEVALIER DES GRIEUX	*Tenor*
COMTE DES GRIEUX	*Bass*
GUILLOT DE MORFONTAINE	*Tenor*
DE BRETIGNY	*Baritone*
POUSSETTE	*Soprano*
JAVOTTE	*Mezzo-Soprano*
ROSETTE	*Mezzo-Soprano*

First Performance
Paris, 19 January 1884.

son and voice that he allowed her to make her debut in Brussels as Manon and then wrote three operas expressly for her — *Esclarmonde, Le Mage,* and *Thaïs.* For several years she was the darling of Paris, and her voice was acclaimed for its "Eiffel Tower" notes.

Massenet remains a supreme figure in France, although many other countries find his music bland, even saccharine. This is perhaps unjust, for the real quality of his melodies remains — what one critic called "at once graceful, suave, warm, elegant, and flowing." His one venture into the world of *verismo,* inspired by Mascagni's *Cavalleria Rusticana,* was *La Navarraise,* which first starred Emma Calvé in London in 1894. She sang it at the Metropolitan in 1895 and it was revived for Geraldine Farrar in 1921. Dramatic sopranos love the role, as their lyric sisters yearn for Manon and Thaïs.

It is interesting to note that one of the works Massenet would have liked to set was the Murger story of Paris Bohemians that made such a success for Puccini. But he did beat Puccini by 12 years to the Abbé Prévost story about Manon Lescaut.

Massenet composed 27 operas, many now neglected. One of his last works was *Panurge,* written expressly for the glamorous baritone Vanni Marcoux. This most French of composers, whose influence extends even to Debussy, died full of honors in 1912.

THE FAMOUS SOPRANOS who have sung Massenet's appealing heroine are legion: Hauck, Edvina, Melba, Garden, Farrar, Bori, Grace Moore, Sayao, De los Angeles, Moffo, Scotto, and Sills. Noted tenors singing Des Grieux include Jean de Reszke, Clement, Caruso, Gigli, Schipa, Tagliavini, Gedda, and Molese. *Manon* contains some spoken dialogue, and is therefore termed an *opéra-comique,* but Massenet used the orchestra as accompaniment instead of the dry harpsichord and thus brought something new into opera.

ACT I.   In the courtyard of an inn in Amiens, the crowd awaits the stagecoach from Arras. Among the passengers is the young Manon Lescaut, who is being escorted to a convent by her cousin, the guardsman Lescaut. Her fresh young beauty attracts the attention of the old roué Guillot de Morfontaine and his companion, the tax assessor De Brétigny, who are giving supper to the nobleman's three mistresses, Poussette, Javotte, and Rosette. Manon expresses her delight and bewilderment at her new surroundings in a charming air, "Je suis encore toute étourdie" (I am still so giddy). Lescaut suspects her of light behavior and cautions: "Ne bronchez pas, soyez gentille" (Be a good girl), and leaves to join fellow guardsmen. The Chevalier des Grieux, a handsome young man who has missed the coach, comes on the scene and immediately falls in love with Manon. She responds to his ardent pleas, and the two run off to Paris in the coach so conveniently provided by the old Guillot, who vows revenge.

ACT II.   The love birds are happily ensconced in a nest in Paris, where Des Grieux is writing to his father for permission to marry Manon. Lescaut and De Brétigny interrupt; the former scolding until he learns Des Grieux's intentions, and then pretending to agree; while De Brétigny tells Manon that her lover is to be abducted by his father that

Enrico Caruso as Chevalier Des Grieux. Caruso first appeared in this role at the Metropolitan Opera in 1913 with Geraldine Farrar playing opposite him as Manon under the baton of Arturo Toscanini.

Geraldine Farrar as Manon.

Victoria de los Angeles as Manon.

*Richard Crooks as the Chevalier
Des Grieux.*

very night — however, he himself will protect her.

Des Grieux goes to mail his letter; Manon sings ruefully of the joys they have experienced: "Adieu, notre petite table" (Farewell, dear little table). Des Grieux returns and sings of the rosy dream he has had of their future: "Le rêve" (The dream), one of the most beloved lyric tenor arias. Their idyll is rudely broken by the kidnapers, and Manon is left grief-stricken.

ACT III, Scene 1 (sometimes omitted). At a popular fête in the Cours la Reine, Manon reigns as queen. De Brétigny is with her, and Lescaut comes and goes. Manon notices the Comte des Grieux, father of her former lover, and discovers from him that Des Grieux is even then entering the seminary of St. Sulpice. Distracted, she snubs Guillot, who has brought the entire Paris Opéra ballet for her diversion, and runs off to find Des Grieux.

*Tito Schipa as Chevalier
Des Grieux.*

Scene 2. In the Seminary, Des Grieux has just delivered a sermon, which is much appreciated by the nuns and visitors. His father comes to plead with him to return to secular life; the son is still determined, although tormented by thoughts of Manon, which he expresses in "Ah, fuyez, douce image!" (Ah, be gone, sweet image!). Manon enters as if on cue, and gradually, by her soft wiles — "N'est-ce plus Manon? (Is it no longer your Manon?) wins him from his determination. After a passionate duet, they flee.

ACT IV.   In the gambling rooms of the Hotel Transylvanie, Des Grieux, against his better judgment but to please Manon, gambles his last money against Guillot and wins, whereupon the old man accuses him of cheating and summons the police. Manon is arrested as his accomplice, but the Chevalier is rescued by his father.

ACT V.   Manon is about to be deported from Havre, when Lescaut and Des Grieux bribe the guard and intercept her on the road. She is, however, too ill to be rescued, and dies pitifully in her lover's arms, crying: "Et c'est là l'histoire de Manon Lescaut!"

THE LOVE-STRUCK poet drawn from Goethe's "The Sorrows of Young Werther" has much to offer a lyric tenor with a passionate mien, as well as drawing considerable drama from the Charlotte, a luscious mezzo-soprano part. The earlier pair were German, for the opera had its premiere in Vienna (it is laid in Frankfurt). When *Werther* came to the Metropolitan in 1894, the two were portrayed by Jean de Reszke and Emma Eames, and it may have been the latter's vaunted "coldness" that prompted W.J. Henderson to write that the opera seemed to have no genuine depth. However, the climate grew warmer in the 1909-10 revival with Edmond Clément, that most French of tenors, and Geraldine Farrar. Not until 1971 was it again heard at the Met, Enrico Di Giuseppe and Franco Corelli sharing the title role, their partner Christa Ludwig; later Placido Domingo or Alfredo Kraus and Elena Obraztsova or Régine Crespin took over (and Julius Rudel crossed the plaza from the New York City Opera to make his Met debut in the pit, replacing the indisposed Massenet specialist Richard Bonynge). Tatiana Troyanos and Neil Shicoff later explored the joys and sorrows of the couple. Meanwhile, many years ago the superb Supervia played Charlotte to Lucien Muratore's Werther in Chicago, while Coe Glade and Tito Schipa, Giulietta Simionato and Cesare Valletti were San Francisco partners.

Werther

Text by Edouard Blau, Paul Milliet, and Georges Hartmann after Goethe.

CHARLOTTE	*Mezzo-Soprano*
WERTHER	*Tenor*
SOPHIE	*Soprano*
ALBERT	*Baritone*
BAILIFF	*Bass*
SCHMIDT, HIS FRIEND	*Tenor*
JOHANN, ANOTHER FRIEND	*Bass*

First Performance
Vienna, 16 February 1892.

Scene from the first act of Massenet's Werther with Marie d'Isle and Léon Beylé, 1904, Opéra Comique, Paris.

Spanish mezzo-soprano Conchita Supervia had great success with the role of Charlotte in Massenet's Werther.

WERTHER'S LAST two acts are the ones that hold the most interest. Previously, Charlotte has become engaged to Albert because of the wishes of her late mother, although she is strongly attracted to Werther, with whom she goes to a dance. Her father, the bluff Bailiff, and her sprightly sister Sophie suspect nothing. The Bailiff's younger children rehearse carols, although it is still summer. Albert and Charlotte are married, but Werther still remains in town. Charlotte sends him away, saying that he may return at Christmas. In the meantime, he writes her impassioned letters, which she cherishes guiltily, and which precipitate her splendid aria in the third act. Sophie tries to cheer her sister, but Charlotte breaks down at the mention of Werther. The poet himself appears; he cannot stay away from his love. He reads some of the verses

Tatiana Troyanos and members of the children's chorus of the Lyric Opera of Chicago as Charlotte and her young brothers and sisters in a scene from Werther.

of Ossian that he had begun to translate—the powerful, tragic aria, "Pourquoi me réveiller?" (O, why dost thou waken me?), and Charlotte can resist no longer. However, she pulls herself together and dismisses him. Albert, entering, sees her distress and guesses the reason for it when he receives a note from Werther asking for the loan of duelling pistols. He coldly bids his wife take them to the poet. Trembling with fear, she finds Werther about to die. Sobbing out her love for him, she cradles his head in her arms, as the sound of the children singing "Noël" reaches her.

THAÏS WAS first sung by Sanderson, but for many years after, Mary Garden was the embodiment of the Alexandrian courtesan. Jeritza, Farrar, Leontyne Price, and a few others have draped Thaïs's mantle about their shoulders, Carol Neblett in recent days causing a sensation in a Southern town by dropping this cloak to reveal the lady in the buff. Beverly Sills at the Metropolitan luxuriated on a gilded swan-couch under full-sized mirrors. With all the extravagances of certain productions, the opera retains its charm—many years ago, W.J. Henderson, who had unkind words for Werther, thought Thaïs a "highly finished piece of stagecraft

Jeritza as Thaïs.

Leontyne Price as Thaïs, 1959,
Lyric Opera of Chicago.

[with] special feeling for theatrical expression." Recent critics have not
been so kind.

Athanaël is a lusty baritone part, and has been sung notably by
Amato, Whitehill and John Charles Thomas in the past; nearer the pres-
ent Sherrill Milnes made a *tour de force* of the tarnished monk at the
Metropolitan.

Thaïs

Text by L. Gallet after the
novel by Anatole France.

THAIS	Soprano
ATHANAEL	Baritone
NICIAS	Tenor
PALEMON,	Bass
OLD CENOBITE	
CROBYLE, A SLAVE	Soprano
MYRTALE, A SLAVE	Mezzo-Soprano
ALBINE, AN ABBESS	Contralto
SERVANT OF NICIAS	Baritone

First Performance
Paris, 16 March 1894.

Scene from Thaïs with Sherrill
Milnes in the role of Athanaël.

Beverly Sills in her widely acclaimed performance in the title role of Massenet's Thaïs, 18 January 1978, Metropolitan Opera, New York.

Cendrillon

(*Cinderella*)

Text by Henri Cain after
Charles Perrault's fairy tale.

CENDRILLON	*Soprano*
PANDOLPHE, HER FATHER	*Bass*
MME. DE LA HALTIERE	*Contralto*
NOEMIE, HER DAUGHTER	*Soprano*
DOROTHEE, THE OTHER DAUGHTER	*Mezzo-Soprano*
FAIRY GODMOTHER	*Soprano*
PRINCE	*Tenor*
MAJOR DOMO OF ENTERTAINMENT	*Baritone*
DEAN OF FACULTY	*Tenor*
KING	*Baritone*
PRIME MINISTER	*Bass*
HERALD	*Speaker*

First Performance
Paris, 24 May 1899.

ATHANAËL, WHO has known Thaïs in Alexandria in earlier days, sees her once more after he has left the carnal world and joined the rigidly religious Cenobites. He attempts to wean her away from her debauchery — she is currently the mistress of Athanaël's former friend, Nicias — but Thaïs scornfully rejects him. After a time, however, she repents and agrees to go to a convent. Athanaël escorts her there, then finds himself unable to forget her. A voluptuous dream reveals to him his true feelings; then he dreams that she is dying. He rushes to her to find that she has indeed achieved a state of purity and dies in ecstasy, while he, all too enslaved by human love, fights the angel of death in vain. There are several arias, both dramatic and touching, and the famous "Meditation," with its plangent violin solo, is a concert favorite, slightly out-of-date.

Mary Garden brought the role of the Prince in Cendrillon (Cinderella) to the Chicago Lyric Opera in 1911-12.

THE PART OF Cinderella was originally written for a soprano and that of the Prince for a dramatic soprano, the type called in French "falcon" after the impressive soprano of the Paris Opéra, Marie Cornélie Falcon.
Nowadays with mezzo-sopranos reaching for high and yet higher realms, it is not surprising to find the charming Frederica Von Stade singing the part on a recording. Her Prince is the tenor Nicolai Gedda, also a departure from Massenet's intention. The New Orleans Opera, noted for its quick follow-up of European novelties, gave the American premiere in 1902.
When Mary Garden brought the opera to Chicago for the first time in 1911-12, *she* sang the Prince, while Cinderella was the dainty Maggie Teyte. The Fairy Godmother is another important role, full of coloratura passages.

THE STORY follows Perrault's tale as far as Cinderella's return from the ball. The two sisters are quarreling over the unknown who has captured the Prince's fancy, and rudely tell Cinderella that he had said she was ugly enough to be hanged. Cendrillon's sympathetic father takes

Maggie Teyte, shown here in the role of Mélisande from Debussy's Pelléas and Mélisande, sang the role of Cinderella opposite Mary Garden's performance as the prince, 1911-12, Lyric Opera of Chicago.

her to the country, and the scene changes to the Godmother's domain. The Prince and Cinderella meet, but are separated by a high hedge. When she returns home, Cinderella talks in her sleep about the Prince, but only her father hears. He persuades her that she has dreamed it all. But it becomes very real when all the girls in the kingdom are summoned to the palace and the slipper fits only one — Cinderella.

GIAN CARLO MENOTTI (Cadegliano, 7 July 1911 –) is widely thought of as American in the U.S.A., although he has retained Italian citizenship and lives in a castle in Scotland. One of the most prolific of contemporary opera composers, the theatrically gifted Menotti has been represented in opera houses all over the world, from the tiniest church group that gives *Amahl and the Night Visitors*, to the European houses that offered several premieres and the Metropolitan, which mounted his frivolous *Amelia Goes to the Ball* a year after its premiere at the Curtis Institute in Philadelphia in 1937. The Met followed this with *The Island God* in 1942, Menotti's only real failure, although his madrigal opera, *The Unicorn, the Dragon, and the Manticore* (1958) met with little favor. His more recent works too, have showed little of the fresh inventiveness, the drama, and the excitement of several earlier efforts, notably *Amahl, The Medium, The Consul*, and *The Saint of Bleeker Street* — the latter two won Pulitzer Prizes. Most of Menotti's operas have been commissioned; his latest, *La Loca*, being written to celebrate Beverly Sills's 50th birthday and given its premiere in San Diego, then heard at the New York City Opera. In spite of the prima donna's virtuoso acting, the work had no musical profile.

Other operas are: *The Old Maid and the Thief* (commissioned for radio, 1939); *The Telephone* (1947), a giddy little curtain raiser whose heroine seems permanently attached to an ear-piece; *Maria Golovin* (1958), a melodrama that achieved little success and yet perhaps deserves revival; *Labyrinth* (1963), a television fantasy that has its hero and heroine chin-deep in water a good deal of the time; *The Last Savage*, a socio-comedy

Teresa Stratas as the Mother with Robert Sapolsky as Amahl in Amahl and the Night Visitors.

Scene from the premiere of Menotti's Help! Help! The Globolinks, 1969, Santa Fe Opera.

concerning a wealthy American girl who imports and exploits a pseudo-savage from the Himalayas (premiere in Paris in 1963 and brought to the Met in 1964); *Help! Help! The Globolinks!* (1968), a trifling absurdity that made Judith Blegen's reputation as violinist as well as soprano; and *The Most Important Man* (1971), which attempted a seriousness beyond the composer-librettist's depth. He has written all his texts, departing from his own invention only with *La Loca*, which features real history—the Queen of Spain who endured persecution from her husband, father, and son, and eventually went mad.

Fundamental character development is perhaps the greatest lack in Menotti's copious output. Only the *Consul's* Magda Sorel, Maria Golovin, and the Mother in *Amahl* seem at all rounded characters, with human emotions and potentials for suffering. His people are more often caricatures and line drawings—even the operatic characters, who may be considered a special breed. With the exception of the three listed above, Menotti's women are most often sluts, flibbertigibbets, fanatics, or sadists. They dominate the weak, vacillating, shallow men. They project bitter-tasting comedy or venomous melodrama—seldom tragedy of the human spirit.

THE MEDIUM was a role made famous by Marie Powers. Madame Flora cynically preys on her clients with fake spiritual effects until something happens she cannot explain—she hears voices and is touched by a cold hand. Her daughter Monica is very fond of the mute boy Toby, who assists in Flora's machinations, and sings for him while he mimes. Later, he hides as Flora is sunk in a drunken stupor, from which she wakes wildly, thinking she has heard "the ghost." She shoots at the puppet theater, Toby's blood appears on the curtain, and he falls dead into the room. "I've killed the Ghost!" Flora cries, as Monica pounds on the door.

Menotti has directed an excellent film of *The Medium*, which had its premiere at Columbia University, New York, on 8 May 1946, and was later revised for Broadway. The opera is frequently performed with the composer's *The Telephone*.

THE CONSUL is one of Menotti's most successful efforts; it is the quality of tragedy which sets it apart from much of his other work.

ACT I.   In an unspecified European country after World War II, John Sorel is forced to leave his wife, Magda, his baby, and his mother, and try to escape across the border. He has been to a secret meeting with his freedom-loving friends, and has been shot, wounded in the leg. He hides as the secret police enter to question the family, and utter baleful threats. John returns to say that a signal will be given—a rock through the window—whereupon Magda must summon Assan, the glass-cutter, who will have news. He leaves.

The Consul

Text by the Composer.

JOHN SOREL	*Baritone*
MAGDA SOREL	*Soprano*
THE MOTHER	*Contralto*
SECRET POLICE AGENT	*Bass*

147
MENOTTI

TWO PLAIN-CLOTHES MEN	*Silent*
THE SECRETARY	*Mezzo-Soprano*
THE FOREIGN WOMAN	*Soprano*
ANNA GOMEZ	*Soprano*
VERA BORONEL	*Contralto*
THE MAGICIAN (NIKITA MAGADOFF)	*Tenor*
ASSAN	*Baritone*
VOICE ON THE RECORD	*Soprano*

First Performance
Philadelphia, 1 March 1950.

Design for a poster for The Consul (detail).

Patricia Neway (c.) as Magda in the first per-formance of The Consul, Philadelphia, 1950.

Scene 2. Magda goes to the Consul's office to secure a visa in order to join John, but meets with unyielding bureaucracy and indifference on the part of the secretary. Everyone waiting tries in turn to move this cold woman, even the Magician, who plays some fancy tricks to no avail. It is a question of papers, papers, papers—and none of them suffice.

ACT II, Scene 1. The signal is given; Assan arrives on the heels of a secret agent from whom Magda has her visa; she tells Assan to reassure him. During the scene, the baby dies.

Scene 2. Again the consulate; again frustration. Magda sings the dominant aria in the work: "To this we've come: that men withhold the world from men." When an "important visitor" comes out of the consul's office, it is the secret agent. Magda faints.

ACT III, Scene 1. At the consulate, Assan hurries in to tell Magda that John is rejoining her, having heard of the deaths of the baby and his mother. She leaves, and just misses John, who has been followed to the office and is now arrested and taken away.

Scene 2. Magda prepares to commit suicide by inhaling gas, but first sees visions of all the people she has met. As she dies, the telephone rings and is unanswered.

AMAHL AND THE NIGHT VISITORS, which has become so popular, was based on a real experience of Menotti's. As a child in Italy, he was taken by a nurse to a shrine, and his crippled leg was cured. The work was commissioned by the National Broadcasting Company for television, and had its premiere on Christmas Eve, 1951. It was the first to

Scene from NBC Television performance of Amahl and the Night Visitors, 1951, NBC Opera Company, New York.

gain commercial sponsorship, and was repeated year after year at Christmas time, eventually being shot in color. As a stage production, *Amahl* knows hardly a rival in popularity in America.

A crippled boy sees a bright star in the sky; his mother will not believe him until the three Kings appear on their way to visit the Holy Child. They take shelter for the night, the villagers come to dance for them, and the Mother, tempted by their gold, tries to steal a piece. She is caught, but forgiven, and the boy is cured as if by a miracle and accompanies the Kings on their journey.

Scene from Menotti's The Saint of Bleecker Street with Gabrielle Ruggerio in the title role, Metropolitan Opera, New York.

THE SAINT OF BLEECKER STREET, after some dissension with the New York City Opera, had its premiere on Broadway, 27 December 1954. It was then heard in Milan, seen on British television, and eventually came to the New York City Opera. In New York, a poor Italian girl, Annina, receives the stigmata and yearns to be a nun. Her brother

Michele is violently opposed, and during the wedding festivities of a neighborhood couple, shows his unhealthy affection for his sister by refusing to let his sweetheart go into the party. She protests and accuses him of being in love with Annina. Enraged, he stabs her. Then in hiding, he meets Annina, who tells him she is dying and is going to a nunnery. In a desperate attempt to stop her, Michele appears as she is taking the veil. But the ritual is completed just before death claims her.

GIACOMO MEYERBEER (Berlin, 5 September 1791 — Paris, 2 May 1864). The famous composer's name was in reality Jacob Liebmann Beer, but a legacy from a wealthy relative named Meyer caused him to place that name in front of his own. The eldest son of a rich Jewish banker in Berlin and a cultivated mother, young Jacob became a child piano prodigy, and for a long time thought to make his career as a performer. But the talent for composition gradually took over. He experienced several distinct periods, changing

Portrait of Giacomo Meyerbeer by Von Kriehuber.

Ballet scene from Meyerbeer's French operetta L'Étoile du Nord (Star of the North).

styles with ease and assurance. His earliest operas, written for German centers, and a middle period, when he turned out Italian works for Padua, Turin, Venice, and Milan, are now buried in history books. The turning point in his life came with *Il Crociato in Egitto*, produced in Venice in 1824, and creating a sensation. This enormous work, only recently revived in concert form, to great acclaim in New York, combined his early German traits with his later Italian "wild oats" (as he called them). When it was given in Paris in 1826, a new era opened up for Meyerbeer—and for opera in Paris. *Robert le Diable* (Robert the Devil), *Les Huguenots,* and *Le Prophète* each created its own wave of success. A German opera, *Ein Feldlager in Schlesien* (The Camp in Silesia), produced in Berlin, where he had been appointed director of the Opera in 1842, carried enormous prestige because of the presence in the cast of Jenny Lind. It also served as a basis for his French operetta, *L'Étoile du Nord* (Star of the North), produced at the Opéra-Comique in 1854. Another lighter work was *Le Pardon de Ploërmel* (Dinorah) in 1859. *L'Africaine,* on which he worked intermittently for a long time before abandoning it in favor of *Le Prophète,* brought disagreement with his faithful librettist, Eugène Scribe, and was only finished at the time of Meyerbeer's death; it was produced posthumously in 1865.

Throughout his life, Meyerbeer enjoyed the friendship of Carl Maria von Weber, and produced his *Euryanthe* in Berlin. He also gave a splendid production to *Rienzi,* and paved the way for a Berlin mounting of *Der Fliegende Holländer* although Wagner was later to become an enemy.

Meyerbeer may be said to have been the founder of truly "grand" opera, with the extravagance of his plans, the sheer size of his productions, and the enormously taxing demands on his casts. To this day, his four most notable works are not too often heard because of these difficulties: *Robert* requires at least four virtuoso singers; *Prophète* an equal number as well as several difficult smaller parts; *Africaine,* five; and *Huguenots* seven! All suffer without elaborate staging and the ballets which were an absolute requisite in Paris.

Robert le Diable
(*Robert the Devil*)

Jenny Lind in her London debut as Alice in Meyerbeer's Robert the Devil with Joseph Staudigl as Count Bertram, Her Majesty's, 1847.

PREMIERE: PARIS Opéra, 22 November 1831, with a libretto by Scribe and Delavigne. Jenny Lind made her sensational London debut as Alice in 1847 when the opera was sung in Italian. New York heard *Robert* (in English) in 1834. The Metropolitan gave it for the first time in its first season, 1883, with Fursch-Madi, Alwina Valleria (the first American to sing at the Met), Stagno, and Mirabella. A Florence Festival revival in 1968 had Renata Scotto and Boris Christoff.

ROBERT, THE SON of Bertram (in reality the Devil), is never free from his father's Satanic influence. His love for Isabella, Princess of Sicily, is thwarted at every turn. The pleas of his foster-sister Alice cannot turn him from his wild, wicked ways; he loses his fortune at gambling and his honor by failing to appear at a tournament. Bertram promises the evil spirits that Robert will join them. In a spectacular scene, the fiend summons up nuns who have broken their vows, and they entice Robert to break off a branch of a mystic cypress which will give him his desires. He forces his way into Isabella's chamber, but her tears move him to break the talisman and the spell. Bertram saves him from Isabella's soldiers and takes him to the cathedral, where he hopes for Robert's signature on a fatal contract for his soul before midnight. But Alice delays him by invoking Robert's mother's spirit, and he is at last redeemed to marry Isabella. Alice now can be wed to Raimbaut, the minstrel. A final trio for Alice, Robert, and Bertram is one of the most noble pages in Meyerbeer's work, which also contains some fine arias and ensembles — and the ballet by the depraved nuns.

Picture of a scene from Robert the Devil from the Parisian version as it appeared at Her Majesty's in 1862. Thérèse Tietjens sang the role of Alice in this production.

THE SOPRANO Marie Falcon (whose name is attached to a particular type of voice) and the tenor Adolphe Nourrit headed the cast at the premiere at the Paris Opéra on 29 February 1836. Covent Garden heard the opera first in German in 1841; New York in French in 1845 (New Orleans had, as usual, beaten the Northern capital to a premiere, in 1839). The Metropolitan had the singers for it in the first season, 1883-84: Nilsson, Sembrich, Campanini, Mirabell, Kaschmann. But long before that, London had considered *Huguenots* a staple, with such singers as Pauline Viardot-Garcia, Marietta Alboni, the famous husband and wife Mario and Grisi, Pauline Lucca, Thérèse Tietjens, Ilma di Murska, and Adelina Patti. Occasionally sopranos would trade the roles of Valentine and Marguerite de Valois. The casts of Meyerbeer operas read like all-star lists—indeed, seven-star, for *Huguenots* is called the opera of "sept étoiles." Melba, Sembrich, Hempel, Kurz and Tetrazzini were notable Marguerites of other days; Sutherland tackled it once in Milan, with Giulietta Simionato doing her first soprano stint as Valentine and the young Franco Corelli as Raoul, Nicolai Ghiaurov as Marcel, and Fiorenza Cossotto as Urbain.

Famous Valentines have been Nilsson, Materna, Lilli Lehmann, Nordica, Albani, Litvinne (the enormous sister-in-law of Edouard de Reszke), Bréval, Gadski, De Macchi, and Destinn. For these Raouls they have died: Campanini, Schott, Jean de Reszke (he, at least, was considered worth it), Saléza, Alvarez, Zenatello, and Caruso.

These Urbains have rattled off their brilliant cavatinas (originally as sopranos, then transposed for lower voices): the indomitable Sophia Schalchi, Alboni, Olitzka, Mantelli, Homer, Walker, and Garrison. Even the little Fritzi Scheff (noted more for *Mlle. Modiste* but a charmer for three seasons at the Met, earning the enmity of Sembrich) sang the page one time. Baritones (or basses) had their nights as well, singing Valentine's father St. Bris: Kaschmann, Lassalle, Plançon, Journet, and Rothier among them, while Journet, Edouard de Reszke, and Kipnis were three who boomed out Marcel's battle song with its "piff, paff, piff." Other dark voices have assumed the role of De Nevers, including Del Puente, Ancona, Maurel, Scotti, and Gilly.

The opera persisted in Metropolitan annals only until 1915, which may say something about the recent availability of *"sept étoiles."* Beverly Sills sang Marguerite in a concert performance, and bits were revived for a cheering, stamping audience in Carnegie Hall by the Friends of French Opera not too long ago when Nicolai Gedda raised the roof—still, one waits for a full-dress presentation with the stars shining in their Meyerbeer heaven.

THE HISTORICAL element of the plot concerns the massacre of the Huguenots by the Catholics on St. Bartholomew's Day in Paris in August 1572. Leading up to the tragic event were the fortunes of the Catholics—Valentine, her betrothed Count de Nevers, her father, Count de St. Bris—and Raoul de Nangis, the Huguenot Valentine has come to love after he has rescued her from molestation by a gang. She arrives at a banquet given by the De Nevers with a request from Marguerite de Valois that De Nevers release Valentine from her engagement. Valentine is seen by the only Huguenot guest, Raoul, who believes her to have a liaison with De Nevers. When Marguerite proposes, in hopes of uniting the Huguenots and the Catholics, that Raoul

Les Huguenots
(*The Huguenots*)

Program for The Huguenots, 29 February 1836, Académie Royale de Musique, Paris.

153
MEYERBEER

Marie Falcon, creator of the role of Valentine in The Huguenots.

take Valentine as a wife, he refuses. Shamed and broken-hearted, she marries De Nevers. She overhears the Catholics plotting to ambush Raoul, and warns him, so that his soldier-servant Marcel can gather enough men to defeat the plot. Now Raoul learns from Queen Marguerite the truth about Valentine's visit to De Nevers, and seeks her out in her home. They are interrupted, and Raoul hides, overhearing the plan for the massacre of Huguenots. Priests bless the swords of the Catholics in a spectacular scene. Resisting Valentine's attempts to hold him, he rushes off to inform the Huguenot leaders. But he is too late; the massacre has already begun. Valentine determines to die with her lover, and the two, with the faithful Marcel, are slain. St. Bris discovers too late that he has wreaked vengeance on his own daughter.

The opera, originally in five acts, can be played in three. The libretto is by Scribe.

Pauline Viardot as Valentine.

Nilsson as Valentine.

Grisi as Valentine and Mario as Raoul in a scene from the fourth act of The Huguenots, *1858, Covent Garden, London.*

Le Prophète
(*The Prophet*)

DAMROSCH'S
ERAND ✳ GERMAN ✳ OPERA
FROM THE
METROPOLITAN OPERA HOUSE, NEW YORK,

New York Symphony Orchestra

MR. WALTER DAMROSCH - - - Director

THIS EVENING
MEYERBEER'S Opera, in 5 Acts,

LE PROPHETE

JEAN OF LEYDEN	. . . . HERR SCHOTT
FIDES, Mother to Jean of Leyden	. . . . . FRL. BRANDT
BERTHA	. . . . MISS MARTINEZ
COUNT OBERTHAL	. . . . . . HERR STAUDIGL
JONAS . . . . } Anabaptist	. . . . HERR KEMLITZ
MATHISEN . . . . } Preachers	. . . . HERR MILLER
ZACHARIAS	. . . . HERR KOEGEL
TWO CAPTAINS	. . . . HERR WOLF
	. . . . HERR PACHE
Chorus of Nobles, Citizens, Peasants, Soldiers, Prisoners, etc.	

The Incidental Divertisement will be supported by . Signora ISOLANI TORRI

Director of the Opera and Conductor . . . . Mr. WALTER DAMROSCH
Stage Manager . . . . With Im Hock
Second Conductor . . . . Herr Lund

Program for a performance of Le Prophète, 6 April 1885, Boston Theater.

WITH A ROSTER of important singers as long as that of *Les Huguenots* and *L'Africaine, Le Prophète* can also boast some recent revivals, among them the Metropolitan's in 1977 with Marilyn Horne, Renata Scotto, and James McCracken. Pauline Viardot and Gustave Roger were the original stars in the Paris Opéra premiere on 16 April 1849, and the mezzo sang again at Covent Garden in 1849 with Mario as hero. Although New York heard performances in 1853, more important showings were at the Metropolitan, the first in German in 1884. The overweening prophet has been sung by Stagno, Schott, Sylva, Niemann, Jean de Reszke, Tamagno, Alvarez, Caruso, and Martinelli. His mother Fidès has called for the services of such distinguished mezzos as Schalchi, Brandt, Mantelli, Schumann-Heink, Matzenauer, Homer, and Branzell. The young sweetheart Bertha has been sung by Valleria, Seidl-Kraus, Lehmann, De Lussan, Muzio, and Easton. Edouard de Reszke and José Mardones were among the basses. The opera was neglected by the Metropolitan until the recent revival.

SCRIBE ALSO fashioned this elaborate plot. The premiere was in Paris on 16 April 1849. Jean of Leyden, a poor innkeeper in Dordrecht, Holland, is not the first anti-hero in opera, but he is a significant one. Because of his religious fanaticism and his strong resemblance to King David, he is exploited by three fanatical Anabaptists and named a prophet of God. He begins to believe in his own myth and is even crowned Emperor at Münster, Germany. His fiancée Bertha has been forbidden by count Oberthal, of whom she is a vassal, to marry Jean,

Enrico Caruso as Jean with Claudia Muzio as Bertha in Le Prophète.

and is taken away by the count himself. When she escapes, Jean's mother, Fidès, is threatened by Orberthal unless Jean will give up Bertha, which he does. After his glorious coronation at Münster, his troubles multiply. The legitimate Emperor seeks to oust him; his mother, believing him dead, reviles the "prophet," only to discover that he is her son. He will not acknowledge her at first, but repents at her tears. Bertha also seeks revenge on the prophet, and when she discovers his true identity, stabs herself. In the meantime, she has set fire to the castle, which blows up in the midst of a bacchanal, killing Jean and Fidès as well as his enemies.

Familiar music is Fidès' grand aria, "Ah, mon fils" (Ah, my son), the ballet of skaters, and the Coronation March. Additional stirring passages are in the penultimate scene: a glorious *scena* for Fidès, a duet between the two women, and a trio with Jean. Needless to say, a spectacular production is indicated, including the famous skating scene, originally done on roller skates, and faked with false skates on boots at the Met.

L'AFRICAINE, like *Les Huguenots*, boasts its huge complement of stars, but in even greater number, for although not as many are required for one performance, Meyerbeer's posthumous opera has persisted for a longer time in the repertory. As recently as 1972 a splendid performance was mounted in San Francisco (and in the original French instead of the usual Italian), with Shirley Verrett as Selika and Placido Domingo as Vasco da Gama. The Metropolitan carried it until 1934 for such singers as Hauk, Nordica, Lilli Lehmann, Litvinne, Bréval, Fremstad, Ponselle, and Rethberg as the heroine, and Dippel, Tamagno, Caruso, Gigli, and Martinelli as Vasco. The baritone role of Nelusko saw Robinson, Ancona, Lassalle, Maurel, Scotti, Danise, Stracciari, and De Luca through the years, while the bass "villain" was assumed by Fischer, Edouard de Reszke, Plançon, Didur, Ludikar, and Lazzari. The lesser soprano role of Inez had its own distinction, with Suzanne Adams, Rappold, Queena Mario, Guilford, and Nina Morgana. Note that many of these are the same as in the *Huguenots* and *Prophète* lists—the great voices were imperative for Meyerbeer.

THE COMPLICATED story was hashed over many times in the composer's first labor with Scribe on it, and again when he resumed. It

Victor Maurel sang Nelusko.

L'Africaine
(*The Indian Maid*)

157
MEYERBEER

Beniamino Gigli as Vasco da Gama,
Metropolitan Opera, New York.

Lilli Lehmann sang the role of Selika in L'Africaine.

makes a little less sense than many another; libretto reading in advance of listening is advised. Inez, daughter of the Portuguese Admiral Don Diego, loves Vasco da Gama, who returns from shipwreck with a captive Indian Queen, Selika, and her attendant Nelusko. Don Pedro, who is favored by her father as Inez's husband, jails Vasco for insulting the council which has refused him permission to explore the land he has discovered. Don Pedro sets out himself on that mission, first having secured Inez's agreement to their marriage, given in order to free Vasco. Selika, who has fallen in love with Vasco and incurred the jealousy of Nelusko, embarks with the two men on a following ship. Don Pedro, when overtaken, captures Vasco. But his ship is wrecked, and the natives at Nelusko's command kill all but Vasco, Selika proclaiming him her husband. As queen of this land, she then frees him to return to Inez, and breathes deeply of a poisoned tree (à la Lakmé) to take her life. Nelusko joins her in death.

Don Pedro's vessel from Act III of L'Africaine, The Verona Festival, Verona, Italy.

ITALO MONTEMEZZI (Vigasio, near Verona, 4 August 1875 – Vigasio, 15 May 1952). Without much formal education, Montemezzi produced several operas popular in Italy, of which his third, *L'amore dei tre re* (The Love of Three Kings) is his masterpiece. His first opera was *Giovanni Gallurese,* an enormous success in Italy after its premiere in 1905; his second, *Hellera,* was less popular. After *L'amore,* Montemezzi produced a block-buster, *La nave,* with a libretto by Tito Ricordi based on D'Annunzio (1918; produced in Chicago in 1919 at enormous cost, with Rosa Raisa and Giacomo Rimini, Montemezzi conducting.) It calls for a grandiloquent production with a huge ship and, as one writer put it, singers of "unflinching larynx and hottentot charisma." More modest were his one-act works, *La notte de Zor-*

ina (1931) and *L'Incantesimo* (1943). Montemezzi lived for a time in California, and conducted *L'amore dei tre re* in San Francisco and at the Metropolitan in 1941.

THE OPERA HAD its premiere in Milan in 1913, and the Metropolitan, quicker in those days to take advantage of European successes, brought it to New York the following year, on 2 January, with Lucrezia Bori and Edoardo Ferrari-Fontana (Matzenauer's husband and the original Avito), Toscanini conducting. But Henry Russell in Boston was equally alert, and managed to secure the new opera on 19 February, then opening his Paris season with it, the singers there being Edvina, Fontana, Cigada, and Vanni Marcoux. The Met performed the attractive work quite often in the days when there were the singers for it — the Fiora (a role coveted by the spinto who could act): Muzio, Easton, Bori, Ponselle, Jepson; the tenor Avito: Caruso, Martinelli, Gigli, Edward Johnson, and Tokatyan; the baritone husband Manfredo: Amato, Danise, Tibbett, Bonelli; the old King Archibaldo: Didur, Mardones, Rothier, Ludikar, Pinza. Grace Moore starred in the 1941 revival which Montemezzi conducted, along with Kullman, Bonelli, and Pinza. The emphasis meanwhile shifted to Chicago, where in

Italo Montemezzi.

Virgilio Lazzari and Dorothy Kirsten in a scene from The Love of Three Kings.

L'Amore dei Tre Re

(*The Love of Three Kings*)

Text by Sem Benelli, from his play.

ARCHIBALDO	*Bass*
MANFREDO	*Baritone*
AVITO	*Tenor*
FIORA	*Soprano*
FLAMINO	*Tenor*

First Performance
Milan, 10 April 1913.

Florence Easton and Edward Johnson in a scene from The Love of Three Kings, Metropolitan Opera, New York.

Lucrezia Bori sang the role of Fiora.

1915 Edvina, Fontana, and Whitehill graced the cast. Then Mary Garden took over the heroine, with Johnson and Lazzari — Garden had a fierce battle with the old King, who strangles her and hoists her over his shoulder. Lazzari used to show her the scratches she inflicted on his hands. Muzio and Bori later sang Fiora, and it was Moore's first appearance anywhere. Kirsten, Weede, and Pinza dominated the later San Francisco casts.

The opera is one of those rareties that uses a play virtually intact. Sem Benelli, the playwright, himself made what condensation was necessary. The music is highly expressive, dramatic, and passionate. . . ."a medieval tapestry, the colors of which have not faded, but still glow with their original depth and color," according to Gustave Kobbé. As for the story, if a deeper meaning is looked for, Kobbé adds, "the three kings are in love with Italy, represented by Fiora, who hates and scorns the conqueror of her country, Archibaldo; coldly turns aside from Manfredo, his son and heir apparent with whose hand he sought to bribe her; hotly loves and dies for a prince of her own people, Avito. Tragic is the outcome of the conqueror's effort to win and rule over an unwilling people. Truly, he is blind."

THE TRAGEDY begins as Archibaldo suspects his daughter-in-law, Fiora, of treachery while her husband is away. Avito has stolen in to be with her, but leaves as a signal tells him Manfredo is returning. The husband, unsuspecting, asks Fiora to wave a long white scarf until he is out of sight as he sets forth again — this she does for a short time but is distracted by the presence of Avito. The blind old king nearly catches the lovers, but Avito escapes. However, vengeance is not denied the old man: he finds Fiora, strangles her, and carries her body off on his shoulders. Archibaldo rubs a fatal poison on her lips as she lies entombed. Certain death comes to Avito, who steals in and kisses her for one last time, but the same fate meets Manfredo. The old man's triumph turns to dust.

CLAUDIO MONTEVERDI (Cremona, (May?) 1567 — Venice, 29 November 1643) joins a trio of composers who revolutionized the art of music in their times — Beethoven, Wagner, and Debussy. In fact, he was the first real startling innovator. With him, the strict polyphony of the 16th century gave way to expression of poetic speech, thus creating *secco recitativo*, thoroughbass, and the new style of *bel canto*. He was also responsible for the *da capo* aria, the first use of *pizzicato* and the tremolo, first heard in *Combattimento di Tancredi e Clorinda*, for although he never wrote a purely instrumental piece, he enlarged and made subtle the accompaniments for his stage and religious works, and was the first to use the violin in the orchestras. He had already become known for his magnificent madrigals, of which he wrote hundreds.

Of the nearly two score operas he wrote, most are lost (twelve, written for Parma and Mantua, were destroyed in the Sack of Mantua). Of his second, *L'Ariana*, only the famous "Lament" remains. We are privileged to hear today, in one or another of the many editions fashioned through the years by composers of varying merit, the *Orfeo* (first titled *La favola d'Orfeo*); *Il combattimento*; *Il ritorno d'Ulisse in patria*; and *L'incoronazione di Poppea*.

Very little is known of Monteverdi's life in Cremona. Only after he was summoned to the court of the Gonzagas in Mantua do we document him. The famous family (the name usurped by Piave for Verdi's licentious Duke in *Rigoletto* when the censors forbade the use of a French King) had been patrons of the arts for quite a while — in their service were Petrarch, Palestrina, Tasso, Galilei, and the painters Rubens and Mantegna (whose splendors are still visible in the Mantua castle). Also to be seen is the great room where *Orfeo* was first performed (later scholarship has placed it there instead of the Accademia first supposed to be its venue). The Gonzagas were not always generous patrons; Monteverdi underwent many years of hardship and was at last dismissed. He was soon invited to Venice, where he exercised his genius chiefly in religious music.

The outbreak of plague in Northern Italy in 1630 undoubtedly affected Monteverdi deeply, and he took holy orders about this time. When the first real opera house opened to the public in Venice in 1637, his interest was reawakened, and he wrote some operas for that city and Parma.

The very name of this "proud and passionate scholar" (as one writer has called him) seemed to have been forgotten for almost two hundred years. Then some interest stirred, and *Orfeo* occasionally came forth in various editions. Only just before and after the First World War did a real renaissance begin, and today we are familiar with what remains of this vital personality, who led music out of the Renaissance into broader, more fertile fields.

Another Fiora, Rosa Ponselle sang the role at the Metropolitan Opera, New York.

Monteverdi with his bass viol, seventeenth-century Italian painting.

Detail of an engraving of Fiori Poetici, a work of Monteverdi's published 1644, Milan.

La Favola
d'Orfeo (Orfeo)

(*The Fable of Orfeo*)

Contralto Adriana Basile (c.1580-1640) was well known throughout Italy. Monteverdi may have written the part of Orfeo for her.

"A DRAMA OF the strangest kind, with all of the actors delivering their lines in music" was the description of the newest entertainment in the Gonzaga palace, as quoted in Kathleen O'Donnell Hoover's *Makers of Opera.* That unprecedented work of art followed closely on the Florentine "Camerata" experiment of Peri's *Euridice*, which Duke Vincenzo of Mantua supposedly had witnessed and thought to imitate. It was Monteverdi's *Orfeo.* Monteverdi had quite outstripped Peri in the fusion of music and poetry, with no loss of dramatic force on the one hand and lyricism on the other. He used a thirty-six piece orchestra — all the resources he could call on — for his setting of the Alessandro Striggio libretto based on the famous legend. The startled ears of the Mantuan court experienced the new sensation first on 23 (or 24) February 1607. The nearest modern approximation of that memorable first night was probably Leopold Stokowski's resurrection of the work for the New York City Opera on 29 September 1960, when the celebrated conductor endeavored to duplicate the original orchestration, and every effort was made to follow the original performance in style. Gérard Souzay sang the title role. The Juilliard American Opera Center staged a revival in 1979, although with comparatively modern instruments. A concert performance was given at the Metropolitan in 1912, while the first American staged production (the Malipiero version) took place in Boston in 1941.

ORFEO WAS preceded by the first opera overture in history. Originally in five acts and a prologue, the opera opens with the Spirit of Music, who commands silence from nature as she tells the story of Orfeo. Nymphs and shepherds celebrate the wedding of the poet to Euridice, but their joy is short lived, for the bride is stung to death by a serpent. Orfeo charms his way into Hades by his song, and Persephone persuades Pluto to release Euridice. But, fatefully, the rescued woman begs her husband to look at her; against the promise he has made, he does so. Euridice disappears, and the infernal chorus gloats. Orfeo wanders

Title page for Orfeo.

in the fields of Thrace; his lament is repeated by Echo. (The story here departs, as does Gluck's work on the same subject, from the original myth which has Orfeo torn to pieces by the Thracian women for grieving too long.) Orfeo is taken to Olympus by Apollo, his father, and general festivity prevails.

Il Combattimento di Tancredi e Clorinda

(The Duel between Tancredi and Clorinda)

CALLED BY Monteverdi a "madrigal" opera, the work is based on Torquato Tasso's verses in *Gerusalemme liberata*; the principal role is that of Testo, the Narrator, a tenor. The one-act work had its premiere in Venice in 1624. After its American premiere at Smith College in 1928, it has been heard a number of times.

The new devices Monteverdi used in this score to illustrate passion and anger were rapidly repeated notes, string *tremolo*, and *pizzicati*, all too familiar today, but a revelation in the early seventeenth century.

TANCREDI, a Christian knight, has fallen in love with the Saracen maiden Clorinda, who, dressed as a man, has led a successful attack on a Christian fortress. Tancredi, believing her to be a man, challenges her to a duel. The music emotionally describes the battle, which is carried out in dance. At last, Tancredi is victorious, only to discover that his victim is his beloved. Both performers have dramatic recitatives. When performed as a ballet, the work is very effective.

Il Ritorno d'Ulisse in Patria

(*Ulysses's Return Home*)

Text by G. Badoarto.

THERE HAS been some doubt that Monteverdi was the composer of this score, but most of that is cleared away, and Luigi Dallapiccola, responsible for a definitive edition in 1942 (performed at the Florence Festival) claimed that the work is a masterpiece. Several well known musicians have made versions, chiefly D'Indy, Kraack, and Raymond Leppard, the last-named giving his adaptation at Glyndebourne in 1972 with Janet Baker and Benjamin Luxon. The premiere was in Venice in February, 1641.

The American premiere was as recent as 19 January 1974, a production by the Opera Society of Washington, in the realization by Leppard, starring Frederica von Stade and Richard Stilwell. The New York City Opera mounted the same production on 29 February 1976, a New York premiere.

THE STORY follows fairly closely the legend of the hero returning from the Trojan War, his inspiration by the gods, his disguise as an old man, and his triumph over the suitors who have plagued Penelope during his absence. The determining feat is his employment of his old bow, killing each of the suitors with an arrow. There is some splendid music, notably a lament for Penelope and one for Ulysses; also a comic element is introduced in the suitors' jester, Iro, who has an aria reflecting the *buffo* element Monteverdi introduced into opera.

Richard Stilwell as Ulysses and Frederica von Stade as Penelope, 1979 Glyndebourne Festival.

Autographed score from Monteverdi's The Coronation of Poppea.

L'Incoronazione di Poppea
(*The Coronation of Poppea*)

WRITTEN WHEN Monteverdi was seventy-six to a libretto by G.F. Busenello, this opera can well be called the first "music drama," presaging the grander works of Wagner and others. Although there are arias and other set pieces, the drama relies largely on a declamation that is passionate speech raised to a high power. It holds the boards today as the masterpiece it is. First heard in Venice in 1642, the work later was revived in Naples, and 250 years later began a scattered round of performances that included the American premiere at the hands of the devoted forces of Smith college in

Tatiana Troyanos sang the role of Poppea in the 1975 San Francisco Opera production of the opera.

Janet Baker as Poppea and
Robert Ferguson as Nero.
1971, Sadler's Wells,
London.

1926. Because of the scanty original material (obviously authentic), various "realizations" have been made from time to time, the most recent being that of the indefatigable Raymond Leppard. This was first performed at Glyndebourne in 1962 and was the version of the New York City Opera in 1973. The American Opera Society performed concert versions in 1953 and 1961. Other useful "arrangements" are by Ghedini, Krenek, and Malipiero.

POPPEA portrays real people instead of gods and goddesses in this tragedy centered around the lascivious Emperor Nero. Earthly passions flame; vengeance is sought and exacted; all does not end in justice. Poppea, who has given herself to Nero and is eventually crowned Empress, is still married to Ottone, who cannot renounce her. Drusilla's love for Ottone is rejected, and he, dressed in Drusilla's clothes, endeavors to carry out the order of Ottavia, Nero's spurned wife, to kill Poppea. But he cannot. Confessing, to save Drusilla because of the masquerade, Ottone and Drusilla are sent into exile. Seneca, who has given unpalatable advice to Nero, is sentenced to death.

DOUGLAS STUART MOORE (Cutchogue, N.Y., 10 August 1893 – Greenpoint, N.Y., 25 July 1969). One of the most beloved educators and composers in the United States, Moore wrote a number of operas, of which *The Ballad of Baby Doe* has earned the greatest lasting success. Moore's earlier operas were *The Headless Horseman* (1936); *The Devil and Daniel Webster* (1939); *White Wings* (1949); *The Emperor's New Clothes* (1949), and *Giants in the Earth* (a Pulitzer Prize winner in 1951). After *Baby Doe*, Moore wrote a short satirical piece, a "soap opera," *Gallantry* (1958); set Henry James's *The Wings of the Dove* (1961), an honorable yet not entirely satisfactory attempt at a libretto of more sophisticated weave than the others, which had mostly been American homespun; and reverted to "just plain folks" with *Carry Nation* (1968) endeavoring to paint a more sympathetic picture of the hatchet lady who wrecked saloons.

THE BALLAD OF BABY DOE was commissioned in honor of the Columbia University Bicentennial by the Koussevitzky Foundation of the Library of Congress. Original in concept, vital in expressiveness, John Latouche's libretto for Moore's opera is exemplary. The story is based on a good deal of reality: the characters existed, and their milieu is still preserved. Appropriately, the opera had its premiere in the mining town of Central City, Colorado, on 7 July 1956. Leadville lies not too many mountains away, the Matchless Mine preserved as a tourist attraction, the opera house built by Horace Tabor presumably still standing (there was talk of restoring it). Opera companies all over the United States have picked up the work for successful performance, most notably the New York City Opera in 1958, when Beverly Sills scored one of her greatest triumphs as the heroine.

ACT I (in several scenes). Tabor and his cronies escape the concert in the opera house, and play up to the girls from the next-door saloon. Soon, Tabor's wife, Augusta, and the other wives corral them, but Horace remains outside, thus witnessing the arrival of Mrs. Elizabeth (Baby) Doe, whom he directs to the Clarendon Hotel. After

The Ballad of Baby Doe

Text by John Latouche.

Scene from The Ballad of Baby Doe with baritone Clifford Harvuot (with cigar) as H.A.W. Tabor and mezzo-soprano Frances Bible (with fan) in the role of Augusta Tabor, Central City Opera, Central City, Colorado.

Beverly Sills (c.) as Baby Doe in the New York City Opera production.

Walter Cassel as H.A.W. Tabor.

the concert, the women gossip about Baby — she has apparently left her husband in Central City. The lady in question sits at her window and sings a charming aria, the "Willow Song." Tabor is entranced, and impulsively kisses her hand. Augusta discovers gloves meant by Horace as a present for Baby; her jealousy brings on a storm of reproach and self-pity, and a confrontation with Tabor. Baby intends to leave, and writes her mother a long letter explaining the situation, but when Augusta harangues her on her lowly state and Horace's weakness, she determines to stay. The women gossip in a fine ensemble about the state of things. Tabor divorces Augusta, and is celebrating his wedding to Baby Doe in Washington. The guests are about to leave, scandalized by the news of the divorce, when President Chester A. Arthur walks in, clearly a close friend of Tabor's. All toast the bride and groom and silver, which is obviously going to lose out to gold.

ACT II. Ten years later, Augusta's friends are still commiserating with her and reviling Baby in Denver. Baby's mother consoles her, and Baby sings reminiscently about her happy life with Tabor. Augusta comes to warn Baby that Horace is on the brink of financial disaster, urging her to persuade him to sell the Matchless Mine. Horace overhears, and puts his ex-wife out the door. Baby remains loyal, giving Horace her jewels to sell, and promising to keep the Matchless Mine no matter what. Tabor's cronies gossip over a poker game, which Horace joins, asking them for help — he has lost everything. They turn him down and Horace ruminates about their "treachery." At the Matchless Mine, a crowd gathers to hear William Jennings Bryan make one of his famous orations about silver. He christens the Tabors' little daughter Silver Dollar. A few weeks later, he is defeated for the Presidency by McKinley, and silver is doomed. Baby Doe's mother comes to plead for help from Augusta, who turns her away, then reproaches herself bitterly. Now it is too late for help: 1899, and Tabor, ghostlike, returns to the Leadville Opera stage, dressed as a laborer, and recalls his former grandeur. He has visions of people formerly important to him, and at last, Baby Doe comes to take him home. Now she is seen to have snow-white hair, and sits, lonely and dying, beside the Matchless Mine, faithful, waiting for death.

WOLFGANG AMADEUS MOZART (Salzburg, 27 January 1756 — Vienna, 5 December 1791). Genius is practically impossible to define — certainly the bromide "one part inspiration and nine parts perspiration" will hardly do. Applying the word to human beings is dangerous; the gold coin can become too easily sullied. But Shakespeare comes to mind, as does Albert Einstein — and obviously, Mozart. He was an expert performer at five; wrote an opera at twelve, and never stopped during his pitifully short span of life turning out a stream of wonderful music unique in our experience. His is the one name you will find in everybody's ivory tower, as well as on the street among the fanatics in whatever "new" kind of music comes along.

Mozart wrote almost two score works for the stage. He yearned passionately for this kind of expression, but was always forced to wait for commissions to come his way — free-lancing was impossible. His first genuine opera was *La finta semplice* (The False Simpleton), ordered by the Emperor Josef II, with a text based on Goldoni. While he was waiting for Josef's impresario to put on the work, he composed the little *Bastien und Bastienne*, a

Mozart at age twenty-six, after an unfinished painting by Joseph Lange.

Mozart the child prodigy shown at the piano with his father Leopold and sister Marianne in Paris, 1763. Painting by Louis de Carmontelle.

The Empress Maria Theresia (seated right) and her family, husband Francis I (seated left) and their eleven children, painted c.1754.

Mozart's wife Constanze.

Singspiel (with spoken dialogue) based on Rousseau's *Devin du village*. It is still a favorite with workshops. Next came *Mitridate, Re di Ponto* (Milan, 1770) written at the instance of Count Firmia, governor-general of Lombardy, for Empress Maria Theresia during the Austrian occupation of Italy. *Lucio Silla*, called a "dramma per musica," honored Archduke Ferdinand (who came late to the performance in 1772). The elector of Bavaria commissioned *La finta giardiniera* (The Girl in Gardener's Disguise) in 1775, but didn't even attend the Munich performance. The same year, Mozart honored Maria Theresia's youngest son, Archduke Maximilian, with *Il re pastore* (The Shepherd King), a dramatic festival play given in Salzburg.

All this while, Mozart had to contend with captious monarchs and librettos thrust at him by his patrons. There was still another trial, when the elector of Bavaria wanted him to compose an Italian opera for the carnival season of Munich in 1781, and himself chose a librettist, Giambattista Varesco, chaplain to Archbishop Colloredo of Salzburg, who continued to make life miserable for the Mozarts and never relaxed his enmity. The opera was *Idomeneo, Re di Creta*, and in spite of its stiff formality in the *opera seria* style, (already becoming oldfashioned), the series of arias and ensembles offered Mozart the opportunity for some very beautiful music. Recently accorded a considerable number of performances and revivals, it can be said to be the first work that truly showed the way to the riches in store, although the next opera in sequence really opened the door.

This was *Die Entführung aus dem Serail* (The Abduction from the Seraglio), which Alfred Einstein called a "springboard." During these few years, so frustrated was Mozart at the scant opportunities in Salzburg that he wrote, but left unfinished, a work in the "Turkish" style popular at the time, called *Zaïde*. The style extended into *Entführung*, which was produced in Vienna in 1782—a breakthrough for the composer. With the exception of two unfinished works, *L'Oca del Cairo* and *Lo sposo deluso* (1783), the half-dozen operas that followed were masterpieces—even the one-act comedy, *Der Schauspieldirektor* (The Impresario), which makes fun of warring prima donnas. It was produced at Schönbrunn Palace for the Austrian court in 1786, the same year that *Le Nozze di Figaro* put the authentic stamp on Mozart's genius.

It is a wonder that Mozart retained his happy spirit in spite of his trials: first an overbearing father for whom he lost affection; then a flighty wife, Constanze, the sister of the Aloysia Weber whom Mozart had originally loved, and who never gave him the understanding he needed. Her constant illnesses, many pregnancies which ended in miscarriages, and love of luxury should have defeated another man, but Mozart bore with her whims till the end. Never prosperous, there were times when he could hardly scratch up a few coins, and his begging letters to friends caused a forfeiture of dignity. But with all these afflictions, and himself only too prosaic, he poured out a stream of music that reveals only his pure artistic soul, his flashing humor, and deep tenderness.

In the midst of his work on his final masterpiece, *Die Zauberflöte*, a mysterious man called on him to request the composition of a Requiem for his wife and was prepared to sign his own name to it—and not the messenger of Death. Working feverishly on this, as well as the interjected opera for Prague *(La clemenza di Tito)*, and putting the finishing touches on *Magic Flute*, Mozart spent his last days between agony of illness and satisfaction at the success of the *Flute*. He never finished the Requiem, which was taken over by his pupil Süssmayr—it was indeed performed under the

Aloysia Weber Lange, sister of Constanze, Mozart's wife, a leading soprano of the time. Mozart was in love with her but when she spurned him he turned his affections to her younger sister Constanze.

Drawing for the design of the 1970 New York City Opera production of The Magic Flute by designer-director Beni Montresor.

Idomeneo, Re di Creta

(Idomeneo, King of Crete)

Text by Abbé Giambattista Varesco.

IDOMENEO	*Tenor*
IDAMANTE	*Soprano*
ILIA	*Soprano*
ELECTRA	*Soprano*
ARBACE	*Tenor*
HIGH PRIEST OF NEPTUNE	*Tenor*
VOICE OF NEPTUNE	*Bass*

First Performance
Munich, 29 January 1781.

Count's name in 1793 — but Mozart had been dead two years. On that bitter December day, his body, unattended by mourners, was buried in a common grave and lost forever.

IDOMENEO enjoyed some European revivals in the early half of the century, then had a splendid performance at Glyndebourne in 1951, conducted by Fritz Busch, with Sena Jurinac, Birgit Nilsson, Richard Lewis, and Leopold Simoneau. Richard Strauss had a revision which was performed in Europe and in the American premiere at Tanglewood in 1947. A notable revival was by the Opera Society of Washington in 1961, and the New York City Opera also produced the opera. It is an occasional favorite of the larger university opera groups as well. The roles all demand florid, classical style, for the succession of arias and display pieces. The role of Electra is especially demanding.

The Italian libretto is by Abbé Giambattista Varesco, based on Danchet's libretto for *Idoménée* by André Campra.

IDOMENEO, King of Crete, is buffeted by storms on his way home from the Trojan War, and rashly promises Neptune to sacrifice the first

Robert Mackie as Arbace (l.), William Blankenship as Idomeneo, 1955 Juilliard production, New York.

person he meets on land. This turns out to be his son Idamante. Loath to keep his vow, Idomeneo tries to send his son, together with the Greek princess Electra, to Greece, but their departure is foiled by a wild tempest. Idomeneo confesses his duplicity to the High Priest. Meanwhile, Idamante ignores the lovesick Electra for Ilya, a captured Trojan princess, and incurs the flaming wrath of the Greek. Learning of his father's plight, Idamante offers to sacrifice himself, but Neptune relents, Idomeneo abdicates, Idamante and Ilya take over the kingdom, and everyone is joyful — except Electra.

Anton Raff (1714-97), the German tenor who created the title role of Idomeneo in Munich.

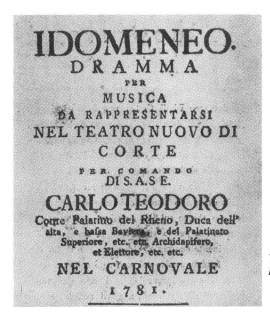

IDOMENEO.
DRAMMA
PER
MUSICA
DA RAPPRESENTARSI
NEL TEATRO NUOVO DI
CORTE
PER COMANDO
DI S. A. S E.
CARLO TEODORO
Come Palatino del Rheno, Duca dell'
alta, e bassa Baviera, e del Palatinato
Superiore, etc. etc. Archidapifero,
et Elettore, etc. etc.
NEL CARNOVALE
1781.

Title page from the libretto for the 1781 Munich premiere of Idomeneo (detail).

ENTFÜHRUNG, Mozart's first staged work in Vienna, had its premiere at the Burgtheater on 16 July 1782, and marked a turning point in the reputation of the composer. The libretto was by Gottlieb Stephanie (who would also do the text for *Der Schauspieldirektor*) after a play by Bretzner. There were some performances in England in the early 1800s, and New York heard it first in 1860. Many performances are registered by American companies of all degrees of proficiency in the first three-quarters of the century. Eleanor Steber sang Constanze at the Met in 1946, its only showing there until a lavish revival in 1979. Phyllis Curtin made an appealing Constanze at the New York City Opera in 1957, while Beverly Sills took over in subsequent revivals, making the most of the elaborate aria "Martern aller Arten." It is interesting to note that here for the first time, in the role of the lecherous overseer Osmin, Mozart has created a flesh-and-blood human being instead of a mythical or royal creature. This is the first step towards the humanity so vividly expressed in his operas to follow.

ORIENTAL influence is quite prominent in the music throughout, the setting being in Turkey in the sixteenth century. Constanze, a Spanish lady, and Blonde, her English maid, together with Pedrillo, the servant of Belmonte, a Spanish prince, are being held captive by Selim Pasha, who intends to marry Constanze. Her fiancé, Belmonte, finds them out,

Die Entführung aus dem Serail

(*The Abduction from the Seralgio*)

Text by Gottlieb Stephanie.

CONSTANZE	*Soprano*
BLONDE	*Soprano*
BELMONTE	*Tenor*
PEDRILLO	*Tenor*
SELIM PASHA	*Speaker*
OSMIN	*Bass*

First Performance
Vienna, 16 July 1782.

Scene from *The Abduction from the Seraglio, 1935 production for the Maggio Fiorentino, Bruno Walter conductor, with the cast of the Vienna Opera.*

Kurt Böhme as Osmin (l.) and Murray Dickie as Belmonte in The Abduction from the Seraglio, 1955, Salzburg.

and gains admittance to the palace through a ruse, fooling Osmin, the overseer of the Pasha's harem. Constanze, loyal to Belmonte, continues to put off the Pasha, while Osmin crudely woos Blonde, much to the distress of Pedrillo. In spite of his religion, Osmin is beguiled into drinking himself into a stupor, and the quartet of young people endeavors to escape. But they are thwarted as Osmin awakes, and takes them before his master. Unexpectedly, the Pasha shows mercy and allows the four to go free, even supplying a boat for their transportation.

ALTHOUGH *FIGARO* was a smashing success at its premiere in 1786 — Mozart being called out numberless times after he had conducted the opera, and encores so plentiful that the Emperor finally had to call a halt — it was soon off the boards, not to gain steady favor in Vienna until 1789, after its journey to Prague. Mozart could write his own ticket in the Czech capital, where he received the commission for *Don Giovanni*. Meanwhile, the conflict between the Italian influence and the desire to create a truly German opera persisted, not really resolved for a considerable time. The Emperor Joseph II, who initiated the move toward a national spirit, of which Mozart's *Entführung* was a standard bearer, himself grew bored, and even accused Mozart of writing too many notes in his *Singspiel*. Mozart's retort to the ruler's ignorant petulance was that he had written exactly as many notes as were necessary. The Emperor was not amused.

Figaro marked the beginning of a partnership that was to last through two subsequent operas—*Don Giovanni* and *Così fan tutte*. Lorenzo da Ponte (called Abbé, because he had taken minor holy orders, but in reality named Emanuele Conegliano), was an Italian *intrigueur*, boon companion of Casanova, extremely facile with his pen. During the same year that he worked on *Figaro*, he executed three other librettos, one for Salieri (music director of the court theater and considered to be Mozart's deadly rival—literally. He was falsely accused after Mozart's death of poisoning his colleague; the story was so prevalent that Rimsky-Korsakov composed an opera on the subject).

Da Ponte overcame initial reluctance to set the play by Pierre Augustin Caron de Beaumarchais, the French playwright, whose two plays were the basis of operas by Rossini and Mozart (*Il Barbiere di Siviglia* having appeared in its most famous musical form in 1816) as well as by several other composers. Da Ponte was wary of the political implications of the story, which ridiculed nobility while praising the cleverness of the "lower classes." But Mozart, who originally had the idea of setting the play, smoothed over the dangerous spots and the opera was permitted.

The opera today is one of the most popular in the literature, produced worldwide. English versions have flourished in America, and workshop productions are not unknown. The list of noted singers who have taken its

Right, top: Playbill for the premiere of The Marriage of Figaro, March 1978, Vienna (detail).
Right: Dietrich Fischer-Dieskau as the Count Almaviva with Evelyn Lear as Susanna in a scene from The Marriage of Figaro.
Left: Sena Jurinac as Cherubino.

Lorenzo da Ponte (1749-1837), librettist for The Marriage of Figaro, Don Giovanni and Cosi fan Tutte.

seven leading roles is endless; it may serve to mention only the casts that revived the opera at the Metropolitan for several seasons after 1939: Brownlee as the Count; Rethberg or Steber as the Countess; Sayao or Albanese as Susanna; Pinza as Figaro; Stevens or Novotna as Cherubino; Petina as Marcellina; Lazzari or Baccaloni as Bartolo. Needless to say there were American performances long before this (the first in 1824 in English).

Da Ponte's last years, spent in straitened circumstances in the United States, aroused some interest in his former accomplishments, especially during the visit to New York in 1825 of an Italian troupe headed by Manuel Garcia, when *Don Giovanni* was performed.

ACT I.   In Count Almaviva's castle near Seville (where the master's infatuation with the Rosina of *The Barber of Seville* has cooled considerably after a brief span of marriage), Figaro, the Count's valet, and Susanna, his promised bride, are arranging the room the Count has designated as their living quarters. Susanna complains that, although it is convenient for her to reach her mistress, it is equally handy for the Count to get to *her*—and that is his prime objective at the moment. He had abolished the *droit du seigneur* (the master's right over a new bride on her wedding night), but proposes to reestablish it. Figaro is appalled, and reacts violently in the aria "Se vuol ballare"—if his master wishes to dance, Figaro will call the tune. Bartolo and Marcellina

---

176
MOZART

Le Nozze di Figaro

(*The Marriage of Figaro*)

Text by Lorenzo da Ponte
after Beaumarchais.

COUNT ALMAVIVA	*Baritone*
FIGARO	*Baritone*
COUNTESS ALMAVIVA	*Soprano*
SUSANNA	*Soprano*
CHERUBINO	*Soprano or Mezzo-Soprano*
DON BASILIO	*Tenor*
ANTONIO	*Bass*
BARBARINA	*Soprano*
DON CURZIO	*Tenor*
BARTOLO	*Bass*
MARCELLINA	*Soprano*

First Performance
Vienna, 1 May 1786.

Scene from the Juilliard production showing the Count and Countess (left), Cherubino (center) and Figaro and Susanna (right), New York.

now take the stage. Rosina's former guardian has come to Seville at the bidding of Marcellina, previously his housekeeper, who informs him that Figaro has borrowed money from her and promised to marry her if he does not repay. The two scheme to revenge themselves, Bartolo singing a patter song to that effect. Then Marcellina and Susanna engage in a duet of left-handed compliments, won temporarily by the younger woman.

Nancy Storace sang the role of Susanna in the premiere of The Marriage of Figaro, *1786, Vienna.*

The Count finds Cherubino hiding in an armchair in Susanna's chamber, scene from Act I of The Marriage of Figaro.

177
MOZART

Now complications enter in the form of the young page, Cherubino, distressed because the Count has found him in the house of Barbarina, Figaro's young cousin, and dismissed him. In love with all womankind, he snatches from Susanna a ribbon belonging to the Countess, and sings his new love song, "Non so più cosa son" (I can't explain these new and troubling sensations). He hastens to hide as the Count approaches, and overhears his master's fervent approaches to Susanna. When the voice of Don Basilio, the music master, is heard, the Count himself hides, displacing Cherubino (most often accomplished in a huge arm chair over which Susanna throws a cloak or curtain). But at Basilio's injudicious comments, the Count emerges, enraged, to Basilio's further delight. Then Cherubino is exposed, and the Count embarrassed. He orders Cherubino to join his army in Seville. Figaro breaks the tension by leading in a band of villagers who serenade the Count. The Count temporizes on his promise to further the wedding. Left alone, Figaro taunts Cherubino with his new military status in a sprightly aria, "Non più andrai" (From now on, my adventurous lover, no more romantic excursions).

Music for Cherubino's Act II love song "Voi che sapete" in Mozart's own handwriting.

Cherubino singing his song to Susanna and the Countess.

ACT II. The Countess Rosina sorrowfully sings of the loss of her husband's love in the touching aria "Porgi amor" (God of Love). Susanna enters, confiding the latest development in the Count's behavior, soon followed by Figaro, who schemes to foil his master. The plan is to smuggle a note to the Count indicating that the Countess is to have a rendezvous with a lover, and at the same time Susanna will promise to meet the Count in the garden. Only for Susanna, Cherubino, dressed as a girl, will substitute. Cherubino comes in, excited at being so close to the mistress he adores, and in a rollicking scene, the two women dress him in girl's clothes after he sings another love song, "Voi che sapete" (You know the answer). The Count, who has supposedly gone hunting, unexpectedly interrupts this comical scene, and Cherubino is forced to hide in a closet. Susanna also hides. The flustered Countess, refusing to open the closet after a noise had been heard from within, is made to accompany the Count in search for tools to pry open the door. The interlude gives time for Cherubino to escape by the only means — jumping out the window — while Susanna takes his place, thus confounding the Count when he returns. Figaro complicates the situation when he enters by refusing to recognize the note the Count has received, but attempts to take the blame for jumping from the window, a feat that has been discovered by Antonio, the gardener. Prompted by the women, Figaro identifies the paper the fleeing boy has dropped — it is Cherubino's commission to the army, which lacks an official seal. All

Elisabeth Schwarzkopf as the
Countess.

seems straightened out — except for the Count's frustration — when Marcellina and Bartolo enter, armed with Figaro's debt to Marcellina. The finale that ensues is one of the glories of the opera, in which the Count stands between the two disputing factions and vows to have things his way.

ACT III.   The Count muses on the series of baffling events, and sends Basilio to check on Cherubino. Then Susanna, on the pretext of borrowing smelling salts, seduces the Count into believing that she will meet him after all. He is completely taken in until he overhears her boasting remark to Figaro. Infuriated, he bursts out in a splendid aria, "Vedrò mentr'io sospiro" (Why must I forgo my pleasure while my serf rejoices?). Now he gives judgment in favor of Marcellina, but again he is foiled when Marcellina turns out to be Figaro's mother — and Bartolo is his father. This marvelous, intricate scene is joyful for all concerned except Almaviva. In a quiet moment, the Countess sings her sec-

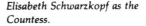

Susanna (Mirella Freni, left) dressing
Cherubino as a girl (Frederica von
Stade, right), Paris Opéra.

ond sad aria, "Dove sono" (Where are the days long departed?). She is joined by Susanna, and in a ravishing duet, she dictates to Susanna a plan for the meeting which will finally confound the amorous Count. They seal the note with a pin. As the bridal festivities are about to begin, a crowd of girls come forward to present flowers to the Countess. Among them is Cherubino, once more dressed as a maiden. Discovery is certain, but Barbarina saves the situation by gentle blackmailing of the Count, who has not neglected her in his comprehensive search for female felicity. She elicits a promise that she may marry Cherubino. Now the wedding festivities may go forward—a double wedding, as Marcellina and Bartolo are finally united. As she steps forward to receive the Count's blessing, Susanna slips him a note. He pricks his hand on the pin that holds it, and Figaro, noticing, jeers at his clumsiness. The act ends with the chorus proclaiming the Count's generosity.

Elisabeth Schwarzkopf and Rita Streich as the Countess and Susanna singing the famous third-act "letter duet," Lyric Opera of Chicago.

Ilva Ligabue (left) and Graziella Sciutti at the Rome Opera in Lincoln Center.

Luchino Visconti's set for the Act IV garden scenes, Marriage of Figaro, 1968 Rome Opera at Lincoln Center production.

ACT IV.   Now comes a confusion of identities and confrontations that is almost impossible to describe. But before the madness begins, Barbarina comes searching for Susanna's pin, which she has lost after the Count has given it to her to return to Susanna. Figaro catches her at it; his dismay at his wife's treachery, expressed in a denunciation of women, deepens when she appears to sing an entrancing song, "Deh vieni non tardar" (Then come, my love). (There have been arias for Marcellina and Basilio before this, but they are most often omitted, as adding further complexity and little musical value to the already confusing situation.)

Now, one after another, occur confrontations between Susanna and Cherubino, the masked Countess and Figaro, and the Count, blundering in on other "assignations." Susanna and Figaro are reconciled, after she explains the masquerade and Figaro proceeds to complete the Count's exasperation by making love to the pretended Countess. Everything is smoothed out as true identities are revealed, and the Count humbly begs Rosina's pardon, promising to behave himself in the future. His penitence (for the moment) is accepted gracefully, and the entire company rejoices.

DON GIOVANNI. Just as there is a pair of operas whose perplexities of jigsaw-like construction are forever with us — *Boris Godunov* and *Les Contes d'Hoffmann* — so two opera characters, Carmen and Don Giovanni, continue to arouse controversy and excitement. The strengths and weaknesses of the Don have been dissected *ad infinitum* and even, *ad nauseam*, to the point of Freudian speculation. Is he the Devil incarnate? a

homosexual *manqué*? actually impotent at the time of the play? — after all, he never quite succeeds in an outright seduction during its course (although there is some doubt about Donna Anna), though his failures are more the fault of chance mishaps than his own — or is he merely the dashing playboy, irresistible to women and anathema to men? Whatever interpretation of this character is chosen, Giovanni has held unbounded fascination for basses and baritones of all countries. The list of Dons encompasses such brilliant names as Faure, Maurel, Lablache (who also sang Leporello), Jean de Reszke (while still a baritone), Scotti, Stabile, Renaud, Pinza, Brownlee, Siepi, London, Gobbi, Fischer-Dieskau, Ghiaurov and some more recent young blades. Annas and Elviras and Zerlinas are also legion, while tenors vie for the two arias and otherwise rather bleak fate of Ottavio. One priceless cast remains in memory: that of Glyndebourne in 1936, when Fritz Busch conducted an ensemble made up of Ina Souez, Luise Helletsgruber, Audrey Mildmay, John Brownlee, Koloman von Pataky, and Salvatore Baccaloni.

The Don Juan legend is very old and widespread, but there is little evidence that such a person really existed. Da Ponte derived his libretto chiefly from a seventeenth-century play by Gabriel Tellez, a Spanish monk whose pen-name was Tirso de Molina. The title may be popularly translated as "The Playboy of Seville and the Stone Guest." The amiable Lorenzo dipped

Left, top: Playbill for the premiere of Don Giovanni, 29 October 1787, Prague (detail).
Left, bottom: Soprano Kiri Te Kanawa as Donna Elvira in the Joseph Losey film version of Don Giovanni, a Gaumont-New Yorker Films release.
Right: Giuseppe Ambroggetti (with glass) as the Don with Giuseppe Naldi as Leporello, Kings Theater, London, 1817.

into it freely, as well as boldly stealing from Bertato's libretto (no copyright laws to bother him!). The subject has frequently been chosen for other operas, but Mozart's reigns supreme in the field.

Another point of dissension is Mozart's own description of the work as a *"dramma giocoso"* — a "jolly play." Tragedy and comedy exist side by side, but when the final sextet is omitted, as occasionally used to be the case, the former element might be said to prevail, for the sextet combines semi-

Nineteenth century stage design for Don Giovanni's castle.

serious moralizing with a merry approach, and is needed for balance. It was first omitted in the Vienna performance of 1788, when the opera grew to inordinate length by additions of a long aria for Elvira (Catarina Cavalieri), "Mi tradì quell'alma ingrata," which seems to fit nowhere comfortably and although retained today is shifted from spot to spot. Another addition was a duet between Leporello and Zerlina after his capture while masquerading as the Don, almost invariably deleted today although still printed in scores. The suppression of "Il mio tesoro" because it was too difficult for the tenor and the substitution of "Dalla sua pace" made little difference in timing; both are included today as recompense for the otherwise rather arid territory of Ottavio.

The patchwork quality of the work remains to plague producers, whose solutions, sometimes far-fetched or absurd, are not always satisfactory. Still, with all its built-in faults and lapses of comprehensible continuity, Don Giovanni is the bright jewel of any repertory. Mozart's music is treasure enough.

The overture, a masterpiece in itself (written at the last moment, as Mozart's often were), reflects the tragic element first with portentous chords and an ominous scale, then breaks into gaiety and leads directly into the action. It is likely that the opera was first divided into four acts, as evidenced by strong scenes midway in each of the two into which current practice assigns the story.

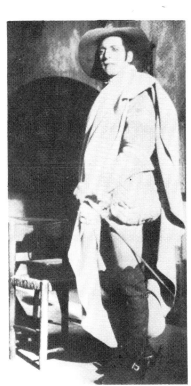

Ezio Pinza as Don Giovanni.

Don Giovanni

Text by Lorenzo da Ponte after
the play by Tirso de Molina and the
opera *Don Giovanni Tenorio* by
Giuseppe Gazzaniga with libretto
by Giovanni Bertati.

DON GIOVANNI	*Baritone or Bass*
LEPORELLO	*Bass*
DONNA ANNA	*Soprano*
DON OTTAVIO	*Tenor*
THE COMMENDATORE	*Bass*
DONNA ELVIRA	*Soprano*
ZERLINA	*Soprano*
MASETTO	*Bass or Baritone*

First Performance
Prague, 29 October 1787.

184
MOZART

ACT I.   Leporello, waiting outside Donna Anna's house for his master, who has entered for obvious purposes, grumbles at his lot and swears to leave his bondage. Suddenly the Don emerges, his face hidden in his cloak, pursued by the indignant Donna Anna. (It is never clear whether the seduction has been accomplished; one school believes that it has, and that Anna's life is changed, causing her to put off her fiancé Ottavio indefinitely. This view is enhanced by a story by E.T.A. Hoffmann. The argument still rages.) As Anna goes to seek Ottavio, her father, the Commendatore, emerges and challenges Giovanni to a duel. Reluctantly, for he has been recognized, he fights, and kills the old man. When Anna and Ottavio return, she makes him swear to revenge her father. The villain and his servant have escaped; they find themselves in a public square where a beautiful woman has just entered. At once, the Don makes advances, only to discover that the lady is not unknown, is, in fact, Donna Elvira, whom he has loved and left. She indulges in an aria expressing her grief at the betrayal: "Ah, chi mi dice mai quel barbaro dov'è" (Ah, where shall I find the traitor?), but her sorrow turns to joy as she recognizes Giovanni. He, on the other hand, is appalled, and makes a furtive escape, leaving Leporello to offer dubious consolation in the "Catalogue" aria, "Madamina," in which he lists the number of the Don's conquests—2,065 in many countries, 1,003 in Spain alone—and of course, she is one of them. Outraged, she stalks off the scene.

Nicolai Ghiaurov as Don Giovanni.

Gabriella Tucci as Donna Elvira singing her famous opening aria "Ah, chi mi dice mai."

185
MOZART

Now the infamous pair chance on a peasant wedding in the country near the Don's castle, and that nobleman loses no time in captivating the gullible bride, Zerlina, while her intended, the clumsy Masetto, looks on helplessly. At last alone, after Masetto has sung, not stupidly, that he understands, the seducer almost succeeds, as his willing victim joins in the delicious duet, "Là ci darem la mano." No doubt that Zerlina

(L) Henriette Sontag as Donna Anna, 1826, Paris.

(R) Nicolai Gedda as Don Ottavio.

Don Giovanni (center) telling Don Ottavio and Donna Anna (left) that Donna Elvira (right) is crazy, in a scene from Act I of the Opera, Tyl Theater, Prague.

Édouard de Reszke as Leporello.

is a minx, but she is saved this time by the intrusion of Elvira, wh warns her against the Don, sends her away, then reappears to join A na and Ottavio, who have found Giovanni and unknowingly asked fc his help in tracing the traducer. Elvira tries to break this up as well, su ceeding only in making a part of a marvelous quartet, in which the Dc accuses her of a mad passion for him that has unhinged her mind. As I follows her offstage, Anna recognizes his voice and is stunned. Whe she tells Ottavio that the supposed friend, Don Giovanni, is the re villain, he cannot breathe until she assures him that nothing happened This is, at least, her story. She embarks on one of the monumental glo ies of the score, the recitative and aria "Or sai chi l'onore" (Now yc know who attacked me). After she storms off, Ottavio sings the mo placid aria, "Dalla sua pace" (On her my peace depends), and leaves tl stage to the Don and Leporello. All is in readiness for the party the Dc has planned around Zerlina's seduction, and the Don celebrates in th famous little showpiece, called the "champagne" aria: "Finch' han d vino." (The exact locales of these scenes is questionable; one or two ma take place in a nook of some "unit" set that endeavors to be all places t all situations.) In the garden near the palace, Zerlina placates Masett with the charming song, "Batti, batti, o bel Masetto" (Beat me, beat m dear Masetto), but he is soon wary again as the Don tries to resume h wooing, only to acknowledge Masetto's presence and summon them bo to the party.

Now three masked figures appear before the castle: Anna, Elvira and Ottavio. They are invited in by Leporello and join the festivitie Three orchestras are playing at once—a Mozart masterstroke, for th noble minuet, the middle-class country dance, and the peasant ländl clearly differentiate who should dance to which music. Masetto is isc ted by Leporello while the Don drags Zerlina into an inner room, ...om where her screams are soon heard. The Don, attempting to put the ...lame on Leporello, is accused by the three avengers, but makes a dar-...g escape as a storm breaks.

ACT II.   Giovanni has taken a fancy to Elvira's maid, and forces Leporello to change apparel with him to lure Elvira out while he ...erenades the maid. The discontented Leporello has to be placated with ...our gold pieces, but his plea that his master give up women is only ...aughed off. Reluctantly, the servant sets about his task in a comic ...cene, and with Elvira uttering some plaintively beautiful strains from ...er balcony, succeeds in luring her outside. The Don's serenade to gui-...ar accompaniment, "Deh, vieni alla finestra" (Come to the window) ...rings the maid, sure enough, but before she can join the serenader, ...Masetto and a band of peasants intervene, bent on vengeance. Mistak-...ng the Don for Leporello, Masetto enlists him only to rue the confi-...ence, for the Don takes his weapons and beats him unmercifully. He is ...eft to moan until Zerlina finds him, soothing with the balm of her ...aresses and the lovely song "Vedrai, carino" (You will see, beloved) his ...urts that all appear to be in non-vital spots.

Elisabeth Schwarzkopf
as Donna Elvira.

187
MOZART

Don Giovanni serenades the maid
of Donna Elvira with the famous
aria, "Deh vieni alla finestra,"
engraving by Luigi Bassi, 1787.

In a dark courtyard, Leporello and Elvira appear, then Anna and ...Ottavio, finally Zerlina and Masetto. They unmask Leporello and threat-...n him, but he escapes. Don Ottavio sings his elaborate paean to his ...ove, "Il mio tesoro," and Elvira at last manages to get in her "Mi tradì (I ...was betrayed). Who listens to them is up to the producer, who will try ...o make some sense out of this most troublesome patch.

Now the Don and Leporello meet (probably by appointment un-...poken in the libretto) in the cemetery near the statue of the Commen-

Cesare Siepi (seated) as Don
Giovanni with Fernando Corena
as Leporello in the supper
scene, near the end of the last
act of Don Giovanni.

Rosa
Ponselle
as Donna
Anna.

Tito Schipa
as Don
Ottavio.

datore. Each brags about his prowess through the night (unfounded o
not), until the voice of the statue is heard in solemn tones reinforced by
trombones in their first use in the score. The Don fearlessly prods Lep
orello into inviting the statue to dinner! The awesome figure nods it
head. (Sometimes this statue is mounted on a horse, sometime merely
standing; the effect can be terrifying either way.) We are taken next to
room in Anna's palace where the gloomy heroine receives Ottavio's spir
ited accusation of cruelty with another tremendous outpouring of reci
tative and song: "Non mi dir, bell' idol mio" (Say no more). But she stil
puts him off.

The Don is enjoying his supper, to the accompaniment of his privat
orchestra, which plays tunes from two operas well-known in Mozart'
time, as well as his own "Non più andrai" from Figaro. Leporello com
ments on the familiarity of the last. In the midst of the merriment, El
vira bursts in, still trying to "reform" her erstwhile lover. He insults he
by his indifference, and she stumbles out, to return shrieking to find
another exit — she has met the statue at the main door. Giovanni send
Leporello to open this door, but the servant retreats in horror, leaving
his master to greet the spectral stone guest. At first Giovanni is flippan
and unrepentant, but when he accepts the statue's handclasp, the chil
of marble penetrates his soul, while the flames of hell mount around
him, and the sinner is cast into the depths. (Productions vary in the
amount of spectacular effect brought to this scene that can be fearsom
indeed.) But it is certain that the libertine has received his proper pun
ishment, and the other six members of the cast come before the curtain

o preach us a little sermon: evil doers will meet evil ends. Anna puts off Ottavio once more — for at least a year; Elvira heads for a convent; Zerlina and Masetto go home to dine, and Leporello will seek another master. Life goes on.

MOZART WAS in one of the all-too-frequent periods of hardship, even though he had been appointed to a small court position after the death of Gluck, when Emperor Joseph II commissioned him to do an *opera buffa*. The trifling remuneration went to pay debts; Constanze was in one of her habitual spells of ill health and indulging it at a costly spa. In the midst of Mozart's work on *Così fan Tutte*, she gave birth to her fifth child, which died almost immediately. None of these troubles showed in Mozart's sparking score, one of his most enchanting, to Da Ponte's outwardly frivolous tale, said to have been inspired by a real-life lover's swap. Although the libretto was considered quite licentious, the Emperor made no objection. The premiere was a happy success for Mozart, but disaster soon set in, for the Emperor died less than a month afterwards, and the theater was closed for two months. *Così* appeared only briefly after the reopening, and then faded from view. Meanwhile, the opera suffered practical dismemberment as far as the libretto was concerned, a dozen different mutilations being performed upon Da Ponte's delightful text. Worse still, as far as the composer was concerned, Da Ponte was forced to leave Vienna after the Emperor, his protector, died. The loss of his best collaborator was a severe blow to Mozart.

First performed in London in 1811, *Così* disappeared until exactly 100 years later, when Beecham revived it. The Metropolitan ventured two brief series of productions in the twenties, accomplishing the American premiere on 24 March 1922, with Easton, Peralta, Bori, Meader, De Luca, and

Così Fan Tutte
(*Women Are Like That*)

Text by Lorenzo da Ponte.

FIORDILIGI	*Soprano*
DORABELLA	*Mezzo-Soprano*
FERRANDO	*Tenor*
GUGLIELMO	*Baritone*
DON ALFONSO	*Bass or Baritone*
DESPINA	*Soprano*

First Performance
Vienna, 26 January 1790.

189
MOZART

Marcello Cortis as Don Alfonso, Nan Merriman and Teresa Stich-Randall as Dorabella and Fiordiligi; Graziella Sciutti as Despina from the Festival Aix-en-Provence production of Così fan Tutte.

Didur, under Bodanzky. But it took Glyndebourne revivals in 1934, 1948 and 1950 to reawaken interest in Mozart's treasure. Rudolf Bing engaged Alfred Lunt to direct a stylish production in English in 1951, with Steber, Thebom, Munsel, Tucker, Guarrera, and Brownlee. Subsequent revivals have been popular, and the opera is a favorite with smaller companies.

The overture, one of Mozart's most spirited, contains the phrase which embodies the title.

ACT I.   In a Naples cafe, two officers, Ferrando and Guglielmo, argue with their cynical friend Don Alfonso about the virtue of their fiancées. Alfonso insists that women are not to be trusted, and proposes a wager to prove it. After firmly protesting the constancy of their inamoratas, the two agree.

The scene changes to the garden of the two ladies in question: Fiordiligi, the beloved of Guglielmo, and her sister Dorabella, affianced to Ferrando. (Note that the pairs go by contrary voice: soprano with bari-

Christa Ludwig as Dorabella.

Anne Howells as Dorabella and Margaret Price as Fiordiligi.

Walter Berry (Don Alfonso), Anneliese Rothenberger and Rosalind Elias (Fiordiligi and Dorabella) in a scene from Così fan Tutte, 1969, Salzburg Festival.

tone; mezzo with tenor.) Their somewhat sentimental rapturing over their lovers is rudely interrupted by Don Alfonso, who brings the news that the men will have to go off to war. The two young men come in to verify the bulletin, and tearful farewells are exchanged. Although momentarily impressed by the apparent sincerity of the girls' emotion, Alfonso, left alone, engages in a bitter tirade against all women.

As if to justify his opinion, the ladies' maid, the pert Despina, joins his plot for a consideration. She counsels the despairing sweethearts to forget their troubles; the absence of their lovers should be a chance for diversion, not melancholy. The sisters violently reject her cynical advice, and stalk off.

Alfonso now produces the crux of his plot — two fantastically garbed "Albanians," really Ferrando and Guglielmo — and introduces them as his friends. The ladies are horrified at the idea of entertaining strangers. Fiordiligi emphasizes her indignation and determination to remain faithful in the ultimate display aria, "Come scoglio" (Firm as a rock). Guglielmo counters with a delightful song that turns into laughter as the girls leave the stage. The two men joyously believe they have won, but Alfonso persuades them to let a day go by; he will prove his point by then. Ferrando sings tenderly of his love: "Un' aura amorosa" (A breath of tenderness).

For the finale of the act, the sisters rush into the garden at a commotion, to find the two Albanians taking "poison" and collapsing. Despina goes for a doctor and returns disguised as a Mesmerist, who brings the "corpses" to life with a magic magnet. The sisters are moved to pity at the weakness of these strong men, and their insistence that they have reached heaven as they are restored. But when they demand kisses, Fiordiligi at least regains her previous adamantine stance, and lets go with some vocal fireworks in which Ferrando joins her. The act ends with the question in doubt: Will the women yield?

Reri Grist as Despina.

Ferrando and Guglielmo disguised as the two Albanians, Teatro San Carlo, Naples.

ACT II. Despina is quick to pursue the weakness she has detec[t]ed in her mistresses' defenses; she scolds them for not behavin[g] like normal women. Her brilliant aria, "Una donna a quindici anni" (A[t] fifteen, a girl should know), ends in a flirtatious "Come to Despina, she[']l[l] show you how!" which always brings down the house. Certainly it a[f]fects the two wavering ladies, Dorabella first, although Fiordiligi goes s[o] far as to join her sister in a delicious duet specifying which of the tw[o] lovers each shall choose — of course, the balance is in favor of the switc[h].

So they are ready for the serenade of the two suitors, accompanie[d] by a small chorus and wind instruments. Now the women are more fo[r]ward; the men are caught in embarrassment at their success. At la[st] they pair off, and Guglielmo's triumph (and despair) is complete, as h[e] exchanges a heart amulet for Dorabella's locket containing Ferrando[']s portrait. This duet is one of the most felicitous moments, with its simu[]lation of a pitty-patty heartbeat.

Fiordiligi is still made of sterner stuff. Although she confesses in [a] dramatic recitative and aria that she has weakened and begs pardon c[f] the absent Guglielmo, her terms are so difficult of execution that sh[e] seems to have set herself an impossible task.

The men foregather to compare notes. Guglielmo is jubilant at Fio[r]diligi's resistance, while Ferrando gives way to despair. Don Alfonso in[]sists there are still some hours remaining before the wager can be se[t]tled, and the intrigue continues.

Dorabella's complete capitulation and Despina's glee only harde[n] Fiordiligi's resolve, although she admits she has been touched at heart[.] Still, one more resource remains. She sends Despina to a storeroom t[o] bring uniforms the lovers have left there (why, one can only surmise[)], and determines to dress up in Guglielmo's and join her fiancé at th[e] front. Perhaps inadvertently, or because, as she apologizes, Ferrando[']s uniform fits her better, she is donning it when its owner intrudes; in [a] final burst of passion, he convinces her of her own feelings. She falls in[]to his arms. Now it is Guglielmo's turn to rage — but Don Alfonso sly[ly] suggests that they marry the girls, forgetting their weakness. After al[l], he reiterates, "Così fan tutte!"

A wedding contract and celebration are quickly arranged; Despin[a] will once again oblige with a disguise as the Notary. The ceremony i[s] about to be performed when the "Albanians" are hastily removed a[s] martial strains are heard presaging the return in their proper guise of th[e] officers, who accuse their faithless sweethearts.

The girls beg forgiveness, but of whom it is not clear. Indeed[,] Mozart has left us with no hint of whether the original couples ge[t] together again, or the new partners are accepted. The more conven[]tional viewers will opt for the former alternative; the more venturesom[e] will argue that the four have only found true depth of emotion in th[e] later encounters, and have learned from their new partners what tru[e] love can be. At any rate, the puzzle is a delightful one to ponder. A[t] least, if the switch is accepted, it brings tenor and soprano, mezzo an[d] baritone together.

MOZART SUFFERED two interruptions during his summer labor on *The Magic Flute*. First came the ominous summons from an unknown, who wanted a requiem. The composer, already ill and with premonitions of death, began to believe that the work would be his own Requiem. (In reality, the emissary, as we have seen, was from a Count who wanted it for his late wife.) Next, Mozart was commissioned to write an opera for the coronation of Emperor Leopold II as King of Bohemia on 6 September, 1791. This entailed a trip to Prague, which Mozart and his pupil Süssmayr undertook with great hardship, the composer working feverishly during the journey and completing the new work in eighteen days. The libretto, a creaking old vehicle by the famous Metastasio, was modified by the poet to the Saxon court, Caterino Mazzolà, and gave some delight to Mozart, as he had long wished to do another *opera seria*, although the form was by that time virtually obsolete. The composer's late genius touched the string of arias and ensembles and produced a work of great beauty, although considered stilted and unplayable by later generations. However, it has been recently revived and found to be a vital and expressive work. One of the latest incarnations is by the New York City Opera under Julius Rudel in the fall of 1979.

La Clemenza di Tito
(*The Clemency of Titus*)

Text by Mazzolà
Adapted from Metastasio.

TITUS	*Tenor*
VITELLIA	*Soprano*
SEXTUS	*Contralto*
SERVILIA	*Soprano*
PUBLIUS,	*Bass*
GUARD CAPTAIN	

First Performance
Prague, 6 September 1791.

Carol Vaness as Vitellia in the 1979 New York City Opera production of La Clemenza di Tito.

193
MOZART

Thomas Moser in the title role of La Clemenza di Tito, 1979, New York City Opera.

Emanuel Schikaneder, the librettist for Mozart's The Magic Flute.

Two "grand" arias have long been concert favorites, with clarinet and basset horn obbligatos originally designed as a favor to Mozart's friend, the famous clarinetist Anton Stadler. The chorus is an active factor, even sharing with the principals the first act finale—an unusual feature for Mozart.

VITELLIA, daughter of the deposed Emperor of Rome, is herself deposed in the affections of the present Emperor Titus, who announces his determination to marry Berenice, daughter of Agrippa I of Judea. She ensnares Sextus, who is madly in love with her, in a plot to kill Titus and burn the Capitol. Then she learns too late that Titus has sent Berenice home and plans to marry a Roman. But it is Servilia he chooses, further complicating matters, as this lady is betrothed to Annius, Sextus's friend. When the Emperor learns of this, he renounces Servilia and settles on Vitellia. But Sextus has already embarked on his deadly mission—only, he kills a substitute instead of the ruler. Still, he sets fire to the Capitol. When caught and tried, he does not implicate Vitellia. But just as he is about to be thrown to the lions, Vitellia repents, and confesses her part in the intrigue. The Emperor exercises extremely unlikely mercy, and all are forgiven.

(Mozart originally intended the part of Sextus for a tenor, but when none was available in Prague, changed it to a contralto.)

THE MAGIC FLUTE is not only magical, but it is mysterious. The magic, of course, is not only in the fairy-tale aspect of the story but the profoundly beautiful music Mozart wrote for it. The mystery remains: why does the plot seemingly reverse itself in midstream, and the villains and heroine change places? It is possible to slide over the difficulty and merely listen to the opera for its musical beauties, not bothering to figure it all out. But there is another possibility: an explanation that goes to the heart of the mystery and finds its answer in the prevailing atmosphere and symbolism of Freemasonry. No doubt exists that Mozart and his librettist Schikaneder were deeply influenced by the principles of the order to which both belonged, and which were adopted by many men of learning, while suppressed by several authorities, among them the Empress Maria Theresia herself.

The importance of the Masonic element in *Flute* was not emphasized at first, for secrecy shrouded the order, and certain punishment was inevitable if too many revelations were made. Today, it is rather amusing to note that those who deny absolutely that there is such influence in the opera are Masons themselves, still bound by secrecy. The theories of one Jacques Chailley, who wrote a book on the subject in 1971, have been pooh-poohed, for he does go overboard in his detailed examination of the text and score, but many of his observations seem sound when honestly confronted.

Early in 1791, when Mozart's fortunes were at their lowest, and his health deteriorated to the point where he felt the imminence of death, he was approached by his old friend Emanuel Schikaneder with a strange proposal. Schikaneder, an actor, manager, vagabond, poet, had secured the management of the Theater auf der Weiden, in a large compound outside the gates of Vienna, and had won some success with a fairy-tale spectacular. The Viennese public was hungry for "native" works, after the large dose of Italian opera prescribed by the Emperor Leopold. Schikaneder thought Mozart would be the man to write for him another work of the same genre.

Unfortunately for the project, the fairy-tale they chose for a libretto was brought out by another theater just ahead of theirs. Its central theme, the abduction of the daughter of the Queen of Night by a wicked sorcerer, was retained in its essence by Schikaneder, but with the modifications that admitted Masonic ideals and turned the picture around. Egyptian influence was also introduced (Masonry is supposed to have originated in that country).

There is one school of thought, led by Goethe and several other writers, that it was Schikaneder's and Mozart's intention all along to show the Queen as only posing as the virtuous mother, with Sarastro as the villain. Or we can consider the plot from Tamino's point of view: he is taken in by the Queen's laments for her daughter, and so are we, only to be enlightened as the action proceeds and Sarastro's noble character is revealed. Viennese comments at the time, circulated rather privately, compared the Queen to the Empress Maria Theresia; Tamino to Josef II, the Empress's son who favored Masonry; Pamina to the Austrian people, led into the light by Sarastro, who was probably based on Hofrath Ignaz von Born, a distinguished founder of the prestigious Vienna Lodge Zur wahren Eintracht ("True Harmony"). Masonic symbolism is carried further in that Sarastro represents the Sun; the Queen, his opposite, the Moon; Tamino, Fire; Papageno, Air; Pamina, Water; and Monastatos, Earth. Papageno and the Moor change

Playbill for the premiere of The Magic Flute, 30 September 1791, Vienna.

Curtain design for a 1937 Munich Staatsoper production of The Magic Flute, painting by Ludwig Sievert.

Backdrop for the Metropolitan Opera production of The Magic Flute designed by Marc Chagall.

Ignaz von Born, intellectual and sci-
entist of Mozart's time, a Freemason
who was the inspiration for the
character Sarastro in The Magic
Flute.

masters, and each achieves his own place in the division between light and darkness, the central theme of the opera.

There is one patch of dialogue (this is a *Singspiel*, with the exposition of the plot spoken), frequently omitted, that makes clear several tricky places which defy understanding. In it, the Queen explains that her former husband was one of the Initiated, the leader of the priesthood which Sarastro now commands. He left the "all-powerful seven-fold shield of the sun" to Sarastro, who wears it on his breast. To the Queen he left nothing really important, rebuking her for trying to concern herself in men's weighty matters. So she was relegated to the Kingdom of the Night, and has been trying to get revenge on Sarastro ever since. She employs Tamino to this effect, and will even use her own daughter, commanding her to kill Sarastro. Of course this appears in the second act, after the "gear-shift" has already occurred.

But it also touches on another aspect of the plot that confirms Masonic principles—anti-feminism. Time after time the abilities of women are decried. Men must be the leaders. Pamina is brought to truth and light by a man.

As we have seen, Mozart was interrupted twice during the composition of the *Flute*, once by the commission for a Requiem, again by the summons to Prague for *La Clemenza di Tito*. When his final work opened at last, on 30 September, the composer conducted. He was thrilled and excited by its success, and fondly sang snatches of its music to himself in his last illness. His death occurred two months later.

Let us plunge into the story, with Masonic sidelights falling where they occur (to be ignored, if so wished, pondered if of interest).

The Overture begins with portentous chords, usually designated as three, and distinctly Masonic (depicting the three knocks of apprentices at the initiation door) but in reality a group of three plus two. Men's mystic number was three; women's two. Women did form separate lodges, called Lodges of Feminine Adoption. But the number three occurs constantly throughout the opera, as will be noted. (The combination of three and two may indicate that women are led to the light by men.)

ACT I.   As the curtain opens, a young Prince, Tamino (he is called Japanese or invested with some other "exotic" nationality), rushes in, pursued by a fearsome serpent. He has a bow, but no arrows, (no experience), and he appears very timid indeed, fainting when no help comes. (This is probably his first trial, his contact with Earth, the first element. The serpent is also a Masonic symbol.) Three veiled ladies appear, kill the serpent with their spears, and admire the beautiful youth, each one wishing she could be left alone with him. Their deceitful, lustful feminine nature thus appears very early. Since none will agree, all three go off together to tell the Queen of the Night, whose servants they are. Tamino revives, sees the serpent dead, and is willing to attribute his rescue to the strange being who now appears and claims the heroic feat — it is Papageno, the bird man, who catches birds for the Queen. He tells us about himself in a little song Schubert might have written. The Ladies catch him in his lie and padlock his lips, giving him a stone instead of the bread he expected. (Padlock and birds: also Masonic symbols.) Then they show Tamino a portrait of Pamina, and

Die Zauberflöte
(*The Magic Flute*)

Text by Emanuel Schikaneder.

TAMINO	*Tenor*
THREE LADIES	*2 Sopranos, Mezzo-Soprano*
PAPAGENO	*Baritone*
QUEEN OF THE NIGHT	*Soprano*
MONASTATOS	*Tenor*
PAMINA	*Soprano*
THREE BOYS	*Boys Voices or 2 Sopranos, Mezzo-Soprano*
THE SPEAKER	*Bass*
SARASTRO	*Bass*
TWO PRIESTS	*Tenor, Bass*
PAPAGENA	*Soprano*
TWO MEN IN ARMOR	*Tenor, Bass*

First Performance
Vienna, 30 September 1791.

197
MOZART

Emanuel Schikaneder as Papageno from the premiere of The Magic Flute, 1791, Vienna.

The three Ladies of the Queen of the Night (Ann Hood, Anne Conoley, Anne Collins) after they have rescued Prince Tamino (John Brecknock) from the serpent, 1979, English National Opera.

Theodor Uppman as Papageno.

tell him the Queen has chosen him to rescue her daughter from Sarastro. He falls immediately in love with the portrait, expressing his emotion in one of the most beautiful of Mozart arias, "Dies Bildnis ist bezaubernd schön" (O, loveliness beyond compare). The Star-Flaming Queen herself appears in a clap of thunder. In her first wildly difficult aria, she expresses her grief at Pamina's loss, but it seems somewhat artificial, with rather obvious sobbing and sighing in the orchestra—particularly if we are looking for this kind of evidence. The Ladies unlock Papageno's lips but command him to accompany Tamino—an adventure he wants no part of. But he is given a set of chiming bells, a symbol of earth; while Tamino receives the magic flute (air), which the Queen has never been able to use since her husband left it. Now who has a map showing Sarastro's realm? The Ladies call in three Genii as guides. (They may appear in a circular swing that suggests the Sun, showing roses, a feminine Masonic flower, which is also suggestive—as youths, they have soprano voices but may grow into manhood. Thus they should always be sung by boys, although this has not been honored in many cases because of the slight carrying power of treble voices.)

Off they go. The scene changes to "a luxuriously furnished Egyptian room." Pamina has tried to escape her imprisonment, and has been dragged back by Monastatos, who threatens her. Papageno, who has become separated from Tamino, finds his way into Pamina's quarters, and is confronted by Monastatos. Both are terrified, each thinking the other the devil, and both exit. Papageno creeps back, to engage in conversation with Pamina. He arouses in her a love for Tamino equal to the

Prince's for her; Pamina assures the lovelorn birdman that such love will also be his one day, and they sing a melodious duet, "Bei Männern, welche Liebe fühlen" (The man who feels sweet love's emotion will always have a kindly heart). "We live by love alone," they carol joyously, then depart.

Tamino meanwhile is led into a palm grove wherein stand three temples: Reason, Wisdom, Nature (all Masonic symbols). The three Genii pipe up, adjuring Tamino to remain silent, steadfast, forbearing. This is the beginning of the Prince's initiation. He is told in stentorian tones to "Go back!" at each of his attempts to enter a temple; at last a Priest appears, telling Tamino that he has been told a lie about Sarastro, and not to trust a woman, a creature of "few deeds, much chatter." Tamino begins his conversion by asking: "When will this veil of darkness be lifted?" and is answered: "Soon, soon, or never!" Reassured that Pamina lives, he plays his flute to attract her. The magic strains draw out a coterie of enchanting animals instead of Pamina. Again he plays his C-major tune, to be answered by Papageno's five-note, pan-pipe scale. But they miss each other this time. All this has been accomplished in beautiful recitative, some of the strongest and most supple Mozart ever wrote, approaching the "through-composed" status of later music drama. Papageno and Pamina enter, but are immediately intercepted by Monastatos and his fellow slaves, who are put off only by Papageno's resort to the magic bells, which hypnotize the Moors and send them

Frieda Hempel sang the Queen of the Night in 1912 at the Metropolitan Opera, New York.

Edda Moser made her Metropolitan Opera debut as the Queen of the Night in 1970.

Raymond Gibbs (r) as Tamino and Richard Stilwell (l) as Papageno, 1974, Santa Fe Opera.

Tenor Stuart Burrows currently includes the role of Prince Tamino in his repertoire.

dancing off. An offstage chorus heralds Sarastro, who receives Pamina's confession of trying to escape with kindness. Still, he will not set her free. He brushes aside her plea for her mother's cause with the decree that a man must guide her destiny. Monastatos drags Tamino onto the scene, but is himself punished for his wrongdoing by the sentence of seventy-seven lashes on the soles of his feet. Pamina and Tamino recognize one another, but Sarastro separates them, and veils their heads so that they may enter the temple. The act ends with a chorus in praise of virtue and justice.

Otto Goritz as Papageno from the Metropolitan Opera premiere of The Magic Flute.

ACT II.   Sarastro and the Priests enter to a solemn March, which includes the three long chords played, as punctuation to Sarastro's pronouncements, by Priests on their trumpets. Tamino must undergo the prescribed trials; Pamina may accompany him; if they come through successfully, they may marry and Tamino will gain an exalted position. Sarastro sings his noble aria, "O Isis und Osiris" (the Egyptian touch). In a temple courtyard Tamino and Papageno are led in by the Speaker and the Second Priest, who receive Tamino's assurance of bravery and silence, but make little impression on the cowardly birdman. The couple must not speak, and Papageno is persuaded to obedience only after being promised a suitable bride. They are warned to withstand temptation from wily females—and that temptation immediately appears in the form of the Three Ladies, who are rebuffed by Tamino, although Papa-

The Queen of the Night, 1840, stage design by Karl Friedrich Schinkel.

geno is terrified at their threats. They disappear in thunder as unseen voices warn them.

Pamina is sleeping in a bower of roses when Monastatos once more makes advances, singing a complaint about his black skin which sets him apart. He is foiled by the appearance of the Queen, who presents her daughter with a dagger and commands her to kill Sarastro. The aria that follows is the height of coloratura ambition; the malevolent Queen hurls her wrath at virtue: "Der Hölle Rache kocht in meinem Herzen" (The wrath of hell burns within my heart).

Monastatos creeps back, snatches the dagger, and commands Pamina to love him. Sarastro forestalls the danger, and sends him away snivelling that he will seek the Mother since the Daughter refuses him. Sarastro's aria now proclaims his creed in a splendid aria: "In diesen heil'gen Hallen kennt man die Rache nicht" (Within these hallowed halls is no vengeance).

Tamino and Papageno await their fate, Tamino stoically, Papageno chattering away. An old crone brings the latter some water at his wish, and calls him "My angel." Their colloquy is silenced by a thunderclap. The three Genii bring the two their magic instruments (which have been taken from them—how, we do not know.) Papageno receives a sumptuous feast, but Tamino merely tries his flute, which summons Pamina. Her joy is cooled by Tamino's refusal to speak to her. She sings of her

Marcella Sembrich sang the Queen of the Night in the 1900 Metropolitan Opera premiere of The Magic Flute in New York.

Johanna Gadski (l) as Pamina in 1901; Andreas Dippel (r) as Tamino in the Metropolitan Opera premiere of The Magic Flute, 1900, New York.

Donald Shanks (center, rear) as Sarastro unites the two lovers Pamina and Tamino, Joan Cardin and Anson Austin, 1973, Australian Opera, Sydney.

Pol Plançon sang Sarastro in the 1900 Metropolitan Opera Company premiere of The Magic Flute.

grief in the poignant, exquisite aria, "Ach, ich fühl's es ist verschwunden" (Ah, I feel it—the joy of love has vanished), and sadly contemplates suicide. She is comforted by the three Genii. Two Men in Armor show Tamino the gate he must enter to pass through fire and water. Pamina is allowed to go with him—in fact, with her new maturity and insight, leads him through the trials.

Elizabeth Hallston as the Queen of the Night with Wilma Lipp as her daughter Pamina, 1962, Theater on the Wein, Austria.

Papageno's great comic scene is inserted here. In despair, he thinks to hang himself, but gives himself the benefit of every doubt, and is restrained by the three Genii, who advise him to use his magic bells. Their merry tune summons Papagena, throwing off her disguise as the old crone, and appearing as his charming counterpart. They sing a delightful patter duet. (This, of course, was the crowning moment for Schikaneder, who played the birdman's part to the hilt.)

In the vaults beneath the temple, the Queen and her Ladies make a last attempt to overthrow goodness and light, but are vanquished. In the Temple of the Sun, Sarastro welcomes Tamino and Pamina, and proclaims that "Darkness has yielded to the power of light," while the chorus chants: "Courage has won; beauty and wisdom are the prizes." And Mozart himself triumphed over the dark forces that threatened him, by leaving this testament to goodness and beauty.

German baritone Hermann Prey, who is known for his singing of Mozart, did the role of Papageno in 1970, with the Vienna Philharmonic under Sir Georg Solti.

THEA MUSGRAVE (Edinburgh, 27 May 1928 –). The composer of many received orchestra, chorus, chamber, and solo works, Musgrave is equally respected for several operas already heard in the United States. Earlier works are the chamber one-act *The Abbot of Dimrock* (1955), and *The Decision* (1964-65), a harrowing tale of a mine disaster. *The Voice of Ariadne*, with a libretto by Amalia Eiguera based on Henry James's "The Last of the Valerii," was commissioned by the Royal Opera of Covent Garden with assistance from the Gulbenkian Foundation, and had its premiere at the Aldeburgh Festival, conducted by the composer, in 1974. Musgrave also con-

Ashley Putnam in the title role of Musgrave's Mary, Queen of Scots, in the American premiere of the work, 1978, Virginia Opera Association.

ducted when the chamber opera came to the New York City Opera in the fall of 1977. Almost simultaneously, her newer work, *Mary Queen of Scots*, was having its first performance at the Edinburgh Festival. The composer was her own librettist. This opera was given at Norfolk, Va., by the Virginia Opera Company of which Musgrave's husband, Peter Mark, is artistic director, in 1978. It is a well-constructed, intensely dramatic account of Mary's troubles, vividly orchestrated and with a superior feminine lead, played on this occasion by Ashley Putnam in one of her first triumphs. Musgrave's next dramatic work, *A Christmas Carol*, based on Dickens, the libretto by the composer, was scheduled for a premiere by the Virginia Opera on 7 December 1979.

MODEST PETROVICH MUSSORGSKY (Karevo, Govt. of Pskov, 21 March 1839 – St. Petersburg, 28 March 1881). Mussorgsky's father was the illegitimate son of a serf woman and a respected officer in the famous Preobrazhansky regiment, but according to Russian law, he was legitimized, and so could inherit his father's estate. After Mussorgsky's parents moved to St. Petersburg, the boy studied music and in 1857 fell under the influence of Alexander Dargomizhsky, with whom he met Cui and Balakirev, the latter two becoming part of the group known as 'The Mighty Five" that also included Mussorgsky, Borodin, and Rimsky-Korsakov. Of these, Mussorgsky was by far the most original, as well as most closely expressing "national" aims through his treatment of folk lore and his setting of the Russian language. All five were virtually amateurs at music, each following a separate profession.

Modest Mussorgsky, painted near the end of the composer's life by I. Repin.

One of the deepest influences on Mussorgsky was the critic Vladimir Stassov, whom the composer consulted about everything. When he met little success at music after giving up his job as a clerk, Mussorgsky began to drink heavily. He was an epileptic as well; his miserable physical condition took him to an early death, at forty-two.

In addition to *Boris*, his operas are the comedy *The Fair at Sorotschinsk*; *The Marriage* (set to Gogol's comedy); and the mamoth *Khovanshchina*, a tale of the Old Believers' sect and their martyrdom. All were unfinished, and had to be completed by another hand. His piano work, *Pictures at an Exhibition*, has retained popularity both in its original and in Ravel's sumptuous orchestration. *A Night on the Bald Mountain* is a favorite orchestral piece, and *Songs and Dances of Death* are in singers' programs, while basses dote on *The Song of the Flea*.

BORIS GODUNOV and Offenbach's *Les Contes d'Hoffman* are the only two operas current in the repertory to suffer so grievously from "versionitis". *Boris* has been the victim of this disease from its very beginning. The cause is easy to spot; the solution murky. Mussorgsky's first version of the sprawling music-drama fashioned on history (as mainly seen through the eyes of the poet Alexander Pushkin) did not please the officials at the St. Petersburg Maryinski Theater in 1869; he revised it, and this second try became known as the "original." Finished in 1872, it too was rejected, but found acceptance, with some cuts, in 1874. Steadily dwindling in popularity, it was removed from the repertory in 1881. Then in 1896 appeared a version by Rimsky-Korsakov; his second revision in 1906-08 was to spread over the world, obscuring the "real" score by Mussorgsky until 1928. That year, the Russian State Publishing House brought out an edition by Paul Lamm, who had access to both the "first" and the "original." Lamm himself made another attempt, and in more recent years there have been concoc-

Mussorgsky in his early thirties.

Scene near the Novodievich Monastery, stage design for the first performance of Pushkin's tragedy, Boris Godunov, which was also used for the first performance of Mussorgsky's opera, 1874, Moscow.

Backcloth for a production of Boris Godunov mounted by Sergei Diaghilev, 1908, Moscow.

The Russian bass Melnikov as Boris Godunov in the first performance of the opera, 1874, Moscow.

tions by many another, including Karol Rathaus, Dimitri Shostakovich (both performed at the Metropolitan), and in 1975 the conductor Thomas Schippers tinkered with a new layout made by David Lloyd-Jones of England and given a splendid production at the Met. This latest fitting of the jigsaw puzzle pieces still left much to be desired structurally. It is probably impossible to reach heart's desire in any production of *Boris*; some favorite part is sure to be eliminated, for if all scenes were included, the opera would stretch from early evening to unconsciousness.

Perhaps the reader can best understand the difficulty by consulting a scheme of the first two Mussorgsky versions side by side.

"First" Version	"Original" Version
1. Outside the Novodievich Monastery in Moscow (the crowd begs Boris to accept the crown).	1. Same, except final section is deleted.
2. A square inside the Kremlin (Coronation Scene).	2. Same.
3. Cell in the Tchudov Monastery (Pimen tells of his work and relates the murder of Tsarevich. Grigory vows vengeance).	3. Same, except Pimen's narrative of the murder of the Tsarevich is deleted.

4. Inn on the Lithuanian border (Grigory escapes).	4. Same, except that the Hostess's song is added.
5. A room in the Kremlin palace of the Tsar.	5. Same, except for addition of two songs for the children and the parrot episode; Tsar's monologue is expanded.
6. Outside St. Basil's Cathedral (the crowd begs for bread; the Simpleton accosts Boris, who bemoans loss of coin and Russia's fate).	6. Omitted. Added: two Polish scenes (6 and 7).
7. Death of Boris in the Duma.	7. (now 8.) Same, slightly cut.
	9. Added: The Forest of Kromy; part of Simpleton's scene from "First" scene 6.

Nicolas Figner as the first Pretender Dimitri from the 1874 Moscow premiere of Boris Godunov.

Rimsky, in his well-intentioned way, smoothed over Mussorgsky's "rough" orchestration, and added bits and pieces to "clarify" the score. This lush outpouring of sound has seduced listeners' ears for a half-century and more. Return to Mussorgsky's more primitive, but infinitely more original, scoring has been the aim of all the restorers. Mussorgsky's is truly a revelation, rhythmically inventive, harmonically piquant, seeming to reflect closely the time and place it illustrated.

Unique, too, at least at the time, was the composer's driving thought—to set the Russian speech as it sounded. This gift of genius slowly penetrated into the world outside. Debussy was influenced by it—indeed, *Boris* may be said to stand on a mountain peak equal in height to that occupied by *Pelléas et Mélisande*—they are two of a kind, no matter how different their ambiance and idiom. Therefore it is wise to be grateful for whatever version is presented to us, while always wishing for the "ideal."

We choose here to outline the story at its fullest, including all the bits one meddler or another leaves out. The reader can easily tell, therefore, what he is missing in any performance he hears.

Some historical facts are useful before the plot is outlined. Tsar Ivan the Terrible was succeeded in 1584 by his feeble-minded son, Feodor. The rightful heir, Ivan, had been killed by his father in a fit of anger. A third son, Dimitri, was also murdered in 1591; the assumption (at least in the libretto) is that Boris, the regent, was responsible for the deed, although later research has acquitted him. Boris had been Ivan's friend, and his sister was married to Feodor. After Feodor's death in 1598, Boris was elected to the throne. His rule began well, and he was responsible for some improvement, but his capitulation to the wishes of the boyars by establishing serfdom alienated the peasants, who were all too ready to rise up against him when the Pretender Dimitri laid claim to the throne. Dimitri reigned for a time after Boris's death in 1605, murdering Boris's widow and son, and taking the former Tsar's daughter as a mistress. He did marry a Polish princess, but his reign was cut short when Prince Shuisky slew him. Shuisky seized power for a short time, but was deposed in 1610. There was no respite to the bloody battles for the throne until 1613, when the first Romanov was elected.

Nicolai Ghiaurov as Boris Godunov, Lyric Opera of Chicago.

Neil Warren-Smith as
Boris (center) and Robert
Gard as Prince Shuisky
(extreme left), 1969,
Australian Opera,
Sydney.

Julia Platanova as the Polish
Princess Marina from the 1874
Moscow premiere of Boris
Godunov.

The later prevalence of performances in Russian has gone a long way toward establishing the opera in its proper place as a "nationalistic" masterpiece. The Metropolitan's latest is a case in point. The American premiere was in Italian, at the Met, in 1913, with Adamo Didur in the title role. Needless to say, it has been Feodor Chaliapin who stands in memory as the greatest of all Tsars. Others who have ruled nobly on his throne have been Alexander Kipnis, George London, Boris Christoff, Vanni Marcoux, Ezio Pinza, Cesare Siepi, Jerome Hines, Norman Treigle, and Martti Talvela. Mezzos have made a glamorous thing of Marina, while tenors strive for passion and conviction as Dimitri, and there are a half-dozen roles of marvelous character.

(Footnote to the "version" battle. Mussorgsky added the two Polish scenes in order to include a "love interest." The music is quite different from the rest of the score; conventionally melodious, with Italian leanings. In order to retain the best of the two disputed scenes, St. Basil and Kromy — one or the other invariably suffers with each new incarnation — why not drop the Poles for a change? This writer has suggested it, to the predictable horror of certain critics. But it might be fascinating to let the tragedy proceed in an orderly and mountingly exciting fashion, without the machinations of the Jesuit and the vacillations of the Polish princess. It seems a pity that the love duet, however basically out of place in the musical scheme, invariably draws the loudest ovations. Is the public always right?)

(The outline will proceed by scenes, as various productions differ in act numbers and divisions.)

SCENE 1. After a brief prelude, the people assemble in the courtyard of the Novodievich Monastery near Moscow, exhorted by the police to pray that Boris will accept the throne. Thoroughly bewildered, they turn to one of their number, Mityukh, who answers them scornfully both about what they are praying for and, after a band of pilgrims has passed by on its way to hail the Tsar, just which Tsar they mean. Shchelkalov, secretary of the Duma, appears with the news that Boris has refused the crown; the people must pray harder. And they are ordered to gather at the Kremlin at the next dawn. "We might as well howl there as anywhere!" they decide. The choruses here, as elsewhere, are magnificent, representing what many consider to be the hero of the opera — the Russian people.

Boris Godunov

Text by the composer, based on the play by Alexander Pushkin and *The History of the Russian Empire* by Nikolai Karamzin.

BORIS GODUNOV	*Bass-Baritone*
FEODOR	*Mezzo-Soprano or Boy Soprano*
XENIA	*Soprano*
NURSE	*Contralto*
SHCHELKALOV	*Baritone*
PIMEN	*Bass*
GRIGORY OTROPIEV, LATER THE PRETENDER DIMITRI	*Tenor*
MARINA MNISHEK	*Mezzo-Soprano*
RANGONI	*Baritone or Bass*
MISSAIL	*Tenor*
VARLAAM	*Bass*
HOSTESS OF THE INN	*Mezzo-Soprano*
PRINCE SHUISKY	*Tenor*
NIKITICH	*Bass*
SIMPLETON	*Tenor*
MITYUKH	*Baritone*

209
MUSSORGSKY

LEVITSKY, CHERNIKOVSKY	*Basses*
FRONTIER GUARD	*Bass*
BOYAR KRUSHCHOV	*Tenor*

First Performance
St. Petersburg, 27 January 1874.

Set design by Léon Bakst for Sergei Diaghilev's 1913 Paris production of Boris Godunov.

SCENE 2. The clangor of the many-toned bells heralds the coronation of Boris in the Kremlin Cathedral. The people wait outside to acclaim him, but he appears gloomy with foreboding, begging God to help him rule wisely. Rimsky's scoring is full and rich; Mussorgsky's leaner but effective.

SCENE 3. Five years after the coronation, an aged monk, Pimen, sits in his gloomy cell in the Monastery of the Miracle of Tchudov, writing a history of Russia. Chanting offstage is followed by a wild cry from the young monk, Grigory Otropiev, who has dreamt for the third time that he stands high above the crowd, then falls. At Pimen's calming advice, Grigory recalls that the old man has been valiant in his youth,

The Coronation scene from Boris Godunov.

The Pretender Dimitri.

and listens with interest to the long narrative (sometimes cut) about the Tsars, and about Tsarevich Dimitri's murder. Grigory learns that he himself would be exactly the same age as the slain boy. After Pimen has gone, Grigory springs to his feet with a ringing denunciation of Boris. The idea of pretension to the throne originates here.

SCENE 4. The Hostess in an inn near the Lithuanian border is singing a charming little folk song when voices are heard outside. Two itinerant monks enter — Varlaam and Missail, accompanied by the fugitive Grigory. The vagrants drink themselves into a stupor after a rousing ballad about the battle of Kazan sung by the fat, red-nosed Varlaam. Grigory learns from the Hostess that the border is guarded, but that there is a side road free. Police officers enter rudely; one of them holds a warrant for the arrest of Grigory. The only one who can read, Grigory fakes the description of the wanted man to resemble Varlaam. The latter, enraged, manages to spell out the true description, but Grigory escapes through a window.

SCENE 5. In the Tsar's study in the Kremlin, Boris's daughter Xenia mourns her dead fiancé, while her brother Feodor pores over a map of Russia. Their Nurse tries to cheer up the girl by singing the "Song of the Gnat and the Bug," but Feodor doesn't like the unhappy ending, and starts a clapping game. Boris interrupts their jollity, tries to console Xenia, then sends the girl and the Nurse away. He compliments Feodor on his studies, and promises the boy that he will rule one day. The boy usually leaves at this point. Boris soliloquizes on his reign; he has supreme power, but can find no peace or happiness. He is haunted by nameless terrors and grieved by the famine and poverty of the land. Feeling guilt on his soul, he envisions the murdered Dimitri, and cries out for mercy from God.

A Boyar enters to announce the visit of Prince Shuisky, and warns Boris that this noble is among the conspirators against the Tsar — has even heard secretly from Poland, where the Pretender Dimitri is gathering forces. Boris's fury is interrupted by Feodor, who explains a commotion outside by a chase after a parrot that escaped (this episode is frequently omitted). Shuisky is admitted, and tells of Dimitri. Boris sends Feodor away, then betrays his fears by questioning Shuisky about the murder of the Tsarevich Dimitri. The wily prince swears that he saw the corpse, and that it was serenely beautiful, "like an angel." Boris is devastated. After Shuisky has gloatingly departed, the Tsar reveals the first onslaught of madness, attributing the moving figures of a clock to the ghost of Dimitri. This powerful monologue ends with Boris's cry for mercy.

The most famous Boris of them all, Feodor Chaliapin as Boris Godunov.

Costume design sketch for Princess Marina by Peter J. Hall for 1974 Metropolitan Opera production of Boris Godunov.

Martti Talvela as the mad Tsar Boris, 1975-76 season, Metropolitan Opera, New York.

SCENE 6. The Polish princess Marina is surrounded by her maids, who praise her beauty. She dismisses them abruptly; she is bored and hopes that her visitor, Dimitri, will entertain her. The Jesuit Rangoni enters and accuses her of faithlessness to the Roman church, threatening excommunication if she does not accept the Pretender and convert the Russians to the true faith. She cringes in horror, and accedes.

SCENE 7. In the garden of the castle at Sandomir, Dimitri impatiently waits for Marina. Rangoni assures him of Marina's love, but counsels him to be patient. (This colloquy is sometimes omitted.) Marina enters on the arm of an aging courtier, and leads her court in a splendid Polonaise. At its end, she joins Dimitri, who pleads his love. Goading him on to an affirmation of his determination to be Tsar, she at last accepts his suit and falls into his arms, joining in a duet that brings down the house, while Rangoni gloats in the background.

SCENE 8. In a square outside St. Basil's Cathedral in Moscow, the starving peasants argue about Dimitri, who, it is rumored, has been seen in the Forest of Kromy. An anathema is being pronounced upon the Pretender inside the Cathedral. A Simpleton runs in, pursued by boys, who steal his only coin. He wails his anguish in a poignant song, then, as Boris emerges from the Cathedral, asks plaintively why the Tsar does not punish the thieves as he murdered Dimitri. The guards would seize him, but Boris bids them desist, asking the Simpleton to pray for him. "I cannot pray for a murderer," says the poor fool sadly. One of the great choral moments of the opera occurs in this scene, when the populace cries in one voice: "Bread! Bread! Give us bread!"

SCENE 9. In the Duma, the Boyars are gathered to discuss the troubling matter of the Pretender. Shuisky enters, describing Boris's agitation. The Tsar stumbles in on the heels of this speech, uttering the same

words: "Go, child!" reflecting his agonizing vision of Dimitri's ghost. He
recovers himself enough to mount the throne and to receive Pimen,
whom Shuisky slyly presents. The old monk describes the miracle he
had seen at Uglich, where a blind pilgrim regained his sight at Dimitri's
tomb. The tale unhinges Boris's reason, and he swoons. When he recovers, the Tsarevich is brought to him, and the Tsar commends his crown
to the boy in the poignant, "Farewell, my son, I am dying." The chorus
intones prayers for the dying as Boris, with his last breath, points to
Feodor as the future Tsar.

(In the Rimsky version, this death scene concludes the opera; the
newer "reforms" put the Kromy scene last, as shown in the "Original" —
see outline.)

Robert Tear as the Simpleton surrounded by children in the last scene of Boris Godunov, Covent Garden, London.

SCENE 10. In the Forest of Kromy, a rampaging crowd taunts the captured Boyar Krushchov, bringing him an old crone for a bride, mocking him and taking out their resentment of the Tsar's regime in some of the most beautiful chorus music ever written. The Simpleton stumbles in, although part of his scene can be cut if both this and the St. Basil's scene are given. Varlaam and Missail join the throng, and assist as two Jesuits, Levitsky and Chernikovsky, are captured and taken off to be hanged. Now the Pretender approaches (sometimes on a stately white charger) and the crowd noisily acclaims him, following his progress to Moscow. The Boyar and the Jesuits are released and join the procession. Only the Simpleton is left, bewailing the fate of Mother Russia. (The entire scene is Mussorgsky's invention; only the barest passage about the Simpleton appears in Pushkin.) While this finale is poetically effective, its extremely quiet last moments commend it less highly to some producers than the tremendous finale offered by the death of Boris.

(CARL) OTTO (EHRENFRIED) NICOLAI (Königsberg, 9 June 1810–Berlin, 11 May 1849). At sixteen, Nicolai ran away from home, studied in Berlin, and went to Rome in 1833 as organist in the chapel of the Prussian Embassy; then in 1837 moved to Vienna, where he was Kapellmeister and singing master of the Kärntnertor Theater, returning to Rome the following year. Later he was chief conductor at the Vienna Court Opera, founded and conducted the Berlin Philharmonic, and became head of the Berlin Opera. Before the resounding success of *Die lustigen Weiber von Windsor* (The Merry Wives of Windsor), Nicolai had composed several operas which gained him comfortable reputation: *Rosmonda d'Inghilterra* (Turin, 1838; Trieste as *Enrico II d'Inghilterra*, 1839); *Il Templario*, after Scott's *Ivanhoe* (Turin, 1840; Naples as *Teodosia*, 1845; Vienna as *Der Templer*); *Odoardo e Gildippe* (Turin, 1841), and *Il Proscritto* (Milan, 1841; Vienna as *Der Heimkehr des Verbannten*, 1844). He conducted the premiere of his *Merry Wives* in March and died the following May.

Nicolai's operas show the Italian influence — lightness, clarity, humor — mixed with the German solidity of his birthright. The *Merry Wives* has never lost its popularity in Germany.

NICOLAI'S *MERRY WIVES* follows Shakespeare more closely than does Verdi's *Falstaff*, although the plot is virtually the same. Page (Herr Reich) appears in Nicolai, not in Verdi; Bardolph and Pistol are not in Nicolai's cast, but Slender (Junker Spärlich) is, and is promised the hand of Anne (the Pages' daughter, not the Fords' in Nicolai).

America first heard the opera in Philadelphia in 1863; the Metropolitan listed it solely in 1900-01, with Sembrich and Schumann-Heink as the merry wives, and Fritz Friedrichs as Falstaff, sung in German. London heard it it Italian in 1864. A centenary production was hailed in Berlin in 1949.

The sparkling overture is a perennial favorite on concert programs, and embodies some of the most charming music in the score. Arias and lively ensembles are plentiful. When given by a young and sprightly cast, the opera has many sure-fire elements.

Otto Nicolai.

Scene V from Nicolai's The Merry Wives of Windsor, 1956, State Theater of Karlin, Prague.

Jacques Offenbach.

JACQUES OFFENBACH (Cologne, 20 June 1819 – Paris, 5 October 1880). Offenbach's father, a cantor named Eberst, took the name of his town, Offenbach-am-Main, when he moved to Cologne, where his son Jakob was born. "O. de Cologne" was the favorite nickname of Jacques (Jakob). His father took him to Paris when he was fourteen, and he studied cello at the Conservatoire for a year, then entered the Opéra-Comique orchestra. He began to compose at about the same time that he became conductor of the orchestra at the Théâtre Français, and from then on turned out a steady stream of works, most of them light and frothy to suit the Parisian taste. In 1855 he became proprietor of the tiny Bouffes Parisiens, later moving to another small theater. For both he wrote pieces with no more than four characters, usually three, and only expanded with his first great hit, *Orphée aux Enfers* (Orpheus in the Underworld) in 1858. By then he had become the rage of Paris, and could do no wrong with the sophisiticated public, which greeted each succeeding operetta with wild acclaim. These included *La Belle Hélène* (1864), *La vie Parisienne* (1866), *La Grande Duchesse de Gérolstein* (1867), *La Périchole* (1868), and *Le Voyage dans la lune* (1875), all of which are still great favorites. A dozen or more of his almost one hundred smaller works are steady fare in workshops and school performances.

But of course it is his only "serious" work, *The Tales of Hoffmann*, for which he is most fervently regarded all over the world. He began to consider Hoffmann's tales as a subject after he returned from a visit to America in 1876 – the play by Barbier and Carré had held intrigue for him as early as 1851, but he never found time for it in the intervening years.

Caricature of Offenbach conducting his own compositions.

The real Hoffmann, who changed his third Christian name Wilhelm to Amadeus for love of Mozart, was a character in his own right. Born in Königsberg in 1776, he had considerable experience as organist, theater and opera conductor before settling in Berlin, and composing a number of operas, of which *Undine* (1816) is probably the best. But it is for his fantastic tales that he is most remembered. He influenced the entire school of Romantic writers, notably among them Poe, Hawthorne, Longfellow, Hugo, Hans Christian Anderson, Dumas Fils, and Gautier. Credited with the invention of the "whodunit," his creepy tale, *Das Fräulein von Scudery* inspired another Offenbach opera, *The Goldsmith of Toledo*, as well as Paul Hindemith's *Cardillac*.

Hoffmann and Offenbach were virtual "look-a-likes," which tempted the composer to stress the resemblance in the person of his hero, Hoffmann. But it is hard to imagine any tenor relishing the description of his namesake: "Hair *à la* weeping willow, mischievous, mocking countenance, with a crooked nose and a perpetual sneer; corkscrew whiskers; hands deformed by rheumatism—a skeleton draped in flowing robes."

No, indeed; our Hoffmanns are made as personable as possible.

E.T.A. Hoffmann.

Two characters from Orpheus in the Underworld.

Character from La Périchole.

Ballet scene from Orpheus in the Underworld.

Program for the Metropolitan Opera premiere of The Tales of Hoffmann.

METROPOLITAN OPERA HOVSE

GRAND OPERA SEASON 1912~1913
GIULIO GATTI-CASAZZA, General Manager.
SATURDAY AFTERNOON, JANUARY 11TH, AT 2 O'CLOCK

THE TALES OF HOFFMANN

FANTASTIC OPERA IN THREE ACTS
(IN FRENCH)
MUSIC BY JACQUES OFFENBACH

OLYMPIA	FRIEDA HEMPEL
GIULIETTA	OLIVE FREMSTAD
ANTONIA	LUCREZIA BORI
NICKLAUSSE	JEANNE MAUBOURG
UNE VOIX	MARIA DUCHENE
HOFFMANN	UMBERTO MACNEZ
COPPELIUS	ADAMO DIDUR
DAPPERTUTTO	DINH GILLY
MIRACLE	LEON ROTHIER
SPALANZANI	
SCHLEMIL	ANDREA DE SEGUROLA
LINDORF	BASIL RUYSDAEL
CRESPEL	GIULIO ROSSI
COCHENILLE	
FRANZ	ALBERT REISS
PITICHINACCIO	ANGELO BADA
NATHANAEL	PIETRO AUDISIO
HERMANN	PAOLO ANANIAN
LUTHER	BERNARD BEGUE
CONDUCTOR	GIORGIO POLACCO

STAGE MANAGER, JULES SPECK   CHORUS MASTER, GIULIO SETTI
TECHNICAL DIRECTOR, EDWARD SIEDLE

Joan Sutherland as Olympia.

OFFENBACH'S *chef d'oeuvre* has endured more battering and mayhem from the hands of "inventive" producers than any other opera except perhaps *Boris Godunov*. There can never be a really "authentic" version, although each new attempt is claimed to "come as close to Offenbach's intentions as possible." The reason that such an ideal is not possible is that Offenbach died too soon, while the opera was still in rehearsal. Man of the theater that he was, all kinks would have been smoothed out by performance time, the characters and the acts in place, the choice between spoken dialogue and recitatives established, necessary cuts or substitutions made. The fact that the premiere went on without the Giulietta act threw the first monkey-wrench. The question became: where to put it, when it was restored. Evidence exists today that it was planned as the closing act, not the middle one. Arguments pro and con are rife; we need not go into them here, but the story outline will follow the order that is indicated in the libretto: "artiste (Olympia); jeune fille (Antonia); courtisane (Giulietta)."

The other sore point is the recitatives. It has always been assumed that Ernest Guiraud (Bizet's friend who performed like services for *Carmen*), as well as assisting in orchestration, had written recitatives to take the place of dialogue—works at the Opéra-Comique, where Offenbach was to have his first "serious" fling, always had dialogue; they were, in fact, labeled *"opéras comiques."* But we cannot doubt that Offenbach wanted this to be his glorious entry into the "grand" opera world. And the latest evidence, unearthed by the conductor and Offenbach expert, Antonio de Almeida, makes it quite clear that recitatives were to be used—had, in fact, been composed by Offenbach himself. This rather puts out of joint the well-intentioned noses of the estimable Walter Felsenstein, Paris Opéra producers, the English National Opera team, and Richard Bonynge, among other lesser lights. Tricky problems in casting have also plagued those who want to be "authentic." That Offenbach intended to have all his heroines sung by one soprano seems sure; certainly Adele Isaacs accomplished the feat at the premiere. But too often in later years the roles were parceled out among various contenders. It is true that each lady demands a different type of voice—Olympia a high coloratura, Antonia a spinto soprano, Giulietta with luscious mezzo tones (Stella seems to be little considered anyway, except in Bonynge's version, which gives her a soaring part, considering that he had Joan Sutherland to sing it). But it can be done, and has been by Vina Bovy first at the Metropolitan, followed by Anna Moffo and Sutherland; and Frances Yeend and Beverly Sills at the New York City Opera, for example.

The four villains seem to have been encompassed by a single bass or bass-baritone more often. Maurice Renaud, with the Hammerstein company, was the first to do it in the U.S. Dapertutto's high G-sharp occasionally brings a baritone, such as Martial Singher, to the single role (his Metropolitan debut). He sang all four later, as did Tibbett, London, Morley Meredith and Thomas Stewart. The four servants have usually been played by the same buffo tenor. Other opera companies have produced some weird casting: Lindorf and Schlémil doubled, Stella as a dancer, and even Olympia as a dancer, while her music was sung from below stage. There is nothing too bizarre for *Hoffmann*, it seems.

Another sore point—and one that goes to the core of the story—is the presence or absence of the Muse. Evidence in the early printed scores makes it clear that the Muse intended Hoffmann to be her own property, and, after a short *mélodrame* (speech over orchestra) in the Prologue, she throws off her cloak to reveal that she is Nicklausse, Hoffmann's boon companion—and watchdog—through his three adventures. Then, standing by while he drinks himself to soddenness in the Epilogue, she claims him—his art will rule his passions. When the Prologue and Epilogue are omitted, the whole plot falls to the ground.

Sketch of Giulietta by José Varona.

219
OFFENBACH

Conductor Richard Bonynge (l) with Joan Sutherland and Henri Wilden (r) in the final curtain call of The Tales of Hoffmann, 1974, Australian Opera, Sydney.

Sketch of Coppélius by Allen Charles Klein.

Sketch of Councillor Lindorf by designer José Varona.

This writer has pursued *Hoffmann* around the world and grieved over the many assaults on its corpus. The characters might be conceived as a five-strand necklace: Hoffmann and Nicklausse each a single strand; the four villains another, the four heroines a fourth, and the four servants, a fifth. Thus the story achieves cohesion, and we can follow quite clearly the foregone fate of the hapless hero.

Notwithstanding all of the revelations in each layer of research that comes to light, we are likely never to see a "perfect" Hoffmann — certainly not as "Offenbach would have intended," — not until that inventive man of the theater comes down to direct its course. And then we might be surprised even out of the current state of revelation — Offenbach was ruthless in cutting and reshaping his works so that a contemporary theater audience would appreciate them immediately, and go away happy, not confused or jaded.

The latest adventure of our hero was scheduled by Almeida himself, who conducted a performance based on his discoveries with the Miami Opera in January 1980. The recitatives are performed, and there is considerable new music, especially important arias for Nicklausse.

Drawing of the Tavern scene from the prologue of The Tales of Hoffmann.

PROLOGUE. In Luther's tavern in Nuremberg, next to the opera house, the voices of the Spirits of Wine and Beer are heard. The Muse enters, proclaims her intention of saving Hoffmann for his art, and reveals herself to be Nicklausse, the poet's companion. The Councillor Lindorf, first of Hoffmann's adversaries, bribes Andrès, the servant of the prima donna Stella, to give him a letter meant for Hoffmann. Lindorf determines to take the poet's place as Stella's escort. In an intermission of the performance of *Don Giovanni*, in which Stella is singing, a crowd of students swarms into the tavern, followed by Hoffmann and Nicklausse. Hoffmann is persuaded to sing the rousing ballad, the "Legend of Kleinzach", but in the middle, he wanders off into a rapt description of his lady-love. Brought back to the present, he finishes the song, trades insults with Lindorf and also with two students, Hermann and Nathanael, then at a unanimous request, begins the stories of his three loves. (Several productions fancy the device of leaving a framework of the tavern throughout the three episodes, suggesting that these are but dreams, figments of the poet's imagination.)

ACT I.   A sprightly minuet opens the act. In the atelier of the "scientist" Spalanzani, preparations are under way for a party at which his latest invention, an automated doll, will be introduced. Hoffmann enters, and is bewitched by the apparition, aided by rose-colored spectacles sold him by the charlatan Coppelius, who has furnished the doll's eyes and demands payment from Spalanzani. The latter puts him off with a due-bill on Elias, the banker (who, however, is broke, as Cop-

Les Contes d'Hoffmann
(The Tales of Hoffmann)

Text by Jules Barbier after a play by Barbier and Michel Carré, based mainly on stories by E.T.A. Hoffmann.

HOFFMANN	*Tenor*
NICKLAUSSE/MUSE	*Mezzo-Soprano*
LINDORF	*Bass*
COPPELIUS	*Bass*
DAPERTUTTO	*Bass**
DR. MIRACLE	*Bass*
OLYMPIA	*Soprano*
ANTONIA	*Soprano*
GIULIETTA	*Soprano***
STELLA	*Soprano*
SPALANZANI	*Tenor*
ANDRES	*Tenor*
COCHENILLE	*Tenor*

221
OFFENBACH

PITTICHINACCIO	*Tenor*
SCHLEMIL	*Tenor*
VOICE OF ANTONIA'S MOTHER	*Mezzo-Soprano*
CRESPEL	*Bass*
FRANZ	*Tenor*
HERMANN	*Baritone*
NATHANAEL	*Tenor*
LUTHER	*Bass*

*Baritone, when villains' roles are separated.
**Occasionally Mezzo-Soprano, when heroines' roles are separated.

First Performance
Paris, 10 February 1881.

Nicolai Gedda and Ashley Putnam as Hoffmann and Antonia from Offenbach's The Tales of Hoffmann.

Joan Sutherland as Olympia
in a scene from Act I of The
Tales of Hoffmann, 1974
Australian Opera, Sydney.

222
OFFENBACH

222
OFFENBACH

Graeme Ewer as Franz.

pelius learns later). Now the guests arrive, and Olympia is produced, to
the delight of the crowd and Hoffmann's mounting infatuation. To a harp
accompaniment by Spalanzani, the captivating creature sings a high-
flying ballad, "Les oiseaux dans la charmille" (The birds in woods and
bowers), delighting everyone. Occasionally, her machinery runs down,
and has to be rewound — audibly and ludicrously — by Cochenille. When
the guests go in to supper, Olympia is allowed to remain with Hoffmann,
who makes ardent love to her. Occasionally he touches her on the shoulder, which produces a "Yes." Then they dance, she so violently that he is
thrown to the ground, while she whirls off the stage. Meanwhile, Coppelius has entered, furious — the banker's note was no good. The guests are
horrified as the doll's limbs are thrown down from a balcony — the magician's revenge is complete, and Hoffmann is devastated.

ACT II.   Hoffmann has fallen in love with the young Antonia,
whose mother was a famous singer, and who now herself has
been forbidden to sing because of her failing health. Her devoted father,
Crespel, has brought Antonia to Munich to escape Hoffmann, on
whom he blames the girl's illness. He gives orders to his deaf servant
Frantz to admit no one. When left alone, Frantz sings a comic song
bewailing his troubles, a certain success with an audience. Hoffmann
has managed to find Antonia, and persuades Frantz to summon her.
They sing a passionate duet, but are interrupted by Crespel's return.
Hoffmann hides and witnesses the macabre scene that follows. The
mysterious and sinister Dr. Miracle appears, lures Antonia into singing
by summoning up the voice of her dead Mother. The ensuing trio is one

of the highlights of the act, with Hoffmann observing from his hiding place as Miracle feverishly plays a violin accompaniment. Antonia's voice rises higher and higher, until, at a wonderfully wild climax, she falls, dying. Crespel rushes in as the girl's final, pitiful words are uttered. The father furiously blames Hoffmann, while the latter repeats in anguish the name of his beloved.

Left: Joan Sutherland as Antonia, Henri Wilden sing a love duet from Act II of The Tales of Hoffmann, 1974, Australian Opera, Sydney.

Bottom: The death of Antonia from the 1913 Metropolitan Opera premiere of the work with Lucrezia Bori as Antonia, Umberto Macnez (l.) as Hoffmann, Léon Rothier (c.) as Miracle and Giulio Rossi (r.) as Crespin, New York.

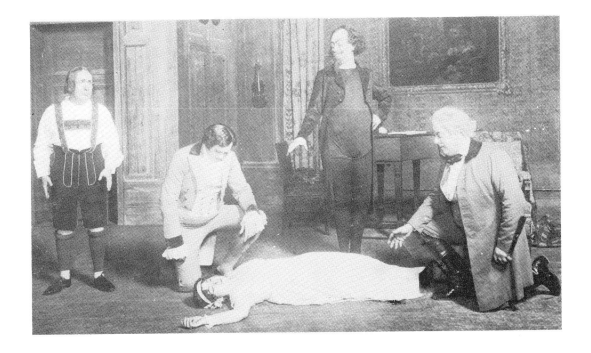

The Gondola scene from Act III of The Tales of Hoffmann

Dapertutto.

ACT III. In Venice, the courtesan Giulietta is entertaining guests, among whom are Hoffman and Nicklausse. The latter joins the hostess in the voluptuous Barcarolle (a song lifted from a former Offenbach failure, *Die Rheinnixen*, and originally sung by two chorus members. It still seems strange to pair Nicklausse with his avowed enemy, Giulietta.). Giulietta bids Hoffmann sing, and he responds with a lively ditty in which the guests join. As the hostess invites her guests for a game, Nicklausse warns Hoffmann that he intends to take him away as soon as possible. Hoffmann vows that he will not fall in love with the courtesan, and invokes the Devil if he yields. As if on cue, Dapertutto appears, bearing a huge diamond which shall be Giulietta's reward if she captures Hoffmann's shadow to add to a similar trophy from Schlémil — one look in a magic mirror will deprive him of his soul. Hoffmann soon forgets his resolve and makes passionate love to Giulietta in a beautiful aria, "O Dieu de quelle ivresse" (What intoxication possesses my soul!). He gives up his reflection in the mirror. A septet (possibly not Offenbach's) ensues*, then Hoffmann fights with Schlémil for the lady's favor. Through Dapertutto's intervention, Schlémil is slain, and the key to Giulietta's chamber is taken from his corpse by Hoffmann. But the fickle lady has fled, and once more the poet is betrayed. (In some versions, Giulietta mistakenly drinks poison prepared for Nicklausse in order to get Hoffmann's protector out of the way. There is, in this newly reconstructed act, also a gambling scene in which Schlémil and Hoffman confront each other.)

EPILOGUE.   After an intermezzo recalling the Barcarolle, the action in the tavern is resumed. As Hoffmann concludes his narrative, the opera ends, and the crowd rushes in again. When Stella appears, Nicklausse, who has termed her the embodiment of all of Hoffmann's fantasies, shows her that the poet is too drunk to accompany her. Lindorf, gloating, obliges. Nicklausse once more emerges as the Muse, placing her hand protectively on the shoulder of the drink-sodden poet, whom she has rescued from his temptations.

*This septet is another debatable point in the Offenbach saga. Almeida thinks it may have been an invention of Guiraud's. Richard Bonynge revamped it as a quartet and placed it in the Epilogue, where it gave Stella an opportunity to shine. It may have been designed to be there in the first place—perhaps further research may clear this up. Another point that has come to light is the switching of arias between Coppelius and Dapertutto. The latter's famous "Scintille, diamant" seems to have been taken from Offenbach's *Le Voyage dans la Lune*, when the aria first planned was disliked by the director of the Monte Carlo Opera.

Huguette Tourangeau sang the role of Nicklausse and the muse of poetry in the 1974 Australian Opera production of The Tales of Hoffmann.

225
PASATIERI

Jobin as Hoffmann back in Luther's Tavern for the Epilogue of the opera.

THOMAS PASATIERI (New York, 20 October 1945 –). Probably the most prolific of contemporary American opera composers, Pasatieri has had a dozen works to his credit before the age of 35. He studied at the Juilliard School with Vittorio Giannini and Vincent Persichetti, receiving the first doctorate ever given by that school. In 1965 he studied with Darius Milhaud at Aspen, where his opera, *The Women*, won the Aspen Festival Prize. *La Divina, a satirical comedy*, was given at Juilliard in 1966.

Thomas Pasatieri.

Padrevia, based by the composer on a tale from Boccaccio's *Decameron*, had its premiere at Brooklyn College in 1967. *Calvary*, an exact setting of the religious music drama by W.B. Yeats, was given in Bellevue, Washington, in cooperation with the Seattle Opera, in 1971.

Pasatieri came to national attention in 1972, when *The Trial of Mary Lincoln* was telecast over N.E.T., commissioned by the network, and with libretto by Anne Howard Bailey. It won an Emmy Award. *Black Widow*, to a libretto based on the novel *Dos Madres* by Miguel de Unanuno, was Pasatieri's first long opera, given its premiere on 2 March 1972 by the Seattle Opera. In 1974, three works by the young composer were performed. Commissioned by the Houston Grand Opera, *The Seagull*, with a libretto by Kenward Elmslie after the Chekhov play, was heard in Houston on 5 March, with Frederica von Stade, Richard Stilwell, Evelyn Lear, Patricia Wells, and John Reardon. *Signor Deluso*, a one-act *opera buffa* based on Molière's *Sganarelle*, commissioned by the Juilliard School for the Lincoln Center Student Program, had its first performance on 27 July 1974 at Wolf Trap, Vienna, Virginia. The story is one of those mixed-up affairs where everyone suspects everyone else and it takes the maid to straighten out pairs of lovers.

Anne Howard Bailey again wrote a libretto for *The Penitentes*, a grim story of the religious sect of Indians known by that name, who celebrate Easter with self-flagellation, and on this occasion, revive the supreme suffering, crucifixion. Goaded by his former mistress, a has-been correspondent becomes the figure on the cross, while the intended victim, an Indian named Felipe, is seduced by the white woman and fails to appear at the appointed time. In abject repentance, he hangs himself. This three-act work was performed at Aspen on 3 August 1974.

Commissioned by the Baltimore Opera for the Bicentennial year, *Ines de Castro* had a libretto by Bernard Stambler. Laid in fourteenth-century Portugal, the story involves Pedro, the heir to the throne, and his illicit love Ines, by whom he has two sons. When his wife Constanza dies, Pedro would marry Ines, but his father the king insists on a marriage with the Infanta of Navarre, to prevent war. He refuses, and is secretly married to his love. But there is no happiness for the couple; when the marriage is revealed, two courtiers kill Ines. In revenge, Pedro ravages the land, until he finds and brings to cruel justice the two murderers. By this time, he is himself to be crowned king. Maddened by the tragic series of events, he causes the corpse of Ines to be crowned Queen.

Pasatieri's next full-length opera was *Washington Square*, its libretto by Kenward Elmslie following the novel by Henry James. Commissioned by the Michigan Opera Theater, it had its premiere in Detroit on 1 October 1976.

A shorter work, *Before Breakfast*, with a libretto by Frank Corsaro based on the Eugene O'Neill play, was scheduled for a premiere in 1980 by the New York City Opera, as part of a triple bill.

The young composer has written in many other forms than opera, but the lyric stage commands his chief interest.

KRZYSZTOF PENDERECKI (Debica, Poland, 3 November 1933 –). There was considerable outcry in the United States (not the least from American composers) when it became known that in 1973 the Lyric Opera of Chicago had commissioned a Polish composer to write a work for the Bicentennial Celebration. But General Manager Carol Fox was not perturbed, and scheduled the work by Penderecki for the appropriate season. Based on the immense epic of Milton's *Paradise Lost*, the assignment proved too mammoth for completion at the appointed time, and did not reach performance until the fall of 1978. Although its reception was slightly mixed, there could be no doubt that the Polish master had created a magnificent spectacle. Miss Fox and her cohorts felt justified in their choice.

Only one stage work by Penderecki had previously been seen in the United States. Shortly after its premiere in Hamburg, *Die Teufel von Loudun* (The Devils of Loudun) was brought by the enterprising Santa Fe Opera to America, on 14 August 1969.

Like other major works, including *Magnificat*, for the Salzburg Cathedral, 1974 and *St. Luke's Passion* (in Latin), Münster, 1966, *Devils* and *Paradise* are strongly based in religion, for the composer is a devout Catholic. He wrote his own libretto for *Devils*, based on John Whiting's dramatization of Aldous Huxley's novel. The worldly Vicar, Urbain Grandier, is sent to the stake, his many indiscretions topped by accusations of hysterical nuns, who believe him responsible for their possession by the

Krzysztof Penderecki.

A child leads the blind poet Milton, stage design for Paradise Lost.

227
PENDERECKI

Choreographer John Butler and Director of Ballet Maria Tallchief collaborated on the dance elements for the world premiere of Paradise Lost, 29 November 1978, Lyric Opera of Chicago.

In Act I of the opera, Adam names the animals. Stage designs for Paradise Lost.

Satan's flight through chaos, stage design for Paradise Lost by Gustave Doré.

Devil. One of these nuns, Jeanne, is hopelessly in love with Grandier, and confesses that he came to her as a demon. Grandier is tortured before going to the stake, and Jeanne realizes too late that it is her unrequited love that has been the source of her possession.

Penderecki calls *Paradise Lost* a *sacra rappresentazione* — sacred performance, even "happening" — rather than an opera. It can be performed in concert form in churches as well as in regular opera houses. The entire Chicago production was shipped to Milan for a La Scala showing. A tremendous effort on the part of all Chicago elements had to be exerted to get the work on stage; unprecedented numbers of everything were called into play. The long-awaited premiere was on 29 November 1978. The forces involved included an actor as narrator in the character of Milton and the Voice of God; singers, solo dancers, a huge chorus and ballet. Adam and Eve were both sung and danced. The noted playwright Christopher Fry made the adaptation of Milton's twelve-book verses, using for the most part the poetic language of the original, but more strongly emphasizing the story of Adam and Eve. Jesus, in his war against Satan, is central to the plot, in which Adam and Eve are expelled from the Garden of Eden after visions of what the world will be, and with the warning that man shall wander until he learns the secret power of harmony.

GIOVANNI BATTISTA PERGOLESI (Jesi, Italy, 4 January 1710 — Pozzuoli, 16 March 1736). In his unhappily short life, Pergolesi accomplished a great deal, turning out numerous comic operas as well as *opera seria*, and the famous *Stabat Mater*. A quarter of a century after his death, his most popular work, *La serva padrona*, caused havoc in Paris, where it polarized the musical world into two camps — Italian *vs*. French — the "Guerre des Bouffons." Adherents to the new form bitterly scorned those who still clung to Lully and Rameau.

Pergolesi's merry little work, composed, as were many of his others, as an intermezzo between two other works, has survived till today, and thrives in workshops. Others, notably *Lo frate innamorato* (1732); *Il geloso schernito* (1731); *Il Maestro di musica* (1731); *Olympiade* (1735) and *Flaminio* (1735) are occasionally performed.

Engraving of a scene from Pergolesi's opera Olympiade, from a 1792 London production of the work.

ch a choleric

La Serva Padrona

(*The Maid as Mistress*)

Text by G.A. Federico.

SERPINA	*Soprano*
UBERTO	*Bass*
VESPONE	*Mute*

First Performance
Naples, 28 August 1733.

THE CRUSTY BACHELOR, Uberto, set in his ways, employs a very attractive maid-servant, Serpina, who makes repeated attempts to gain his attention. He resists her, although the idea of marriage does enter his head. The clever girl introduces Vespone in the disguise of a choleric soldier, and claims him as her fiancé. Uberto begins to feel jealousy, and asks if the engagement can be broken. Only if he refuses to pay the four thousand crowns her fiancé demands as dowry, says the girl demurely. This completely wins Uberto, and he agrees to marry her himself, even after Vespone is unmasked.

JACOPO PERI (Rome, 20 August 1561 — Florence, 12 August 1633). In reality father of opera as we know it — his setting to music of the play *Dafne* to a text by Ottavio Rinuccini was produced in 1597, and his *Orfeo* in 1600 preceded Monteverdi's by seven years — most of Peri's work is lost, and the *Orfeo*, occasionally revived, loses out woefully to Monteverdi's. Nevertheless, Peri was a commanding figure in his day: court musician to the Medicis; singer (he took leading parts in both operas named above), and familiar for his long golden hair, which won him the nickname of "Il

Jacopo Peri.

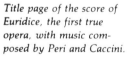

Title page of the score of **Euridice**, the first true opera, with music composed by Peri and Caccini.

Zazzerino"; and a member of The Camerata, the group of noble Florentines who started opera on its centuries-long journey by endeavoring to approximate the styles and methods of the Greeks. The words were held to be most important; frivolous music was abandoned, and long, graceful, dramatic recitatives were the order of the day. Monteverdi, of course, brought this style to its highest form, but several Camerata members contributed greatly — notably Vincenzo Galilei (father of the astronomer), and Giulio Caccini, in addition to Peri.

AMILCARE PONCHIELLI (Paderno, Fasolaro, 31 August 1834 — Milan, 17 January 1886) is another of those composers who survive in only one work, although they produced others, some of them highly considered in the composers' lifetimes. *La Gioconda* is, of course, Ponchielli's enduring work, although it does not find favor in all countries at all times. With an enormously complicated libretto by Arrigo Boito (who did much better a few years later by Verdi), there are some fine musical passages, notably the arias "Cielo e mar" and "Suicidio," and the perpetual favorite Dance of the Hours.

Gioconda had its American premiere as the only novelty in the first Metropolitan Opera season, 1883-34, with Nilsson, Fursch-Madi, Schalchi, Stagno, Del Puente, and Novara, and Malvina Cavalazzi as prima ballerina. The Metropolitan revival of 1966 was one of nine new productions in the first season at the new house; it featured Tebaldi, Corelli, MacNeil, and Siepi. Met performances of 1979 had Grace Bumbry, who had previously sung Laura, in the title role. San Francisco put on a new production also in 1979, with Scotto and Pavarotti.

The "Joyful Singer" of Venice provided Maria Callas with her first international success, in Verona in 1947. Zinka Milanov, Rosa Ponselle, Emmy Destinn, and Lillian Nordica (who opened the new Boston Opera in 1909 with the role), also favored Gioconda.

Amilcare Ponchielli.

Maria Callas as La Gioconda from the 1947 La Scala performance which first brought her international acclaim and also marked the beginning of her association with conductor Tullio Serafin who was to have great influence on her career.

231
PONCHIELLI

Conductor Tullio Serafin.

Program for La Gioconda featuring Maria Callas, 1947, La Scala, Milan.

La Gioconda
(*The Joyful One*)

Text by Arrigo Boito.

LA GIOCONDA	*Soprano*
LA CIECA	*Contralto*
ALVISE BADOERO	*Bass*
LAURA	*Mezzo-Soprano*
ENZO GRIMALDO	*Tenor*
BARNABA	*Baritone*
ZUANE	*Bass*
ISEPO	*Tenor*
A PILOT	*Bass*

First Performance
Milan, 8 April 1876.

THE PLOT OF *La Gioconda*, based on the turgid play by Victor Hugo (*Angelo, Tyran de Padoue*), has been said to be even more incomprehensible than that of Verdi's *Il Trovatore*. Certainly, Arrigo Boito, who wrote the libretto under the anagram of Tobia Gorrio, was decidedly less successful than in his collaborations with Verdi—*Otello* and *Falstaff*. As in *Trovatore*, each of the opera's four acts bears its own title. The overall title seems hardly justified: La Gioconda has little to be joyful about.

ACT I. "The Lion's Mouth." On one side of the grand courtyard of the Ducal Palace in seventeenth-century Venice is a sculptured "Lion's Mouth," with this inscription cut into the stone: "For Secret Denunciations to the Inquisition Against Any Person, with Impunity, Secrecy, and Benefit to the State." Barnaba, a spy of the Inquisition, watches the lively scene preceding the regatta. Gioconda leads in her blind mother, La Cieca, and converses tenderly with her. Barnaba, whose advances to Gioconda have been repulsed several times, again forces himself upon her, but she runs away. She is secretly in love with Enzo, a nobleman who has been banished from Venice, but who has slipped back into the city disguised as a sea captain, hoping for a glimpse of his former love, Laura. Barnaba incites the loser of the regatta, Zuane, to vengeance on La Cieca, whom he calls a witch. As the crowd is harrassing the blind woman, the doors to the Ducal Palace open and Laura appears, masked, on the arm of her husband Alvise, one of the heads of state. She insists that the terrified old woman be released, and in gratitude, La Cieca gives her a rosary. Laura and Enzo exchange glances of recognition. When the others have departed, Barnaba exposes Enzo, but promises him that Laura shall come to his ship that night, to elope with him. Then Gioconda overhears Barnaba dictating a letter to the scribe Isèpo, informing someone that his wife is unfaithful with Enzo. He drops the letter in the Lion's Mouth as Gioconda vanishes, realizing that her love for Enzo is hopeless.

Scene from Act I of La Gioconda from a performance given at Verona.

Enzo's vessel from Act I of La Gioconda.

ACT II: "The Rosary." Enzo's ship is being readied for departure. In an ecstasy of anticipation, he sings the famous aria apostrophizing the sky and sea: "Cielo e mar." Barnaba brings Laura to him, and the lovers exchange rapturous vows. Then Enzo goes below to give final orders, and Laura is suddenly confronted by Gioconda. The two engage in a wonderfully dramatic duet; then, just as Gioconda is about to stab Laura, she sees the rosary her mother has bestowed on her savior, and generously spirits her rival away. When Alvise and his Venetians appear, the women have gone, and Enzo, rather than have his ship fall into enemy hands, sets it afire.

Left: Lillian Nordica as La Gioconda.

Right: Caruso as Enzo.

José Mardones as Alvise.

Rosa Ponselle as La Gioconda.

ACT III. "The House of Gold." Alvise sings of the vengeance he contemplates, then summons Laura, accuses her of faithlessness, and demands that she take poison before a serenade sung outside shall end. She is saved by Gioconda, who is in the palace for the entertainment to follow, and who substitutes for the poison a sleeping draught. Alvise is tricked into believing his wife dead, and exposes her "corpse" to the guests, among whom are La Cieca and Enzo. Meanwhile they have enjoyed a great spectacle, which includes the Dance of the Hours. But all merriment is stilled at the denouement of the act.

ACT IV.   "The Orfano Canal." Gioconda has brought the sleeping Laura to her hideaway, a ruined palace on the island of Giudecca. She has promised Barnaba to be his if he will save Enzo. Now she sees no way out, and passionately sings the "terrible" aria, "Suicidio!" in which she will find her solution. When Enzo enters and is led to believe that the corpse of Laura has been smuggled out of the burial vault, he turns his dagger upon Gioconda, who wishes only to die by his hand. But Laura rouses, and the lovers are reunited, escaping in a boat provided by Gioconda. The singer awaits her fate, but when Barnaba comes to claim his privilege, she stabs herself. In his rage, he cries out, too late for her to hear, that he has strangled her mother.

Giuseppe De Luca as Barnaba.

FRANCIS POULENC (Paris, 7 January 1988 – 30 January 1963), whose earlier compositions bore the stamp of popular "boulevardier," but who developed a serious, if often witty and always brilliant style, outranked in reputation the other five members of the experimental group known as "Les Six." Of these, only Darius Milhaud's works retain some currency; we seldom hear those of Arthur Honegger, and almost never the compositions of Louis Durey, Georges Auric, or Germaine Tailleferre. Poulenc is easily the most famous composer of French song in modern days; his other works are also popular. He scored a *succès scandale* twice — with his first and third operas. *Les Mamelles de Tirésias* (The Breasts of Tiresias), on a text by Apollinaire, created a furor at the Opéra-Comique in 1947, with its bold satire on the battle of the sexes. Tiresias becomes a man, and her husband a woman — the latter, with an incubator, produces hundreds of children. Eventually the two are reunited, returning to their proper roles, and all participants urge the audience to go and have children.

Ten years afterward, Poulenc produced his masterpiece, *Dialogues des Carmélites*, and in 1959 his second sensation, the one-act monodrama, *La Voix humaine*, to a play by Jean Cocteau. He wrote this for Denise Duval, who had starred in the two previous operas. It is a highly dramatic, even feverish monologue of a woman who is talking to her faithless lover on the telephone, knowing that he is to be married the next day. Produced first in America in concert form, then by the New York City Opera in 1977 (with Maralin Niska), *La Voix humaine* restored Magda Olivero, who had taken over Duval's crown, to an adoring public in San Francisco in the fall of 1979. The work requires just such a singing actress to be effective. The latest stage actress in the play is Liv Ullmann.

One writer has called Poulenc's personality a "characteristic ecstasy of personal expression like a form of musical poetry," while his biographer Henri Hel wrote of him: "Sacred or profane, serious or flippant, mocking or moving, he is as intensely himself in the one as in the other." *Dialogues* established him firmly in the small band whose operas remain unique examples of a singular art — *Pelléas et Mélisande*, *Boris Godunov*, *Wozzeck* and *Peter Grimes* are members of this exclusive club. His goal was to "translate into music all that language conceals without depriving the word of its first position." This is eminently personified in *Dialogues*, which as a play attracted him, and which he set almost word for word. Bernanos had fashioned his play from a script written for a film that had never been used. He had been asked for it by the Reverend Fr. Bruckberger and Philippe Ago-

Francis Poulenc.

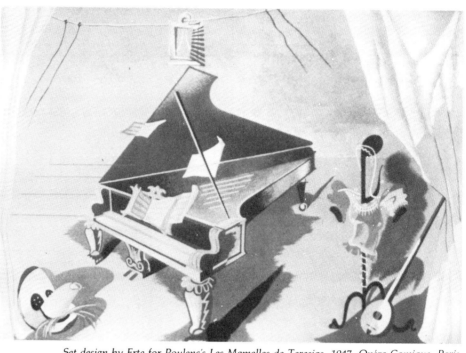

Set design by Erte for Poulenc's Les Mamelles de Teresias, 1947, Opéra-Comique, Paris.

stini, who had based a scenario on a short novel by a German writer, Gertrud von le Fort, titled "Die Letzte am Schaffot" (The Last on the Scaffold). A real incident lay behind it: the guillotining of sixteen Carmelite nuns in 1794. The author invented the character of Blanche, and Father Bruckberger added Blanche's brother.

The story goes that the director of the Italian publishing firm Ricordi commissioned a ballet from Poulenc, who, however, was bored with the idea and suggested an opera instead. The publisher offered *Dialogues* as a subject; Poulenc was convinced only after seeing a copy of the play in a bookstore window, a coincidence he deemed fated, as he had long admired the play.

Denise Duval in Poulenc's La Voix humaine with scenery and direction by Jean Cocteau, 1958-59, Piccola Scala, Milan.

AFTER ITS PREMIERE at La Scala (in Italian) in 1957, *Dialogues* was given shortly in Paris, with Denise Duval, Regine Crespin, and Rita Gorr in the cast. A Cologne performance and the American premiere in San Francisco (in English) followed in the same year, the latter with Dorothy Kirsten, Leontyne Price, Blanche Thebom, and Claramae Turner. Covent Garden produced it in 1958; Vienna in 1959. Since then, the opera has appeared in many houses; a notable revival was the Metropolitan's in 1977, with Maria Ewing, Crespin, and Shirley Verrett.

ACT I, Scene 1. Beset by fear of events that portend riots and revolution, Blanche de la Force asks permission of her father, the Marquis de la Force, to join a Carmelite convent. Her father and brother, the Chevalier, have strong objections, but yield.

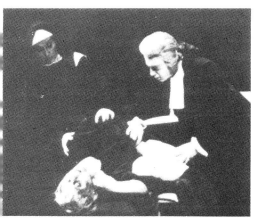

The death of the Prioress, Act I, Dialogues of the Carmelites, Mignon Dunn (l.) as Mother Marie, Régine Crespin (c.) as the Prioress and Jon Garrison as the Chaplain.

Maria Ewing as Blanche and William Dooley as the father, Act I, Dialogues of the Carmelites.

Scene 2. In the Convent at Compiègne, the old Prioress warns Blanche of the rigors of her order.

Scene 3. Blanche, who has chosen the name of Sister Blanche of the Agony of Christ, is closely associated with the other young novice, Constance, a merry girl whose high spirits are not easily restrained, but whose religious fervor is obvious. She tells Blanche of a dream she has had that the two will die together.

Scene 4. The Prioress, on her deathbed, fears the end and is not reassured by the Assistant, Mother Marie of the Incarnation, to whom she entrusts the care of Blanche. After a violent scene in which she virtually utters blasphemy and predicts the desecration of the convent, the Prioress dies.

Dialogues des Carmélites

(Dialogues of the Carmelites)

Text by Georges Bernanos after the play made from his script for a film, with authorization by Emmet Lavery. Bernanos was inspired by a novel by Gertrud von le Fort.

MARQUIS DE LA FORCE	*Baritone*
CHEVALIER DE LA FORCE	*Tenor*
BLANCHE DE LA FORCE	*Soprano*
THIERRY, A FOOTMAN	*Baritone*
MME. DE CROISSY, THE PRIORESS	*Contralto*

237
POULENC

SISTER CONSTANCE	*Soprano*
MOTHER MARIE	*Mezzo-Soprano*
M. JAVELINOT, DOCTOR	*Baritone*
MME. LIDOINE, NEW PRIORESS	*Soprano*
MOTHER JEANNE	*Contralto*
SISTER MATHILDE	*Mezzo-Soprano*
FATHER CONFESSOR	*Tenor*
FIRST COMMISSARY	*Tenor*
SECOND COMMISSARY	*Baritone*
OFFICER	*Baritone*
JAILER	*Baritone*
ELEVEN CARMELITES	*Soprano, Mezzo-Soprano, Contralto*

First Performance
Milan, 26 January 1957.

Costume sketches for the revolutionary mobs by Jane Greenwood.

ACT II, Scene 1. Blanche is confused and terrified at the bier of the Prioress. She and Constance take flowers to the grave, and Constance wonders at the difficulty the Prioress had in dying — it is as if she had experienced the wrong death by mistake, like being given someone else's cloak in a cloakroom. Perhaps someone else will find it comfortable to die. "We die not for ourselves alone, but for one another, even instead of each other."

Scene 2. It is not Mother Marie who has been chosen to succeed the Prioress, but a comparative stranger, Madame Lidoine. In an aria, she warns the nuns to be wary of even the joy of martyrdom. The nuns sing an Ave Maria. Suddenly the side doorbell rings. The Chevalier has come to see his sister before he goes abroad.

Scene 3. In a bitter scene, the Chevalier accuses Blanche of staying in the convent because of fear, and Blanche counters with the claim that her "battle" is as dangerous as his. Irreconciled, they part.

Scene 4. The Father Confessor relates that the priesthood is to be scattered; he must hide. At the Prioress's remark about martyrs taking the place of men, Mother Marie speaks wildly about the duty of the nuns to give their lives. She is rebuked, and the nuns are left bewildered. A mob enters, and two commissaries tell the nuns that they are to be expelled. The first commissary shows pity, and gets rid of the mob. Mother Jeanne gives Blanche a small statue of the Christ Child, but at noise from the crowd outside, Blanche drops it, and it shatters. She is terrified.

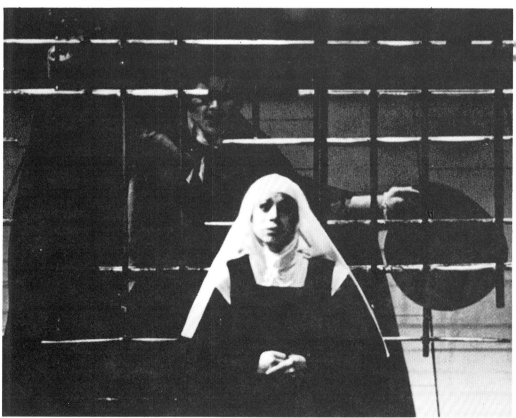

Raymond Gibbs as the Chevalier de la Force, Maria Ewing as his sister Blanche, Act II, Dialogues of the Carmelites.

The final scene from Dialogues of the Carmelites, 1956, La Scala, Milan.

ACT III, Scene 1. Mother Marie at last speaks out firmly on the need for martyrdom. They must take a vote, and it must be unanimous. But one vote is missing; Constance, to save Blanche (who, she is sure, is the culprit), confesses that it was she, and retracts, so that the vote is complete. Blanche takes advantage of the ensuing confusion to escape as the nuns, in civilian dress, file out of the ruined convent, each to her own destination.

Scene 2. Blanche has sought refuge in the ruin of her own house as a servant. Her father has been guillotined the week previously. Mother Marie finds her, but cannot persuade her to leave and join the others. Later, Blanche learns that all the members of the convent (except Mother Marie) have been arrested.

Scene 3. The Prioress places the nuns under a vow of obedience. They have been condemned to die, and she will share their fate. Constance is certain that Blanche will join them — she has seen it in a dream. In an interlude, Mother Marie learns from the Confessor of the nuns' condemnation and desires to join them, but is dissuaded by the priest, who says she made her vow to God, not to man. Thus the most ardent for martyrdom is the only one not to experience it. True to Constance's dream, Blanche appears at the last moment. After singing a fervent "Salve Regina," the nuns go one by one to the scaffold, and the thud of the falling guillotine punctuates, at horrifying — and irregular — intervals, the music — it *is* the music, as one writer insisted. The voices diminish, one by one, until there is only Blanche to take up the hymn where Constance has left off.

*Shirley Verrett as Mme. Lidoine heartens
the condemned sisters.*

Portrait of Sergei Prokofiev by Matisse.

SERGEI SERGEIVICH PROKOFIEV (Sontsovka, Ekaterinoslav, 23 April — Moscow, 5 March 1953). Although he is perhaps best known for his brilliant piano sonatas and several concertos and symphonies, as well as ballets, the cantata *Alexander Nevsky*, and the universally popular children's fantasy *Peter and the Wolf*, Prokofiev wrote a half dozen major operas, most of which have been performed in the United States with some frequency. The best known is probably *The Love for Three Oranges*, which had its premiere in Chicago in 1921; the least, *Semyon Kotko*, the tale of a working man, which earned the composer only mild favor after he had returned to his birthplace in 1933. Truly a cosmopolitan, with years spent in Paris, London, and the United States, Prokofiev nevertheless yearned for acceptance in Soviet Russia, and resumed citizenship there. He was one of the victims of a Soviet condemnation in 1948, and his last opera, *The Story of a Real Man*, written as a kind of apology, added nothing to his stature. That he was capable of a light comedic touch is apparent in *Three Oranges* as well as *Betrothal in a Monastery (The Duenna)*. His technical perfection is evident in *The Gambler*, and his mastery of the large canvas in War and Peace.

The Gambler, revised in 1928 after its original composition a decade previously, and given its premiere in Brussels on 29 April 1929, was based in the composer's libretto on Dostoyevsky's story about the young tutor Alexei who gambles to win enough money to marry Pauline, daughter of an impoverished General. The General hopes for a windfall from his rich Grandmother, but she gambles away all her fortune. Now Pauline is faced with marriage to a Marquis. Alexei, having broken the bank, brings the money to Pauline, but she hysterically throws it into his face.

The opera had its American premiere at the 85th Street Playhouse on 4 April 1957, to a two-piano accompaniment. After several European per-

Scene from Prokofiev's The Gambler with Vera Soukupóva, Jirí Berdych, Oldrich Spisar and Jiri Novotný, 1957, Tyl Theater, Pilsen.

Scene from The Flaming Angel, 1966.

formances, it was heard at the Edinburgh Festival in 1962, and the Bolshoi Opera Company brought it to New York in 1975.

L'Ange de feu (The Flaming [or Fiery] Angel), suffered a lapse between composition and performance. It belongs to Prokofiev's "Western" period, when he was living in Paris and other cities. He wrote the libretto, based on a so-called historical novel by Valery Bryusov, and spent eight years revising the work. Still it was not performed, and then only in concert form, until 1954 in Paris. Its stage premiere occurred in Venice on 14 September 1955; then Spoleto, Cologne, the Paris Opéra-Comique, and the New Opera Company of London picked it up. The New York City Opera gave its American premiere on 22 September 1965, with Eileen Schauler and Sherrill Milnes.

The story is one of religious fanaticism. The emotional and unstable girl, Renata, has had visions from childhood of an Angel of Fire, and later transfers these visions to a German knight, who has loved her but abandoned her. She ends her life at the stake after driving a convent of nuns into hysterics.

Prokofiev wrote this opera after what was considered to be the failure of *Love for Three Oranges* in Chicago, but his hopes that Mary Garden would produce it in the mid-west city were dashed when the prima donna left the directorship of the opera after a single financially disastrous year.

Betrothal in a Monastery (The Duenna) was based on Sheridan's play, *The Duenna*, adapted by Mira Mendelson. Plans for its premiere were postponed because of the German invasion of Russia in 1941, and again put off in 1943. The opera finally saw the light in Leningrad on 30 November 1946.

Scene from Betrothal in a Monastery (The Duenna) with Karl Diekmann and Fritz Ollendorf, 1959, Deutsche Oper am Rhein, Düsseldorf.

Costume design for the Prince from The Love for Three Oranges.

Its first performance in New York was a drastically cut, two-piano accompaniment affair by the Lemonade Opera on 1 June 1948. Later representations were in Leipzig, East Berlin, Naples, Zagreb, and Strasbourg. America heard the comedy again at the Hartt College of Music, directed by the gifted Elemer Nagy on 29 April 1970. It is the usual story of confused identities, enormously complicated, with the two older fellows discomfited by two younger couples, all in bubbling good humor.

THE LOVE FOR THREE ORANGES premiered in Chicago; the opera had been commissioned for the company, newly under the guiding hand of Mary Garden, who insisted on being known as "directa." Chicago was somewhat bewildered by the new piece, which had only two performances, and was taken to New York with a similar reception. It remained for the hilarious revival in 1949 with Val Rosing as director of the New York City Opera ensemble to spark interest in the charming work, which was later popular at the Edinburgh Festival, Sadler's Wells, and other centers. Beverly Sills brought it again to the New York City Opera in 1979, a production borrowed from Tito Capobianco's staging in San Diego. The composer's libretto is a reworking of the comedy by Carlo Gozzi, and parodies the commedia dell'arte antics of that play.

ACT I.   The King, informed that his son cannot be cured of a possibly fatal illness unless he can be made to laugh, fears that his throne may go to his hateful niece Clarissa. He takes Pantaloon's advice, and summons the jester Truffaldino as well as his prime minister Leandro, commanding them to prepare feasts and jolly performances.

Now magic takes a hand. Celio, the King's protector, and the baleful witch Fata Morgana, protector of Leandro, play a game with gigantic cards. Celio loses.

Once again in the palace, Clarissa and Leandro plot mischief. She will marry him after he has managed the death of the Prince, so that she may succeed to the throne. Leandro plans to bore the Prince to death with long speeches. But Clarissa wants action — poison, stabbing, or shooting. The black Smeraldina, discovered eavesdropping, advises calling her mistress Fata Morgana. During some of this activity, the spectators in boxes alongside the stage have come down to take part, to advise, and to demand comedy or tragedy or whatever is in their minds.

The Love For Three Oranges

Text by the composer after a comedy by Carlo Gozzi.

THE KING OF CLUBS	*Bass*
THE PRINCE	*Tenor*
PRINCESS CLARISSA	*Contralto*
LEANDRO	*Baritone*
TRUFFALDINO	*Tenor*
PANTALOON	*Baritone*
FATA MORGANA	*Soprano*
CELIO	*Bass*
PRINCESS LINETTA	*Contralto*
PRINCESS NICOLETTA	*Mezzo-Soprano*
PRINCESS NINETTA	*Soprano*
CREONTE, THE COOK	*Bass*
FARFARELLO	*Bass*
SMERALDINA	*Mezzo-Soprano*
MASTER OF CEREMONIES	*Tenor*
HERALD	*Bass*

243
PROKOFIEV

TRUMPETER	*Bass Trombone*
TEN SPECTATORS	*Five Tenors, Five Basses*

First Performance
Chicago, 30 December 1921.

Karl-Friedrich Hölzke as Truffaldino tries to amuse Harald Neukirch as the Prince, Act I, The Love for Three Oranges; set by Gerhard Schade, Staatsoper, Dresden.

The Prince, Truffaldino and the Three Oranges in Act I of the Tito Capobianco production of *The Love for Three Oranges*, 1979, New York City Opera.

Costume design for The Love for Three Oranges by Isaac Rabinovitch, 1927, Moscow.

ACT II.   The Prince mopes in his room; nothing cheers him up.

Truffaldino persuades him to come out and watch the festivities. The gay and witty little march that is one of the memorable bits of the score accompanies them to the second scene, where all the comedy presented is to no avail. Only when Fata Morgana is discovered and turned upside down by the guards does the Prince begin to laugh. But the witch curses him, and predicts that he will fall in love with three oranges, pursuing them to the ends of the earth. As he sets forth with Truffaldino, the little devil Farfarello blows his bellows to help them along.

ACT III.   Celio tries to help the wanderers by warning them that the oranges are in the custody of a fierce Cook, the terrible Creonte. He also advises them that if they open the oranges, to be sure water is near. Farfarello the while is using his bellows to transport the travelers. They arrive at Creonte's kitchen, and Truffaldino distracts the hefty cook by producing a pretty ribbon while the Prince steals the oranges—no inconsiderable task, as they are larger than life. (The comic effect is enhanced by casting a burly buffo bass as Creonte.)

In the desert, the oranges have grown even larger. Truffaldino, parched with thirst, cuts one open, only to find a beautiful girl, who promptly dies for lack of water. The Princess in the second orange meets the same fate. When the Prince awakes, he orders burial of the two dead girls and liberates the third. She at least is saved by the intervention of one of the box occupants, who produces a pail of water. This is the Princess Ninetta, who consents to become the Prince's bride; but she insists that he must fetch her a suitable bridal gown. Foolishly, he leaves her alone, to the apprehension of the box-holders, who fume as Smeraldina appears and sticks a magic needle into Ninetta's head, turning her into a rat. Smeraldina is to take her place. The King and the Prince appear at the head of a procession, but the Prince refuses to marry this black girl who calls herself Ninetta. The King, however, insists, and they all go back to the palace.

ACT IV. Fata Morgana and Celio are squabbling again, but the spectators dispose of the witch for the moment. In the throne room, a large rat is seated in the Princess's place but Celio eventually manages to transform it back into Ninetta. The traitors are discovered and pursued, but manage to escape with Fata Morgana. Happiness now reigns. (In the New York City Opera 1949 version, the last scene took place in the kitchen, and Ninetta was transformed from a white dove back into her own form.)

Scene from Act IV, the final act of The Love for Three Oranges, from a production of the work by B. Dmitri, 1926, Maryinski Theater, Leningrad.

AFTER *WAR AND PEACE* was read aloud to Prokofiev by his young second wife, Mira Mendelson, the composer set aside plans for an opera on Tolstoi's *Resurrection*. The tremendous task of composing the opera —which, in thirteen scenes, took more than four hours of music—was finally finished, and the first part was performed in Leningrad in 1946; but the reactionary action on the part of the government toward composers in 1948 prevented performance of the second part. The composer made many revisions before his death in 1953, but the final form remains thirteen scenes, with a choral Epilogue of great strength often used to open the opera instead of a relatively weak overture. Considering its length and the demands made upon an opera house's resources, *War and Peace* has been performed more often than might be expected. Its subsequent Russian productions were in Leningrad in 1955, Moscow in 1957 and 1959. Also in 1957, the NBC-TV Opera gave the American premiere, cut to 150 minutes. The first performance outside Russia was in Florence in 1953. Others were Leipzig and Zagreb in 1961; Sadler's Wells, 1972; Opera Company of Boston under Sarah Caldwell, 1974. The opera was chosen to open the new Sydney Opera House in 1973. The Bolshoi Opera brought a stunning production of the opera to New York in its visit of 1975.

Dozens of prominent singers have filled the roles. Mention may be made only of Caldwell's principals: Arlene Saunders, William Neill, Donald

Robert Gard as Anatol leads the waltz, from Scene 2 of Prokofiev's War and Peace, 1972, Australian Opera, Melbourne.

War and Peace

Text by Mira Mendelson-Prokofieva
after Tolstoi.

Cast (Principals only).

PRINCE ANDREI BOLKONSKY	*Baritone*
COUNT ROSTOV	*Bass*
NATASHA	*Soprano*
PIERRE	*Tenor*
HELENE	*Mezzo-Soprano*
ANATOL	*Tenor*
DOLOKHOV	*Bass*
DENISOV	*Baritone*
KUTUZOV	*Bass*

(There are more than fifty
additional lesser and bit roles)

First Performance
Leningrad, 12 June 1946.

Gramm, Lenus Carlson. The British conductor Edward Downes has been closely associated with the opera, both in England and Australia.

The title of the opera should really be *Peace and War*, since the episodes before the conflict take up the first half. The characters, motives, and internal struggles are adapted from the novel as closely as possible; the result is a full-bodied, deeply moving musical tale.

THE FIRST SEVEN scenes are devoted to the period before war. A brief synopsis follows.

1. Prince Andrei Bolkonsky is captivated by the voice of Natasha, whom he overhears in a duet with her cousin Sonya in Count Rostov's garden.

2. Andrei's determination to marry Natasha is crystallized at a New Year's ball in the palace at St. Petersburg.

3. Count Rostov and Natasha seek permission for the marriage from the old Prince Nicolai, Andrei's father. They are rudely received, in spite of the intervention of Andrei's sister, Princess Marie. Andrei is sent abroad.

4. Natasha becomes the object of the attentions of the dissolute Anatol, Prince Kuragin, brother of Hélène, who is married to Count Pierre Bezukov. Natasha is reluctantly persuaded to elope.

5. Anatol's friend Dolokhov tries to prevent the rash elopement; Anatol is already married and in addition has a faithful mistress.

The Ballroom scene, Scene 2 of War and Peace, 1974, Australian Opera, Melbourne.

Scene 8 of War and Peace, showing the Russian troops massing for the Borodino Battle, 1946, Little Opera House, Leningrad.

6. Natasha has been confided to the care of Princess Maria Akhrosinova, and is visited by Pierre, who is already more than half in love with her. He tells her of Anatol's perfidy, to her dismay and remorse.

7. Pierre's study, he orders Anatol to leave Moscow. But all personal matters are thrust aside when his friend Denisov brings news of Napoleon's invasion.

8. The battle of Borodino. Pierre meets Andrei, already under arms. General Kutuzov reviews his troops. Andrei refuses to join his staff, preferring to go into battle.

9. In Napoleon's camp, the Emperor receives news of defeat, but determines to invade Moscow.

10. A hut near Fili, in which Kutuzov decides to abandon Moscow.

11. Refugees are fleeing Moscow. In a crowded street, the Rostovs take several wounded officers in their carriages; one is Andrei, unbeknownst to Natasha. Pierre and a soldier, Platon Karateyev, are arrested. Napoleon is deeply affected by the Russian spirit.

12. Andrei lies delirious in a hut outside the city. Natasha comes to him, begging forgiveness. Andrei dies, after their brief reconciliation.

13. On the road to Smolensk, the French are in full retreat. Pierre and Platon are freed by partisans. The unbroken Russians sing a hymn to their general and their country.

Tatiana Larova as Natasha at the New Year's Ball, Scene 2 of Prokofiev's War and Peace.

Giacomo Puccini.

GIACOMO PUCCINI (Lucca, 20 December 1858 — Brussels, 29 November 1924). The family of Puccini yields only to that of Bach in length of "dynasty" — five generations to seven. Giacomo was the namesake of the founder, his great-great-grandfather, who settled in Lucca in the early 1700s. Spurred by his beloved mother's ambition, the boy joined the conservatory and soon had posts as organist; he also began to compose. He received a subsidy from a grand-uncle and a grant from Queen Margherita, and entered the Milan Conservatory in 1880, where one of his teachers was Amilcare Ponchielli. His first opera, *Le Villi*, was refused in a competition held by Sonzogno, who later accepted Mascagni's *Cavalleria Rusticana*. Nevertheless Puccini's maiden effort had a performance at the Teatro dal Verme in Milan in 1884. During the five years that elapsed before his next opera, *Edgar*, was composed, personal affairs occupied the young man. His mother died, and he fell in love and eloped with Elvira, the wife of a former school friend. The couple lived "without benefit of clergy" until the husband's death in 1904, but their subsequent marriage was stormy, and at one time threatened to ruin Puccini's life and career (see *Fanciulla del West*). Never one to reject the attentions of beautiful ladies, the handsome composer also made many woman friends, chief among them the Englishwoman Sybil Seligman.

Puccini's great luck came in the presence at the *Villi* premiere of Giulio Ricordi, head of the famous publishing house, who took an immediate interest. The composer was paid a regular stipend for a long time, and only

Puccini at rehearsal, caricature by Enrico Caruso.

one of his operas does not bear the Ricordi imprint — *La Rondine*, which was brought out by Sonzogno after the composer had quarreled with Giulio Ricordi's successor, Tito. The dissension occurred over a legal squabble over the rights to Ouida's *Two Little Wooden Shoes*. After winning, Tito gave the work to Puccini, who, bored by the delay, refused to set the piece, which Tito promptly gave to Mascagni.

This was only one of many Puccini discards which were picked up by other composers — Puccini liked to hedge his bets, and always kept two or three projects going at once like juggler's balls, dropping those in which he lost interest. Among these abortive attempts were *Anima Allegra*, a Spanish comedy later set by Franco Vittandini (Metropolitan, 1922); and *Sly*, made into a play by Giovacchino Forzano which was set by Ermanno Wolf-Ferrari in 1927.

Ljuba Welitsch in the title role of Puccini's opera Tosca.

Puccini (l.) with Giuseppe Giacosa (c.) and Luigi Illica (r.), the librettists for La Bohème, Manon Lescaut and Madama Butterfly.

Puccini had librettist trouble from the start. With his insistence on intervention at almost every juncture (following Verdi's customary procedure), he displeased several writers, and succeeded in fixing a firm team only for the "Big Three" — *La Bohème*, *Tosca*, and *Madama Butterfly*. After Giuseppe Giacosa's death in 1906, Puccini alienated Giulio Ricordi by dropping Luigi Illica, the remaining member of the winning combination.

Most of his famous works were composed at a villa in Torre del Lago, near his birthplace. After the war, he moved to Viareggio nearby. In 1924, a throat ailment that had plagued him for quite some time was diagnosed as cancer, a fact known only to his son Antonio, who persuaded him to go to Brussels for treatment. Nothing availed, and after a painful operation which affected his heart, he died on the morning of November 29.

(Note: Particular circumstances and incidents will be found under the various opera sections which follow. *Le Villi* and *Edgar*, although they have attracted some attention in recent years in the wave of "revivals" of neglected or forgotten works, are not analyzed in detail; *La Rondine*, the least

Frontispiece for the published version of Puccini's Manon Lescaut.

Manon Lescaut

Text by Leoncavallo, Praga, Oliva, Giacosa, Ricordi and Illica.

MANON LESCAUT	*Soprano*
LESCAUT	*Baritone*
CHEVALIER DES GRIEUX	*Tenor*
GERONTE DE RAVOIR	*Bass*
EDMONDO	*Tenor*
INNKEEPER	*Bass*
DANCING MASTER	*Tenor*
MUSICIAN	*Mezzo-Soprano*
LAMP LIGHTER	*Tenor*
NAVAL CAPTAIN	*Bass*
WIG MAKER	*Mime*
SERGEANT OF ARCHERS	*Bass*

First Performance
Turin, 1 February 1893.

popular of the later works, although it too is in for revival, notably at the New York City Opera, is only briefly treated.)

THE FACT THAT Massenet had brought out in 1884 an enormously succesful French version of the Abbé Prévost's novel about the little country girl who became the leading courtesan in Paris did not bother Puccini at all He went right ahead, first rejecting Ricordi's choice of librettist — Ruggiero Leoncavallo. *Pagliacci* had not yet been written, and the two composers' feud over *La Bohème* was also in the future, but unpleasant vibrations wer already aroused. The final writers chosen were Marco Praga and Domenicc Oliva, but Giacosa and Illica also had little fingers in the pie, although unacknowledged — in fact, not even the Abbé Prévost got a credit line originally. Ricordi and Puccini himself had the final say. The result was a story based truly enough on the book, but avoiding some duplication with Massenet.

The premiere in Turin's Teatro Regio on 1 February 1893 brought Puccini instant success, but never again did he receive such unanimous acclaim and the opera itself has never attained the height of popularity of the "Big Three."

Covent Garden heard the opera in 1894; the same year the Philadelphia Grand Opera gave the American premiere. The Metropolitan's first performance was in 1907, with the beautiful Lina Cavalieri in the title role opposite Gigli and Scotti. Other fascinating Manons have been Bori, Kirsten, Caniglia, Albanese, Steber, and in the Metropolitan 1980 revival, Scotto, with Domingo as Des Grieux.

ACT I, like Massenet's opera, takes place in the courtyard c an inn at Amiens, with the anticipated arrival of a coach cor taining Manon, her brother Lescaut (in Massenet her cousin), and o Treasurer-General Géronte. The Chevalier des Grieux, immediatel smitten with Manon, elopes with her in Géronte's carriage after Edmor do, a student, warns him of the old man's plot to kidnap Manon.

Lina Cavalieri as Manon Lescaut from the Metropolitan Opera premiere of the work, 1907, New York.

Set for Act III of Manon Lescaut from the Metropolitan Opera premiere, 1907, New York.

ACT II.   Manon has been "rescued" from the poor surroundings of her liaison with Des Grieux and is established in the luxury of Géronte's Paris house. But she repents her abandonment of her young lover in the aria "In quelle trine morbide;" still, she is cheered by the madrigal singers and the dancing master, who gives her a lesson in minuet. She sings the brilliant aria, "L'ora, o Tirsi, e vaga e bella," while Géronte and his friends admire her. When they leave, Des Grieux enters, and the two engage in a passionate love duet. Manon resolves to run away with him, but cannot resist lingering to gather up her jewels. She is caught by Géronte and sent to jail as an abandoned woman.

ACT III.   Manon is to be deported with other women convicts; an instrumental intermezzo depicts the journey to Le Havre. In a square near the harbor, Des Grieux and Lescaut fail in their attempt to rescue Manon, but Des Grieux makes such an impassioned plea that the ship's captain allows him to accompany his loved one on board.

ACT IV.   The libretto specifies "a vast plain on the borders of the territory of New Orleans." Manon and Des Grieux have escaped the others and wandered this far, but there is no relief in sight. When the man goes off to seek help, Manon laments her fate in the powerful (and presently popular) aria, "Sola, perduta, abbandonata" (Alone, lost, abandoned!). He returns, and she dies in his arms.

Richard Tucker as Des Grieux.

Nellie Melba as Mimi.

SCÈNES DE LA VIE DE BOHÈME, Henri Murger's novel, entranced Puccini from his first encounter with it. The struggling artists in their shabby milieu appeared infinitely romantic, offering plentiful opportunity for both tears and laughter and for both melody and dramatic excitement — ingredients that the composer was to draw on henceforth. Restless after the success of *Manon Lescaut*, he seized on Murger's work as his next firm project, first, however, rejecting a libretto on the subject sent him by his fellow composer Leoncavallo, who had worked initially on *Manon Lescaut*. Believing that Puccini was not interested in Bohemian life, Leoncavallo proceeded to set the story himself, and so there were two *Bohème*'s racing to the starting line, with their respective composers no longer friends. Puccini won, not only in the timing (by more than a year), but also in lasting reputation. Leoncavallo's opera follows Murger more closely and contains some charming moments, but so far has lost the race. It was not given in New York until 1960, and has had few revivals.

Arturo Toscanini conducted the first performance of La Bohème, 1896, Turin.

At first, it seemed as if Puccini's bohemian band had nowhere to go but offstage. Reception of the premiere in Turin was lukewarm, even with Toscanini conducting. Not until its third production in Palermo several months later did the future of the opera seem secure. An obscure traveling troupe introduced it to America in Los Angeles in 1897; it did not reach the Metropolitan until 1900. There its reception was not an unmixed success. The words of Henry E. Krehbiel of the *Tribune* amuse us today, but created a fearful row at the turn of the century. *Bohème*, he said, was "foul in subject and fulminant but futile in its music. . .silly and inconsequential incidents and dialogues designed to show the devil-may-care life of artistic Bohemia . . .daubed over with splotches of instrumental color without reason and without effect except the creation of a sense of boisterous excitement and confusion."

Nellie Melba was the Mimi of those years. The placid prima donna felt that the little Parisian seamstress didn't show off her talents quite flamboyantly enough, so after each performance she would appear in flowing robes, with hair wildly streaming, and trill her way through the Mad Scene from *Lucia*. Audiences felt cheated without this bonbon.

Needless to say, *La Bohème* has gone on to become the center of the ABC's of popularity in opera—at least at the Metropolitan—the "A" being *Aida*, the "C," *Carmen*.

Murger's characters were drawn from life: a parallel exists for almost every person in the story, although they have been reshaped and combined by the author and still further changed by the librettists and composer.

Helen Jepson as Mimi.

Caricatures by Enrico Caruso.

Caruso as Rodolfo.

Antonio Scotti as Marcello.

Andrés De Segurola as Colline.

La Bohème
(*The Bohemians*)

Text by Giacosa and Illica.

RODOLFO	*Tenor*
MARCELLO	*Baritone*
SCHAUNARD	*Baritone*
COLLINE	*Bass*
BENOIT	*Bass*
MIMI	*Soprano*
MUSETTA	*Soprano*
ALCINDORO	*Bass*
PARPIGNOL	*Tenor*
SERGEANT	*Bass*

First Performance
Turin, 1 February 1896.

ACT I. In a Paris garret, the four Bohemians gather for companionship in the perilous life they lead in France of the 1830s. It is not entirely clear how many of the four actually live there, since there seems to be only one single bed, but Marcello, the painter, takes it upon himself to pay the rent (when, as, and if), and Rodolfo, the poet, also seems a fixture. The other two—Colline, the young philosopher, and Schaunard, the feckless musician, appear to be only visitors, but constant ones. As the curtain opens after a brief prelude that characterizes the four (and will appear whenever their antics are called into play), Rodolfo and Marcello are bewailing the bitter cold. They have no money to feed their heartless stove. Marcello would even break up the furniture, but Rodolfo suggests that his (rejected) manuscript will make a hotter fire. Even after two acts have been consumed, the shivering artists are not much better off. Colline joins them, followed by Schaunard, who has encountered a windfall and distributes largesse all over the place—wine, firewood, food, and best of all, money. They fall to, but are interrupted by the landlord, Benoit, who is persuaded to join them in drink and becomes so befuddled that he loses sight of the rent he had come to collect. Three of the four go to spend their new cash in the

The four Bohemians gather around a cold stove, scene from Act I of La Bohème, left to right: Jan Peerce, Francesco Valentino, Italo Tajo and George Cehanovsky, San Francisco Opera Company.

Grace Moore as Mimi.

Ferruccio Tagliavini as Rodolfo.

Luciano Pavarotti and Ileana Cotrubas as the two lovers, Rodolfo and Mimi, 1977, Lyric Opera of Chicago.

restaurant Momus for a Christmas Eve feast, leaving Rodolfo to complete an article for a magazine. The poet is not alone for long—a timid knock at the door heralds Mimi, the pretty, frail little seamstress who apparently lives in an even less comfortable cranny in the building and has come to get a light for her candle. Rodolfo, enchanted by her beauty, gives her a light, then, when a gust of wind extinguishes it, blows out his own. She returns to search for the key she dropped. In the gloom, groping on the floor, he finds it, but will not tell her. Their hands meet, and this calls forth the beautiful and beloved aria, "Che gelida manina" (Your tiny hand is frozen), in which he describes his life as a poet, ending by asking her for the same revelation. She answers (after applause), "Mi chiamano Mimi" (I am called Mimi), telling of her simple life as a flower maker. The infatuation between the two develops rapidly. Telling his friends who shout from below that he will be down soon, he turns to her and in the most meltingly lovely duet, "O soave fanciulla" (O beautiful maid), they confess their love and end the scene with (it is hoped) a pair of high C's from just outside the door.

Jussi Björling as Rodolfo.

Left to right: Florence Easton as Musetta, Dahn as Alcindoro, Brongeest as Marcello, Maclennan (seated) as Rodolfo, and Freda Hempel as Mimi, Act II of La Bohème, 1907, Berlin Opera.

Renata Scotto as Musetta.

ACT II.   The bustling crowd in the square where stands the Café Momus does not seem to mind the chilling cold of Christmas Eve, but wanders joyfully about. The three companions wait at a table for Rodolfo, who brings Mimi to them, to their evident pleasure. A vendor of children's toys, Parpignol, makes a brief appearance, and draws a throng after him. Only Marcello is gloomy, for his former sweetheart, Musetta, appears on the arm of an old boulevardier, Alcindoro, and plants herself down at an adjoining table, determined to bedevil Marcello to the limit. She succeeds, first by singing her famous waltz, "Quando me'n vo' soletta per la via" (As I wander here and there), boasting of her attractiveness. Marcello is infuriated; Mimi wonders at such brashness; Rodolfo cautions her that he is jealous; the comrades enjoy Marcello's discomfiture. At last, Musetta can stand it no longer — she screams with assumed pain and sends the tottering Alcindoro off to get her slipper repaired. Hopping on one foot, she reaches Marcello, throws her arms around his neck, and is carried off amid a marching patrol. Alcindoro is left to pay not only his own bill, but also that of the Bohemians.

ACT III.   In a cold February dawn, with snow on the ground, Mimi comes to find Rodolfo at an inn near the Barrière d'Enfer, a gate just outside the city. Marcello and Musetta have taken refuge there, in exchange for some of Marcello's paintings. Rodolfo has come to visit them. It is apparent that the two lovers have disagreed. Mimi refuses to let Marcello call Rodolfo, and hides when the poet appears, overhearing Rodolfo tell his friend that his love is dying, but that he wants to leave her not only because of their frequent quarrels, but also because the cold studio is undermining her health. Her coughing now reveals her presence, and Rodolfo runs to her, remorseful. But they decide to part, in a heart-rending duet. Mimi's farewell, "Donde lieta uscì", which ends with the whispered phrase, "Addio, senza rancore" (Farewell, without ill will), leaves the audience sobbing as loudly as she. Marcello and Musetta reappear, quarreling vigorously. Their rough accusations contrast strongly with the other pair's tenderness in the quartet that follows. The climax comes with Musetta storming off, followed by Marcello's imprecations, while Rodolfo and Mimi believe they may try to last out till spring.

Frances Alda as Mimi.

Scene from Act III of La Bohème, V. Heroldová as Musetta and R. Svozil as Marcello (background), M. Safránková as Mimi with L. Prochazka as Rodolfo (foreground), 1949, State Theater at Ostrava, Czechoslovakia.

The final scene of La Bohème with José Carreras as Rodolfo and Ileana Cotrubas as Mimi, 1976, Teatro alla Scala at John F. Kennedy Center for the Performing Arts, Washington, D.C. Inset: José Carreras as Rodolfo with Katia Ricciarelli as Mimi.

Alma Gluck as Mimi.

ACT IV.   True love has hit a rocky road for both couples. Rodolfo and Marcello are alone in the studio, fuming at the absence of their loved ones, and finding no consolation in work. Their plaintive duet, "Ah, Mimi, tu più non torni" (Ah, Mimi, you will never return), expresses their genuine sorrow. But they are cheered temporarily by the advent of their two companions; this time, Schaunard brings much scantier provender, and they must be content with a dried fish and water to drink. They engage in some horseplay to lighten their spirits, but are violently interrupted by the entrance of Musetta, who gasps out that Mimi is below, terribly ill. She has expressed the wish to die where she was so happy. Quickly they bring the slender girl up and put her on the bed. Everyone is solicitous: Colline goes out to sell his beloved coat (and sings about it in a charming aria, "Vecchia zimarra"), Musetta gives her earrings to Marcello to sell in order to buy medicine while she runs out to get a little muff to warm Mimi's hands. Rodolfo and the dying girl are left alone. She recalls the happier days, and he comforts her. When the others return, they sense the truth before Rodolfo does: Mimi is gone. With a despairing cry, he throws himself upon her lifeless form, as the others turn away in sorrow.

TROUBLES BEHIND the scene bothered Puccini at intervals through the ten-year period during which *Tosca* occupied some portion of his thoughts. The play by Victorien Sardou, first suggested to the composer by Ferdinando Fontana, his librettist for *Edgar,* held great appeal. Ricordi stepped in as usual and handed the libretto to Illica, incurring Fontana's enmity. Then the publisher discovered that Alberto Franchetti already had the rights from the playwright. Ricordi, serving both composers, tricked Franchetti into relinquishing *Tosca,* and Puccini went ahead.

All this intrigue was complicated at rehearsals by a bomb threat, which unnerved the sensitive conductor, Mugnone. The performance was postponed a day. When it did occur, interruptions were frequent and disrupting, and the audience was divided in its opinions. Queen Margherita, who had given Puccini an early subsidy, was present. In spite of a great deal of adverse criticism, *Tosca* (the "La" was dropped from the play's title) became an immediate popular success. Milka Ternina and Antonio Scotti made the roles of Tosca and Scarpia notable in England and America, and all three leading roles commanded the greatest of singers from then on. Famous Toscas have been Cavalieri, Destinn, Eames, Muzio, Jeritza, Garden (her performance with Vanni Marcoux in Boston almost caused the mayor to ban the opera because of the sizzling near-rape scene between them), Farrar, Caniglia, Moore, Welitsch, Tebaldi, Callas, and Nilsson. Much has been

Above: the Ricordi poster for Tosca designed by Alfred Hohenstein.

Right: Mary Garden as Tosca.

Left: Vanni Marcoux as Scarpia.

made of the part of Scarpia by Baklanoff, Marcoux, Stabile, Tibbett, Gobbi, Warren, London, and Siepi. Caruso sang Cavaradossi as early as 1900 at Treviso, and in his first season at the Metropolitan. Other tenors have assumed the painter's smock and luscious arias with relish.

Krehbiel had not recovered from his attack of jaundice at beholding *La Bohème* at the Metropolitan only two months previously. The *Tribune* critic, whose morals were outraged by the story, also called the score "shreds and patches. . .phrases of real pith and moment mixed with phrases of incredible balderdash. . .out of Wagner's logical mind." After some consoling words, W.J. Henderson concluded in the *Times:* "Puccini will do better work with a better story."

One complaint with the libretto is that it omits so much that is essential to understanding the story. Sardou, who helped reduce the five-act play to a three-act libretto, must have approved. This is the background: Italy has been invaded by Napoleon at the head of the French Republican Government and the Austrians, who occupy Italy, have just won a victory at Marengo. At this news, Marie Caroline, Queen of Naples (daughter of Empress Maria Theresia and sister of Marie Antoinette), who is visiting Rome, orders a celebration, at which Tosca is to sing a new cantata by Paisiello.

Rumanian soprano Hariclea Darclée, the first Tosca, 14 January 1900, Rome.

260
PUCCINI

Milka Ternina as the first American Tosca, 1901, Metropolitan Opera, New York.

Caruso as Cavaradossi, 1903, Metropolitan Opera, New York.

Cavaradossi, who has been exposed to "liberalism" in Paris through association with Voltaire and other "disreputable" characters, is in Rome on family business, but intends to leave with Tosca when she goes on tour. He has found refuge by painting a madonna in the church of Sant' Andrea. Angelotti, who seeks a change of clothing in the family chapel and calls on Cavaradossi for help, has escaped from the imprisonment caused by his revolutionary activities. He has also won the enmity of the famous Lady Hamilton, wife of the English Ambassador to the court of Naples, by revealing that she was previously of highly dubious repute—she also became, of course, the paramour of Lord Nelson.

Angelotti's sister has married into the illustrious Attavanti family, which keeps a chapel in the church. It is she whom Cavaradossi has used as a model unbeknownst to her. The fan that is later found was possibly left by her as part of Angelotti's disguise.

Baron Scarpia is an old enemy of Angelotti's, having been only recently sent from Naples to Rome as Chief of Police. His own shaky position is imperiled by Angelotti's escape. In the play, Angelotti and Cavaradossi are strangers, but the painter is moved to help his fellow republican.

ACT I.   The curtain opens upon the pronouncement of three ominous chords, depicting the evil Scarpia. Angelotti stumbles into the church, finds the key to the family chapel, and hides. The Sacristan, the only figure with any pretense to comedy (although he is not really funny, only stupid), comes in, complaining about Cavaradossi, who has not cleaned his brushes or eaten the food left him in a basket. When Mario enters and begins to paint, the Sacristan continues to grumble and mutter imprecations at the painter's ungodliness. Mario compares the blonde beauty of his model to the dark handsomeness of Tosca in the "Recondita armonia" (Strange harmony), which all tenors linger over. Tosca enters and there is a tender love scene, ruffled momentarily by her jealousy of the blonde lady in the painting. They exit hastily as the cannon booms, announcing a prisoner's escape. The Sacristan has news of the defeat of Napoleon. The antics of choir boys around the Sacristan are interrupted by the arrival of Scarpia and his henchmen, Spoletta and Sciarrone, who find the empty food basket and

Tosca

Text by Illica and Giacosa
after the play by Sardou.

FLORIA TOSCA	*Soprano*
MARIO CAVARADOSSI	*Tenor*
BARON SCARPIA	*Baritone*
CESARE ANGELOTTI	*Bass*
SACRISTAN	*Baritone*
SPOLETTA	*Tenor*
SCIARRONE	*Bass*
JAILER	*Bass*
SHEPHERD	*Contralto*

First Performance
Rome, 14 January 1900.

PUCCINI

Scene from Act I of Tosca with Tito Gobbi (foreground, left) as Scarpia; set design, Pier Luigi Pizzi, Lyric Opera of Chicago.

Zinka Milanov as Tosca.

the fan in the chapel. Tosca comes back to tell Mario she cannot meet him because she must sing at the palace, and Scarpia cleverly uses the fan, obviously the Attavanti's, to arouse her jealousy. Scarpa escorts her out, then returns to engage in a lustful outburst of desire and hatred mingled, while the choirs chant a prayer behind him. "Tosca, you have made me forget God!" he exclaims.

(Two acts, omitted from the play, further explore the jealousy of Tosca and her determination on revenge, her revelation to Scarpia that Mario had left the church too soon, and some incidents with the Attavanti family. Tosca is quieted by Mario's account of the true happenings, the police arrive and torture Mario, after which Angelotti is discovered in the well, dead. The political situations are far more important in the play than in the opera, where the love interest is paramount.)

ACT II.   At supper in his apartment in the Farnese Palace, Scarpia sends a note to Tosca, who will be singing in the salon just below, demanding that she come to him for Mario's sake. Then he abandons himself to brutal thoughts of taking Tosca by force — no romantic frills for him. Spoletta brings news that Angelotti has not been found at Mario's villa, but that he has forced the painter to accompany him. As Mario is questioned, the music of the cantata being sung by Tosca (not

Renata Tebaldi as Tosca with Tito Gobbi as Scarpia, Lyric Opera of Chicago.

John Reardon as Scarpia with Eleanor Lutton as Tosca, Santa Fe Opera.

Paisiello's, as Puccini had first intended) comes through the open window. Scarpia slams the window to shut out the music. Mario resists his inquisition, until Tosca rushes in. He warns her not to give away anything about the villa before he is taken into the adjoining room, from where his screams of pain emerge as the torturers tighten the band around his brow. Tosca at last yields — she can bear it no longer — and tells Scarpia to look in the well at the villa. Mario, released, is horrified to discover that Tosca has betrayed him. The tense scene is heightened by the news that Napoleon has been victor after all at Marengo. This causes the outburst of Mario, who cries "Victory!" at the top of his voice. Now he can legitimately be arrested as a traitor and is dragged away. Pouring wine, Scarpia calmly discusses the manner in which Cavaradossi may be saved. The price is Tosca herself. Desolate, she sings her most famous aria, "Vissi d'arte, vissi d'amore" — she has lived for art and for love, and why should such degradation be demanded of her? It is a heart-breaking plea, to which the cold Scarpia is indifferent. When Spoletta enters to say that Angelotti has taken poison and Cavaradossi awaits Scarpia's decision, Tosca numbly nods her head. Scarpia instructs Spoletta to stage a mock execution — "like that of Palmieri." Spoletta understands. Now Tosca demands a safe conduct for herself and her love, and while Scarpia is writing it, takes a sip of wine. There on the table is the sharp knife with which the police chief has peeled an apple. Clutching it behind her back, she awaits the villain's approach. With open arms, he gloats: "Tosca, at last thou art mine!" As she stabs him full in the breast, she cries: "It is thus that Tosca kisses!" Cursing her, he dies. Horrified at her deed, she yet takes the time to find the safe conduct crumpled in his dead hand, and to place two candles at either side of his head and a crucifix upon his breast. Then she creeps away. It is one of the eeriest, most effective scenes in opera.

Lawrence Tibbett as Scarpia.

Antonio Scotti as Scarpia.

Maria Jeritza as Tosca reaching for the knife to kill Scarpia.

ACT III.   At the approach of dawn, a shepherd sings his plaintive song as on the battlements of the Castle Sant' Angelo Cavaradossi awaits his execution. The condemned man begs to write a letter and is granted permission by the jailer. He pens the lovely poem to Tosca, singing it the while: "E lucevan le stelle" (The stars were brightly shining), and has barely finished when Tosca herself appears. Joyfully she tells him of the bargain she has struck with Scarpia and the outcome; he marvels that such fragile hands could do such a bloody deed. Their voices join in a rapturous duet, then Tosca warns her lover to

Maria Callas as Tosca with Renato Cioni as Cavaradossi from the last act of Tosca, 1964, Covent Garden, London.

play dead when the firing squad carries out its mock execution. But it is the real thing, as she discovers after a few exultant moments. Her lover lies dead, and she is being sought for the murder of Scarpia. With nothing left to live for she casts herself from the parapet as Spoletta and soldiers burst into view.

MADAMA BUTTERFLY was a resounding failure at its premiere in Milan on 17 February 1904, incredible as that may seem to us now. The fiasco was probably engineered by his enemies, who resented his former successes. Tito Ricordi wrote of the outrageous behavior of the audience: "Growls, shouts, groans, laughter, giggling, the usual single cries of *bis* [these calls for encores undoubtedly sarcastic]. . .the spectacle in the auditorium seemed as well organized as that on stage." Puccini, of course, was heartbroken. He had been so sure that his lovable and pitiful little heroine would be a success. Withdrawing the opera after one performance, he made many revisions, so that we have not lost this most treasurable of operas.

Salomea Krusceniska sang Madama Butterfly at the first successful performance of the opera, 29 May 1904, Brescia.

Chiefly he cut the long second act, which had induced a certain understandable restlessness in the spectators, into two. Then, and also later, he dispensed with some of the unnecessary "family" details in the first act. The new version had a triumph in Brescia on 28 May 1904. Rosa Storchio, the first Cio-Cio-San, had gone to Buenos Aires, where she would sing the role for the first time outside Italy on 2 July. Her successful substitute in Brescia was Salomea Krusceniski. Arturo Toscanini replaced Cleofonte Campanini

Poster for Madama Butterfly.

Lucrezia Bori as Madama Butterfly.

as conductor. Toscanini, who would later be in the pit when Geraldine Farrar and Enrico Caruso teamed up for the first time at the Metropolitan, thought the music too "sugary." It was probably during a *Butterfly* rehearsal that the classic encounter between conductor and prima donna occurred. Farrar proclaimed: "Maestro, *I* am the star!" He retorted: "Signorina, there are no stars except in the heavens!" A temporary coolness fell between these two, who certainly experienced warmer feelings for each other for a period.

Whether or not kimonos were becoming, Butterfly has been a favorite role of sopranos large or small, tall or tiny, black, white, and Oriental. Maria Callas sang it only a few times and created the illusion that she was just right and others were too small when she appeared in Chicago in 1955.

Lucrezia Bori's adorable Cio-Cio-San was heard in America only in Boston in 1913. The scoundrelly Lt. B.F. Pinkerton, eagerly assumed by tenors although it is not the most grateful of roles, was made more palatable by a later Puccini addition, the *romanza*, "Addio fiorito asil" (Farewell, flowery refuge).

Henry W. Savage, who ambitiously took an English-singing company throughout the United States in the early years of the century, beat the Metropolitan to the American premiere, playing the opera in Washington, D.C., on 15 October 1906. The Met premiere was on 11 February 1907. Covent Garden had heard it in 1905, with Destinn, Caruso, and Scotti.

Puccini saw David Belasco's play in London in 1900 and, although he couldn't understand a word, immediately fell in love with the heroine. (This was a necessary process for the composer in all of his earlier operas, although he couldn't be said to have felt so deeply for Minnie, Giorgetta in

Tabarro, or Turandot.) One wonders if he would have been so enraptured if he had read first the story by John Luther Long on which the play was based (and which in turn drew on a true incident as well as Pierre Loti's exotic *Madame Chrysantheme*). Long had the delicate Butterfly utter some of the most atrociously mangled English on record. A sample: "How many time I tellin' you, no one shall speak anthin' but those Unite' States language in these Lef-ten-ant Pik-ker-ton's house!" Or: "I am mos' bes' happy female woman in Japan—mebby in that whole worl'—what you thing?"

And the whole business about returning robins. Pinkerton is supposed to have said: "I come back to my Japanese sweetsheart. . .w'en robins nes' again. But robins fly away. Sa-ay, see if you don' fin' one that's more in-dus-trial and domestics." Then, when she is nobly dying by her own hand, she murmurs: "Too bad those robins di'n't nes' again!"

Belasco dithered over giving the rights to his play and meanwhile Illica had only the Long story to work on. No wonder that he was upset when Puccini presented his ideas, which were based on the play. A great deal of juggling had to be done to whip it into some sort of coherent story. Puccini, endeavoring to bring out the contrast between East and West, used many Japanese melodies and employed a kind of harmony that suggests the Orient, although the overall atmosphere is decidely "Puccinian." One or two unfortunate touches remain: the quotation of "The Star-Spangled Banner"

John McCormack as Pinkerton.

Geraldine Farrar as Madama Butterfly.

Set for Acts II and III of Madama Butterfly, Metropolitan Opera, New York.

Licia Albanese as Madama Butterfly.

and the reference to "milk punch or whisky." But these are not half so jarring as the attempts on producers' part to restore the vulgarisms of Long and Belasco, which clash with the true poetry of the libretto and the sensitively revealing music.

Early in 1907, Puccini traveled to New York, where, as the guest of the Metropolitan, he was paid $8,000 by Heinrich Conried, the general director, to "supervise" the premieres of *Manon Lescaut* and *Madama Butterfly*, which occured within a month of one another. His ship was delayed by fog, so that he reached port only two hours before the *Manon Lescaut* premiere on 18 January, and therefore could not exercise much "supervision." But his presence caused a furor, and he received a standing ovation. Many incidents crowded his stay, including the rich autograph hunter's payment of $500 for the opening bars of Musetta's Waltz Song, which Puccini immediately used as a down payment on a new motor boat. He had suffered an almost fatal accident when his "horseless carriage" overturned, and he suffered from inhaling gasoline fumes, as well as sustaining a broken thigh which left him with a limp. He also contracted diabetes at this time.

Caruso paid him a visit in his hotel and was struck by the composer's tall handsomeness, his strongly built frame, his bushy mustache and crop of chestnut curls, his very prominent nose and sleepily sensuous eyes with the drooping left lid. Puccini's own description of himself was typical: "A mighty hunter of wild fowl, beautiful women, and good libretti." He is also supposed to have said: "On the day I am no longer in love, you can hold my funeral."

This cheerful boast almost got him in real trouble. Caruso, ever the prankster, is supposed to have told the jealous Elvira, who accompanied Puccini on this trip to his frequent discomfort, that her husband was flirting with a lady in a prominent opera box, who was wearing a big diamond ring, presumably a gift of Puccini's. Elvira stalked into the box, demanded the ring, and created a *scène scandale!* Then she went through all of Puccini's clothes, until she found a note from a lady hidden in his hat band. The fury resounded up and down Broadway!

Puccini was happy at his success, but not entirely satisfied with the performance of *Butterfly*, even though the *Times* attributed its beauty to the composer's "super-vision." Vigna's conducting was "asinine," he disliked the beauteous Farrar, and Caruso wouldn't learn anything, he wrote Mrs. Seligman. "Your god is lazy and too pleased with himself; all the same, his voice is magnificent." Scotti he liked. Both men had also performed in *Manon Lescaut* and had previous experience in London with *Butterfly*.

ACT I.   After a short prelude, we see the marriage broker Goro escorting Lt. B.F. Pinkerton to view the tiny house Pinkerton has rented for his honeymoon with Butterfly. The servants are introduced, chiefly the maid Suzuki. The American Consul Sharpless puffs up the hill, and is offered a drink of whisky by the host. Pinkerton reveals his shallow nature — he is all for a girl in every port, and this one is especially charming — he is even willing to go through a Japanese ceremony with her, which, of course, will not be binding, as he intends to marry (legitimately) an American. The men toast "America forever." Sharpless warns Pinkerton not to mistreat the lovely Butterfly, whose voice is now heard approaching. She is surrounded by her friends and relatives, all brightly dressed, and sings of her happiness. To the consul's questions she replies that she is fifteen, but falls silent when her father is mentioned. She shows Pinkerton the little treasures she has collected; chief among them is the sharp knife which, we learn, has been used by her father to commit honorable hara-kiri. The Imperial Commissioner and the Registrar officiate at the ceremony, which Pinkerton takes very lightly; but Butterfly shows that her whole soul is wrapped up in this love. After the officials and Sharpless leave, the ominous voice of The

Madama Butterfly

Text by Giacosa and Illica
after the play by David Belasco.

CIO-CIO-SAN, MADAMA BUTTERFLY	*Soprano*
SUZUKI	*Mezzo-Soprano*
LT. B.F. PINKERTON	*Tenor*
KATE PINKERTON	*Mezzo-Soprano*
U.S. CONSUL SHARPLESS	*Baritone*
GORO	*Tenor*
PRINCE YAMADORI	*Baritone*
THE BONZE	*Bass*
IMPERIAL COMMISSIONER	*Bass*
REGISTRAR	*Baritone*
TROUBLE	*Mute Child*

First Performance
Milan, 17 February 1904.

269
PUCCINI

Butterfly's entrance, Act I, with Theodor Uppman as Sharpless and Barry Morrell as Pinkerton (l.), Teresa Stratas as Butterfly.

Bonze, Butterfly's uncle-priest, is heard. He advances majestically and furiously anathematizes Butterfly for abandoning her faith. This terrifies the girl, but she is soon soothed and persuaded to join her lover in a passionate duet, after which he carries her into the bridal house.

Dennis Cunningham as Pinkerton with Elaine Malbin as Butterfly, NBC Television, New York.

ACT II.   Three years later, Butterfly is still confident that her lover will return, but Suzuki is gloomy, pointing to the last few coins in their possession. (In some productions, as many Americanisms as possible have been introduced into the room in Butterfly's house.) The girl-wife expresses her hope in the most renowned aria in the opera, "Un bel dì vedremo" (One fine day he will come). The tender sentiment of the libretto's language contrasts strongly with the mediocrity of Belasco's language: "He get angry, say all kinds of 'Merican language — debbils — hell!"

Goro brings Sharpless, who tries to tell the fluttering Butterfly that he has had a letter from Pinkerton — she will not listen to its contents, but presumes that Pinkerton is coming to her, whereas he is bringing his new American wife to Nagasaki (highly unlikely on a tour of duty for the American navy). Goro produces Yamadori, the wealthy prince, who wants to marry Butterfly. But she furiously turns them out, showing Sharpless her blonde, blue-eyed child Trouble, and saying that she would rather die. (Casting the part of the baby has always been troublesome, for any to behave well must be older than three years; once a midget played the part, but lived up to his name in an entirely adult

Paul Althouse as Pinkerton.

270
PUCCINI

Leontyne Price (r.) as Butterfly, watched by Mildred Miller (l.) as her maid Suzuki, sings the famous Act II aria, "Un bel dì vedremo," Lyric Opera of Chicago.

way when his "mother" held him on her lap.) She sings an extended aria to the boy, and sends Sharpless away, still never having heard the entire contents of Pinkerton's letter. Her little lullaby to the baby is punctuated by Suzuki's "Poor Butterfly."

Now the long wait begins. But first the house must be adorned with flowers, accompanied by a beautiful duet between mistress and maid. Then they settle down to the night watch. Voices come to them from the harbor below, exquisitely harmonious.

Lucrezia Bori as Madama Butterfly shown with her son, Trouble.

Felicia Weathers as Madama Butterfly waits for Pinkerton's return, Lyric Opera of Chicago.

The death of Butterfly with Renata Scotto in the title role.

ACT III. Butterfly is still awake as the dawn comes, but is persuaded to take some rest. While she is out of the room, Pinkerton and Sharpless arrive. Suzuki learns the truth, and the three engage in a fine trio, after which Pinkerton sings the farewell to his former love nest, and dashes away. Butterfly's hopes are crushed as she enters, but with pathetic dignity she greets Pinkerton's wife, Kate, who has already told Suzuki that she would like to take the child. Butterfly asks her to send Pinkerton for Trouble in a half hour. Then she makes her preparations, reading the works on her father's dagger: "Death with honor is better than life with dishonor." Suzuki sends the baby in as a last hope of saving her mistress, but the distracted woman binds his eyes and seats him (sometimes with an American flag in his hand, center stage), while she retires behind a screen. We hear the dagger fall, as Butterfly staggers out to join her son, dying just as his father comes for him.

PUCCINI SAW David Belasco's play, *The Girl of the Golden West*, during his 1907 visit to New York (described in the section on *Madama Butterfly*), and thought it had possibilities, but did not meet the playwright. His enthusiasm for the project was diluted by pursuit of other ideas, but later in the summer, he became single-minded about it. A new librettist had to be found, as Giacosa was dead and Illica dismissed, so Ricordi suggested Carlo Zangarini, a poet who had done several librettos. In his favor was the fact that he had an American mother, who could assist him with the thorny spots in Belasco's strange use of the English language. But he lagged in performance, and Puccini grew so impatient that a second writer was called in, one Guelfo Civinini. The composer's enthusiasm persisted in spite of these difficulties, but in late 1908, a tragic incident occurred that shut off his creative powers as well as embittering his personal life. The jealous Elvira accused a pretty serving girl of having an affair with her husband, persisting so cruelly that the poor Doria Manfredi committed suicide. An autopsy proved her innocence, and the girl's family sued Elvira, who was fined and threatened with imprisonment. Puccini paid a large sum to the parents to settle out of court, but his household was shattered, and it was many months before he and his wife and son would live again under the same roof.

Creative powers came back slowly, and he finished the new opera on 28 July 1910. Gatti-Casazza had bid successfully for the world premiere, the Met's very first. Seldom had excitement run so high around Thirty-ninth Street and Broadway. The press had a field day and Puccini an unending fête, catered to by operatic deities, petted and lionized by society ladies (Elvira had been left at home this time), and summoned for dozens of curtain calls, during one of which Gatti-Casazza placed a silver wreath on his brow, decorated with ribbons in the colors of Italy and the United States.

Poster for Puccini's La Fanciulla del West.

273
PUCCINI

Giulio Gatti-Casazza, David Belasco, Arturo Toscanini with Puccini.

Pasquale Amato as Jack Rance.

La Fanciulla Del West

274
PUCCINI

(*The Girl of the Golden West*)

Text by G. Civinini and C. Zangari after the play by David Belasco.

MINNIE	*Soprano*
JACK RANCE	*Baritone*
RAMERREZ, ALIAS DICK JOHNSON	*Tenor*
NICK	*Tenor*
SONORA	*Baritone*
TRIM	*Tenor*
SID	*Baritone*
HANDSOME	*Baritone*
HARRY	*Tenor*
JOE	*Tenor*
HAPPY	*Baritone*
LARKENS	*Bass*
ASHBY	*Bass*
BILLY JACKRABBIT	*Bass*
WOWKLE	*Mezzo-Soprano*
JAKE WALLACE	*Baritone*
JOSE CASTRO	*Bass*
COURIER	*Tenor*

First Performance
New York, 10 December 1910.

Scalpers got as much as $100 for a ticket. The opera itself was received with some reservations by the press, and did not persist in public and critical affections as had previous Puccini favorites. Belasco had been largely in charge of the stage, and had minimized some of the arm-waving, chest-beating antics of the Italian chorus who made paisanos out of gold miners, but still a few awkwardnesses crept in. At more recent revivals, we have been able to accept the West as just another fantasy land, but in those days, it was very real — 1849 was only a little more than a half-century behind us, and we could not accept "caricatures" readily.

The Met cast was exemplary: Destinn, Caruso, Amato in the leads, and Toscanini giving one of his incandescent performances. Campanini conducted when Chicago had its premiere on 27 December, with Carolina White, Bassi (who was borrowed by the Met when Caruso was ill in March), and the fabulous Maurice Renaud as Rance. Famous later "Girls" have been Jeritza, Steber, Magda Olivero, Carol Burnett, and Marilyn Zschau. One of the most bizarre performances had both a black and white Minnie, when in the Chicago production borrowed by the Met in 1961-62, Leontyne Price became ill and Dorothy Kirsten rode in on her horse in the third act. (Incidentally, Puccini had asked for eight horses in the original production — and got them.)

Fanciulla has another Metropolitan distinction — it was the first opera ever to be performed in the new house in Lincoln Center. One fine April day, busloads of children drew up in front of Lincoln Center Plaza and wondering loads of children entered the new portals — a complete surprise to everyone but the management and a few selected press representatives. The object was to test the acoustics with a full house. It was splendidly done; the performance with Beverly Bower and a young cast satisfied everybody, and the success of the acoustics was assured. To start it all off, a gun was fired — the real test, an appropriate one for pistol-packing Minnie.

Notable Ramerrez-Johnsons have been Jagel, Edward Johnson, Martinelli, Tucker, Konya, Corelli, del Monaco, and Domingo. Properly menacing Sheriff Rances: Tibbett, Weede, Danise, Colzani, Guarrera, and Milnes.

ACT I.   In the barroom of The Polka Inn, in a mining camp at the foot of California's Cloudy Mountains, the forty-niners gather for a game of faro and a song, led by Jake, revealing their homesickness. Larkens in particular is affected, and the bartender Nick tells Sheriff Rance that the miner has got gold fever. Sonora takes up a collection to send Larkens home. (Jake's song, which in the play was *Old Dog Tray*, has become "Che faranno i vecchi miei" in the opera, strongly hinting at *Old Folks at Home*. Many songs were inserted in the play; Puccini has absorbed some of the atmosphere but the overall fabric is more European than "American," and more particularly even advancing into Debussy and Strauss.)

The mood is broken as Handsome catches Sid cheating. Rance saves the culprit from the miners' threat of hanging by pinning a card to his shirt to show to the camp that here is a cheat. Ashby, the Wells Fargo agent, enters with news that he is close on the trail of the bandit Ramerrez. Nick pours drinks on the house as a gift from Minnie, and they all toast their mentor. Rance boasts that she will soon marry him, but the

Maria Jeritza as Minnie.   Lawrence Tibbett as Sheriff Jack Rance.

others protest. Their quarrel is halted by the appearance of the lady herself. All crowd around to offer her little gifts, and Sonora hands her a bag of gold, which she enters towards his account. Ashby is horrified that so much gold is kept there, virtually at the mercy of bandits. Minnie pays no attention, but draws the "boys" around for their regular lesson—a reading from the Bible. (This is the *classe de asèn* [class of asses] which Puccini insisted be retained from the play's third act, although there the book was "Old Joe Miller's Jokes.")

Another flurry is caused by the discovery that Billy Jackrabbit has stolen some cigars. Minnie scolds the Indian, and commands him to marry her servant Wowkle, who has a six-month-old baby by him. The post-boy brings a letter for Ashby from one Nina Micheltorena, the former sweetheart of Ramerrez, who betrays his presence near them.

Rance makes advances to Minnie, who repulses him, singing wistfully about her happy parents and her own determination to marry for love. A stranger enters, and is immediately suspect for his citified ways. He gives his name as Dick Johnson. Minnie recognizes him as the gallant man she had once met and never forgotten. The miners accept him and watch with pleasure as he dances with Minnie in the dance hall adjoining. Now Castro is brought in. Noticing "Johnson's" saddle, he presumes his leader captured, but learning that Ramerrez is free, promises to take the sheriff to his (false) hiding place. They follow him out, leaving Johnson alone with Minnie. There is a scene of tentative avowal and tenderness, interrupted by Castro's whistle. Minnie is disturbed at being alone with the gold, and vows to give her life protecting it. Johnson must go now, but promises to visit her in her cabin on the mountain side. Minnie laments her illiteracy and uselessness, but Johnson tells her she has the face of an angel. She repeats his words, wonderingly. (The play had her adding, in reversion to type, the ejaculation, "Oh, hell!" Puccini softened that, as well as some bizarre turns of her speech.)

ACT II. In Minnie's cabin, Wowkle is rocking her papoose and singing a lullaby. Billy enters, and they converse and sing together, with frequent punctuations of "Ugh!" which the Italians considered Indian patois. Minnie comes in, excited at the prospect of Johnson's visit, and turns the place upside down in her efforts to put on fancy clothes and tidy up for her visitor. At first, ill at ease in his presence, she chatters away, evading his attempts to embrace her, until finally, after sending Wowkle away, she yields to her first kiss. Now it is snowing heavily, and Johnson is persuaded to stay. Minnie gets into her night clothes and wraps herself up in a blanket by the fire — Johnson is to take the bed. But Rance, Nick, Ashby, and Sonora demand entrance, telling her that Ramerrez is in truth that fellow Johnson — who is hiding at the moment behind the curtains. When they have gone, Minnie furiously denounces Johnson for his deception and sends him out into the storm.

Emmy Destinn as Minnie cheats Pasquale Amato as Sheriff Rance at poker in order to save the life of Enrico Caruso (head down) as Ramerrez, from Act II of the premiere performance of La Fanciulla del West, 1910, Metropolitan Opera, New York.

Scene from the final act of La Fanciulla del West, from the premiere performance of the work, starring Emmy Destinn as Minnie, Enrico Caruso (about to be hanged) as Ramerrez and Pasquale Amato (far right) as Sheriff Jack Rance, 1910, Metropolitan Opera, New York.

But shots are heard, and he staggers back in, wounded. She helps him up the ladder to hide in the loft, and admits Rance. His suspicions are lulled and he is about to leave when a drop of blood falls on his hand. (The incident, seemingly so coincidental, was based on a true happening in Belasco's father's adventures.) But Rance is once more gulled. Agreeing to play three hands of poker for the possession of Johnson, he loses — to Minnie's cheating.

ACT III.   Rance is not through with his vengeance — Johnson has been caught and is about to be hanged by the inflamed crowd. He makes an impassioned plea that Minnie shall never know of his disgrace, in the most famous piece of the opera: "Ch'ella mi credi libero e lontano" (Let her believe I am free and far away). The noose is already around his neck when shots are heard and the heroine enters — preferably on horseback. First by intimidation, then by reminders of all she has meant to them, she persuades the rough miners to let her have her man. They agree, and only Rance is left embittered as the lovers ride off into the sunset — a typical "Horse-opera" ending.

La Rondine
(*The Swallow*)

Text by G. Adami.

MAGDA	*Soprano*
LISETTE	*Soprano*
RUGGERO	*Tenor*
PRUNIER	*Tenor*
RAMBALDO	*Baritone*
PERICHAUD	*Baritone or Bass*
GOBIN	*Tenor*
CREBILLON	*Bass-Baritone*
YVETTE	*Soprano*
BIANCA	*Soprano*
SUZY	*Mezzo-Soprano*
A STEWARD	*Bass*

First Performance
Monte Carlo, 27 March 1917.

ORIGINALLY INTENDED as a Viennese operetta but postponed because of World War I, *La Rondine* was based on an original libretto by Willner and Reichert, and although the music is lighter in tone than other Puccini works, it is by no means an operetta. As we have seen, it is the only one of his works not to bear the Ricordi imprint, and it is also the most neglected of his later output. However, revivals occur periodically. The Juilliard Opera produced it in 1979, and the New York City Opera had it on schedule.

ACT I.   Magda is entertaining in the luxurious salon where Rambaldo has installed her, and takes up the poet Prunier's song about the dreams of one Doretta where he left off—the one aria in the opera that remains thoroughly current, known as Doretta's song. A young man, Ruggero, is shown in, as Magda reminiscences about her earlier carefree days and the lover she had once had—this newcomer reminds her of him. Everyone goes off to the bohemian cafe, Bullier's, except Prunier, who waylays Magda's maid Lisetto, embraces her, and takes her off to the party. Magda also decides to go, and dresses as a simple grisette.

ACT II.   Magda finds Ruggero, enchants him, and goes away with him after Rambaldo has discovered them together.

ACT III.   The lovers are blissfully happy in a little cottage near Nice, but when Lisette and Prunier arrive with a message stating that Rambaldo will take Magda back, she renounces Ruggero and his honorable intentions and the swallow returns to its well feathered nest.

Lucrezia Bori and Beniamino Gigli in Puccini's La Rondine (The Swallow), Metropolitan Opera, New York.

THE METROPOLITAN'S second Puccini world premiere came in a package of three: *Il Tabarro*, a gruesome tragedy of extreme *verismo*; *Suor Angelica*, a sentimental tragedy; and *Gianni Schicchi*, a rollicking comedy. The last scored the most resounding success and has remained a fixture in world repertoire; the other two appear fitfully. All three, however, make a stunning triple bill, every so often appearing as such in the larger houses. The parade of top singers at the premiere entranced a Met audience: Muzio, Crimi, and Montesanto in *Tabarro*; Farrar as Sister Angelica; and De Luca, Easton, Crimi, and Didur in *Schicchi*. Moranzoni was the conductor. Among later singers who shone in the various roles were Tibbett and Gobbi in *Tabarro*, Sutherland as Angelica, and Baccaloni as Schicchi. Edward Johnson sang the tenor roles under his early assumed name, Di Giovanni, in Rome in 1919.

Trittico
(*Triptych*)

Il Tabarro
Suor Angelica
Gianni Schicchi

First Performance
as Triple Bill
New York, 14 December 1918.

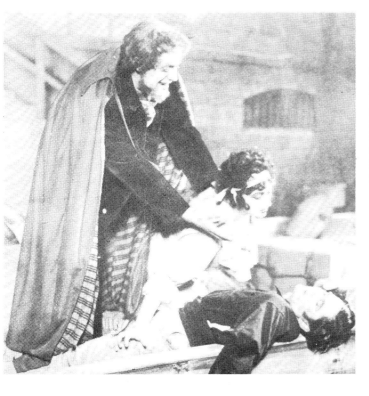

Scene from the first performance of Il Tabarro with Luigi Montesanto as Michele (l.), Claudia Muzio as his wife Giorgetta and Giulio Crimi as her lover, 1918, Metropolitan Opera, New York.

279
PUCCINI

MICHELE, AGED fifty, is the owner of a barge docked on the River Seine. His young wife, Giorgetta, has taken as a lover one of the young bargemen, Luigi. They drink at the end of a day, with the others— bargemen Tinca and Talpa. Talpa's wife, Frugola, sings of her life as a rag-picker. When the lovers are alone, they arrange a rendezvous for later—a lighted match will be the signal. Michele wants to restore a warm relationship with his wife—why does she not ask for refuge beneath his cloak any more? She is indifferent, and goes off to bed. But Michele's suspicions are aroused when he sees she has not undressed. He lights his pipe, and Luigi, thinking it is the signal, creeps on board. Michele, with a cry of rage, strangles him and hides the corpse beneath his cloak. When Giorgetta comes on deck, he flings aside the cloak to show her what it is hiding.

Gold's play was titled *La Houppelande* (The Greatcoat).

Il Tabarro
(*The Cloak*)

Text by G. Adami after the play by Didier Gold.

MICHELE	*Baritone*
GIORGETTA	*Soprano*
LUIGI	*Tenor*
TINCA	*Tenor*
TALPA	*Bass*
FRUGOLA	*Mezzo-Soprano*

Suor Angelica
(*Sister Angelica*)

Text by G. Forzano.

SUOR ANGELICA	*Soprano*
THE PRINCESS	*Contralto*
THE ABBESS	*Mezzo-Soprano*
ALMS COLLECTOR	*Soprano*
MISTRESS OF NOVICES	*Mezzo-Soprano*
SUOR GENEVIEVE	*Soprano*
SUOR OSMINA	*Soprano*
SUOR DOLCINA	*Mezzo-Soprano*

BECAUSE OF THE scandal she caused her noble family by giving birth to an illegitimate child, Sister Angelica has done penance for seven years in a convent near Siena. The Princess, her aunt, arrives, but instead of bringing forgiveness, she demands that Angelica sign a paper which turns over her inheritance to her young sister, who is about to be married. The wretched girl learns that her son, for whom she has longed all this time, has died two years before. In despair, Angelica drinks a poisonous brew she makes of herbs and flowers. She begs the Virgin to forgive her this last and most grievous sin. In a vision, the Virgin appears with a child, which she sends toward Angelica. An invisible chorus sings of salvation as she dies. Angelica has one aria which remains famous: "Senza mamma" (Without a mother).

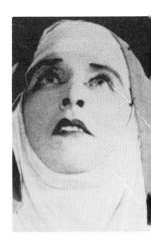

Left: Puccini's sister Giulia Enrichetta, in whose honor he wrote Suor Angelica.

Right: Geraldine Farrar created the role of Suor Angelica, 1918, Metropolitan Opera, New York.

Scene from Suor Angelica.

Donati's greedy relatives feign grief over his corpse in this scene from Gianni Schicchi, scenery and costumes, Zdenek Rossman, 1957, North Bohemian Theater at Liberec, Czechoslovakia.

THE STORY WAS suggested by a passage from Dante concerning a probable real-life scoundrel. In Florence in 1299, Buoso Donati has just died and left his considerable estate to charity. His greedy relatives despair, until young Rinuccio advises them to summon the crafty Gianni Schicchi—the boy is in love with Schicchi's daughter Lauretta and knows the old man well. Schicchi wastes no time; the corpse is removed from the deathbed and the rogue takes his place, to testify to the notary in disposition of his wealth. What is the rage of the rapacious crew when Schicchi bequeaths all the best bits to himself. They dare not protest, as he reminds them by a wave of the arm and a chant of the "old refrain," for bearing false witness means amputation of a hand and banishment from Florence. He sends the whole pack flying, and gives his blessing to the young couple, asking the audience if they will applaud a verdict of "Extenuating Circumstances." Not only does the audience agree, but it invariably applauds the delightful music that accompanies the comedy at every juncture. Lauretta's aria, "O mio babbino caro" (O, my beloved father), in which she begs her parent to reconsider his first impulse to storm out in disgust at the rapacious relatives, has become one of Puccini's jewels, as often performed as those from more widely favored operas. It was one of Maria Callas's last attempts to recall the greatness of her career as she sang in a final round of concerts.

Gianni Schicchi

Text by G. Forzano.

GIANNI SCHICCHI	*Baritone*
LAURETTA	*Soprano*

RELATIONS OF BUOSO DONATI:

ZITA	*Contralto*
RINUCCIO	*Tenor*
GHERARDO	*Tenor*
NELLA	*Soprano*
GHERARDINO	*Alto*
BETTO DI SIGNA	*Bass*
SIMONE	*Bass*
MARCO	*Baritone*
LA CIESCA	*Mezzo-Soprano*
SPINELLOCCIO	*Bass*
DI NICOLAO	*Baritone*
PINELLINO	*Bass*
GUCCIO	*Bass*

Poster for the La Scala premiere of Turandot, 1926, Milan.

Rosa Raisa, the first Turandot.

PUCCINI'S LAST opera is thought by many to be his masterpiece. Certainly it reveals a new mastery of musical thought, the amalgamation of exotic elements into the fabric of the orchestra more smoothly than in *Madama Butterfly* or *Fanciulla del West,* and a sure melodic sense that produced a beautiful line. The Gozzi fairy tale was accepted by the composer only after several other projects fizzled, among them *Oliver Twist.* Puccini's librettists concentrated on the central elements of the story involving the icy princess and her eventual subjugation to love for the prince who dared to answer her three riddles — and got them all right. The addition of the pathetic little slave girl Liù provided a foil to the adamant Turandot, and the only remaining vestige of the commedia dell'arte that Gozzi favored was the deportment of the three ministers, Ping, Pang, and Pong. *Turandotte* was the fourth of the ten Gozzi fables; this original spelling suggests that the final "t" of the opera's title be pronounced. Puccini also relied on a Persian legend from the *Thousand and One Nights,* as his biographer Vincent Seligman, has said, as well as a Chinese fairy tale, a Venetian Masque, a play of Schiller, and an overture of Weber.

Before the last act could be completed, Puccini died. Franco Alfano, the composer of several operas, was chosen to complete *Turandotte,* but Toscanini, who was to conduct, did not approve his first version and sent it back for revision. At the first performance, when the place in the music occurred where Puccini had dropped his pen, Toscanini laid down his baton, and delivered the only speech he ever made in public, saying that here death overcame art. He walked out, leaving the ending unplayed. So Alfano's music was not heard until the second performance. It begins after the sorrowful accompaniment to Liù's funeral cortege, with Calaf's "Principessa di morte," and includes the love duet.

Rosa Raisa was the first Turandot, Miguel Fleta the Calaf. Three important performances were given in the same year, 1926: in Rome, Buenos Aires (with Muzio and Lauri-Volpi), and at the Metropolitan with Jeritza, Lauri-Volpi, Martha Attwood, and De Luca, Serafin conducting. Covent Garden heard it in 1927, then 1929 brought another famous Turandot in London, Eva Turner. The Metropolitan revival of 1967 starred Birgit Nilsson and Corelli, with Stokowski conducting in his Met debut.

ACT I.   The expectant populace hears from a mandarin that the Prince of Persia has failed to answer Turandot's three riddles, and must die, as have all previous suitors — their heads are plainly to be seen on poles atop the high walls. Out of the crowd emerges an old man, led by a pretty young slave girl — he is Timur, the deposed Emperor of Tartary, who has been guided here by the faithful Liù. They seek — and to their amazement, find — Timur's son, Calaf, but their reunion is interrupted by the arrival of the Executioner's assistants, who sharpen a huge sword for their master. The temper of the bloodthirsty crowd changes as the young Persian Prince appears, going to his doom. In answer to the many cries for pardon, Turandot appears on a balcony, and with a wave of the hand, bids the execution to proceed. But now a new victim is at hand — Calaf, smitten with Turandot's cold beauty, determines to try his luck at the riddles. In vain do Timur and Liù, and even the ministers, try to dissuade him. Liù's entreaty, especially, is piti-

Scene from the first act of Turandot.

ful and beautiful – the aria, "Signore, ascolta" (Milord, hear me!) – but even though touched, he will not heed. He bids her take care of his father and tries to comfort her in "Non piangere, Liù". Then, as mysterious voices predict death, Calaf strikes the great gong as a summons to Turandot.

ACT II. Scene 1.   The three ministers engage in nostalgia for the happier days when China was not a matter of three riddles and "off with his head." They hope the newcomer will succeed and rid the kingdom of this scourge. Each of them has a secret hideaway, to which he wishes to retire. They go out, accompanied by the sound of trumpets calling them to the newest trial. This is a wonderfully executed scene, with glittering orchestration, and a colorful Oriental atmosphere.

Scene 2. The Emperor Altoum sits on his throne atop a huge stairway in the vast square before the Imperial Palace. Eight ancient wise men each hold three scrolls which contain the answers to Turandot's riddles. The old Emperor weakly begs Prince Calaf to reconsider, but Calaf thrice stubbornly proclaims his intention to persist. Turandot, drawing a mammoth train behind her, appears with her retinue, and begins, in a cruelly high tessitura, to relate the story of her ancestor's rav-

Turandot

Text by Adami and Simoni
based on Gozzi's fable.

PRINCESS TURANDOT	*Soprano*
PRINCE CALAF	*Tenor*
LIU	*Soprano*
TIMUR	*Bass*
EMPEROR ALTOUM	*Tenor*
PING	*Baritone*
PANG	*Tenor*
PONG	*Tenor*
MANDARIN	*Baritone*

First Performance
Milan, 25 April! 1926.

Birgit Nilsson as Turandot in Act II, Scene 2, stage design by Nicola Benois, 1958, La Scala. Milan.

Giacomo Lauri-Volpi as Calaf.

ishment by invading Tartars — a fate that inspired her descendant's campaign of revenge against men. "In questa reggia," she begins — in this palace, Princess Lo-u-ling was despoiled. "Never shall a man possess me!"

She proclaims the first riddle: A phantom that disappears at dawn to be reborn each night within the heart of man. The Prince unhesitatingly replies: "Hope." The Wise Men agree, and the crowd murmurs. Slightly upset, the Princess gives the second riddle: "A fever, it spurts like a flame and yet is not a flame; inertia transmutes it to languor; it grows cold with loss of life." After a pause, the Prince shouts: "Blood!" and the crowd acknowledges he is right. But the furious Turandot confronts Calaf, and in a pitch a half-tone higher than before, propounds the final

Left to right: Grahame Clifford, Edgar Evans and Hubert Norville as Ping, Pang and Pong with the slaves of seduction, from Act III of Turandot.

riddle: "Ice which gives thee fire. And from thy fire takes ice. . ." Now the Prince seems desolate, and Turandot taunts him. But he soon raises his head, and exclaims: "My fire thaws thee — TURANDOT!" The crowd is jubilant, but Turandot is a spoilsport. She begs the Emperor to release her from the vow she has made, and asks Calaf if he would have her full of hate. Magnanimously, he promises to release her if she can discover his name before sunrise.

ACT III. The populace is restless, for Turandot has ordered that no one shall sleep until the unknown's name shall be discovered; the penalty is death. Calaf takes up the injunction in the ravishingly beautiful aria, "Nessun dorma" (None shall sleep), and vows that when the sun shall rise, he will be the victor. Ping, Pang, and Pong try to tempt him to flee with beautiful maidens and priceless treasures, but to no avail.

Now the crowd menaces him, but is mollified when Timur and Liù are dragged in — they know the unknown's identity, it is said. To save Timur, Liù says she is the only one who knows, but she will not tell. Turandot arrives and orders the girl tortured. Liù makes her last plea: "Tu che di gel sei cinta" (Thou who in ice are girded), and, snatching a dagger from a soldier, stabs herself. In the ensuing confusion, Turandot's maidens cover her face with a white veil (perhaps symbolical?)

This is where Puccini's music left off and Alfano's begins. The Prince kisses Turandot passionately, and her stony heart is melted. She admits that her first tear marks his victory in an aria, "Del primo pianto;" he entrusts her with his name, and the opera ends in a burst of glory as the sun rises on the assembled court. Turandot tells her father: "I know his name; it is Love."

Eva Turner as Turandot.

Portrait of Henry Purcell by Jean Clostermann.

Dido and Aeneas

Text by Nahum Tate based on
Book IV of Virgil's "Aeneid."

DIDO	*Soprano or Mezzo-Soprano*
AENEAS	*Tenor*
BELINDA	*Soprano*
FIRST WOMAN	*Soprano*
SECOND WOMAN	*Mezzo-Soprano*
SORCERESS	*Mezzo-Soprano*
FIRST WITCH	*Soprano*
SECOND WITCH	*Soprano*
SPIRIT	*Soprano*
SAILOR	*Tenor*

First Performance
London, probably 1689.

HENRY PURCELL (London, c1659 – 21 November 1695). The English claim to a true Baroque master, Henry Purcell revealed his genius as opera composer only in *Dido and Aeneas,* although he wrote several masques and incidental music for plays which held the stage magnificently. Chief among these are *King Arthur,* to words by Dryden, *The Fairy Queen,* based on *A Midsummer Night's Dream,* and *The Tempest.* His other work – songs, instrumental and sacred pieces – number in the hundreds. The son of a Gentleman of the Chapel Royal, he was a boy chorister and studied with John Blow, then became "keeper of the instruments," composer for the King's band, and organist in prestigious situations.

THE EXTRAORDINARY fact about this opera is that it was composed for girls' voices – for, in fact, Josias Priest's School for Young Ladies, located in the Chelsea district of London. After its first hearings, it languished until 1895, when the Royal College of Music revived it. New York waited until 1923 to hear the work, and then only in a concert performance at the Hotel Plaza, by a Connecticut girls' glee club. Other performances, some of them professional, were scattered through the years and the countries, with a notable revival in 1951 by the Mermaid Theater of London, in which Kirsten Flagstad took the title role. Other Didos of recent years have been Giulietta Simionato, Janet Baker, Irmgard Seefried, Gloria Davy, Teresa Berganza, and at the New York City Opera in 1979, Sandra Browne.

A version by Benjamin Britten, which the composer himself conducted several times, is often used.

ACT I.   Dido, Queen of Carthage, is surrounded by her court and counseled by her lady-in-waiting, Belinda, to marry the stranger, Aeneas, who has sought refuge in Carthage on his flight from

Kirsten Flagstad as Dido, Queen of Carthage.

Troy. Dido at last accepts the hero's suit, and the court rejoices.

Scene 2. A Sorceress plots the downfall of Dido and Aeneas in some very beautiful music.

ACT II.   A pastoral moment during the hunt on which the lovers are embarked. Distant thunder scatters the company, but Aeneas is left behind. The spirit of Mercury, in reality one of the Sorceress's minions, appear to him and says he brings Jove's command that Aeneas shall set forth immediately to resume his true mission, the founding of Italy.

ACT III.   In the harbor at Carthage, the Trojan sailors make ready to sail, and sing a bawdy ballad. The Sorceress and her band of witches appear, two of them sing a macabre duet, and there is a dance of spirited revelry. The merrymakers disperse as Dido and Belinda come to look for Aeneas. When it is apparent that her lover is truly leaving her, the Queen takes to a fiery bier, first singing the famous aria by which the opera is most remembered: "When I am laid in earth . . Remember me, but ah! forget my fate!" The mourning chorus closes the opera.

MAURICE RAVEL (Ciboure, 7 March 1875 – Paris, 28 December 1937). Although Ravel's two operas have suffered some neglect, possibly in the case of *L'Enfant et les Sortilèges* because of its inherent difficulties, both are rapidly gaining ground, especially *L'Heure espagnole*, and abundantly deserve place in the repertoire of opera companies of all degrees of eminence. Both show the individual genius of the composer who had to outlive the unjust comparison with Debussy. Ravel is secure in the Hall of Fame for his many delectable piano pieces, ballet, chamber and orchestral works — we have only to mention *Daphnis et Chloé*, *Boléro*, *Ma Mère l'Oye*, *La Valse*, *Shéhérazade*, *Chansons madécasses*, the *String Quartet*, *Trio*, and a dozen others in all genres.

It was a loss to the world that he did not complete three operatic projects on which he was working: *The Sunken Bell*, *Jeanne d'Arc*, and *Don Quixote*.

Maurice Ravel (r.) at the piano with Nijinsky, who choreographed Ravel's ballet Daphnis and Chloe.

L'Heure Espagnole
(*The Spanish Hour*)

Text by Franc-Nohain.

CONCEPCION	*Soprano*
GONSALVE	*Tenor*
TORQUEMADA	*Tenor*
RAMIRO	*Baritone*
DON INIGO GOMEZ	*Bass*

First Performance
Paris, 19 May 1911.

288
RAVEL

ABOUNDING IN charming light music, the opera shows few opportunities for extended solos. Delightful Concepcions have been Bori, Supervia, Albanese, Duval, and Berganza, while the burly muleteer Ramiro was admirably interpreted by Tibbett, among others.

The story concerns an absent-minded clock-maker, Torquemada, who goes off each week to wind all the clocks in Toledo. His flirtatious wife Concepcion takes advantage of his absence to receive her lovers, who include Gonsalve, a poet, and Don Inigo Gomez, a banker. But before they can arrive, the muleteer Ramiro enters the shop to have his watch repaired. To get rid of him, she asks him to carry a heavy clock up to her bedroom. His return foils her attempt to greet Gonsalve, whom she hides in a huge grandfather's clock. Don Inigo also meets the same fate, both men being carried upstairs or down at intervals by Ramiro, until the exchange of clocks becomes farcical. At last, Concepcion casts her eye on the muscular Ramiro, and takes him upstairs. But Torquemada comes back unexpectedly—Concepcion explains the two gentlemen hidden in the clocks as customers, and Torquemada promptly sells each one his "prison," then, goodhumoredly accepting the situation, joins the other four in a sparkling quintet.

Scene from a La Scala production of Ravel's L'Heure Espagnole.

L'Enfant et les Sortilèges
(*The Bewitched Child*)

Text by Colette.

ORIGINALLY INTENDED as a ballet, the Colette libretto was set by Ravel over a period of years, during several of which he was in the French Army at the front. It was not finished until 1924. The parts of The Child and his various tormentors are brilliantly written, and the fantastic story points its moral in enchantingly vivid terms.

The destructive Child, too lazy to work, smashes the cup and saucer, bedevils the caged squirrel, pours water from the teakettle onto the fire, vandalizes the wallpaper with a poker and breaks the grandfather clock, then tears up his books. All animals—including a pair of lovesick cats, and the wild beasties in the garden—and the inanimate objects, coming to life, return his viciousness in good measure, until, isolated in

Child's drawing of her impressions of Ravel's opera L'Enfant et les Sortilèges from a Santa Fe Opera production of the work.

THE CHILD	Mezzo-Soprano
THE MOTHER	Contralto
THE LOUIS XV CHAIR	Soprano
THE CHINESE CUP	Contralto
THE FIRE	Soprano
THE PRINCESS	Soprano
THE CAT	Mezzo-Soprano
THE DRAGONFLY	Mezzo-Soprano
THE NIGHTINGALE	Soprano
THE BAT	Soprano
THE LITTLE OWL	Soprano
THE SQUIRREL	Mezzo-Soprano
SHEPHERD GIRL	Soprano
SHEPHERD	Contralto
THE ARMCHAIR	Bass
THE GRANDFATHER CLOCK	Baritone
THE TEAPOT	Tenor
THE LITTLE OLD MAN	Tenor
THE TOM CAT	Baritone
A TREE	Bass
THE FROG	Tenor
SETTLE, SOFA, OTTOMAN, WICKER CHAIR	Children's Chorus
NUMBERS	Children's Chorus

First Performance
Monte Carlo, 21 March 1925.

289
RAVEL

loneliness, he cries for his mother. Now all his enemies surround him with growing menace. At last a little squirrel whom he has wounded limps toward him. The child, suddenly remorseful, binds up its paw. This act of mercy changes him and now he is forgiven by the world he has so thoughtlessly torn apart. All the animals help him toward the house, where his mother is waiting.

Nicolai Rimsky-Korsakov.

Antonia Nezhdanova as Volkhova the sea king's daughter from Rimsky-Korsakov's opera Sadko, 1906, Bolshoi Opera, Moscow.

NICOLAI RIMSKY-KORSAKOV (Tikhvin, 18 March 1844 — St. Petersburg, 21 June 1908) was entirely absorbed in a naval career until he met Mili Balakirev, one of the "nationalistic" composers who were destined to become known as the "Mighty Five" (also including Borodin, Cui, Mussorgsky, and Rimsky himself). So inspired was Rimsky that he began to compose a symphony, although he had no training whatsoever. Naval engagements prevented his embracing his new profession entirely until after he had completed that symphony, and composed another, as well as his first opera, *The Maid of Pskov* (1873), when he was relieved of all but the most nominal naval duties. Self-taught until now, he soon became one of the most distinguished orchestrators, and even taught courses at the St. Petersburg Conservatory and wrote a definitive book on the subject. He is justly famous for his orchestral works, high among them *Shéhérazade*, and his second symphony, *Antar*, as well as choral and chamber works and pieces for voice. And he is also noted, and occasionally reviled, for his reorchestrations and rearrangements of other composers' works, notably Mussorgsky's *Boris Godunov*.

Of his thirteen subsequent operas, the last, *Le Coq d'or*, has been the steadiest favorite in the United States, although several of the others are occasionally heard. Most are based on Russian themes. All of these but two, *The Maid of Pskov* (or *Ivan the Terrible*, twice revised) and *The Tsar's Bride* (1890), which deal with real people, are laid in the world of fantasy and supernatural forces.

The operas are: *May Night* (1880), a version of the "Undine" theme, concerning water nymphs, a wicked stepmother who drove her daughter to drown herself and become a nymph; revenge, and a happy ending for the mortal hero and his beloved.

Snow Maiden (1882), the tale of a fairy maid who epitomizes Winter, and whose pleas to be loved by a human bring about her destruction as she melts, thus bringing summer back to the land.

Mlada (1892), revised as a lyric stage work from an unfinished ballet score by Rimsky with Cui, Borodin, Mussorgsky, and Minkus projected twenty years before.

Christmas Eve, (1895), written after a two-year period of inertia, and in reality but a forerunner of *Sadko*.

Sadko (1898), one of the composer's most colorful stories and scores. Sadko, a singer of Novgorod, boasts that he can make the town merchants rich if they will sail to the far seas. He is ridiculed, but, aided by the daughter of the King of the Ocean, Volkhova, who has fallen in love with him, he makes good his boast. However, his luck does not hold, and he is thrown overboard. But Volkhova takes him to her kingdom at the bottom of the sea, and they live happily until an apparition sweeps away the undersea kingdom and returns Sadko to land and to his mourning wife. Volkhova changes herself into a river to be near him always, and his ships return, bearing riches. The opera contains the celebrated "Song of India," sung by one of three exotic merchants who describe their various countries.

Mozart and Salieri (1898), in one act, is based on Pushkin's dramatic poem which takes as true the legend that Salieri poisoned his rival, Mozart.

The Tsar's Bride (1899). The Novgorod merchant Sobakin's daughter, Martha, has been promised to the boyar Lykov, but the wild Griaznoi covets

Feodor Chaliapin (r.) and V.P. Shakaker as Salieri and Mozart, in a scene from the opera Mozart and Salieri, 1898, Moscow.

her and orders a love potion from the Tsar's physician. Griaznoi's mistress, Lyoubacha, overhears and substitutes a poison for the love potion. At a party celebrating her betrothal, Martha drinks the poison Griaznoi has put in her drink. To everyone's consternation, a messenger brings news that Martha has been chosen as the Tsar's bride. But she soon languishes and dies. Griaznoi names Lykov as the poisoner, and the latter is executed. Then Lyoubacha confesses the truth, Griaznoi stabs her and is led off to be executed.

Tsar Saltan (1902). Two elder sisters (à la Cinderella) drive the younger, who has been married to the Tsar, out of the kingdom. She and her son find refuge on a magic island, where a beautiful swan befriends them — naturally a Princess, who marries the young Prince. He is sent back to his father as a bumblebee (the famous "Flight of the Bumblebee" occurs here), and the truth is revealed.

Kaschei the Immortal (1902). A darkly hued fairy tale, rewarding music- ally but not often performed; nor is *Pan Voyevoda* (1904).

The Legend of the Invisible City of Kitezh (1907). A rather moralistic fairy tale, with a beautiful and saintly maiden, a Prince who falls in love, a village that mocks her, a Tartar invasion, a kidnaping of the maid, a search for the mysterious citadel city foiled by a mágic fog, the death of the Prince, and the final conveyance of the maid to Kitezh and Paradise. The convolutions of the story need not detract from some entrancing music.

Le Coq d'or
(*The Golden Cockerel*)

Text by V. Bielsky after Pushkin.

KING DODON	*Bass*
PRINCE GUIDON	*Tenor*
PRINCE AFRON	*Baritone*
GENERAL POLKAN	*Bass*
AMELFA	*Contralto*
THE ASTROLOGER	*Tenor*
THE QUEEN OF SHEMAKA	*Soprano*
THE GOLDEN COCKEREL	*Soprano*

First Performance
Moscow, 7 October 1909.

The arrival of the King and Queen from Act I of Le Coq d'or.

Cover design for the vocal score of Le Coq d'or by Ivan Biliban.

PERFORMANCES ALL over the world have brought coloratura sopranos (Barrientos, Pons, Dobbs, Sills, etc.) to the role of the high-flying Queen, and notable basses (Didur, Pinza, Treigle and Co.) to sing the foolish King Dodon. Censors prohibited it at first in Russia (no reason given) and it was not performed until after the composer's death. Then it was thought to be too difficult for singers to dance as well. This problem has been solved in certain productions by separating the two functions, but it is not entirely satisfactory. We need draw no moral from the story; only rejoice in its brilliant musical setting and comic antics.

A piercing high trumpet call establishes the Cockerel's motive, which occurs whenever the bird appears. The other characteristic music belongs to the Queen, who has the famous "Hymn to the Sun."

ACT I. The doddering old King Dodon is worried that his kingdom will be invaded by his enemies, and asks advice of his stupid sons, but is comforted by the advent of the Astrologer, who brings a magic Cockerel that will warn of danger. The Cockerel soon lets out his clarion call, and the warlike general wakens the King to the need for mobilization. Somehow, a ragged army is got together, and the King goes back to sleep tended by the housekeeper Amelfa. But now the bird is more raucous than ever, and the King himself sets out to do battle.

ACT II. The war is lost, the princes slain. The King finds himself in strange territory, where a beautiful woman appears and seduces the King so thoroughly that he takes her home with him.

ACT III. The Astrologer reappears and demands the Queen as payment for his services. Dodon refuses and kills the Astrologer. Then the Queen turns on Dodon and the Cockerel descends and fells the King with a blow of his beak. In a peal of thunder, the Cockerel and the Queen disappear, and the Astrologer, restored to life, declares the whole story merely a fairy tale.

NED ROREM (Richmond, Indiana, 23 October 1923 –). One of the most felicitous American composers for the voice, Rorem has written several small operas, but his chief operatic work is *Miss Julie*, which, with a libretto by Kenward Elmslie, is based on Strindberg's play and follows the action closely. The story concerns a spoiled young woman who antagonizes her fiancé, then begins a flirtation with John, valet to the Count, her father. John takes it rather seriously, although Christine, the cook, has been very friendly with him. Julie is trapped in John's room by roistering peasants, who occupy the kitchen. Next morning, John offers to take her away if she will find him the money to start his own business. But she has none, so steals it from her father. John reveals the darker side of his nature by killing her pet canary. She slashes her wrists, but John cannot help her – his master has rung for him. He obeys the summons, and Julie walks off into the garden to finish her life.

Rorem revised the opera after its premiere by the New York City Opera on 4 November 1965. Donald Gramm was an effective John in that production.

Other Rorem operas include *A Childhood Miracle* (1955); the grim *Robbers*, after Chaucer (1958); *Bertha*, a legendary drama; *Fables*, four short tales based on La Fontaine (1971), and *Three Sisters Who Are Not Sisters*, on Gertrude Stein's fantasy (1971).

Ned Rorem

GIOACCHINO ROSSINI (Pesaro, 29 February 1792 – Paris, 13 November 1868). "The Swan of Pesaro" wrote his first opera, *Demetrio e Polibio* at fourteen. His first professional work was the buffo *La cambiale di matrimonio* (Marriage by Promissory Note), given in Venice in November 1810, later neglected, but more recently restored to favor in American workshops. Only one opera appeared in 1811, *L'equivoco stravagante* (The Strange Misunderstanding), but he wrote five in 1812. Of these, only *La scala di seta* (The Silken Ladder) and *La pietra del paragone* (The Touchstone) are remembered. This last was a real touchstone in Rossini's career: it brought him a commission for three operas and helped obtain for him an exemption from military service.

Of all the operas Rossini composed before *Il Barbiere* (1816), those most likely to be heard today are *Il Signor Bruschino*, *L'Italiana in Algeri* (The Italian in Algiers) (both from 1813), and *Il Turco in Italia* (The Turk in Italy) of 1814. The remainder have joined the ranks of honorably forgotten stage works, although a few points of interest might be mentioned: *Tancredi* (1813) achieved a measure of success in 1952 at the Florence Maggio Musicale and has been revived as a vehicle for Marilyn Horne; the overture from *Aureliano in Palmira* (1813) served two years later for *Elisabetta, Regina d'Inghilterra* and today is heard as the Overture to *Barbiere*.

Elisabetta (1815) provided the first of the many roles Rossini composed for Isabella Colbran, the glamorous soprano who was to share his life as interpreter, mistress, and wife. *Otello*, produced in December, 1816, ten months after *Barbiere*, also gave Colbran the highly dramatic role of Desdemona – in a version of Shakespeare that would barely be recognized by Verdians, let alone devotees of the Bard. A third work, *La Gazzetta*, is also dated 1816.

Gioacchino Rossini.

Drawing of Rossini with the characters from his operas, by an unknown artist of his time.

Giuditta Pasta as Tancredi from the Rossini opera of the same name.

La Cenerentola (Cinderella), whose charm has come to be appreciated once more, belongs to 1817. Three other operas date from 1817. *La gazza ladra* (The Thieving Magpie), Rossini's first for Milan since *Il Turco*. It won immediate success.

The spectacular *Armida* found favor in Naples in 1817, but *Adelaide di Borgogna*, hastily produced in Rome on 27 December, barely seven weeks after *Armida*, was frankly a potboiler.

In 1818 Rossini produced for Naples one of his most ambitious works, *Mosè in Egitto* (revised for Paris as *Moïse* in 1827). Also belonging to 1818 were a one-act opera-buffa called *Adina*, and *Ricciardo e Zoraide*.

In 1819, Rossini turned out four works: *Ermione*, a tragedy whose fate equalled its heroine's; *Edoardo e Cristina*, bits from earlier Rossini operas not previously heard in Venice; *La donna del lago* (Naples), based—loosely—on Scott's *Lady of the Lake*; and, unhappily for Milan, *Bianca e Faliero*, with a lame libretto by Felice Romani, who had better served Rossini in *Aurelio*, and even more so in *Il Turco*.

This stream of creativeness became sluggish in 1820. Thereafter, Rossini would produce only four more operas for Italy, and those but once a year. First came *Maometto II* (1820, Naples), less successful than a later reworking, *Le Siège de Corinthe*, for which Rossini lifted certain parts from the former for a Paris production; next, a patchwork not only of music but of libretto in *Matilda di Shabran* (1821, Rome); and last, *Semiramide* (1823, Venice). Also in 1823 he visited Vienna for performances of his works, paying the celebrated call on Beethoven.

When the Rossinis went to Paris in 1823, it was, to all intents and purposes, for good. Although Paris was divided in its admiration for the Italian, enough honors were heaped on him to satisfy him. He was made director of the Théâtre des Italiens, where his scenic cantata with ballet, *Il viaggio a Reims* (The Journey to Rheims), was produced in 1825. The final four operas, all given at the Opéra, were *Le Siège de Corinthe* (1826), *Moïse* (1827), *Le Comte Ory* (1828), and the great finale *Guillaume Tell* (1829).

No one has yet discovered why Rossini abruptly stopped composing operas after *Tell*. He spent his remaining thirty-nine years without creating a single stage work, although he added to his store of cantatas, orchestral works, and other lesser compositions—notably the one hundred and eighty pieces call *Péchés de vieillesse* (Sins of Old Age). (Always an enigmatic character, despite his open conviviality and worldly sophistication, it is now considered certain that the composer suffered from a venereal disease contracted in his youth, and that his physical condition greatly influenced his later mental and spiritual attitudes.)

The Rossinis' home was a center for the artistic celebrities of the age. In 1860, one of the highlights of Rossini's eventful retirement was a visit from Richard Wagner; their conversation, taken down by a friend, revealed a growing admiration and mutual respect between the two vastly different artists.

After the death of Colbran in 1845, Rossini acquired a new female companion, Olympe Pélissier, the former mistress of a Parisian painter. He married her in 1846. His last word, on his deathbed in 1868, was said to have been her name.

Henriette Sontag as Elena in Rossini's La Donna del Lago, 1828.

295
295
ROSSINI

CONTRALTOS HAVE found Isabella extremely congenial in the revivals of *L'Italiana* from time to time—Supervia, Castagna, Simionato, and Horne among them.

The action takes place in Algiers, where the Bey Mustafa, weary of his wife Elvira, sends Haly, the captain of his guard, to find an Italian wife for him. At his court, a captive Italian, with the favorite name of Lindoro, is bewailing the loss of his wife, Isabella, when that lady is conveniently shipwrecked on the shores of Algeria. She brings with her

L'Italiana in Algeri
(*The Italian Girl in Algiers*)

Text by Angelo Anelli.

MUSTAFA	*Bass*
ELVIRA	*Soprano*
ZULMA	*Contralto*
HALY	*Bass*
LINDORO	*Tenor*
ISABELLA	*Contralto*
TADDEO	*Baritone*

First Performance
Venice, 22 May 1813.

Costume sketches for The Italian Girl in Algiers, showing two versions of Elvira and one of Zulma (c.).

Costume sketch for Mustafa from The Italian Girl in Algiers.

the foolish old Taddeo, who is in love with her. The joy of Isabella and Lindoro is unbounded as they meet in the Bey's palace, but is shortlived, as the Bey commands Lindoro to take Elvira off his hands and plans to marry Isabella immediately. Isabella, emitting flights of elaborate coloratura singing, refuses to marry the Bey unless he will go through an absurd ritual, the ancient Italian order of the "Pappatacci," to show that he will be a docile husband. This requires that he consume an immense amount of spaghetti. While he is engaged in this pastime, Isabella and Lindoro board a boat that has been prepared for them, and sail away. The discomfited Bey forgives Elvira and takes her back as his wife.

Mariano Stabile as the old poet in The Turk in Italy, 1955, La Scala, Milan.

Il Turco in Italia
(*The Turk in Italy*)

Text by Felice Romani.

SELIM	*Bass*
FIORELLA	*Soprano*
GERONIO	*Bass*
NARCISO	*Tenor*
ZAIDA	*Mezzo-Soprano*
ALBAZAR	*Tenor*
PROSDOCIMO,	*Baritone*
A POET	
ISAURA	*Soprano*

First Performance
Milan, 14 August 1814.

IL TURCO was long neglected—partially because it suffered unfavorable comparison with *L'Italiana in Algeri*—but regained favor in many centers after its revival in 1950 in Rome with Callas, Valletti, and Stabile. A recent performance at the New York City Opera starred Beverly Sills and Donald Gramm.

In Naples, Fiorella, married to the old Don Geronio, is restlessly searching for some diversion, preferably amorous. Fortuitously, Sultan Selim of Turkey lands on the shore near Naples, and is at once the object of Fiorella's attentions. Let it be said that he is willing. But there are objections not only from Don Geronio, but also from Narciso, who loves the errant lady. Furthermore, the gypsy Zaida is revealed as a former flame of the Sultan's. The confusion mounts at a masked ball where the ladies are dressed alike—and so are the men. A poet, who has acted as *deus ex machina* throughout, now believes he has an ideal plot for a play, and contrives to straighten out the tangle, Fiorella returning to her doting husband and the Sultan to Zaida.

HISTORY RECORDS few such stunning fiascos as that experienced by Rossini's *Barbiere* at its premiere in 1816. Howls, laughs, whistles (*not* expressions of approval, as in America) created such bedlam that the music could hardly be heard. The Basilio sang his Calumny aria through a bloody handkerchief, having sustained a nasty fall at his entrance. He was popularly supposed to possess the "evil eye" anyway. To cap the horrors, a cat wandered around the stage, completely stealing the scene. No doubt all the brouhaha was caused by partisans of Giovanni Paisiello, whose own *Barbiere* had been popular since 1782. All of Rossini's apologies and endeavors to avoid setting exactly the same material failed. The rift was absolute, but Rossini was the survivor. Even by the second night the opera was assured of success, and it rapidly gained entree to the rest of the world. London heard it in 1818 in both Italian and English; New York followed a year later with an English production, then in 1825 it was the first Italian opera to be heard in New York, by a company headed by Manuel Garcia and including his son Manuel and two daughters, Maria Malibran and Pauline Viardot. *Barbiere* was a highlight of the Metropolitan's first season, 1883-4, with Sembrich and Del Puente.

Coloratura sopranos who have soared into Rosina's realms form an international company; mezzos who sing the part as it was originally intended are more scarce, but their tribe is increasing and already includes Supervia, Simionato, Tourel, and Berganza. Famous Figaros are also legion.

Rossini's facility was fabulous, never more apparent than in the composition of *Barbiere*, which is said to have been completed in nineteen or twenty days. He was aided by the fact that the playwright Beaumarchais had conceived the play as an *opéra comique*, with appropriate divisions for solos and ensembles.

Maria Malibran, shown here as Desdemona from Rossini's Otello, sang Rosina in the first New York production of The Barber of Seville, 1825, New York.

Scene from a performance of The Barber of Seville on the occasion of a state visit by Queen Victoria and Prince Albert to Her Majesty's Italian Opera House. In the cast were Grisi as Rosina and Mario as Count Almaviva (at the piano) and Lablache as Bartolo, 1843, London.

Giulietta Simionato as Rosina with Tito Gobbi as Figaro.

Il Barbiere di Siviglia

298
ROSSINI

(*The Barber of Seville*)

Text by Cesare Sterbini
after the Beaumarchais play.

COUNT ALMAVIVA	*Tenor*
FIGARO	*Baritone*
ROSINA	*Mezzo-Soprano or Soprano*
DOCTOR BARTOLO	*Bass*
BASILIO	*Bass*
BERTA	*Mezzo-Soprano*
FIORELLO	*Baritone or Tenor*
SERGEANT	*Tenor*
AMBROGIO	*Bass*
NOTARY, MAGISTRATE	*Mute*

First Performance
Rome, 20 February 1816.

Borrowing from one's own works was an accepted practice, and plenty of examples can be found in this composer's output. The most notable in *Barbiere* is, as previously noted, the overture.

Rossini had the opportunity just before he died to show the magnanimity denied him by Paisiello, and in exactly parallel circumstances. A young composer, Costantino Dall'Argine, asked permission to dedicate to the master his own setting of *Il Barbiere*. Ill as he was, Rossini wrote courteously, accepting the dedication, and remarking that they should not be the victims of the adage: "Between two contending parties, the third party benefits." When Dall'Argine's *Barbiere* was performed on 11 November 1868, a hot controversy arose, similar to the earlier one between Paisiello and Rossini. But the master lived only two days after, and never knew that he need not have worried about this new competition—if, indeed, he ever had.

ACT I, Scene 1. The pretty Rosina is being kept virtually a prisoner in the Seville home of her crusty old guardian Doctor Bartolo, who plans to marry her. The dashing Count Almaviva, visiting from his estate nearby, has spied her and determines to win her, taking his servant Fiorello and a group of musicians to accompany him as he sings under her window the serenade, "Ecco ridente in cielo" ("Behold, the dawn is breaking"). Figaro approaches, caroling his blithe challenge to the world, the celebrated "Largo al factotum," in which he relates how he, as the town barber and intriguer, is required to be everywhere at once. Almaviva recognizes him as his former valet, and accepts his advice in the matter of winning Rosina. The young lady appears briefly on her balcony and drops a note to her suitor, asking his name. He sings that it is Lindoro—a name she will cherish.

Scene 2. In a room in Doctor Bartolo's house, Rosina is musing on her new love, and sings the famous "Una voce poco fa" ("A voice I heard just now"). She has written a letter to "Lindoro," but lacks a messenger. Figaro enters, but any confidences are interrupted by the return of Bartolo, who is disturbed by premonitions. His annoyance is deepened by

Hermann Prey as Figaro and Marilyn Horne as Rosina, Lyric Opera of Chicago.

Amelita Galli-Curci as Rosina.

Don Basilio, who brings the news that Count Almaviva is in town and confirms Bartolo's suspicion that Rosina is the target. Basilio proposes to ruin the Count by slander, in the hilarious aria, "La Calunnia" ("Calumny"). When the two cronies depart, Figaro, who has been in hiding, emerges, and suggests Rosina write her lover. To his surprise, she produces the letter she has already penned. Bartolo comes back and cross-questions Rosina about the note she has dropped, but is not satisfied with her evasive answers and lectures her in a buffo aria. Now the Count forces his way into the house in the disguise of a soldier who demands that he be billeted there. In the ensuing mêlée, Almaviva is discovered and arrested, but shows the Sergeant proof that he is a Grandee of Spain. There is a fine sextet and rousing finale.

Feodor Chaliapin as Don Basilio in The Barber of Seville.

Scene from *The Barber of Seville, production by Franco Enriquez, sets by Giulio Collellacci, 1964-65, La Scala, Milan.*

Fernando Corena as Don Bartolo.

ACT II. The Count adopts another disguise, as a music teacher, claiming to be Basilio's assistant as Basilio is ill. There is a great deal of byplay at the piano, as Rosina sings her "lesson," habitually a show piece chosen by the prima donna herself, although Rossini wrote an aria for this spot. Figaro comes in opportunely to shave Bartolo so that he cannot observe the lovers, and the barber also obtains the keys to the balcony so that an elopement can be managed that night. But to everyone's dismay, the real Basilio enters, not ill at all, although Almaviva, with the aid of a full purse, manages to persuade him that he should take to his bed. The scene is extremely comic, with its series of "Buona sera's"—it is difficult to get rid of the cadaverous music master. The false music master has convinced Bartolo of his good intentions by producing the letter Rosina has written to him, and saying he has purloined it from Almaviva. Now Bartolo shows it to Rosina, leading her to believe her lover is false. She agrees to marry Bartolo. While he has gone for the notary, Figaro and the Count come to effect the elopement, and the situation is soon straightened out. When Bartolo returns, he is forced to agree to Rosina's marriage to her true lover. In the last scene, before the elopement is about to take place, one of Rossini's typical storms occurs, with appropriate music.

A LAST-MINUTE suggestion by the librettist Ferretti for something to please Rome in Carnival season, the *Cenerentola* libretto was handed piece by piece to Rossini, who completed the music in twenty-four days. His prevalent practice of cannibalizing his own works operated here: he borrowed the overture from the forgotten *La Gazzetta* and the heroine's pyrotechnical aria, "Non più mesta," which he had dropped from *Barbiere*, where it was intended for Almaviva. He also had help from the composer Agolini for Clorinda's aria and the introduction to the second act.

The opera's reception was almost as disastrous as *Barbiere's*, and *Cenerentola* did not recover as fast nor hold international favor as firmly as its predecessor, possibly because Rosina was easily transferable to a higher voice while Cenerentola is not, and contralto coloraturas are rare birds. One of the most charming of more recent revivals was the earlier production of the New York City Opera with Frances Bible in the title role, and a hilarious ballet set to the dances from *Guillaume Tell*, which was later dropped. Its garlanded youths and maidens in languishing poses and "classical" steps provided a picture not soon to be forgotten. *Cenerentola* does well today, what with singers such as Frederica von Stade.

IN THE SHABBY castle of the Baron of Mountflagon, Don Magnifico's two daughters Clorinda and Tisbe constantly quarrel and abuse their step sister Angelina, whose only place seems to be in the cinders by the fireplace. "Cinderella" sings a sad little song as she makes coffee. When

La Cenerentola
(*Cinderella*)

Text by Jacopo Ferretti based on Étienne's libretto for Isouard's "Cendrillon" after the fairy tale.

DON RAMIRO	*Tenor*
DANDINI	*Bass*
DON MAGNIFICO	*Bass*
CLORINDA	*Soprano*
TISBE	*Mezzo-Soprano*
ANGELINA (CINDERELLA)	*Contralto*
ALIDORO	*Bass*

First Performance
Rome, 25 January 1817.

The Ball scene from Rossini's La Cenerentola, Veniero Colesanti and John Moore, designers, 1969, Rome Opera at Lincoln Center, New York.

a beggar enters, she alone takes pity on him—the sisters are frightful snobs. The beggar is in reality the philosopher Alidoro, confidant of Prince Ramiro. He is seeking a bride for the Prince, who has been told that he must marry immediately or be disinherited. Upon Alidoro's advice, Ramiro comes to Don Magnifico's castle, but exchanges roles with his valet Dandini, who is immediately beset by the two sisters thinking he is the Prince. Ramiro and Cinderella fall in love at first sight. But she is not allowed to go to the ball, although she begs. When Alidoro returns as himself and demands to see a third daughter, Magnifico denies that he has one and threatens Cinderella with a beating when she timidly steps forward. Alidoro then appears à la fairy godmother, and arranges for Cinderella to go to the ball.

At the palace, Don Magnifico makes free with the royal wine cellar, while Dandini, still disguised as the Prince, diddles the two sisters with rash promises. When an unknown lady is announced, and her beauty immediately captivates the Prince, the two girls are bitterly chagrined. As in the fairy story, Cinderella must leave by midnight, but she gives the Prince a bracelet, one of a pair, rather than dropping a slipper. Of course, the bracelets match, and the Prince claims his own true love. Cinderella generously forgives the Baron and his odious daughters.

The musical score is a delight, abounding in dazzling ensembles and solos. Notable: the long dream aria of Magnifico, florid passages for Dandini and Ramiro, an extremely difficult aria for Clorinda, Cenerentola's famous "Non più mesta," the ensemble trilling "r's" all over the place in "Questo è un grrup-po rrrintrrrecciato" as Cinderella is discovered and the sisters repudiated, and the "Zitto, zitto, piano, piano" in which Dandini tells Ramiro "in the softest of whispers" just how awful the Baron's two daughters are.

Semiramide

Text by Gaetano Rossi, based on Voltaire.

SEMIRAMIDE	*Soprano*
ARSACE	*Contralto*
GHOST OF NINO	*Bass*
OROE	*Bass*
ASSUR	*Baritone*
AZEMA	*Soprano*
IDRENO	*Tenor*
MITRANE	*Tenor*

First Performance
Venice, 3 February 1823.

AT ITS FIRST performance, *Semiramide* ran four hours, but Rossini shortened it for subsequent hearings. It was his last Italian opera, and also the swan song of his wife, Isabella Colbran. One of the notable early revivals was at the Metropolitan in 1893, with Melba and Schalchi; a later production at Milan, 1962, starred Sutherland and Simionato.

THE STORY, based on Voltaire, relates how Queen Semiramide of Babylon, having killed her husband King Nino with the assistance of Prince Assur, has fallen in love with a young army commander Arsace, not realizing that he is her own son Ninia. But Arsace is already pledged to Princess Azema. When the Queen is about to announce her choice of husband in the temple, the ghost of Nino appears, proclaiming Arsace as his successor and commanding the boy's presence at midnight, when he will learn the truth about the old King's assassination. Assur, who had expected to be chosen by the Queen, confronts her in a rage. She has learned from the high Priest Oroe about Arsace's true identity, and steps between him and Assur to receive the death blow meant by the youth for the prince.

Among the music that glorifies this score are the marvelous example of *bel canto* in the duet, "Giorno d'orrore" for soprano and contralto; the soprano aria "Bel raggio lushinghier," a stately priests' march, and the Overture, which has retained popularity on concert programs.

Marilyn Horne as Arsace (l.) with Joan Sutherland as Semiramide (r.), 1971, Lyric Opera of Chicago.

303
ROSSINI

ALREADY ESTABLISHED in Paris as "The Voice of Opera" by reason of the success of *Le Siège de Corinthe* and *Moïse* (both adapted from earlier works), Rossini decided that it was time to give the French capital a sample of his predominant style, the opera bouffe. Even now he did not write a completely original work, but borrowed copiously from a "vaudeville" (a show with popular tunes) that he had produced in 1816 on the subject of Count Ory. Then he added four numbers from his spectacular cantata, *Il viaggio a Reims*. That this was quite a dish to set before the Paris public was proved by 400 performances in the next half century. It came to New York within a few years, but languished until recently, when revivals have been frequent. One amusing performance at the Juilliard School boasted hilarious moving scenery by the cartoonist Saul Steinberg. A St. Louis production of the late seventies moved on to Santa Fe and then to the New York City Opera. The music is sparkling, among Rossini's lightest and most expert, with parts of great difficulty for tenor and soprano.

THE STORY IS farcical. Count Ory, a young rake, has disappeared from his customary haunts, and is sought by his page Isolier and his Tutor. They find him disguised as a hermit, posting himself outside the

Le Comte Ory
(*Count Ory*)

Text by Scribe and Delestre-Poirson.

RAIMBAUD	*Baritone*
ALICE	*Soprano*
COUNT ORY	*Tenor*
RAGONDE	*Contralto*
TUTOR	*Bass*
ISOLIER	*Mezzo-Soprano*
YOUNG NOBLEMAN	*Tenor*
COUNTESS ADELE	*Soprano*

First Performance
Paris, 20 August 1828.

Scene from Le Comte Ory, with sets by Jean-Pierre Ponnelle based on the 15th century illuminated manuscript Les très riches de Jean Duc de Berry, 1957, Berlin.

castle of Countess Adele, all of whose men kin have gone off to the Crusades. Isolier, consulting this bogus hermit on the subject of his love for the Countess, thus betrays himself. Adele also hopes to learn from the hermit a way out of her vow to remain widowed, in order to marry Isolier. But now Ory is exposed. And at the same time, the imminent return of Adele's brother and his men is announced. Ory must hurry if he can succeed in seducing the beautiful Countess. With Raimbaud, his bawdy companion, and a group of adventurers, he manages to gain entrance to the castle during a storm—all the men are disguised, somewhat unrealistically, as nuns. There is a scene of rivalry in which the "nuns" sample the vintages of the castle storeroom, then Ory manages to find his way into the bed of the Countess—only it is Isolier, already in occupancy, to whom he makes love in the dark. The entire deception is revealed, and the culprits are smuggled out just as the castle men arrive.

THE SHEER LENGTH of *Guillaume Tell*, which many consider to be Rossini's masterpiece, has militated against its performance in recent years—if uncut, it would run five hours. Also, several of the roles are very demanding: a baritone, tenor, and soprano of exceptional strength, range, and agility are mandatory. It has languished in America since the last Metropolitan Opera revival in 1931 with Lauri-Volpi, Danise, and Fleischer; in 1923 Ponselle, Martinelli, and Danise had assumed the three leading parts. The Overture, of course, has been immortalized not only in concert but also as a theme for a leading radio show of other years. The Schiller play from which the opera was drawn perpetuates the famous Swiss legend.

TWO SWISS PATRIOTS, Guillaume Tell and Walter Furst, struggle to free their country from Austrian oppression, led by the tyrant Gessler. At the Shepherd Festival, Ruedi, a fisherman, sings of the beauty of the country. The patriarch Melchthal blesses all lovers but omits his son Arnold, who has fallen in love with Gessler's daughter Mathilde after rescuing her from drowning. Austrian guards seek a shepherd, Leuthold, who has killed a soldier to protect his daughter. Tell helps Leuthold escape, and the soldiers take Melchthal as a hostage. Arnold renounces his passion for Mathilde when he learns that his father has been killed, and joins the rebels. Tell and his son Jemmy refuse to bow to Gessler's hat as a sign of sovereignty, and Gessler, as punishment, orders Tell to shoot an apple off the head of Jemmy. He skillfully does this, then tells Gessler that a second arrow was ready for him if the first failed. Jemmy goes to tell his mother Hedwig to light beacons as a signal to the revolutionaries, but, failing this, she sets fire to their own house. Tell is arrested, but shoots Gessler with his second arrow, and the victorious Swiss rejoice.

Guillaume Tell
(*William Tell*)

Text by De Jouy and Bis, based on the play by Schiller.

GUILLAUME TELL	*Baritone*
HEDWIGE	*Soprano*
JEMMY	*Soprano*
ARNOLD	*Tenor*
MELCHTHAL	*Bass*
GESSLER	*Bass*
MATHILDE	*Soprano*
RUDOLPH	*Tenor*
WALTER FURST	*Bass*
LEUTHOLD	*Bass*
RUEDI	*Tenor*

First Performance
Paris, 8 August 1829.

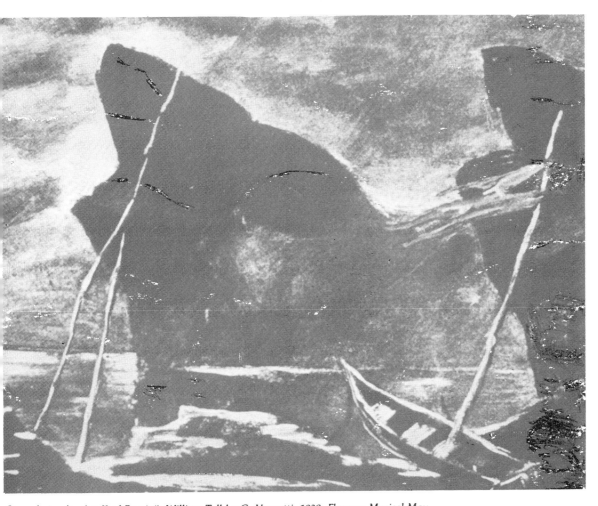

Stage design for Act II of Rossini's William Tell by G. Vagnetti, 1939, Florence Musical May Festival.

Caricature of Camille Saint-Saëns by fellow composer Gabriel Fauré.

CAMILLE SAINT-SAËNS (Paris, 9 October 1835 – Algiers, 16 December 1921). Virtuoso pianist and organist, composer in virtually every field, author, man of the world, *bon vivant*, greatly honored, Saint-Saëns composed thirteen operas, of which only *Samson et Dalila* has survived. He was naturally endowed, extremely facile, and noted for the form, style and workmanship of his music, although he did not plumb great emotional depths. Although himself a conservative, and enemy of contemporary composers, he yet was a founder of the Société Nationale de Musique, designed to promote French music. He toured throughout the world, winning fame as a composer-performer and friends for his genial nature. Many of his works remain current, among them four symphonies, many concertos, the witty *Carnival of the Animals*, chamber music, songs and other vocal music, and, among his four tone poems (in which he took Liszt as a model), *Danse macabre*. Liszt was indeed a great influence, and it was through him that *Samson* was produced at Weimar after being rejected by Paris. Rouen heard the opera in 1890, but it did not reach the Paris Opéra until 1892. The later operas were all accorded Paris premieres.

Margarete Matzenauer as Dalila.

Rita Gorr as Dalila and Gabriel Bacquier as the High Priest of Dagon, 1962, Lyric Opera of Chicago.

Samson et Dalila

(*Samson and Delilah*)

Text by Ferdinand Lemaire.

DALILA	*Mezzo-Soprano*
SAMSON	*Tenor*
HIGH PRIEST	*Baritone*
ABIMELECH	*Bass*
OLD HEBREW	*Bass*
MESSENGER	*Tenor*

First Performance
Weimar, 2 December 1877.

BECAUSE OF ITS Biblical origin and its somewhat static nature, *Samson* has often been considered as an oratorio, and given in concert form. Indeed, its premiere at Weimar, and its first hearings in London and New York were as concerts. New Orleans gave its first staged performance in 1893, while the Metropolitan produced it two years later, with Mantelli, Tamagno, Campanari, and Plançon. A revival in 1915 brought Matzenauer and Caruso to the title roles, while later temptresses and tempted have been Wettergren or Risë Stevens and Maison or Vinay, Thebom and Del Monaco, Rita Gorr and Jess Thomas, Grace Bumbry and Richard Tucker, and Obraztsova and Chauvet.

SAMSON, LEADER of the captive Israelites in Gaza, arouses his people to active resistance against the Philistines. The High Priest of Dagon persuades Dalila, a young priestess, to try to find Samson's secret—his strength has made him invulnerable to the Philistine army. Dalila captivates the hero, and he becomes so infatuated with her that he reveals his secret—his strength is in his long hair. While he is asleep, Dalila summons assistance and the hair is cut, rendering Samson powerless. He is imprisoned and blinded, then, forced to entertain the enemy, he enlists a small boy to guide him to the temple pillars. At the height of the festivity, Samson regains his strength and pulls down the pillars, so that the temple crushes the celebrants. He dies with them.

Among the famous musical moments are Dalila's two arias, "Printemps qui commence," and "Mon coeur s'oeuvre a ta voix," and a sensuous bacchanal.

Arnold Schönberg, photograph by Man Ray, 1925.

Moses und Aron

(*Moses and Aaron*)

Text by the composer
based on the Old Testament.

MOSES	*Bass*
ARON	*Tenor*
YOUNG GIRL	*Soprano*
INVALID WOMAN	*Contralto*
YOUNG MAN	*Tenor*
NAKED YOUTH	*Tenor*
MAN	*Baritone*
EPHRAIMITE	*Baritone*
PRIEST	*Bass*
FOUR NAKED VIRGINS	*2 Sopranos,*
	2 Contraltos
VOICE FROM BURNING BUSH, SIX SOLO VOICES IN ORCHESTRA	*Several Voices*

First Performance
Concert version: Hamburg, 12 March 1934.
Stage Premiere: Zürich, 6 June 1957.

ARNOLD SCHÖNBERG (Vienna, 13 September 1874 — Los Angeles, 13 July 1951). The "father" of the twelve-tone system of composition wrote four operas, of which *Moses und Aron* is the only long work. *Erwartung* (Expectation, 1909 — produced 1924) is an eerie monodrama in which a woman searches for her lost lover, only to find him dead. It is an extraordinarily nightmarish psychological exploration of a woman's mind. *Die glückliche Hand* (The Lucky Hand, 1913 — produced 1924), is another venture with but one character, and concerns an artist's quest for truth. This theme runs throughout Schönberg's stage works, although it is not so evident in *Von Heute auf Morgen* (From One Day Till the Next, 1930), which is the first twelve-tone opera, a comedy of surprising accessibility, showing the difficulties between a husband and wife as they seek other partners, but eventually reach a charming reconciliation.

ONLY TWO ACTS were completed by the composer. A third consists of text alone, and is sometimes recited, but the two-act version is very effective. It has received a stage premiere in America by the enterprising Opera Company of Boston under Sarah Caldwell, and has been heard in concert by the Chicago Symphony under Georg Solti.

The use of *Sprechstimme* (speech set to a definite pitch) is notable here; it was introduced by Schönberg in an earlier opera and remains a distinctive feature of his work. The opera is difficult in all phases: orchestral, vocal, chorus, production.

A spiritual argument rages between Moses, the law-giver, and his brother Aron, exponent of action. God speaks to Moses out of The Burning Bush, and he takes the message to his skeptical and inconstant

The dance around the golden calf from Schönberg's Moses and Aaron; scenery and costumes by Michel Raffaelli, 1959, Saädische Oper, Berlin.

people. The Israelites become impatient at Moses's forty-day sojourn on the mountain of revelation and fall into sinful ways. Aron is forced to restore their former god in the form of a golden calf. The people worship wildly and ever more bloodily, until the orgy is unrestrained. When Moses returns, he destroys the idol with a terrible curse. Aron attempts to temporize. Then Moses smashes the tablets he has brought down from the mountain, crying, "O Word, Word, that I lack!" The third act shows Aron a prisoner unable to defend himself against Moses's abstract vision of God. When freed, Aron falls dead, showing that his embodiment of falsehood is self-destructive.

DIMITRI SHOSTAKOVICH (St. Petersburg, 25 September 1906 — Moscow, 9 August 1975). *The Nose,* Shostakovich's first experiment with opera, a satirical takeoff on the old Russian regime, was a factor in the establishment by Stalin of "Socialist Realism" in music, a doctrine that bedeviled many Soviet composers from then on, and, after the original success of Shostakovich's *Lady Macbeth of Mtsensk* in 1934, caused the withdrawal of that opera and a long period of uncertainty about the composer's status. *The Nose* has seldom been heard outside of Russia, but a Santa Fe production in 1965 aroused considerable excitement. *Lady Macbeth* was heard with that title in Cleveland under Artur Rodzinski in 1935 and also in New York and Philadelphia, and aroused some moral indignation not only because of its subject matter but also because of some suggestive orchestral passages. This version was also revived in Düsseldorf in 1959, but the composer then issued a revision, entitled *Katerina Ismailova* after the heroine, and it was in this form that the opera was heard in Moscow and Covent Garden in 1963. The next year San Francisco gave the American premiere of the version, and it was heard at the New York City Opera in 1965 and 1970, with Eileen Schauler in the title role. The later version, let it be said, is not vastly different from the original, but the offending trombone passages have been smoothed out.

KATERINA, BORED and beautiful, despises her rich provincial husband Zinovy Borisov and his father Boris Timofeyevich. Forced into wrestling with Sergei, one of her husband's workmen, she conceives a passion for him, and he is discovered leaving her bedroom by her father-in-law. Katerina poisons the old man with mushrooms, but her seemingly sincere mourning fools the priest. A powerful entr'acte follows. When Zinovy returns from a trip, the lovers murder him and hide his body in the cellar. At the wedding of Katerina and Sergei, a drunk stumbles into the cellar and discovers the body. The culprits are arrested and sent off to Siberia. On the road, Sergei flirts with a convict, Sonyetka; whereupon the jealous Katerina drowns her rival, and jumps in after her. The other convicts move on. The orchestral interludes, several of them composed for the new version, are among the most interesting portions of the score. Katerina's role is especially difficult, calling for a highly dramatic action and sustained vocalism.

Dimitri Shostakovich.

Katerina Ismailova

Texts by A. Preiss and the composer based on a story by Nikolai Leskov.

BORIS TIMOFEYEVICH ISMAILOV	*Bass*
ZINOVY BORISOVICH ISMAILOV	*Tenor*
KATERINA LVOVNA ISMAILOVA	*Soprano*
SERGEI	*Tenor*
A DRUNK	*Tenor*
SONYETKA	*Contralto*
MANY SMALLER ROLES	

First Performance
Lenigrad, 22 January 1934.

Bedřich Smetana.

BEDŘICH SMETANA (Lytomysl, 2 March 1824 — Prague, 12 May 1884) became the leading exponent of nationalism after the Austrian yoke was lifted from his country, and *The Bartered Bride* was and is the patriotic as well as musical pride of the Czechs. Others of his operas reflect this ardent patriotism as well, although several are light in character. His first, *Brandenburgers in Bohemia*, struck this patriotic note, combining a love story with the freeing of Bohemia from her oppressors. It was composed in 1862-63, but not produced until 1866. *The Bartered Bride*, immediately following, eclipsed the earlier work, which is not often revived except in Czechoslovakia. Next came the heroic *Dalibor* (1868), based on a legend but also owing its central theme to *Fidelio*. A production by the English National Opera in recent years and a concert performance by the Opera Orchestra of New York under Eve Queler have kept this noble opera alive. *The Two Widows* (1874) is a complete contrast, a comedy of manners, with great elegance of style. *The Kiss* (1876) is likewise a comedy, but of peasant stock and very frothy indeed. *The Secret* (1878) also has comic elements, but is of a more romantic and folkloristic style. Smetana was almost deaf at the time it was composed. *Libuse*, composed earlier but not produced until 1881, was designed by Smetana as a splendid festival piece, and it inaugurated the National Theater, but its delayed production submerged the pageant-like work, and Smetana never heard it — he was completely deaf. *The Devil's Wall* (1882) was Smetana's last opera, completed in spite of the mental illness which overwhelmed him.

Elizabeth Rethberg as Marenka and Marek Windheim as Vašek in a scene from The Bartered Bride.

Scene from Act III of The Bartered Bride, 1951, Bolshoi Theater, Moscow.

The Bartered Bride
(*Prodaná Nevesta*)

Text by Karel Sabina.

KRUSINA	*Baritone*
LUDMILA	*Mezzo-Soprano*
MARENKA	*Soprano*
MICHA	*Bass*
HATA	*Mezzo-Soprano*
VASEK	*Tenor*
JENIK	*Tenor*
KECAL	*Bass*
RINGMASTER	*Tenor*
ESMERALDA	*Soprano*
CIRCUS INDIAN	*Tenor*

First Performance
Prague, 30 May 1866.

IN VARIOUS LANGUAGES (the Metropolitan gave it in German for a long time), Smetana's enchanting opera has gone round the world captivating audiences everywhere. Many Marenkas have been bartered for the better, including Destinn, Jurinac, Rethberg, Novotna (most appropriately, for the lady was a Czechoslovakian Baroness), and Stratas. The stuttering part of Vasek has been a favorite of buffo tenors, and even a heldentenor such as Jon Vickers desired to do it — and did, although it was far out of his accustomed realm. The dances are traditionally charming, a polka and the Dance of the Comedians in the circus act.

Marenka has been ordered by her father Krusina to marry Vasek, the son of the landowner Mìcha and his second wife Hata. But Vasek is a stuttering simpleton and Marenka despises him. The youth she truly loves, Jenìk, is something of a mystery in the Bohemian village, and he further earns Marenka's distrust, even her fury, when he allows himself to be bribed by the marriage broker Kecal so that he will give up his claim on the girl. The condition is that she shall marry no one but Mìcha's son. Of course, this turns out to be Jenìk himself, but a good deal of misunderstanding, confusion, and misery must be gone through before the denouement. At a circus performance, dominated by the Ringmaster and his charming dancer Esmeralda, Vasek is persuaded to wear a bearskin, replacing a departing performer, and discovers that he likes circus life, while the happy lovers are reunited and their respective parents satisfied. Only Kecal is left out of the merrymaking.

Johann Strauss, Jr.

Die Fledermaus

(*The Bat*)

Text by Carl Haffner and
Richard Genée after Meilhac and
Halévy's "Le Reveillon" from
Benedix's play "Das Gefängnis."

GABRIEL VON EISENSTEIN	*Tenor*
ROSALINDA	*Soprano*
ADELE	*Soprano*
DR. FALKE	*Baritone*
ALFRED	*Tenor*
DR. BLIND	*Tenor*
FRANK	*Baritone*
PRINCE ORLOFSKY	*Mezzo-Soprano*
IDA	*Soprano*
FROSCH	*Comedian*

First Performance
Vienna, 6 April 1874.

JOHANN STRAUSS, JR. (Vienna, 25 October 1825 – 3 June 1899). Nowhere was the Waltz King more captivating than in his operetta *Die Fledermaus*, which is welcome everywhere in the operatic or musical comedy world. *The Gypsy Baron* has not managed to rival *The Bat*, at least in America, which claims a *Fledermaus* tradition if not equal to at least as enthusiastically pursued as the Viennese. New York heard it as early as 1874 in German, and San Francisco's popular Tivoli produced it in English in 1880. Heinrich Conried caused a near scandal by giving the operetta (the first time at the Metropolitan and the first time in the country using singers of operatic caliber) as his "benefit" in 1905 – all the proceeds of the ticket sale at double the usual price went to him. W.J. Henderson commented in the *Sun* about the procedure of introducing practically all of the important members of the company in the party scene: "The truth seems to be that people were asked to be astonished at the general lavishness of expenditure and to gape at the appearance of Caruso, Nordica, Fremstad and the rest in a cafe chantant spectacle at a masquerade ball."

Rudolf Bing created a stir almost as vociferous when he placed the operetta in a series of gala performances in his opening season, 1950-51, with the unlikely casting of Ljuba Welitsch as Rosalinda and Set Svanholm as Eisenstein. The whole romp was, however, vastly amusing, and the other singers received their due: Patrice Munsel, Richard Tucker, Risë Stevens, and John Brownlee.

A particularly lively production at Covent Garden on New Year's Eve, 1977, was beamed by satellite out to the world. It featured a tenor as Count Orlofsky, a part claimed mostly by mezzos, and the dialogue lapsed from German into English whenever someone seemed to feel like it. Kiri Te Kanawa was a particularly enchanting Rosalinda.

By the heroine's name the operetta has been seen in a version by Max Reinhardt, the latest incarnation in Miami in 1980.

DR. FALKE PLANS revenge after his friend Eisenstein has abandoned him, drunk and dressed as a bat, after a fancy-dress ball. His opportunity comes when Eisenstein, convicted of kicking a policeman (or tax collector in some versions) is sentenced to eight days in jail. He visits Eisenstein's house, where just a few moments before, Adele, the maid, has received a letter from her sister Ida suggesting that she come to a masquerade ball in the house of the rich Prince Orlofsky. And Rosalinda, Eisenstein's wife, has been excited by the appearance of a former lover, the tenor Alfred, who still makes her heart flutter with his high C's. Now Falke proposes that Eisenstein, instead of reporting to jail immediately, go to the same party disguised as a French Marquis. The two go off in high merriment, leaving Rosalinda to the tender mercies of Alfred, who eats Eisenstein's dinner, kisses his wife, and puts on his smoking jacket. He is arrested as Eisenstein when Frank, the head of the jail, comes to escort the culprit to jail.

Everyone ends up at Orlofsky's where the fun is "each to his own taste." Adele dares Eisenstein to recognize her in a charming song, our hero falls in love with a beautiful and masked Hungarian Countess (of ourse his own Rosalinda), and everyone salutes champagne as the ource of all merriment. At last in jail, Eisenstein discovers his rival and xposes him, excoriating Rosalinda. But that lady has stolen her husand's favorite chiming watch at the ball, and now produces it—a tandoff. Frosch, the jailer, who is always a comedian of somewhat road humor, has his night center stage, the inebriated Frank once gain makes up to Adele, who comes to visit, and the whole company ventually admits that it all was a joke—in the very best of taste.

Kiri Te Kanawa sang the role of Rosalinda in 1977 at Covent Garden, London.

osalind Keene (r.) as Adele, Peter Grant as Eisenstein and Mary O'Brien (l.) as osalinda from Act I of Die Fledermaus, 1963, Australian Opera, Melbourne.

Richard Strauss conducting.

RICHARD STRAUSS (Munich, 11 June 1864 — Garmisch-Partenkirchen, 8 September 1949) had already become celebrated as the foremost composer in Germany, as well as a notable conductor, before he began to write operas. Composing symphonic works, songs, solo piano works, and chamber music occupied him simultaneously with acting first as assistant conductor of Hans von Bülow's orchestra in Meiningen then as conductor at the Court Opera in Munich and first conductor of the Court Orchestra in Weimar where he brought out his tone poems *Don Juan* and *Macbeth*. He continued this special form with *Tod und Verklärung* (Death and Transfiguration) in 1890; *Till Eulenspiegels lustige Streiche* (Till Eulenspiegel's Merry Pranks), 1895; *Also sprach Zarathustra* (Thus Spake Zarathustra, after the philosopher Nietzsche), 1896; *Don Quixote*, 1898; and *Ein Heldenleben* (A Hero's Life), 1899, the first of three works which reflected his own life, career, and personality. The second of these was the *Sinfonia Domestica*, which he led for the first time in a Carnegie Hall concert in 1904 during the first of two visits to the United States. The third would be the opera *Intermezzo*.

Strauss's father, a noted horn player in the Munich Opera orchestra, was famous for having made the horn call in Wagner's *Siegfried* playable. His mother was one of the brewing family Pschorr. One of the precocious youth's first compositions was a chorus from Sophocles' *Elektra*.

During convalescence from a serious illness in 1892, he voyaged to Egypt and Sicily, where he conceived his first opera, *Guntram*. Rather woolly and diffuse in subject matter and characterization, the opera contained many musical weaknesses; but the promise later to be fulfilled is shown. Later revision also failed. Still, from it he acquired a wife, the fine soprano Pauline de Ahna, who sang the part of Freihild, written specially for her. Frau Strauss was a controversial character, but her husband never deviated from his love and loyalty for her.

In 1898, Strauss was appointed conductor at the Royal Opera in Berlin, where he became acquainted with Ernst von Wolzogen, who provided a libretto on a folk tale entitled *Feuersnot* (Fire Famine). It concerned the punishment a young suitor inflicted on a cruel girl who had induced him to mount to her room in a basket, then left him dangling halfway up all night. The original tale proved too indelicate, for she was punished by a wizard who caused flame to spurt from her backside. All sources of fire having been magically extinguished from the town, the burghers had to line up to relight their candles. The libretto modified the punishment to her yielding her maidenhood in penance, but even this proved shocking.

After Berlin and Vienna showed reluctance, the premiere was given to Dresden and Ernst von Schuch, the first in a succession of Strauss premieres in that city. The reception on 21 November 1901, was polite, and thereafter Frankfurt, Vienna, and Berlin accepted. But the Kaiser withdrew the opera after malicious gossip, and the ensuing scandal caused the Royal Opera's Intendant to resign. Performances abroad have been few and scattered. Philadelphia boasted the American premiere in 1927. A notable feature of *Feuersnot* is the love scene that seems to portray sexual experience musically. Strauss has written similar passages in *Ein Heldenleben*, the Introduction to *Der Rosenkavalier*, the Recognition scene in *Elektra*, and the Prelude to Act III of *Arabella*. This graphic unbridled sensuality, causing sensation in early

Stage design by Salvador Dali for a controversial production of Strauss's Salome, mounted by Peter Brook, 1947, Covent Garden, London.

days, has been accepted in more recent times, as have the suggestive musical passages of Wagner's music dramas.

With the production of *Salome* in 1905, Strauss came into recognition of his full powers. For many years, it was the fashion to consider practically everything written after *Der Rosenkavalier* as "uninspired rehashing." But more recently, especially since the composer's death, this judgment has been revised, with approval for such exquisite writing as *Capriccio*, his last opera, and the *Four Last Songs*. There is scattered enthusiasm for later works — *Die Aegyptische Helena*, *Die schweigsame Frau* (The Silent Woman), with a libretto by Stefan Zweig based on a play by Ben Jonson, but less for the three operas for which Joseph Gregor wrote librettos — *Friedenstag* (Peace Day), a stern one-acter that attempts to "instruct rather than entertain," *Daphne*, and *Die Liebe der Danae*, the two latter reversions to classical mythology.

Capriccio, the final opera, for which Clemens Krauss wrote the libretto, is an adaptation of Salieri's *Prima la musica e poi le parole* (First Music, Then Words), and had its premiere in double bill with Mozart's *Der Schauspieldirektor* (The Impresario) in Vienna in 1786. It concerns a countess who must choose between a poet and a musician.

Strauss's collaboration with the poet and playwright Hugo von Hofmannsthal provided the determining operatic influence in his life until the poet's death. Strauss himself wrote: "Hofmannsthal was the one and only poet who, besides his strength as a poet and his gifts for the stage, had the sympathetic ability to present a composer with dramatic material in a form suitable for setting to music — in short the ability to write a libretto that was simultaneously stageworthy, satisfying at a high literary standard, and composable. . . .He not only had the inventive gift of discovering musical subjects, he had — although he himself was scarcely musical (like Goethe he had a clairvoyant intuition for music) — a simply astounding flair for the sort of

Drawing of Richard Strauss with librettist, poet, playwright Hugo von Hofmannsthal.

Richard Strauss and his wife, soprano Pauline de Ahna.

material which, in given circumstances, corresponded to my needs." Many instances of disagreement between the partners are recorded—Strauss begging for something "sensational," or a modern "neurasthenic" subject, or a "really wild Renaissance plot with someone like Savonarola." Or he would insist on a "light" subject to contrast with previous serious works—usually unfortunately just as the poet had retreated into meditation and immersion in the abstract, the symbolic, and the obscure.

Often Strauss found himself in a welter of symbolism he hardly understood. The self-glorification in *Intermezzo,* written during a separation from Hofmannsthal, infuriated the poet, who frankly could not bear the composer's wife. His avoidance of her brought forth the great accumulation of correspondence since compiled into a volume entitled *A Working Friendship.* Hofmannsthal, the sensitive genius, showed a sensibility almost too delicate for the bourgeois Strauss, who, although no genius, was a supremely talented craftsman and one of the most effective composers of the century.

Strauss was addicted to a popular German card game "Skat." Sometimes he would hurry through conducting an opera or a concert, sink into a chair, beam at his partners, pick up his cards, and murmur happily: "Now all is cozy." ("Jetzt ists gemütlich!")

Strauss has been condemned for his association with Nazi Germany. Perhaps it stemmed from three of his characteristics: a willingness to compromise, a cool, businesslike regard for the financial side of his craft, and a real disregard for politics. His defense of Stefan Zweig, who had been forced to flee before the completion of *Friedenstag* (for which Zweig suggested Gregor as his successor), may have been inspired by his own needs, but it did not disturb his position in Germany, which the Nazis were careful to guard. Only their banning of *Die schweigsame Frau* after its first few performances showed their displeasure at Strauss's interference when officialdom excised the Jewish librettist's name from the program. Strauss became increasingly restive, declaring before his eightieth birthday that "if I had had my way, there never would have been glorious war heroes to be

lleted on me, because there would never have been a war" (quoted in
William Mann's critical study of the operas).

Strauss cheerfully — perhaps half-jokingly — acknowledged his limitations,
calling himself "a first-class second-rate composer." Nevertheless, in spite of
his self-deprecation (with which many have agreed), there is so much inventiveness, beauty, and sensuous delight to be found in his music that we
must accord Richard Strauss a high place in the annals of opera. His genius
for setting conversation to apt and exquisite melodious line, as opposed to
dry recitative, has never been equalled. Nor has his subtle and cunning portrayal of human character in music.

*Painting of Salome by Moreau
which inspired both Oscar
Wilde's play and the Strauss
opera Salome.*

Salome

Text by the composer
after Hedwig Lachmann's German
translation of Oscar Wilde's play.

HEROD ANTIPAS	*Tenor*
HERODIAS	*Mezzo-Soprano*
SALOME	*Soprano*
JOKANAAN	*Baritone*
NARRABOTH	*Tenor*
PAGE TO HERODIAS	*Contralto*
TWO NAZARENES	*Tenor, Bass*
FIVE JEWS	*Four Tenors, Bass*
TWO SOLDIERS	*Basses*
CAPPADOCIAN	*Bass*
SLAVE	*Soprano*

First Performance
Dresden, 9 December 1905.

SALOME HAD A sensational success at its premiere in spite of initial difficulties. The conductor, Ernst von Schuch, had heard that the music was
considered too difficult for him; stung, he took extra pains to follow
Strauss's suggestion to play it as if it were fairy music by Mendelssohn —
after all, the composer remarked, it was "only a Scherzo with a fatal conclusion!"

Moral scruples troubled the heroine, Marie Wittich, and she did not attempt the Dance of the Seven Veils at the premiere — perhaps wisely, as
she did not resemble a girl of sixteen. Attempts at censorship cropped up
here and there even though the opera rapidly became popular in almost
every European center. The Kaiser in Berlin demanded that the Star of
Bethlehem be shown at the close (even though the opera presumably is
laid thirty years after Christ's birth), and Vienna would have it not at all
until 1911.

Salome's fate at the Metropolitan is well known: Heinrich Conried had
planned it as a jewel in his 1907 season, and Olive Fremstad had gone so
far as to ask the morgue how much a severed head would weigh. But Conried made the mistake of holding the dress rehearsal on a Sunday and the
horrors of the grim work repelled J.P. Morgan's daughter. The magnate in-

*Marie Wittich (far right) as Salome just before the famous dance of the seven veils. Ka.
Burian is seated (with crown). Premiere of Salome, 1905, Dresden.*

*Aïno Acté, London's first
Salome, 1910.*

sisted that the opera be withdrawn after its first performance, and it did
not reenter the sacred portals until twenty-seven years had elapsed. In the
meantime, however, Oscar Hammerstein introduced Mary Garden in the
voluptuous role at his Manhattan Opera House, and gradually the opera
took its rightful place without eliciting such epithets in the prudish press a
"degeneracy," "moral stench," "gruesome," "abhorrent," "diseased,"
"polluted," and "bestially perverted," which first greeted it. Henry E. Kreh
biel, always the guardian of musical morals, wrote that the finale beatifie
"an impulse which can only be conceived as rising from the utmost pit of
degradation."

London remained timorous for quite a while, allowing the work on
stage only after it had been changed beyond recognition. Whether or no
to require the heroine to do the actual dance has remained moot, as has
the question of just how far she goes in making love to the head of John
the Baptist on the silver salver. Aïno Acté, a Finn who had the figure
for it, was the first to throw off her veils, in London in 1910. At the
Metropolitan the dance has been attempted more or less by Göta Ljung-
berg, Marjorie Lawrence, Lily Djanel and Ella Flesch, all of whom appeared before the advent of the incandescent Ljuba Welitsch in 1949. As
trid Varnay, Christel Goltz, Inga Borkh, Birgit Nilsson, Leonie Rysanek,
and Grace Bumbry were later Salomes, while at the New York City Opera Phyllis Curtin, Brenda Lewis and Maralin Niska offered individual
characterizations.

Television solved the dance problem fairly well, NBC inserting a dancer who resembled the singer Elaine Malbin, while Teresa Stratas in a British production was her own terpsichorean.

Strauss came to believe that the part should be played as a young and innocent girl at the beginning, gradually overcome and finally corrupted at the moment her sexuality was aroused. The part is doubly effective when conceived and played this way. Josephine Barstow, the English soprano who sang the role at Santa Fe, is notable in this respect.

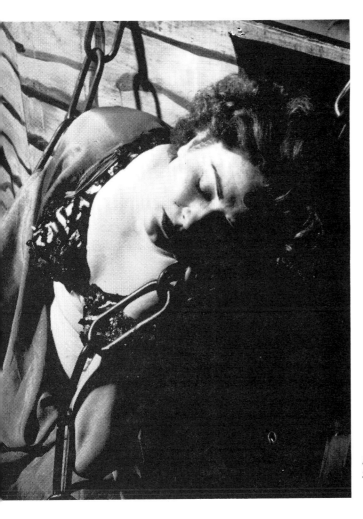

Ljuba Welitsch as Salome.

Strauss used the Wilde play, which he saw in 1903 in the Max Reinhardt production in Berlin, virtually intact after its translation. In this he paralleled *Pelléas et Mélisande*, *L'Amore dei tre re*, and *Wozzeck*. Wilde, with an obsession about Salome, had been particularly influenced by the painting of Gustave Moreau, which is the very soul of early Art Nouveau. At least two other composers beat Strauss to the subject: Massenet had written his *Hérodiade* (based on Flaubert's tale) in 1881, and Antoine Mariotte set the original French play of Wilde earlier than Strauss, although it was not performed until 1908, and did not survive in the competition with its stronger rival.

Strauss's horn-playing father reacted violently to his son's score: "God! What nervous music! Like having your pants full of Maybugs!" Strauss's

William Dooley as the Prophet Jokanaan, 1969, Santa Fe Opera.

Set Svanholm as Herod.

large orchestra — even more players (110) than Wagner's — poses problems for smaller opera companies, but that does not stop them from mounting what is probably the composer's most impressive and successful work for the stage.

THE CURTAIN RISES on the courtyard of Herod's palace in Judea, where a silver moon illumines the quiet scene. There is a banquet going on offstage, and the young Syrian guard Narraboth is watching Princess Salome intently, commenting on her fairness, all to the distress of the Page, who warns him that something terrible is likely to happen. Suddenly, the voice of the prophet Jokanaan is heard from the cistern where he has been imprisoned, telling of the coming of another "mightier than I." His words puzzle the soldiers and the Cappadocian, but Narraboth pays no attention, for Salome has left the banquet and enters the courtyard, troubled by Herod's attentions and the gabble of the Jews quarreling over their religious beliefs. Jokanaan cries out again, and the Princess is immediately curious. In mounting excitement, she at last persuades Narraboth, who is powerless to resist her, to open the cistern and let the strange man emerge. Enraptured and repelled at the same time, she entreats Jokanaan in the only way she knows — to allow physical contact. At last he repulses her, calling down a curse on her and her sinful mother. She falls dazedly on the lid of the cistern as it closes over him. Narraboth, horrified at her perverse words, stabs himself. When Herod emerges and slips in Narraboth's blood, he is distraught and calls it an ill omen, wildly searching for Salome, petulantly ignoring Herodias's protests, demanding that Salome drink with him, eat with him, sit beside him. To these requests Salome responds indifferently. Jokanaan's voice is heard again and Herodias demands that he be silenced or delivered to the Jews, for he is insulting her. But Herod uneasily refuses, and the Jews begin their quarrel again. The Nazarenes join in the discussion of the coming of a Savior and chatter away until Jokanaan again is heard, this time cursing the "harlot of Babylon." Despite all Herodias's protests, Herod asks Salome to dance for him. When he swears that he will give her anything she asks, she consents. Her maids invest her with the seven veils, and she begins the sensuous dance that so inflames Herod that he is ready to keep his promise. But when she asks for the head of the Prophet Jokanaan on a silver salver, and repeats the grisly command after each alternative he proposes — the most beautiful emerald in the world, white peacocks, marvelous jewels, even the mantle of the high priest, the veil of the sanctuary — he sinks,

Mary Garden as Salome.

Drawing by Aubrey Beardsley showing Salome with the head of Jokanaan, inspired by the Oscar Wilde play which forms the basis for the Strauss opera.

apparently oblivious; and Herodias, who is delighted by the turn of events, slips the ring of death from his finger and gives it to the executioner.

Now ensues the breathless, tingling wait in a silence broken only by deep basses and bass drum, with an eerie screech by a single bass on a pinched string struck sharply by the bow. Salome, inflamed to the breaking point, thinks she hears the executioner's sword drop, and after several frustrating moments, a huge black arm emerges from the cistern, bearing the salver on which rests the severed head.

In a finale that crowns all sensuous and spine-chilling effects, Salome croons to the head, mourning that the Prophet should have loved her. In a final spasm of ecstasy, she kisses the dead lips. Herod, deeply revolted by this monster, ignores Herodias's glee and orders the soldiers to "Kill that woman!" With their heavy shields, the men crush the entranced girl as the moon sheds a pallid beam over the horrid scene.

Marilyn Richardson as Salome with the severed head of Jokanaan, 1975-76, Australian Opera, Melbourne.

Elektra

Text by Hugo von Hofmannsthal based on the plays by Sophocles, Aeschylus, and Euripides.

ELEKTRA	*Soprano*
CHRYSOTHEMIS	*Soprano*
KLYTEMNESTRA	*Mezzo-Soprano*
AEGISTHUS	*Tenor*
ORESTES	*Baritone*
KLYTEMNESTRA'S CONFIDANTE	*Soprano*
TRAINBEARER	*Soprano*
OVERSEER OF SERVANTS	*Soprano*
YOUNG SERVANT	*Tenor*
OLD SERVANT	*Bass*
GUARDIAN OF ORESTES	*Bass*
FIVE MAIDSERVANTS	*2 Sopranos, 2 Mezzo-Sopranos, Contralto*

First Performance
Dresden, 25 January 1909.

WITH ERNST VON Schuch conducting, *Elektra's* first cast included Annie Krull as Elektra, Ernestine Schumann-Heink as Klytemnestra, Margarethe Siems as Chrysothemis, Carl Perron as Orestes, and Johannes Sembach as Aegisthus. The portly Schumann-Heink refused to sing the part again, calling the opera "frightful, a set of mad women. We have reached the furthest boundary in dramatic writing for the voice with Wagner, but Strauss goes beyond. His singing voices are lost. We have come to a full stop. I believe Strauss himself sees it."

Later when Mariette Mazarin sang the first American Elektra with Oscar Hammerstein in 1910, she fainted after the performance, but managed later to sing Elektra in the afternoon and Salome in Massenet's *Hérodiade* that same evening. Emulating Schumann-Heink, Jeanne Gerville-Réache, Hammerstein's Klytemnestra, abjured the part after one attempt. Famous Elektras thereafter were Edyth Walker in Beecham's London production in 1910; Gertrud Kappel, who sang it first with Bruno Walter in London in 1925 and at the Metropolitan premiere in 1932, with Karin Branzell as her demented mother; Rose Pauly (with Kerstin Thorborg), Astrid Varnay (with Elisabeth Hoengen), Inge Borkh (with Jean Madeira), and more recently, Birgit Nilsson, whose return in the part in 1980 marked her first opera appearance at the Metropolitan for several years.

The indignation with which some critics received this latest scandalous example of Strauss's genius reached almost as high a pitch as that provided by *Salome*, with Krehbiel in the forefront of the outraged. The *Tribune* thought the opera's music the strongest proof of its decadence: "The age of the greatest skill—'virtuosity' as it is called—is the age of the greatest decay in really creative energy." The impact had not softened even twenty-two years later for the same paper's critic, Lawrence Gilman, who remarked "the pitiful outcries of dismay, blended with deafening explosions of indignation" in the town. Later audiences have become conditioned, more sophisticated, more tolerant of violence, whether it be on the stage or in the pit—or in life.

Hofmannsthal provided the inspiration for *Elektra*, keeping after Strauss, with whom he had wished to collaborate since their first meeting in 1900, and wearing down the composer's reluctance to accept a subject so near to *Salome*. Even after he had started work on *Elektra*, Strauss flirted with other ideas, hoping to find a lighter subject. But the Greek tragedy drew him ineluctably, and he found for the savage house of Atreus the most savage music written to that day—Stravinsky's *Sacre du printemps* did not appear until 1913. He produced his most sophisticated, meaningful, and technically perfect score in *Elektra*. Turning to the more frivolous world of *Der Rosenkavalier* immediately afterward, he never looked back at the venture he had made into what might have, if he had pursued it, rivalled Schönberg and equalled Berg.

Hofmannsthal was accused by one critic of dragging "the powerful subject of the ancient myth down from the lofty realm of tragedy. . .to the pathologically perverse." As if that myth did not itself represent the bloodiest, most horrifying tale of human perversity!

Knowledge of the myth is useful in absorbing the story of the opera. Elektra came from a family that incurred trouble from the beginning. The founder, Tantalus, repaid the favors of the gods by serving them his own son Pelops at a banquet. Their omniscience prevented them from becoming cannibals, and they doomed him to eternal thirst and hunger—"tantalized" him. Pelops was restored to life, the only issue of Tantalus who was not cursed. His daughter Niobe boasted arrogantly of her power and praised

Ernestine Schumann-Heink (l.) as Klytemnestra with Annie Krull as Elektra in the premiere of Strauss's Elektra, 1909, Dresden.

Astrid Varnay (l.) as Elektra with Hildegard Hillbrecht as Chrysothemis, Bayerische Staatsoper, Munich.

her seven sons and seven daughters so vaingloriously that Apollo and Artemis killed them all. Niobe was turned to stone; only her tears flowed forever. Pelops's sons were Atreus and Thyestes. The latter seduced his brother's wife; in revenge, Atreus served him a stew in which his sons were the chief ingredient. Thyestes ravished his own daughter, Pelopia; but the son resulting from this union was legitimized by Atreus, who unknowingly married Pelopia. This child of compound incest was Aegisthus, who may be seen to be distantly related to Klytemnestra by marriage. Aegisthus was set to kill Atreus by his real father, Thyestes, at that time ruler of Mycaenae. But Atreus's son Agamemnon succeeded to the throne, while his brother Menelaus ruled in Sparta. The brothers married sisters, Klytemnestra and Helen (daughters of Leda and the swan that was Zeus in disguise). Agamemnon's wife was the widow of a man he had killed, therefore she did not love him from the first. While the brothers were away for the duration (ten years) of the Trojan War (caused by the abduction of Helen by the Trojan prince Paris), Klytemnestra took Aegisthus for a lover. She had hated her husband the more for sacrificing their daughter Iphigenia to bring a favorable wind to Troy. One version has Iphigenia spared to become a priestess at Tauris; these stories are told in the Gluck operas. Menelaus and Helen spent some time in Egypt on their return home from Troy, providing the locale for Strauss's *Die Aegyptische Helena*. When

Rose Pauly and Irene Jessner in Strauss's Elektra.

Agamemnon returns, Klytemnestra, with Aegisthus's help, plans to murder him in his bath. She throws a towel over him, her lover delivers the death blow with his sword, and Klytemnestra beheads him with an ax. Aegisthus has all the while cherished hatred for the descendents of Atreus, and Orestes, the son of Klytemnestra and Agamemnon, has been sent into exile. Aegisthus, however, has spared Agamemnon's remaining two daughters, Elektra and Chrysothemis (the latter an invention of Homer and Sophocles).

Poor Orestes is doomed, no matter what he does. If he murders his mother to avenge his father, he will be pursued by the Furies for shedding a parent's blood. If he refrains, he will be assailed by a dreadful disease for failing to obtain revenge for a slain parent. Sophocles ends his tale with Aegisthus's death. Mythology has it that Elektra lives and marries Pylades, a friend of Orestes, but Hofmannsthal has her dance a wild dance, collapse, and die.

Strauss vetoed his librettist's idea of appending to the opera an explanatory ballet based on Orestes and the Furies. Strauss detested placing either *Salome* or *Elektra* in tandem with another work. Indeed, *Elektra* usually stands alone, but *Salome* is subjected to all kinds of strange stage-fellows, from saccharine ballets to *Gianni Schicchi* to (Heaven forfend!) *Pagliacci*.

Inge Borkh as Elektra.

IN THE GLOOMY courtyard of the great palace at Mycenae, five maidservants and their overseer are gossiping viciously about the mad antics of Elektra, when the Princess herself appears, running into the shadows and crouching like a wounded beast. One maid shows pity, but the others jeer at her and the object of her compassion, then the girl is taken inside and beaten. Elektra, completely consumed by the lust for vengeance, cries out to her dead father Agamemnon in a superb monologue, then in her degradation vows to avenge him. Her sister Chrysothemis enters, and warns Elektra of a plot to shut her away in a tower. Elektra tries to enlist her sister in her search for vengeance, but all Chrysothemis wants is a peaceful and domestic life. She further warns Elektra not to confront Klytemnestra just now; the mother has suffered a frightful dream and is on the point of breakdown. To a fearful and savage cacophony, Klytemnestra appears, a debauched harridan, one of the most hateful of Strauss's characters. Hofmannsthal has described her: "Her sallow, bloated face appears, in the lurid glare of the torches all the more pale above her scarlet robe. She is leaning on her Confidante (dressed in dark violet) and also on an ivory stick, and is decked with jewels and talismans. Her arms are hung with bangles, her fingers glisten with rings. Her eyelids appear unnaturally large, and it seems to cost her a fearful effort to keep them open." Strauss thought rather that she should not be old, but a proud, handsome woman of about fifty. The woman is at least hag-ridden with dreams.

She appeals to Elektra to tell her what blood sacrifice will bring her relief from her haunted sleep. Elektra replies: "When the right blood flows under the hatchet, all thy dreams shall end." Then Elektra prophesies that a man shall shed this blood—a stranger, "yet of this house." She is still hoping for Orestes's return. This cat-and-mouse dialogue

Conclusion of Strauss's Elektra, production by Herbert Graf, 1938, San Francisco Opera.

ends with Elektra's direct threat to her mother; Klytemnestra seems
thoroughly cowed until the Confidante rushes in and whispers news
that brings the woman back to triumphant mien. It seems that Orestes is
dead. Chrysothemis confirms the dire news. Elektra is overcome, then
rallies to the thought that she and her sister must do the awful deed she
has hoped for from her brother. But the more timorous sister again
shrinks away. Elektra creeps along the side of a wall, searching for
something (the ax she has hidden). Suddenly she notices a stranger,
who says that he is a former companion of Orestes and has a message
for the Queen. But it is Orestes himself. The brother and sister do not
recognize each other, for he is disguised and she is pitifully ragged and
animal-like. When recognition dawns, the music embodies the intensity
of emotion that each feels; it is in character more like lovers music than
siblings. Strauss seldom excelled these few moments. But they are soon
over; Orestes and his guardian are received in the palace, from whence
a scream is soon heard, bloodcurdling and, to Elektra, the realization of
her deepest desire. When Aegisthus appears, she playfully urges him to
go inside, and in spite of his distrust at her sudden change of manner, he
enters, and is in turn murdered. Now vengeance is complete, but
Elektra does not live to enjoy it. After a mad dance of joy, she collapses
and dies.

ERNST VON SCHUCH, with *Der Rosenkavalier*, conducted his third Strauss premiere. The cast included Margarethe Siems as the Marschallin, Carl Perron as Ochs, Eva von der Osten as Octavian, and Minnie Nast as Sophie. Nuremberg had the second performance the very next night; Munich, Hamburg, and Berlin followed. The censor in Berlin insisted on changes in the text to avoid the word "bed" and certain vulgarisms of Ochs; the results were faintly ridiculous. Covent Garden exercised over Sir Thomas Beecham the same "moral" proscriptions in 1913; he simply eliminated the actual bed.

The opera did not reach the Metropolitan until 1913, when Alfred Hertz led a cast that included Frieda Hempel (Marschallin), Otto Goritz (Ochs), Margarete Ober (Octavian), and Anna Case (Sophie). When the United States entered the First World War, *Rosenkavalier* shared the banishment of other German operas, returning in 1922. Lotte Lehmann made the role of the Marschallin peculiarly her own, singing it many times in world centers, retiring from the opera stage after a particularly affecting performance at the Metropolitan in 1945. She had sung both the other feminine roles in her early career.

Eleanor Steber, who made her debut as Sophie in 1940, later assumed the Marschallin's role; Astrid Varnay, Lisa Della Casa, and Elisabeth Schwarzkopf (who made her belated debut in 1964) were others who graced the role. Helen Traubel was given the part briefly by Rudolf Bing. Later Marschallins were Evelyn Lear, Teresa Zylis-Gara, and Johanna Meier, who also sang the role at the New York City Opera. Celebrated as

Der Rosenkavalier
(*The Rose Cavalier*)

Text by Hugo von Hofmannsthal.

MARIA THERESA, PRINCESS OF WERDENBERG (THE FELDMARSCHALLIN)	*Soprano*
BARON OCHS AUF LERCHENAU	*Bass*
OCTAVIAN ROFRANO	*Mezzo-Soprano*
HERR VON FANINAL	*Baritone*
SOPHIE	*Soprano*
MARIANNE LEITMETZERIN	*Soprano*
VALZACCHI	*Tenor*
ANNINA	*Contralto*
COMMISSARY OF POLICE	*Bass*
MARSCHALLIN'S MAJOR-DOMO	*Tenor*

FANINAL'S MAJOR-DOMO	*Tenor*
NOTARY	*Bass*
INNKEEPER	*Tenor*
SINGER	*Tenor*
THREE NOBLE ORPHANS	*Soprano, Mezzo-Soprano, Contralto*
MILLINER	*Soprano*
ANIMAL VENDOR	*Tenor*
FOUR SERVANTS OF THE MARSCHALLIN	*Two Tenors, Two Basses*
FOUR WAITERS	*Tenor, Three Basses*
FLUTE PLAYER; HAIRDRESSER; SCHOLAR; NOBLE WIDOW; MOHAMMED; LEOPOLD, OCHS'S BODY SERVANT	*Silent Roles*

First Performance
Dresden, 26 January 1911.

Lotte Lehmann as the Marschallin.

Richard Mayr as Baron Ochs.

Ochs were Michael Bohnen, Richard Mayr, Alexander Kipnis, Emanuel List, Otto Edelmann, Walter Berry, and, more recently Aage Haugland. Most Sophies are entrancing; they include Elisabeth Schumann, Erna Berger, Hilde Gueden, Roberta Peters, Reri Grist, Judith Raskin, Judith Blegen, and Gianna Rolandi. Risë Stevens commanded the part of Octavian at the Metropolitan for many years, spelled by Jarmila Novotna and Blanche Thebom and succeeded by Yvonne Minton, Brigitte Fassbänder, Tatiana Troyanos, and Agnes Baltsa. Frances Bible was the indispensable City Opera's Octavian, partnered by its Marschallins, who included Wilma Spence and Rose Bampton among others. The small but demanding part of the Italian singer has called on expert talents, among them Giuseppe di Stefano, Kurt Baum, Sandor Konya, Nicolai Gedda, and Luciano Pavarotti.

Strauss is said to have wished to write "a Mozart opera" after the gloom of *Salome* and *Elektra*.

Hofmannsthal, after some evasiveness, finally caught fire on the idea of a comedy with echoes of Beaumarchais, Molière, and another French playwright, Louvet de Couvray. He pursued his own research, delving, as was later learned, into the diaries of Prince Johann Josef Khevenhüller-Mensch, the Imperial Lord High Steward at the court of Leopold II, from which he derived many names and situations embodied in the libretto.

Frieda Hempel as the Marschallin from the Metropolitan Opera premiere of Der Rosenkavalier, 1913, New York.

Originally the opera was conceived to center around a baritone (Ochs) and a young and graceful girl ("the type of a Farrar or a Garden"), but the role of the Marschallin began to grow in importance until she became the dominating figure.

Pre-production difficulties included the trouble in casting Ochs, for Richard Mayr was busy elsewhere, although he later took it over. Both Strauss and Hofmannsthal disliked the Dresden stage manager, Georg Toller, and they contrived to smuggle in Max Reinhardt, who lent valuable assistance although he received no credit. The usual censorship operated, in that much of the Baron's vulgarity was cut, and the controversy about the bed arose for the first time; it would haunt the opera. The original length of the work rivalled that of *Die Meistersinger*; other resemblances have been pointed out. There is the renunciation of a young lover by an older person, the proud father, young love, the grotesque wooer, and the opposition of distorted art and nobility.

The music is among Strauss's subtlest, and the pervading waltz idiom that never grows tedious is a buoyant success. Strauss composed extra music for a silent film produced in 1926 in Dresden and even conducted the orchestra at its showing in London. It was seen in America at Yale University a half-century later.

In 1936, Ernst Lubitsch, the celebrated Hollywood director, passionately desired to make a film of *Rosenkavalier*. He would have cast Jeanette MacDonald (!) as the Marschallin and, more appropriately, Emil Jannings ·as Ochs. But he ran into trouble with Octavian—Hollywood would not have accepted a girl. His plans evaporated.

ACT I.   The passion that opens the overture with its upsurging theme characterizing the young Octavian has subsided as the curtain rises. Octavian, youthfully boasting, is gently reproved by the Marschallin, and has to hide when the little Blackamoor Mohammed brings in the morning chocolate. After an exchange of endearments with Maria Theresa, his high spirits mount again, and his injudicious remarks about enjoying his lady's favors in her husband's absence disturb the Marschallin, who does not love her elderly husband but respects him and his position as Feldmarschall. In fact, she has dreamed of him, she says. This outrages Octavian, who is further inflamed by her inadvertent admission that, one time. . .obviously meaning that once before she had almost been caught in a similar situation. She finally calms the boy down, but their intimacy is interrupted by voices outside. Hastily hiding, Octavian is reassured by her relief that it is only a visitor, not her husband. The boy emerges dressed in feminine attire— presumably a maid's which he has found in a dressing room. Now the Baron Ochs storms in, scattering the restraining attendants behind him. He has sent a letter to his cousin Maria Theresa, but she has hardly glanced at it. Before he gets down to the business of asking for a cavalier

Margarethe Siems as the Marschallin with Eva von der Osten as Octavian from the premiere of Rosenkavalier, 1911, Dresden.

Eva von der Osten as Octavian.

Octavian's entrance from Act I of Der Rosenkavalier with Ingeborg Hallstein as Octavian, Bayerische Oper, Munich.

to convey his traditional silver rose to his intended bride, he is irresistibly drawn to the young "Mariandel" and he can hardly keep his eyes — and hands — off "her." There is a great deal of by-play as Octavian attempts vainly to escape, and is finally told by the Marschallin to fetch his own miniature portrait, as she proposes that he should be the Rose Cavalier. The Baron notices the resemblance to the maid, and remarks that she must possess some blue blood — he himself has a byblow as a body servant. He manages a short colloquy with "Mariandel," after which the boy escapes just as the Marschallin's morning levée is announced. The Baron is introduced to the Princess's notary and sits at the side drawing up marriage contracts. One after another, suppliants vie for the Marschallin's attention — a mother and three noble orphans; a milliner; an animal vendor (his pets usually afford some extracurricular amusement); the intriguer Valzacchi and his niece Annina; a singer, who, accompanied by a flutist, launches into the extremely difficult "Italian" aria; and a fussy hairdresser, who is eventually accused of making the Marschallin look old. The Baron's servants are admitted, and the bodyservant, the ludicrous Leopold, brings the case containing the silver rose. In the midst of a second stanza from the singer, the

Baron explodes with rage at the notary. The levée is over; the intriguers, last to leave, offer their services to the Baron, who asks them to find "Mariandel." The Marschallin, left alone, begins the lovely monologue, one of the most moving scenes on the opera stage. Her mood is black; she excoriates the vulgar roué who will accept the person and fortune of a young girl so complacently — she remembers that she was just such a girl married right out of the convent, and now she is forced to consider herself no longer young. How can this be? In her darkest moment, Octavian returns, brash and cheerful at having escaped so handily. He cannot understand his Bichette's mood, and she is irritated by his ardent possessiveness. At last she sends him away, dismayed and hurt — then remorseful, would call him back, but he has galloped off like the wind, her footmen tell her. She sends for Mohammed and entrusts the silver rose to him, to be delivered to Octavian.

ACT II. In the palace of the rich, newly ennobled Herr von Faninal, all is a-bustle awaiting the arrival of the Rose Cavalier. The Major-domo firmly banishes the father; he must by tradition not be present. The duenna Marianne flutters about while the young Sophie, in mixed dread and exaltation, waits for the messenger. At last, to great

Frances Bible as Octavian with Lorenzo Alvary as Baron Ochs

331
STRAUSS

Lorenzo Alvary as Baron Ochs with Régine Crespin as the Marschallin, 1957, Paris Opéra.

Risë Stevens as Octavian.

flourishes and enchanting music, he arrives, costumed in white and silver and bearing the silver rose, which he presents to the maiden. There is immediate sympathy between the two young people. She tells him she knows all about him, even knows all his names, and recites them, even to the affectionate nickname Quinquin—so well he does not himself remember them. He is enraptured, even by her effusiveness and her brash statement that no one will get the better of her. But she is quickly cast down when the Baron appears and treats her so familiarly that she is repelled. No sympathy is forthcoming from her father or duenna, but Octavian begins to simmer, and after several misadventures, takes things into his own hands, challenging the Baron to a duel and wounding him in the arm. The boy is banished from von Faninal's house, but manages to enlist Valzacchi and Annina, who have previously been on the Baron's side, in a scheme to ruin the roughneck. Sophie is threatened with a convent if she doesn't obey. Everyone leaves the Baron alone to rest, but Annina comes in to a famous waltz strain and brings a note from "Mariandel" setting an appointment for supper. The Baron refuses to give Annina a tip, and gleefully waltzes around the stage, uttering his characteristic refrain: "With me, with me, no night is too long."

ACT III.   This act caused some trouble in the making, and it still shows weaknesses. There is apt to be utter confusion at certain junctures, and the humor is occasionally rather heavy. The scene is an inn, where Octavian and his accomplices are arranging a calamity

Lisa Della Casa as the Marschallin.

Frances Bible as Octavian with Virginia Haskins as Sophie.

for the Baron. He will be frightened by sinister apparitions, badgered by a woman and a dozen children claiming him as "Papa," frustrated by "Mariandel" in his efforts to get her into a bed which is behind a curtain in the room, and humiliated by the police who arrive because of the hullabaloo. His last blow is the double arrival of Faninal and Sophie, and of the Marschallin, summoned by Leopold who thinks to help his master. Faninal collapses at the outrageous behavior of the Baron trying to pass off "Mariandel" as Sophie; the Marschallin, spotting Octavian behind the bed curtains (where he has resumed his own attire and amused the informed Commissary of Police by tossing the maid's undergarments over the curtain), takes in the situation at a glance and firmly forbids the Baron to have anything more to do with Sophie. Ochs has spotted the identity of Octavian-Mariandel, but is reproved by the Marschallin and allowed no leeway. Disgruntled, he pushes his way out of the crowd who thrust bills for services at him, and is gone forever. Now it remains for the three concerned characters to resolve their problem. They begin by singing a glorious trio, in which the women's voices blend in unearthly beauty, combining motives of each: Sophie's admiration for the Marschallin gradually giving way to the certainty of her love for Octavian; Octavian at first bewildered and torn between the old love and the new, finally not even noticing as the Marschallin, angered but rueful and at last resigned, leaves the room. The lovers rush into each other's arms and sing a rapturous duet, interrupted only by the exit of the Marschallin and von Faninal, the latter remarking fatuously that youth must have its way, and the great lady murmuring a final and sorrowful "ja, ja." At last, the two young ones run offstage. But the opera is not over. To the most delicate and sparkling music, the tiny Mohammed patters in, carrying a lantern. Sophie has dropped her handkerchief. With a final flourish, the Blackamoor finds it, waves it high, and vanishes.

Maria Jeritza as the first Ariadne in Strauss's Ariadne auf Naxos.

ARIADNE WAS first conceived as an appendage to a one-act play, which Hofmannsthal adapted as *Der Bürger als Edelmann*, based on Molière's *Le Bourgeois Gentilhomme*, to which Strauss composed incidental music, now often played as an orchestral suite. The first Ariadne, named Mizzi, soon afterward became known as Maria Jeritza. Hermann Jadlowker was Bacchus, and the tremendously difficult role of Zerbinetta was undertaken by Margarethe Siems, the first Elektra and Marschallin. This version had several European performances and Beecham conducted it in London in 1913, then revived it for the Edinburgh Festival in Glyndebourne in 1950. But the play proved awkward to produce, and the opera itself seemed too short for an entire bill, so Hofmannsthal wrote a Prologue, for which Strauss composed some entrancing music, especially for the character known simply as the Composer. Selma Kurz was the Zerbinetta in the Vienna premiere, Jeritza was again the Ariadne, and Lotte Lehmann substituted at short notice for Marie Gutheil-Schoder as the Composer. Again the opera went the rounds; in London Lehmann was Ariadne, Elisabeth Schumann the Composer, and Maria Ivogün, Zerbinetta. Strauss himself conducted the Dresden Opera performance in London in 1936.

The Philadelphia Civic Opera, with Alexander Smallens conducting, had the honor of the United States premiere in 1928, and further honors went to the minor singers, Helen Jepson (Echo) and Nelson Eddy (Harlequin), who sang from the pit while the characters were mimed on stage. Eddy doubled as the Wigmaker in the Prologue. The Juilliard School gave the first New York performance in 1934, in an English translation by Alfred Kalisch, but the first professional production in the metropolis belonged to the New York City Opera in 1946. The Metropolitan did not mount it until 1962.

Some noted Ariadnes: Leonie Rysanek, Maria Reining, Eileen Farrell, Montserrat Caballé, Leontyne Price, Carol Neblett, Johanna Meier; Zerbinettas: Rita Streich, Roberta Peters, Ruth Welting, Reri Grist, Virginia

Scene from Ariadne auf Naxos, 1938 Munich Festival.

MacWatters, Edita Gruberova; Composers: Sena Jurinac, Kerstin Meyer, Evelyn Lear, Maralin Niska, Susanne Marsee, Tatiana Troyanos; Bacchuses: Jess Thomas, Sandor Konya, James King, Alberto Remedios.

PROLOGUE.   As the curtain opens, the backstage room in the nobleman's castle is revealed. The rich man's Major-domo is arguing with the Music Master, who resents the news that a vulgar opera buffa has been scheduled to follow the *Ariadne* his pupil has specially composed for a festive occasion. Both entertainments must be ended by nine o'clock, when a fireworks display is planned. As the two exit, a Lackey shows in a young Officer and indicates Zerbinetta's dressing-room. Suddenly the Tenor's door bursts open and the Wigmaker staggers out, accompanied by invective from the singer, who ignores the agitated Composer and goes back inside. Now Zerbinetta emerges with the Officer, telling him that it is going to be hard to raise a laugh after the tedious opera. They go to the back of the stage as the Prima Donna comes out of her room with the Music Master. As the Dancing Master enters and goes to Zerbinetta, the Composer spots her for the first time and asks the Music Master who she is. The Music Master evades the question. The Composer is much taken with Zerbinetta's appearance, but reacts furiously when the Music Master tells him of the comedy and the part she will play in it.

The four comedians enter in goosestep and Zerbinetta introduces them to the others, then sends them to fetch her make-up accoutrements. The Composer is aghast — the Music Master must have known this desecration all along. He tears up his composition in a rage. There is a great deal of dissension between the two factions; then the Major-domo announces that the schedule has been changed — not the order reversed, as both sides think, but that both pieces shall be played simultaneously to save time. To the general consternation, he adds that furthermore the noble lord is greatly displeased that the opera scene is a barren desert island — surely in such a magnificent mansion, more luxurious settings could have been found. In the babble of protest that ensues, the Music Master restrains the Composer by reminding him of the fifty-ducat fee. The stricken Composer is persuaded to cut portions of his music, whereupon both Tenor and Prima Donna approach him surreptitiously, each suggesting that the other's part be shortened.

The Dancing Master flippantly instructs Zerbinetta in the opera plot, and she flusters the Composer by insisting that it is not Death Ariadne wants, but a new admirer. But the Composer will not give up, and explains his idea of Bacchus reaching godhood through ennobling experience with Ariadne so passionately that Zerbinetta is quite carried away. For a few precious moments, she persuades the Composer that she is a gentle, loving woman and not the coquette she so often portrays, and leaves him in a blissful daze, which though inspired by human, feminine attraction, turns into an apostrophe to music, the holiest art. He is rudely awakened by a shrill whistle from Zerbinetta, who musters her quartet. "Offensive creatures!" cries the Composer, and, emitting a final burst of despair at the philistine world, dashes off. The curtain falls as the Music Master shakes his head sadly.

Ariadne auf Naxos
(*Ariadne on Naxos*)

Text by Hugo von Hofmannsthal.

CHARACTERS IN THE PROLOGUE:

MAJOR-DOMO	*Speaking Role*
MUSIC MASTER	*Baritone*
COMPOSER	*Soprano*
TENOR	*Tenor*
(LATER BACCHUS)	
OFFICER	*Tenor*
DANCING MASTER	*Tenor*
WIGMAKER	*Bass*
LACKEY	*Bass*
ZERBINETTA	*Soprano*
PRIMA DONNA	*Soprano*
(LATER ARIADNE)	
HARLEQUIN	*Baritone*
SCARAMUCCIO	*Tenor*
TRUFFALDINO	*Bass*
BRIGHELLA	*Tenor*

335
STRAUSS

CHARACTERS IN THE OPERA:

ARIADNE	*Soprano*
BACCHUS	*Tenor*
THREE NYMPHS:	
NAIAD	*Soprano*
DRYAD	*Contralto*
ECHO	*Soprano*
ZERBINETTA	*Soprano*
HARLEQUIN	*Baritone*
SCARAMUCCIO	*Tenor*
TRUFFALDINO	*Bass*
BRIGHELLA	*Tenor*

First Performance
First Version: Stuttgart, 25 October 1912.
Second Version: Vienna, 4 October 1916.

Ariadne, surrounded by her three attendants, laments the loss of her lover Theseus, Staatsoper, Dresden.

THE OPERA. The grief-stricken Ariadne has been abandoned by Theseus after their escape from Crete. The daughter of the King, she had helped him slay the Minotaur, half-man, half bull, and led him and other Athenians out of danger. Ariadne is in a state of perpetual grief, commented on by her three attendants, Naiad, Dryad and Echo. The comedians peep at her, but she pays them no attention, and continues her plaint in a series of arias. The four men dance to a merry little quartet, until Zerbinetta dismisses them and tries her own prescription in "Grossmächtige Prinzessin," the show-stopping aria, in which she quotes her own experience of welcoming each new lover as a god, she captive to his arts.

This ravishing coloratura piece was shortened and lowered for the second version, but it still remains a glittering jewel. Toward its end, Ariadne disappears into her cave. Harlequin appears, and manages to persuade Zerbinetta that he is the man for her. They go off to hide, as the other three clowns vainly seek Zerbinetta in a sprightly ensemble, in which she eventually joins them, flirting with each one in turn.

To a brass fanfare, the nymphs return to herald the ship of a "comely boy, a youthful god," and proceed to tell of Bacchus's entrapment by Circe, from which he has just escaped. The voice of the god himself is heard, drawing Ariadne out of her cave as if by magic. Bacchus is hailing his escape from Circe. Ariadne thinks at first that the new arrival is Theseus, then the messenger of Death. Their beautiful and extended duet gradually clears up these mistaken identities, and as Bacchus kisses her, Ariadne is finally prepared to face life with this new-found joy. The couple retires into the cave as the nymphs chant a hymn of rejoicing. Zerbinetta comes gaily from the wings and repeats her frivolous philosophy: "When a new god comes to woo us, captive are we, helpless, dumb!" Bacchus's rapturous apostrophe to love brings down the curtain.

DIE FRAU OHNE SCHATTEN had been in the minds of Hofmannsthal and Strauss as early as 1911, simultaneously with *Ariadne*. But the work on the latter and the advent of World War I postponed definitive action for six years. Hofmannsthal found himself unable to work steadily on this "terribly delicate, immensely difficult task." He got at it again in 1913, also writing the long short story of the same name, but did not complete the libretto until April 1915. The revision of *Ariadne* then occupied both men, so that Strauss did not finish composing the third act until September 1916, and the scoring took until the following June. Then they laid it aside until after the War. Vienna was chosen for the premiere because Strauss had been invited to become co-director with Franz Schalk, and assumed the post in May 1919.

Franz Schalk conducted the first performance, and in the cast were Maria Jeritza as the Empress; Lotte Lehmann as the Dyer's Wife, and Richard Mayr as Barak. Subsequent performances were in Dresden twelve days later and Berlin in 1920. The first hearing in the Western Hemisphere was in Buenos Aires in 1949. The distinction of a United States premiere fell to San Francisco in 1959, with Leopold Ludwig conducting and Edith Lang, Sebastian Feiersinger, Marianne Schech, Mino Yahia, and Irene Dalis in the cast. A repetition the following year brought Leonie Rysanek as the Empress, Ticho Parly as the Emperor, and Paul Schoeffler as Barak.

In 1964, the 100th anniversary of Strauss's birth, New York heard the work for the first time in a concert performance by Thomas Scherman's Little Orchestra. The Metropolitan at last mounted the work on 2 October 1966, four months after London heard it for the first time through the visit of the Hamburg Opera. As one of nine new productions to celebrate the first season in the new Lincoln Center house, the Metropolitan production was designed by Robert O'Hearn and directed by Nathaniel Merrill, an elaborate fantasy that called on all the resources of the new house. Karl Böhm conducted, and the cast included Rysanek (Empress), James King (Emperor), Dalia (Nurse), Walter Berry (Barak), and Christa Ludwig (Dyer's Wife). Covent Garden at last got its *Frau* premiere in 1967.

The opera is so complex, with its action on three levels—the spirit world, the human world, and the plane in which the Emperor and Empress move between them—and its philosophy of life expressed through so many symbols, that the libretto should be studied in advance of a hearing.

Only two characters possess proper names: Barak, the Dyer, and Keikobad, Ruler of the Spirit World.

That Barak is a Dyer is no accident; Hofmannsthal set great store by the symbolism of color. Keikobad was a real-life Turkish ruler, but Hofmannsthal thought of him as a successor to Sarastro. Another derivation from Mozart's *Die Zauberflöte* was the idea of the two couples who find their way to wisdom through trials.

All the other characters are known by their title, station, or attributes. Barak's Wife was inspired by Strauss's notoriously tactless wife. Hofmannsthal wrote the composer: "Your wife might well, in all discretion, be taken as a model. . .she (the Wife) is a bizarre woman with a very beautiful soul, *au fond*, strange, moody, domineering, and yet at the

National-Theater

München, Sonntag den 9. November 1919
Plätzmiete aufgehoben
Zum ersten Male:

Die Frau ohne Schatten

Abendkasse ab 4¾ Uhr Anfang **5** Uhr Ende gegen 9 Uhr

Program for the second performance of Strauss's Die Frau ohne Schatten in Dresden (detail).

Leonie Rysanek as The Empress.

same time likeable." Strauss, who loved his wife deeply in spite of her shortcomings, evidently ignored this, for the character remains shrewish at first. The others are all types: the Emperor, Empress, Nurse, Messenger, and so on.

Strauss's music emphasizes and distinguishes the three levels of the story. The differentiation is also emphasized by the use of a chamber orchestra for the spirits and a full orchestra for the humans. The Nurse is the liaison between the two worlds. The Prelude consists of three statements of Keikobad's sinister theme.

Before the opera, the Emperor of the Southeastern Isles, while hunting on the slopes of the "Moon Mountains," has watched his falcon attack a white gazelle. As the bird clawed at its victim, the animal disappeared and in its place stood the daughter of Keikobad. Although like her mother she was a peri and immortal, she shared her mother's strong attraction to the world of mankind. Her father had given her a talisman which had the power to transform her into any shape, thereby allowing her to go about among mankind unobserved.

The Emperor, dazzled by her beauty, drove the falcon from her with his knife. Wounded and bleeding, the bird snatched the talisman in his beak and flew off with it. The Emperor carried the Princess to his mountain-top palace and made her his wife and Empress.

According to certain Eastern mythologies, a man who marries a peri will turn to stone unless within twelve months she ceases to be a creature

338
STRAUSS

Costume design for the Empress and Emperor by Alfred Roller.

of light and becomes solid flesh, able to cast a shadow. The possession of this shadow is therefore the symbol of mortality and the ability to bear children.

Keikobad sent his daughter's Nurse to care for her, and this Nurse receives each month from him a spirit messenger to inquire whether her charge has been transformed into a mortal. The Nurse—a half-demonic creature—loathes all mankind, and longs to return to the spirit realm. As the opera begins, only three days remain of the year of the Empress's freedom.

ACT I, Scene 1. The Nurse prepares to greet Keikobad, but it is merely another Messenger who appears. He inquires if the Empress casts a shadow. "No," replies the Nurse, "light passes through her body as through the clearest crystal." The Empress seems to have no life except when she is with her husband; she exists only for the sexual aspect of human relationships. The Empress must get a shadow within three days.

The Emperor emerges from the bedchamber and informs the Nurse that he is going on a three-day hunting trip to the Moon Mountains to try to retrieve his sorely missed falcon. Charging the Nurse to guard his wife, he strides off.

The Empress enters and breaks into a dazzling *scena*, accompanied by an orchestra that suggests awakening nature. Suddenly the Falcon, its wing dripping blood, floats overhead, bearing in its beak the Empress's talisman, and intoning in a weird phrase, "Wherefore should I not weep? The woman casts no shadow; the Emperor must turn to stone." At last the Empress understands her dilemma. She implores the Nurse's help in finding a shadow. Although the Nurse is reluctant, she accompanies the Empress to the world of men; the only place her quest can succeed. A vivid interlude leads to:

Scene 2. In the hovel of Barak, his three deformed brothers—the One-Eyed, the One-Armed, and the HunThback—quarrel furiouso:

Scene 2. In the hovel of Barak, his three deformed brothers—the One-Eyed, the One-Armed, and the Hunchback—quarrel furiously. Barak's wife screeches at them to be silent and throws a pail of water on them. The Wife is a pretty woman, but shallow and selfish; her only thought is of personal comfort. She loathes Barak's brothers, and even dislikes her husband, a good and gentle man. Barak enters with a load of dyed clothes, and his wife turns angrily on him. He tries to calm her, and says that she will attain contentment when she fulfills her destiny as a woman by bearing him children. But she no longer wants children.

Barak gathers up a load of dyed materials and bears it off to market. As soon as he has left, the Wife is surprised to see two veiled women enter. It is the Empress and her Nurse. The former gazes with longing at the woman's shadow, while the Nurse flatters the bewildered Wife, and says that if she will accept their services for three days, and foreswear motherhood forever, she will be rewarded with riches beyond her dreams. To prove her point, she conjures up a vision of slaves and scantily clad, bejeweled dancing girls who deck the Wife in sumptuous raiment, while the voice of a beautiful youth praises her. Convinced of the strangers' powers, she consents to barter her shadow and fertility in exchange for earthly riches. The Nurse promises that she and the Empress

Die Frau ohne Schatten
(*The Woman Without a Shadow*)

Text by Hugo von Hofmannsthal.

THE EMPEROR	*Tenor*
THE EMPRESS	*Soprano*
NURSE	*Mezzo-Soprano*
SPIRIT MESSENGER	*Baritone*

339
STRAUSS

GUARDIAN OF THE THRESHOLD	*Soprano or Countertenor*
APPARITION OF A YOUTH	*Tenor*
VOICE OF THE FALCON	*Soprano*
VOICE FROM ABOVE	*Contralto*
BARAK, THE DYER	*Bass-Baritone*
HIS WIFE	*Soprano or Mezzo-Soprano*

BARAK'S BROTHERS:

THE ONE-EYED	*Bass*
THE ONE-ARMED	*Bass*
THE HUNCHBACK	*Tenor*

SIX CHILDREN'S VOICES	*3 Sopranos, 3 Contraltos*
VOICES OF NIGHT WATCHMEN	*3 Basses*
SERVANTS	*2 Sopranos, Mezzo-Soprano*

First Performance
Vienna, 10 October 1919.

Inside the Dyer's hut, scene from Die Frau ohne Schatten with (left to right) Marianne Schech, Irene Dalis, Mino Yahia, Raymond Manton, Lorenzo Alvary, Eugene Green, 1957, San Francisco Opera.

will return on the morrow to begin their servitude. They disappear, leaving the Wife bewildered. Suddenly, to her consternation, the voices of her unborn children are heard, begging to be let in from the cold and dark. Their wailing ceases when Barak enters. The Wife now insists that henceforth Barak must sleep alone, and flounces off to her bed. Barak muses that she is indeed a strange creature. Voices of Watchmen intone a hymn to conjugal love that is one of the most beautiful passages in the opera.

ACT II, Scene 1. In the Dyer's hut the next day, the Nurse and the Empress have begun their servitude. Seeking to further tempt the Dyer's Wife, the Nurse conjures up the image of a Youth. As the Wife is about to succumb to his embraces, Barak is heard returning, and the Nurse dismisses the phantom. Barak and the three Brothers enter, surrounded by a crowd of beggar children. The Dyer has sold his goods and bought food and drink, which he intends to share with his poor neighbors. He kindly offers the Empress food, but when he approaches his wife with sweetmeats, she dashes the plate from his hand and bewails the fact that she must suffer contact with beggars and other rabble. The Empress, however, is deeply touched. This scene is characterized by intricate ensemble writing, with a folklike theme sung by the crowd as they rejoice with Barak over his good fortune.

Scene 2 takes place in a deep forest outside the Emperor's falcon lodge. The orchestral interlude has sounded the harsh theme of the falcon, which has returned to the Emperor and led him to the place where his wife had informed him by messenger that she would spend the three days of his hunting trip. He is aghast to find it empty. Believing that his wife has deceived him, the Emperor vows to kill her, but can not bring himself to the deed.

Scene 3, again the interior of Barak's hut, finds the Dyer working while the Wife nags him and the Nurse is impatient to get on with her plot. She gives Barak a sleeping potion, and when he succumbs, tempts the Wife again with a young lover. Still resentful of interference, the Wife resolves to go out on her own, and the Nurse is forced to dematerialize the phantom. On awakening, Barak sees his tools scattered and broken, and is further devastated when his Wife goes out with the Nurse, leaving the Empress to help restore order. This acquisition of human sympathy is bringing her closer to deserving a shadow.

An interlude enlarges on the themes of the Empress's conscience, and her attitudes toward the conniving Nurse, the Emperor as lover, and the knowledge of his fate. As the curtain rises on:

Scene 4, the Empress rises from her bed in the Falcon House, disturbed by a nightmare in which she realizes her sin against Barak in seeking his Wife's shadow. The wall of the room becomes transparent to reveal a great cave with a bronze door at one side. The Falcon cries, and the Emperor approaches the door, pauses, and knocks. Voices from behind the door are bidding him draw near to the water of life, to the brink of death. The Falcon intones the warning on the talisman: "The woman casts no shadow, the Emperor must turn to stone!" The door opens to the Emperor and closes behind him. The Empress rises from her dream and wishes that she might endure her husband's trial in his place.

Ingrid Bjoner as the Empress.

341
STRAUSS

The Empress (Ingrid Bjoner, r.) and her nurse (Martha Mödl, c.) plot to take the shadow from the Dyer's wife (Inga Borkh, l.), Bayerische Staatsoper, Munich.

The Empress rises from her bed in the Falcon House, Ingrid Bjoner as the Empress, Martha Mödl as the nurse, Bayerische Staatsoper, Munich.

The interlude carries on the nightmare themes, dominated by Keikobad's motif.

Scene 5 returns us to Barak's hut. The emotions of all characters are revealed in a splendid ensemble: Barak bewildered; his Wife on the verge of hysterical outburst; the Brothers ignorantly terrified; the Nurse worried over supernatural manifestations that seem superior to her own; and the Empress's anxiety mixed with appreciation of Barak's fine character. At last, the Wife blazes out at Barak that she will now foreswear motherhood. The Nurse, who has been waiting for this climax, urges the Empress to steal the shadow, for at Barak's order, a huge fire is built up, revealing that his Wife is shadowless. But the Empress protests that she does not want the Shadow at such a price. There is blood on it, she cries, for Barak is threatening to kill his wife. A sword leaps magically to his hand. But the Wife repents: she says she has not yet sold her Shadow, although she is willing to die for having contemplated it. The earth opens and swallows up the Dyer and his wife, and the hut is submerged in raging waters, as the Brothers rush out, and the Nurse and the Empress escape in a little boat providentially provided. The orchestra rages to a cataclysmic conclusion. Higher powers, as the Nurse remarks, have taken over.

ACT III, Scene 1. An underground vault is divided by a thick
wall, with Barak seated on one side and his Wife on the other,
neither knowing of the other's presence. The introductory music is solemn, reminding us of the unholy bargain the Empress would have
made. Then the motif of the unborn children drives the Wife to distraction. Barak's voice joins hers as he sings of his love for her, and then as
she falls silent, he goes on with his beautiful melody alone.

A voice mysteriously bids Barak climb a magic stairway which suddenly appears. The Wife is also bidden to climb.

The scene changes to a rocky terrace over a river, with steps leading
up to a bronze door, where Keikobad's Messenger is waiting with attendant spirits. The boat with the Nurse and the Empress is moored at the
foot of the steps.

The Empress remembers the stairway and the bronze door from her
dream, and knows that her father is sitting in judgment over her husband and that she must share his fate. She is committed to human morality and to her own trial. She dismisses the Nurse angrily, realizing at
last that the woman has tricked her all along for her own selfish interest.
The bronze doors open and the Empress goes within.

The Nurse is left to renew her curses on mankind, and is able to take
out some of her spite on Barak and his Wife, urging each to revenge on
the other. Then she calls on Keikobad for help for her mistress. But it is
the Messenger who appears, implacably cold. He peremptorily orders
her away, as a fierce storm breaks out. Their voices are joined in a wild
ensemble by those of Barak and his Wife. Then the music comes to a
halt and the Messenger pronounces the Nurse's appropriate doom: she
is to wander endlessly through the realm of man, hateful. The storm
breaks out once more in the orchestra, the already large orchestra aug-
mented by a wind machine, a thunder machine, and assorted loud percussion. The voices of Barak and his Wife at last are heard. Spirits behind the scenes counsel them to courage and reverence.

Scene 3, the interior of the Temple, with a curtained niche in the
center. The Empress stands before the niche, calling on her father to
mete out her proper punishment for having returned without a shadow.
A fountain of golden water (mortal life) springs up. The Guardian of
the Threshold appears, urging her to drink, but Barak and the Wife are
heard calling to each other, and the Empress recoils, exclaiming that
there is blood in this water, and she will not drink. The fountain subsides, as the Empress calls on Keikobad to appear and judge her. The
niche brightens, and to the Empress's horror, the figure of the Emperor
is revealed, seated on a throne, frozen except for his eyes.

The Guardian of the Threshold repeats the tempting offer of the
shadow, but the plight of Barak and his Wife haunts the Empress, who
has almost collapsed, but she manages to utter: "I will *not!*" and the
fountain sinks down forever.

The music becomes unearthly, with high violins, and shimmering
tones from the glass harmonica, as a light begins to grow and spread,
bathing the Empress in radiance. From her feet a shadow springs. The
Emperor rises from the throne, and sings an exalted passage proclaiming that the prophecy made to him when he was in death's grip has been

*Dietrich Fischer-Dieskau as Barak the
Dyer surrounded by beggar children.*

*Costume design for the Guardian
of the Threshold by Alfred
Roller.*

Final scene of Die Frau ohne Schatten with Leonie Rysanek, Walter Berry, James King and Christa Ludwig.

Blanche Thebom as Adelaide from the Metropolitan Opera premiere of Strauss's Arabella, 1955, New York.

fulfilled; the voices of the Unborn Children chime in. The Emperor tells of their identity and meaning. They will make love fruitful. The curtain falls on the jubilant scene, and in the interlude we hear not only the motifs of the reunited couple, but also those of Barak and his Wife, whose fate must yet be resolved.

Scene 4, a landscape of great beauty and tranquility, with the golden fountain turned to a waterfall, above which the royal couple stands. Mysterious beings guide the Dyer and his Wife to a bridge at mid-level. The woman is still fearful, but as a shadow springs to her feet, and her husband approaches with love and humility, she accepts her fate with gratitude and joy. The climax is a great ensemble, built up in the orchestra to grand heights, with the four principals joined by a chorus of Unborn Children, actual children's voices and solo sopranos.

THE PREMIERE OF *Arabella* was conducted by Clemens Krauss; in the cast were Viorica Ursuleac and Margit Bokor as the sisters; Frederick Plaschke and Camilla Kallab as their parents; and Alfred Jerger as Mandryka. Strauss had wanted Fritz Busch, but the conductor had been forced to flee at the advent of the Nazis in March. In protest, Strauss withdrew the score, but eventually allowed the July premiere.

A half-dozen cities picked the opera up soon after, but *Arabella* came late to the Metropolitan, on February 10, 1955, with Eleanor Steber in the title role, and a cast including Blanche Thebom, Hilde Gueden, Walter Herbert, George London, Brian Sullivan, and Roberta Peters. Rudolf Kempe conducted. Later performances found Lisa Della Casa as Arabella—she had starred in the role in Europe. The Met has heard the opera in English only, with a translation by John Gutman.

Hofmannsthal was to do no more librettos for Strauss. The poet found his inspiration for *Arabella* in a carnival of Vienna cabbies, where the mascot was a tavern singer known as Fiakermilli. He also consulted one of his short stories, *Lucidor,* from which he derived the ideas and characters of this opera. Hofmannsthal died of a stroke on July 15, 1929, just before the funeral of his son Franz, who had committed suicide two days previously. The librettist never saw the telegram of congratulation sent him by Strauss, who was very pleased with the words for Arabella's aria at the end of the first act.

Strauss felt the death of his partner very keenly, and suspended work on *Arabella* for a while, working on an adaptation of Mozart's *Idomeneo* and seeking a new librettist in the person of Stefan Zweig. Some gaps remained in Hofmannsthal's work, but Strauss left them, notably two ensembles that were never finished.

Hofmannsthal derided the opinions that professed to find *Arabella* a copy of *Der Rosenkavalier,* although they persisted.

ACT I.   In a richly furnished salon, the Waldner family is uneasily contemplating the future. The Count is a gambler, and has lost heavily. The only hope for redeeming the family status is seemingly to marry off the eldest daughter, Arabella, to a rich suitor. To this end, the younger sister, Zdenka, has been forced to wear boy's clothing and been brought up as a boy. She is not in the least resentful, but worships Arabella. This afternoon, the mother, Adelaide, has received a fortune teller, while Zdenka is fending off creditors. When the young girl is alone, Matteo arrives—a suitor for Arabella's hand, but passionately

Arabella

Text by Hugo von Hofmannsthal

COUNT WALDNER	*Bass*
ADELAIDE	*Mezzo-Soprano*
ARABELLA	*Soprano*
ZDENKA	*Soprano*
MANDRYKA	*Baritone*
MATTEO	*Tenor*
COUNT ELEMER	*Tenor*
COUNT DOMINIK	*Baritone*
COUNT LAMORAL	*Bass*
FIAKERMILLI	*Soprano*
FORTUNE TELLER	*Soprano*
A HUSSAR	*Speaker*

First Performance
Dresden, 1 July 1933

345
STRAUSS

The Cabman's Ball, scene from the premiere of Arabella with Viorica Ursuleac, Margit Bokor, and Alfred Jerger, 1933, Dresden.

Lisa Della Casa as Arabella with Anneliese Rothenberger as her sister Zdenka.

loved by Zdenka. Matteo is ready to commit suicide if Arabella will not notice him. He rushes off as Arabella enters. She has received presents from three suitors, but says she is not interested; the right man has yet to show up: "Aber der Richtige," and she will instantly recognize him. The two sisters sing a charming duet. Elemer, one of Arabella's suitors, comes to take her for a sleigh ride, and promises to return in a half hour. Arabella asks Zdenka if she has noticed the stranger who has passed below their window frequently — he goes by just at that moment, but does not look up.

Now the daughters leave as the parents return. The Count confesses that in his extremity he has written to an old friend, Mandryka, and sent a picture of Arabella, hoping to interest the rich and eccentric man. Just then, a stranger is announced — it is the man Arabella has seen. His name is also Mandryka; he is the nephew and heir of the Count's friend, and he is mad to marry Arabella. The Count can hardly believe his good fortune, but Mandryka makes good his promise by leaving a great deal of money as a pledge of his intentions.

Meanwhile, Matteo asks Zdenka when he will get the letter she has told him Arabella has written. She promises that he will receive it at the ball that night — the Fiakerball (the Fiaker was a two-horse cab). Then Arabella and Elemer leave for their sleigh ride.

ACT II.   At the ball, Arabella, very popular, leaves the throng and joins her mother to be introduced to Mandryka. She recognizes the stranger and is charmed by his proposal. They engage in a passionate duet, in which Mandryka tells her that in his country it is

Margit Bokor as Zdenka with Martin Kreuier as Matteo from the premiere of Arabella, 1933, Dresden.

Scene from the last act of Arabella; in the hotel lounge Arabella (Lisa Della Casa) and Man-dryka (Dietrich Fischer-Dieskau) declare their love, 1958, Salzburg Festival.

customary for an engaged girl to give her betrothed a glass of water as a sign of her purity and her acceptance. But Arabella is not willing just yet to give up her gaiety, and begs for an hour of dancing, during which the frisky Fiakermilli presents her with a bouquet, sings a lively polka, and tells her she has been chosen Queen of the Ball. Arabella distributes the flowers, and goes off to dance. Matteo does not learn of the engage-ment, and is excited at the letter Zdenka gives him, containing, she says, the key to Arabella's room. Mandryka overhears, and is stricken. But when he is handed a note from Arabella saying she has gone on to their hotel, he determines to confront her and leaves with her parents.

ACT III.   In the hotel lounge, Arabella enters in time to notice Matteo coming down the stairs. He is amazed to see her, for he believes he has just been with her. The misunderstanding is gradually cleared up, Arabella presents a glass of water to Mandryka, and Matteo realizes that Zdenka is the girl he has made love to — and now loves. A duet between Mandryka and Arabella closes the opera.

IGOR STRAVINSKY (Oranienbaum near St. Petersburg, 17 June 1882 — New York, 6 April 1971). We know Igor Stravinsky better for his ballets and his instrumental music than for his operas, although these latter are highly respected, and *The Rake's Progress* is considered a contemporary masterpiece. The ballets are frequently performed, notably by the New York City Ballet, for its director, George Balanchine, has long been a close friend and exponent of Stravinsky's work. *Petruchka* and *Fire Bird*, from his early years, have never been out of the repertoire, and although *Sacre du printemps* caused a scandal when it was first unveiled in Paris in 1913, it

Portrait of Stravinsky by Picasso.

too has gained respectability. *Les Noces, Apollo Musagetes, Pulcinella, Jeu de cartes, Orpheus,* and *Agon* have also attained the stature of classics. Stravinsky was stimulated to write several of these by his close and often stormy association with Sergei Diaghilev, the erratic genius who held monarchial sway over Le Ballet Russe in the early part of this century.

Stravinsky was destined to be a lawyer by the will of his father—a famous bass at the St. Petersburg Opera—who did not want his son to join his own profession. The young Stravinsky stood it until he was twenty-three, then broke free to follow his own bent. Rimsky-Korsakov exerted an early influence, but Stravinsky soon left the older composer far behind in his quest for individuality.

The majority of Stravinsky's short operas were written before the composer came to America in 1945, where he became a citizen and made his home. These operas are: *Le Rossignol* (The Nightingale—1914), a fairy tale based on the story of the bird who sang for the Chinese Emperor; *Mavra* (1922), a folk opera; *Oedipus Rex* (1927), called an "opera-oratorio," and given at the New York City Opera; and *Persephone* (1934), a melodrama with an important part for a narrator. *L'Histoire du soldat* (The History of

Stage design for a production of Stravinsky's ballet Firebird, the first performance of which brought Stravinsky acclaim as a composer.

Drawing by Jean Coc-
teau of Stravinsky in
rehearsal for his ballet
The Rites of Spring,
1913, Paris.

a Soldier) dates from 1918; a work which calls for acting and dancing and
is not genuinely operatic, although it is given by opera groups. Stravinsky
was a great favorite in Santa Fe, and conducted several of his works there
in what amounted to a festival.

A little work called *The Flood*, which enlisted song, ballet, drama and
oratorio, was based on a medieval play about Noah, and was broadcast
over a CBS network in 1962.

The Rake's Progress was inspired by Hogarth's engravings in the
Chicago Art Institute. Shortly after Stravinksy had finished it, he turned to
the twelve-tone system, which he had previously forsworn, and then
adopted what is called "neo-classicism."

ELISABETH SCHWARZKOPF was the first Anne Trulove; Jennie Tourel,
the Baba; Robert Rounseville, the Tom; Otakar Kraus, the Nick. Stravinsky
conducted. There were performances the same year (1951) in Zürich, Stuttgart, and Milan; in 1952, Vienna heard the opera and it was broadcast from
London. In 1953, Fritz Reiner, with Stravinsky looking over his shoulder,
conducted the work at the Metropolitan, with Hilde Gueden, Blanche
Thebom, Eugene Conley, and Mack Harrell as the principals. Santa Fe,
where Stravinsky was a favorite, has also performed it.

ACT I, Scene 1. Tom Rakewell is not acceptable to Trulove as a
suitor for his daughter, but Trulove offers him a job. Tom airily
says he has other prospects; Trulove is still dissatisfied. Left alone in
Trulove's garden, Tom determines not to be a slave all his life, and invokes Fortune. Nick Shadow appears (*à la* Mephistopheles), and with
Anne present, tells Tom he has inherited a fortune; the terms will be settled in a year and a day. Tom hastens off to London, while Nick confides to the audience: "The progress of a Rake begins."

Scene 2. In Mother Goose's brothel, the Roaring Boys and Whores
toast Venus and Mars. Tom is catechised by Mother Goose and answers
that pleasure is the goal. The question: "What is love?" brings a rebirth

The Rake's Progress

349
STRAVINSKY

Text by W.H. Auden
and Chester Kallman

TOM RAKEWELL	*Tenor*
TRULOVE	*Bass*
ANNE TRULOVE	*Soprano*
NICK SHADOW	*Baritone*
BABA, THE TURK	*Mezzo-Soprano*
MOTHER GOOSE	*Mezzo-Soprano*
SELLEM	*Tenor*
A KEEPER	*Bass*

First Performance
Venice, 11 September 1951

of conscience, but Nick intervenes, and Tom drinks wildly, singing a plea to love. Mother Goose claims him, while the company engages in a singing game.

ACT II, Scene 1. Tom is weary of the good life in his pleasant town house and begins a long scene: "Vary the song, O London!" Nick persuades him to marry the bearded Baba the Turk as a piquant change.'

Scene 2. Anne comes to Tom's house, and watches as servants take many packages indoors; a sedan chair is borne to the door, disgorging Tom. He urges Anne to return to the country. Now Baba pokes her head out from the chair and Tom is forced to acknowledge her as his wife. After a mournful trio, Anne departs, Tom helps Baba from the chair, and she takes off her veil, revealing the notorious beard to the gathering crowd.

Scene 3. Baba dominates Tom's household, never stopping her babbling talk, displaying dozens of possessions. At last, Tom cannot stand it any more, and claps a huge wig over his wife's head. His relief is shattered by Nick's arrival with a contraption that he boasts will make bread out of stones. Of course it is a fake. But Tom is gulled into believing that he can relieve suffering mankind with this miracle.

ACT III, Scene 1. Tom's house is now in complete disarray, musty and thick with cobwebs. Baba is still sitting at the table with the wig over her head. A crowd of citizens is picking over objects to be auctioned. When Anne enters and asks for Tom, they give her silly answers. She leaves to search for him. The auctioneer, Sellem, begins

Elisabeth Schwarzkopf was the first Anne Trulove.

350
STRAVINSKY

Poster for a 1962 production of Stravinksy's The Rake's Progress, Santa Fe Opera, by Randall Davey.

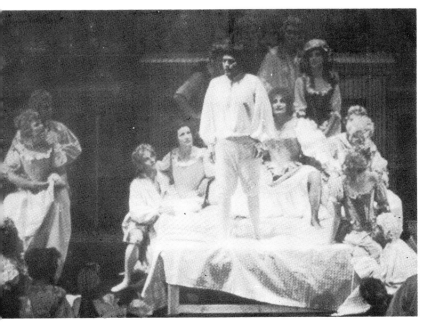

The brothel scene from Act II of The Rake's Progress, 1975, Glyndebourne Festival.

his spiel, and when he comes to Baba asks: "Is it a cake? An organ? Golden Apple Tree? A block of copal? Mint of alchemy? Oracle? Pillar? Octopus?"

When he snatches off the wig, Baba finishes the word she began when Tom cut her off—"...ever." Nick and Tom sing offstage, and Anne rushes in, recognizing Tom's voice. Baba kindly tells Anne that Tom still loves her, but to beware of his servant. As for herself, she will go back to the stage. After Anne goes out to find Tom, Baba tells the crowd that the next time they see her, they will pay.

Scene 2. Nick and Tom enter a graveyard, where there is a freshly dug grave. Nick tells Tom his year and a day are up, and he must pay with his soul. He has only to choose among a dagger, a rope, a gun, or poison, all of which Nick produces from a bag. Midnight is the final hour. At the stroke of eight, Tom prays to Heaven. Nick stops the clock and offers Tom a game—he shall guess three cards. Tom, with the help of Anne's voice from a distance, guesses all three correctly, and Nick falls senseless. But he still has the power to curse Tom, and condemns him to madness. When the lights come up, Tom is proclaiming himself Adonis, loved by Venus.

Scene 3. In Bedlam, Tom is madder than the ones who surround him. The keeper brings Anne to visit, and, prewarned, she addresses him as Adonis. Their reunion is touching, but Anne knows that Tom no longer needs her, and goes with her father when he comes to fetch her. However, Tom wakes to a terrible longing, and cries out for his lost Venus. The inmates deny that anyone has been there, and Tom falls dead, while the others mourn for "Adonis, ever young."

EPILOGUE. Before the curtain, with the house lights up, the principals point out a moral (Baba is without her beard, the men without wigs). The moral is: "Good or bad, all men are mad; all that they say or do is theater," and, "For idle hands and hearts and minds the Devil finds a work to do."

Robert Gard as Tom Rakewell and John Pringle as Nick Shadow, Australian Opera, Melbourne.

Peter Ilyich Tchaikovsky.

Tchaikovsky's patron Madame Von Meck.

PETER ILYICH TCHAIKOVSKY (Votinsky, 22 December 1840 – St. Petersburg, 6 November 1893). Like several other Russian composers, Tchaikovsky turned to music only after pursuing another career, that of jurisprudence. It was not until he was 21, after seeing a performance of *Don Giovanni,* that he determined to become a musician, entering a school headed by Anton Rubinstein. Although his father could not help him (his mother had died of cholera in 1855), the young man soon made his way, first getting a position at the Moscow Conservatory, where he lived with Nicholas Rubinstein and made the acquaintance of a young publisher, Jurgenson.

Before he produced *Eugene Onegin,* Tchaikovsky wrote four operas: *The Voyevode* (1869), after a play by Ostrovsky, later abandoned; *Undine,* written in the same year but destroyed by the composer; *The Oprichnik* (1874), a historical subject; and *Vacula the Smith* (1876), revised as *Tcherevichky* **(The Little Shoes) in 1887.**

Tchaikovsky felt such sympathy for Tatyana in Pushkin's poem that he immediately wrote the letter scene when he began to consider *Onegin* for an opera. Then, because he was so revolted at Onegin's heartlessness, he himself accepted a passionate avowal of love from a young student and married her in 1877 – an act characterized as "rash" by his brother Modest, who knew of Peter's problems – both men were homosexuals. The marriage was inevitably a disaster, and in his effort to escape from it, Tchaikovsky suffered increasingly bad health. The girl eventually ended up in an asylum, where she outlived her miserable husband by a quarter of a century.

In addition to Modest, a favorite sister, and a faithful servant to whom he bequeathed his country home, Tchaikovsky made one "Beloved Friend," the wealthy Nadezhda von Meck, with whom he carried on a fervent correspondence (they never met face-to-face) until three years before his death, when she inexplicably withdrew her support and stopped writing. This embittered his last years, and her name was on his lips when he died.

Pique Dame **(Queen of Spades) was produced in 1890. Before that, he** had written other operas, which are infrequently performed: *The Maid of Orleans* (1881), *Mazeppa* (1884), and *The Sorceress* (1887). *Iolanthe* (1892) has been occasionally revived.

ALTHOUGH the stage so greatly occupied his creative mind, Tchaikovsky is perhaps better known for his six symphonies, the Fourth, Fifth, and Sixth *[Pathétique]* being repertoire staples; his ballets, *Nutcracker, Swan Lake,* and *Sleeping Beauty;* the concertos and several orchestral pieces, as well as songs, piano pieces, and chamber music.

His visits to other lands brought great réclame, but the composer invariably suffered from homesickness and hurried home. He participated in the opening concert of Carnegie Hall in 1891, and gave concerts in Philadelphia and Baltimore. In 1893, he visited London, then returned to his country place and in October went to St. Petersburg for rehearsals of his Sixth Symphony. On the first of November, he drank unboiled water and immediately contracted cholera, from which he died five days later.

THE POET Alexander Pushkin was a natural choice by Tchaikovsky for two opera librettos, *Onegin* and *Queen of Spades.* Idolized in Russia, he wrote with such dramatic passion that the stage inevitably took over –

Drawing of a scene from the first production of Tchaikovsky's ballet Swan Lake, 1877, Moscow.

almost three dozen of his works have been set by numerous composers, most of them Russian, to be sure. Also prominent among these latter are Mussorgsky, Glinka, Stravinsky, Rimsky-Korsakov, Dargomizhsky, and Rachmaninov. Only Tchaikovsky seems to have tackled *Onegin*, and even he was criticized at first, so reverently did his fellow countrymen regard Pushkin's long narrative poem. Tchaikovsky concentrated on the emotional content and the behavior of its chief characters, and ignored the social comment and cynical overview which the poet had made central in the story. He could have reasoned, in omitting several scenes crucial to the understanding of Tatyana's later demeanor, that the audience could supply the missing action and motivation without conscious thought. (One of these omissions concerned a visit by Tatyana to Onegin's library while he was away, and her realization of his character from the books he had read and the passages marked in them.)

Prague picked up the opera in 1888, Hamburg in 1892, with Gustav Mahler conducting. That same year, London heard it in English, and Covent Garden produced it in 1906, with Destinn, Kirkby-Lunn, Battistini, and Journet, Campanini conducting. Two years later New York heard a concert performance, but the Metropolitan did not give it stage space until 1920, when Claudia Muzio, Giuseppe De Luca, and Giovanni Martinelli sang it in Italian. English was the language for the 1957 production with Lucine Amara, George London, and Richard Tucker.

Subsequent revivals (the latest sung in Russian, perhaps to challenge the Bolshoi Opera's stunning production during its recent New York visit) have brought several charming Tatyanas: Leontyne Price, Makvala Karashvili, Raina Kabaivanska, and Teresa Zylis-Gara. Sherrill Milnes was an imposing Onegin, Yuri Mazurov of the Bolshoi an impassive one; Michael Devlin sang the role in Santa Fe. Nicolai Gedda has been one of the most admired Lenskys.

Eugene Onegin

Text by the composer and
Konstantin Shilovsky after
Pushkin's poem

MADAME LARINA	*Mezzo-Soprano*
TATYANA	*Soprano*
OLGA	*Contralto*
EUGENE ONEGIN	*Baritone*
LENSKY	*Tenor*
FILIPIEVNA	*Mezzo-Soprano*
TRIQUET	*Tenor*
PRINCE GREMIN	*Bass*
ZARETSKY	*Bass*
CAPTAIN	*Bass*
GILLOT	*Mute*

First Performance
Moscow Conservatory, 29 March 1879
Professional: Moscow, 23 January 1881

Because of his reluctance to offend Pushkin partisans, Tchaikovsky called *Onegin* "lyrical scenes in three acts." Whatever its designation, the work has a powerful appeal, its score a never-ending web of communicative sound, its action the result of proud and passionate characters.

ACT I, Scene 1. A prelude introduces a theme that will always be associated with Tatyana. In Madame Larina's country home, the voices of the two sisters, Olga and Tatyana, are heard singing a romantic duet, while Larina reminisces upon her own girlhood; she has been forced to make a loveless marriage of convenience, but has made the best of it. Peasants approach, and sing of their joy at the end of a day's work. The girls appear, and it is at once evident that Tatyana is a dreamy romantic, while Olga is practical and worldly. Lensky, a poet and Olga's fiancé, brings his friend Eugene Onegin, whose uncle has left him a country estate nearby.

Tatyana is immediately smitten, while Onegin remains curious but coolly polite. After a brief quartet, Lensky and Olga go off for a walk, and Onegin, conversing with Tatyana, reveals his bored and cynical outlook on life.

Scene 2. In her room, Tatyana confesses to Filipievna that she has fallen in love, and bids her bring writing materials. Then she begins to

Act I, Scene 2 from Eugene Onegin, Tatyana (Patricia Wells, standing) tells the servant Filipievna (Batyah Godfrey) of her love for Onegin, 1978, Santa Fe Opera.

The Duel scene from Eugene Onegin with Anton Dermota (l.) as Lensky and George London (r.) as Onegin.

compose a declaration of love to Onegin, in the famous letter scene. Between her hesitations, day-dreaming, and uncompleted attempts, she has barely finished the letter by dawn, when the nurse finds her still awake. Feverishly the girl tells Filipievna to deliver the note secretly to Onegin, and gazes out at the rising sun, fearing and hoping for an answer to her impassioned plea for love and understanding.

Scene 3. In the garden, girls are picking berries and singing a charming song. Tatyana enters as they leave, and watches Onegin approach. In words that could not be better chosen to wound her sensibilities, he tells her that he honors her sincerity, but that he cannot feel anything for her except the affection of a brother. He caps this arrogant declaration by advising her to show more self-control. Tatyana is stunned, and picks up the letter from the bench where he has contemptuously placed it.

ACT II, Scene 1. Tatyana's birthday is being celebrated at a country ball, to which Lensky brings the bored Onegin. After one dance with Tatyana, Onegin cannot abide the gossip he hears all around him, and determines to make some mischief. He flirts with Olga, who seems to respond, thereby arousing Lensky's fierce jealousy. Matters are calmed down for a few moments while the Frenchman Triquet sings a little couplet in honor of Tatyana, but soon there is no turning back — Lensky challenges Onegin to a duel. The scene ends with a big ensemble in which Lensky repents but does not forgive Onegin; Onegin is brought to his senses and regrets the whole prank; the girls and the company mourn the turn of events.

Scene 2. In a bleak winter landscape at sunrise, Zaretsky, Lensky's second, complains that Onegin is late. Lensky meditates on his love for Olga in the one extended aria in the opera. Onegin finally appears with his second. The two principals sing together, each wishing that the duel need not take place, but it is inevitable. **Onegin** kills Lensky.

Scene from the ball in Act II of Eugene Onegin, 1957, New York.

Giuseppe De Luca as Onegin with Claudia Muzio as Tatyana in the last scene of Eugene Onegin, 1920-21, Metropolitan Opera, New York.

ACT III, Scene 1. Tatyana has married a rich Prince, and is an admired hostess in St. Petersburg. At a great ball, Onegin seeks out his former friend, Prince Gremin, only to discover that the Prince's glamorous wife is the Tatyana he once spurned. The Prince sings warmly of his love for Tatyana. She greets Onegin coolly, although it is evident that his presence has stirred her. He bursts out into a stormy realization that he loves this woman who is so different from the bashful girl he had dismissed so cruelly.

Scene 2. Tatyana has received a letter from Onegin, and is deeply troubled. When he arrives in her boudoir, she at first repulses him coldly, but eventually breaks down and admits that she still loves him. However, her sense of honor and her affection for her husband will not permit her to go away with him, as he wildly pleads. She tears herself from his embrace and rushes out, leaving him to bewail his fate in Tatyana's own music — condemned to wander forever without love.

MAHLER conducted the first performance of *Pique Dame* at the Metropolitan (in German) in 1910 with Destinn, Slezak, Forsell, and Meitschik. La Scala had heard it in Italian in 1906, but it did not reach London until 1915, when it was sung in Russian. Russian was also undertaken by the cast for Thomas Scherman's Concert Opera performance in New York in 1965, when Jennie Tourel was the Countess. The Met resorted to English in 1966, with Felicia Weathers, Jean Madeira, and James McCracken in leading roles, but tried Russian in 1972, with Teresa Kubiak, Regina Resnik, and Nicolai Gedda, under a Polish conductor, Kazimierz Kord. Elaine Bonazzi made a deep impression as the Countess in an Opera Society of Washington performance in 1961; the legendary Magda Olivero did wonders with the characterization at the Spoleto Festival of 1976.

ACT I, Scene 1. On a spring day in the court of St. Petersburg's Summer Garden, children are at play, nurses and governesses gossiping. Herman, a young officer, is teased by his friends Tchekalinsky, Sourin, and Tomsky for his melancholy. He confesses that he is in love with a girl of high station whom he has never met. Prince Yeletsky enters, announcing his betrothal to Lisa, who soon appears, in company with her crochety grandmother, the old Countess. Herman, distraught at the discovery of his beloved's betrothal to another, is distracted by Tomsky's tale of the Countess's past — she had been a great belle in Paris, known as the Muscovite Venus, and is said to have sold herself to the Count St. Germain for the secret of three cards that would inevitably win at faro. She later told the secret to her husband and to a young lover; then a ghost appeared and warned her that if she told a third impassioned man, she would die. Both Lisa and the Countess regard Herman with foreboding — he seems to follow them wherever they go. Left alone, Herman vows to win both Lisa and the secret of the three cards.

Scene 2. In Lisa's room, Lisa and Pauline entertain their friends with songs and duets. As the merriment grows, the Countess enters, reprimanding them for being "too Russian." Later, in solitude, Lisa is troubled by her attraction toward the stranger who regularly stands below her balcony. Suddenly Herman appears before her, avowing his love. He hides as the Countess appears, then tells Lisa he will die without her love. She bids him live.

ACT II, Scene 1. At a masked ball in Prince Yeletsky's palace, Lisa too obviously shows her melancholy, and the Prince questions her. Then a pastoral entertainment is announced. Chloe, a shepherdess, plights her troth to Daphne, a shepherd, despite the gifts offered by the wealthy Plutus. Herman meets Lisa surreptitiously, by now obsessed with the idea of the three cards. She gives him the key to her room and asks him to come there after the ball. The scene ends with the surprise entrance of the Empress, Catherine the Great.

Scene 2. Herman finds his way to the Countess's boudoir, where he hides as Lisa and the Countess return from the ball. Lisa retires, and the Countess, after being prepared for the night by her maids, sings an old French air, and falls asleep. Herman awakens her, pleading for the secret of the three cards. When she does not answer, being speechless with

Pique Dame
(*The Queen of Spades*)

Text by Modest Tchaikovsky and the composer, after Pushkin

LISA	*Soprano*
COUNTESS	*Mezzo-Soprano*
HERMAN	*Tenor*
COUNT TOMSKY	*Baritone*
PRINCE YELETSKY	*Bass*

357
TCHAIKOVSKY

PAULINE	*Mezzo-Soprano*
GOVERNESS	*Mezzo-Soprano*
MASCHA	*Soprano*
TCHEKALINSKY	*Tenor*
SOURIN	*Bass*
TCHAPLITSKY	*Tenor*
NARUMOV	*Bass*
MASTER OF CEREMONIES	*Tenor*

CHARACTERS IN THE PLAY:

CHLOE	*Soprano*
DAPHNIS (PAULINE)	
PLUTUS (TOMSKY)	

First Performance
St. Petersburg, 19 December 1890

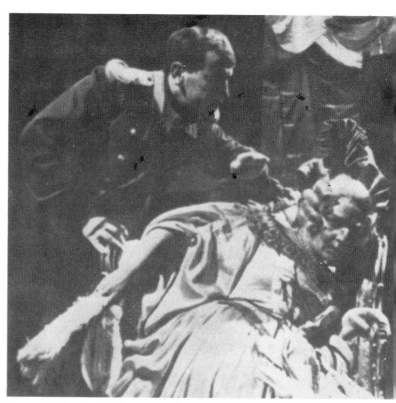

Herman frightening the Countess to death in Act II of Tchaikovsky's The Queen of Spades, 1935 Meyerhold production, Maly Theater, Leningrad.

fear, he threatens her with a pistol. Her heart fails, and she dies. Lisa enters, and realizing that Herman is responsible, accuses him of murder and insists that he leave her forever.

ACT III, Scene 1. Herman, in his room in the officers' quarters, reads a letter from Lisa, saying that she realizes he did not mean to kill her grandmother, and asking him to meet her that night by the quay on the River Neva. Herman recalls the funeral of the Countess, when he thought that the corpse smiled and winked at him. In terror, he quails now before the apparition of the Countess, who tells him the three cards: three, seven, ace.

Scene 2. Lisa waits for Herman on the quay, but when midnight strikes, she fears he will not come. However, he does appear, breathless and hurried — they will go away, he says, but he must first go to the gaming room. The three cards have become his only reality. Lisa, in despair, throws herself into the Neva.

Scene 3. The gambling house. A scene of revelry, with Tomsky singing a drunken song. Prince Yeletsky enters, vowing vengeance on Herman, who now arrives, and to everyone's surprise, joins the game. He wins on the first two cards, three and seven. But the third, on which he stakes everything, turns out to be the Queen of Spades, the nickname of the old Countess, whose ghost once more appears to Herman. With nothing left, the unfortunate man stabs himself, and, dying, begs forgiveness of Prince Yeletsky and calls Lisa's name.

Adamo Didur as Count Tomsky in the Queen of Spades.

AMBROISE THOMAS (Metz, 3 August, 1811 — Paris, 12 February 1896). Said to have learned his notes with his alphabet, Thomas showed musical traits very early and won a constant stream of prizes. As early as 1837, he began a string of works for the Opéra-Comique, then graduated to the Opéra, where he brought out more than a dozen works, including his most famous, *Mignon*, in 1866. *Hamlet* followed two years later. It is because of these two operas that Thomas is known at all today, but it has been suggested that a richer vein of his dramatic talent lies hidden.

CÉLESTINE GALLI-MARIÉ scored a triumph at the premiere of *Mignon*, and a thousand performances were racked up within Thomas's lifetime. He wrote recitatives to replace the spoken dialogue for the London premiere in 1870, when Christine Nilsson sang. New Orleans had the American premiere in 1871. Nilsson was also the Mignon in the Metropolitan's first season, 1883-84. More recent favorites have been Jennie Tourel and Risë Stevens.

The opera is more notable for several high spots than for continued interest. Philine's Polonaise, "Je suis Titania," always brings down the house, and Mignon's plaintive "Connais-tu le pays?" brings out the handkerchiefs.

Ambroise Thomas.

Mignon

359
THOMAS

Text by Michel Carré and
Jules Barbier based on
Goethe's "Wilhelm Meister"

MIGNON	*Mezzo-Soprano or Soprano*
PHILINE	*Soprano*
WILHELM MEISTER	*Tenor*
LOTHARIO	*Bass*
FREDERIC	*Tenor or Contralto*
LAERTE	*Tenor*
GIARNO	Bass

First Performance
Paris, 17 November 1866

*Jennie Tourel as
Mignon with Charles
Kullman as Wilhelm.*

Luisa Tetrazzini as Philine in Thomas's Mignon.

THOMAS

Hamlet

Text by Michel Carré and
Jules Barbier after Shakespeare

HAMLET	*Baritone*
CLAUDIUS	*Bass*
OPHELIA	*Soprano*
GERTRUDE	*Mezzo-Soprano*
LAERTES	*Tenor*
HORATIO	*Bass*
POLONIUS	*Bass*
MARCELLUS	*Tenor*
GHOST	*Bass*
TWO GRAVEDIGGERS	*Baritone, Tenor*

PANTOMIME: PLAYER KING, PLAYER QUEEN,
PLAYER VILLAIN, PAGES

First Performance
Paris, 9 March 1868

The story concerns a girl of noble birth who has been kidnapped by gypsies, and is abused by their leader, Giarno. Her father, Lothario, has become a wandering minstrel, ever searching for her. Lothario, with the help of a young student, Wilhelm Meister, rescues her. She becomes passionately fond of Wilhelm, but he has eyes only for Philine, the giddy young actess who with her partner Laerte is to perform in Frédéric's castle. The girl remains dressed in boy's clothing and watches Wilhelm's courtship with growing anger until at last she wishes Philine would be burned alive. Lothario takes her at her word and fires the building where Philine is playing, but it is Mignon who is trapped. Wilhelm saves her and takes her to an Italian castle which he intends to buy. Lothario recovers his memory — it is his castle. Mignon and Wilhelm are happily united.

THOMAS originally intended Hamlet to be a tenor, but none being available, he chose Faure, the eminent baritone, and rewrote the role. The American premiere was in Italian at the Academy of Music, New York, on March 22, 1872. The Metropolitan produced it in French in 1892 with Jean Lassalle as the hero and Edouard de Reszke as Claudius. It was heard for a few seasons afterward and then dropped. In San Diego, Tito Capobianco revived the opera in 1978, with Ashley Putnam and Sherrill Milnes, in an English translation by Andrew Porter. The same production is listed in the New York City Opera repertoire.

THE LIBRETTISTS follow Shakespeare on general lines, with one rather horrendous departure, the insertion of a happy ending: Hamlet does not die but is crowned King. When the opera played in Covent Garden in 1869, the English insisted on reverting to the original tragedy, and Thomas had to write music accordingly.

Hamlet broods bitterly at the festivities marking the crowning of his mother after her marriage to his uncle Claudius, who has murdered Hamlet's father. Nevertheless, Hamlet assures Ophelia, daughter of Polonius, of his love. Her brother Laertes announces his departure on a mission for the King. Horatio and Marcellus tell Hamlet of the ghost they have seen. This ghost, of Hamlet's father, reveals his murder and urges his son to take revenge. Hamlet, preoccupied, shuns Ophelia, who asks permission to leave the court. The King is convinced Hamlet is mad. When a troupe of players arrives, Hamlet coaches them in a scene that shall bring his uncle to light as a murderer, and leads them in a Bacchic drinking song. When the court ignores the message of the play, Hamlet ponders his future in an abridged version of the famous soliloquy. Suspecting Polonius of complicity, he vents his anger on Ophelia, and on Queen Gertrude. The Queen is spared by the intervention of the Ghost, who chides Hamlet for his lassitude. The distraught Ophelia wanders among the guests at a *fête champêtre* and walks into the lake. Hamlet muses near a grave; his questions to the philosophical gravediggers are interrupted by Laertes, who engages Hamlet in a duel. A funeral cortege enters — it is Ophelia's. Hamlet kills the King, then stabs himself (Covent Garden ending).

VIRGIL THOMSON (Kansas City, Mo., 25 November 1896 –). One of America's most popular, and still controversial figures, Thomson was greatly influenced by periods of residence in Paris, where he encountered many of the great ones of the period. His close acquaintance with the writer Gertrude Stein produced the librettos for his two operas, which have come to be considered American classics. Wit and erudition spiced his reviews for the New York *Herald-Tribune* during several years, and he has been in demand for lectures. His ballet, *Filling Station,* and his multitude of works in all forms are consistently before the public.

Four Saints in Three Acts (really in four acts) was first heard in concert form in Ann Arbor, Mich. in 1933, then staged in Hartford on February 8, 1934 by the Society of Friends and Enemies of Modern Music. Alexander Smallens conducted, Frederick Ashton directed, and the costumes were by Florine Stetheimer. The cast was entirely black, and became notable when the opera moved to Broadway later in February, causing a sensation because of its utter freshness and beguiling surrealism. The setting is 16th-century Spain, and the acts were described by Stein: "A narrative of prepare for Saints. Act I: Avila: St. Theresa half indoors and half out of doors. Act II: Might it be mountains if it were not Barcelona. Act III: Barcelona: St. Ignatius and one of two literally. Act IV: The Sisters and Saints re-assembled and reenacting why they went away to stay."

The action is a series of highly stylized vignettes, most often with no concrete meaning, but nevertheless evocative. Fictional but typical incidents from the lives of St. Theresa and St. Ignatius Loyola are intertwined kaleidoscopically with imaginary doings of imaginary characters like St. Settlement and St. Chavez. There are also a Commère and Compère, who comment on the action.

361
THOMSON

Above and left: Two characters from a 1952 production of Virgil Thomson's Four Saints in Three Acts, ANTA Play Series, New York.

Giuseppe Verdi.

The Mother of Us All had its premiere in New York on May 7, 1947, and has since been performed in several centers, most recently in Santa Fe. Based on historical and imaginary characters, the Stein libretto centrally concerns the career of Susan B. Anthony, whose life is shown in private and public as she crusades for women's rights. Characters from a century of American history and from imagination are all treated as contemporaries in the 19th century.

GIUSEPPE VERDI (Le Roncole near Busseto, 10 October 1813 – Milan, 27 January 1901). Without doubt, Verdi is the most favored opera composer in the world. Oddly enough, his reputation rests on only about one-third of his entire output of twenty-six operas – *Rigoletto, La Traviata, Il Trovatore,* and *Aida,* with the more recent additions of *Un Ballo in maschera, La Forza del destino, Otello,* and *Falstaff.*

Lately joining this core, however, have been *Simon Boccanegra, Don Carlos, Luisa Miller, Ernani, Nabucco, Macbeth,* and *I Vespri Siciliani,* while the still more neglected operas are coming into their own in early-Verdi festivals and single performances. That there is indeed gold in these long-neglected mines is pointed out by several authorities, notably Charles Osborne and Julian Budden.

Verdi, born of poor parents, listened to church music, then acquired an old spinet and learned to play both it and the organ. He went to live in Busseto, where he was befriended by Antonio Barezzi, who made it possible for the young man to try for the Milan Conservatory. Although he was rejected, he stayed in Milan and studied conducting, once substituting as con-

Verdi's first wife Margherita Barezzi was the daughter of his patron Antonio Barezzi.

ductor for Haydn's *The Creation* with the Filodrammatico, which asked him for an opera. This work was possibly, after being modified by Solera, *Oberto, Conte di San Bonifacio*—which became Verdi's first work to be produced, on November 17, 1839. Verdi had just turned 26.

Already he had experienced sorrows. In 1836 he was married to Margherita Barezzi, daughter of his patron. She had borne him a son and a daughter. Both children died within a year and a quarter of each other, the boy just before the premiere of *Oberto*. Margherita was to die while he was working on his next commission, *Un Giorno di regno*. The impresario Bartolomeo Merelli insisted that he finish the work, but Verdi's health broke down and he was not to tackle another work in comic spirit until *Falstaff*, fifty years later.

Both his early operas were hindered by poor librettos—*Oberto's* by Piazza and *Giorno's* by Felice Romani, who had successfully collaborated many times with Rossini, Bellini, and Donizetti. Romani never again worked for Verdi. Instead, the next libretto was by Temistocle Solera, who had helped complete *Oberto*. Although he had vowed never again to write an opera, Verdi was excited by the story of Nebuchadnezzar, and was lured back to the stage. *Nabucco* was an instantaneous success, not only for its undoubted musical value, but also because the chorus which had attracted Verdi in the first place became the rallying point for patriotic Italians who longed for the unification of their country against the opposing Austrians and French. Italians identified themselves with this chorus, "Va pensiero," which proclaimed the suffering of the Jews under Babylonian rule, and Verdi thus became the symbol of the *Risorgimento* or liberation.

Nabucco marked another milestone in Verdi's career, for it was the first of his operas in which Giuseppina Strepponi starred. The prima donna was at the time Merelli's mistress, but she would later be Verdi's, and would eventually become his wife.

Twelve operas intervened between *Nabucco* in 1842 and *Rigoletto* in 1851—more than one per year. Verdi later referred to this decade as his "galley years." *I Lombardi alla prima crociata* (The Lombards at the First Crusade) came first, at La Scala, in 1843; it was later reworked as *Jérusalem* by Alphonse Royer and Gustav Vaëz from Solera's original for the Paris Opéra in 1847. Then came *Ernani*, at the Teatro Fenice in Venice in 1844, to a libretto by Francesco Maria Piave, based on a play by Hugo. Piave was also the librettist for *I due Foscari*, based on Byron's play, *The Two Foscari*, in 1844. (New York heard a rare performance of this opera in 1968 by the Rome Opera as part of the Lincoln Center Summer Festival.) In this gloomy but powerful work, Verdi made notable progress in the expressiveness of the orchestra.

Verdi and Solera returned to Milan for *Giovanna d'Arco*, based on Schiller's play about Joan of Arc. First heard in 1845, it is not often performed in America, but was given in San Diego in 1980.

If careful and appropriate productions are given them, most of the neglected works are viable. Among these are five of the next half dozen: *Alzira* (Naples, 1845) with libretto based on Voltaire by Salvatore Cammarano (later of *Trovatore* fame); *Attila* (Venice, 1846), libretto by Solera based on a play by Werner; *I masnadieri* (London, 1847, with Jenny Lind), libretto by Count Andrea Maffei, based on Schiller's play, *The Brigands* (due for

Antonio Barezzi helped the young Verdi further his studies.

Giuseppina Strepponi, Verdi's second wife.

Program from the La Scala production of Verdi's first opera, Oberto.

Australia with Joan Sutherland); *Il Corsaro* (Trieste, 1848), libretto by Piave, based on Byron's *The Corsair*; and *La battaglia di Legnano* (Rome, 1849), libretto by Cammarano, which received an ecstatic reception because of its patriotic fervor, but was soon censored. The sixth in this group was *Macbeth* (1847).

Between *Luisa Miller* (Naples, 1849) and *Rigoletto* (1851) came *Stiffelio*, with libretto by Piave, based on a French play. It was given in Trieste in 1850 and was rewritten by Piave as *Aroldo* for performance in Rimini in 1857.

From *Rigoletto* on, the road seems to us all upward, although many hollows existed for the composer in spirit. The man suffered while the creator forged ahead. In 1849, he took Giuseppina with him to Busseto and bought the Villa Sant' Agata nearby. The neighborhood was scandalized. But Verdi married her, and the couple would live there until Giuseppina's death. There may have been an affair with the prima donna Teresa Stolz; at least, friction occurred between the two women, and Stolz remained close to Verdi after his wife's death.

Verdi's modesty is well known, but under it he was fiercely proud of his own worth and integrity; and while he was all too quick to resent a supposed injury or slight, he was also too slow to forgive and forget — witness

Painting of La Scala by Inganni at the time of Verdi's early successes there.

the long disaffection with Boito. He cherished few illusions and possessed a dry wit. Attributed to him and often quoted by Giulio Gatti-Casazza, general manager of La Scala and the Metropolitan, was the remark: "The theater was intended to be full, not empty," indicating a seeming preoccupation with box-office receipts.

Verdi made the fortune of the Ricordi publishing firm while furthering his own. The composer was seldom absent from their catalogue after the publication of *Oberto*. He knew three generations of Ricordis—Giovanni, Giulio, and Tito.

Of the works not composed for the opera house, the *Requiem Mass* in honor of the hero Manzoni, performed in 1874, is well loved, possibly because it is distinctly operatic. Other sacred works are also important, particularly four pieces that were the last he wrote: the *Ave Maria*, *Stabat Mater*, *Laudi alla Vergine Maria*, and *Te Deum*. The *Inno delle nazioni* (Hymn of the Nations) with words by Boito is occasionally revived. There are also a string quartet and two collections of charming songs.

Of the operas that are lesser known, several have been omitted here.

NABUCCO, with Giuseppina Strepponi in the cast, was Verdi's first real success. It had some currency in Europe, and has been revived when the appropriate singers are found. New York heard it in 1848, but the Metropolitan did not pick it up until 1960, when Thomas Schippers conducted and Leonie Rysanek "made a brave attempt" at the fiendishly difficult part of Abigaille, the most imposing figure in the opera.

The opera takes place in pre-Biblical Jerusalem and Babylon. Zaccaria, a Hebrew prophet, brings Fenena, daughter of Nabucco (Nebuchadnezzar) to the Temple of Solomon as a prisoner. The Hebrews have been defeated by Nabucco. Fenena is put in the charge of Ismaele, the

Frontispiece for the published edition of Nabucco.

Nabucco

Text by Temistocle Solera.

ABIGAILLE	*Soprano*
FENENA	*Soprano*
ISMAELE	*Tenor*
NABUCCO	*Baritone*
ZACCARIA	*Bass*
HIGH PRIEST OF BABYLON	*Bass*
ABDALLO	*Tenor*
ANNA	*Soprano*

First Performance
Milan, 9 March 1842.

Leonie Rysanek as Abigaille.

Cornell MacNeil as Nabucco.

King's nephew, who is already in love with her; she has allowed him to escape from Babylon and now he proposes to do the same service for her. But her sister Abigaille, leading a band of Babylonians disguised as Hebrews, captures the Temple. Abigaille is smitten with Ismaele and offers him freedom if he will love her, but he refuses. Nabucco arrives and plunders the Temple, taking the Hebrews as prisoners to Babylon.

Abigaille discovers that she is not Nabucco's daughter after all, but a slave who has been adopted. Infuriated, she is out for revenge, and assumes the throne when it is rumored that Nabucco has been killed. Fenena frees the Hebrews and defies Abigaille, but Nabucco arrives and changes the picture. He proclaims himself God, orders the Hebrews killed, including Fenena. But he is dashed to the ground by a thunderbolt from Heaven, and Abigaille again takes command. Nabucco, however, is not finished; once more he makes his presence known, this time revealing Abigaille's lowly birth. She tears the proof into pieces and is for the moment triumphant. The Hebrews in chains sing of their homeland ("Va, pensiero," the famous chorus which so inflamed the suppressed Italians). Nabucco regains his sanity and is converted to the Hebrew faith, frees Fenena and Ismaele, and orders a new Temple built. Abigaille takes poison, and, on her deathbed, repents.

I Lombardi
(*The Lombards*)

Text by T. Solera.

ARVINO	*Tenor*
PAGANO	*Bass*
VICLINDA	*Soprano*
GISELDA	*Soprano*
PIRRO	*Bass*
PRIOR OF MILAN	*Tenor*
ACCIANO	*Bass*
ORONTE	*Tenor*
SOFIA	*Soprano*

First Performance
Milan, 11 February 1843.

THE FULL TITLE is *I Lombardi alla prima crociata* (The Lombards at the First Crusade). This was the first Verdi opera to be heard in New York, in 1847. It was given in London in 1846, then in Paris as *Jérusalem* in a revised version in 1847, and in Italian in Milan in 1950. There have been sporadic revivals, but America has heard very little of the opera to date, although a performance by the Opera Orchestra of New York under Eve Queler whetted the appetites of Verdi fans, and *I Lombardi* is on the regional circuit in several early-Verdi festivals.

The libretto is not the clearest; in fact, it is one of the most complicated in opera. Pagano, son of Folco and brother of Arvino in Milan, loses Viclinda to his brother and attempts to kill him, for which he is banished. But Pagano returns to Milan, seemingly penitent, then plots with his henchman Pirro to abduct Viclinda, after killing Arvino. Instead, he slays his father. Now he seeks absolution by becoming a hermit in a cave near Jerusalem.

Arvino embarks on the first crusade. In Antioch, King Acciano's wife Sofia attempts to console her son Oronte, who has fallen in love with Giselda (the daughter of Arvino), who has been captured by the Moslems. Pirro, who has also repented and joined his master Pagano, guides the Crusaders to victory. Giselda has repudiated her father for his cruelty, and wanders in the Valley of Jehoshaphat. She finds Oronte, who has been wounded, and they repair to a grotto for refuge.

Meanwhile, Arvino seeks the help of the hermit, not knowing his identity. Through a miracle, the fountain of Siloam flows, ensuring the victory of the Crusaders. Arvino forgives the fatally wounded hermit, his brother Pagano.

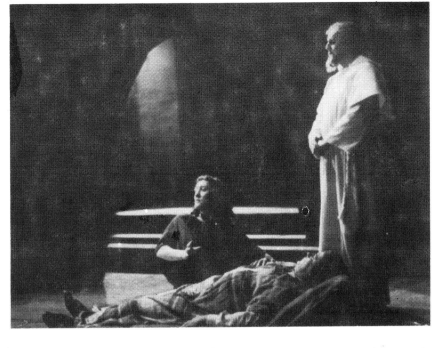

Oronte's death scene from *I Lombardi* with Chloë Owen as Giselda, Theodor Bitzos as Oronte, and Gottfried Fehr as the hermit.

LONDON HEARD *Ernani* the year after its premiere and it reached New York in 1847. The Metropolitan mounted it for Sembrich, De Marchi, Scotti, and Edouard de Reszke in 1903; it has been revived several times. The Metropolitan has brought it back with some regularity: in 1921 and 1928 for Ponselle, Martinelli, Danise or Ruffo, and Hines; in 1956 for Milanov, del Monaco, Warren, and Siepi; in 1962 and 1964 for Price, Corelli or Sergi, MacNeil, and Hines; and in 1970 for opening night, with Arroyo, Bergonzi, Milnes, and Raimondi. San Francisco heard *Ernani* in 1968.

Hugo's play *Hernani* was famous for Sarah Bernhardt's performance of the heroine, and Hugo objected bitterly when the opera was proposed for Paris; it had to appear under another title, *Il Proscritto* (The Proscribed). Italy exercised the all too usual censorship as well, so that the conspiracy scene had to be modified. But the opera holds the boards surprisingly well, its lively melodies and rousing ensembles more than compensating for its somewhat unbelievable plot. The soprano aria, "Ernani involami" (Ernani, fly with me!") is justly famous.

Don Ruy Gomez de Silva hopes to marry his ward Elvira, but she is also sought by two others: Ernani (in reality John of Aragon), her favorite, and Don Carlos, the King. The King saves Ernani on one occasion, but Elvira, believing her lover dead, consents to marry Silva. However, Ernani returns disguised as a monk, and Silva protects him by reason of the laws of hospitality. He hides Ernani from the King, who demands that he surrender his sword, and threatens to execute him. The King carries off Elvira as a hostage.

Ernani goes to rescue her, first giving Silva his hunting horn and promising to kill himself if Silva shall ever blow it. The King is proclaimed Emperor and forgives everybody. Ernani, whose land and titles have been restored, is about to marry Elvira when the horn is sounded.

Ernani

Text by Francesco Maria Piave after the play by Victor Hugo.

DON CARLOS	*Baritone*
DON RUY GOMEZ DE SILVA	*Bass*
ERNANI	*Tenor*
DON RICCARDO	*Tenor*
JAGO	*Bass*
ELVIRA	*Soprano*
GIOVANNA	SOPRANO

First Performance
Venice, 9 March 1844.

Scene from the first London production of Ernani in 1845 with Ernani and Elvira on the right. The principal singers shown are Botelli, Fornasari, Napolean Morian and Rita Borio.

True to his promise, Ernani stabs himself, and Silva gloats over his body and that of Elvira, prostrate upon the form of her lover. Revenge is complete.

Attila

Text by T. Solera.

ATTILA	*Bass*
ULDINO	*Tenor*
ODABELLA	*Soprano*
EZIO	*Baritone*
FORESTO	*Tenor*
POPE LEO I	*Bass*

First Performance
Venice, 17 March 1846.

LONG NEGLECTED since its American premiere in New York in 1850, *Attila* now shares in the restoration of interest in early Verdi operas. It was given in New Orleans in 1969 and Newark in 1972, and is on several major opera house calendars in the early '80s. London, Berlin, Buenos Aires, Edinburgh, and Florence have all sampled its showy arias.

Attila the Hun captures the Italian city of Aquileia and intends to make Odabella, daughter of the late ruler, his wife. The girl pretends to love the conqueror, thus leading her beloved Foresto to believe her faithless. She convinces him, however, that she is true. Ezio, envoy of the Roman Empire, tries to bargain with Attila for Italy's freedom, but the conqueror presses on until a warning vision stops him, and he declares a truce. He entertains the Romans in spite of another warning vision, and Ezio and Foresto poison his wine. Odabella prevents him from drinking, then persuades him to spare Foresto, who, however, again misunderstands her motives and leaves her. Neither Ezio nor Foresto believe in Odabella's loyalty until Attila discovers her in the company of Romans, when she stabs him.

SHAKESPEARE and Schiller exerted twin influences on Verdi, and although he set more plays by the latter, it was the Bard who dominated much of Verdi's thought and imagination. *King Lear* obsessed him throughout his active composing life, although he was never to complete it. And when, after the Paris premiere of the revised *Macbeth*, a critic accused him of not knowing his poet, he reacted in fury. "It may be that I have not done justice to *Macbeth*, but to say that I do not know, understand, and feel Shakespeare—no, by God, no! He is one of my very special poets!"

When he accepted a commission from the opera in Florence for a work to be done in the Carnival season of 1847, and chose *Macbeth* (which he deemed "one of the greatest creations of man"), he sent a complete synopsis to Piave. Many were his suggestions and criticisms, some of them quite cutting, before the libretto was finished to his satisfaction. Entirely true to the play it is not, for Verdi dwelt more concentratedly on Lady Macbeth than on her husband, who was shown to be little more than a pawn in the hands of his ambitious wife and of the Witches who predicted his fate. The other characters in the play are reduced to veritable comprimario or even walk-on parts.

In Lady Macbeth, Verdi achieved his deepest penetration into human character thus far. Neither is Macbeth, for all his weakness, a cardboard figure. Verdi wanted his anti-heroine's character to be portrayed vocally as well, specifying that her voice should be "rough, hoarse, and gloomy, with something diabolical about it." Maria Callas used this injunction to the letter, providing an unforgettable portrait of the domineering lady.

When Verdi the theater man took over, changes in Shakespeare (himself a man of the theater too, of course, but not always providing for operatic needs) were inevitable. Verdi the politician had little to worry about here, although in Venice there was some trouble after Macduff had sung bitterly about his betrayed country.

Macbeth remained one of the composer's favorites all through his life. It has not enjoyed the popularity of the other great ones, although when a so-

Program for Verdi's Macbeth at La Scala featuring Maria Callas, 1952, Milan.

Right: Maria Callas as Lady Macbeth.

Left: Birgit Nilsson as Lady Macbeth.

Shirley Verrett as Lady Macbeth.

Macbeth

prano of sufficient gifts takes it on, it can become a theater evening of blazing interest. Verdi revised it extensively for Paris in 1865. The revised version, translated back from French into Italian, has become the one universally produced.

Havana heard the opera as early as 1849, and it reached New York in 1850. Pauline Viardot-Garcia sang Lady Macbeth in the original version in Dublin in 1859. Revivals were scarce thereafter until the '20s and '30s, but many other companies—even a production with Florence Kirk and Jess Walters in New York in 1941-42, the Hartt College in Hartford in 1953, San Francisco in 1955, the New York City Opera (directed by Margaret Webster) in 1957, and a concert performance in New York—beat the Metropolitan to its first mounting in 1959. Covent Garden followed in 1960.

Leonie Rysanek, who had sung the New York concert performance, took over the Met premiere from Callas when that fiery singer was summarily dismissed by Rudolf Bing. Birgit Nilsson and Shirley Verrett have since given stunning portrayals of Lady Macbeth.

ACT I, Scene 1. After a Prelude which touches on several of the important themes in the score, the curtain rises on a desolate heath, where groups of three witches each (Verdi specified the multiplicity) are brooding over their cauldrons. They greet Macbeth and Banquo, who enter, and begin the chain of events that are to lead to tragedy, for they hail Macbeth as Thane of Glamis, Thane of Cawdor, and King of Scotland. Banquo they call lesser than Macbeth, and

370
VERDI

Text by the composer and Piave with additional verses by Andrea Maffei; after Shakespeare.

MACBETH	*Baritone*
LADY MACBETH	*Soprano*
BANQUO	*Bass*
DUNCAN	*Mute*
MACDUFF	*Tenor*
MALCOLM	*Tenor*
FLEANCE	*Mute*
LADY-IN-WAITING	*Mezzo-Soprano*
A MURDERER	*Bass*
A PHYSICIAN	*Mute*

First Performance
Florence, 14 March 1847.
Revised for Paris
21 April 1865.

Macbeth (Burg) and Lady Macbeth (Burkhardt), Staatsoper, Dresden.

The Witches' chorus from Verdi's Macbeth, Staatsoper, Dresden.

greater, for he shall be father of kings. The second promotion of Macbeth is almost immediately announced by mesengers who proclaim the death of Cawdor (the first, to Glamis, is never explained, although Macbeth later mentions it). Banquo is understandably disturbed.

Scene 2. Lady Macbeth at home reads aloud a letter from her husband (in the speaking voice traditional at the time). When she begins to sing, her character is revealed—she will "fire that cold, that rigid heart... to act this bold, this glorious part." When a servant announces that King Duncan is accompanying Macbeth and will spend the night there, his hostess plans a bloody welcome for him. But once the monarch is established in guest quarters, and the lady has urged her mate to the fateful deed, he quails. In the famous soliloquy, "Is this a dagger which I see before me," he sings *sotto voce* (or is ordered by Verdi to do so), convinces himself of his murderous intentions, and leaves to carry them out. When he returns, he finds his lady, who has heard the portentous shriek of an owl. The two engage in a sombre duet, which embodies some famous lines: "Glamis has forever murdered sleep; therefore, oh! Cawdor, thou shalt sleep no more!", but omits the equally famous "innocent sleep that knits up the ravell'd sleave of care." Lady Macbeth chides all three—Macbeth, Glamis, and Cawdor—for their cowardice, and returns the dagger herself to the murder room. Then the hosts join in the horrified clamor at the discovery of Duncan's murder.

The banquet scene from Act II of Macbeth with Tito Gobbi as Macbeth and Amy Shuard as Lady Macbeth, Covent Garden, London.

ACT II, Scene 1. Uneasy is the head that wears the crown. Although Duncan's son Malcolm has been convicted of his father's murder because he has fled England, Macbeth cannot forget the Witches' nomination of Banquo as father of kings. He determines to kill Banquo. The entire scene was new for Paris, including Lady Macbeth's aria, "La luce langue" (Light wanes and pales the torch).

Scene 2. Murderers (in multiples, like the Witches) await Banquo and his son Fleance in a park near Macbeth's castle. When the two intended victims enter, they are at once set upon, but Fleance escapes. (In the play, Lady Macbeth is ignorant of this murder; the opera makes her a full conspirator.)

Scene 3. At a grand banquet, Macbeth is entertaining Macduff and a merry company. Lady Macbeth sings a brilliant but rather brittle brindisi. Then Macbeth holds his not altogether satisfactory conversation with the murderers and the merriment resumes, to be interrupted by the appearance of Banquo's ghost, and Macbeth's terrified words: "Thou canst not say I did it; never shake thy gory locks at me!" Lady Macbeth tries to calm him and repeats her drinking song, but once again the apparition frightens Macbeth, and at his outburst, which Lady Macbeth cannot quell, the guests vanish.

ACT III. The Witches again hold sway, with their "venomous toad," "tongue of viper," and "finger of a child," while their cauldrons bubble. Once more Macbeth seeks their wisdom, and they grant him a parade of apparitions, which warn him to beware Macduff, add that no man born of woman can harm him, and pronounce him invincible until the wood of Birnam rises against him. When Macbeth pursues his question about Banquo's son, the Witches vanish, and an eerie procession of Kings appears, Banquo the last. The spirit points to the other seven, and Macbeth realizes that he means they are his progeny, all to reign. He faints. (Here the ballet for Paris was inserted, with Hecate a prominent character.) When he recovers, Lady Macbeth is with him, scouting his fears. They plan that "the blood of all our foes be shed," and sing their vow resoundingly.

ACT IV, Scene 1. A contingent of Scottish refugees joins Macduff (whose wife and children have been murdered by Macbeth's orders) and is supplemented by Malcolm and his followers. Near Birnam wood, they take branches to bear in front of themselves, thus fulfilling the prophecy. This is a fine choral scene, inserted for Paris, and placed before the sleep-walking of Lady Macbeth.

Scene 2. This is the famous "Out, damned spot!" soliloquy that has engaged the talents of the greatest actresses. Verdi has set the entire text with a vividness of expression he had never before attained, and seldom equalled afterward. It is very difficult, extreme in range, and demanding an extraordinary control of vocal resource and shading.

Scene 3. Macbeth awaits his foes, the more fiercely when he learns that his wife is dead. Originally the opera ended with a *scena* for Macbeth, and occasionally is produced this way. But, for Paris, Verdi added a splendid finale, with a fugue and chorus, and short passages for Macduff and Malcolm.

Maria Callas as Lady Macbeth in the sleepwalking scene.

The finale of Macbeth, Glyndebourne Festival production.

Frontispiece for the published edition of Luisa Miller.

Luisa Miller

Text by S. Cammarano from
Schiller's play "Kabale und Liebe."

COUNT WALTER	*Bass*
RODOLFO	*Tenor*
MILLER	*Baritone*
LUISA	*Soprano*
FEDERICA	*Contralto*
LAURA	*Soprano*
WURM	*Bass*

First Performance
Naples, 8 December 1849.

THE NEW WORLD heard *Luisa Miller* three years after its premiere, in Philadelphia. Some European performances followed, and the Metropolitan mounted it for Rosa Ponselle in 1929, then revived it in 1968 with Caballé, Tucker, Milnes, and Tozzi, and again in 1971 and 1978.

Verdi cherished two projects that were never realized—the omnipresent *King Lear* and *The Siege of Florence*, a historical novel. But when he proposed the latter to Salvatore Cammarano, the librettist refused, knowing it to be a politically dangerous subject, sure to meet censorship. Schiller's play *Kabale und Liebe* was chosen instead when Verdi grudgingly returned to Naples in order to help Cammarano, who had suffered when Verdi had previously cancelled his contract with the Naples Opera house. Schiller offered no political problems, but the story of *Luisa Miller* concerned the oppression of lower classes by the wealthy, and several adjustments had to be made to smooth over possible trouble. Thus the opera is not as strong medicine as the play, but the libretto served Verdi well enough for melodious and ensemble purposes.

The overture is a giant step forward in Verdi's mastery of this form. Julian Budden calls it "a tour de force of musical science," and adds that "in no other of his overtures is so much musical thought concentrated in so few notes."

LUISA, THE daughter of an old soldier in the Tyrol, has fallen in love with Rodolfo, whom she knows as Carlo and takes to be a peasant like herself. In reality, he is the son of Count Walter. This information is

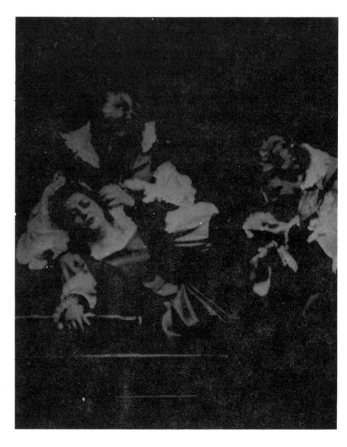

The death of Luisa at the end of the opera with **Montserrat** *Caballé as Luisa, Sherrill Milnes (l.) as her father and Richard Tucker as Rodolfo, 1968, New York.*

conveyed to Miller by Wurm, one of the Count's retainers. The Count wants his son to marry a childhood sweetheart, his own niece, the Duchess Federica, who has recently been widowed. Wurm tells the Count of Rodolfo's love for Luisa, and the Count determines to break up the romance. Rodolfo, not realizing the depth of Federica's love for him, tells her that he loves Luisa, whereupon she becomes enraged. The Count breaks up a meeting between Luisa, her father and Rodolfo, during which the young man has confessed his true identity. The Count arrests both father and daughter. Rodolfo resorts to his knowledge of the foul means by which his father came to his high position, and threatens to expose him. Luisa is spared, but her father is taken off to prison. To save his life, Luisa consents to Wurm's insistence that she write a letter of love to him; she even manages to convince the Duchess that she only pretended to love Rodolfo. This so infuriates the young man that he rushes off to hear these "truths" from Luisa's own lips; bound by her oath to Wurm, she admits them. Rodolfo then puts poison in her wine, and drinks the poisoned wine as well. Freed by impending death, Luisa confesses the real truth and the lovers die in each other's arms—but not before Rodolfo has run Wurm through with his sword.

One of Verdi's loveliest melodies is Rodolfo's aria: "Quando le sere al placido" (When at evening in the calm light).

SOON AFTER its premiere, *Rigoletto* was being performed all over Italy; occasionally, because of censors, it appeared under other names: *Viscardello*, *Clara di Perth*, and *Lionello*. Other important premieres: Covent Garden, May 13, 1853; Academy of Music, New York, February 19, 1855; Théâtre Italien, Paris, January 19, 1857. The first Metropolitan Opera performance was on November 16, 1883. The famous singers who have interpreted the various roles are legion. Enrico Caruso made his American debut as the Duke at the Metropolitan on November 23, 1903, with a cast that included Marcella Sembrich, Louise Homer, and Antonio Scotti. It is seldom absent from world repertoires.

When the management of the Teatro la Fenice in Venice commissioned an opera from Verdi, he decided on what he later called the best libretto ever to come his way—a story based on Victor Hugo's *Le Roi s'amuse*. The play had provoked a scandal in Paris in 1832 on moral grounds—although Hugo maintained that politics had caused its banning. King Francis I of France was Hugo's "anti-hero," depicted as a profligate whose debaucheries were abetted by his jester Triboulet. Hugo, at first infuriated by the opera, came to champion it fervently.

Censorship, at this period of Austrian occupation so soon after the February Revolution of 1848, was extreme. Verdi perhaps should not have taken the word of his librettist, Francesco Maria Piave, that such *lèse-majesté* would be acceptable. The blow fell when the Royal Imperial Council of Public Order in Venice prohibited the opera. There was altogether too much for the censor to swallow: the very title, *La Maledizione* (The Curse), was unacceptable. (Verdi believed the father's curse lay at the heart of the story.) The plot itself generated opposition: "so revoltingly immoral and so obscenely trivial." Piave, realizing the political implications, tried to substi-

Titta Ruffo as Rigoletto.

Galli-Curci as Gilda in Rigoletto.

tute a French prince for the King and to tone down the text. The censors of Venice suggested that the hideous humpbacked jester be turned into a presentable, upstanding man. All this offended Verdi so deeply that a complete breach seemed inevitable. There was no time to choose a new subject, and the censors understandably rejected Verdi's suggestion to substitute his *Stiffelio*, which had just had its premiere in nearby Trieste.

Resolution came from a most unexpected corner. The General Director of Public Order, Carlo Martello, loved Italian opera. He proposed a change of place and title: the King should become a Duke of an extinct Italian line. The Dukedom of Mantua was chosen, who knows why. The famous family of Gonzaga no longer existed, but in the sixteenth century, during which the opera takes place, Francesco II and his wife Isabella d'Este, patrons of Mantegna and many other artists, and their descendant Vincenzo, mentor of Monteverdi, were alive. Neither Duke seems to have been as profligate as the nobleman in the opera. Mantua later returned the somewhat dubious compliment with imagination and humor, conferring a commemorative plaque on a small dwelling, designating it as "Rigoletto's House," and on an outlying inn as "Sparafucile's."

The opera's title was changed to *Rigoletto* in this pacific move (the similarity to Triboulet is apparent). Verdi was allowed to retain the sack in which Gilda's body is placed, but had to relinquish the door key used by the Duke to enter the room where his courtiers had sequestered the heroine —so much for moral values.

The *Gazzettino di Venezia* accounted the opera "a most complete success." Verdi himself was delighted; he told the Rigoletto, Felice Varesi, that

Program from an early Italian production of Rigoletto showing the famous fourth act quartet scene (detail).

he thought he would never do anything better. He cannily withheld the music to the Duke's song, "La donna è mobile," from Raffaele Mirate until a few hours before dress rehearsal, begging him and the rest of the cast to refrain from whistling or singing the tune. The audience, caught up instantly by the simple melody and catchy words, went away singing them, and the song swept through Venice and the operatic world.

Rigoletto, the masterpiece of Verdi's younger period, marks a definite division between the earlier and later works. The depth of characterization, the probing of the human spirit, and the dramatic interplay of motives, emotions, and actions were new, and he set them to music that fitted like skin, for the most part. These attributes would flower into *Otello* and *Falstaff,* as well as infusing all the operas in between. The music of *Rigoletto* is masterly. Verdi claimed that he thought of it as a series of duets, and the effect can be one of closely woven ensemble. Particularly fine are the ominous colloquy between Rigoletto and Sparafucile, and the pitiful exchange between Gilda and her father after she confesses her plight. The famous Quartet in the last act is one of the two greatest ensembles in all opera (the other is the Sextet from *Lucia di Lammermoor*), where Verdi exercises one of his most telling devices: each character voicing his own private thoughts and emotions while blending with the others in a glorious musical tapestry.

The short prelude begins with six low, ominous strokes followed by equally grave measures that foretell the incipient tragedy.

ACT I. In a magnificent hall, the courtiers and ladies of the Court of Mantua dance and flirt and await their master. He enters immediately, confiding in the courtier Borsa that he intends that night to finish an adventure — he has observed a lovely girl, a commoner, in church each Sunday and has followed her to a remote corner of the city, where a mysterious man visits her each night. This preoccupation does not deter him, however, from pursuing a flirtation with the Countess Ceprano, although her jealous husband is nearby. The Duke confirms his unprincipled, fickle character in a blithe aria, "Questa o quella," saying that one woman or another, all please him equally.

During the dance that follows, the Duke leads the Countess away as his jester Rigoletto observes them cynically and comments to the courtiers that Ceprano is boiling with rage. Another courtier, Marullo, bursts in with the news that Rigoletto is keeping a mistress. The Duke and Rigoletto return and Rigoletto suggests ways in which a husband may be put out of the way — poison, exile, or even beheading — while the libertine approaches the wife. All this has been carried on in a light patter of conversation over the frothy, rhythmic music beneath. Now Ceprano and the others withdraw and plan vengeance on Rigoletto in a big ensemble.

The Duke's merriment is abruptly halted by the entrance of Count Monterone, who rails at the Duke for the seduction of his daughter. Before the Duke can reply, Rigoletto taunts the old man until his rage can no longer be contained. Bitterly he curses the Duke and his panderer. The Duke orders Monterone imprisoned. The Duke is not affected, but the superstitious Rigoletto recoils in horror from the father's curse — for he, too, is a father.

Enrico Caruso as the Duke of Mantua, the role in which he made his Metropolitan Opera debut in 1903.

Rigoletto

Text by Francesco Maria Piave, after Victor Hugo's play, "Le Roi s'amuse."

RIGOLETTO	*Baritone*
GILDA	*Soprano*
THE DUKE OF MANTUA	*Tenor*
SPARAFUCILE	*Bass*
MADDALENA	*Mezzo-Soprano*
COUNT MONTERONE	*Bass*
MARULLO	*Baritone*
BORSA	*Tenor*
COUNT CEPRANO	*Baritone*
COUNTESS CEPRANO	*Soprano*
GIOVANNA	*Mezzo-Soprano*
A PAGE	*Mezzo-Soprano*

First Performance
Venice, 11 March 1851.

Leonard Warren as Rigoletto.

Louise Homer as Maddalena.

ACT II.   Rigoletto stumbles into the deserted cul-de-sac where his humble home lies across the alley from the back of Count Ceprano's castle. He mutters, still dismayed by the curse: "Quel vecchio maledivami!" A sinister stranger approaches and offers his skill with the sword to rid a customer of any enemy. The jester, though protesting that he has no need for such services, nevertheless asks pointedly about the cost and method of the possible murder of a nobleman. The stranger mentions twenty crowns, and suggests that his home is the best setting, to which his attractive sister can lure a victim. He tells his name and where he may be found — "Sparafucile,...here any evening." This colloquy takes place against a spare accompaniment in the deep tones of solo cello and double bass. When the villain has gone, Rigoletto reviles himself for his own black deeds in a vitriolic aria, "Pari siamo!" (We are alike — murderers; I with my tongue, he with his dagger!) Then he recalls the curse, but shrugs it off as he enters his home to be greeted by his affectionate daughter.

He demands to know if she has been out of the house; she says only to Sunday church. Then she asks: Who was her mother? Has he no homeland, no family, no friends? In a duet of considerable pathos and beauty, he recalls her mother as the only one ever to give him love and pity. Rigoletto summons the duenna Giovanna, asks her if anyone observed his arrival, accepts her denial, and charges her to guard his treasure closely. He thinks he hears a noise outside and goes to investigate. As the door is unguarded, neither he nor Gilda sees the stealthy entry of a young man (the Duke in disguise), who tosses a purse to the venal Giovanna and hides himself. Rigoletto returns and once more cautions Giovanna not to open the door to anyone.

The Duke is doubly startled to learn that the mysterious man he has seen is his jester and that the supposed lady-love is in truth a daughter. Rigoletto, not quite convinced that all is secure, departs. Gilda confesses to Giovanna that she can love the handsome stranger who has cast amorous glances at her in church. The Duke emerges and soon, overcoming her shyness, she joins her lover in pledges of undying affection. At her question, he invents a name for himself — Gualtier Maldè. Giovanna hears footsteps in the street outside. The Duke slips away, leaving Gilda with his name on her lips, the "beloved name" of the "Caro nome", with its dreamy moments contrasted to girlish flights of coloratura.

The furtive noises outside increase; it is the courtiers, come to abduct Rigoletto's "mistress." Seeing her on the staircase, they remark upon her angelic beauty. Rigoletto himself, still uneasy, returns and surprises the group, but it is too dark for him to see that their leader is Ceprano. They trick the jester by telling him it is the Countess Ceprano they mean to abduct. They blindfold him effectively, and he holds the ladder for the abductors to mount his own wall. Gilda utters despairing cries as she is carried off, but her father cannot hear. After a few moments, he tears off the blindfold, and by the feeble light of an abandoned lantern recognizes a scarf Gilda has dropped. Frantically, he cries out: "Ah! la maledizione!" ("The curse!") as the curtain falls.

*Lily Pons as Gilda with Giuseppe **Valdengo** as Rigoletto.*

ACT III. The Duke enters the large antechamber where hang portraits of himself and his Duchess (his wife is surely the most neglected spouse in opera). He is greatly agitated, having returned to Gilda's house only to find her gone. In an apparently sincere aria, "Parmi veder le lagrime", imagining the tears that drop from her eyes, he wins momentary sympathy. And as the courtiers come to inform him of their splendid jest, and he realizes that their captive is the beloved he mourns, he bewilders them by his emotional reaction. The cabaletta in which he expresses this, "Possente amor mi chiama" (The power of love calls me) is usually omitted, so that the Duke's haste to join the prisoner is attributed to his customarily lustful nature, which indeed soon reasserts itself.

Now Rigoletto enters, feigning gaiety but replying to the courtiers' taunts abstractedly. The Duchess's page comes to ask for an audience with the Duke; they answer that he is asleep but immediately contradict it by saying the Duke is out hunting. The page is not satisfied but is forced to withdraw. Rigoletto has spotted the discrepancy and guesses the truth. "Give me back my daughter!" he begs. The courtiers are amazed at the revelation of this relationship and a few show uneasiness, but most turn deaf ears to the jester's pleas, which change into invective in the powerful aria, "Cortigiani, vil razza dannata" (Courtiers, vile race of the damned!). As he concludes, Gilda rushes in and throws herself into his arms. The courtiers leave the room. A moving scene, in which the duet that ends with "Piangi, fanciulla" (Weep, my child) expresses

Gianna D'Angelo as Gilda with Ettore Bastianini as Rigoletto, 1962, Lyric Opera of Chicago.

Rigoletto's pity for Gilda and fury at her abductors. Now the old Monterone passes through the hall on his way to prison. Addressing the Duke's portrait, he laments that his curse has not taken effect. "No, old man!" vows Rigoletto, "I will avenge you!" Gilda pleads with him for mercy as the curtain falls.

ACT IV.   To persuade Gilda of the Duke's perfidy, Rigoletto leads her to the door of Sparafucile's hut, where she can see through a crack the entrance of the Duke, dressed as a cavalry officer. He asks Sparafucile for a room and some wine. Then he embarks on a frivolous toast to women, calling them fickle as a feather, but indispensable to man's happiness ("La donna è mobile"). Sparafucile brings wine and knocks on the ceiling to summon his sister Maddalena. He then slips outside to conclude his business with Rigoletto, but the latter asks him to wait. Now with Rigoletto and Gilda outside, and the Duke and his paramour inside the inn, the quartet that follows is a masterly revelation of the inner thoughts of each, blended into a musical ensemble of great beauty and effectiveness. The Duke begins, "Bella figlia dell' amore", and continues a passionate avowal to Maddalena, who voices disbelief in his protestations; Gilda sings of her betrayal, Rigoletto of vengeance. Rigoletto then bids Gilda flee to Verona, where he will join her. Sparafucile creeps in, and Rigoletto gives him ten crowns, the other half to be paid upon delivery of the Duke's body. Rigoletto will drag it to the river himself.

As the jester departs, a storm gathers, and at its height, a humming chorus behind the scene adds to the eeriness of the music. Sparafucile reenters the inn, warns the Duke about the wild night, and offers his own room, which the young man lightheartedly accepts, hoping for a rendezvous with Maddalena. Sparafucile ironically wishes him God's protection. When he has mounted the stairs, Maddalena, who has succumbed to the Duke's charm, begs Sparafucile to spare him. But the cutthroat has his own creed: "Am I a thief? Have I ever betrayed a client?" They finally agree that any stranger who knocks will be the victim. Gilda has crept back and overhears. She offers herself as a sacrifice. When Rigoletto returns at midnight, Sparafucile has the sack ready. He urges Rigoletto to go upriver to deeper water and reenters the dark inn. The gloating Rigoletto suddenly hears, to his horror, the voice of the supposedly dead Duke, lightly singing "La donna è mobile" as he leaves the inn, possibly warned off by Maddalena. Feverishly, the hunchback tears open the sack, and by a wan ray of moonlight sees his daughter. Gilda, not yet dead, begs his forgiveness. As she expires, her despairing father utters a wild cry: "La maledizione!" The curse has struck home.

ONE OF THE most popular operas in the world, *Il Trovatore* was heard, in the two years after its premiere, in Paris, New York, and London. The New York premiere was at the Academy of Music in 1855. The Metropolitan gave the opera on the third night of its season, October 26, 1883, with Alwina Valleria, the first American to sing at the Met, as Leonora. The opera has seldom been absent from the repertoire since. The great singers who have sung leading roles are beyond listing. One has only to mention

Maurice Renaud as Rigoletto.

381
VERDI

Title page for the published edition of Il Trovatore (detail).

Leontyne Price as Leonora in Il Trovatore.

Il Trovatore

(*The Troubador*)

Text by Salvatore Cammarano based on the play "El Trovador" by Antonio García Gutiérrez. Completed by Leone Emmanuele Bardare.

LEONORA	*Soprano*
MANRICO	*Tenor*
COUNT DI LUNA	*Baritone*
AZUCENA	*Mezzo-Soprano*
FERRANDO	*Bass*
INEZ	*Soprano*
RUIZ	*Tenor*
GYPSY	*Baritone*
MESSENGER	*Tenor*

First Performance
Rome, 19 January 1853.

the Metropolitan production of 1968-69, which starred Leontyne Price, Placido Domingo, Grace Bumbry, and Sherill Milnes.

The idea of Gutiérrez's *El Trovador,* a play popular in Spain since 1836, had occurred to Verdi in 1850. He asked Salvatore Cammarano for a synopsis, and began to work at it while recovering from the depression caused by the death of his mother. But Cammarano died in 1852 and Leone Bardara was called in to write additional verses. The unprecedented gap between *Rigoletto* and *Trovatore* (two years) was caused by the lack of an offer of performance for the latter.

There is a factual basis behind the melodrama that permeates the opera. Spain did endure a civil war, and among the antagonists in Aragon and Catalonia was a prince who counted Di Luna in his retinue. One of the prince's rivals was the Count of Urgel, Manrico's patron. Both love and politics were causes of the animosity between the protagonists.

The plot of *Il Trovatore* has been cited for its obscurity, but is not really so difficult to understand, given a little knowledge of the events that occurred before the curtain goes up. Also it is well to study the narrative parts of the libretto, and to realize that Azucena is central to the plot (Verdi at first called the opera after her); and to remember that the two men are in fact brothers.

The music has been enough excuse for the opera's popularity. Such a string of melodies exists nowhere else in Verdi's work—or in that of any other composer, for that matter.

ACT I. The Duel. Scene l. In the Castle of Aliaferia, seat of the Court of Aragon, Ferrando, captain of Di Luna's guard, regales the sleepy soldiers and servants with an oft-told story that nevertheless always arouses excitement. The old Count di Luna, it seems, had two sons, Garcia and the Count we know. In their infancy, a fearsome gypsy was discovered near Garcia, and chased away. From then on, the child sickened. At last, the gypsy was captured and burned alive, although her daughter Azucena escaped. In revenge, Azucena kidnapped the baby. Later, on the very spot where the witch was burned, the charred corpse of a child was found. Everyone but the old Count believed that Garcia had died. The old man charged his other son to seek his brother, and this quest has become the young Count's reason for living—aside from his love for Leonora. Ferrando remembers the gypsy very well and would know her daughter again. His dark vision of the gypsy's haunting the castle still terrifies the others, who shudder as the clock strikes midnight.

Scene 2. Leonora has come out into the moonlit gardens of the palace with her companion, Inez. She hopes for another visit from the mysterious Troubador who has serenaded her previously. She tells Inez (as if that close confidante did not already know) about the royal tournament at which a black knight won all the honors. She had placed the wreath of victory upon his head, and had fallen in love on the instant. But then, the civil war had intervened, and she had seen him no more until one night he had appeared as a minstrel below her balcony. She expects him again. Her "Tacea la notte" (The night was still) is one of the jewels of the opera, long-breathed, intensely lyrical. Inez's murmurs of

Act I, Scene 2 from Il Trovatore with Franco Corelli (r.) as Manrico and Gabriella Tucci (l.) as Leonora.

Fiorenza Cossotto as Azucena.

dismay at her mistress's infatuation are swept away in Leonora's brilliant cabaletta, "Di tale amor" (There are no words for such a love), and the two women exit as the Count appears.

Di Luna's fervent protestations of love for Leonora are cut short by the appearance of the Troubador, Manrico. Leonora, hearing the notes of his harp, rushes out to meet her lover, but mistakes the Count for the serenader and is caught in mid-embrace by Manrico. The Count recognizes his enemy, a follower of the rebel Urgel. The two men rush off for a duel after a heated trio, leaving Leonora to faint.

ACT II. The Gypsy. Scene 1. The gypsy encampment at the foot of a mountain in Biscay. Azucena is seated near a huge fire, Manrico at her side. The gypsies begin their chattering chorus, accompanied by blows on their anvils, the strong rhythms and catchy tune making this one of the most popular and easily recognized bits of operatic music. As it subsides, Azucena begins to sing to herself, reliving the awful night when her mother was cast into the flames. "Stride la vampa" (The flames roll upward) is another of the justly acclaimed arias in the opera. It depresses the gypsies, who wander off. Manrico is fascinated and horrified by the story, which apparently he has not known, and immediately questions his supposed mother when she hints that she has felt pity for the Count's infant. Her reassurance that she is really his mother cannot wholly satisfy Manrico, but he accepts it.

The atmosphere is changed as a messenger arrives from Ruiz, one of Manrico's soldiers, bringing news that Urgel has captured the fortress at

Count Di Luna's encampment below Castellor, scene from Act III of Il Trovatore, scenery and costumes by Alessandro Benois, 1952-53, La Scala, Milan.

Leo Slezak as Manrico.

Castellor; Manrico is needed. Also, that Leonora, believing Manrico dead, is about to take the veil. Manrico rushes off to save his love, in spite of Azucena's protests.

Scene 2. Near the convent in the vicinity of Castellor, Di Luna and his followers have come to bear Leonora away. The Count also believes Manrico dead, and glories in a moment of victory, hailing his love in the beautiful and tender aria, "Il balen del suo sorriso" (In the light of her smile). His joy is soon turned to fury, as Manrico and his band appear, and, triumphing, carry off the heroine themselves, accompanied by a great deal of emotional music.

ACT III. The Gypsy's Daughter. Scene 1. The Count is encamped for a siege on Castellor, whence Manrico has taken Leonora. Soldiers bring in Azucena, and the gypsy cannot forestall Ferrando's recognition, in spite of her lies about her identity. She cries to **Manrico for aid, which only enrages the Count further, and she is led** away to prison, fated to be burned at the stake.

Scene 2. The only peaceful moment the lovers are destined to enjoy, enhanced by Manrico's beautiful lyric aria, "Ah, si ben mio" (Ah, yes, **my love), is shattered by Ruiz, who breathlessly tells of Azucena's cap-**ture. Manrico is determined to rescue her, but first tosses off the heaven-storming "Di quella pira" (The flaming pyre), with the famous **high C's interpolated, it is said, by the tenor Tamberlik with Verdi's per-**mission. No tenor would think to omit them, but few have the stamina to sing this cabaletta twice, as is indicated in the score.

ACT IV. The Torture. Scene 1. Ruiz conducts Leonora to the tower of Aliaferia where Manrico is imprisoned; there he leaves her. She is unafraid, for her ring contains poison, to which she can resort in an extremity. Her lovely aria holds out some hope, as she bids her love fly on rosy wings to Manrico : "D'amor sull'ale rosee." Funeral bells toll, and a chorus of monks prays for the souls of those about to die. Against this "Miserere," Leonora's broken-hearted phrases are followed by Manrico's mournful apostrophe to death, the whole scene one of the most famous in opera. Now the Count enters, troubled at the thought that he is exceeding the authority vested in him by the Prince in his condemnation of Azucena and her son, and longing for news of Leonora. She appears before him, but only to plead for Manrico. The more tearful she becomes, the harder is his heart. At last she agrees to give herself to him only if the Troubador may be spared. As the Count gives orders to this effect, she swallows the poison, and breaks into a joyous cabaletta (which may seem out of place in this gloomy setting, but only reflects her joy that her lover will live). The Count returns and joins her in a dramatic duet.

Scene 2. Azucena lies in a cell, Manrico by her side. Half-crazed, she once again lives in the horrible past, then begins to sing still another justly beloved melody, "Ai nostri monti" (Home to our mountains), in which Manrico joins most affectingly. Leonora enters, and Manrico greets her rapturously (and melodiously), then becomes increasingly suspicious as Leonora will not tell him how she achieved the pardon she extends to him. Only when she dies in his arms does he realize the truth, and then it is too late. The Count enters, realizes that Leonora has tricked him, and orders Manrico to his execution. Azucena wakes, and the Count drags her to the window to see the ax fall. She screams: "He was your brother. Mother, you are avenged!" And the desolate Di Luna cries out: "And I live on?" as the curtain falls.

Placido Domingo as Manrico with Fiorenza Cossotto just before the tragic dénouement of the opera.

LA TRAVIATA. There was much vacillation about the choice of subject before Verdi settled on Dumas's play, *La Dame aux camélias* (sic; based in turn on Dumas's novel of the same name), for the Venice Carnival Season of 1853. He had been dissatisfied with the selection of prima donnas available, and indeed, should have been, for the final choice for the heroine, Salvini-Donatelli, was, to put it mildly, stylishly stout, and made of Violetta's consumptive death throes a ridiculous spectacle. The word "fiasco" was in the air and the public prints; Verdi echoed it in a letter to Emmanuele Muzio, and added: "Is the fault mine—or the singers'?"

We know where the fault lay—certainly not with the composer. In addition to the corpulent soprano, the tenor was hoarse, the baritone scornful of the "minor" role of Germont père. The accusation that critics found fault with the contemporary setting (for the events take place in the decade just before the premiere) seems unfounded, because the first performance transferred the action back a century. When to set it and how to costume La Traviata is pretty much up to the directors—it may be entirely "contemporary," or be set in the period of Louis XIV—nobody seems to mind. But the customary usage is to place the action in the 1850s when it occurred.

Alphonsine Duplessis, a celebrated courtesan of Dumas's time, was the real-life inspiration for the heroine of his play on which Verdi's La Traviata is based.

Scene from Act III of the London premiere of La Traviata with Marietta Piccolomini as Violetta and Calzolari as Alfredo, 1856.

Amelita Galli-Curci as Violetta.

Fact and fiction blend in the libretto. Violetta Valéry had her origin in Dumas's heroine, Marguerite Gauthier, who was based in turn on the real Alphonsine Duplessis, a celebrated courtesan of the time, and Dumas's mistress for a short while. This famous beauty, who also counted Liszt among her conquests, was the embodiment of grace and charm, although perfectly capable of joining in the ribald merriment of her lowlier companions. (None of this, of course, appears in the opera, where Violetta's character is altogether noble, although a director now and then manages to introduce a semi-orgy into the party scenes.)

Another point in the plain-speaking novel which is ignored in the play and opera (although a prima donna or two sometimes takes note of it and dresses accordingly) is the circumstance that the camellia-loving heroine wore white flowers every day except at certain times of the month, and, giving Alfredo (or Armand) a flower and bidding him to return when it is wilted, acknowledges her bondage to the cycles of the moon.

The moral outrage that greeted this opera would be unthinkable today. But in mid-19th century, to portray on stage a veritable prostitute, no matter how "reformed," and pit her against respectability in the form of her lover's father—even though virtue could be said to have triumphed in the end—was scandalous. Certainly everything seemed against *La Traviata.* There were even those who thought that Verdi was too facile. After all, he had barely finished and produced *Il Trovatore* when this opera was put on the stage.

But revivals soon showed the opera's true worth. And today it is more often performed, perhaps, than its more rugged, passionate fellow work, *Il Trovatore.* The singers who have undertaken the complex heroine (musically she requires at least two voices, a flashing coloratura and a throbbing lyrico-spinto) are too numerous to mention—they reach from Albanese to Zeani, while tenors and baritones cover a similarly extensive ground, and conductors cherish the opera as a vehicle for intensely personal interpretation.

ACT I.   In Violetta's elegant salon, a party is in full swing, only revealed to us after a Prelude of exquisite sensibility that characterizes Violetta's charm. The gaiety is at its height as Gaston enters, bringing along young Alfredo Germont, who is introduced as an admirer of the hostess. At his attentiveness, Violetta's current protector, Baron Duphol, is immediately alerted. He glowers throughout the scene. Gaston tells Violetta that all during her recent illness, Alfredo has come every day to enquire about her. She taunts the Baron with this faithfulness, and he replies that he himself has known her but a year. "*He* has known me only a minute," she retorts. The scene is set for jealousy. Violetta breaks the tension by calling for a toast, and, the Baron rather churlishly refusing, she turns to Alfredo. He responds with the brindisi, "Libiamo, libiamo," to which Violetta adds a verse and in which the chorus joins. Then as a band begins to play in the next room, all start to go, but Violetta is seized with a fit of coughing. She motions the others to leave, but Alfredo lingers, begging her to give up her shallow life, and confessing his deep love for her in "Un di felice" (One happy day), telling her of his constant vigil. She lightly puts him off, but is undoubtedly touched, for she gives him a flower, telling him to return when it is faded. "Oh, joy! Tomorrow, then!" he exclaims, and she agrees. The guests stream in to say farewell, and Violetta is left alone.

No doubt remains that she is deeply affected, and in her marvelously emotional aria, "Ah, fors' è lui," she wonders at this new feeling that has overcome her—can it be real? Is this the man who will change her life? Then she dismisses the thought as folly, plunging into the brilliant coloratura aria of greatest appeal to sopranos, "Sempre libera." She must be free, she insists, and even though some melting tones come from Alfredo, who is still outside her window, she persists in her defiance of love and her determination to pursue her frivolous life until the last high D-flat.

ACT II.   Violetta has changed her mind and joined Alfredo in a country retreat. To keep this up, she is forced to sell many of her belongings, and has sent her maid Annina to Paris to accomplish this. Alfredo, coming in from a morning's excursion, rejoices in his present happiness in the aria, "De' miei bollenti spiriti" (She tempered my rebellious passion). His joy is dissipated at Annina's news of her mistress's disposition of her resources. Pausing only for a cabaletta (which is often omitted), he rushes off to Paris himself, to raise some money. Violetta comes in and learns of his departure from Annina. She receives an invitation from her former crony, Flora Bervoix, to a party that evening, but she puts it aside as her servant Giuseppe announces a visitor. Thinking it is her business representative, she is shocked at the entrance of the gentleman who announces with dignity that he is Alfredo's father. The scene that ensues is the heart of the opera, revealing the pitiless respectability of the conventional gentleman, the initial defiance and eventual yielding of the unfortunate woman. Alfredo's sister must marry, the older Germont says, and the knowledge of her brother's liaison would ruin the marriage. He demands a sacrifice. Even when he learns that it is Violetta, not Alfredo, who has maintained their hideaway, his growing sympathy for Violetta does not cause him to relent.

La Traviata
(*The Fallen Woman*)

Text by Francesco Maria Piave after Dumas's play "La Dame aux camélias."

ALFREDO	*Tenor*
VIOLETTA	*Soprano*
GERMONT	*Baritone*
GASTON	*Tenor*
BARON DOUPHOL	*Baritone*
ANNINA	*Soprano*
FLORA BERVOIX	*Mezzo-Soprano*
DOCTOR GRENVIL	*Bass*
MARCHESE D'OBIGNY	*Bass*
GIUSEPPE	*Tenor*

LADIES AND GENTLEMEN; SERVANTS AND MASKS; DANCERS AND GUESTS

First Performance
Venice, 6 March 1853.

387
VERDI

Antonio Scotti as Germont.

*Above: Lawrence Tibbett
as Germont.*

*Left: Beverly Sills as
Violetta.*

Gradually she realizes that it is no temporary parting he insists upon, but a permanent one. He leaves it to her to find the means. She exclaims in the sad and beautiful melody, "Dite alla giovane" (Say to thy daughter), that she will make this sacrifice, tells him to wait in the garden for Alfredo, and begs him to tell Alfredo of her sacrifice when she is dead.

When Germont is gone, Violetta writes a note to Alfredo, telling him that she is going back to her old life. She barely has time to conceal it as Alfredo enters. Then she begs Alfredo to say he loves her, in a scene so tender, so impassioned and strained, that it is difficult to see why the young man is not alerted to trouble. But he happily settles down when she leaves, only to be jolted out of his complacency by Violetta's note, delivered by a gardener. His anguished cry is heard by his father, who attempts to console him in the rather placid aria, "Di Provenza il mar," urging his son to return to the familiar and peaceful land of his birth. But Alfredo will not be comforted; with a cry of rage he rushes out to seek revenge.

Stuart Burrows as Alfredo (far left) and Beverly Sills as Violetta (seated, far right) in a scene from Act III of La Traviata.

ACT III.   In Flora's extravagant villa, the party is under way. A ballet of gypsies delights the guests, among whom Gaston and his friends appear as matadors. Alfredo enters, and in spite of the whispering around him (the grapevine works quickly in these circles and all know of his parting from Violetta), he sits down to gamble. He is on a winning streak as Violetta enters on the arm of Baron Duphol. The latter challenges Alfredo's luck at cards, and loses. When supper is announced, all repair to an adjoining room. But Violetta returns, sends for Alfredo, and begs him to leave. Only if she goes with him, Alfredo responds. When she refuses, he summons the others back, taunts Violetta, and throws his winnings at her feet, crying that it is in payment for her services. Of course the Baron challenges Alfredo immediately, and there is a moment of high tension, not relieved by the entrance of Germont, who excoriates his son for his graceless behavior. The ensemble works up to a feverish high point, dominated by the soaring tones of the hapless heroine.

ACT IV.   The Prelude is yet another piece of ethereal beauty. Violetta, her resources almost gone, lies ill in a hotel room, watched over by the faithful Annina. Carnival preparations are being made outside the window. An old friend, Dr. Grenvil, who has observed Violetta's life throughout, now comes to predict, sorrowfully, its ending. Of course he does not tell her, but indicates to Annina that there is little hope. When he is gone, Violetta sends Annina out with the last of her money for the revelers. Then Violetta gets out the letter she has received from Germont, and in throbbing tones, reads it aloud. Alfredo has been told of her sacrifice; the duel has spared him, but the Baron was wounded; Alfredo will come to her soon. "But it is late," she utters in low tones. Looking at herself in the mirror, she realizes how dreadfully she has changed. "Addio del passato," she sings in melodious sorrow—farewell to the past. The carnival chorus breaks in on her wretchedness, and Annina returns in great excitement—Alfredo has ar-

Nellie Melba as Violetta.

Program for a 1951 La Scala production of I Vespri Siciliani featuring Maria Callas, Milan.

I Vespri Siciliani
(*The Sicilian Vespers*)

Text by Scribe and Duveyrier.

ELENA	*Soprano*
ARRIGO	*Tenor*
GUIDO DI MONFORTE	*Baritone*
GIOVANNI DI PROCIDA	*Bass*
DE BETHUNE	*Bass*
COUNT VAUDEMONT	*Bass*
NINETTA	*Soprano*
DANIELI	*Tenor*
TEBALDO	*Tenor*
ROBERTO	*Bass*
MANFREDO	*Tenor*

First Performance
Paris, 13 June 1855.

rived. Violetta rouses herself to greet him, and they passionately reaffirm their devotion, planning to leave Paris ("Parigi, o cara").

But it is too late. She bursts out vehemently: "Oh, God! to die so young!" and falls back. The Doctor and Germont arrive just in time to witness the end. One moment she rises to her feet, proclaiming that she lives again; the next, she has fallen in death.

VERDI'S FIRST WORK for the Paris Opéra had been *Jérusalem*, a reworking of *I Lombardi*, but when he was called on for another, he decided it must be truly "grand," to rival the spectacular long pieces of the reigning Meyerbeer. He had trouble in getting a suitable libretto from his specified poet, Eugène Scribe, but after several abortive attempts, they settled on the *Vespers*. Verdi presumably did not know at the time that it was a rehash of *Le Duc d'Albe*, which Scribe and his colleague Charles Duveyrier had written for Donizetti, but which remained unfinished at Donizetti's death. There were many fits and starts and acrimonious confrontations, and other alarms and excursions before the opera was produced, in French of course, and under the title *Les Vêpres siciliennes*. One circumstance which drove Verdi to the boiling point was the sudden disappearance of the designated soprano, Sofia Cruvelli, during rehearsals. She was not heard from for several weeks, during which the entire opera house fumed, but she quietly reappeared one day, having been on a premarital honeymoon with her husband-to-be, Baron Vigier.

The opera is based partly on history, partly on legend. There was an uprising in Sicily, but it was from general discontent rather than the result of a conspiracy. The character of Procida as conspirator is fictional,

Sophia Cruvelli in the role of Elena which she created for the 1855 Paris premiere of I Vespri Siciliani.

Magazine illustration of a scene from Verdi's I Vespri Siciliani which appeared around the time of the opera's premiere (detail).

and his role is not developed as thoroughly as Verdi had wished. But the opera, in spite of some unfavorable views (partly stimulated by the complaints of Verdi himself at the time), has many beauties and can be produced very effectively.

Italy's first performance was at Parma in 1855; Milan heard it the next year as *Giovanna di Guzman* and Naples in 1857 as *Batilde di Turenna*. London and New York both had performances in 1859. A Palermo production in 1937 must have aroused some patriotic heart-burnings. John Dexter and Josef Svoboda brought their striking production from Hamburg in 1969 to the Metropolitan in '73-'74, with Caballé, Gedda, Milnes, and Tozzi. This version opened the 1974 season as well. Previously, the Metropolitan had given a concert performance in Newport, R.I., in 1966, and even before that, a concert version had been performed by Thomas Scherman in New York in 1964.

The length of the opera—five acts, as specified by Paris, was burdensome even to Verdi. There were of course ballets—two of them—omitted in the Met's production. The overture is one of Verdi's most accomplished, featuring a motive from the duet between Arrigo and his father.

Sicily is ruled severely by the French, with Guido di Monforte as governor. A conspiracy among Sicilians, of which Giovanni di Procida, a noble physician, is a leader, is afoot to overthrow their oppressors. He has returned from exile and joins Arrigo, a young Sicilian, and Duchess Elena, his beloved. Elena demands as a price of marriage that Arrigo shall kill the governor. Monforte discovers that Arrigo is in reality his son by a Sicilian woman. When he tells Arrigo, the young hothead is torn between Elena and filial responsibility. Though he scorns attempts at reconciliation, he protects his father from assassins at a ball. The governor offers to pardon Elena and Procida if Arrigo will acknowledge his paternity, but Arrigo consents only when those two are about to die. Procida is not reconciled; he still plans revenge. The Sicilians will strike at the very peal of the wedding bells for Elena and Arrigo. Elena

Carlo Negrini as Gabriele.

Luigia Bendazzi as Amelia.

Leone Giraldoni as Boccanegra.

The three who created these principal roles for the first performance of Simon Boccanegra, 1881, Milan.

knows this, but does not tell Arrigo, so that the massacre takes place. Arrigo dies with his father and Elena stabs herself. No one alive remaïns on the stage — but Sicily is freed.

Outstanding moments in the score: Procida's "O tu Palermo," in which he apostrophizes his native land; Monforte's soliloquy, "In braccio alle dovizie" (Given over to riches); Arrigo's gloomy aria, "Giorno di pianto" (Day of weeping); Elena's Bolero, a brilliant show piece, and several fine ensembles.

CONVERTING HIS failed *Simon Boccanegra* to the opera as we know it today was, for Verdi, "like turning a stage-coach to a steam train," wrote Julian Budden. The original libretto by Piave, taken from the play by Gutiérrez (from whose work *Il Trovatore* had been drawn), seemed over-complicated and severe to the Venice public and critics, who distrusted Verdi's stern and relatively unlyrical music as well. Almost a quarter century went by before a revision was accomplished, and then only after overcoming first Verdi's indifference and second the reluctance of Boito, who had already embarked on the *Otello* project that was to mark a pinnacle in operatic history. The details of the revision are much too thicket-like to be recounted here; nor is a comparison of first and second versions practical. Suffice it to say that the entirely new material includes the opening scene of the Prologue (aside from a speech by Paolo) up to Fiesco's aria, the introduction to Act I, the duet for Gabriele and Fiesco, the climax of the "recognition" duet, Boccanegra's solo in Act II and Paolo's preceding soliloquy, the opening of Act III up to the entrance of Boccanegra, and much of the final quartet and chorus. All this in addition to the central piece, the scene in the Council Chamber, which was to be the jewel of the opera.

Verdi was not too happy about the singers chosen for the revival, and sneaked into Milan to hear them secretly. He was satisfied — indeed, who would not have been, with Victor Maurel, Edouard de Reszke, and Francesco Tamagno! Maurel and Tamagno, in fact, were chosen for Verdi's Iago and Otello, and Maurel for his Falstaff.

The opera is unusual with its preponderance of male voices and only one woman. Boccanegra is one of the greatest characters ever developed by Verdi; noble, far-sighted, compassionate, balanced. It is a part to be relished by any ambitious baritone, and several have made a glory of it. We can cite Lawrence Tibbett, Leonard Warren, Tito Gobbi, Eberhard Wächter, Cornell MacNeil, and Ingvar Wixell; basses have made the most of Fiesco's "Il lacerato spirito" on every opportunity.

Perhaps one reason for the earlier lack of enthusiasm for the opera lies in the relatively unimportant part given to "love interest." Simon is a political being; the division between plebeian and patrician forces is most important — the key to the entire action. The Prologue is indeed gloomy, but the rest of the opera has life and motion, although there are some situations that need to be explained.

PROLOGUE. In a fourteenth-century Genoa piazza on which border the church of San Lorenzo and Fiesco's palace, the plebeians Paolo and Pietro are arguing about who should be newly elected as Doge, the ruler of this maritime city. Patricians have always been

Simon Boccanegra

Text by Francesco Maria Piave
after a play by Gutiérrez.
Revised by Arrigo Boito.

AMELIA	*Soprano*
GABRIELE ADORNO	*Tenor*
SIMON BOCCANEGRA	*Baritone*
JACOPO FIESCO	*Bass*
PAOLO ALBIANI	*Baritone*
PIETRO	*Bass*
CAPTAIN	*Tenor*

First Performance
Venice, 12 March 1857.
First performance revised version
Milan, 14 March 1881.

Lawrence Tibbett as Simon Boccanegra.

chosen, the most recent being Fiesco. Now it is proposed that the naval hero Simon Boccanegra be a candidate—the first plebeian. Boccanegra has in the past fallen in love with Maria, the daughter of Fiesco, and they have had a child, who has disappeared. Simon agrees to be a candidate. Pietro brings on a mob, tells them that another candidate has sold out to the patricians; they agree to the candidacy of Boccanegra and curse Fiesco and the patricians. After they leave, Fiesco emerges from his palace, torn with grief. Maria has just died. He sings the famous "Il lacerato spirito" (Spirit torn by grief), and begs Maria in heaven to pray for him. Boccanegra enters, drops to his knees and asks for mercy. But Fiesco angrily says it is too late, and only the presence of Maria's child by Simon can appease him. He exits, leaving the palace door ajar. Simon, entering, discovers Maria's body and is inconsolable, not even rousing to the acclamation of the returning mob, which hails him as Doge.

ACT I.   It is twenty-five years later. Boccanegra has banished many patricians, but Fiesco has returned to Genoa disguised as Andrea Grimaldi, bringing with him a foundling whom he has named Amelia and given the surname Grimaldi (no one, including the girl herself, knows that she is Fiesco's own granddaughter). Amelia is rejoicing in the beauty of the day, and welcomes her lover, Gabriele Adorno. Their rapturous duet is followed by the entrance of Pietro, who begs audience for the Doge. Gabriele is astounded that the Doge should visit

Amelia, but Amelia tells him she is sure the ruler means to ask her guardian to permit her marriage to Paolo. She begs Gabriele to intervene with his own proposal. When Fiesco enters, the young man does this, but is put off by Fiesco, who explains that the girl is a foundling and will not inherit the Grimaldi fortune. Andrea protests that he loves the girl, not the money, and Fiesco agrees to their marriage. Both leave as the Doge enters and confronts Amelia. He tells her he will pardon her brothers (the Grimaldis, whom he has banished), and asks if she has thought of marriage. She forestalls him by saying that she is in love with one man but pursued by another who seeks only the Grimaldi fortune. He quickly guesses this to be Paolo. She then confides that she is not a Grimaldi, and that her only clue to her identity is a locket containing the portrait of her mother. (Why Fiesco has never seen this is one of the minor mysteries of the plot.) Boccanegra immediately recognizes his dear Maria and embraces his lost daughter. Their duet is both impassioned and tender, one of the lovely lyrical moments of the score. Of course, marriage with Paolo is out of the question, and the Doge lets that wily man know it. Paolo immediately plans to abduct Maria and sets Pietro about it.

The Council Chamber (one of the finest in all Verdi). A body of patricians and another of plebeians sit at either side, as Boccanegra presides. The Doge calls for an agreement to a treaty with Tartary,

Fiesco (Ruggero Raimondi) and Amelia (Mirella Freni) return to Genoa, scene from Act I of Simon Boccanegra from the Giorgio Strehler production, 1971, La Scala, Milan.

Scene from the beginning of Act II of Simon Boccanegra; in the Grimaldi Villa father Andrea tells Gabriele about the origin of Amelia; scenery, Gustav Oláh, 1956, State Opera, Budapest.

whereby the latter promises to keep its waters open to the ships of Genoa. They agree. Then he asks for a more difficult "Yes" — peace between Venice and Genoa. He quotes a letter from Petrarch urging the reconciliation. At once all are on their feet, swords drawn, with shouts of disagreement — only Genoa is to be considered. This tumult is interrupted by another from outside, which is caused by Andrea and Gabriele battling a mob of plebeians. Boccanegra summons them all inside and demands an explanation. Gabriele confesses that he has killed a certain Lorenzino, who, he says, has abducted Amelia. Simon suspects the truth, but before he can act, Gabriele tries to attack him and is restrained. Now Amelia enters, and clears up the story — she has been seized and taken to Lorenzino, but has so terrified him with threats of the Doge's vengeance that he has freed her. She looks meaningfully at Paolo, and the Doge understands. But the patricians are ready to riot again against the plebeians, and only a strong speech from the Doge quiets them. Then Simon turns to Paolo and exacts from him a curse on the man who has abducted Amelia. Paolo does not dare refuse; trembling with fear and rage, he utters the curse, but staggers from the room, disgraced.

ACT II.   Paolo has entered the Doge's chamber, sending Pietro to bring in Gabriele and Andrea, who are still in custody. Then he pours poison into the cup usually used by the Doge — he will ensure death one way or another. When the two prisoners appear, Paolo shows that he knows Fiesco's identity and offers him freedom if he will kill the Doge in his sleep. Fiesco, too noble for such an underhanded deed, refuses, and is led away. Gabriele too is about to refuse when Paolo fires his jealousy by telling him that the Doge loves Amelia and she

*Tito Gobbi as Boccanegra
with Ilva Ligabue as
Amelia, 1965, Lyric Opera
of Chicago.*

*Robin Donald as Gabriele
and Joan Cardin as Amelia
lament over John Shaw as
the dead Boccanegra at the
opera's conclusion, 1976,
Australian Opera, Sydney.*

returns his love. When Amelia appears, Gabriele confronts her with treachery, but Amelia does not yet reveal the truth. She hides Gabriele as the Doge enters. When the Doge learns that it is his enemy whom she loves, he refuses permission to marry, but she wins him by swearing to die with her lover. Simon takes a drink from the poisoned goblet, then lies down for a rest. He is disturbed by Gabriele, who creeps in to kill him. Only Amelia has kept watch and now prevents the deed. The truth about Amelia's parentage finally comes out. Simon forgives Gabriele, then sends him out to quiet a gathering mob with a message of peace.

ACT III.   Andrea is released, but learns to his sorrow that the patricians have been defeated in a struggle. Paolo, under guard, tells Andrea of the poison, and the old man is horrified. Paolo is led away, and Andrea waits for the Doge as a Herald goes to the balcony outside the great hall and bids the populace cease their celebration of the victory. The Doge, already feeling the effects of the poison, enters and sits reminiscing over the days of his sea exploits. Fiesco enters, and in a dramatic scene learns of Amelia's true identity—she is his own granddaughter. There is peace between the old enemies at last, and Simon lives long enough to tell Amelia of her true heritage, and to appoint Gabriele as his successor.

UN BALLO IN MASCHERA. When it came to a new opera for the San Carlo in Naples, Verdi ran into more trouble with censors than ever before, even with *Rigoletto*. Not only that, but the venture ended in a lawsuit and more recriminations than could be heaped on a platter. A veritable cabal existed in the southern city, where Saverio Mercadante had reigned for so long and now furiously resented the incursion of this man from the north—and the best-loved composer in Italy at that.

Several abortive tries ensued. Once again the *King Lear* project absorbed Verdi, but he gave up when the singer chosen for Cordelia did not please him. He thought of Victor Hugo's *Ruy Blas*, considered for a time another play by Gutiérrez (author of the plays that inspired *Il Trovatore* and *Simon Boccanegra*) and even had in mind the play by Scribe that eventually became *The Masked Ball*. But the last-named occurred to him only after Naples had refused reworkings of *La Battaglia di Legnano* or *Stiffelio (Aroldo)*; neither did San Carlo wish to mount the all-too-recent *Simon Boccanegra*.

Verdi and Antonio Somma set out on the *Ballo* voyage sanguinely; they expected no trouble. After all, the play by Scribe, the opera written on the play by Auber, and even an earlier opera by Mercadante himself had met with no murmur from the censors. But the times were touchy; the revolution of 1848 haunted the minds of the upper classes, and kings trembled on their thrones.

Mercadante feared, hated, and mistrusted Verdi, with some reason. Although the latter's *Alzira* and *Luisa Miller* had not been entirely successful in the San Carlo stronghold, Verdi had borrowed the name of Violetta, which Mercadante considered his property, for *La Traviata*, and had even borrowed (permanently, as it turned out), Mercadante's prima donna. That Giuseppina Strepponi accompanied his northern rival to Naples and even posed as his wife added fuel to Mercadante's fury. No doubt he influenced the censors, who immediately pounced on the subject Verdi finally selected, to be called *Gustavus III*. No sovereign could be assassinated on stage, to be sure, so the title and the title role had to be changed—the former to *Una vendetta in domino* (Masked Vengeance), the latter to the "Duke of Pomerania." The locale was moved to Stettin. But Verdi balked at changing the time of the action to the thirteenth century. He proceeded to write the music, leaving only the completion of the orchestration and the submission of the libretto to the censors for his arrival on January 13.

This was one day after an Italian anarchist, Felice Orsini, attempted to kill Napoleon III as he was leaving the Paris Opéra. This unfortunate coincidence only inflamed the censors further. A hack writer, Domenico Bolognese, was brought in, the title was changed to *Adelia degli Adimari* (which would have put Verdi into the position of straggling along with a third *Adelia* after Mercadante's own and Donizetti's—which had, in fact been written for Strepponi in 1840. The insult to Giuseppina was also doubtlessly intentional.) Other changes made of the new concoction a monstrosity. Amelia became the sister of Renato—adultery was forbidden. Florence was now the setting, in the fourteenth century. No witch, please, and certainly not a black. No Creole for Renato, either. And no masked ball. No masks, no dancing. Oscar became a lackey with the name Arpino,

Program from the premiere of Un Ballo in Maschera, 1859, Rome.

Drawing of the final scene of Verdi's Un Ballo in Maschera.

which reflected on Verdi's lawyer Arpino. The thing would have been farcical, if it had not been so outrageous.

Verdi tried for months, but nothing would give. He refused to go on; was sued; countersued. The case was settled out of court with the result that Verdi promised to return to Naples in the fall, to mount *Boccanegra*. Meanwhile, he found a sympathetic ear in Jacovacci of the Rome Opera. This man had known all the circumstances of Donizetti's and Strepponi's alliance, had produced Donizetti's *Adelia*—had commissioned it—and engaged Strepponi many times. He accepted *Una vendetta in domino*..

But Verdi's troubles were not over. Rome had censors too, and they wouldn't hear of regicide on stage. The title was changed to the present one, and the choice of Boston as the setting was eventually confirmed. Verdi did not object. The hero became Richard, Count of Warwick, but Verdi held fast to the idea of the gallows hill, which caused some uneasiness. Verdi also prevailed in retaining the black Ulrica, the frisky page Oscar, and the Creole Renato.

The opera was liked by audiences, but various members of the cast fell ill, and only a few performances marked its first season. Performances in Lisbon, Paris (where the locale was changed to Florence), and London followed.

Verdi's political affiliations were well known at this time, and added to his difficulties. Crowds would gather to shout "Viva Verdi!" which signified to the patriots who wanted a unified Italy an acronym: **V**(ittorio)**E**(mmanuele)**R**(e)**D'I**(talia). It has often been stated that these uprisings occurred in Naples at the time of Verdi's struggle for *Ballo*, but Frank Walker (*The Man Verdi*) establishes them in Rome just before *Ballo's* premiere.

In 1861, New York witnessed its first *Ballo*. On February 11, although an attack on Fort Sumter was threatened, the Academy of Music drew a glamorous audience for the newest Verdi work. In the cast were Pauline Colson, Adelaide Phillipps, and Isabella Hinckley. Daring members of the audience climbed to the stage during the masked ball to join the company in a galop specially composed by the conductor, Emmanuele Muzio, one of Verdi's rare pupils.

Nine days later, Abraham Lincoln, on the way to his inauguration in Washington, was present for the first act. He received wild applause, but left soon after the entire company came on stage to sing the national anthem and to cheer him. Thus he did not witness the assassination of a head of state.

The first Metropolitan performance came in the midst of the German seasons, in 1889, so that the emotions of a Swedish king transported to Boston by an Italian composer were sung in German. Verdi's language took over in 1903.

The five leading roles have enjoyed stellar representatives. Think of the tenors: Jean de Reszke, Caruso, Martinelli, Bonci, Björling, Di Stefano, Tucker, Bergonzi, Domingo, Gedda, Pavarotti. Consider the sopranos:

Maggie Teyte as Oscar.

Richard Bonelli as Renato with Elisabeth Rethberg as Amelia, 1940, San Francisco Opera.

Price, Rysanek, Caballé, Arroyo, Ricciarelli. Remember the baritones: Merrill, Milnes, Quilico. And the light sopranos for Oscar, recently among them Reri Grist, Roberta Peters, Judith Blegen. Then possibly the most famous Ulrica of all: Marian Anderson, who made her belated debut in the role in 1955. Many other singers have graced these roles, of course. It is charming to think of Lilli Lehmann singing the German Amelia in those early Metropolitan years.

Ragnar Ulfung as Gustav III (Riccardo) and Anne Lund-Christiansen as Amelia in the Stockholm Opera production which took Verdi's opera back to its original Swedish setting, 1958, Stockholm.

Un Ballo in Maschera

(A Masked Ball)

Text by Antonio Somma, based on Scribe's libretto for Daniel Auber's *Gustave III, ou Le Bal masqué.*

RICCARDO	Tenor
RENATO	Baritone
AMELIA	Soprano
ULRICA	Contralto
OSCAR	Soprano
TOMMASO	Bass
SAMUELE	Bass
SILVANO	Bass
JUDGE	Tenor
AMELIA'S SERVANT	Tenor

First Performance
Rome, 17 February 1859.

In 1958-59, the original Swedish names appeared after the Italian ones in the Metropolitan programs, and the scene was set in Stockholm, where it should have been in the first place. And although performances which have occasionally attempted to resore this milieu did not really work, the plot appeared stronger and more completely believable. A recent Stockholm Opera production went further toward historic veracity, showing the king as an elegant homosexual. This makes the love affair with Amelia ridiculous, however, and destroys the central motive. (The king was, in fact, unhappily married to a Danish princess, but this is ignored in the opera.)

Because the Italian names are now generally used and appear in scores, recordings, and most librettos, they are retained in the synopsis below.

Ballo is one of the most elegant of Verdi's operas, and presents as well a coherent plot and motivations that need no reference to offstage or prior happenings. The music is dazzling, though enigmatic; the roles are musically and dramatically satisfying. Luciano Pavarotti, the effulgent tenor, has said that of all the Verdi roles he would rather sing Riccardo—it has everything. Renato and Amelia are also perfectly rounded characters, with hidden depths revealed in highly emotional outbursts.

ACT I, Scene 1. In the Governor's mansion in Boston, citizens await Riccardo. The malcontents Samuele and Tommaso brood over the Governor's injustices and plot to assassinate him. When the Governor enters, he is immediately handed by Oscar a list of those invited to a masked ball. The young page is an obvious favorite (many implications were noted about this attraction when the central character was portrayed as a homosexual). But the Governor's real attention is focused on a name he sees on the list—Amelia, the wife of his secretary Renato, and he indulges in a reverie about her. Renato arrives, and tells Riccardo of a plot on his life. The Governor lightly dismisses the threat, and forbids Renato to reveal any names of conspirators.

Oscar returns, bringing a judge who wants condemnation of the fortuneteller Ulrica. But Oscar defends the black woman in a lilting aria, "Volta la terrea." This page's sprightly character marks a new side of Verdi's mastery, one of the first injections of true light-heartedness into his galaxy. Riccardo determines to visit the seeress in disguise.

Scene 2. In Ulrica's den, the seeress, presiding over a smoking cauldron, calls on Satan to inspire her. Then as a crowd enters, she predicts good fortune for the sailor Silvano. Riccardo arrives in time to overhear this, and, writing out a promotion, slips it into Silvano's pocket. When the sailor finds it, Ulrica's reputation is ensured. Then Riccardo notes the presence of Amelia's servant, as Ulrica bids everyone depart. The Governor hides as Amelia herself enters, and he overhears her plea to be released from a guilty love for the Governor. Ulrica says Amelia must go to a lonely heath and at midnight pluck an herb that grows under the gallows. Riccardo determines to follow her. But meanwhile, the throng reenters, among them Samuele and Tommaso. Riccardo breaks out into a cheerful sailor's ballad. Then he asks his own fortune. Ulrica reluctantly tells him that he will die by the hand that first clasps his in friendship. Riccardo is only amused, but no one will shake his hand until Renato enters. Hands are clasped, and fate is sealed.

Photo by Beth Bergman.

Luciano Pavarotti as Riccardo.

Ulrica's den with Marion Anderson (far left) as Ulrica, the role in which she made history in 1955 as the first black performer to sing at the Metropolitan Opera, New York.

Scene from Act II of Un Ballo in Maschera, scenery, Alan Barlow and Alix Stone, 1952, Covent Garden, London.

 402
VERDI

ACT II.   Amelia appears on the lonely heath and confesses her terror ("Ecco l'orrido camo"). Riccardo startles her by his appearance and his confession of love, but she gradually yields and admits that she loves him in return. A passionate duet ensues, interrupted by Renato, who warns Riccardo that the conspirators are approaching. Amelia in terror has hidden her face beneath a veil. Riccardo entrusts the lady to her own husband, making him swear that he will not ask her identity. But the conspirators appear, and in the ensuing scuffle, Amelia unveils to prevent bloodshed. The villains are vastly amused, and their hollow laughter echoes as the husband's rage mounts. Renato bids Samuele and Tommaso visit him the next morning on serious business.

ACT III, Scene 1.   At home, Renato threatens Amelia with death, but when she pleads tearfully to see her son once again, he yields to that request, and sends her out of the room. When he is alone, he ruminates that it is not Amelia, but Riccardo who should die. Gazing at a portrait of his friend and benefactor, he sings the stirring aria of embitterment, "Eri tu," (It was you who defiled that soul). The conspirators enter, and Renato informs them that he knows of their plot, and wishes to join it. They engage in a rousing trio, then try to decide who shall commit the deed. Renato places three pieces of paper, each with a name written on it, in a vase. Amelia enters, with the news that Oscar is waiting to see Renato. Renato takes advantage of her presence to force her to draw the name of the man who shall kill her lover. Fearfully, she does so—and it is Renato whose name is chosen. His triumph is cut short by Oscar's entrance, the page caroling an invitation to the masked ball. The conspirators hail the occasion as perfect for their deed, while Amelia determines to warn Riccardo.

Scene 2. Riccardo muses at his desk on the unfortunate events of the recent past, and determines to renounce his guilty love and send Renato and Amelia back to their home. He signs a paper to that effect. Oscar brings a note from a mysterious woman, warning of the plot, but Riccardo dismisses it.

Scene 3. The ballroom, with dancing couples, costumed and masked. The three conspirators wear identical dominoes, and try to discover the Governor's costume. Oscar unwittingly enlightens them. When Amelia appears, Riccardo approaches her and tells her of his plan. They engage in passionate farewells, rudely interrupted by Renato's appearance with a gun. (In some versions, Riccardo is stabbed, but the original plot calls for a firearm.) The shot is fatal, but before he dies, Riccardo nobly reveals his proclamation to send Renato and his wife home, and forgives everyone before he dies. We are left with a sense of high tragedy, and a wonder if Renato and Amelia can ever forgive each other.

The death of Riccardo, the final scene of Un Ballo in Maschera, 1944, Metropolitan Opera, New York.

Zinka Milanov **as Leonora in La Forza del Destino.**

LA FORZA DEL DESTINO. For two years after the premiere of *Un Ballo in Maschera,* Verdi seemed to forget about music, devoting his time to personal matters—he married Giuseppina Strepponi and, always a fervent patriot, allowed his idol Cavour to persuade him to become a member of parliament from his district. After Cavour's death, the composer attended meetings irregularly and was probably relieved when a chance to compose once again was offered to him.

One day a letter arrived from the tenor Enrico Tamberlik, who was singing in St. Petersburg. It contained a commission from the Imperial Theater for an opera, with the fee of 20,000 rubles. The money appealed to the thrifty Verdi, who could very well use it in repairs to his house, but the idea of the cold weather of the Russian capital intimidated him. Giuseppina, however, was delighted at the whole thing, and wrote to a friend that she would do everything in her power to get Verdi to agree: "I shall employ a method which I have been assured succeeds even at the gates of Paradise with St. Peter, and that is to insist and make a nuisance of oneself until one gets what one wants." (Quoted from Julian Budden's 'The Operas of Verdi.")

His attentive wife also saw to it that Verdi would be able to feast on his accustomed Italian cuisine, ordering among other comestibles the following: rice, cheese, salt, pasta, 100 bottles of light Bordeaux, 20 bottles of fine Bordeaux, and 20 bottles of champagne.

The subject Verdi chose was Victor Hugo's *Ruy Blas.* But he did not count on censorship in Russia as well as in Italy—the Tsar objected violently to the idea of a peasant rising to power. The verdict was communicated to Verdi by telegram, which antagonized the touchy composer completely. He, however, suggested a meeting with Tamberlik, but the tenor's son Achille made the pilgrimage instead. With the utmost tact, he insisted that Verdi could do anything he liked—even *Ruy Blas*—with the possible exception of asking Tsar Alexander to declare a republic. Verdi was mollified, but by that time had tired of *Ruy Blas.* After fussing a great deal about finding another subject, he hit on the one that eventually became St. Petersburg's only Verdi opera premiere.

But all this to-do proved useless, for when the Verdis arrived in Russia and rehearsals began, the prima donna fell ill. There was no one to replace her, so Verdi and Giuseppina went back to Italy, promising to return the following September. There was a new soprano this time, and a very good cast, but the opera was not a total success. The Verdis went on to Madrid for the Spanish premiere, which was greeted coolly. New York heard *Forza* at the Academy of Music in 1865, London in 1867. Then Verdi, dissatisfied with the work, asked Ghislanzoni to revise it for La Scala. Piave, the old, trusted librettist, had suffered a stroke. The Milan version has been generally given since, but occasionally an "original" performance will crop up, such as the one at the University of California at Irvine in April 1980. This production boasted an English translation by Andrew Porter, and was staged to approximate as nearly as possible the original Russian showing, even to its five-hour length. The Metropolitan mounted an "original," but not to that extent.

Forza has always demanded the very best singers, and their names will be found scattered through world casts. It was in just such company that

Leonard Warren, himself revered among baritones, fell dead upon the Metropolitan stage on March 4, 1960, leaving aghast his colleagues, Renata Tebaldi, Richard Tucker, Jerome Hines, and Salvatore Baccaloni. It was the first death during a Met performance since the collapse of Armand Castelmary while singing the part of Sir Tristan in *Martha* on February 10, 1897.

Forza will always take an honored place in Metropolitan annals as being the vehicle for Rosa Ponselle's debut, in 1918, with Caruso and De Luca. It was also the Met premiere of the opera. Revivals have included one by Bruno Walter, who used a libretto reworked by Franz Werfel. Milanov, Baum, Tibbett, Pinza, and Petina were the singers.

The play chosen by Verdi for Russia was Spanish—*Don Alvaro*, or *La Fuerza de Sina*, by Angel Perez de Saavedra, Duke of Rivas, himself a romantic character. His central figure is supposed to be an aristocrat, son of a Viceroy of Peru, whose mother is the last descendant of Inca kings. But to the haughty Marquis of Calatrava, with whose daughter the young man has fallen in love, he is unworthy. This Spanish pride is the root of the entire tragedy, for Don Carlo, Leonora's brother, shares it, and would kill for it.

The opera is the most loosely structured of any of Verdi's later period. The revised overture is probably the most popular of any of Verdi's for concert use, embodying several of the most prominent themes, especially Leonora's aria, "Pace, pace."

ACT I.   In Leonora's room in a castle in Seville, the girl says goodnight to her father, the Marquis of Calatrava, then confesses to her maid Curra her repentance for the step she is planning—an elopement with the stranger Alvaro—and her terror at the thought of the obscure future. Alvaro enters through the window over the balcony, and succeeds in persuading Leonora to fly with him, but the delay and the noise they make bring the Marquis. He denounces Alvaro and will not listen to the young man's protestations of honorable intentions. To show his good faith, Alvaro throws down the pistol with which he has threatened to take his own life. It lands at an unfortunate angle and goes off, the bullet striking the Marquis. The lovers hastily escape, with the Marquis's curse in their ears.

ACT II, Scene 1. Leonora's brother, Don Carlo, is in search of his sister and her lover, determined on revenge. The two young people have lost each other in their flight and each believes the other dead. Don Carlo, disguised as a student, has come to an inn in the village of Hornachuelos where a variegated company makes merry. The Mayor asks the student to say grace before dinner, and he obliges. As he is speaking, Leonora, who is staying at the inn in men's attire, peers from her room, but recognizes her brother and withdraws. The scene is enlivened by the entrance of the gypsy Preziosilla, who launches into a song of recruitment for soldiers to fight against the Germans in the war just begun. As she promises to go along, the volunteers are many—her saucy, seductive appearance is attraction enough. She tells fortunes all around, surprising Carlo by penetrating his disguise, although she does not know his identity. Pilgrims now enter, and a great chorus ensues, in which Leonora, still unobserved, joins. Carlo questions the muleteer Trabuco about the companion he has traveled with (apparently Leo-

La Forza del Destino
(*The Force of Destiny*)

Text by Francesco Maria Piave, after the play by the Duke of Rivas.

405
VERDI

LEONORA DI VARGAS	*Soprano*
CURRA	*Mezzo-Soprano*
DON ALVARO	*Tenor*
MARQUIS DI CALATRAVA	*Bass*
DON CARLO DI VARGAS	*Baritone*
PADRE GUARDIANO	*Bass*
FRA MELITONE	*Baritone*
PREZIOSILLA	*Mezzo-Soprano*
TRABUCO	*Tenor*
MAYOR OF HORNACHUELOS	*Bass*
SURGEON	*Tenor*

First Performance
St. Petersburg, 10 November 1862.

Rosa Ponselle as Leonora dressed as a man, in Act II of the opera in which she made her Metropolitan Opera debut, 1918, New York.

Renata Tebaldi as Leonora.

nora), but the surly fellow evades his questions. Baffled, Carlo suggests that they break into the stranger's room and paint mustaches on his face, but the Mayor forbids the prank. Instead, he asks Carlo to explain himself. Carlo relates his story in a ballad, giving false names. Then the company disperses.

Scene 2. Leonora has found her way to the monastery of the Madonna degli Angeli, where she has been promised refuge. Introduced by the "destiny" theme so prominent in the overture, the recitative and aria she sings are the most extensive in the opera, the aria justly famous: "Madre pietosa vergine" (Holy Mother, hear my prayer). She believes Alvaro has deserted her and sailed home, and she longs only for seclusion from the world. This she is promised by Padre Guardiano, in a duet that ranks high among Verdi's accomplishments in this form.

Scene 3. In the church, the Father Superior, who knows Leonora's history, pronounces a curse upon anyone who will disturb her seclusion in a solitary cave on the mountain, where the Father will himself bring her food every day. Dismissed from the earlier scene has been the crusty, grumbling monk Fra Melitone, whose antics provide the few brief moments of humor in the story.

ACT III, Scene 1. In Italy, the war is in progress. Don Alvaro and Don Carlo, each under different names, have enlisted. Alvaro sings of his loneliness in a beautiful aria, "O tu che in seno agli angeli," praying that Leonora will be his guardian angel. His meditation is shattered by noise outside and calls for help. He rushes off, bringing back with him the wounded Don Carlo, whose life he saves. The two men exchange histories (false) and swear eternal friendship.

The battle is joined. Alvaro is wounded and carried into the house of a senior officer. A surgeon accompanies him, and Don Carlo enters, distressed at his friend's condition. A soldier lays a small case on a nearby table. Carlo leans over Alvaro and, as Alvaro recovers consciousness, Carlo promises him the order of Calatrava for bravery. He is astounded at Alvaro's reaction of horror. Alvaro sends the surgeon away. He begs Carlo to take the small case, and, if he dies, to burn the letter within, unopened. Carlo swears to do this. Their duet, "Solonne in quest' ora," is a favorite with tenors and baritones, and was a famous recording by Caruso and Scotti.

Don Alvaro and Don Carlo sing the duet "Solonne in quest' ora," drawing of a scene from Act III of La Forza del Destino.

But after Alvaro has been taken out, Carlo cannot restrain his curiosity. He opens the casket, and though he does not read the letter, finds a portrait of Leonora. Now he knows his enemy! And when a messenger brings the news that Alvaro will live, Carlo rejoices that he can at last achieve vengeance.

Scene 2. (This scene underwent several changes before it settled into the following pattern, which is adopted by the Metropolitan.) A few weeks later, on the battlefield, Preziosilla, Trabuco, and other camp followers try to cheer up the soldiers with a tarantella and some low comedy. Fra Melitone has found his way here, and tries to hold the company's attention with a lecture on their vices, but the soldiers react violently, and Preziosilla has to quiet them with a vigorous Rataplan, which gives the mezzo-soprano a chance to ply a drumstick if she wishes.

The death of Leonora at the end of the opera, left to right, Carlo Bergonzi, Floriana Cavalli and Nicolai Ghiaurov, Covent Garden, London.

Alvaro is now seen, and soon is challenged by Carlo, who reveals his identity and demands a duel. When he learns that Leonora is still alive, Alvaro fights to prevent Carlo from tracking her down and murdering her. But soldiers separate the two, and Carlo is taken away. Alvaro resolves to join a monastery.

ACT IV, Scene 1. In the cloister of the Madonna degli Angeli, Fra Melitone grudgingly serves beggars out of a huge cauldron of soup, grumbling the while. The crowd compares his testiness unfavorably with the gentle demeanor of Fra Raffaelo (in reality Alvaro), which annoys the old monk still further. He kicks over the cauldron in disgust, spilling the soup. The Father Superior rebukes him, and he trots off to answer the ring at the door. It is Carlo, who has tracked down Alvaro. When Raffaelo appears, Carlo immediately tries to provoke a duel, but the new monk refuses, until Carlo's insults to his blood and nationality and his accusation of cowardice goad Raffaelo too far. The two rush out to settle this long and bitter feud. This duet is one of the splendid Verdi examples of writing for high and low male voices.

Scene 2. Leonora emerges from her cave and sings her plea for peace in the renowned aria, "Pace, pace, mio dio." But peace is not for her. The clash of swords is heard nearby, and she returns to her cell. Alvaro wounds Carlo, and seeks the hermit to hear the dying man's confession. When the lovers confront each other, having each believed the other dead, it is a terrible and tremulous moment. But Alvaro has to confess that he has mortally wounded her brother, whereupon Leonora goes quickly to Carlo. Leaning over his body, she hopes for his forgiveness, but he, with his last strength, stabs her to the heart. Alvaro curses the fate that has brought him to such extremes, but Padre Guardiano, coming upon the scene, bids him rather seek the mercy of Heaven, and submit to the force of destiny.

DON CARLOS is considered by many to be Verdi's noblest work. Grand in structure, glorious in music, revealing depths and intricacies of character in its six great roles, it sweeps throughout its not inconsiderable length to powerful climaxes and breathtaking moments of sublimity. In this generation we are privileged to hear a fully considered work, restored to some of Verdi's original intentions while blessed by his thorough revisions.

The opera has experienced a checkered history, for its original version, produced in Paris with an eye toward the eminent Meyerbeer (which accounts for much of its grandeur), did not achieve an especially warm success. Verdi's revision for Italy came more than fifteen years later, when *Otello* was already in his thoughts, and the maturity of his outlook and style pervades the newer *Don Carlos*. As written for Paris, the great length of the work had to be compressed for Italy, so Verdi dropped the first act, retaining only the aria by Don Carlos. When this act is restored, the length of the opera is insupportable. Scissors and paste have been applied by many revisers, so that a "definitive" version is hard to come by, but some recent restorations of material discovered by Andrew Porter bring the *corpus* as near to perfection as it probably will ever be. Mr. Porter has said that he occasionally regrets having exhumed these bits, which Verdi himself may have excised, but asserts that in no case has he left material that Verdi obviously revised. At any rate, we need not concern ourselves with the tiny pieces of this jigsaw puzzle, but may easily follow the story line as it develops.

Although there was no threat of censorship in Paris, Verdi felt a chill when the Empress Eugénie pointedly turned her back to the stage at one moment she obviously considered heretical; still this incident did not halt the procession of a dozen performances. The opera was neglected thereafter in Paris until the 1960s, when the Italian version was given at the Opéra.

Italian seemed to have been the preferred language for performances in other countries, although the Paris structure remained in London and New York productions, the latter in 1877 at the Academy of Music. But at least one New York critic loathed the work, saying that Verdi "was robbing Meyerbeer and had not yet begun to pilfer from Wagner." Any comparison with Wagner inevitably aroused Verdi's hackles. The Paris version (but in Italian) obtained at the Metropolitan's first production in 1920, which even included the five-part ballet with Rosina Galli as soloist. The stars were Ponselle, Matzenauer, Martinelli, De Luca, Didur, and D'Angelo, with Papi conducting. James G. Huneker dismissed the work in his *Tribune* review as "a transitional type, with inchoate plot and score of unequal merit." That was the only time the Fontainebleau scene has been included until 1979-80, for it was dropped in two subsequent seasons in the '20s, although the ballet remained. In 1922, Chaliapin scored a heavy success as King Philip, and twice entranced audiences (although the management disapproved) by repeating the famous Act III monologue.

Thirty years after the Metropolitan premiere, *Don Carlos* returned in splendor, inaugurating Rudolf Bing's first season, with Margaret Webster directing, sets by Rolf Gérard, and a sumptuous cast including Cesare Siepi (in his debut) as King Philip, Jussi Björling as Don Carlos, Robert Merrill as Rodrigo, Delia Rigal as Elisabetta, Fedora Barbieri as Eboli, and Jerome Hines as the Grand Inquisitor. (Bing dropped the final "s" on *Don Carlos*.)

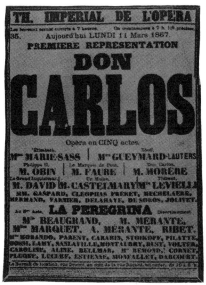

Program from premiere of Don Carlos, 1867, Paris.

Portrait of the historical Don Carlos, son of Philip II of Spain.

Don Carlos

Text by François-Joseph Méry and
Camille du Locle, based on Schiller.
Revised by Verdi and
Antonio Ghislanzoni.

Chaliapin as King Philip.

DON CARLOS	*Tenor*
ELISABETTA DI VALOIS	*Soprano*
PHILIP II, KING OF SPAIN	*Bass*
RODRIGO, MARQUIS OF POSA	*Baritone*
PRINCESS EBOLI	*Mezzo-Soprano*
GRAND INQUISITOR	*Bass*
TEBALDO	*Soprano*
COUNT LERMA	*Tenor*
FRIAR	*Bass*
FORESTER	*Bass*
HERALD	*Tenor*
CELESTIAL VOICE	*Soprano*
COUNTESS OF AREMBERG	*Mute*

First Performance in French
Paris, 11 March 1867.
First Performance, Revised Version, in Italian
Milan, 10 January 1884.

Mr. Hines has remained since to do both bass roles, and was the Inquisitor in the revival of 1979-80. Other singers in this production were Gilda Cruz-Romo or Renata Scotto, Giuseppe Giacomini or Vasile Moldoveanu, Sherrill Milnes, Tatiana Troyanos, and Paul Plishka or Nicolai Ghiaurov.

It is just as well not to look back at the facts of history when considering *Don Carlos*. This son of Philip and grandson of Charles V, Emperor of the Holy Roman Empire, was not the handsome youth who loved his stepmother, but a misshapen epilepsy victim, clumsy and unappealing. After a bad fall and an operation which cut away a part of his skull, he even showed spells of extreme violence—not at all a lovable stepson, although he is said to have formed an attachment to Elisabetta. This lady, of Carlos's age, was married at fourteen to Philip, and lived apparently happily with him, bearing him two daughters. Although feared and hated for his tyranny and closeness to the Inquisition, the monarch showed tenderness to his family, not an uncommon trait among villains. It is good to know these facts, but better to dismiss them when contemplating Schiller's romantic play and Verdi's tremendous setting of it.

ACT I, Scene 1. In the forest of Fontainebleau, Don Carlos waits and watches for a glimpse of Elisabetta di Valois, to whom he is betrothed, and whom he has never seen. He has come to France incognito and without the knowledge of his father, King Philip II. Elisabetta appears on horseback accompanied by her page Tebaldo; they are lost. She gives alms to the peasants, and goes on her way. Carlos comes forth, exultant at the beauty of his betrothed, who is known as Isabella in Spain. He sings the lovely romanza, "Io la vidi" (I have seen her).

When the Princess returns, he throws himself at her feet, begging to serve her, and finally handing her a medallion which contains his portrait. Thus does she know that it is Carlos in the person of the unknown who so attracts her. They vow their new-found love in a meltingly tender duet. Their bliss is cut short when Tebaldo returns and hails her as Queen of Spain. Her protests are silenced as Count Lerma, the Spanish ambassador, tells her that King Philip is to be her husband, in order that peace may be signed between Spain and France. Bitterly, she agrees, and so, perforce, must Carlos. The assembled company rejoices, while the two lovers bewail their fate.

Scene 2. In the Monastery of St. Just, where Emperor Charles V had retired after his abdication, and where he is now buried, his grandson Don Carlos comes to mourn his loss. A chorus of monks prays behind the scenes, and Carlos notes with terror a Friar who closely resembles his grandfather. Rodrigo, Marquis of Posa, enters. When Carlos confesses that he loves his stepmother, Rodrigo urges him to forget his sorrow by championing the cause of the oppressed peoples of Flanders, who are ground under Philip's heel. The two men dedicate themselves to freedom in one of those rousing tenor-baritone duets Verdi so loved: "Dio che nell'alma infondere" (Oh, God, by His infinite love). The King and Queen appear and kneel before the tomb of the Emperor. Carlos is transfixed by the appearance of his beloved, and is restrained by Posa as the monarchs retire.

Scene 3. In the garden of the Monastery, the attendants await the Queen. Among them is Princess Eboli, who with Tebaldo joining in and accompanying on the mandolin, sings the somewhat daring Moorish song, "Canzone del Velo," which describes the predicament of a King who does not recognize his boring wife under her veil and makes love to

Giovanni Martinelli as Don Carlos.

411
VERDI

Lauris Elms as Princess Eboli, 1968 Australian Opera.

Antoinetta Stella as Elisabetta.

Gertrud Palson-Wettergren as Eboli.

her as a possible successor. When Elisabetta emerges from the chapel Eboli remarks her sad and withdrawn appearance, but is distracted from further speculation by the entrance of Posa, who brings news from France and a letter for the Queen. Together with this missive he smuggles a note from Carlos to Elisabetta, who is visibly disturbed on reading it. Eboli's curiosity is averted by Posa, who takes her away and pays her extravagant compliments. Carlos has begged for a last interview, and the Queen grants it, allowing her ladies to realize that she would be alone. They drift away, Eboli still being attended assiduously by Posa, and Carlos begins the interview quietly, but soon loses control and throws himself at the Queen's feet. In a beautiful duet, he begs her to intercede with the King to send him to Flanders, and she promises to try. At first carefully preserving propriety, she at last softens to his ardor, and confesses her feelings for him, though she will not yield to his embrace, even after he has fainted with emotion and recovered to further passionate avowals. She rebukes him, demanding that he behave as a son to his mother, and, his senses returning, he flees. Now Tebaldo hurries in to announce the arrival of the King, but it is too late to summon the ladies-in-waiting, who straggle in, conscience-stricken. Philip immediately singles out the Countess of Aremberg as responsible for leaving the Queen alone, and banishes her. The Queen tries to console the weeping lady in a tender little aria, and all the women depart. The King retains Posa for a conversation, which reveals the Marquis's passionate desire for the freedom of Flanders. The King sternly refuses. Philip admires Posa deeply and requests his close presence, trusting him with the observation of his wife and Carlos, whom he suspects, but warning him to beware the Grand Inquisitor.

ACT II, Scene 1. Carlos has received a note bidding him come to the Queen's garden at midnight, and believes it to be from Elisabetta, but it is Eboli who has written it and who meets him in the gloom. Still under a misapprehension, he pours out his love, and is aghast when the lady drops her veil and he discovers Eboli. Sensing his astonishment, she immediately jumps to the conclusion that it is the Queen he expected. She upbraids him, threatening to tell the King. Posa enters, and threatens in return, but is prevented from killing the woman by Carlos. After an exciting trio, Eboli leaves in a fury, and the two men reaffirm their friendship. Posa asks Carlos to give him any incriminating papers, in case Eboli tries to carry out her threat, and Carlos agrees, although by this time he is wary of Posa's growing intimacy with the King.

Scene 2. (This is the only scene left unrevised by Verdi.) In the great square before the Church of Our Lady of Atocha, preparations are under way for an auto-da-fé, the burning of the heretics at the stake, for which the entire court will gather, along with an eager crowd. The King is in the Cathedral assuming the crown as a token of the solemnity of the occasion. A procession of monks brings in the accused who are to be burned. Elisabetta leads a large retinue from the palace. Representatives from all over Philip's domain form a colorful throng, under flying banners. Now the King emerges and is about to join Elisabetta when a del-

Act II, scene 2, the great square in Madrid, scene of the auto-da-fé. Drawing from the Covent Garden premiere of Don Carlos with Pauline Lucca as Elisabetta, Petit as King Philip, Grazziani as Posa and Emilio Naudin as Carlos, 1867, London.

egation from Flanders, led by Carlos, bars his way, begging for clemency for their beleaguered country. Carlos asks for the governorship of Flanders. Philip is highly incensed, and his fury grows when Carlos desperately draws his sword in defiance. No one dares disarm the Infante until Posa steps forward and demands his friend's sword. Stunned at this apparent treachery, Carlos yields his weapon, and the King confers a Dukedom upon Posa. The procession resumes, and as the pyre is lit, a Heavenly Voice promises the victims life beyond death. "Glory to heaven above!" shout the crowds, as the flames mount.

ACT III, Scene 1. This scene contains some of the most moving and beautiful music Verdi ever wrote. From beginning to end it is one glorious segment after another. It begins with Philip's monologue, "Ella giammai m'amò" (She never loved me), in which he gloomily meditates on his Queen's coldness, his own loneliness, and his inability to read the innermost depths of the human heart. At its close, Lerma announces the Grand Inquisitor. In the ensuing dialogue between the two powerful rulers, and in the marvelous deep bass voices which never sing together but follow one another in rising agitation, Verdi's highest artistry is displayed. The King asks if he may condemn his own son with impunity from the Church. The Inquisitor, a towering old man, almost totally blind, but with the weight of all of the Church's authority

Boris Christoff as the brooding King Philip of Act III, scene 1.

Rosemary Gorden as Elisabetta.

upon him, replies that God gave his only Son. Philip is rebellious at the other's power, but is quickly humbled when the Inquisitor reminds him of higher powers. Then the fierce old man demands that Posa be handed over to him. Philip cries: "Never!" But he has been warned. The Inquisitor summons his acolytes and angrily walks out. Hardly has the door closed when it opens again to admit Elisabetta, who asks for justice in three explosive cries. Her jewelry box has been stolen. The King calmly shows her the box, which has been brought to him, and asks her to open it. She refuses, whereupon he breaks it open, revealing the medallion with the portrait of Carlos that had been given her in Fontainebleau. He immediately accuses her of infidelity. She protests in vain that she was betrothed to Carlos before marrying his father. He calls her an adulteress, and she faints. He summons help, and when Eboli and Posa arrive, the four engage in one of the greatest quartets Verdi ever wrote—some prefer it even to the famous example in *Rigoletto*. Then the men exit, and Eboli is left with the Queen and her own remorse. Eboli explains, in halting phrases, that it was she who betrayed the Queen; and not only by giving the King the jewel box, because of her jealousy over Carlos, but also by being the King's mistress. Elisabetta, frozen by these revelations, bids Eboli in a deadened monotone to return the cross she had given her, then offers her the choice of exile or a nunnery. Left alone, Eboli bursts into the blazing aria, "O don fatale" (Oh, fatal beauty), cursing the endowment that has led her to ruin. Then she quietly and melodiously bemoans her loss of the Queen's trust. Finally, she realizes that one way remains for her to salvage something out of the calamity—she will save Carlos from the prison where he has been immured. This *scena* is the goal of all mezzo-sopranos.

Raina Kabaivanska (l.) as Elisabetta with Grace Bumbry as Princess Eboli in Act III, scene 1 of Don Carlos.

Frontispiece of the piano-vocal score of Don Carlos showing the death of Posa at the hands of the Inquisition, Act III, scene 2.

Scene 2. In Carlos's prison cell, Posa comes to see his friend, urging him to escape by virtue of his own sacrifice — Carlos's papers have been discovered and Posa is marked for death. His noble aria, "Per me giunto" (My life will soon be ended), is all too prophetic; a soldier of the Inquisition has stealthily entered and shoots Posa in the back. As he dies, Philip and his grandees enter, but the crowd outside demands the release of the Infante, and seems to menace the King. The Grand Inquisitor intercedes, sternly commanding the people to kneel before the King, the highest earthly authority. Thus is Church once more superior to throne, saving the King for its own purposes. In the mêlée, Eboli in disguise smuggles Carlos out, telling him Elisabetta awaits him in the Monastery.

Scene 3. Once more in the seclusion of the Monastery, Elisabetta waits for Carlos and in a long and beautiful aria, "Tu che le vanità" (You who knew the vanity of the world), prays to the spirit of the Emperor to intercede with God for her salvation. She mourns her lost love, and longs only for death. When Carlos enters, the two renounce their earthly love in an exquisite duet, "Ma lassù ci vedremo" (Beyond, up in Heaven). Hardly have they said farewell when Philip storms in, demanding that both be given to the Inquisitor. This personage sternly agrees that the Inquisition will perform its task, but at the last moment, the gates of the Emperor's tomb open, and Carlos is drawn within by the Friar to escape (presumably) to Heaven. The awe-stricken crowd recognizes Charles V — is he a ghost? Still alive? This ending is Verdi's; Schiller had concluded bleakly with the Inquisition claiming Carlos. Elisabetta's fate is left uncertain. (In real life, she died the same year as Carlos.)

Frontispiece for the piano-vocal score to Aida.

Teresa Stolz as the first La Scala Aida, 1871, Milan.

AIDA DID NOT RECEIVE its premiere at the opening of the opera house in Cairo, although it was commissioned by Ismail Pasha, Khedive of Egypt. Nor did the opera have anything to do with the opening of the Suez Canal, as is often claimed. Verdi refused the first commission, which was to be a hymn of celebration for the opening. But later he agreed to write an opera, having been lured from his indifference by Camille du Locle, who presented him with an outline for an exotic plot laid in Egypt. This was discovered to be the work of Mariette Bey, a famous Egyptologist, who later concerned himself intimately with details of scenery and costumes, recreating the Egypt of the Pharaohs. (The actuality of the characters has never been established, although there have been many scholarly efforts to do so.) Du Locle, who was director to the Opéra-Comique, was asked to write a scenario, which Ghislanzoni versified in Italian, Verdi taking more than ordinary pains in revising and correcting. The opera was ready by 1870. By then, the Cairo Opera had opened (in November 1869) with *Rigoletto*, and the gala had been dedicated to the Suez Canal, opened at the same time.

But the Franco-Prussian War intervened in the plans for *Aida*. The scenes and costumes, executed in Paris, could not be shipped out. So the new opera was postponed from January 1871 to December of the same year.

The only notable participant in that illustrious occasion was the conductor, Giovanni Bottesini, a celebrated performer on the double bass, as well as a composer. He had become known in America as a soloist, and as conductor at the New Orleans Opera in 1856.

The Aida who had originally been scheduled for Cairo but had to defect because of the delay was Teresa Stolz, whom Verdi admired greatly—and for whom he entertained even warmer feelings, it was said—causing Giuseppina some anxious moments. Stolz finally sang the role in the Milan production which followed on February 8, 1872. Verdi, who had not been able to attend the Cairo premiere, had his watchful eye on Milan, and saw to every detail, even conducting the performance. New York and London heard the new Verdi success shortly after, but the Metropolitan did not pick it up until its third German season, 1886, when, although the cast was the best the company could offer, the language did not seem to convey the complete expression of Verdi's genius. A true representation had to wait until 1891, when Italian management returned, although the heroine was the German Lilli Lehmann (singing in Italian, of course). There has hardly been a season since when this most popular of Verdi operas has been absent, and it has been chosen for the honor of opening nights more often than any **other opera. One such illustrious event was the 1908 opening, when** Giulio Gatti-Casazza made his debut as general director; it was also a first time for Arturo Toscanini. Responding to the imperious baton were Emmy Destinn and Adamo Didur (in debuts), Enrico Caruso, Louise Homer, and Antonio Scotti. It was *Aida* on the bill in Rio di Janeiro the night Toscanini stepped in for an ailing conductor, leaving his post as cellist. The title role has been the choice of virtually every lyrico-spinto-dramatic soprano in history; even Adelina Patti tried it. And tenors fail—or don't even try—to achieve the *pianissimo* that Verdi wanted on the last high B-flat of "Celeste Aida." Mezzos or contraltos glory in the lush vengeance of Amneris, while baritones eagerly don the customary tiger skin of the Ethiopian King Amonasro, and bass-

Two Aidas, Emmy Destinn (left) and Elisabeth Rethberg (right).

es are happy with either Ramfis or the Egyptian King. Here are a few famous names at random: Nordica, Eames, Rethberg, Raisa, Muzio, Ponselle, Giannini, Milanov, Welitsch, Price, Hunter; Tamagno, Martinelli, Zenatello, Slezak, Lauri-Volpi, Vinay, del Monaco, Tucker, Bergonzi, McCracken; Matzenauer, Onegin, Stignani, Castagna, Wettergren, Simionato, Horne, Obraztsova; Merrill, Quilico, MacNeil, Managuerra, Milnes; Siepi, Hines, Plishka, Morris, and so on forever.

No opera house since has matched the opulence of Cairo's *Aida* investiture: real gold for Amneris's crown and real silver for Radames's armor, for example; but every company that has undertaken the production of the opera has lavished as much extravagant scenery as possible on this most durable of stage works—even to elephants and camels in the outdoor performances in Italy.

ACT I, Scene 1. The brief Prelude opens with a high, plaintive theme that will suggest Aida henceforth, and also includes a passage that refers to the priests. We are in Memphis in the time of the Pharaohs; the first scene depicts a hall in the King's palace.

The High Priest Ramfis informs the young patriot Radames that he has been chosen to lead the Egyptian armies against a new invasion by the forces of Ethiopia. Radames, overjoyed at the news, is left alone, and reflects that his new glory may enable him to free the Ethiopian slave, Aida, for whom he cherishes a passionate—and requited—love. He expresses his emotion in the aria, "Celeste Aida" (Divine Aida). The King's daughter, Amneris, surprises him in his reverie, wondering at his happy expression. He disguises his feelings by attributing them to the possibility of his army command, but she begins to suspect that he does not return her love for him, and has cast his eyes elsewhere. When Aida enters, he betrays his agitation and Amneris's suspicions are confirmed. Aida tries to temporize by saying that her unhappiness is caused by rumors that Ethiopia is once again going to try her fortunes against the Egyptians, and when the three join voices, each expresses individual emotions in one of those marvelously wrought Verdi ensembles.

Aida

Text by Antonio Ghislanzoni from a French scenario by Camille du Locle after a prose sketch by Mariette Bey.

RAMFIS	*Bass*
RADAMES	*Tenor*
AMNERIS	*Mezzo-Soprano*
AIDA	*Soprano*
THE KING	*Bass*
AMONASRO	*Baritone*
MESSENGER	*Tenor*
PRIESTESS	*Mezzo-Soprano*

First Performance
Cairo, 24 December 1871.

Campanini as Radames.

The King enters, followed by his court and priests, headed by Ramfis. A messenger brings news of the Ethiopian invasion, whereupon Ramfis announces Radames's appointment and bids the soldier go to the temple to be blessed. The crowd cries for war: "Guerra! Guerra!" and a great chorus ensues, in which the solo voices are heard above all, Aida's soaring in her confusion—whether to pray for her country or her beloved. The climax is a great wish for victory: "Ritorna vincitor!" And Aida is left alone to echo it: "Return victorious?" Can she possibly wish that Radames will conquer her own father? For she, unbeknown to the Egyptians, is the daughter of the Ethiopian King, Amonasro. The concluding words of her high, spun-out aria are: "Numi, pietà!" as she begs the gods to pity her plight.

Scene 2. In the Temple of Vulcan, priestesses evoke the gods and perform a solemn dance as a mysterious chant rises from on high. Ramfis places a sacred veil on Radames's head; thus he is consecrated to his mission. This is the most Egyptian-like of all the scenes, heavy in atmosphere and "oriental" in musical color.

ACT II, Scene 1. In her sumptuous room in the palace at Thebes, Amneris reclines on a couch while her slaves prepare her for the return of the victorious army—Radames has bested the Ethiopians. Little Moorish slaves dance triumphantly. The Princess sighs a long-breathed melody, summoning her loved one, as the slave girls sing the praises of the hero. As Aida enters, Amneris watches her narrowly to see her reaction to the news she is about to fling at her. After pretending to console her for the possible loss of her father and brothers, Amneris suddenly says: "Radames has been killed in battle." Amneris's deepest suspicions are confirmed; then, to make doubly sure, she reveals that Radames does indeed live. Aida's outburst of joy is the final proof; Amneris accuses her of loving the hero and commands that she be present to witness his triumphant return and her own betrothal to Radames.

Marilyn Richardson (l.) as Aida with Elizabeth Connell as Amneris, 1975, Australian Opera, Sydney.

Act II, scene 2, the famous Triumphal March with Richard Tucker as Radames (center on sedan chair).

Scene 2. The resplendent scene of the return of the victorious army is introduced by the famous Triumphal March; the chorus of Egyptians rejoices as the hero is brought on with great pomp, and soldiers parade past the twin throne on which sit the King and Amneris. The spoils of war are proudly displayed; a wild ballet expresses the overwhelming joy of the moment. Then the prisoners are brought in. Among them is Amonasro, Aida's father, dressed in soldier's garb (in some cases this consists solely of a wild animal's skin), and Aida runs to him at once. "Do not betray me," he utters hoarsely. When the King honors Radames with the highest laurels and promises to grant him any request, he asks that the prisoners be freed. Ramfis objects fiercely—this will only lead to further insurrection.

But the King agrees, with one provision suggested by Ramfis: that they keep Amonasro under guard. Then the King astounds Radames by

Adelina Patti as Aida.

Gilly as Amonasro.

Emma Eames as Aida.

Louise Homer as Amneris.

bestowing upon him the hand of Amneris. Aida is as desolate as her lover. The act ends with a tremendous chorus, over which the voices of the principals are heard in individual outpourings of very different emotions.

ACT III. Near a temple on the banks of the Nile, the moon shines down on a peaceful scene. Amneris comes with Ramfis to the temple to give thanks for the victory. After they have disappeared, Aida creeps into view, singing the plaintive aria of unworldly beauty: "Oh, patria mia," lamenting that never again will she see her native ·land. She is there to meet Radames, but it is her father who confronts her, after having eluded his guards. He demands that, to save her country, she elicit from her lover the route that he intends to take to put down yet another uprising by the Ethiopians. She bluntly refuses, but when he curses her as no longer his daughter and no longer a loyal Ethiopian, when he summons her mother's ghost to chastise her, she submits. Radames now joins her, and their duet is highly dramatic, with its forceful melody and propulsive thrust. Then it subsides into a throbbing avowal of love, into which Aida interjects the fatal question, and suggests that they flee together. Although appalled by the thought of leaving his country, Radames does tell her the path he intended to take, so that they may avoid it in their flight. At this moment, Amonasro appears; Radames, completely dishonored, gives up his sword as Amneris and Ramfis confront him. He is arrested; Aida and Amonasro slip away.

Left: Rosa Raisa as Aida.

Right: Marie Brema as Amneris.

Left: Caruso as Radames.

Right: Gadski as Aida.

ACT IV, Scene 1. Amneris is seen near the temple where the priests will gather to determine the fate of Radames. As the hero passes her under heavy guard, she asks to be left alone with him, and pleads with him to retract his confession; she still loves him and would have him for a husband. Their heated duet ends in defeat for the Princess and sure death for Radames, as the priests are heard pronouncing judgment: three times they cry "Traditor!" (Traitor!). Radames is conducted to the subterranean cell where he will be left to die.

Cover of the original published edition of Aida,
showing Radames and
Aida imprisoned in their
tomb, based on the stage
design for the original 1872
Milan production.

Arrigo Boito, composer of the opera
Mefistofele, wrote the librettos for
Verdi's last two operas, Otello and
Falstaff.

Scene 2. In his underground tomb, Radames bewails the fact that he
will never see Aida again—but to his amazement, Aida herself emerges
from the shadows. She has managed to hide herself here in order to die
with her lover. Their duet is one of the most affecting in opera, as they
bid farewell to earth in almost unearthly voices: "O terra addio!" From
above, Amneris, casting herself on the great stone slab that seals the
tomb, pleads for peace for her soul and for Radames.

IT IS SOBERING to think that *Otello* might never have come to performance—so many unfortunate events stood in the path of its completion. In
the first place, Verdi began to believe, after *Aida,* that he was too old to
write more music. He had been acquainted with Arrigo Boito, the young
Italian-Polish poet, since 1861, when Boito supplied the text for the *Hymn
of the Nations,* performed at the International Exhibit in London the following year, a great success and very pleasing to the composer. But one es-
trangement after another occurred subsequently: first, Boito wrote a letter
that was unfortunately made public, in which he reviled the current state of
Italian music. Verdi, as the prime exponent of the nation's opera, was deeply offended. He shunned Boito and his friend, the young conductor Franco
Faccio, from that time, even though the unwitting Boito wrote warmly in
praise of Verdi's works in several publications. There was also a leaning
toward Wagner among Italians of that day, and this was anathema to Ver-

di. Furthermore, one of Faccio's friends got the post at the Milan Conservatory for which Verdi had suggested his old librettist, Piave.

Then Boito and Faccio drifted away from each other, the latter becoming a conductor and the former completing his opera *Mefistofele*, based on *Faust*, which had a successful premiere at La Scala in 1868. Verdi was scornful. Verdi was not mollified even by Boito's defense of the older composer after an imbecilic letter from one Emilio Broglio, Minister of Public Instruction, caused Verdi to return his recently received decoration as Commendatore.

Now Faccio conducted a splendid performance of *La Forza del destino*, and Verdi's publisher Giulio Ricordi got Boito to abandon work on his own opera, *Nerone*, to allow Verdi to compose it. Still, the breach was not healed, and Verdi lost interest in *Nerone*. The noble Boito had made his gesture in vain, and although he resumed work on *Nerone*, it was never really completed and not performed in the composer's lifetime. He also worked on a libretto, *Ero e Leandro*, which Luigi Mancinelli later set.

Things began to look a little brighter for a collaboration between the estranged friends. Faccio had become quite a Verdi expert, so the onus was off him. And *Mefistofele* was revived quite successfully. Still, it required all of the tact of Giulio Ricordi to accomplish the reconciliation. He planted the thought of Shakespeare's *Othello* and Boito in Verdi's mind; Faccio brought Boito around to meet the composer, and Boito came up with the outline of a libretto. Verdi reacted favorably, but was still capricious,

Tamagno as Otello from the 1887 premiere of the work.

Frontispiece for a program from an early Italian performance of Verdi's Otello.

Verdi and Victor Maurel as Iago after the 1887 premiere of Otello, La Scala, Milan.

Emma Albani as Desdemona in the 1891 Covent Garden production, London.

causing one postponement after another. It seemed as if the unborn *Otello* would find a resting place beside that other unattainable Shakespearean effort, *King Lear.*

But the sly Ricordi knew what to do; he got Verdi to work with Boito on the revision of *Simon Boccanegra,* which roused great enthusiasm at its La Scala performance in 1881. Still, five more years were to go by before the *Otello* project came to fruition, marked by several crises and much backing and filling.

The great night came at last. So tumultuous was the applause at the premiere, said to be one of the longest ovations ever at La Scala, that Verdi pulled Boito on the stage, acknowledging him as an equal partner. As we shall see, the friendship and mutual respect persisted, resulting in the finest accomplishment of both men in *Falstaff.*

Boito adhered to Shakespeare's text as closely as possible, but compressing, and omitting the Venetian scenes, then adding two very important sections: the "Credo" of Iago which establishes his villainy plainly, and the "Ave Maria" of Desdemona. Shakespeare before him had done the same sort of thing when he adapted a tale by a sixteenth-century author, Giovanni Cintio.

Faccio conducted the premiere in 1887, and the two chief male characters were of Verdi's own choosing: the celebrated stentorian tenor, Francesco Tamagno, as Otello, and the supremely gifted baritone, Victor Maurel, as Iago. The tenor Italo Campanini (who had opened the Metropolitan's first night as Faust) joined his brother Cleofonte, a fiery conductor, in forming a company to bring the opera to America, where New York heard the premiere in 1888, at the Academy of Music. Eva Tetrazzini, wife of Cleofonte, was the Desdemona; Antonio Galassi, a well known baritone with Mapleson's company, sang Iago. The venture did not last long. Henry E. Abbey brought the opera to the Metropolitan in 1891 after its regular German season closed, climaxing a long tour with a company that starred Patti. *Otello* was a smashing success, with Tamagno, Emma Albani, and Giuseppe Del Puente, foreshadowing the return to Italian opera at the house under Abbey. He, indeed, gave *Otello* in his first season, with Jean de Reszke in the title role. Later Otellos have included Alvarez, Slezak, Martinelli, Zenatello, Vinay, del Monaco, McCracken, Vickers, and Domingo. Desdemona has been sung by Eames, Melba, Alda, Rethberg, Caniglia, Albanese, Tebaldi, Kiri Te Kanawa, Scotto, and Cruz-Romo, among others. Succeeding Maurel (who made his Metropolitan debut as Iago in 1894) have been Scotti, Amato, Tibbett, Warren, Merrill, MacNeil, Stewart, and Milnes.

ACT I.   The curtain rises on a stormy scene, with crashing music depicting the wild sea and winds through which Otello must guide his ship back to Cyprus, where he is governor, after a battle with the Turks. The crowd on shore sings a splendid ditty about the roaring bonfire, then joins Iago in a drinking song; but Iago is without mirth. He despises Otello, who has promoted Cassio above himself, and plots to undo him. Insidiously he works on Roderigo, who loved Desdemona before she married Otello; and he fills Cassio's cup over and over until the young man is quite drunk. Suddenly the ship appears, a great shout of victory is heard from the returning Otello, and he goes into his castle. Iago now provokes a fight between Cassio and the former governor, Montano, the noise of which brings Otello out. Cassio cannot explain his behavior, and is demoted by the outraged Otello. The crowd disperses as Desdemona joins her husband, and a tender love scene ensues, in which the motive accompanying Otello's request for a kiss, and yet another kiss, is memorable.

ACT II.   Iago continues his diabolical plot in the castle garden, counseling Cassio to seek the intervention of Desdemona in an effort to regain his position with Otello. Iago, alone, bursts into the fearful "Credo in un Dio crudel," proclaiming that he believes only in a wrathful God, and that after death there is nothing. At the rear of the stage, Desdemona is seen with Emilia, Iago's wife, receiving flowers

Otello

Text by Arrigo Boito
after Shakespeare.

OTELLO	*Tenor*
DESDEMONA	*Soprano*
IAGO	*Baritone*
CASSIO	*Tenor*
RODERIGO	*Tenor*
LODOVICO	*Bass*
MONTANO	*Bass*
EMILIA	*Mezzo-Soprano*
HERALD	*Bass*

First Performance
Milan, 5 February 1887.

425
VERDI

Otello's waterfront Cyprus palace, 1961, Rome Opera.

Scene from Act II of Otello, left to right, Mario del Monaco as Otello, Renata Tebaldi as Desdemona, Irene Kamarich as Emilia and Tito Gobbi as Iago, Lyric Opera of Chicago.

Victor Maurel as Iago.

and compliments from the populace. This is the time to seek favor, Iago whispers to the returning Cassio. Then as Otello enters, Iago has the perfect gambit—he insinuates that Cassio has won Desdemona's love. Otello is not at first willing to believe this, but when the lady herself importunes him in Cassio's behalf, the wicked seed is planted. Desdemona attempts to soothe his angered brow with her handkerchief, but he casts it aside. This is Iago's moment—he wrests the handkerchief from Emilia, who has retrieved it. Then, as the women depart, Iago continues to instill the poison of suspicion in Otello's mind, saying that he has seen that self-same handkerchief in Cassio's possession, and heard him murmur Desdemona's name in his sleep. Roused to fury, Otello compels Iago to join him in a fearsome duet of vengeance.

ACT III.   A Herald announces the imminent arrival of the Ambassador from Venice to Otello and Iago. The latter advises Otello to hide and watch Cassio. Desdemona comes timidly to Otello, fearing the wrath she cannot understand. She makes the fatal mistake of choosing this moment to press Cassio's cause—he reacts violently, demanding her handkerchief. Of course she cannot produce it. His fury grows, and to her protestations of innocence, he retorts only that she is a strumpet. Barely controlling his rage, he sends her away. He sings of his despair, then follows Iago's advice to hide. Iago enters with Cassio, who innocently plays with the handkerchief which Iago has previously planted in his chamber. Just out of earshot, the jealous husband sees Cassio's lighthearted actions and occasionally catches a word or two as Iago and Cassio approach him. He is now convinced of Desdemona's faithlessness and he determines to kill her. Iago counsels strangling instead of poison, and in the bed she has defiled. They are interrupted by the arrival of the retinue from Venice, headed by Lodovico, who proclaims the return of Otello to Venice and the appointment of Cassio as governor in his place. Otello shows his fury at Desdemona, throwing her to the ground, as the others protest. When all have withdrawn, the Moor falls unconscious in a fit (he was thought to be an epileptic). Iago stands over the recumbent form, ironically pointing to the fallen Lion of Venice.

ACT IV.   In Desdemona's chamber, she prepares for bed with Emilia's assistance, and sorrowfully sings a song about a forsaken lover — the Willow Song, "Salce, salce." She embraces Emilia, then in a sudden heartbreaking outburst, calls her back for a final farewell. Once alone, she sinks to her knees before a priedieu and sings the affecting "Ave Maria," after which she slowly lies down on the bed. In a moment, Otello stealthily enters, and in the colloquy between them — he still accusing her and claiming to have killed Cassio, she tremulously begging for pity — the climax is reached, and he strangles her.

Emilia's cry is heard at the door, and when admitted, she tells Otello that Cassio has murdered Roderigo. Desdemona's faint voice is heard,

Desdemona is unable to understand Otello's fury, Act III, with Mario del Monaco as Otello and Renata Tebaldi as Desdemona, 1957, Lyric Opera of Chicago.

Frances Alda as Desdemona singing the famous Willow Song and Ave Maria, just before she is strangled by her jealous husband in Act IV of Otello.

Victor Maurel as Falstaff, a role he created at the premiere performance in 1893.

claiming she has been killed unjustly. Emilia is horrified and, turning on Otello, calls for help. When Iago appears, she confronts Otello with the truth; Cassio confirms it, and Montano adds further evidence from the lips of the dying Roderigo. Iago escapes (in some versions, first stabbing Emilia), and Otello determines to join Desdemona in death. Lodovico takes his sword, but the crafty Moor draws a concealed dagger and plunges it into his heart. Dying, he crawls to the bier, sobbing a request for a kiss, and yet another kiss, to the music of a similar request in the first act; and he expires upon that kiss.

As a postscript, here is a quotation from George Bernard Shaw: "Instead of *Otello* being an Italian opera written in the style of Shakespeare, *Othello* is a play written by Shakespeare in the style of Italian opera...With such a libretto, Verdi was quite at home."

THERE IS STILL a great deal of mystery surrounding the composition of *Falstaff*, Verdi's final masterpiece. Very little material has been unearthed to date that shows the progression of events that led to the composer's crowning effort. After the success of *Otello*, Verdi seemed ready to settle down

One of a series of drawings depicting scenes from Verdi's Falstaff by such notable artists of the time as Reynolds, Romney, and others. Here is shown the famous scene of Falstaff being stuffed into a laundry basket, Act II, scene 2.

into a comfortable old age. It is fairly certain that his publisher Giulio Ricordi and his *Otello* librettist Arrigo Boito were the levers that brought him into action once more—for the last time, as far as the stage was concerned. In 1889 Boito sent Verdi, who was taking the waters at the spa in Montecatino near Florence, an outline for the *Falstaff* libretto. Verdi had at some time close to that date written Boito that he believed himself too old for such a monumental task, but Boito persisted. Then when Ricordi gently nudged Verdi into promising a delivery date, the old gentleman rather coyly replied that he wasn't sure he wanted this work to be made public—he might just show it in Sant'Agata—if he finished it at all!

But there is no doubt that, with all his soul, Verdi yearned to write a successful comedy to make up for the failure of *Un giorno di regno* years before. The choice of the fat knight of Shakespeare's imagining was inspirational. Into *The Merry Wives of Windsor*, in which Falstaff was shown as a mere buffoon, parts of *Henry IV* were interpolated, to give the clown his more serious and knightly aspects. Whatever Verdi's qualms, he created as masterful a comic opera as Wagner had at middle age *(Die Meistersinger)* or Mozart in his prime *(Le Nozze de Figaro, Così fan tutte)*..

Once more Verdi chose Victor Maurel for his protagonist; the incomparable baritone dominated the role in other opera houses at later performances as well. *Falstaff* at the Metropolitan provided one of the most dramatic incidents that could occur in a singer's career, when in 1925 Antonio

Antonio Scotti as Falstaff.

Lawrence Tibbett as Falstaff.

Falstaff

Text by Arrigo Boito
after Shakespeare.

SIR JOHN FALSTAFF	*Baritone*
FORD	*Baritone*
FENTON	*Tenor*
DR. CAIUS	*Tenor*
BARDOLPH	*Tenor*
PISTOL	*Bass*
ALICE FORD	*Soprano*
NANETTA	*Soprano*
MISTRESS PAGE	*Mezzo-Soprano*
DAME QUICKLY	*Contralto*

First Performance
Milan, 9 February 1893.

Scotti in the title role that had previously brought him acclaim had to give way to the roars of applause that summoned Lawrence Tibbett back for many curtain calls after his powerful delivery of Ford's monologue. Tibbett took over the title role thereafter. Other famous Falstaffs have been Leonard Warren, Tito Gobbi, Geraint Evans, and Donald Gramm. The role of Ford has attracted rising young baritones since. Many charming ladies have graced the roles of the Merry Wives and the young Nanetta, and comely contraltos have intoned their "Rev-er-en-za's" as Dame Quickly.

ACT I, Scene 1. At the Garter Inn in Windsor, Falstaff receives Dr. Caius, who complains that the knight's cronies, Bardolph and Pistol, have gotten him drunk and robbed him. Falstaff grandly dismisses the crochety doctor, and finishes the two letters he is writing, which he asks Pistol and Bardolph to carry to two ladies in the town, Mistress Ford and Mistress Page. In lordly fashion, he would woo them both. When the two henchmen refuse with false pride, Falstaff sends the notes off with a messenger and furiously lets Pistol and Bardolph know what he thinks of their "honor." This monologue, directly out of Shakespeare, is set with sparkling irony and relish. At its close, Falstaff chases the two scoundrels out of the inn with a broom.

Scene 2. Mistress Page meets Mistress Ford in front of the latter's home, and both discover that the letters they have received are identical. With them are Dame Quickly and the Fords' daughter Nanetta. Their sprightly quartet is the first of this form to spring in this score like quicksilver from Verdi's pen, soon to be matched by a fivesome of gentlemen—Ford, Caius, Bardolph, Pistol, and young Fenton, who is in love with Nanetta. Sometimes the women are heard alone, sometimes the men; occasionally they all mingle in a delightful web of sound, each group singing in a different time measure. Fenton and Nanetta twice manage a moment alone, time for a snatch of love song whose tender melody recurs and lingers in the memory. Vengeance is in the air, formulated by both men and women.

ACT II, Scene 1. Back at the Inn, Bardolph and Pistol play false with Falstaff, asking his pardon and promising to reform. They introduce Dame Quickly, who makes deep bows accompanied by her stentorian "Reverenza" until Falstaff impatiently tells her to get about her business. He is happy when he hears it—Alice Ford will receive him but Meg Page is kept indoors by her husband and cannot. The hour of the rendezvous is from two till three ("Dalle due alle tre' "), repeated comically several times. Falstaff tips Quickly a paltry coin and she retires, leaving Falstaff to anticipate with delight the coming meeting in bubbling measures, and a comic little march, "Va, vecchio John" (Go, old John).

Now another visitor is announced—Mister Brook. In reality it is Ford, who has learned of the letters from Bardolph and Pistol. He poses as a man wildly in love with Mistress Ford, who will not listen to him; he has heard of Falstaff's prowess, and begs him (with the inducement

Regina Resnik as Dame Quickly.

Left to right: Oralia Dominiguez as Dame Quickly, Margaret Roggero as Mrs. Page, Elisabeth Schwarzkopf as Mrs. Ford and Audrey Schub as Nanetta, Act I, scene 2 of Falstaff, San Francisco Opera.

Sketch of Act II scene 2 showing Falstaff being stuffed into the laundry basket (far right) and Dame Quickly's famous 'reverenza,' or curtsy, done at the time of the 1893 La Scala premiere of the opera, Milan.

Judith Raskin as Nanetta.

of a fat purse) to go before him, seduce the lady, and thus open the door for him. Falstaff replies with glee that he has an appointment that very afternoon and will certainly pave the way for the generous Mister Brook. Ford hears himself described in the most unflattering terms, which increases his rage. Then Falstaff goes off to adorn his huge person and leaves Ford to indulge his fury in the famous monologue. When the gaudily clad Falstaff waddles back in, the two men outdo each other in false courtesy, but at last manage to leave the room together.

Scene 2. In Ford's house, the four women are plotting Falstaff's downfall. In the course of the conversation, it is made plain that Ford intends to marry Nanetta to Dr. Caius, but Alice Ford is determined to thwart this outrageous marriage. Their ensemble is vivacious, but soon Quickly warns of Falstaff's approach, and all hide but Alice, who sits pensively playing the lute as the fat suitor enters. Falstaff sings an extravagant paean to her beauty, and tells of his youth in the graceful "Quand' ero paggio" (When I was page to the Duke of Norfolk). But they are interrupted by Quickly, who says Ford is on his way home. Falstaff is hidden behind a screen as the men storm in, and as they scatter to search the house, the fat man is smuggled into a huge laundry basket brought in by servants, and is covered with soiled linen, to his vast discomfort. Nanetta and Fenton manage to conceal themselves behind the screen, and are discovered by Ford. Then in the absence of the searchers, the servants dump the basket into the river outside the window. When Ford returns, his wife treats him to the spectacle of her erstwhile suitor's humiliation. The Fords are reconciled in hilarity.

ACT III, Scene 1. Sneezing, wrapped in blankets, with his bare feet in a tub of warm water, the disgruntled Falstaff calls for more wine, hoping that it will counteract the horror of the river water within his paunch. At least it has the effect of cheering up the old rogue. But his sanguine mood is darkened by another visit from Quickly—with her multiple curtseys and greetings that Falstaff now finds tiresome. She at last persuades him that the two ladies will in reality meet him, but it must be at midnight at Herne the Hunter's Oak in Windsor Forest. All the others watch from hiding and plan Falstaff's discomfiture. The gullible knight arrays himself in a helmet with great horns, the disguise of the black huntsman who was supposed to have hanged himself from the oak tree, and repairs to the rendezvous.

Scene 2. Fenton sings a beautiful aria, in which he expresses his love for Nanetta, then midnight strikes. Falstaff's meeting with Alice is brief—they are interrupted by elves, goblins, and other mysterious beings, while dragonflies dance about. Falstaff hides, but all eventually discover and torment him unmercifully. In this mêlée, Alice's plot is working—she has managed to so disguise the principals that when Ford witnesses the marriage of his (supposed) daughter to Caius, it is Bardolph who is disclosed as the "bride," and the real lovers are united in their disguises. At the end, everyone happily joins in a magnificent fugue, led by Falstaff, who claims that "jesting is a man's vocation. Wise is he who is jolly." This unlikely musical form for the end of an opera was Verdi's rare accomplishment; he had managed it once before in *Macbeth*, and his mastery of the difficult form, while keeping a melodic and dramatic sheen over the musical fabric, was his final operatic triumph.

Thomas Stewart as Falstaff, 1975. Santa Fe Opera.

Frank Guarrera as Falstaff and Charles Anthony as Bardolph.

Richard Wagner, painting by F. von Lenbach.

Josef Tichatschek as the first Rienzi, 1845, Dresden.

RICHARD WAGNER (Leipzig, 22 May 1813 — Venice, 13 February 1883). Wagner remains one of the most — perhaps the most — controversial composers in history, polarizing opinions for and against his music and his character. The great innovator of the nineteenth century, he virtually split the atom of music, creating the fission that is known as chromaticism. His work opened the door to the twelve-tone music that was to become in its way as much a center of dissension as his own when launched by Arnold Schönberg and his disciples.

Wagner was the first to write his own texts exclusively, and is still the most eminent composer to claim this distinction. One of the latest to develop a real and apparent talent, he began formal studies only in his late teens, having rather recklessly spent his time and efforts in many abortive ventures in youth and early manhood.

His life was a succession of schemes and scandals — indeed, it has always been difficult for some to separate the man from the artist, to revile the person while adoring his genius. Scoundrel is not too strong a word for the man; nor is genius for the artist. The darker side of this phenomenon was described by Deems Taylor in a radio talk entitled "The Monster." A liar, a cheat, a profligate; a supreme egoist who believed the world owed him a living; a libertine whose pursuit of women was ruthless and self-serving; a betrayer of close friends; an unscrupulous borrower of money and a laggard repayer — in short, amoral to the core.

The young Wagner moved from town to town as his stepfather, Ludwig Geyer (who may have been his real father) found engagements as a playwright and actor. Wagner's musical education was patchy indeed, but he began serious study in 1831 and feverishly devoured symphonic scores by Mozart and Beethoven. A year later he wrote his first opera, *Die Hochzeit*, but abandoned it because his sister thought the story too bloody. The first completed stage work (in 1883) was *Die Feen* (which, however, was not produced until 1888). By this time he was chorus master in Würzburg, but moved to Magdeburg in 1834, to take a position as theater conductor. Here his second opera, *Das Liebesverbot* (The Love Ban), was unsuccessfully given in 1836. This same year he met and married the actress Minna Planer, and moved to Königsberg, conducting there for a year. Riga came next in his migrations; *Rienzi* was composed there, but the Wagners, in the first of a series of escapes from debt, fled to London. Then the exploits of Meyerbeer in Paris attracted him, and in hopes of rivalling that genius, he and Minna set forth for the French capital. The stormy voyage in a small boat from Riga to London, together with his knowledge of the legend of the Flying Dutchman, had already planted the inspiration for that opera, which he worked on even while in debtor's prison for a short time in 1840. *Rienzi*, now complete, was sent to Dresden, and eventually being accepted, brought the Wagners back to Germany. Meanwhile, however, the libretto for *The Dutchman* suffered a sad fate: it was bought outright for 500 francs, set by an inferior musician, and produced at the Paris Opéra in 1842, a failure. *Rienzi's* success in Dresden led to an equally good production of his own *Dutchman* there in 1843 and his appointment as music director for the Saxon court. For six years he produced other men's operas with distinction, and completed his own *Tannhäuser*, which was produced in 1845. But he could not secure production for the next work, *Lohengrin*, except for a

Franz Liszt, who encouraged Wagner early in his career, was the father of Wagner's second wife Cosima, the illegitimate child of Liszt and the Countess Marie d'Agoult.

fragment. Franz Liszt rescued the new work, producing it at Weimar in 1850, although Wagner did not hear it until much later.

By the middle of the century, the composer became restless and dissatisfied with the "bourgeois" life around him, and allowed himself to become involved with revolutionary groups. During the May uprising of 1848, he was forced to flee Saxony, taking refuge first in Weimar, then in Jena, and finally in Zurich. Minna joined him there, and he began to delve deeply into literary pursuits, concocting the philosophical studies that aroused ridicule in some quarters, reverence in others. Here was coined the term, "Music of the Future," which was to cause endless argument on the continent and elsewhere.

In 1852, Wagner completed the poems of the Nibelung Trilogy. He had become involved in a love affair with a married woman, Jessie Laussot, and attempted to desert Minna, but eventually returned to her in Zurich. Still another amorous adventure befell him; he became enamored of the wife of a wealthy merchant, Otto Wesendonck. Wagner and Minna went to live on the Wesendonck estate where Richard could be near his beloved Mathilde, for whom he wrote the famous five songs set to her poems.

In 1854 he completed *Das Rheingold* and, influenced by Schopenhauer, began to work on *Tristan und Isolde*, carrying it with him at the same time he was completing *Die Walküre* (1856) and working on *Siegfried* (1856-57). The situation with Mathilde, meanwhile, was explosive. Minna left Wagner, and he went to Venice, where he completed the second act of *Tristan*.

Mathilde Wesendonck.

King Ludwig II of Bavaria, one of Wagner's most loyal benefactors.

Things began to look up about this time: Wagner conducted a series of successful concerts of his own music in London in 1855, which added to his world fame and to the arguments for and against his compositions. Paris became interested again, under the influence of Napoleon III, and he conducted concerts there, then saw *Tannhäuser* produced at the Opéra in 1861. But it aroused such fierce opposition that only three performances were given.

Germany accorded him an amnesty in 1860, although Saxony did not **reprieve him until two years later. Minna had come back to him in 1859,** but separated decisively from this erring husband in 1861, and died in Dresden in 1866. Wagner went to Vienna in 1861 and heard *Lohengrin* for the first time. But there was no hope of a *Tristan* production, so he returned to Paris and worked on the libretto for *Die Meistersinger* (which had been in his thoughts for many years). The music was not finished until 1867.

Tristan was finally accepted in Vienna, but given up—after seventy-seven rehearsals—as "impossible." Although Wagner had some success in concerts in Russia, his finances now became impossibly muddled. Two things happened at this juncture that were to change the currents of his artistic and personal life. King Ludwig II of Bavaria became fanatically interested in the composer's output, and Wagner fell in love with Liszt's illegitimate daughter by the Countess Marie d'Agoult. Not only was Liszt the benefactor of his profligate colleague, but the husband of Liszt's daughter Cosima, Hans von Bülow, befriended Wagner even after his wife had left him and gone to live with Wagner. Cosima bore three of Wagner's children before obtaining a divorce and marrying her lover.

Wagner now began to work seriously on his last operatic venture, *Parsifal*, and to dictate his autobiography to Cosima. Munich became impossible for the couple, because of court intrigues and complaints about Wagner's private life, so they moved to Switzerland. Munich however gave the premieres of *Meistersinger* (1868) and *Das Rheingold* (1869). Wagner fell

In 1872 Wagner's dream of a theater of his own was realized when King Ludwig offered him Bayreuth for this purpose.

Richard and Cosima Wagner.

under the influence of the philosopher Nietzsche at this time. And his long-cherished dream of a theater of his own was about to be realized.

King Ludwig, who never lost faith in his protégé, offered Bayreuth as a site for this theater, and the Wagners moved there in 1872. The cornerstone of the famous Festspielhaus was dedicated on May 22 of that year, and the house, Wahnfried, that later became the Wagner shrine, was built.

Finally, in 1876, the dream came to fruition. Three complete performances of *Der Ring des Nibelungen* were produced in the house that was to become the Mecca of Wagnerites from then on. Hans Richter conducted the performances, which brought réclame but little salve to Wagner's sore bankroll. *Parsifal*, his last work, the "Bühnenweihfestspiel" (sacred festival drama), was finished in 1882, and performed in Munich that year under Wagner's supervision. He and Cosima left in the autumn for Venice, where Wagner died suddenly on February 13. His remains are buried in the garden at Wahnfried.

It is unfortunate that Wagner's grandiose ideas of the egoistic superman proved so attractive to Hitler, who went often to Bayreuth and cultivated the friendship of Wagner's daughter-in-law, the English Winifred, who had married Wagner's son Siegfried. The resulting stigma in the eyes of the rest of the world was slow to disappear, and the Festival was discontinued at Bayreuth for a period during World War II, resuming only in 1951, when Wagner's grandsons, Wieland and Wolfgang, restored its prestige with sweeping reforms. Wieland was the more adventurous of the two, and after his death, Wolfgang returned to more traditional presentations.

Wagner lived, as John Russell of the New York *Times* wrote, speaking of Picasso, during the lifetimes of Darwin and Marx and Nietzsche, and "believed what they believed: that we are sent into the world to change it, rather than to add an amusing garnish to the way things had always been... [and] thought of his career as a duel to the death between himself and the status quo.

Cosima Wagner in later years.

Program for the premiere performance of Rienzi, 1842, Dresden.

438
WAGNER

Rienzi

Text by the composer
after Bulwer-Lytton's novel.

COLA RIENZI	*Tenor*
IRENE	*Soprano*
STEFFANO COLONNA	*Bass*
ADRIANO	*Mezzo-Soprano*
PAOLO ORSINI	*Bass*
RAIMONDO	*Bass*
BARONCELLI	*Tenor*
CECCO DEL VECCHIO	*Bass*
MESSENGER OF PEACE	*Soprano*

First Performance
Dresden, 20 October 1842.

RIENZI, WHICH Hans von Bülow wittily called "Meyerbeer's best opera," has had a sketchy performance record in the United States. Indeed, it was not heard here for the first time until 1878 (at the New York Academy of Music), thirty-six years after its premiere in Dresden, when Joseph Tichatschek created the title role, and Adriano, Wagner's only "trouser" role, was sung by Wilhelmine Schröder-Devrient. In the Metropolitan's German years, the opera was given in 1885-86, 1886-87, and 1889-90, the first two years starring Lilli Lehmann as Irene and Marianne Brandt as Adriano. Eloi Sylva sang Rienzi the first year, and Anton Schott the second. Anton Seidl conducted. The other revival was notable only for a change of conductor: young Walter Damrosch presided. After that, silence from the Metropolitan, although a German company gave New York performances in 1923. Forty years after, Thomas Scherman revived the work in concert form, and a similar presentation was given by Eve Queler and her Opera Orchestra of New York in 1980.. Meanwhile, San Antonio, among other rare cities, staged Rienzi fairly completely in 1977 with distinctive results. German cities have heard it more often, as was to be expected, but it is impossible to find it listed in Covent Garden annals.

Uniquely, it is the only surviving piece of Wagner's for which he used another man's original work, in this case the novel by Bulwer-Lytton. Thereafter, he was his own man with words.

In spite of its inordinate length (five acts, if uncut), it is a pity that the opera is not more often heard. The acute ear can find in it the cells from which practically every musical structure of Wagner's sprang (except perhaps the work immediately following, the so-called "Italianate" *Dutchman*). It is fascinating to trace the beginnings of great things.

The overture, of course, is a concert staple, and enables listeners to identify many leading themes. Particularly prominent is Rienzi's "Prayer," which tenors occasionally put on concert programs, if they dare. The part is a truly heroic one, but also exacting are those of the two ladies involved.

The hero is Niccolo Gabrini, a papal notary known as Cola di Rienzi, and the full title of the opera is *Cola Rienzi, der Letzte der Tribunen*, for he will be the last of the Roman tribunes.

ACT I.   In the street outside San Giovanni Laterano in Rome, it is apparent that Paolo Orsini, a Roman nobleman, is attempting to abduct Rienzi's sister Irene from her house. But the abduction is foiled by the arrival of Steffano Colonna, another noble, and the followers of the two men begin fighting. Steffano's son, Adriano, rushes in to defend Irene, with whom he is in love, and Rienzi also comes upon the scene. Outraged at the behavior of the nobles, he is further inflamed by Cardinal Raimondo and passionately vows to curb the aristocrats' power. Adriano joins him in overpowering the nobles and the people hail Rienzi as their deliverer.

ACT II, Scene 1. In a large hall in the Capitol, Rienzi, now the sole ruler in Rome, receives a procession of youths dressed in white, messengers of peace. They assure him that the countryside is indeed peaceful. He receives foreign representatives and the subdued nobles, whom he reminds of their promise to be peaceful.

Act II, scene 3 of Rienzi, stage design from the first English production of the work, 1879, by the Carl Rosa Company. The leading role of Cola Rienzi was sung by the English tenor Joseph Mass.

Scene 2. The nobles, chiefly from the houses of Orsini and Colonna, are deeply resentful and plot Rienzi's downfall. Adriano, overhearing their plan to kill Rienzi, hurries to warn him.

Scene 3. A procession of people approaches the great hall of the Capitol, where Senators and nobles are waiting. Rienzi enters with Irene, and orders entertainment to proceed. Adriano takes this opportunity to warn the tribune of the plot against him. During the festive dances, Orsini and his fellows approach and Orsini attempts to stab Rienzi; but the shirt of chain mail he is wearing under his tunic saves him. Now Adriano pleads for Orsini's life, and Rienzi, touched, agrees to spare the nobles on condition that they take a new oath of allegiance. They agree, but rebel in secret.

ACT III. Rienzi's soft treatment of the nobles is resented by the people, who once again are called upon to fight. Rienzi leads them to triumph in battle. Adriano, torn by his two loyalties, pleads in vain for his father's life. When the corpses of Orsini and Colonna are brought in, Adriano turns against Rienzi in anguish, and is rejected by the tribune as the victory bells sound.

ACT IV. The nobles have not given up, but have appealed to the Emperor, saying that Rome is being ruled by a dangerous rebel. They also seek the Pope's intercession so that Rienzi is confronted by two enemies as he approaches the Lateran Church for a thanksgiving service. Adriano has made up his mind to kill Rienzi, but his courage

Anton Seidl conducted the Metropolitan Opera's 1885-86 premiere of Rienzi, New York.

Program from the premiere of The Flying Dutchman, 1843, Dresden.

fails as Rienzi addresses the crowd. As Rienzi is about to enter the church, he is confronted by Raimondo, the Papal Legate, in full regalia, who pronounces a Papal ban on the tribune. Rienzi is stunned, and the people recoil in horror. Adriano tries to persuade Irene to leave her brother, but she will not listen. The young man leaves, as a final sombre chorus of priests and monks is heard.

ACT V.   In a room in the Capitol, Rienzi kneels and prays. He still has faith in God and in the people. Irene enters and attempts to console him, but he warns her that if she stays with him she will also be cursed. He leaves for one more attempt to rouse the people. Adriano enters, trying to persuade Irene to go with him — the Capitol is in danger of being burnt, he says, and Rienzi's life is in grave danger. But she persists in her loyalty, and, joined by Rienzi and the repentant Adriano, stands stoically on a balcony of the Capitol as the flames mount and eventually envelop the scene.

THE DUTCHMAN got off to a slow start, and has never quite caught up in popularity with Wagner's later works, although occasional new productions — such as the startling one by Jean-Pierre Ponnelle for San Francisco in 1975 (and the Metropolitan in 1979) — occasionally arouse public excitement. Even Dresden did not take warmly to the opera with which it launched the young composer, until a revival in 1865. The fact that it was sung in Italian in both London (where it was the first taste of Wagner for the British public) in 1870 and in Philadelphia in 1876 cannot have been the best auspices. Its original language was restored for a performance in New York's Academy of Music in 1877, but Tannhäuser and Lohengrin, both of which had preceded it, held the boards more firmly.

Still, The Dutchman was chosen by Anton Seidl to open the Metropolitan season of 1889, but once again the Italian language prevailed for an 1892 revival, with Emma Albani singing her last appearance in America and Jean Lassalle his first Dutchman, with Edouard de Reszke as Daland. Senta was sung by Milka Ternina and Johanna Gadski, and Schumann-Heink was Mary.

A revival in 1930 brought Friedrich Schorr and Maria Jeritza; another in 1937 starred Flagstad. Rudolf Bing mounted the opera in his first season, 1950-51, with Hans Hotter and Astrid Varnay. Later revivals were several, with, among other singers, Rysanek, London, Dooley, and Tozzi. The "scandalous" Ponnelle production at the Metropolitan featured Carol Neblett, José van Damm, Paul Plishka, and William Lewis singing the combined parts of the Steersman and Erik — one of Ponnelle's fantasies that outraged the critics.

The theme of "redemption through love" appears in Wagner's works for the first time here. It was to be central to the others. The adoption of legendary subjects for the composer's own librettos (broken only in the case of Die Meistersinger) also found its first outlet here. And the beginning of "the music of the future" is in The Dutchman, although a few "set pieces" remain in the flow of orchestral music that was to dominate from now on, making the music serve the text. Another innovation was the use of the leitmotif, the phrase that would distinguish a particular character, mood, emotion, or idea, whenever it appeared. This usage, not exclusive to Wagner by any means, but closely identified with his music dramas, permeated his works from now on.

Various sources exist for the legend that Wagner chose. There was the story of the doomed Vanderdecken, who recklessly vowed to sail his ship around the Cape of Good Hope if it took until eternity and was condemned to do just that. A story in *Blackwood's Magazine* in 1821, an English play **inspired by it, and a novel on the same subject by Captain Maryatt in 1839** may all have contributed. But a more direct influence was Heinrich Heine's novel, *Memoirs of Herr von Schnabelewopski*, which appeared in 1839. In it is the first indication of a woman's true love redeeming the condemned man. The calamitous voyage from Riga to London in 1839 crystallized the idea in Wagner's mind. The ship paused in a Norwegian fjord, and the music of the sailors inspired a similar scene in Wagner's already forming conception.

"The passage among the crags," he wrote, "made a wonderful impression on my fancy; the legend of the Flying Dutchman, as I heard it confirmed from the seamen's mouths, took on within me a distinct and peculiar color which only the sea adventures I was experiencing could have given it."

As we have seen, Wagner's attempt to sell his libretto to Paris only re-sulted in another man's composing the music. After the fiasco it produced, Wagner wrote his own music for the libretto in seven weeks.

Not only did Wagner conduct the Dresden premiere, but he occupied himself with every detail of the staging. He wanted the opera to be played

Anton Van Rooy as the Flying Dutchman, 1907 Metropolitan Opera, New York.

in one act, but various considerations prompted the separation into three. Ponnelle's production restored it to the original single act, which consumed almost two and one-half hours. But the cumulative effect of the unbroken line showed the advantage of the original conception.

There are two principal themes to be noted: the motif of the Dutchman himself which opens the Overture, and the theme of redemption, which is first heard after the cessation of the fury of the storm and the sea. The Overture was written last, so that the chief themes of the opera were included. Wagner later rewrote the conclusion, expressing the "transfiguration" idea later employed in *Tristan* and *Götterdämmerung*.

ACT I.   Daland's ship comes ashore on a rocky coast as a storm rages. His sailors make the ship fast, singing a joyful chanty, and Daland inspects the landing place. It is at Sandwike (the very village where Wagner's ship had found refuge in the fjord), and only seven miles from Daland's home. He goes below for a nap, sending the sailors within, and leaving the Steersman on guard. The Steersman sings a song to his "Mädel," then falls asleep. As the storm picks up again, a phantom ship appears, its sails blood-red, and coasts silently to port just beside Daland's ship. The Dutchman emerges, as his ghostly crew makes the ship fast. Sadly, the Dutchman sings of his fate: one more seven-year portion of his penance is at an end, and he is free for a short time to seek the woman's love that shall redeem him. His monologue begins with the orchestral motif that characterizes his wandering. He has tried by many means to find death, but in vain. Unless he can find a woman who will be faithful to him, he is doomed to wait for the end of the world for his own demise. The crew echoes his last phrases, welcoming eternal death.

Der Fliegende Holländer

(*The Flying Dutchman*)

Text by the composer.

442
WAGNER

DALAND	*Bass*
SENTA	*Soprano*
ERIK	*Tenor*
MARY	*Mezzo-Soprano*
STEERSMAN	*Tenor*
THE DUTCHMAN	*Baritone*

First Performance
Dresden, 2 January 1843.

The Flying Dutchman meets Daland, the ship captain, in a scene from Act I of the Flying Dutchman.

The Dutchman's phantom ship.

Daland now comes on deck and spots the strange ship, scolding the Steersman for not waking him. He goes ashore to speak to the Dutchman, who answers his questions evasively, but promises him great reward for a night's lodging. Does Daland indeed have a daughter? Who might be eligible for marriage? Daland, overcome by the promise of great treasures, joins the Dutchman in a duet, each congratulating himself on his find. Then Daland sets off for home, the Dutchman to follow.

ACT II.   The orchestral prelude was lengthened from a relatively brief interlude when the opera was divided into three acts. The curtain rises to show a room in Daland's house, where the girls of the village are at their spinning wheels, led by Mary, Daland's housekeeper. Their song is very popular; the orchestra emulates the whirr of the spinning wheels under a sweet vocal harmony. Senta, Daland's daughter, sits apart, gazing at the portrait of a strange man on the wall. She has heard the legend of the Dutchman, whose portrait this is, and is enraptured by it. The girls tease her and warn that Erik, her humble suitor, will be jealous. She asks Mary to sing the ballad of the Dutchman, but Mary superstitiously refuses. Senta thereupon sings it herself, launching into the three wild verses with great force and abandon. At its close, she leaps to her feet and vows that she will be the one to save this unfortunate soul. Erik, entering at that moment, overhears, and distractedly relates a dream that he has had in which he has seen Daland returning with a stranger—the very man in the portrait—who will win Senta. Now, bringing the news of Daland's safe landing, he realizes that his dream may come true. He leaves in dismay.

Daland enters, and in a jolly aria tells his daughter that he has promised her hand to the stranger who follows him into the room. He shows her the jewels he has received in return. Senta and the stranger meanwhile are gazing deeply into each others' eyes, riveted by the recognition of their destiny. (It has always been a mystery why Daland does

Joel Berglund as the Flying Dutchman.

Kirsten Flagstad as Senta.

not recognize in the stranger the portrait of the Dutchman which has hung on his wall for such a long time. This is one of the unexplained curiosities of opera plots.)

Left alone, the two stand motionless while the orchestra comments on the themes of the Dutchman and redemption. Then the man begins a recitative which develops into a melody fraught with passion. Senta joins in a duet which expresses their deepest emotions. Daland reenters, gives them his blessing, and calls for a celebration as the curtain falls.

ACT III.   The scene shows a rocky strand, with the two ships anchored near Daland's house. The Norwegian sailors are making merry, singing boisterously, and jollying the girls of the village. The Dutchman's ship is dark and silent, and only begins to show signs of life after the girls have left, frightened by its menace. Weird sounds are heard, and the ghostly crew sings a taunt to their captain, predicting that once again he will fail in his quest. The two groups of sailors sing in opposition, but at last the Norwegians, frightened by the others, go below decks, accompanied by jeering laughter from the other ship.

Senta comes from her house, followed by Erik, who is desperately pleading his cause once more. She repels him, but the Dutchman overhears part of their dialogue and immediately suspects Senta of unfaithfulness. All her protests are in vain. Her saturnine lover summons his crew and prepares to sail. At the conclusion of the trio (Erik pleading, Senta protesting her faithfulness, the Dutchman sadly renouncing her and releasing her from her vow), the doomed pilgrim tells the girl of her sad fate should she go with him. He mounts to his ship, which sails on the instant. Senta breaks from the restraining arms of Erik and throws herself into the sea, whereupon the phantom ship sinks, and Senta and the Dutchman are seen, transfigured.

TANNHÄUSER has suffered from "versionitis" more than any other of Wagner's operas, chiefly because of its revision for the Paris Opéra. To be sure, the Dresden premiere was not entirely satisfactory; several weak spots were clarified for a performance two years later, but it was the acceptance by Paris that caused the major shake-up, which was the addition of the elaborate and sensuous Venusberg music as a ballet in the first act. Paris of course had to have its ballet. But by that time, Wagner was already writing in a chromatic "Tristan-esque" style and the contrast with his earlier work was notable. Companies occasionally revert to the Dresden version, which has the virtue of coherent style, but which somehow seems drab after the lushness of the Paris setting. The ending, too, was modified, for at first Venus's reappearance was signalled only by a red light, and Elisabeth's death by the tolling of bells.

The premiere cast in Dresden hardly lived up to the opera's potential, although Wagner's niece, Johanna Wagner, sang Elisabeth prettily, and Wilhelmine Schröder-Devrient was a powerful Venus. Tichatschek and Mitterwurzer were the other principals, the latter as Wolfram at least trying to understand Wagner's "endless melody."

The *scandale* of the second night in Paris is well known. The first night had been fiasco enough, what with an incompetent conductor (Wagner was not allowed to preside) and the tenor Albert Niemann, who on this occasion did not give evidence of his future accomplishments as a Wagnerian singer. But the audience was the culprit on the second night, particularly that segment known as the Jockey Club, a coterie of fashionables who virtually ruled the opera. It was they who demanded ballets so that they could visit their favorite ballerinas in the Green Room at intervals. Wagner had provided the ballet, sure enough, but in the first act. The Jockey Club arrived in force for the second act, and immediately kicked up a row at missing the ballet. They were already prejudiced against the German composer, whom they accused of hating their favorite, Meyerbeer, and against Wagner's patroness, Princess Metternich. The second night degenerated into a shambles of shouts, insults, and interruptions, a scene of utter pandemonium. After a third night that showed little improvement, Wagner withdrew the opera, and it was not seen again in the French capital for many years.

Germany accepted the Dresden version immediately, and this was the manner in which New York first heard it in 1859—and incidentally, it was the first Wagner opera to be played in America. Leopold Damrosch chose the opera to open the 1884-85 season, the first of seven German years at the Metropolitan, and it persisted into the ensuing regimes, gradually becoming a staple, although not an invariable choice, of managers to follow. But the Paris version was not given until 1889, when Lilli Lehmann was the Venus and her husband, Paul Kalisch, sang the title role. Melchior and Svanholm were notable Tannhäusers in the 1940s. The Dresden version was reinstated in 1953-54, when George Szell returned to conduct, and the cast included Vinay, Harshaw, Varnay, and Hines. New productions by Wieland Wagner at Bayreuth stirred controversy, and in 1961 there was much talk about the "black Venus," sung by Grace Bumbry. The Metropolitan's new production in 1977 restored a traditional approach, with beautiful, romantic, yet realistic scenery by Günther Schneider-Siemssen that still took advantage of

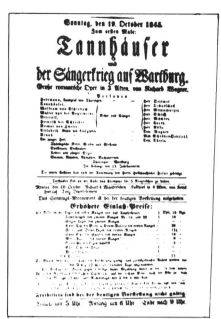

Program from the premiere of Tannhäuser, 1845, Dresden.

445
WAGNER

Josef Tichatschek as Tannhäuser from the opera's premiere.

Wilhelmine Schröder-Devrient sang Venus in the 1845 Dresden premiere of Tannhäuser.

Tannhäuser

Text by the composer.

446
WAGNER

LANDGRAVE HERMANN	*Bass*
TANNHAUSER	*Tenor*
WOLFRAM VON ESCHENBACH	*Baritone*
WALTHER VON DEN VOGELWEIDE	*Tenor*
BITEROLF	*Bass*
HEINRICH DER SCHREIBER	*Tenor*
REINMAR VON ZWETER	*Bass*
ELISABETH	*Soprano*
VENUS	*Soprano or Mezzo-Soprano*
YOUNG SHEPHERD	*Soprano*

First Performance
Dresden, 19 October 1845.
Paris Performance of revised version
13 March 1861.

modern technology to work magic transformations. James Levine conducted, and the hero was James McCracken, with Leonie Rysanek as Elisabeth and Grace Bumbry, no longer startling, as Venus. Bernd Weikl sang the "Evening Star" of Wolfram mellifluously.

After completing the poem in 1843, Wagner did not finish the score until two years later. The original title was *The Venusberg,* but it engendered inevitable ribaldry, and was changed to *Tannhäuser and the Contest of Song on the Wartburg* (generally shortened). A combination of two legends seems to have inspired the composer: one about the contest of minnesingers at Wartburg, the other clustering around Tannhäuser himself, a real person. There is also a story by E.T.A. Hoffmann which concerns a singers' contest in Thuringia, in which a Wolfram and a Walther take part — the latter was to serve as inspiration for Wagner's hero in *Die Meistersinger.* Both were also real people. One of the Brothers Grimm's stories also concerns Tannhäuser and his search for absolution, but the flowering of the Pope's staff is too late to save him, as he has already returned to Venus.

THE OVERTURE has become a well-worn concert piece, and is played complete in itself. It depicts the chief elements in the story: first, the Pilgrims' song, then the atmosphere in Venusberg, Tannhäuser's song in praise of Venus, and her plea for him to remain with her. All of this was contained in the original Overture. But now the material added for Paris enters to provide a different ambiance, fully sensual and, as we have seen, thoroughly "Tristan-esque."

ACT I, Scene 1. In Venusberg, the goddess reclines on a couch with her lover nearby, while the dancers grow more and more animated and orgiastic around them. The bacchanal is interrupted for a soft sirens' song, then resumed with increasing excitement, until at last all dancers cease in an atmosphere of fatigue and ennui. Enticing visions appear before the lovers, but Tannhäuser is weary of the languor and yearns to return to the world of spring and green grass. Although Venus employs all her charm and artifice, and three times succeeds in rousing

Albert Niemann as Tannhäuser from the 1861 revised Paris version of Tannhäuser.

Venus and Tannhäuser in Venusberg, Act I scene 1 of Tannhäuser, Herbert Graf production, Vienna State Opera.

him to a song of praise for her, she at last must let him go back to the world of men. Her fury is unleashed. She warns him not to tell of his sojourn with her or he will be reviled and scorned, and he must then return to her. But he vows never to return, and cries that his salvation is with the Virgin Mary.

Scene 2. The Venusberg has dissolved into a peaceful scene in the Thuringian valley, where Tannhäuser reclines on a grassy bank while a shepherd pipes and sings a paean to the lovely month of May. A band of elderly Pilgrims approaches and passes, and Tannhäuser kneels in prayer. His impulse is to join the holy band, but he is restrained by the entrance of a hunting party, headed by Hermann, the Landgrave of Thuringia. Wolfram is the first to recognize his old comrade, and the others welcome him joyously, insisting that he return to the castle, where his songs have, in times past, made him a happy companion. He is still filled with the idea of moving on with the Pilgrims, but the mention of a name stays him—Wolfram tells him that he has been sorely missed by Elisabeth, the Landgrave's niece, who has languished without his singing. He determines to return to her among general rejoicing.

ACT II. Elisabeth, tremulously joyful at Tannhäuser's return, greets the hall of song where he so often entranced her, in the aria "Dich teure Halle." Tannhäuser, entering, evades her questions about his absence from her, and begs her forgiveness. She sings of her gladness at seeing him again, and of her longing to hear him sing. Their duet is one of utter commitment to each other. Wolfram, who overhears, dismisses his own hopes of winning Elisabeth.

The company assembles to a stately march. So confident is the Landgrave that the prodigal will win in a singing contest that he promises Elisabeth's hand to the victor, and Elisabeth is overjoyed. Wolfram is the first to sing. He praises a lofty, serene, and refreshing love; his is a thoroughly noble song. Then Tannhäuser rises, and with growing fervor, sings of a vital, fiery love, hailing a burning passion in terms that

Kirsten Flagstad as Elisabeth.

Drawing of a scene from Act II of the original 1845 Dresden production of Tannhäuser.

Kerstin Thorborg as Venus.

dismay the throng and puzzle Elisabeth. Walther attempts to smooth over the situation by rising to proclaim the sacredness of love, but Tannhäuser, now thoroughly aroused and oblivious to the growing agitation around him, jumps to his feet and wildly extols love as pleasure only. To Biterolf's challenge to combat, Tannhäuser replies defiantly; then as the Landgrave demands peace and Wolfram attempts once more to praise a holy love, Tannhäuser breaks through all restraint and lustily sings a hymn to Venus.

The stunned crowd reacts violently, but Elisabeth protects Tannhäuser from their vengeance, and he, now deeply repentant, is ordered by the Landgrave to join the band of Pilgrims even now on its way to Rome. He falls at Elisabeth's feet, kissing the hem of her robe, then hastens away with a cry of exultation: "To Rome!"

ACT III.   In the Valley of the Wartburg, Elisabeth has sought out a wayside shrine and is praying before it. Wolfram finds her, comments that she comes here to watch the returning pilgrims in the hopes of seeing her banished lover, then watches as she seeks him in vain among the passing band. Elisabeth sinks down and sends her heart-rending Prayer to heaven, beseeching the Virgin to take her soul. She refuses Wolfram's offer of assistance and goes slowly away, leaving him to his sorrow. He expresses this beautifully in the famous "Evening Star" apotheosis, and continues to play his harp as Tannhäuser appears, ragged and pitiful. Wolfram does not at first recognize him, then sorrowfully warns him not to remain unless he has been forgiven by the Pope. Tannhäuser relates his experience in the long Narrative, a taxing passage for a Wagnerian tenor. It is a sorrowful tale, revealing the supplicant's approach to the Pope and the pontiff's rejection of him. The Pope has declared that sooner would the staff in his hand break into fresh green leaves, than will this erring soul be redeemed. Tannhäuser has found his painful way back to the valley, intending to rejoin Venus as once she prophesied he would. Wolfram tries to dissuade him, bu the apparition of the goddess herself seductively beckons him. Only the mention of Elisabeth's name has any effect; Tannhäuser stands bemused as a chorus of men in the distance comes closer, proclaiming the death of that lovely maiden. Tannhäuser sinks dying on her bier as it is borne past him, without witnessing the young pilgrims who enter joyfully, bearing the papal staff that has brought forth fresh green leaves. All hail the miracle that has saved the sinner's soul as the curtain falls.

Ludmila Dvořáková as Elisabeth in Tannhäuser, scenery by F. Tröster, 1955, National Theater, Prague.

Hof-Theater.

Weimar, Mittwoch den 28 August 1850

Zur Goethe-Feier:

Prolog

von Franz Dingelstedt gesprochen von Herrn Jaffe

Darauf

Zum Erstenmale

Lohengrin.

Romantische Oper in drei Akten
nach dem Text von
von Richard Wagner.

Program from the premiere of Lohengrin at Weimar in 1850.

450
WAGNER

WAGNER, unable to go to Weimar for the premiere because of his banishment from Germany for participation in the 1848 revolution, did not hear *Lohengrin* until 1861 in Vienna. He would probably have suffered apoplexy at the ineptitude of the performance, for Liszt did not truly understand the work of the artist he so deeply admired, and his forces were, to say the least, inadequate. But the opera made its way, although slowly, first throughout Germany and then abroad. America heard it first in 1871 in New York, in Italian. That language prevailed throughout performances at the Academy of Music in 1874 and in its first season at the Metropolitan, 1883-84. German was restored only in 1885, when Anton Seidl made his Metropolitan debut on November 23, with his wife as Elsa and Marianne Brandt as Ortrud.

Because *Lohengrin* is probably the most popular of all Wagner's operas, in spite of the cumulative mastery of the later works, the number of famous singers who have taken leading roles is nearly infinite in number. To mention some of them: Eames, Nordica, Fremstad, Farrar, Jeritza, Ternina, **Melba, Lotte Lehmann, Flagstad,** Bjoner, Steber, Créspin, Grümmer, Arroyo, Lorengar, Zylis-Gara as Elsa; De Reszke, Niemann, Slezak, Melchior, Svanholm, Konya, Kollo, Peter Hofmann as Lohengrin; Schumann-Heink, Lilli Lehmann, Matzenauer, Varnay, Thebom, Branzell as Ortrud; and many fine baritones and basses as Telramund and Henry respectively.

Productions have ranged from the tattered to the extremely "modern"; one example of the latter was the Wieland Wagner show at the Metropolitan in 1966, when a huge swan as background (resembling Tiffany glass) replaced the traditional boat drawn by a stuffed bird. This production was scrapped in favor of one by August Everding and Ming-Cho Lee in

The Swan Castle, scene of Wagner's Lohengrin.

*Sketch by Wagner of the
stage design for Lohengrin.*

1979-80 in which there was no swan at all, merely a blinding light. The remark, "What time is the next swan?" after a hitch in the performance had caused the tardy appearance of the bird has been attributed to many tenors since, but it was undoubtedly first uttered by the antic Leo Slezak.

During his exile in Paris and Zurich, Wagner's personal life and fortunes suffered many disruptions. His debts mounted, and Minna had to contend with the affair with Jessie Laussot. He had been working intermittently on *Lohengrin* since 1845, when he went to Marienbad to recuperate from his strenuous months in Dresden. Oddly enough, *Meistersinger* occupied his thoughts at the same time, but the Swan Knight gradually took over and became an obsession. He would get out of the healing baths in a frantic hurry to run to his room and jot down new ideas, at last completing the prose sketch, then versifying it.

Some of the characters in the legend were based on real people: Henry I of Saxony (919-936) chief among them. There were of course many legends about the damsel in distress who was rescued by the mysterious knight, as told, for example, in the Walloon-French epic, *Le Chevalier au cygne*, and the Wolfram poem about the Holy Grail, *Parzifal*, which also inspired Wagner's *Parsifal*. The Knights of the Grail were charged, on their rescue missions, not to reveal their identities for fear of the loss of their power; thus the injunction laid on Elsa by Lohengrin is not an arbitrary bit of fantasy. Wagner finished the third act first; the Prelude was composed last of all.

The Preludes to the first and third acts have become well loved in many performances by symphony orchestras. The first Prelude is an absorbing study in the use of high strings to convey an otherworldly mood. Wagner himself wrote of it:

> Out of the clear blue ether of the sky there seems to condense a wonderful yet at first hardly perceptible vision; and out of these there gradually emerges, ever more and more clearly, an angel host bearing in its midst the sacred Grail. As it approaches earth it pours out exquisite odors, like streams of gold, ravishing the senses of the beholder. The glory of the vision grows and grows until it seems as

Leo Slezak as Lohengrin.

if the rapture must be shattered and dispersed by the very vehemence of its own expansion. The vision draws nearer and nearer, and the climax is reached when at last the Grail is revealed in all its glorious reality, radiating fiery beams and shaking the soul with emotion. The beholder sinks on his knees in adoring self-annihilation. The Grail pours out its light on him like a benediction and consecrates him to its service, then the flames gradually die away, and the angel host soars up again to the ethereal heights in tender joy, having made pure once more the hearts of men by the sacred blessing of the Grail.

Lohengrin

Text by the composer.

LOHENGRIN	*Tenor*
ELSA OF BRABANT	*Soprano*
FRIEDRICH VON TELRAMUND	*Baritone*
ORTRUD	*Soprano or Mezzo-Soprano*
HENRY THE FOWLER	*Bass*
HERALD	*Baritone*

First Performance
Weimar, 28 August 1850.

ACT I. King Henry of Germany has come to seek the help of the nobles of Brabant in his war against Hungary, and has assembled knights and nobles of Saxony and Thuringia to confront those of Brabant on a plain near Antwerp. He asks Count Frederick of Telramund the cause of the unsettled conditions in Brabant. Telramund replies that the young heir Godfrey, entrusted with his sister Elsa to Telramund upon the death of their father, the Duke, has disappeared. He accuses Elsa of murdering Godfrey. Telramund, although he has the right to take Elsa for his wife, has married Ortrud, daughter of the Prince of Freisland, a sorceress and even more fiercely ambitious than her husband, who claims the right to the Dukedom of Brabant. The King sees no reason to distrust this pair, and summons Elsa to give an account of herself. The maiden appears, so pale, so innocent in mien,

Margarete Matzenauer as Ortrud.

The arrival of Lohengrin in Act I of the opera, 1958, Bayreuth.

that it is hard to suspect her. To the King's gentle questioning, she replies that as in a dream she has seen a champion appear to defend her (Elsa's Dream). The music reflects the promise of the Grail.

Telramund jeers at the idea, but the King summons a Herald to sound trumpets in a call to this champion. The Herald's first call is met only by silence; but at the second, given because of Elsa's plea, a stir is seen among the crowd and with growing excitement they watch a boat approaching the bank of the River Scheldt, drawn by a great white swan, and holding a gallant knight in armor so bright that it blinds the eyes of the bewildered watchers. The knight (he is Lohengrin) steps on land and in a tender song bids farewell to his faithful swan, which draws the boat away. Then turning to the King, he offers himself as champion for the the fair lady. Elsa throws herself at his feet in gratitude, and promises to be his bride if he is victorious. He raises her from her knees and exacts from her a promise never to ask his name, his rank, or his origin.

At the King's bidding, the Herald announces the contest between accuser and champion, and the two men draw their swords. Lohengrin **fells Telramund, who lies in disgrace, attended by Ortrud, while the** others rejoice in so happy an outcome.

Florence Easton as Elsa.

Irene Dalis as Ortrud with Ramon Vinay as Telramund, Bayreuth.

Jean de Reszke as Lohengrin.

ACT II.   Ortrud and Telramund sit brooding outside the walls of the women's quarters in a fortress in Antwerp. Frederick accuses his wife of being the cause of his dishonor, and reveals that it is she who has borne false witness to Elsa's drowning of her brother. But Ortrud is not done with her evil plans, and soon convinces him that the one road to their triumph is to persuade Elsa to coax the hero's name from him. Even if this fails, there is another way: simply cut from his body the slightest fingertip and his magic will be dissipated. Their evil duet is accompanied by music of dark, brooding power. Suddenly Ortrud bids Telramund to be silent and leave her. He creeps into the shadows as Elsa appears on a balcony above, rejoicing and thanking Heaven for her happiness. Ortrud calls her plaintively. The gullible girl responds to the woman's false penitence with tenderness and pity, finally escorting her into the palace, while Frederick Telramund gloats over their momentary triumph.

The scene changes to the courtyard of the cathedral, where all assemble. The Herald announces Telramund's banishment and the appointment of the strange knight as Guardian of Brabant and husband of Elsa. There is general rejoicing except for a group of four Brabantian nobles, whom Telramund, revealing himself, persuades to dissent.

As the procession grows, to the accompaniment of stately music, Elsa appears in bridal array. She is about to enter the cathedral when Ortrud breaks loose from her retinue and claims precedence. Her violent outbreak concludes with a taunt to Elsa—she does not even know the name of the man she is marrying. In spite of the protests of the crowd and Elsa's own rejection of the fierce woman, the seed of doubt has been planted. When the King and Lohengrin appear, Ortrud is at once banished, but Telramund now dares to step forward and accuses Lohengrin of sorcery. The knight replies nobly, but notices Elsa's trembling and is perturbed. The King and the assemblage give their trust to Lohengrin, but Elsa is approached furtively by Telramund, who advances the idea that the loss of even a finger will lead her husband to confess his name—he intends to be near the bridal chamber if she should call for him. Lohengrin intervenes, and Elsa is once more reassured. The throng hails the couple as they enter the cathedral, but Ortrud once more appears to menace the shivering Elsa.

ACT III.   This Prelude is a joyous blast of the brass instruments, a festive anticipation of happiness to come. The first scene is the bridal chamber, into which a procession leads the couple to the strains of the famous Wedding March. Left alone, Elsa and Lohengrin rejoice in their bliss, but the worm of doubt once more creeps in, and Elsa begins to question her bridegroom, growing ever more feverish. Who is he? Whence does he come? Will he not vanish as suddenly as he appeared? At the height of her inquisition, to which Lohengrin listens with mounting dismay, Telramund and four other nobles burst in. Hastily snatching the sword handed him by Elsa, Lohengrin strikes Telramund dead. The conspirators flee, and Lohengrin turns to Elsa sternly. He summons her maidens and orders them to take her to the judgment site on the river bank where first we saw them.

Schumann-Heink as Ortrud.

455
WAGNER

Set Svanholm as Lohengrin.

Johanna Wagner, Wagner's niece, shown here as Ortrud, was a leading soprano at the Dresden Court Theater in the mid-1800s.

Now, to the assemblage, the knight at last reveals his origin. His aria, "In fernem Land" (In a distant land), tells of the Holy Grail on Mount Monsalvat, and the company that attends it. He is one of them, a knight charged with doing noble deeds throughout the world, always under the cloak of anonymity. If his name should be revealed, the power of the Grail is dissipated. He must depart, he declares, saying at last that his name is Lohengrin, and that Parsifal is his father. The crowd is awestruck, and Elsa collapses. Tenderly and ruefully he bids her farewell, and turns to the river, where the swan-boat is seen approaching. Sorrowfully, Lohengrin then reveals to Elsa that if she had but waited a single year, her brother would have been returned to her. For him, Lohengrin gives Elsa his own sword, ring, and horn. This is too much for Ortrud, who steps forward to cry, gloating, that she is responsible for Godfrey's disappearance—she has, in fact, turned him into this very swan. Apparently Lohengrin was ignorant of this bit of her trickery. He kneels in prayer, and is answered by the appearance of the Grail's dove, which takes the swan's place, while the young Duke Godfrey suddenly materializes, and embraces his sister. Lohengrin sails away as Elsa sinks lifeless at her brother's feet.

Lohengrin's departure, painting by Wilhelm von Kaulbach.

TRISTAN UND ISOLDE is possibly the greatest love song of all—and probably the longest. We are now in another world from the somewhat four-square, formal plan of *Tannhäuser* and *Lohengrin*, in an onward flowing, never ceasing stream of consciousness, rising and ebbing through strange landscapes. We are with beings shunning the light, seeking the night. For *Tristan* embodies the idea that love finds its fulfillment only in death.

If Wagner had stopped composing with *Lohengrin*, he would still have been hailed as one of the world's great composers, but with *Tristan* and *The Ring* another dimension was added. We consider *Tristan* first because, although it was written after the first two segments, and part of the third of *The Ring*, it was performed before *Das Rheingold*. Wagner habitually wrestled with two problems at once—witness the simultaneous work of *Lohengrin* and *Die Meistersinger*, and now the composition of part of the new cycle before *Tristan* obtruded into his consciousness. Then, even while working on that masterpiece, a theme for the hero of the third *Ring* segment inserted itself into his fertile mind, and the second act of *Siegfried* was finished.

There are many versions of the Tristan legend, but it was probably that by Gottfried von Strassbourg of the 13th century, translated into modern German, that influenced Wagner most. The earliest legends seem lost; Ernest Newman says that the French scholar Joseph Bedier "conjecturally sets forth the main genealogical table" as derived from three main sources, English and French prose and poetry, and that all owe their existence to a lost poet, "perhaps an Anglo-Norman."

Although at one time he contemplated including it, a portion of the legend is omitted from Wagner's final libretto. This concerns the "other Isolde," Iseult of the the White Hands, whom Tristan marries in Brittany after escaping from Marke's court. But memories of Iseult the Fair (as she is called) cling to him, and he is married in name only to Iseult of the White Hands, who grows increasingly jealous. Tristan goes back once more to Cornwall, and the two lovers indulge in many subterfuges to be near one another, outwitting the court by stealth and tricks. But, near discovery, he returns to Brittany. Once more incurably wounded, he sends a messenger to Iseult the Fair asking her to come to him. If she returns, the ship's sail will be white; if not, a black sail will be flown. (This circumstance has been noted in other legends and histories.) But Iseult, his wife, learns of the plot, and tells Tristan that the ship bears black sails, although Iseult the Fair is truly on board. Tristan, informed of the dark omen, turns to the wall and dies. When Iseult the Fair arrives, she joins him in death, as in Wagner's story. Another omission is the tender tale of how King Marke sails to Brittany and takes the lovers' bodies back to Cornwall, burying them in separate tombs. But at night a briar (or an ivy vine) grows from Tristan's tomb and twines across the space to embrace the tomb of Iseult. Three times it is cut back, but it always grows again, until finally Marke commands that it remain.

There are countless variations and mutations of the legend, but while scholars may find them absorbing, we must concentrate on what Wagner's genius made of them.

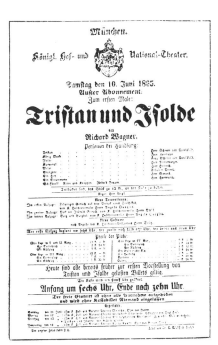

Program from the premiere performance of Tristan and Isolde, 1865, Munich.

457
WAGNER

Olive Fremstad as Isolde.

Hans von Bülow, Cosima Wagner's husband prior to her marriage to Wagner, conducted the premiere of Tristan and Isolde, 1865, Munich.

As Newman points out, it is certain that *Tristan* sprang musically from Wagner's subconscious mind, although usually he was first motivated by the word—a poem or idea. A fragment of music later found seems certain to be the *Tristan* "thread" that haunted the composer while he was working on *Siegfried.* And it is to the music that we must attend most closely. While it is impossible to trace the "threads" here in such a limited study, we should always keep in mind the vivifying force that brings the seemingly rather primitive story to its glorious existence in the opera house.

Although very close emotionally to Wagner during the time of its composition, Mathilde von Wesendonck cannot be said to have been the "inspiration" for *Tristan,* as is often claimed. That inspiration came directly from the genius within him. But it is interesting to note that of the five songs he composed to her poems, the *Tristan* motif is prominent. And he presented her with the finished poem of the opera in September 1857.

The full orchestral score was not completed until July 1859. As we have seen, Vienna rejected the opera as "impracticable," and it remained for Munich to give the premiere in 1865. The pair of lovers were sung by a real husband and wife, Ludwig and Malvina Schnorr von Carolsfield. Hans von Bülow was the conductor. Only the patronage of King Ludwig II saved it from immediate oblivion; as it was, only three performances were given at the time, and the music drama made its way very slowly into world circuits. London heard it in 1882; Bayreuth in 1886; and the Metropolitan gave the American premiere also in 1886, with Seidl conducting and Lilli Lehmann, Brandt, Niemann, Robinson, and Fischer in the cast. The sensation it caused then was repeated in 1895 when Jean and Edouard de Reszke and Lillian Nordica were the principals. Among famous names connected with the opera in ensuing years are Fremstad, Leider, Matzenauer, Flagstad, Traubel, Varnay, Nilsson, Lindholm, and Knie as Isolde; Melchior, Svanholm, Vinay, Windgassen, Thomas, and Vickers as Tristan.

Malvina Garrigues (l.) and her husband, Ludwig Schnorr von Carolsfeld (r.), sang the title roles in the 1865 Munich premiere of Tristan and Isolde.

Conductors who have proved their mettle with this most symphonic of operas are Mahler, Toscanini, Busch, Stiedry, Reiner, Böhm, Karajan, and Leinsdorf. Among the Brangänes may be noted Olszewska, Matzenauer, Thorborg, Branzell, Thebom, and Dunn. As Kurvenal, Paul Schoeffler and Joel Berglund may be singled out, while many distinguished basses have sung King Marke.

An unusual feature about the composition of the work was that Wagner wrote the Prelude first, even before beginning the first act. As a perfect symphonic piece, it remains in the repertoire, furnished with a concert ending when the *Liebestod* is not appended. It is a stunning evocation of love and longing without hope of fulfillment, a never-ending cry of the heart's deepest passion.

It is here that we should consider the matter of *leitmotifs*, those fragments of melody which recur often and always with some meaning attached. It is impossible to go into any detail in limited space, and authorities often disagree upon just which motif means just what emotion, character, or situation, so that we need not worry too much about them. Listening to the music, we will soon sift out certain recurring patterns which may mean "Longing," "Magic Potion," "The Love Glance," and so on—one or another may even carry two meanings—and the student can find them spelled out in several books (Newman's among them) and in a vocal score. It was Wagner's genius that he wove them into the seamless fabric that is the peerless music of *Tristan und Isolde*.

Edouard de Reszke as King Marke.

Jean de Reszke as Tristan.

ACT I. On the ship which, with Tristan at the helm, bears Isolde from Ireland to Cornwall to be King Marke's bride, Isolde reclines on a couch on deck, hiding her face in the pillows. Her serving maiden Brangäne has drawn aside the curtains and is gazing out over the railing. From aloft comes the voice of a Young Sailor, singing with abandon of the Irish maid he left behind. Isolde takes this as an insult to her, calls to Brangäne and orders her to summon Tristan to her side from his place at the helm. It is plain that she is exceedingly angry, but underneath her wrath is the music that tells us the cause is more than her virtual abduction—it is her anguish at the fact that Tristan is the cause of it. When the knight refuses to leave his post, and his henchman Kurvenal has sung a little ditty of defiance, Brangäne returns to her mistress, who has observed it all.

Isolde now pours out the real story (which Brangäne must have known, at least in part—but it is one of those narratives that usefully explains past happenings without an actual flashback). This tremendous solo passage tells of the advent of the wounded knight, who called himself Tantris (a flimsy disguise, but no matter) and sought her out for the vaunted healing powers which she inherited from her mother. As he lay recovering, she found his sword, from which a sliver was missing, and discovered that the missing portion was indeed the fragment which she had recovered from the fatal wound of her champion and betrothed Morold, who had suffered his death from a battle with Tristan on an island near Cornwall, testing the supremacy of Ireland or Cornwall. Furious, she was about to take her revenge with the hero's own sword, when he looked up at her with such longing and love that she could not

459
WAGNER

Tristan
und Isolde
(*Tristan and Isolde*)

Text by the composer.

TRISTAN	Tenor
ISOLDE	Soprano
KING MARKE	Bass
BRANGANE	Soprano or Mezzo-Soprano
KURVENAL	Baritone
MELOT	Tenor
SHEPHERD	Tenor
STEERSMAN	Baritone
YOUNG SAILOR'S VOICE	Tenor

First Performance
Munich, 10 June 1865.

Tristan and Isolde on board Tristan's ship, scene from Act I, Nicola Benois, designer, 1939, Rome Opera.

Lilli Lehmann as Isolde.

help but respond. Great was her dismay when, instead of claiming her for his own bride, he revealed that he had come as the emissary of his uncle, King Marke, who was seeking through this marriage to make peace with Ireland.

Isolde is trapped. Now she vows death to the traitor, and bids Brangäne to fetch the little medicine chest which her mother, mistress of spells and potions, had entrusted to her. It is not the love potion her mother intended for Marke and Isolde, but a certain other vial that she desires. Brangäne in terror realizes that her mistress means to share a draught of death with her traitorous lover. Trembling, she secretly substitutes for it the potion that ensures love, not death, everlasting.

The sailors sing out boisterously from above, as Tristan's arrival is announced by Kurvenal, who has been cowed into submission by an imperious command from Isolde. The hero comes down onto the deck in a series of musical steps that increases in power and intensity until he stands before Isolde, impassive and courteous. To his question, she answers that she wishes to gain forgetfulness and forgiving. Then she begins to count her grievances, concentrating on the slaying of Morold and the treachery of his slayer; all the while her anger simmers just below the surface. Tristan replies with dignity that if Morold was so dear to her, she may slay the man in front of her with his own sword — and draws it partially out of its sheath to offer her. She bids him sheathe his weapon; they will instead drink to atonement. The sailors, meanwhile, are again signalling their approach to land. At Isolde's signal to Brangäne, the maid brings forth the great cup. Isolde hands it to Tristan, who, knowing full well what it portends, sings poignantly of his honor and faith, and attempts to drain it to the bottom. But Isolde is not to be cheated, and snatching the vessel from him, drinks the last drops herself.

A shuddering silence endures for a moment; then the orchestra tells of the emotions that slowly grip the two, who, facing each other, begin to realize what has happened. At last, she tremulously utters his name and he calls hers. Then to the throbbing music they fall on each other's breasts, feverishly acknowledging the love that at last has been revealed to them. We should not attribute this passion only to the effects of the potion, which is merely a key that unlocks the emotion already within their hearts and allows them to bring it into consciousness. It is difficult to tear them apart now. Both Kurvenal and Brangäne endeavor to make them ready to leave the ship, and as King Marke's emissaries come aboard to escort them, the pair are led off, oblivious to their surroundings. (In some productions, the emissaries are led by the knight Melot who thus is able to observe for himself the spell cast upon the two, and later capitalize on his knowledge.)

ACT II.   After a long Prelude in which Isolde's impatience is made clear and the ominous motive of Day is introduced, the curtains open on a moonlit scene in the castle garden. A hunting party is heard in the distance, its horns growing ever fainter. Brangäne, at the head of a flight of stairs, warns her mistress, who is below, of her suspicion that the King hunts more than an animal, and warns her about Melot. But Isolde is blind to danger. She has summoned Tristan by extinguishing the torch (symbolic of the rout of Day, and the reign of Night) on the castle stairs, and now awaits him in agitation. At last he comes, and their bliss mounts higher and higher as they virtually interrupt each other's transports. At last, they sink down on a flowery bank to extol their Night. Many things are made clear now. Tristan reveals that he had resolved to leave King Marke's court after his first trip to Ireland and the dawning of his love for Isolde, but that honor and a

Lillian Nordica as Isolde.

Isolde signals Tristan, scene from Act II of Tristan and Isolde, Cologne Festival production.

Lauritz Melchior as
Tristan.

Milka Ternina as Isolde.

promise to Marke had forbidden him to advance his own cause. He had welcomed the draught which he thought should take him to Eternal Night; but Day had once more claimed him. The many subtleties of this love scene, the tender portion of it beginning with the words "O sink' hernieder, Nacht der Liebe," carries them through their world of rapture, twice warned by Brangäne from the tower that day is near and danger comes with it. Finally, the idyll ends with a crashing dissonance; Kurvenal dashes in to warn the lovers, and the King's party erupts on the scene, headed by Melot.

The King, deeply troubled, reproaches Tristan for his faithlessness in a long monologue, very moving when beautifully sung. Tristan responds that he is going on a far journey and asks Isolde if she will go with him. At her assent, Melot intervenes furiously, drawing his sword. Tristan responds, but allows his weapon to drop, so that Melot deals a savage blow to the hero who chooses death. The curtain closes on the dismay of the court.

ACT III.   The Prelude foretells the sadness that is to come.
Tristan has been brought by Kurvenal to his old home in Kareol, and lies gravely ill in a courtyard under a great tree. Isolde has been sent for, and a shepherd will announce by his piping the news — mournful if no ship can be seen, jubilant when a ship is sighted. The long solo by the English horn reflects the loneliness and despair of the scene. The shepherd inquires about Tristan; Kurvenal gloomily replies that he may live only if the ship brings the woman who can heal him. The tune has awakened Tristan, who asks of the astonished Kurvenal what song is

that, and where does he lie. In Cornwall? No, the faithful servitor replies. I have brought you here to your father's castle.

Now begins the three-part delirium which Tristan suffers; moments of joy and exaltation when he envisions Isolde and longs for her coming; periods of despair and yearning; an interval where he praises the friendship and service of the loyal Kurvenal; an apotheosis of love that centers on the radiant Isolde, and at last, the moment when he is sure she is approaching. Now Tristan springs to his feet, calls on the light to be extinguished, tears the bandages from his wounds, and in delirium expires. Isolde arrives just too late. Sinking down on his body, she is seemingly unconscious as the Shepherd announces another ship. Kurvenal hastens out as Brangäne rushes to her mistress, but the servitor mistakes the friendly advance of King Marke's attendants for enmity, and wages battle, in which he is fatally wounded. His own theme, echoed in a minor key, accompanies his return to his master's side, where he joins him in death. Now Isolde rouses herself from her torpor and begins to sing the "Liebestod," that fateful paean to love and death. As she concludes, she sinks beside Tristan and the lovers are united at last as they wished it to be — in the realms of Night.

Bispham as the faithful Kurvenal.

Isolde on her way to Kareol from Act III of Tristan and Isolde, drawing by Franz Stassen.

Program for Die Meistersinger von Nürnberg.

DIE MEISTERSINGER VON NÜRNBERG. Wagner thought of the possibilities of an opera based on the Mastersingers of Germany as early as 1845, no doubt as a relief from his labors in the world of the Holy Grail as exemplified by *Lohengrin.* At first there was no trace of the seriousness which later was to infuse the character of Hans Sachs and the reverence for German art explicit in the finale of the opera. That development was obvious in the letter Wagner wrote to King Ludwig II just before the first performance in Munich: "It is impossible that you should not have sensed, under the opera's quaint superficies of popular humor, the profound melancholy, the lament, the cry of distress of poetry in chains, and its re-incarnation, its new birth, its irresistible magic power achieving mastery over the common and the base."

Audiences may draw what inferences they will from the opera, but it is at least on the surface a comedy of great gusto and skill. Wagner's mastersingers are mere caricatures of the real personages on whom they were fashioned (he changed several names and professions, but most were authentic). Sachs was a real person (1494-1576), famed for his thousands of poems as well as for his shoes. The ritual of the song-tests, so maddeningly outlined for Walther by the apprentice David was actually proved useful in form and practice, but Wagner shows how such rigidity can be entirely stultifying, and how, as Sachs says, when something new seems to break the rules, its own rules should be sought.

As we have seen, Wagner put aside his comedy in favor of *Lohengrin,* worked on it again in 1861, wrote the Prelude in 1862, but did not complete the score until 1867. He had, during this time, deepened his research, finding several fruitful sources. No doubt these included E.T.A. Hoffmann, but chiefly an old account of Nuremberg by Wagenseil which listed the multifarious rules of "the Gracious Art of the Mastersinger," of which Wagner made such cunning use.

Nuremberg as it looked in the fifteenth century at the time Wagner's opera is set, from the Nuremberg Chronicle, 1493.

The first measures of the prelude to Die Meistersinger, in Wagner's own hand with his signature.

The Prelude has become so well known through concert performances that we do not question why it concentrates on the nobility of the Mastersingers, hints of the Prize Song of Walther, and the antics of the apprentices, and contains no reference to Sachs or to Beckmesser. It seems obvious, according to Newman, that Wagner had not fully developed the parts these two characters were to play when he first approached the musical composition of the opera.

Hans von Bülow conducted the first performance, which was rapturously received by the public, although several critics remained hostile. German cities quickly took it up, and it was popular in Vienna and Prague. London's first experience with the opera was in 1882, when Hans Richter, a young protégé of Wagner, conducted. Italian was the language in 1889 at Covent Garden, when the cast included Jean de Reszke, Albani, and Lassalle. Meanwhile, Seidl introduced a drastically cut version at the Metropolitan in 1886. Almost all the same singers as in Covent Garden presented the work at the Met in 1891, when it was called *I Maestri*. German was restored in 1901 by De Reszke, Gadski, Schumann-Heink, and Bispham.

During World War I, German operas were banned at the Metropolitan, and even after they returned, were sung in English for a few seasons. *Meistersinger* did not enjoy even this translated return, because it so blatantly extolled the holiness of German art in the last act (this long peroration by Sachs has been frequently cut since).

Notable portrayers of Hans Sachs have been Clarence Whitehill, Friedrich Schorr, Joel Berglund, Paul Schoeffler, Otto Edelmann, Thomas Stewart, Norman Bailey, Karl Ridderbush, Theo Adam, and Georgio Tozzi. Evas of distinction have been Emma Eames, Frieda Hempel, Elisabeth Schwarzkopf, Lotte Lehmann, Eleanor Steber, Lisa Della Casa, Ingrid Bjoner, Johanna Meier, and Pilar Lorengar. Singing Walther's Prize Song have been René Maison, Leo Slezak, Set Svanholm, Charles Kullman, Sandor Konya, Jess Thomas, John Alexander, and James King. David Bispham was a famous Beckmesser in olden days; Karl Dönch notable in the role more recently. Beckmesser was originally called "Hans Lick," but the obvious comparison to the anti-Wagnerian critic Hanslick was too blatant.

The seal of the Mastersingers of Nuremberg showing portraits of four famous Mastersingers dating from c1620.

Die Meistersinger von Nürnberg

(*The Mastersingers of Nuremberg*)

Text by the composer.

MASTERSINGERS

HANS SACHS, COBBLER	*Bass*
VEIT POGNER, GOLDSMITH	*Bass*
KÜNZ VOGELGESANG, FURRIER	*Tenor*
KONRAD NACHTIGALL, TINSMITH	*Bass*
SIXTUS BECKMESSER, TOWN CLERK	*Bass*
FRITZ KOTHNER, BAKER	*Bass*

BALTHAZAR ZORN, PEWTERER	*Tenor*
ULRICH EISSLINGER, GROCER	*Tenor*
AUGUSTIN MOSER, TAILOR	*Tenor*
HERMANN ORTEL, SOAP-BOILER	*Bass*
HANS SCHWARZ, STOCKING-WEAVER	*Bass*
HANS FOLTZ, COPPERSMITH	*Bass*

WALTHER VON STOLZING	*Tenor*
DAVID	*Tenor*
EVA	*Soprano*
MAGDALENA	*Soprano or Mezzo-Soprano*
NIGHT WATCHMAN	*Bass*

First Performance
Munich, 21 June 1868.

THE PRELUDE, although supplied with a few bars to end a concert version, goes directly into a beautiful Chorale as the curtain opens on 16th-century Nuremberg.

ACT I. In the Church of St. Catherine, the Franconian knight Walther von Stolzing stands impatiently, watching the girl Eva and her companion Magdalena as the morning service ends. He has fallen in love at sight, having been received by Eva's father, Pogner, the day before. It is plain that Eva returns his feelings, for when the service is over, she sends Magdalena back twice to retrieve possessions so that she may listen to the knight's passionate pleas. But there are too many interruptions, and the women leave Walther to the mercies of David, the apprentice to the cobbler Sachs, who has been told to instruct the knight in the rules of the singing competition to be held immediately. Walther has learned that Eva's hand is to be given to the winner of the contest, and so he determines to enter it—and win. He is abashed by David's lengthy explanation of the complex rules, and sullenly waits as the apprentices set up the arrangements for the "sing-out" and the Mastersingers arrive. Pogner, Eva's father, and Beckmesser, the town clerk, are the first. When Walther greets the former and states his intention to be a contestant, it is plain that Beckmesser, himself a candidate and a rival for Eva's hand, will do everything he can to prevent the stranger from winning. For the cantankerous town clerk is the chosen "marker,"

Statue of Walther von Stolzing by Kaspar Ritter von Zumbusch.

St. Catherine's Church from an old print.

the judge who will note the faults in the contestants' songs—each is allowed seven faults and no more before being pronounced "outsung."

Walther is examined by the other Mastersingers who have arrived, and sings three verses of "Am stillen Herd," proclaiming his Master to have been the poet, Walther von Vogelweide. The freedom of the song leaves the listeners puzzled. Kothner is doubtful, while Beckmesser is openly scornful. Sachs intervenes, and Walther is allowed to continue. He sings a new melody, which still confuses the others. He is shown and read the rules, and is made to sit in the "singer's chair," from which he impetuously rises as his song progresses, earning more and more audible chalk marks on Beckmesser's slate, until his improvised melody extolling spring brings Beckmesser out of his marker's box in fury, his slate covered with fault-marks. The other Masters join in condemning the impetuous contestant, except for Sachs, who tries to bring reason into the mélée, and hints that Beckmesser is perhaps not as unprejudiced as a judge should be.

Beckmesser retorts with an insult to Sachs's poetry, and the Masters protest that they have heard enough. But Sachs insists that Walther be allowed to finish. All through his bright song of the birds of the forest, the Masters keep up an obbligato of complaint until the finale becomes uproarious, with Beckmesser darting about to show the singer's bad marks, and the apprentices joining in a merry dance to their own tune as eventually Walther is rejected and stalks out. The other Masters leave Sachs alone. The apprentices are still capering about as the philosophical cobbler exits, shaking his head in humorous dismay.

ACT II.   At the foot of a steep, narrow street, apprentices are closing the shutters of the houses on one side while David is engaged in the same task at Sachs's house in the foreground. Magdalena approaches, bringing David a basket of goodies, and, learning that the knight has fared badly at the trial that afternoon, leaves him and enters

Bispham as Beckmesser.

Anton Van Rooy as Hans Sachs.

Pogner's house on the opposite side of the street. The apprentices resume their teasing of David, who is always the butt of their jokes, but Sachs's arrival disperses them. The cobbler and David enter the shop. Pogner and Eva come down the street, and in their conversation, it finally dawns on the father what is troubling his daughter about the visiting knight. He goes into the house while Eva questions Magdalena about the trial. Learning of Walther's failure, Eva would try to see Sachs, but Magdalena restrains her, and they go inside. Sachs now comes out to his workbench just inside the half-door of the shop and starts to work on Beckmesser's shoe, but memories of the afternoon and the spontaneous and beautiful song he has heard haunt him. Eva comes out to seek his advice, and tries to get information about Walther. Only after considerable verbal fencing, during which she even asks Sachs why he is not a candidate for her hand (he thinks himself too old), does Sachs give an ironic version of Walther's dismal failure. Thinking that Sachs agrees with the other Masters, Eva leaves him in a fury, which confirms his suspicions about the direction in which her affections are pointed. How to make it come right? He closes his shutter so that he is virtually invisible.

Eva learns from Magdalena that Beckmesser intends to serenade her tonight. She hears footsteps approaching and sends Magdalena to lean out of the window in her stead, while she welcomes Walther with a rapturous cry. The failure of the day has brought their love into focus, and they plan to elope. But the advent of the Night Watchman with his haunting horn peal stays them. Eva goes into the house as Walther hides and the Watchman proceeds on his rounds. Sachs has observed all, and when Eva emerges from the house and the two young people attempt to flee, he places his lamp so that they should have to pass in its light. Frustrated, they withdraw under a lime tree.

Now another figure comes upon the scene. It is Beckmesser, bent on serenading Eva. Mistaking Magdalena for Eva at the window, he begins a ditty in a cracked voice, but Sachs, determined to outwit him, plies his cobbler's hammer at every mistake — and Beckmesser, who so avidly marks the faults of others, himself commits many grievous errors. The elaborately humorous scene finally erupts into chaos as the noise increases and burghers are summoned from their beds into the street. The brawl climaxes as Sachs intercepts the two lovers and draws Walther into shelter, pushing Eva into her own house. At the height of the fury, an immensely complicated many-part chorus, the Watchman's horn is once more heard, and the crowd disperses in a wink. All is peace as the Watchman goes by. But we hear a trace of Beckmesser's discomfiture, he having suffered a severe beating from David, who thought Magdalena the object of the bizarre serenade.

ACT III, Scene 1. The Prelude reflects the deeper side of Sachs's nature, his humanity, the sadness he feels at the loss of Eva, and his eventual resignation. The curtain rises on his workshop. Sachs sits at a large table, reading. David enters, bringing a basket which contains Magdalena's gifts. He is about to eat a sausage when Sachs looks up.

Hurriedly David apologizes for his behavior the night before. He is abashed by Sachs's continued silence, but eventually the Master greets him kindly and asks him to sing his verses. David thoughtlessly begins by using a tune from Beckmesser's serenade, but rights himself and sings a simple tune about St. John baptizing a child and naming it Johannes, which becomes Hans — the very name of his master, he exclaims. After some more chatter, Sachs sends the boy off to dress for the festivities of St. John's Day, and himself falls into meditation about the folly of man in the poignant "Wahn! Wahn!" The monologue ends in a thrilling burst of sound, as the aging cobbler hails Midsummer's Day and pledges to put right the injustices of Midsummer's Eve.

Walther now emerges from an adjoining room, saying that he has had the most wondrous dream. Sachs persuades him to sing about it, and over the young man's objections that any attempt on his part to make a Mastersong would again meet with the scorn of the Masters, counsels him to make his own rules. Sachs takes down the poem as Walther sings, ("Morgenlich leuchtet in rosigem Schein"), and proclaims that the knight has indeed made the first verse of a Mastersong — two stanzas of similar import and an aftersong. But he still expresses some doubt, and asks Walther for a second verse. Walther obliges ("Lieblich ein Quell"), whereupon Sachs remarks that he has achieved the stanzas

Ernestine Schumann-Heink (l.) as Magdalena and Johanna Gadski (r.) as Eva.

Friedrich Schorr as Hans Sachs.

Paul Schoeffler as Hans Sachs.

—and now how about the aftersong to complete it? But Walther demurs, so Sachs bids him remember his dream, for he will have a trial later that day. The two men go off to change into festive raiment (Walther's servant has brought his baggage there). Into the quiet workroom limps Beckmesser, cringing as his aching muscles betray him. He sees the song that Sachs has transcribed, and, thinking it to be the work of Sachs, appropriates it for his own use. Sachs, returning, notes the absence of the manuscript, but after some caustic remarks, cheerfully lets the jubilant Beckmesser keep it, knowing that he cannot possibly do it justice.

After Beckmesser departs, Eva comes cautiously in, ostensibly to ask Sachs to loosen one of her new shoes. While he has turned his back to do the chore, the door opens and reveals Walther in his splendor. Eva utters an ecstatic cry, while Sachs prattles on to cover the lovers' silent gazing into each other's eyes. Eva, in a mood of thanks and remorse, suggests that Sachs himself might have sought her hand, but he humorously rejects the idea—he is no Tristan (and we hear a motive

Two other famous Sachses, above: Emil Fischer, right: Otto Edelmann.

Act III, scene 2 of Die Meistersinger von Nürnberg, from the 1956-58 Bayreuth Festival production.

from that opera). Eva then expresses her love and gratitide for this noble man. David and Magdalena enter, and Sachs promotes his apprentice to journeyman. They join voices in a beautiful quintet, in which we hear the lovely strains of the Prize Song. Then all depart for the festival of St. John's Day.

Scene 2. On the meadow on the banks of the River Pegnitz, the good folk of Nuremberg have gathered, the apprentices and girls dance merrily with David their center, and the various guilds advance, each with its own banner and song. Sachs is given a specially warm tribute, in a song set to a poem by the real Sachs. Touched to the heart, Sachs replies gratefully.

Then Kothner calls on the unmarried men to sing the trial. Beckmesser is to begin. That unfortunate creature, hobbling in pain and surreptitiously consulting the poem he has stolen, endeavors to sing it to the creaky music of his serenade the night before, and is met with increasing ridicule and scorn, until he shambles off in disgrace. Sachs then introduces Walther as the original poet, and the young man begins the famous Prize Song which, although it starts out similarly to the recounting of the dream in the previous scene, soon changes to different music—and words. But by the sixth line, there is no thought of comparing the written poem with the song, for Kothner has dropped the manuscript in astonishment at the beauty of the song, which proceeds to its triumphant close. The knight is awarded the wreath of victory and Eva's hand. In playful joy, the girl takes the wreath from her lover and places it on Sachs's head, whereupon the entire crowd rejoices. Then Walther, remembering his ill treatment at the hands of the Masters, refuses the medallion that Sachs would confer on him; but the cobbler holds forth on the honor of the art which the Masters serve, as does he in his own way. Walther is reconciled, accepts the medal, and the tableau comes to a glorious finale with a universal tribute to Sachs.

Der Ring des Nibelungen

(*The Ring of the Nibelung*)

IT IS NO WONDER that the composition of *Der Ring des Nibelungen*, the most epic achievement of any musical endeavor, took Wagner twenty-two years to complete—even though during many periods of that span he was otherwise preoccupied with *Tristan*, *Die Meistersinger*, and *Parsifal*. What is amazing is that he composed it virtually backwards. His first sketch in 1848 was called *Siegfried's Death* and corresponds roughly to *Götterdämmerung* as we know it. In his revelation of the trials and triumphs of the gods over the cave-dwelling dwarfs and the stupid giants, drawn chiefly from the *Volsunga* and *Thidrek* sagas and the *Nibelungenlied*, the poet-composer realized that he was cramming too much of what we should call today "flashback" technique into *Siegfried's Death*. He made an entirely new opera from this left-over material, called *The Young Siegfried*. Then the material again grew too bulky and too long-winded, so that he started again, and wrote *Das Rheingold* (the prose sketch) in 1852 and the *Walküre* sketch and poem the same year. With all this looking over his shoulder, he realized that the last two segments needed revising. But some rather long "narrative" portions still remain, extremely valuable to listen to in order to grasp the essentials of the plots, and there are a few awkwardnesses of transition. However, the accomplishment remains the single greatest musical monument in history to date, and it will well repay the listener to learn as much as he can about the background and workings of Wagner's mind, in order to enjoy fully the musical masterpiece which is the ultimate reward.

For the serious student, it is recommended that Ernest Newman be read on the subject, and also that some knowledge of the hundreds of motifs be attempted, as they are the keys to the rich and subtly colored tapestry of ideas that unfolds as *The Ring* progresses.

It is interesting to note that Wagner originally intended a happy ending, in which Brünnhilde restores the Ring to the Rhinemaidens, frees Alberich

Stage machinery for the original Rhinemaidens from Wagner's Ring Cycle.

The finale of a space-age design for Die Walküre, given in 1972 by Kassel, Berlin.

and the Nibelungs, and proclaims the hero worthy to go to Valhalla, where the gods still dwell. The change to the sombre finale and the downfall of the gods came about as Wagner's own personality and point of view became darker, more heavily philosophical, and more pessimistic about men and gods—who after all, in his view, shared many of men's weaknesses. This change came about in 1851.

Another point should be made: Wagner discarded rhymed verse in favor of short, uneven lines, unrhymed at the ends but including "sound-alikes"—similar first consonants in words in any place in the line. This is the peculiarly Wagnerian *Stabreim*, an ancient device in German and English poetry, as Newman points out. Note the "r's," "n's," "k's," and "w's" in these lines (quoted from Newman):

> *Was du mir nahmst, nütztest du nicht...*
> *kehrt mir, ein Wissen wieder*
> *erkenn' ich des Ringes Runen.*

The full impact of this "music of the future" was not realized until the first complete performance of *The Ring*, at Bayreuth in 1876. *Rheingold* had been heard in 1869, *Walküre* in 1870, but the last two segments came on succeeding nights in the new house built by Ludwig for his favorite.

Ludwig, whose "madness" alternated with periods of great clarity, should probably not qualify for the former term, but certainly may be regarded as one of the greatest eccentrics of all time. Wagner had every reason for tolerating his benefactor's odd behavior. The composer was an obsession with the monarch from early years, who could not do enough for the man when once they had met. His favoritism even spelled a degree of ruin for Wagner, because court jealousies and intrigues drove the composer out of Munich. But Ludwig remained for Bavaria the symbol of romanticism, with his wild extravagances, his legendary castles (of which Neuschwanstein, the most fantastic, is redolent of Wagnerism, with murals, gold bathroom fixtures in the form of swans, and other evidences of this particular passion), and his never-ending search for beauty.

Program from the premiere of Das Rheingold (detail).

Das Rheingold
(*The Rhinegold*)

Text by the composer.

GODS

WOTAN	*Bass-Baritone*
FRICKA	*Mezzo-Soprano*
FREIA	*Soprano*
FROH	*Tenor*
DONNER	*Baritone*
LOGE	*Tenor*
ERDA	*Mezzo-Soprano*

NIBELUNGS

ALBERICH	*Bass*
MIME	*Tenor*

GIANTS

FASOLT	*Bass*
FAFNER	*Bass*

RHINEMAIDENS

WOGLINDE	*Soprano*
WELLGUNDE	*Soprano*
FLOSSHILDE	*Mezzo-Soprano*

First Performance
Munich, 22 September 1869.

The first complete performance of the cycle in London took place in 1882 under Anton Seidl, who also introduced the huge work to the Metropolitan in 1889. Three segments had been heard in New York previously, but *Das Rheingold* was the last to appear, in this full cycle.

Complete performances were the exception for many years, but of late they are more frequent. Notable is the series by the Seattle Opera, which for several years has produced *The Ring* both in German and in the English translation by Andrew Porter. Details of performances of the separate operas will be given under each heading.

WAGNER INTENDED that *The Ring* should be a trilogy, with three long "days" preceded by a Prologue. But it has gradually become known as a tetralogy, with all four segments being equal—although *Rheingold* has proved to be the least popular of the four if it comes to a question of giving the music dramas separately. It was the last to enter the Metropolitan's repertory, just before the complete *Ring* was given in 1889. At that time, Max Alvary was the Loge and Emil Fischer the Wotan.

BEFORE EMBARKING on a study of the monumental music dramas, it is wise to understand what has gone before. As we have seen, the world is populated by three main groups: the underground dwarfs, the Nibelungs, who mine precious elements; the earthdwelling Giants; and the Gods of the upper regions, who are not immune to the weaknesses of the few humans under their power who inhabit the earth. There is already unease among these three elements. Wotan, chief of the Gods, has visited the spring that comes from the World Ash, a tree guarded by the three Norns, who are the daughters of the Earth-Goddess Erda, and spin the fate of the world. To pay for a drink from the fountain of wisdom, Wotan has sacrificed an eye, and has thereby gained great power and married the Goddess Fricka (he is always seen with a patch or lock of hair over one eye). He has taken a branch from the huge tree for the shaft of his Spear, and engraved upon it a set of runes by which he must govern justly. Any breach of these rules will bring about the destruction of the Gods' power. He soon will yield to temptation and sow the fatal seed of destruction.

The opera opens with a Prelude of impressive magnitude, beginning with a single deep E-flat in the double basses, and gradually adding notes of the dominant chord until a mighty sound swells and undulates, evocative of the Rhine itself, and providing the motif that will connote the river.

Scene 1. We first see the bottom of the Rhine in a deep green gloom, with high jagged rocks shrouded in mist. The Rhinemaidens, Woglinde, Wellgunde, and Flosshilde, are swimming merrily about, only fitfully guarding the Gold that reposes at the tip of the highest rock. Their play is interrupted by Alberich, who has emerged from the depths, and seeks to join them in sport. They alternately flirt with and repel him, until he is completely frustrated. But now the motif of the Gold sounds, and a sudden ray of sun penetrates the water and touches the splendid metal. Two of the maidens witlessly tell of its power if made into a ring, but

The Rhinemaidens, left to right, Lilli Lehmann, Marie Lehmann, Minna Lammert, 1876, Bayreuth.

Flosshilde scolds them. They reply carelessly that no one would want to steal the Gold because he would have to forswear love — no one would choose that, least of all this lusty monster. Alberich's greed, however, overcomes his desire, and to the motif of Renunciation, he plunders the Gold and vanishes as darkness descends on the scene.

Scene 2. Now we seem to float upwards through the water and into mist, to a mountaintop, where Wotan and Fricka lie asleep. Fricka wakens, and rouses her spouse to the vision of the castle Valhalla, which gleams above and beyond them. Their ensuing argument reveals Wotan's thoughtless bargain with the Giants: for building his dream castle, they will receive as a prize the Goddess Freia, symbol of youth and beauty. Wotan has done this without consulting any of the other Gods, especially Fricka, and she is furious. The dialogue is perhaps typical of any husband and wife bickering, but very great things are at stake. Wotan has engraved the bargain in his spear, so that if he breaks it, disaster is sure to follow. Now he temporizes, thinking that the crafty God of Fire, Loge, can always get him out of a predicament. He counter-accuses Fricka of greed; she also wanted the castle. Her riposte is that she thought it would keep him at home. He had been overfond of roaming the earth and impersonating a human — or an animal or bird — in order to seduce various ladies. When she tries to put her womanly love in the scales with his desire for power, he retorts that he sacrificed an eye for her — and furthermore, he intends to break his word with the Giants and never to let Freia go.

Costume design for Alberich.

Emil Fischer as Wotan from the first Metropolitan Opera complete Ring cycle, 1889, New York.

Just then the younger Goddess rushes in, fleeing the Giants Fasolt and Fafner, who are coming to claim her. Wotan sends for Loge, the sly trickster, whom Wotan has tamed, but who is above no ruse, whether to help or confound his masters. Freia in desperation calls on her brothers, Donner and Froh, for help, but the Giants intervene. Fasolt, the less offensive of the two, attempts to reason with Wotan, but when the God refuses, Fafner brutally lays down the ultimatum. He knows that without Freia's golden apples, the Gods will lose their youth, beauty and strength. Freia is being dragged away, in spite of Froh and Donner (who, as God of Thunder, raises his huge hammer threateningly), but finally Loge appears in a flicker of flame, all sly deceit.

He tells the assembled company of the rape of the Gold by Alberich, and of the great hoard that the dwarf has amassed in the bowels of the earth; it is there for the taking. Everyone pauses: Wotan begins to desire the power inherent in the Ring Alberich has forged; Fricka thinks of it as a piece of jewelry, and Loge whispers to her that it would inspire her husband's faithfulness as well as adorn her; the Giants begin to think of accepting the hoard in lieu of Freia.

But Loge imposes another impediment: the man who possesses the Ring must give up love — is Wotan willing? Wotan objects; Loge has more arguments to advance, but says that in any case the Ring must be

Above: lineup of the Gods, l. to r., Hinshaw, Burian, Weil, Matzenauer, Gluck, Murphy, 1912, Metropolitan Opera, New York.

Left: Richard Holm as Loge (c.) with Bengt Rundgren as Fasolt and Hans Hotter as Wotan, 1973, Lyric Opera of Chicago.

Ernestine Schumann-Heink as Erda.

returned to the Rhinemaidens, for he has promised this if he should ever retrieve it. The Giants eventually agree to accept the treasure, but will not let Freia go until the gold is actually in their hands. They drag the goddess away as hostage; the other Gods immediately begin to show signs of age. Loge is the only one not affected, for he is really only a half-God, and never had the benefit of the golden apples anyway. He is, in fact, allied to the powers of darkness as well as to the Gods, feared and distrusted by both, who nevertheless are dependent on his cleverness.

When it seems the only thing to do, Loge leads the way to the nether regions through a sulphurous crevice in a rock. The scene changes as the travelers descend through layers of mist and rocky caverns. We see a huge cave with fiery forges, and hear the noise of hammers rhythmically beating. We are in Nibelheim.

Scene 3. Alberich drags his misshapen brother Mime, scolding him for not finishing the Tarnhelm, a fine-meshed helmet which will let its wearer appear as any living object or render him invisible. Mime, who had hoped to hold out the magic helmet for himself, is forced to give it up. Alberich immediately tries it on, and becoming invisible, beats the poor Mime unmercifully, then goes to supervise, invisibly, the work of his slaves. Wotan and Loge appear at this moment, and by showing sympathy to the cowering Mime, earn his confidence — and the story of the Ring and the Tarnhelm. Alberich now returns in his own shape, driving a horde of dwarfs who pile up treasure before him. He is immediately suspicious of the visitors. But Loge flatters him, reminds him that they are really kin, and that it was he who gave them the fire for their forges. The boastful Alberich tells of the treasure he has amassed and the power that will one day enable him to rule the upper world. Loge silences Wotan's angry protest, and continues to wheedle information out of Alberich, who finally shows the power of the Tarnhelm. Challenged by Loge to prove it, Alberich turns himself into a serpent,

Set Svanholm as Loge.

Costume design for Fricka by Franz Seitz.

Costume design for Freia by Franz Seitz.

which the Gods pretend to fear. Then Loge taunts Alberich into transforming himself into something smaller, and when the gullible dwarf becomes a toad, Wotan pounces on him and entraps him, whereupon he resumes his own shape. They convey him up through the successive layers of scene we have traversed in the other direction, and emerge into the light.

Scene 4. Alberich is told the terms of his release — the treasure. When his right hand is freed, he presses the Ring to his lips and summons the Nibelung horde to bring the treasure up to him. They pile it in a great heap, then disappear at his command. The defeated dwarf attempts to keep the Ring and the Tarnhelm, but Wotan wrests both from him, whereupon Alberich, accusing the God of even meaner motives than his own, pronounces a curse upon any owner of the precious Ring: "Let its owner never be blest; let it draw the slayer to his doom; let death be his portion and fear his daily bread." He laughs crazily and disappears down into the rocky cleft.

Wotan and Loge are not visibly moved by Alberich's curse, and calmly reassure Fricka, Donner and Froh as they appear. When the Giants arrive with Freia, they agree that she will be freed when she is entirely covered by the hoard of treasure. They begin to heap it up in front of her until it is exhausted, but Fasolt, who has been reluctant to give up her youth and beauty, claims he can still see one of her eyes through a small aperture. The Tarnhelm is reluctantly sacrificed to fill the chink, but Fasolt insists he can still see that bright eye, and demands the Ring from Wotan's finger to stop the gap. In vain does Loge protest that the Ring must go back to the Rhinemaidens. Wotan still refuses. The Giants drag Freia out, and Fricka pleads with Wotan to give up the Ring. When he is adamant, the scene darkens, and in a bluish light a figure emerges from the earth, commanding and powerful — the Earth-Goddess Erda. Even Wotan is subdued by her threat of the dire fate that will follow his disobediance. He would learn more, and when she sinks back into the earth, tries to follow her, but is restrained by Fricka and Froh. At last he yields up the Ring, and as Freia is returned, the Gods begin to regain some of their youthful mien.

But the Ring is already bringing trouble for the new owners. Fasolt and Fafner quarrel over sharing the treasure, and the brutal Fafner kills his brother, then departs, dragging his brother's corpse with him.

The seed of dissolution is already sown in Wotan's soul. He immediately begins to plan for the recovery of the Ring, and determines to seek out Erda to learn more of her secrets. Meanwhile, he must enter the castle. Donner strikes the rocks a tremendous blow which produces lightning and thunder, and he and Froh disappear in storm clouds. Then the air clears and they reappear, at their feet a rainbow bridge across the valley. Wotan picks a sword from the treasure left behind by the Giants, raises it, and christens the new castle, now visible, by the name of Valhalla. As the other Gods begin to cross the bridge, Loge remains behind, not willing to share the fate he is sure they will encounter. The Rhinemaidens are heard bewailing the loss of their Gold, and are not satisfied by Loge's cynical response (at Wotan's prompting): "Be happy in the golden glory the Gods shed on you." They continue to wail

The Gods look to Valhalla and the close of the opera, painting by L. Sievert.

but the sound is soon lost in the swelling motives of Valhalla and the Rainbow as the curtain falls. For the time being, the Gods have triumphed.

DIE WALKÜRE was the first of the *Ring* operas to be introduced to America, in a drastically cut version, at the Academy of Music, New York, in 1877. It was the first time the opera had been heard outside Bayreuth, Munich, and Vienna. Since those early days, it has become the most popular part of *The Ring*, often given by itself. The Metropolitan heard it initially in 1885, with Leopold Damrosch conducting, and a cast that included Materna in her Bayreuth role as Brünnhilde, with Seidl-Kraus, Brandt, Schott, and Staudigl.

Ring performances come and go as capable singers become available. The great roles demand the utmost from heroic performers, among whom may be counted Lilli Lehmann, who first was content with a Rhinemaiden and a Valkyrie in Bayreuth, and then became one of the greatest Brünnhildes and Sieglindes. Others since have courageously taken both roles: Florence Easton, Kirsten Flagstad, Olive Fremstad, Johanna Gadski, Helen Traubel, Lotte Lehmann, Astrid Varnay, and Birgit Nilsson. We should mention as famous Brünnhildes Marjorie Lawrence, Lillian Nordica, Frida Leider, Nanny Larsen-Todsen, Margaret Harshaw. Sieglindes were Emma Eames, Rose Bampton, Maria Jeritza, and Elizabeth Rethberg, among others. Siegmund has called on herioc tenors from the early Max Alvary and Jacques Urlus to the mid-point Lauritz Melchior and Set Svanholm to the more recent Jon Vickers and James King. Wotans were Hans Hotter, Friedrich Schorr, Paul Schoeffler, and more recently, Thomas Stewart and Norman Bailey. We have heard as Fricka Ernestine Schumann-Heink,

Program from the premiere of Die Walküre, 1870, Munich.

Die Walküre
(*The Valkyries*)

Text by the composer.

SIEGMUND	*Tenor*
HUNDING	*Bass*
SIEGLINDE	*Soprano*
WOTAN	*Bass-Baritone*
BRUNNHILDE	*Soprano*
FRICKA	*Mezzo-Soprano*

VALKYRIES

HELMWIGE	*Soprano*
ORTLINDE	*Soprano*
GERHILDE	*Soprano*
WALTRAUTE	*Mezzo-Soprano*
SIEGRUNE	*Mezzo-Soprano*
ROSSWEISSE	*Mezzo-Soprano*
GRIMGERDE	*Mezzo-Soprano*
SCHWERTLEITE	*Mezzo-Soprano*

First Performance
Munich, 26 June 1870.

480
WAGNER

Lotte Lehmann as Sieglinde.

Louise Homer, Karin Branzell, Kerstin Thorborg, Blanche Thebom, Christa Ludwig, and Mignon Dunn.

BETWEEN *DAS RHEINGOLD* and the second segment of *The Ring*, a number of years have passed, in which Wotan has sought a way out of his dilemma. In order to remove the curse upon the Ring, it must be restored to the Rhinemaidens; yet he cannot seize it by force from Fafner, who by this time is safely ensconced with the Nibelung treasure in a deep cave in the forest. Such force would only compound the evil Wotan has brought upon himself and the world by his initial theft. He has sought out Erda in the depths of the earth, but has not profited by her advice—instead, he has fathered with her nine war-like maidens, who are to guard the heroes slain in battle after bringing them on winged horses to Valhalla. Of these, Brünnhilde is the leader. But this does not satisfy Wotan's original need: to find some hero who will unwittingly rescue the Ring and—so ambiguous are his thoughts—relieve Wotan of the responsibility of returning the precious gold to its original owners. To create such a hero, Wotan has visited earth in the shape of a mortal, calling himself Wälse, and with a human woman has had twins, Siegmund and Sieglinde. Siegmund is Wotan's hope for the innocent hero. But events occur differently, as we shall see.

ACT I.   A violent storm rages in the music, with Donner's thunderbolts rampant. As it dies down, the curtain rises on the primitive home of Hunding, a Neidung warrior, who has kidnaped Sieglinde while her father and brother were hunting, and has married her. Now Siegmund, driven from his course by the storm, and battered from fighting his pursuing enemies, seeks refuge in this home. He staggers into the courtyard and collapses by the open hearth in which a fire flickers. In the dimness we see a huge ash tree and a table, with benches beside the trunk. Soon Sieglinde appears from the interior of the house, and, spying the stranger, is immediately attracted to him. When he awakens suddenly and calls for water, she gives him a drinking horn. The music here shows plainly that these two lives are intertwined, even though the couple does not yet recognize it. He attempts to leave, learning that this is Hunding's house, but she restrains him. They gaze deeply into each other's eyes.

The mood is broken as Hunding enters. The rough warrior first tells Sieglinde to prepare their meal, then demands from his guest the particulars of his life. Siegmund carefully narrates how he and his father, returning from a hunt, found their hut burned, his mother murdered, and his sister gone. He became separated from his father during a battle, finding only a wolf-skin once the battle was done. The music tells us that his father was Wotan. Siegmund has wandered ever since, accompanied only by misfortune. This very day he has attempted to rescue a maid from a marriage forced upon her by her brothers. He slew the brothers, and the girl denounced him as a murderer, calling on her kinsmen for revenge. Hunding was one of those summoned, and now knows that before him is the object of his vengeance. But the laws of hospitality forbid him to kill his guest, who, he says, is safe for the night; but with the morning, Siegmund must defend himself.

Left: Olive Fremstad as
Sieglinde, right: Burgstaller
as Siegmund.

Left alone by the fire, Siegmund meditates gloomily that he has no
sword, although one has been promised him by his father. As a motive
sounds, the fire flares up and reveals the handle of a sword embedded in
the great tree trunk. Sieglinde glides swiftly in; she has given Hunding a
sleeping potion, and now intends to rescue the visitor. She points out
the sword and relates that an aged stranger who intruded on her wedding feast had implanted the blade of the sword in the tree. Whoever
could draw it out should possess it. All the men tried and failed, and
there it has remained. We hear in the orchestra the motive of the
Wälsungs, but now triumphant. Siegfried takes Sieglinde in his arms.
Gradually they recognize each other as of the same race, the Wälsung,
and of the same father, destined to live or die together.

Suddenly the doors at the back fall open, and a vision of green
forests and flowers appears, while the orchestra tells us that Love and
Spring are one. Siegmund greets his love with the wondrous
"Winterstürme" the "Spring Song." Sieglinde answers, "Thou are the
Spring that long I sighed for." She now names him Siegmund, her twin
brother. With a mighty effort, he wrenches the sword from the tree,
names it Nothung ("Needful"), and clasps Sieglinde in his arms as the
two rush out into the spring night.

ACT II.   The intricately symphonic Prelude reminds us of the
love of Siegmund and Sieglinde, but with a new and vigorous
element, that of flight, and the introduction of the Valkyries, their Ride,
and their leader, Brünnhilde. The curtain opens on a rocky pass in the
mountains. Wotan and Brünnhilde enter, the maid fully armed. The
God instructs her that in the approaching combat between Hunding and
Siegmund, she must aid the young Wälsung. Her joy at this is expressed
in the famous cry, "Ho-jo-to-ho!" and when it is ended, she warns him
to expect trouble, for Fricka is approaching in her ram-drawn cart. The
Goddess appears, simmering with anger. As the protector of marriage,
she demands justice for Hunding, defeat for the despoiler of his house-

Helen Traubel as Brünnhilde.

Friedrich Schorr as Wotan.

hold. Wotan's explanation of his reason for sparing Siegmund — that Siegmund must be the hero who redeems the Ring — does not sit well with this wrathful spouse. She overcomes his protests with sheer force of character — and the argument that, should the Wälsungs go unpunished, she, Queen of the Gods and protector of the marriage vow, would be degraded before mankind. In spite of Wotan's feeble attemts to save his own race, the curse of Alberich still obtains, even though it is through the vessel of the righteous Fricka. Wotan summons Brünnhilde to rescind his order — now she must protect Hunding and allow Siegmund to be defeated. To her pleas he is deaf; he is the pawn of fate, if ostensibly only a henpecked husband.

Brünnhilde muses sadly after he leaves her, knowing that his heart is with the young warrior. Now she sees the couple approaching, Sieglinde almost at the end of her strength, Siegmund supporting her. The warrior maiden watches as Siegmund quiets his sister after her wild outburst of terror. He tells her that he is determined to meet Hunding just here. Then, as Sieglinde dozes fitfully, Brünnhilde engages in a somber duet with Siegmund, punctuated by music that breathes of fate, death, and Valhalla. She promises to convey the hero to that magic home, but he merely asks if Sieglinde may accompany him. If not, he will remain with his bride. So moved is Brünnhilde by his calm resolution and heroic bearing that she resolves to break her vow to Wotan. When Hunding appears to challenge the abductor of his wife, the Valkyrie moves to protect Siegmund. But Wotan intervenes, strikes Siegmund's sword with his spear and breaks it; Hunding kills Siegmund. Then, in rage at what he has had to do, Wotan smites Hunding in turn. Sieglinde, rousing, sees the fate of her lover-brother, and falls to the ground, shrieking. Brünnhilde gathers her up, together with the pieces of Siegmund's sword, and flees.

Right: Lilli Lehmann.
Left: Margarite Mat-
zenauer as Brünnhilde.

Wotan's farewell, the final scene of Die Walküre, production Wieland Wagner, 1956, Bayreuth.

ACT III.   The famous "Ride of the Valkyries" precedes the opening of the curtain, which discloses the high, rocky terrain where the eight warrior-maidens are awaiting their sister Brünnhilde, and crying at the tops of their voices. When Brünnhilde arrives, bearing across her saddle not a hero but a fainting woman, she tells her sisters what has happened and bids them watch for Wotan, who is pursuing her to mete out punishment for her disobedience. She sends Sieglinde off into the forest with the pieces of the sword. The eight try to shield Brünnhilde, but their father finds the erring maid. Sending the sisters away, he confronts his favorite daughter with her grievous act. This great scene between father and daughter is one of pity, terror, and undeniable love. "What did I do that was so shameful?" she asks piteously. He cannot forgive her; she must be punished. He will cast her into a deep sleep, and the first man who finds her will find not a Valkyrie, but a mere woman. But she pleads with him: at least let him surround her with a ring of fire, so that only a true hero may find his way to her. She confides, indeed, that just such a hero may yet be born, for Sieglinde will give birth to one Siegfried, who may fulfill Wotan's desire to save the world—as well as herself. Tenderly, he agrees. He puts her into a deep sleep and carries her to a rocky bed. Covering her with her helmet and shield, he summons Loge (to the strains of the celebrated "Fire Music"), and bids his darling farewell in a moving final passage, "Leb wohl." The fire music mounts higher and higher, mingled with a motif foretelling Siegfried, as Wotan places a spell on the sleeping Brünnhilde with his spear, then sorrowfully departs. As the fire music dies away, the curtain falls.

Karin Branzell as Fricka.

Max Alvary as Siegfried, from the Metropolitan premiere of the opera, 1887, New York.

Siegfried

Text by the composer.

SIEGFRIED	*Tenor*
MIME	*Tenor*
WOTAN (THE WANDERER)	*Bass-Baritone*
ALBERICH	*Bass-Baritone*
FAFNER	*Bass*
ERDA	*Contralto*
FOREST BIRD	*Soprano*
BRUNNHILDE	*Soprano*

First Performance
Bayreuth, 16 August 1876.

AFTER ITS FIRST performance as part of the first complete *Ring* Cycle in Bayreuth in 1876, the third opera in the tetralogy made its way slowly to world centers, never quite achieving the popularity of *Die Walküre*. London heard it in 1882 and again at Covent Garden in 1892. The Metropolitan premiere was in 1887, with Alvary as Siegfried, Lilli Lehmann as Brünnhilde, Seidl conducting. When *Siegfried* returned to the repertory after the new Italian regime was instituted, the De Reszke brothers were starred, and Nellie Melba was ill-starred. That captious prima donna, hitherto content in the realms of lyric and coloratura supremacy, wanted to sing Brünnhilde, and against some better judgment, did. She survived only one performance, after which Felia Litvinne took over. The incident proved disastrous all around, because Lillian Nordica, insulted at being passed over for a part that should have belonged to her, left the company and was not wooed back for two seasons.

Several characters from *Das Rheingold* who did not show up in *Die Walküre* reappear in *Siegfried*: Alberich and his brother Mime, Erda, and Fafner (disguised as a dragon), while Wotan once more appears in the guise of the Wanderer.

The same coterie of leading singers appear throughout the *Ring*, but we can note a few famous Mimes: Albert Reiss, Karl Laufkoetter, and, more recently, Ragnar Ulfung. A new, if less important, character in *Siegfried* is the Forest Bird, whose elevated trills have been accomplished by such lustrous singers as Elisabeth Schumann, Eleanor Steber, and Joan Sutherland.

WHEN SIEGLINDE fled after being rescued by Brünnhilde, it was to the very forest where Fafner, as a dragon, guards the Nibelung treasure in a deep cave. Nearby is the home of the dwarfs Alberich and Mime. Mime found the terrified Sieglinde and helped deliver her child, who,

Jess Thomas as Siegfried.

she insisted before her death, should be called Siegfried. Mime took the child and the pieces of sword to his own dwelling.

ACT I.   The prelude reveals the innermost soul of the scheming Mime, who intends, through Siegfried, to regain the Ring and rule the world after reforging the powerful sword, whose properties he knows. As the curtain rises, he is attempting to make a sword for Siegfried, who has demanded one. But each weapon fashioned by Mime breaks at the first blow delivered by the strong young man. He has tried, but has never succeeded in making whole the pieces that will form the sword Nothung.

Siegfried enters with a shout, dragging in a large bear. The youth is dressed in animal skins, and wears a silver horn around his neck. His youthful theme sounds in the orchestra as he playfully sets the bear on Mime, who cowers in terror. But the dwarf has completed a sword, and Siegfried, after chasing the bear away, tries the new weapon. With one mighty blow on the anvil, he smashes it to bits. Then he turns in rage on Mime, reviling him in a perfect tempest of anger. Mime attempts to calm him by relating all the wonderful things he has done to bring up the boy: he has given him food and shelter and that pretty horn, has watched over him wisely while toiling all the while. Siegfried turns to stare at his benefactor, who cannot meet his eyes. Then, quietly, Siegfried begins to revile his foster father, working himself into a storm of passion, but pausing to wonder why it is that he always returns to this wretched place and this loathsome creature whom he cannot abide. Mime answers, to a strain of lovely music, that it is love which inspires him. Siegfried retorts that he has seen love in the forest, and that it is always two parents who cherish their offspring—why does he not have a mother? Mime replies that he is both father and mother, whereupon the boy, in mounting fury, tries to choke the truth out of him.

At last, the cringing dwarf tells the story of Siegfried's birth, and reveals the name his dying mother gave him. Furthermore, he produces the fragments of the sword. Siegfried exultantly knows that this will be his sword, the one he has longed for, and demands that Mime forge it that very day. Rushing off into the forest, he leaves the perturbed dwarf, who knows very well that he cannot accomplish this task. He broods darkly about his problem: how can he make Siegfried kill the dragon and steal the Ring if he cannot provide the weapon to do it?

Now Wotan enters, dressed as a Wanderer in a long cloak and a broad-brimmed hat which partially conceals the patch over his eye, and carrying his spear. Mime ungraciously greets him, but refuses his offer of wise counsel, saying that he knows all he needs to. The Wanderer ignores this, and proposes a game of wits: his head will be forfeit if he cannot answer three of the dwarf's questions. Mime perks up; he believes he can confound this traveler. But the Wanderer answers all three questions: the beings that dwell below the earth are the Nibelungs; those on earth are the Giants; those above are the Gods—at which he touches his spear to the ground as if by accident, and a light rumble of thunder is heard.

Now it is the dwarf's turn to answer questions. He knows that the race which Wotan dealt wrathfully with while loving them the most are

Reiss as Mime.

Wotan the Wanderer.

Lauritz Melchior as Siegfried.

the Wälsungs; Mime relates their history even as far as Siegfried. He also knows the name of the sword that Wotan fashioned and Siegmund rescued, and that a cunning smith now holds it. But when asked who shall forge the pieces into a whole, Mime trembles, crying wildly that it is he who has the pieces, but that they defy him.

Wotan tells him that his head is forfeit, but that he will leave it for Fafner's destroyer—that fearless being who should himself forge the sword. The God disappears in a blazing orchestral passage, accompanied by musical flickers of fire, Loge's contribution to the scene. Mime utters a terrified shriek, "Fafner! Fafner!" and seeks refuge behind the anvil.

When Siegfried enters, demanding the sword, Mime craftily tells him he must learn to fear because of the many dangers he will encounter. Siegfried remains unaffected by all of Mime's fearful images, and Mime finally promises that the boy will indeed learn to be afraid when he is taken to the Neidhöhle, eastward in the wood, where a fierce dragon repels all invaders. Siegfried is intrigued, but first must have his sword. When Mime confesses that he is not able to forge it, Siegfried takes on the task himself. He resists Mime's instructions, and begins to file the pieces into powder, asking the name of the sword. Mime replies that the boy's mother had called it "Nothung." Happily, Siegfried repeats the name vociferously, while completing the reduction of the metal to powder, which he now plunges into a crucible. When the metal has reaches white heat, he pours it into a mold, tempers the metal by thrusting it into water, and then works the bellows to fan the flames

Kirchoff as Siegfried has just split the anvil with the sword "Nothung" while Heinrich Henke as Mime looks on, 1911, Berlin.

that shall complete the forging process. He sings a lusty song all the while, repeating the phrase, "Hoho! Hohei!" at the top of his voice, accompanied by the motive of Victory.

Mime the while has been preparing a meal, but Siegfried refuses to eat any food the dwarf has concocted. He takes the mold from the fire, completes the forging, and fits the blade into a haft. Now he brandishes the weapon aloft. With a mighty blow, he splits the anvil into halves, as the curtain descends on his triumph and Mime's terror. (A stage manager's nightmare is the vulnerability of the anvil; programmed to fall apart at a blow, occasionally it has either resisted, or has prematurely separated before feeling the might of Nothung.)

ACT II. We are in a different atmosphere, laden with the premonition of disaster, as foretold in the motives of the Dragon, the Curse on the Ring, and the hint of Annihilation predicted by Alberich after the Ring had been stolen from him. When the curtain rises, we dimly perceive Alberich, sitting at the foot of a cliff and brooding over the wrongs done him. His anticipation of the approach of the Dragon-slayer is false, for it is Wotan as the Wanderer who appears before him. The colloquy that follows shows that Alberich knows full well the treachery and ambition of the God, while Wotan threatens the dwarf with the advent of the hero who shall slay the dragon. But perhaps he, the God, can persuade Fafner to give up the Ring. He summons the dragon, who roars sleepily from his cave. While Wotan proposes that he give up the Hoard to save his life, Alberich exhorts Fafner to yield the Ring only, as that is what the approaching hero will want. But the dragon contemptuously refuses, and growls his way back to sleep.

Now Wotan laughs and tells Alberich that all things will be as they must, and that the dwarf must contend with his brother, and with a new menace as well, which the orchestra reveals as Siegfried and his sword. Wotan disappears, accompanied by fitful winds and flickering lights, and Alberich crawls into a cleft in the rock to await the coming events.

As day dawns, Siegfried and Mime appear. After a few futile attempts to arouse the feeling of fear in the boy's mind, and meeting only a flood of contempt, Mime slinks off, hypocritically offering aid if Siegfried should call.

Siegfried sinks down on a grassy knoll, and meditates on his parents; surely he would resemble a true father, as he does not resemble this horrid gnome who claims him; and his mother — was she beautiful? He dreams on, as the forest murmurs ever more distinctly. At last, a Bird breaks into song above him. He cuts a pipe from a tree stem, but its sound is too clumsy to echo the Bird. Then he thinks of his horn, and blows a great sustained call, which arouses the whole forest — but more importantly, stirs Fafner out of his sleep. The dragon pulls his heavy body out of the cave and up onto the knoll, from which he engages in an increasingly fierce dialogue with the boy. Siegfried deals him a wound; angered by it, the dragon raises his body so that his heart is vulnerable. Immediately Nothung finds its target. With his dying breath,

Bispham as Alberich.

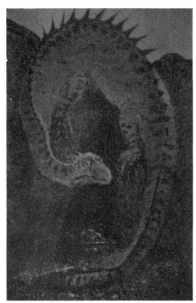

*Drawing of Fafner as a dragon by
Arnold Böcklin.*

Louise Homer as Erda.

Fafner questions the boy about who has set him to do this deed (and we hear the Curse motive), but Siegfried disclaims any provocation but the dragon himself. The dragon dies without revealing anything Siegfried wants to know. As the boy draws his sword from the fatal wound, blood splashes on his hand, and involuntarily he sucks it to relieve the burning sensation it causes. Suddenly he understands the song of the Bird above him.

The Bird reveals that the Tarnhelm and Ring await the hero; Siegfried plunges into the cave to retrieve them. Mime now appears, but Alberich emerges and blocks his way, each fiercely claiming the prizes within the cave. Mime suggests that he keep the Tarnhelm, while Alberich shall have the Ring and all the rest, but Alberich scornfully denies him any part of the Hoard. Now Siegfried comes out, bearing only the Ring and the Tarnhelm; but he does not know what they mean, and still nothing has taught him fear. The Woodbird breaks into song again, warning him against Mime. That one now approaches, cajoling and wheedling, deceitfully offering congratulations along with a flask of broth. But the Bird has enabled Siegfried to read the dwarf's mind, and his real utterances are vile threats of poison and decapitation by Siegfried's own sword. This diatribe ends as Mime proffers the poison, and Siegfried, quiet until now, furiously strikes him dead. Alberich's laughter is heard as Siegfried carries Mime's body into the cave.

With difficulty, Siegfried pushes the dragon's body back into the cave, to guard, with Mime, the treasure that has so corrupted them both. Resting from his labor, he hears the Bird once more, this time directing him to the rock where Brünnhilde slumbers, and promising that he shall penetrate the wall of fire and win her for his bride. For he is the one without fear, the only one who can accomplish this miracle. Exultantly, Siegfried follows the course of the Bird on this momentous journey.

ACT III. Wotan's turbulence of soul is shown in the Prelude, which leads to a scene at the foot of a rocky mountain. Wotan summons the Earth Goddess, Erda; for his confusion of motive and morality has set him into a mood that alternates between resignation and rebellion, and he wants some counsel from this primal being. Slowly she rises out of a cleft in the rock, bathed in greenish light, covered with the frost of long sleep. The dialogue reveals all that has happened, but in a new light. Erda's wisdom is asleep; let him look to Brünnhilde, the bearer of the new wisdom. Learning of Brünnhilde's disobedience and punishment, she ironically says that he, who was responsible, is now angry at his own deed—let him depart. Already reconciled to the doom of the Gods which he has ensured by his greed and rash actions, Wotan now confides the morality of the world to the innocent hero, who knows nothing of him or his plots and who, with Brünnhilde, will found a new world. Wotan bids Erda farewell as she sinks into the earth for the last time. Then he awaits Siegfried.

The young hero appears and is petulant at finding his way barred by the old stranger. Disregarding all caution, he presses on to his goal,

Siegfried waking Brünnhilde in the final scene of Siegfried, Bayreuth.

whose fiery ambience he can see in the distance. Wotan makes a token last effort to stop the forces he himself has set in motion, but when the boy impetuously shatters the potent spear that once broke the sword he now wields, Wotan quietly picks up the pieces and retreats, leaving Fate to take its course.

Siegfried blows his horn and penetrates the wall of flame into a mist-ridden landscape. When the clouds disperse, we are at the scene of Brünnhilde's rock, where she lies sleeping under her great shield, the helmet on her head. When the hero loosens the shield by cutting the straps, and the fulsome figure meets his eyes (it is usually a very fulsome figure indeed), he utters a line that invariably draws a laugh from the audience: "That is no man!" Of course, he has never seen a woman, but he knows somehow that this must be one.

The sight arouses within him emotions hitherto unknown, but somehow longed for. Could this be fear? he wonders. Its strong propulsion leads him to waken her with a kiss.

Slowly the maiden sits up, and, raising her arms to the sun and the world, cries a joyful greeting. Then she confronts her rescuer partly in gladness, partly timidity. They have each gone through much to meet, but she is resentful at being reduced from immortality to mere humanity. Gradually he persuades her that their love will conquer all obstacles, that he himself has no fear, and that theirs is the new day that is now dawning. On this rapturous note, the curtain falls on the third day.

THE FINAL "DAY" of *The Ring* was the climax of the performances at Bayreuth in 1876. It reached London in 1882 and the Metropolitan in 1888. The New York cast included Niemann, Robinson, Fischer, von Milde, Seidl-Kraus, Brandt, and Lilli Lehmann, with Seidl conducting. Most of the singers mentioned in the accounts of the three previous music dramas have taken part in *Götterdämmerung* as well, but a few additional names may be mentioned: Bohnen, List, and Rundgren as Hagen; Whitehill, Hotter, Uhde, and Stewart as Gunther; Weed, Resnik, Bjoner, and Rankin as Gutrune; and Telva, Olszewska, Madeira, Dalis, Ludwig, and Dunn as Waltraute. The productions of portions of *The Ring* by Herbert von Karajan, who also conducted in several seasons, were features of recent Metropolitan history. In early days, the scene with the Norns and the Waltraute scene were omitted, but the current tendencies are toward uncut versions (which make of the "days" very long evenings).

Götterdämmerung
(*The Twilight of the Gods*)

Text by the composer.

SIEGFRIED	*Tenor*
BRUNNHILDE	*Soprano*
ALBERICH	*Bass-Baritone*
HAGEN	*Bass*
GUNTHER	*Baritone*
*GUTRUNE	*Soprano*
WALTRAUTE	*Mezzo-Soprano*
FIRST NORN	*Contralto*
SECOND NORN	*Mezzo-Soprano*
THIRD NORN	*Soprano*

RHINEMAIDENS

WOGLINDE	*Soprano*
WELLGUNDE	*Soprano*
FLOSSHILDE	*Mezzo-Soprano*

First Performance
Bayreuth, 17 August 1876.

THE FIRST SCENE of *Götterdämmerung* is called the Prelude, and is introduced by a short orchestral passage that connotes Primal Nature, the Rhine, Erda, and the Weaving of the Norns. We see these three beings at the foot of the rocky eminence that contains Brünnhilde's cave—essentially the same scene that closed *Siegfried*. The three Norns are manipulating the lines of Fate, tossing them back and forth to each other, winding them around a sharp rock, and singing all the while of events that have led to the present perilous time. We know most of this already, but a few new facts come to light. The great Ash Tree has withered since Wotan cut the branch for his spear, and the spring has dried up. Wotan has had the tree trunk cut into logs which now surround Valhalla, awaiting the torch that will set them alight and burn down the citadel where the God sits gloomily, surrounded by his ineffective warriors. The destroying fire will come from the breast of Loge, into which Wotan will drive the fragments of his splintered spear. At the recollection of Alberich's Curse, the cord of Fate breaks, and the Norns disappear, wailing, into the earth. The end of their world is near.

Dawn breaks, and Brünnhilde and Siegfried emerge from the cave. She is leading her horse, Grane, and he is clad in full armor—Brünnhilde's. They engage in a duet that reveals each as more mature than when he reclaimed her from the fiery circle. She has taught him much, but now he (according to the best principles laid down for heroes) must go forth into the world and perform heri009 deeds. He has given her the Ring in exchange for the horse and armor—neither knows its power.

Siegfried begins to descend the mountain, accompanied by the mighty music that is known as Siegfried's Rhine Journey. He passes out of sight to the themes of the Rhinemaidens, Alberich's Renunciation, the Ring, and the Nibelungs' despair.

ACT I, Scene 1. The Hall of the Gibichungs sits on the bank of the Rhine, sheer cliffs behind it. Alberich has had a son by the Gibichung queen, Grimherd; the son is called Hagen. The queen has also borne twins, half-siblings to Hagen: Gunther and Gutrune. They sit with Hagen at a table, engaged in serious conversation. Hagen is disturbed because neither of the twins has married, and he proposes a solution. For a bride, Gunther will take the heroine Brünnhilde, and as a groom for Gutrune, Hagen proposes Siegfried. He tells the story of the enchantment over the warrior maiden, omitting the fact of her rescue, and states falsely that Siegfried is master of the Nibelungs and their hoard—but, of course, Siegfried has remained ignorant of the magic properties of the Ring and the Tarnhelm. Hagen will give Siegfried a magic potion which will make him love Gutrune. Hagen tells his half-brother that, once enchanted by the potion, Siegfried will rescue Brünnhilde and bring her back for Gunther.

Siegfried providentially appears at this juncture, in a boat he has obtained somehow. Presently he appears at the castle (apparently having tethered Grane somewhere, for the horse accompanied him in the boat). Hagen and Gunther greet him warmly, Hagen questioning him about the Nibelung hoard. Siegfried answers carelessly that he has almost forgotten it; he took only the helmet, which now hangs at his belt, but he has never found any use for it. And the Ring, which rests with a wonderful woman. Hagen quickly explains the magic of the Tarnhelm, and advances the plot by calling to Gutrune to bring the visitor a welcoming drink. The maid advances (to her own rather too-sweet theme) and modestly hands the drinking horn to Siegfried, with whom she has been instantly smitten. Siegfried drinks the potion, and his indifference toward her turns to blazing passion. Quickly the bargain is sealed—he will have Gutrune, and will secure for Gunther the Brünnhilde he has totally forgotten. Siegfried and Gunther drink blood brothership, a serious business in which each drops his own blood from a cut in his wrist into wine, which each then drinks. They start off on their dastardly quest.

Hagen is left alone to gloat over the prospects of success for his ambition. It is a dark and powerful monologue, accompanied by memories of his horrid father Alberich, and of his own hatred for everyone else. As the curtain falls, the gloomy music changes to a lighter tone, signifying Brünnhilde's happiness, but reverting to the themes of the Curse and Annihilation.

Scene 2. Brünnhilde is not to be happy for long, for thunder and lightning announce the approach of a flying horse bearing Waltraute. Brünnhilde immediately presumes that Wotan has forgiven her, but Waltraute interrupts her rapturous outpouring with the sorry tale of Wotan's dissolution into weakness and the general gloom around Valhalla. She begs Brünnhilde to give the Ring back to the Rhinemaidens—it is the only way certain doom can be averted. But Brünnhilde is all too human by now, and passionately refuses—it is the token of Siegfried's love, and the most meaningful thing in her life. Sadly, her sister Valkyrie departs, followed by Brünnhilde's injunction never to return.

Now Brünnhilde notices that her guardian fire is brightening, showing that someone is trying to penetrate its circle. Joyously, she thinks it is Siegfried, but the man who confronts her wears the Tarnhelm and appears to be Gunther, a stranger. He subdues her, wrests the Ring from her finger, and takes her into the cave, using the sword Nothung to

Edouard de Reszke as Hagen.

Kathleen Howard as Waltraute.

Jean de Reszke as Siegfried.

separate them so that she will be untouched for Gunther. Their struggle, physical and emotional, is mirrored in a wonderful mixture of musical motives.

ACT II.   In front of the Gibichung hall, Hagen slumbers fitfully, while Alberich creeps in and harangues his son on the imperative need to regain the Ring, even if it means resorting to murder. Hagen replies groggily to his father's tirade, and we realize that he is in reality dreaming the scene. Alberich vanishes with the dawn. Siegfried appears, enabled by the magic of the Tarnhelm to arrive before Gunther and Brünnhilde. He is wearing the coveted Ring. Gutrune comes out to greet her bridegroom, questioning him about the abduction of Brünnhilde. Siegfried's replies are a bit evasive, but Gutrune is satisfied with his explanation that the sword separated him from her brother's intended bride, even though the two men did not assume their rightful identities until after Siegfried had brought Brünnhilde out through the flames. Preparations are begun for a sumptuous wedding feast.

Hagen sounds his mighty ox-horn in a weird series of calls to the four corners of the territory, summoning Gibichung vassals to the wedding festivities. But he shouts to them to bring weapons and prepare for an emergency. Soon the stage is crammed with followers, and we hear

Olive Fremstad as Brünnhilde.

The gathering of vassals, Act II, Götterdämmerung, 1930, Bayreuth.

the very first chorus in all of *The Ring.* The vassals are surprised to
learn that their weapons are to be used only to slaughter wild animals
dedicated to Fricka, Goddess of Marriage (a bit of irony on Hagen's
part), but also the hint is given that the bride may need protection if she
has been wronged.

Now Gunther and Brünnhilde arrive, to be greeted by a great choral
outpouring. Brünnhilde is sullen; she does not even look up when Siegfried and Gutrune enter. But at the mention of Siegfried's name, she is
aroused to horror and the longing for vengeance. When she sees the
Ring on Siegfried's finger, she breaks into accusation, arousing
Gunther's suspicion, but eliciting from Siegfried only bewilderment. He
remembers only that he gained the Ring after slaying the Dragon.
Hagen intends to seize the opportunity to bring revenge on Siegfried;
everyone is further aroused by Brünnhilde's wild accusation against
Siegfried as the betrayer — the sword was not between them. Siegfried
swears his honesty on Hagen's spear, stating that if he has been false,
this will be the weapon to slay him (the most solemn of oaths, and here
a prophetic one).

Brünnhilde breaks in wildly, replacing Siegfried's hand on the spear
with her own, and swearing her own consecration of the weapon to his
death. Siegfried makes matters worse by handing his former love over
to Gunther. Taking Gutrune by the hand, he leads his new love into the
hall.

Brünnhilde, Hagen and Gunther now brood together over complex
orchestral patterns. Finally, the wronged woman speaks — as a woman,

Gunther.

not the goddess who would have realized that a trick had been played on her. Her powers are gone; she has bestowed them all on the hero. Still bent on vengeance, she lets it slip that Siegfried is vulnerable only on his back, which he would never turn to a foe. "That is where my spear shall strike!" exclaims Hagen.

Hagen urges Gunther to aid in the betrayal, but the weakling feels himself bound by blood brothership; furthermore, Siegfried's death would grieve Gutrune. Brünnhilde excoriates the girl as the cause of the betrayal, but Hagen's arguments are stronger; he plays on Gunther's greed and ambition. Furthermore, the deed will take place away from Gutrune — on a hunting trip. It shall be supposed that a wild boar attacked the hero. A powerful trio ensues in which Brünnhilde and Gunther call on Wotan for aid, but Hagen relies on his wicked father Alberich. Siegfried and Gutrune are brought out on the backs of the vassals in general rejoicing, during which Gunther forces Brünnhilde to a semblance of joy. Hagen's motive rings out over Gutrune's as the curtain falls.

ACT III, Scene 1. In the Prelude we hear Siegfried's horn-call as well as the approaching ox-horn of the Gibichungs, in a wild part of the forest through which the Rhine flows. The Rhinemaidens are present, asking the sun goddess for light, as their Gold is no longer with them. When they hear Siegfried, they rush to the bank, beseeching the hero to return the Ring. They tease him, and when he refuses, accuse him of stinginess. He is irked at their jibes, and is even about to yield the Ring to them, but they turn solemn and tell him to keep it — and they tell him of the Curse that goes with it. This only antagonizes him, especially their prediction of his own murder this very day. They bid farewell to this fool who will not listen to wisdom, and swim away, foretelling that a wise wife will inherit the Ring and will know what to do with it.

Siegfried and the Rhinemaidens, painting by F. Leeke.

Siegfried reveals his changed character by showing amusement at the wiles of women—if he were not married to Gutrune, he jokingly remarks, he might have wooed one of these maidens. Then he turns to join the Gibichung hunting party.

He has no game, he tells Hagen, but he could have bagged three waterbirds who have warned him of his death. Gunther looks guilty, but Hagen says that it would be a shame if some wild beast should attack the hero—a reference only Gunther understands. Then Hagen hands Siegfried a drinking horn, asking him if it is true that he can understand the language of birds. Siegfried replies that he is out of the habit. Gunther remains gloomy, uncheered by Siegfried's efforts to join in a brotherly drink. At last, Hagen asks Siegfried to tell his history. Siegfried obliges, beginning with the forging of the sword and continuing up to the rescue of the Ring and the Tarnhelm. Then, as Hagen pours a different potion into his drinking horn, Siegfried remembers everything. His innocent account of his union with Brünnhilde brings the others to their feet in anger.

A pair of ravens spring up and fly away. They are the messengers of Wotan, and go to report to the God. As Siegfried turns to watch them go, Hagen plunges his spear full into the hero's back. Siegfried tries with his last strength to raise his shield, but it falls, and he falls with it. Hagen strides away, leaving Gunther to raise the fallen hero, who sings of Brünnhilde's glory with his last breath. Gunther and his men bear Siegfried toward the Gibichung Hall as the wondrous fabric of the Funeral March begins to unfold.

Scene 2. Inside the Gibichung Hall, Gutrune comes out of her room, distraught with dreams, and finds Brünnhilde gone. Hagen roughly calls out, telling Gutrune of her hero's death, as Siegfried's corpse is brought in. Gutrune accuses Gunther of the murder of her husband, but he in turn points to Hagen. Then Hagen and Gunther dispute the possession of the Ring, and Hagen strikes Gunther dead. When Hagen attempts to wrest the Ring from Siegfried's finger, the corpse's arm rises as a threat, cowing the superstitious crowd. Brünnhilde comes forward, and bids the men to build a great pyre for the hero. Gutrune begins to revile Brünnhilde as the cause of their sorrow, but to no avail; Brünnhilde is serene in the knowledge of Siegfried's true love, having been told of Hagen's treachery by the Rhinemaidens. Gutrune throws herself upon the body of Gunther. Hagen stands gloomily leaning on his spear.

As the pyre mounts, Brünnhilde begins her long Immolation Scene, one of the most impressive in all opera. She promises the Ring to the Rhinemaidens—they shall retrieve it from the ashes of the pyre, she says, as she takes it from Siegfried and places it on her own finger. Then she summons one of the men to throw a torch on the pyre, and as the fire rises, the heroic maid mounts her horse Grane and leaps into the flames. (Marjorie Lawrence is one of the very few sopranos who have ever dared to attempt this feat, even partially).

The music combines fire and water as the Rhine rises and overwhelms the scene. The Rhinemaidens are seen reclaiming the Ring, and as Hagen plunges into the water to try to recover it from Flosshilde, the

Marjorie Lawrence as Brünnhilde.

Birgit Nilsson as
Brünnhilde.

other two drag him down to his doom. Meanwhile, the flames are
mounting to Valhalla, and as the citadel crashes into ruins, the theme of
Redemption by Love takes over in a stupendous finale to one of the
glories of the operatic stage.

Program from the Bayreuth
premiere of Parsifal, 1882.

WAGNER'S LAST great music drama, *Parsifal* (he called it *Bühnenweihfestspiel,* or Stage Dedication Festival Play) created the most violent up-
heaval throughout the world that any opera had ever known. Because he
considered it highly religious (although those aspects of its nature have been
hotly disputed and are still in question), the composer desired that it be
given only in the shrine of Bayreuth. He relented enough to allow a European tour, but died before arrangements could be completed. His motives
do not seem entirely spotless, for he intended to charge advanced fees for
Bayreuth performances and certainly would have profited from the tour.
But after his death, his widow Cosima carried out the master's expressed
wishes even beyond his intentions—she guarded the sacred work fiercely
—no one outside of Bayreuth should see it.

What was her fury, then, when Heinrich Conried, newly appointed
general director of the Metropolitan, obtained a score somewhere and
pirated the piece, producing it on Christmas Eve, 1903, in his first season.
(A concert performance under Walter Damrosch at the Metropolitan in
1886 apparently did not count.)

The dissension that sprang up came from two opposing camps: the
Clergy and the Law. The "Rape of *Parsifal*" it was called by the former,
who banded their congregations together and heaped fire and calumny on

the head of the Metropolitan's director. The Law argued sensibly that there was no copyright for America, and Conried was justified. This controversy raged for two years, while Conried produced the work in the house and took it on tour. Sixteen cities joined in the excitement—to a barrage of publicity never quite equalled by any single event since—at least in the operatic world. Should you applaud after the first and third acts? "NO!" thundered the purists, although it was permissible to clap your hands after the "secular" second, when Parsifal was tempted by the Flower Maidens and Kundry. How should one dress for an event that began late in the afternoon, broke for dinner, then resumed in the evening? Just how reverent *should* you be?

There seems little justification for the pall of piety that has forever hung over this stupendous work. It is a mélange of legend, pagan and Christian, a concoction of fancy and fable, owing its origins to a French poem, a set of Welsh legends, and the poet-singer Wolfram. When the clergy railed against the portrayal of the Last Supper, as well as of the Savior and the Crucifixion, they obviously had not seen the work. The story concerns the Holy Grail, its guardians, and the young "fool" who shall restore its power. "The Guileless Fool Who Made a Fortune," one might say. *Parsifal* to this day commands its devoted audiences, and has seldom been absent from the Metropolitan's repertory, except in those few World War I years. It is given freely all over the world, and subjected to "modern" interpretations—not the least being the revival by Wagner's grandsons at Bayreuth after World War II.

What we have is a superb work by a genius who has managed to summon all his forces for this last supreme effort. Here he has perfected the use of motifs, weaving them into an orchestral web of superlative beauty and poignance. The singing voices should all be of equal excellence, although the work has been given with success in such seemingly unlikely places as the University of Indiana at Bloomington, where it was an annual delight.

Parsifal was the only work of Wagner's given at the Bayreuth Festival of 1882, the opera's premiere. Alternating casts provided Winkelman, Gudehus, and Jager as Parsifal; Materna, Brandt and Malten as Kundry; Scaria and Siehr as Gurnemanz; Hill and Fuchs as Klingsor. Hermann Levi was the first conductor.

The Metropolitan's first cast included Milka Ternina as Kundry, Aloys Burgstaller as Parsifal; and Anton Van Rooy, Marcel Journet, Robert Blass, Otto Goritz, and Louise Homer. Parsifals in the years since have been Melchior, Ralf, Kullman, Svanholm, Vinay, Konya, Thomas, and Vickers. Singing Kundry have been Flagstad, Thorborg, Bampton, Varnay, Nilsson, Dalis, and Troyanos. Hines has been a notable Gurnemanz through the years, with Siepi occasionally singing the part. Schorr, Hotter, London, Bailey, Weikl, and Stewart sang Amfortas.

Whether or not we take *Parsifal* as a religious experience, it is unquestionably a masterpiece. Wagner, as we have seen, had no particular religious leanings, and certainly drew on myth and legend for his works. He considered *Parsifal* as early as 1845, when, on vacation in Marienbad, he allowed several ideas to simmer at once. *Lohengrin* took over, and the Holy Grail and the jovial Mastersingers had to wait, the former until 1854, when Wagner had a fleeting notion to introduce the Guileless Fool into the last

Heinrich Conried.

497
WAGNER

Parsifal

Text by the composer.

AMFORTAS	*Bass-Baritone*
TITUREL	*Bass*
GURNEMANZ	*Bass*
KLINGSOR	*Bass*
PARSIFAL	*Tenor*
KUNDRY	*Soprano*
FIRST KNIGHT	*Tenor*
SECOND KNIGHT	*Bass*
FOUR ESQUIRES	*Sopranos, Tenors*
SIX FLOWER MAIDENS	*Sopranos*

First Performance
Bayreuth, 26 July 1882.

act of *Tristan*. Mercifully, this came to nothing. In the late 1850s, Wagner became deeply absorbed in the philosophy of Schopenhauer, which, together with the exalted mysticism of *Tristan*, fired him to explore further the idea of salvation through love or suffering which had imbued his consciousness for years. He did not complete *Parsifal* until January 1882.

AS THE PRELUDE OPENS, we are in the land of the Grail. There are three themes to be noted: the Sacrament, the suffering of Amfortas, and the Spear which caused the wound from which he suffers. Next we hear the Grail motif, so-called "Dresden Amen," very solemn. Then strongly enters the theme of Faith. The next portion concerns Amfortas. After soft, high chords, the curtain rises.

ACT I, Scene 1. On the outskirts of a forest near Montsalvat, Gurnemanz, an elderly but vigorous knight of the Grail, sits under a great tree, with two young Esquires asleep at his feet. The peaceful scene is soon interrupted by the advent of the procession from the King's castle. King Amfortas has sinned grievously. Lured into the magic garden of Klingsor, a magician who has been denied entrance into the brotherhood of the Kinghts of the Grail, Amfortas has lost the Holy Spear of the Grail, and been wounded by it at the hands of Klingsor. His wound will not heal until it is touched by the Spear held by a Guileless Fool, pure in heart. Each day Amfortas comes to the lake in the forest to bathe, hoping for a cure.

On this day, a wild creature blunders onto the scene. It is Kundry, who was responsible for Amfortas's betrayal, and who, in another side

Olive Fremstad as Kundry.

of her character, also serves as a messenger of the Grail. She has sought out a potent balsam in a far land and now gives it to Gurnemanz for the King. Amfortas thanks her as he passes by on his return to the castle, but she only laughs wildly. The young Esquires tease and torment her, but Gurnemanz stays them, relating the story of how the Spear was captured from Amfortas. Kundry listens uneasily. Suddenly from the lake come shouts of distress, and a huge bird falls dead at the feet of Gurnemanz. It is one of the sacred swans of the Grail brotherhood. Knights drag in the culprit, young Parsifal, who stands stoically while his motif rings out, and Gurnemanz begins to reprimand him.

At first, he has no sense of wrong-doing, but at last he begins to know what he has done, and his repentance is truly moving. When Gurnemanz questions him about his life, he tells of growing up in the woods, running away from his mother to join a group of knights, and never going back. His mother Herzeleide (Heart's Sorrow) has died of grief. But he knows nothing else, and Gurnemanz begins to hope that he may possibly be the guileless fool for whom they seek. He determines to take Parsifal to the castle, where the Grail is to be unveiled in a celebration.

Andreas Dippel as Parsifal.

Scene 2. In Bayreuth, the scenery here was stretched on two rollers at either side of the stage, so that as Gurnemanz and Parsifal walked along, the scene changed, woods giving way to rocky cliffs, then rising slopes, and finally a great hall which they enter, its lofty ceiling lost in the shadows. This is accompanied by the Bell motif, pronounced solemnly (at Bayreuth, huge bells mounted backstage were struck with great hammers). Parsifal is placed to one side and, with his back to the audience, watches through the entire proceedings.

The knights march into the hall and range themselves around the tables at either side. Esquires follow, while a boys' choir behind the scenes sings of the Savior's grief. Amfortas is carried in and placed on a raised couch at the back. It is his duty to expose the Grail so that all may be blessed in its light, but each sight of the holy vessel makes his wound bleed afresh. He so dreads this duty that he begs his ancient father, Titurel, to take it over, but the former King responds from off-stage that he is too old; it is his son's responsibility. The knights and esquires cry out to see the Grail, and Amfortas must obey. As the cover is taken from the sacred vessel, the stage darkens, and a ray of brilliant light strikes the cup (or it glows blood-red in the darkness). All sink to their knees to receive the blessing. Then, the Grail light dims as the boys cover it again, and each knight finds his cup filled with wine, a piece of bread beside it. As they partake of the consecrated fare, Amfortas collapses, placing his hand over his heart. Parsifal, who has not moved until now, starts, and presses his own heart, but gives no other sign. When Gurnemanz questions him about what he has seen, the youth shakes his head and makes no answer. All he had to do was ask: "What is it that they do here?" But he says nothing, and Gurnemanz, calling him a goose, sends him away.

Perron as Amfortas.

Stage setting for the Grail scene from the Bayreuth premiere of Parsifal, 1882.

Otto Goritz as Klingsor.

ACT II.   In Klingsor's castle, the evil magician summons Kundry out of her slumber. As she wakes with wild cries, she admits that she has served the knights of the Grail, for which Klingsor demands reparation. He has complete power over this side of her nature, and she cannot withstand him. She can be set free only if some victim spurns her. Such a one is now approaching — it is the young Parsifal himself. Calling to his soldiers and to his coterie of temptresses, the magician sinks out of sight and the castle is transformed into a lush garden, in which lightly clad, voluptuous girls are bewailing the loss or maiming of their lovers, Klingsor's soldiers. Apparently the guilty assailant is Parsifal, who stands on top of a wall, regarding them curiously. He admits to the assault on their lovers, but chaffs them lightly and earns from them a flirtatious response. They deck themselves with flowers and prepare to seduce him. But he evades them without trouble, and they disappear as a voice is heard from an arbor, calling Parsifal by name. It is Kundry, now young and ravishingly beautiful. She lures the youth into her net by recalling his mother, who was called Heart's Affection before he left her, but who has since died. Parsifal, moved to anguish, kneels and receives upon his lips his first kiss — the Kiss of Love.

But the effect upon him is quite unexpected. He springs up, pressing his hand to his heart, and he knows that he feels Amfortas's spear wound. It now bleeds within him. But no, it is the Savior's wound, and at last Parsifal realizes what he has seen and what his mission should be. As if gifted with deeper sight, he recognizes the face above him as that which had tempted Amfortas, and he spurns the temptress with horror. She in turn begs his forgiveness, but he will not yield. She makes one more plea for his love, but he promises her redemption only if she will show him the way back to Amfortas. She reveals the theft of the Spear and threatens that even now the weapon awaits him. She shrieks for Klingsor's help. The magician appears on a battlement and hurls the Spear at the young man. Miraculously, it remains poised in the air above the head of Parsifal, who reaches up and grasps it firmly. With it, he makes the sign of the Cross, and the garden withers and vanishes, leaving only ruins. To Kundry, as she sinks to the ground, Parsifal cries: "Thou knowest where only we shall meet again!" as the curtain falls.

Alexander Kipnis as Gurnemanz.

ACT III, Scene 1. After a Prelude of profound psychological meaning, in which Wagner reached even higher summits of chromatic subtelty than in *Tristan*, we see a flowery meadow near a wood. Gurnemanz, grown very old, comes out of a hut as he hears a long and piteous groan — it is Kundry, who has dragged herself hither to render service if she may. But the castle is in a state of disrepair, the knights are starving, and the Grail remains covered. Titurel, deprived of the Grail's beneficence, has died, and Amfortas fills the air with his moans of anguish. But it is Good Friday, and hope still lingers in Gurnemanz's breast. Now seen approaching is a knight clad all in black, helmeted and visored, and carrying a Spear. This weapon he thrusts into the ground, and doffing his helmet and placing it with his other weapons, he kneels in silent prayer before the Spear. Then Gurnemanz recognizes him, rejoicing at his return. Parsifal tells of his constant wanderings in search of the Grail. The Spear he has cherished, never lifting it in battle. Now he has come, Gurnemanz tells him, in time to rescue Amfortas, but not Titurel. Gurnemanz bids Kundry bathe the traveler's feet, and gives him to drink from the sacred spring nearby, whose water he also sprinkles on Parsifal's head, anointing him king of the knights of the Grail. Parsifal in turn baptizes Kundry. Then the two men begin their pilgrimage to the castle as the Good Friday music, a miracle of beauty and light, unfolds, and the scenery once more is transformed.

Scene 2. As they reach the castle, its sad aspect is all too apparent. Knights bear Titurel's coffin into the great hall, and set Amfortas down on the couch beside the covered shrine of the Grail. Amfortas, springing to his feet, begs for death rather than being forced to uncover the Grail. But as he stands in agony, Parsifal, hitherto unnoticed, approaches and touches the wound with the point of the Spear. The boys unveil the Grail, and Parsifal holds it aloft as it glows with a divine light, shedding its blessing on all. Even Titurel is raised for a moment to receive the boon. Then, as Parsifal kneels in contemplation of the holy vessel, Kundry sinks to the ground in death, freed and forgiven at last. Gurnemanz and Amfortas kneel in homage, and all join in praising "the wondrous work of mercy."

Melanie Kurt as Kundry.

SIR WILLIAM WALTON (Oldham, England, 29 March 1902 –). Walton wrote only two operas. He is better known for works in other forms, notably the oratorio, *Belshazzar's Feast*; concertos for violin and viola; the film scores (two of many) for Olivier's *Hamlet* and *Henry V*; and the witty "entertainment," *Facade*, which consists of twenty-one poems by Edith Sitwell set to charming, often skittish music (the poems are recited to an accompaniment by six musicians). Walton was an intimate friend of Dame Edith and her two brothers, Sacheverell and Osbert.

Troilus and Cressida was Walton's first opera, with a libretto based on, Chaucer by Christopher Hassall. It had its premiere in London on 3 December 1954, and was given the following year by the San Francisco and New York City Operas.

The story: Calkas, a Trojan High Priest, deserts his city after ten years of siege by the Greeks, leaving his daughter Cressida in Troy. Troilus, son of Priam, loves Cressida, who is persuaded by her uncle Pandarus to send Troilus her red scarf as a pledge of her love. The idyll of the two young people is rudely interrupted by the arrival of the Greek Prince Diomede, bearing a royal decree for the exchange of Cressida for a captive Trojan warrior. Troilus returns the scarf and promises to communicate secretly, but ten weeks go by with no word from him – the treacherous maid Evadne has intercepted the messages. Cressida heeds her father's plea to marry Diomede to save their lives. She gives Diomede the red scarf. Just before the wedding, Troilus and Pandarus arrive, intending to carry Cressida back to Troy. Seeing Diomede with the scarf, Troilus attacks him but is mortally wounded. Diomede orders Cressida to remain as a common whore, but the disgraced heroine kills herself.

The Bear, Walton's second opera, is a short work based on the Chekhov comedy of the same name (the story has been drawn upon by several composers). It was commissioned by the Koussevitzky Foundation and had its premiere by the English Opera Group at the Aldeburgh Festival on 3 June 1967. The story concerns a young widow who is determined to remain faithful to her departed husband, but finally yields to the strong personality of a neighbor who at first demands payment for a debt incurred by her husband, then gradually succumbs to her charms.

Scene from Walton's Troilus and Cressida, 1954, Covent Garden, London.

CARL MARIA VON WEBER (Eutin, Oldenburg, 18 November 1786 – London, 5 June 1826). Several operas, which Weber later discarded or which proved only faint successes, preceded the great work that made his fame secure – *Der Freischütz*. The acknowledged "father" of German Romanticism, Weber held important posts as early as the age of eighteen, and particularly in Dresden was noted for sweeping reforms, although in earlier positions, his youth and inexperience negated many of them. At the Prague Opera in 1813, he introduced many operas new to the public and created an ensemble worthy to sing them. One of the singers he imported from Vienna was Carolina Brandt, whom he later married.

One opera, *Abu Hassan*, a witty and fresh short work, remains from his early period. *Der Freischütz* was conducted by the composer when the newly reconstructed Berlin Opera summoned him for the honor in 1821.

The immediate success of this fantastic *Singspiel* brought an invitation from Barbaia, the intendant of the Kärnthnerthor Theater in Vienna, for a new opera. Weber put aside a comic opera, *Die Drei Pintos* (which was later completed by Mahler) to work on *Euryanthe*. This sprawling work, Weber's only "grand" opera, with a clumsy libretto by an eccentric woman, Helmina von Chézy, has never made its way satisfactorily, although it contains much stirring music. A similar fate has dogged Weber's last opera, *Oberon*, which he composed specially for London, conducting the first and eleven other performances in 1826. Its libretto was by James Robinson Planché, based on Wieland's tale and an earlier French romance, and is full of dramatic incident and picturesque scenes. Although seldom performed, its overture, as well as those of *Euryanthe* and *Der Freischütz*, is a great concert favorite.

In London, the tuberculosis that had plagued Weber as early as 1812 began to take its toll, and his condition rapidly worsened. Friends found him dead on the morning of June 5, the day before he was to have sailed back to his wife and two sons. He was given a resplendent funeral and buried in London, but in 1844 his body was taken back to Germany and reburied in a vault next to his younger son, who had died of measles just two weeks previously.

A curious fact is that the "von" in Weber's name seems to have been arbitrarily appropriated by Franz, his father, and to have no relation to aristocracy, although his descendants still use it. Alternate generations have had the names of Max Maria and Carl Maria, together with what other names they choose. For example, the fifth and sixth generations are: Hans Jürgen Carl Maria and Christian Max Maria. Musical gifts have not been bestowed on any successor of the first Carl Maria.

HAILED AS THE TRUE representative of the German Romantic spirit, *Der Freischütz* has never lost ground in Germany, and is indeed popular in many parts of the world, although many bowdlerizations of it have been perpetrated, particularly in Paris. Its popularity in London led to the commissioning of *Oberon*. In this century, revivals there have starred Eva Turner and Joan Sutherland. New York heard it first in English in 1825; New Orleans about that time, in French; Philadelphia in German in 1840; and New York again, in Italian, in 1850. It was a feature of the Metropolitan's

Carl Maria von Weber.

503
WEBER

Der Freischütz

(*The Free-Shooter*)

Text by Friedrich Kind.

PRINCE OTTOKAR	*Baritone*
CUNO	*Bass*
MAX	*Tenor*
CASPAR	*Bass*
KILIAN	*Tenor*
HERMIT	*Bass*
SAMIEL	*Speaker*
AGATHE	*Soprano*
ÄNNCHEN	*Soprano*

First Performance
Berlin, 18 June 1821.

504
WEBER

German season of 1884-85, with Schröder-Hanfstängel, Seidl-Kraus, Udvardy, and Kögel. Later revivals had as Agathe Johanna Gadski, Elizabeth Rethberg, and Maria Müller. After 1929, it was not heard at the Met until 1971, when Pilar Lorengar and Sandor Konya were starred.

Central Europe has long cherished the legend of the magic bullets, which, secured from Satan, can invariably find their target. Weber was not the first to set the legend to music, but it is his work that survives, despite a libretto that is not the highest achievement either in fantasy or poetry, and despite the liabilities of spoken dialogue.

THE OVERTURE marked a turning point in such structures, as it embodied an entire section of the opera itself, notably excerpts from arias by Max and Agathe.

ACT I.   Max, the young forester, aspires to succeed Cuno as hereditary forester to Prince Ottokar, and to marry Cuno's daughter Agathe, but he seems to have lost his skill at shooting. He is badly defeated in a match by Kilian, a rich peasant who taunts him unmercifully, joined by the villagers. His plight is worse because there is to be a shoot the next day before the Prince, to settle the succession. Smarting over his shame, he is the more amenable to the offer of Caspar, a comrade forester (in reality a familiar of Samiel, the Devil in disguise). Caspar introduces Samiel, who hands Max his gun and bids him fire it at an eagle in the sky above. Max shoots; the eagle falls dead at his feet. Caspar explains that it was a magic bullet that felled the bird, and suggests that he and Max meet at midnight in the Wolf's Glen, where they will mould more bullets. Caspar sings a wild drinking song and a very difficult aria to end the act.

ACT II, Scene 1. Agathe and her friend Ännchen are together in the former's room; they sing a charming duet. Ännchen tries to cheer Agathe with a merry little song, but the girl remains gloomy, heavy with forebodings about the coming trial. Left alone, she sings the beautiful prayer, "Leise, leise, fromme Weise" (Softly sighing, day is dying), followed by a recitative and a passage that is the most famous in the opera. Max enters, followed by Ännchen, but the man is uneasy, and soon leaves, saying that he must go to Wolf's Glen to retrieve a deer that he has shot. The girls warn him about the place, which is supposed to be haunted.

Nineteenth century costume designs for Der Freischütz.

Gottlob Frick as Caspar (l.) with Peter Anders as Max in the Wolf's Glen Scene, Hamburg State Opera.

Scene 2. In the Wolf's Glen, which is Samiel's place, Caspar plans to turn Max over to his master in exchange for more days on earth, as his time is almost up. When Max enters, the two foresters mould seven bullets, six of which will hit the mark, while the seventh is subject to the will of Samiel. This is one of the eeriest scenes in opera, giving an impression of wildness and the supernatural, accompanied by extremely grotesque music. The ghost of Max's mother appears, warning him. Strange animals and weird creatures flit by; the effect can be overpowering if it is not carried to a ludicrous extreme.

ACT III, Scene 1. In her room, Agathe is dressed for her bridal day, and sings the lovely "Und ob die Wolke" (And though a cloud can obscure the sun). Ännchen in turn sings an arietta, then the chorus of maidens enters and winds the bridal garland.

Scene 2. The shooting test begins with a hunting chorus. Max has only the seventh bullet left after the hunt. When he fires it at a dove according to the Prince's order, Agathe cries out that she is the dove, and falls. But she is only in a faint, and the bullet has instead found Caspar, who has climbed a tree to watch Max's disgrace. It seems that Max is absolved because he did not go to the Glen by his own free will, but was tempted by Caspar, who is therefore the victim. Max, however, confesses, and is banished by the Prince, but saved by the intercession of a Hermit who is revered by everyone. The opera ends happily for the young couple.

KURT WEILL (Dessau, 2 March 1900 – New York, 3 April 1950). The stage works of Kurt Weill have become extremely popular in the seventies, the rush to present several of them amounting almost to a cult. For a long time, only *The Three-Penny Opera* held the boards in America, and that only in an "Americanized" version by Marc Blitzstein. Suddenly, *The Rise and Fall of the City of Mahagonny* was mounted to wild enthusiasm (and some dissension) by the Metropolitan; the New York City Opera revived his Broadway success, *Street Scene,* and later brought out an obscure early work, *Silbersee,* renamed *Silverlake;* there was talk of reviving *Lost in the Stars;* his Second Symphony was played; a cabaret act was based on his music; and two biographies appeared.

Weill and his wife, Lotte Lenya, had to flee Germany in 1933 because of danger from the Nazis. Works produced before that time included: *The Protagonist* (1926), with a libretto by Georg Kaiser; *The Tsar Has His Photograph Taken* (1927), to a libretto by Kaiser; *Die Dreigroschenoper* (the famous *Three-Penny Opera,* a satire based on *The Beggar's Opera,* 1928); *Happy End,* with a libretto by Bertold Brecht (1929); *Aufstig und Fall der Stadt Mahagonny,* to a Brecht libretto (1930) – a shorter version had been produced three years previously; *Der Jasager* (The Yes-Sayer), to a text by Brecht (1930); *Der Bürgschaft,* to a text by Caspar Neher (1932); *Silbersee,* libretto by Kaiser (1933); and the ballet, *The Seven Deadly Sins* (1933), produced in London.

Weill and Lenya also paused in Paris, where *Marie galante,* to a libretto by Jacques Deval, was produced. When he came to America, the composer made every effort to absorb and reflect the American scene, and succeeded beyond any doubt. He wrote many successful shows in the musical comedy idiom, notably (after a relatively unknown *Johnny Johnson* in 1923, and the music for Werfel's *The Eternal Road* in 1937) *Knickerbocker Holiday,* from

Left to right: Robert Allman, Ronald Dowd and Rosina Raisbeck in a scene from Weill's The Rise and Fall of the City of Mahagonny, Australian Opera.

which "September Song" still lingers; *One Touch of Venus, Lady in the Dark* (in which Gertrude Lawrence starred and Danny Kaye was first discovered); *Street Scene*, and *Lost in the Stars.* An opera for workshops, *Down in the Valley*, written in 1948, has had hundreds of performances.

Street Scene was based on Elmer Rice's play, and concerns the lives and misfortunes of the diversely ethnic residents of a tenement house in New York. The differences between Irish, Jews, Italians, Scandinavians, and plain (all too plain) Americans are vividly pointed up. The tragedy involves a laborer, his unfaithful wife—whom he shoots, together with her lover— their daughter, and the two men who love her. The songs range from pure jazz to the lyrical, rising even to aria proportions. The New York City Opera gave it a splendid production in 1959 after its premiere on Broadway in 1947, and later revived it.

Mahagonny, one of the most controversial works of recent times, embodies Brecht's ideas of a corrupt America, set in altogether fictional places, and with some very shady characters. It is a bitter comment on the rougher, rawer sides of human nature, exaggerated to the point of satire, biting, unresolved. It cannot be said that the Metropolitan's sketchy setting in the cavernous stage for the equally cavernous theater, and the operatic voices chosen to elucidate the outworn slang of Brecht's conception, did the work real justice, although it was hailed by fanatics.

Silverlake, too, had its drawbacks, when the contemporary Hugh Wheeler translated Kaiser's turgid prose, and Lys Symonette similarly transformed the lyrics. The staging by Harold Prince, a "wonder-man" of Broadway, eclipsed the content of the play as well as its actor-singers.

The Three-Penny Opera remains the pinnacle of Weill's genius, translated into a dozen or more languages, seen all over the world. Its heroine, Jenny (a favorite name of Weill's), was portrayed by Lenya, who has remained the standard bearer for her husband's work.

Lotte Lenya.

507
WEINBERGER

JAROMIR WEINBERGER (Prague, 8 January 1896—St. Petersburg, Fla., 8 August 1967). Weinberger wrote several operas, of which *Schwanda the Bagpiper* (Svanda Dudek) is the only one current. When it was first produced, it swept the operatic world, being translated into more than a dozen languages. Its only rival among Czech operas in earlier years was Smetana's *The Bartered Bride*. After its premiere in Prague on 27 April 1927, it came to the Metropolitan in 1931 and was heard in Covent Garden in 1934. The Met has not revived it to date. Weinberger came to America in 1939.

The libretto of *Schwanda* is by Milos Kares and Max Brod. The story concerns the adventures of the piper, Schwanda, who is lured away from his wife Dorotka by the wily robber Babinsky. Schwanda melts the heart of the Ice Queen, but is condemned to death when the royal lady discovers he is already married. He charms his judges with his playing and is sent home, but on the way, he lies to Dorotka and goes to the Devil. In Hell, he refuses to play for his host, but is eventually rescued by Babinsky, who wins all the Devil's power in a game of cards. The music from the opera which is most frequently heard is the famous Polka and Fugue, which has a sprightly charm.

ERMANNO WOLF-FERRARI (Venice, 21 January 1876 – 21 January 1948). Of German-Italian parentage, Wolf-Ferrari gave up his idea of becoming a painter after a visit to Bayreuth, and turned to music. His first opera, *Cenerentola* (1901) was produced in Venice, but it was with his second, *Le donne curiose* (Curious Women) that he made his first success, in Munich in 1903. This was based on a Goldoni comedy, as were four other operas: *I quattro rusteghi* (The Four Rustics, or sometimes translated Four Ruffians or School for Fathers); *Gli amanti sposi* (The Loving Spouses); *La vedova scaltra* (The Crafty Widow); and *Il Campiello* (The Campiello). He also wrote the charming short work, *Il segreto di Susanna* (The Secret of Susanne), in which the lady's secret is not infidelity, but smoking. It is often used as a curtain raiser. Several other operas are on his list, all of them written with the highest skill and a delightful sense of lightness and comedy. Only one, *I gioelli della Madonna* (The Jewels of the Madonna) ventures into *verismo,* its libretto by Golisciani and Zangarini dealing with a lover who steals the jewels from the local statue of the Madonna to please his girl, with disastrous results to everyone.

The Secret of Susanne is performed widely; *The Four Ruffians* has been heard at the New York City Opera and is revived in many cities; *The Jewels of the Madonna* is occasionally put on by an ambitious company – the Boston Opera gave it a sizzling production in 1913 with Edvina, Zenatello and Marcoux, and the Metropolitan mounted it in 1925-26 and 26-27, but Chicago beat them both to the American premiere, just a few weeks after its premiere in Berlin in 1911. Bassi, Carolina White, and Sammarco were the principals.

Louise Edvina and Mario Sammarco in Wolf-Ferrari's The Jewels of the Madonna.

RICCARDO ZANDONAI (Sacco, 28 May 1883 – Pesaro, 5 June 1944).
Zandoni was hailed by the publisher Ricordi as the successor to Puccini in
verismo opera, but although he wrote ten major works, only one of them
persists, at least in America, and that sporadically. *Francesca da Rimini*,
which was based on D'Annunzio's play by the same name, with Tito Ricordi as librettist, had its premiere in Turin on 19 February 1914. Its first London performance was at Covent Garden in 1914, with Edvina, Martinelli,
and Cigada; La Scala in Milan produced it in 1916 with Raisa, Pertile, and
Danise. The American premiere was at the Metropolitan on 22 December
1916, with Alda, Martinelli, and Amato. Chicago produced it specially for
Raisa on 5 January 1917, when the soprano's colleagues were Rimini and
Crimi. San Francisco's first performance was on 28 September 1956, with
Gencer, Martell, and Colzani. *Francesca* has been revived several times in
Europe, and is slated for a revival at the Metropolitan.

*Giovanni Martinelli and
Frances Alda as the
doomed lovers Paolo and
Francesca from Francesca
da Rimini, 1916, Metropolitan Opera, New York.*

The story: Francesca, daughter of Guido da Polenta, is being forced to
marry Giovanni, known as Gianciotto, "The Lame," son of Malatesta da
Verrucchio. But because he is so ugly and misshapen, Gianciotto sends his
younger brother Paolo to the bride. The young people immediately fall in
love, but when Francesca discovers the truth, she is desolate. There is a war
between the Guelphs and the Ghibellines, which Francesca watches from a
tower. She bitterly reproaches Paolo for the fraud, but they are interrupted
by a third brother, Malatestino, who has lost an eye in battle and is called
"The One-Eyed." Gianciotto comes to say that the war is won, and that
Paolo is to be sent as Captain of the People to Florence.

Francesca in her tower room is reading the story of Lancelot and
Guinivere to her women, who dance and sing in celebration of spring. A
slave brings word that Paolo wishes to see her – he has returned from
Florence. The lovers at last are united, but their bliss lasts only briefly.
Malatestino, who also cherishes a passion for Francesca, discovers them and
reports to Gianciotto. The outraged husband enters and kills both Francesca
and Paolo.

Index

I. General

Operas are listed on pages 7-8.
Page numbers in italics indicate illustrations.

A

"Ah fors'è lui," 387
"A te, o cara," 27
Abbey, Henry E., 424-25
"Aber der Richtige," 346
"Abscheulicher! Wo eilst du hin?", 21
"Ach, ich fühl's es ist verschwunden," 202
Acté, Aïno, *318*
Adagio for Strings, 13

Sydney Opera House, Sydney, Australia.

Adam, Adolphe-Charles, 9
Adam, Theo, 465
Adams, Suzanne, 157
"Addio del passato," 389
"Addio fiorito asil," 266
Adelia, 397, 398
"Adieu, notre petite table," 140
"Adonis, ever young," 351
Agolini, S., 301
Agostini, Philippe, 235-36
Agoult, Countess Marie d', 435, 436
"Ah, chi mi dice mai quel barbaro dov'è," 184, 185
"Ah, fuyez, douce image!", 140
"Ah, Mimi, tu più non torni," 258
"Ah, mon fils," 156
"Ah, non credea mirarti," 25
"Ah! non giunge," 25
"Ah, si ben mio," 384
Ahna, Pauline de, 314, *316*
"Ai nostri monti," 385
Aida, 40, 253
Alarie, Pierrette, *62*
Albanese, Licia, 176, 250, *268*, 288, 386, 425

Albani, Emma, 153, *424*, 440, 465
Albert, Donnie Ray, 89
Alboni, Marietta, 153
Alda, Frances, 94, *257*, *425*, *428*, *509*
Alexander, John, 465
Alexander Nevsky, 240
Alfano, Franco, 282, 285
Allman, Robert, *506*
Almeida, Antonio de, 218, 220, 225
Also sprach Zarathustra, 314
Althouse, Paul, *270*
"Altra notte in fondo al mare, L'," 47
Alvarez, Albert, 153, 155, 425
Alvary, Lorenzo, *87*, *331*, *340*
Alvary, Max, 474, 479, *484*
"Am stillen Herd," 467
Amara, Lucine, 353
Amato, Pasquale, 143, 159, *274*, *276*, *277*, 425, *509*
Ambroggetti, Giuseppe, *182*
American in Paris, An, 89
American Opera Society, 166
American Spoleto Festival, Charleston, S.C., 13, 14, 122
Amor Brujo, El (Love, the Sorcerer), 84
Amore dei tre re, L', 66, 319
Ancona, Mario, 153, 157
Anders, Peter, *505*
Anderson, Marian, 399, *401*
Angelo, Tyran de Padoue, 232
Anima Allegra, 249
Antar, 290
Anthony, Charles, *433*
Anthony, Susan B., 362
Anvil chorus (*Il Trovatore*), 383
Apthorp, William, 71
Arena, Verona, *524*
Argento, Dominick, 9-11
Arlesienne Suite, *L'*, 39, 45
Aronsen, Rudolph, 135
Arroyo, Martina, 367, 399, 450
Ashton, Frederick, 361
Attwood, Martha, 282
Aubade, 129
Auber, Daniel François, 11-13, 58, 397
"Aura amorosa, Un'," 191
Auric, Georges, 235
Austin, Anson, *202*

Australian Opera House, Sydney, *511*
"Avant de quitter ces lieux," 103, 105
"Ave Maria" *(Otello)*, *424*, 427, 428
Ave Maria (Verdi), 365
Ayars, Ann, *15*

B

Baccaloni, Salvatore, 176, 182, 279, 405
Bacquier, Gabriel, *307*
Bailey, Norman, 465, 479, 497
Baker, Janet, 164, *166*, 286
Baklanoff, George, *104*, 260
Bakst, Léon, 209
Balakirev, Mili Alekseevich, 48, 204, 290
Balanchine, George, 347
"Balen del suo sorriso, Il," 384
"Ballatella," 131
Ballo in maschera, Un, 19, 23
Baltimore Opera, 226
Baltsa, Agnes, 328
Bampton, Rose, 328, 479, 497
Barbaia, Domenico, 503
Barber, Samuel, 13-14

Bayreuth Festspielhaus.

Barbiere di Siviglia, Il (The Barber of Seville), 135, 176
Barbieri, Fedora, 409
"Barcarolle," 224, 225
Barezzi, Antonio, 362, *363*
Barezzi, Margherita, *362*, 363
Barlow, Alan, 402

Deutsche Oper, Berlin.

Bolshoi Theater, Moscow.

Kongelige Theater, Copenhagen.

Old Metropolitan Opera House.

Central City Opera House, Central City, Colorado.

Royal Opera House, Stockholm.

Salzburg Festspielstadt Theater

Hessian State Theater, Wiesbaden.

The Arena, Verona.

Vienna Opera House (Vienna Staatsoper).

Grand Theater, Barcelona.

Opera House, Mantua.

Moscow Theater, Moscow.

Index

II. Librettists and Authors